Sharing Literature with Children

Longman English and Humanities Series
Advisory Editor: Lee A. Jacobus
University of Connecticut, Storrs

Sharing Literature with Children

A Thematic Anthology

FRANCELIA BUTLER

LONGMAN
NEW YORK AND LONDON

For my grandchildren:
Grace Anne, John Cosman, and Jerome Francis Wandell

SHARING LITERATURE WITH CHILDREN
A THEMATIC ANTHOLOGY

MANUFACTURED IN THE UNITED STATES OF AMERICA

Senior Editor: Gordon T. R. Anderson
Developmental Editor: Virginia Hans
Editorial and Design Supervisor: Nicole Benevento
Interior Design: Angela Foote
Jacket and Cover Design: Maurice Sendak
Manufacturing and Production Supervisor: Donald W. Strauss
Composition: Western Publishing Company, Inc.
Printing and Binding: Hamilton Printing Company

Library of Congress Cataloging in Publication Data

Main entry under title:

Sharing literature with children.

(Longman English and humanities series)
Includes bibliographies and index.
SUMMARY: A thematically arranged anthology of folklore, myths, fiction, poetry, biographies, and essays.
1. Children's literature. [1. Literature—Collections] I. Butler, Francelia McWilliams, 1913-
PZ5.S514 808.8 77-3999
ISBN 0-679-30328-6
ISBN 0-582-28114-8 pbk. (previously 0-679-30343-X pbk.)

Acknowledgments

"Skip-Rope Rhymes as a Reflection of American Culture" by Francelia Butler. Reprinted from *Children's Literature,* vol. 5, edited by Francelia Butler. Copyright © 1976 by Francelia Butler (Philadelphia: Temple University Press, 1976).

Selection from *The Velveteen Rabbit* by Margery Williams Bianco used by permission of Doubleday & Company, Inc.

"In Which Christopher Robin Leads an Expotition to the North Pole." From *Winnie-the-Pooh* by A. A. Milne, illustrated by Ernest H. Shepard. Copyright, 1926, by E. P. Dutton & Co., Inc.; renewed, 1954 by A. A. Milne. Reproduced by permission of the publishers, E. P. Dutton & Co., Inc.

Selection from *Impunity Jane* by Rumer Godden. Copyright 1954 by Rumer Godden. Reprinted by permission of The Viking Press.

Selection from *Raggedy Ann and the Paper Dragon* by Johnny Gruelle, Copyright 1926 The Bobbs-Merrill Company, Inc., Copyright renewed 1953 by The Bobbs-Merrill Company, Inc.

"The Steadfast Tin-Soldier." English translation copyright © 1959 and 1961 by Oxford University Press. First published by Oxford University Press in 1961. From the book *Hans Andersen's Fairy Tales,* translated by L. W. Kingsland and illustrated by Ernest Shepard. First American edition published by Henry Z. Walck, Inc., a division of David McKay Company, Inc., in 1962. Reprinted by permission of the publishers.

Selections from *Pinocchio* by Carlo Collodi translated by Walter S. Cramp and published by Ginn and Company in 1904.

Selection from *The Sign on Rosie's Door* by Maurice Sendak. Copyright © 1960 by Maurice Sendak. Reprinted by permission of Harper & Row, Publishers, Inc.

Selection from *The Boy and the Whale* by José Maria Sanchez-Silva published by The Bodley Head.

"Us Two." From *Now We Are Six* by A. A. Milne. Copyright, 1927, by E. P. Dutton & Co., Inc.; renewal © 1955 by A. A. Milne. Reprinted by permission of the publishers, E. P. Dutton & Co., Inc.

"Paper Boats," selection from *Crescent Moon.* Reprinted with permission of Macmillan Publishing Co., Inc. from *Collected Poems and Plays* by Rabindranath Tagore. Copyright 1913 by Macmillan Publishing Co., Inc., renewed 1914 by Rabindranath Tagore. Reprinted also with the permission of the Trustees of the Tagore Estate, Macmillan London and Basingstoke.

"Lines and Squares." From *When We Were Very Young* by A. A. Milne. Copyright, 1924, by E. P. Dutton & Co., Inc.; renewal, 1952, by A. A. Milne. Reprinted by permission of the publishers, E. P. Dutton & Co., Inc.

"The Kite" by Harry Behn. From *Windy Morning,* copyright, 1953, by Harry Behn. Reprinted by permission of Harcourt Brace Jovanovich, Inc.

"The Pickety Fence." Copyright 1952 by David McCord. From *Far and Few: Rhymes of the Never Was and Always Is* by David McCord, by permission of Little, Brown and Co.

"Hiding." Reprinted by permission of G. P. Putnam's Sons from *Everything and Anything* by Dorothy Aldis. Copyright 1925, 1926, 1927 by Dorothy Aldis; renewed.

"Blum." Reprinted by permission of G. P. Putnam's Sons from *Here, There, and Everywhere* by Dorothy Aldis. Copyright 1927, 1928 by Dorothy Aldis; renewed.

"Tiptoe" from *In the Middle of the Trees* by Karla Kuskin. Copyright © 1958 by Karla Kuskin. Reprinted by permission of Harper & Row, Publishers, Inc.

"My Plan." From *Around and About* by Marchette Chute. Copyright © 1957 by E. P. Dutton & Co., Inc., and reprinted with their permission.

"Chanson Innocente." Copyright 1923, 1951 by E. E. Cummings. Reprinted from his volume, *Complete Poems 1913–1962,* by permission of Harcourt Brace Jovanovich, Inc.

"The Centaur" by May Swenson is reprinted by permission of the author from *To Mix With Time, New & Selected Poems* copyright © 1963 by May Swenson and Charles Scribner's Sons, New York.

"Some Remarks on Raggedy Ann and Johnny Gruelle" by Martin Williams. Reprinted from *Children's Literature,* vol. 3, edited by Francelia Butler. Copyright © 1974 by Francelia Butler (Philadelphia: Temple University Press, 1974).

"The Puppet Immortals of Children's Literature" by Michael Michanczyk. Reprinted from *Children's Literature,* vol. 2, edited by Francelia Butler. Copyright © 1973 by Francelia Butler (Philadelphia: Temple University Press, 1973).

"The Sea of Gold" is reprinted by permission of Charles Scribner's Sons from *The Sea of Gold and Other Tales from Japan* by Yoshiko Uchida. Illustration by Marianne Yamaguchi. Copyright © 1965 Yoshiko Uchida.

"Jack and the Beanstalk" by James Reeves. Reprinted from *English Fables and Fairy Stories* by James Reeves by permission of Oxford University Press, London.

"The Madman of Naranath" retold by K. Shankar Pillai ("Shankar") from *A Treasury of Indian Tales* by

Estate, Macmillan London and Basingstoke, and The Macmillan Company of Canada Ltd.

"Sometimes I Feel This Way" by John Ciardi. From *You Read to Me, I'll Read to You* by John Ciardi. Copyright © 1962 by John Ciardi. Reprinted by permission of J. B. Lippincott Company.

"Wild West" by Robert G. Boylan. Reprinted by permission of *Saturday Review.* Copyright © 1957.

"My Aunt" by Ted Hughes. From *Meet My Folks,* copyright © 1961, 1973 by Ted Hughes. Reprinted by permission of the publisher, The Bobbs-Merrill Company, Inc. and Faber and Faber Ltd.

"My Inside-Self" by Rachel Field. Reprinted with permission of Macmillan Publishing Co., Inc. from *Poems* by Rachel Field. Copyright 1924, 1930 by Macmillan Publishing Co., Inc.

"The Old Wife and the Ghost" by James Reeves, copyright © 1952 by James Reeves from *The Blackbird in the Lilac* published 1952 by the Oxford University Press.

"The Listeners" by Walter de la Mare. Reprinted by permission of The Literary Trustees of Walter de la Mare and The Society of Authors as their representative.

"Forgotten," anonymous. From *I Never Saw Another Butterfly . . .* edited by H. Volavkova 1964, McGraw-Hill Book Company. Used with permission.

"Molly Means" by Margaret Walker, from the book *For My People;* Yale University Press, 1942. Copyright 1942 by Margaret Walker. Reprinted by permission of the author.

"The Shadow." M. Esther Harding, *The 'I' and the Not-I': A Study in the Development of Consciousness.* Bollingen Series 79. © 1965 by Bollingen Foundation. Chapter 4, "Projections to Persons of the Same Sex: The Shadow" (abridged), reprinted by permission of Princeton University Press.

"Atalanta" by Betty Miles, from *Free To Be . . . You and Me* by Marlo Thomas and Friends. Copyright © 1973, Free To Be Foundation, Inc.

"Nana Miriam" by Hans Baumann. From *The Stolen Fire* by Hans Baumann, translated by Stella Humphries. Copyright © 1974 by Random House, Inc. Reprinted by permission of Pantheon Books, a Division of Random House, Inc.

"Three Strong Women" by Claus Stamm. Copyright © 1962 by Claus Stamm and Kazue Mizumura. Reprinted by permission of The Viking Press.

"Molly Whipple" by James Reeves. Reprinted from *English Fables and Fairy Stories* by James Reeves by permission of Oxford University Press, London.

"The White Horse Girl and the Blue Wind Boy" by Carl Sandburg. From *Rootabaga Stories* by Carl Sandburg, illustrated by Maud and Miska Petersham, Copyright 1922, by Harcourt Brace Jovanovich, Inc.; renewed, 1950, by Carl Sandburg. Reprinted by permission of the publishers.

Excerpt from *Harriet the Spy* by Louise Fitzhugh. Copyright © 1964 by Louise Fitzhugh. Reprinted by permission of Harper & Row, Publishers, Inc.

"A Taste of Blackberries" by Doris Buchanan Smith. Copyright © 1973 by Doris Buchanan Smith from *A Taste of Blackberries* by Doris Buchanan Smith used with permission of Thomas Y. Crowell Company, Inc., publisher.

Excerpt from *It's Like This Cat* by Emily Neville, illustrated by Emil Weiss. Copyright © 1963 by Emily Neville. Reprinted by permission of Harper & Row, Publishers, Inc.

Excerpt from *Julie of the Wolves* by Jean Craighead George. Text copyright © 1972 by Jean Craighead George. Reprinted by permission of Harper & Row, Publishers, Inc.

Excerpt from *Sojourner Truth, A Self-Made Woman* by Victoria Ortiz. Copyright © 1974 by Victoria Ortiz. Reprinted by permission of J. B. Lippincott Company.

"A Certain Age" by Phyllis McGinley. From *Times Three* by Phyllis McGinley. Copyright © 1956 by Phyllis McGinley. Originally appeared in *The New Yorker.* Reprinted by permission of The Viking Press.

"My Dog Is a Plumber" by Dan Greenburg from *Free To Be . . . You and Me* by Marlo Thomas and Friends. Copyright © 1972, Free To Be Foundation, Inc.

Excerpt from "Fairy Tale Liberation" by Alison Lurie. Reprinted with permission from *The New York Review of Books.* Copyright © 1970 Nyrev, Inc.

Excerpt from "Witches and Fairies" by Alison Lurie. Reprinted with permission from *The New York Review of Books.* Copyright © 1971 Nyrev, Inc.

"Womenfolk and Fairy Tales" reviewed by Susan Cooper. © 1975 by The New York Times Company. Reprinted by permission.

"Some Day My Prince Will Come: Female Acculturation Through the Fairy Tale" by Marcia R. Lieberman. Copyright © 1972 by the National Council of Teachers of English. Reprinted by permission of the publisher.

"Demeter" and "Cupid and Psyche." From *Mythology* by Edith Hamilton. Copyright 1942 by Edith Hamilton. Copyright © 1969 by Dorian Fielding Reid. Copyright © 1969 by Doris Fielding Reid, Executrix of the will of Edith Hamilton. By permission of Little, Brown and Co.

"Round the Mulberry Bush" and "Ring-a-Ring o' Roses." From *Ding Dong Bell, A First Book of Nursery Rhymes* devised by Percy Young and Edward Ardizzone. Reprinted by permission of Dennis Dobson, Publishers, and Dover Publications, Inc.

"St. George and the Dragon" by Diana John. First published by Methuen 1961. Published in Puffin Books 1966. Text and illustrations Copyright © 1961, 1966 by Diana John. Reprinted by permission of Associated Book Publishers Ltd.

"East of the Sun and West of the Moon." First American edition 1956, published by Henry Z. Walck, Inc., a division of David McKay Company, Inc. From the book *Scandinavian Legends and Folk-Tales* by Gwyn Jones. Illustrated by Kiddell-Monroe. Reprinted by permission of Oxford University Press.

"Esarhaddon" by Leo Tolstoy. From *Fables and Fairy Tales* by Leo Tolstoy, translated by Ann Dunnigan. Copyright © 1962 by Ann Dunnigan. Reprinted by arrangement with The New American Library, Inc., New York, New York.

Excerpt from *The Little Prince,* written and drawn by Antoine de Saint Exupéry, copyright 1943, 1971 by Harcourt Brace Jovanovich, Inc. and reprinted with their permission.

Excerpt from *Charlotte's Web* by E. B. White, pictures by Garth Williams. Copyright, 1952, by E. B. White. Reprinted by permission of Harper & Row, Publishers, Inc.

Excerpt from *Waterless Mountain.* Copyright 1931, renewed 1959 by Laura Adams Armer. From the book *Waterless Mountain,* originally published by Longmans, Green and Company, Inc., a division of David McKay Company, Inc. Reprinted by permission of the publisher.

Selection from . . . *And Now Miguel* by Joseph Krumgold. Copyright © 1953 by Joseph Krumgold. From . . . *And Now Miguel* by Joseph Krumgold, illustrated by Jean Charlot. Used with permission of Thomas Y. Crowell Company, Inc., publisher.

The World Is Round by Gertrude Stein. Reprinted from *The World Is Round,* © 1939 & renewed 1967, by Gertrude Stein, a Young Scott Book, by permission of Addison-Wesley Publishing Company, Inc.

"There Was a Child Went Forth" from *Leaves of Grass* by Walt Whitman. Used by permission of Doubleday & Company, Inc.

"Dream Variation" by Langston Hughes. Copyright 1926 by Alfred A. Knopf, Inc. and renewed 1954 by Langston Hughes. Reprinted from *Selected Poems,* by Langston Hughes, by permission of the publisher.

"The Pleasures of Merely Circulating" by Wallace Stevens. Copyright 1936 by Wallace Stevens and renewed 1964 by Molly Stevens Stephenson. Reprinted from *The Collected Poems of Wallace Stevens,* by Wallace Stevens, by permission of Alfred A. Knopf, Inc.

"The Secret Sits" by Robert Frost. From *The Poetry of Robert Frost* edited by Edward Connery Lathem. Copyright 1942 by Robert Frost. Copyright © 1969 by Holt, Rinehart and Winston. Copyright © 1970 by Lesley Frost Ballantine. Reprinted with permission of Holt, Rinehart and Winston.

"The Cat and the Moon" by William Butler Yeats. Reprinted with permission of Macmillan Publishing Co., Inc. from *Collected Poems* by William Butler Yeats. Copyright 1919 by Macmillan Publishing Co., Inc., renewed 1947 by Bertha Georgie Yeats. Also reprinted with permission of M. B. Yeats, Miss Anne Yeats and The Macmillan Company of London and Basingstoke.

"Where the Hayfields Were." From *Collected Poems 1917–1952,* by Archibald MacLeish. Copyright 1952 by Archibald MacLeish. Reprinted by permission of Houghton Mifflin Company.

"The Creation." From *God's Trombones* by James Weldon Johnson. Copyright 1927 by The Viking Press, Inc., © renewed 1955 by Grace Nail Johnson. Reprinted by permission of The Viking Press.

"Even as the Snow Fell" by Issa. From *The Autumn Wind,* Wisdom of the East Series, translated by Lewis Mackenzie. Reprinted with permission of John Murray (Publishers) Ltd.

A Roundabout Turn by Robert H. Charles copyright Frederick Warne & Co. 1930, reproduced by permission of Frederick Warne & Co., Inc. and Frederick Warne & Co. Limited, London.

"Webs of Concern: *The Little Prince* and *Charlotte's Web*" by Laurence Gagnon. Reprinted from *Children's Literature,* vol. 2, edited by Francelia Butler. Copyright © 1973 by Francelia Butler (Philadelphia: Temple University Press, 1973).

Selection from *The Uses of Enchantment: Meaning and Importance of Fairy Tales* by Bruno Bettelheim. Copyright © 1976 by Bruno Bettelheim. Reprinted by permission of Alfred A. Knopf, Inc. Portions of this book originally appeared in *The New Yorker.*

"The Ethics of Elfland." Reprinted by permission of Dodd, Mead & Company, Inc. from *Orthodoxy* by G. K. Chesterton. Copyright 1908 by Dodd, Mead & Company. Copyright renewed 1935 by Gilbert K. Chesterton. Also reprinted by permission of Miss D. E. Collins and The Bodley Head Ltd.

"A Meditation on Children and Their Literature" by Clifton Fadiman. Copyright © 1976 by Clifton Fadiman. This material will be expanded in Mr. Fadiman's forthcoming book to be published by Little, Brown and Company. Reprinted by permission of Little, Brown and Company.

Selection from *Tree and Leaf* by J. R. R. Tolkien. Copyright © 1964 by George Allen & Unwin Ltd. U.S. Rights reprinted by permission of Houghton Mifflin Company. Also reprinted by permission of George Allen & Unwin Ltd.

The author wishes to thank the following contributors whose works were written expressly for this volume: Chinua Achebe, "The Flute"; Jerry Griswold, "The Fool and the Child"; Anne Devereaux Jordan, "Sugar 'n Spice 'n Snips 'n Snails"; K. Narayan Kutty, "A Look at Andersen's 'The Shadow' "; Leonard R. Mendelsohn, "Toys and Literature"; J. D. O'Hara, "Gertrude Stein's 'The World Is Round' "; "Isaac Bashevis Singer: Interview"; Marianne Whelchel, "Achebe's 'The Flute.' "

Preface

This book is designed for use in college classes in children's literature, as a source book in libraries and in elementary schools, and for parents who want to share great literature with their children. Besides being a collection of literature for children, the book offers a theory about children's literature that grows out of something we all have experienced and sensed intuitively—that the most deeply moving literature seems to center in certain basic symbolic themes, which keep recurring like the patterns in music.

Because these basic themes are independent of age and are deeply felt emotionally, they go beyond the naming of genres, such as rhymes, fables, folktales, fantasy, fiction, nonfiction. For this reason, the thematic arrangement of material is the primary arrangement in this book; arrangements by genre are supplied, too, but they are subsidiary to the main movements of the material.

The book is not intended only to acquaint adults with "children's" literature for teaching or sharing purposes; it is intended also to reach or reawaken the "hidden" children in adult readers,* so that they may respond *directly* to the rich literature of fantasy and folktale that has been relegated (wrongly, some feel) to children. Selections have been chosen, therefore, with both actual and "hidden" children in mind.

On different occasions, P. L. Travers, author of *Mary Poppins,* and Maurice Sendak, author of *Where The Wild Things Are,* were asked by members of my class, "How do you know what it is like to be a child?" Fortunately for us, both writers have retained their childlike view of the world. Each answered in turn. "I have been a child." The "hidden" child in the adult is what teachers, parents, and other concerned adults must recapture if they are to work most effectively with children.

A root meaning of fantasy is "to reveal or make clear," and it is through this process of imaginatively re-creating our own childhood attitudes that we can paradoxically arrive at a clearer and more realistic understanding of ourselves and at the same time give more of ourselves to children. The gift without the giver is never very meaningful, and this is why generous-spirited adults become children and so are able to share the child's world. The essays by Bruno Bettelheim, G. K. Chesterton, Clifton Fadiman, and J. R. R. Tolkien in the Afterword of this book all demonstrate the need for this kind of sharing.

Besides the thematic arrangement, four criteria for selection of material have been feeling, values, quality, and balance. I felt that the literature selected must not be coldly antiseptic. If it doesn't move at least some people, if it reveals no "wisdom of heart," then it is not worth either an adult's or a child's time. Adults must feel the literature first, and then so must the children with whom the adults are sharing it—whether in the classroom or library or home.

Many of the selections in this book—all of them in one way or another—have to do with values, some of them more obviously than others. In the largest sense, all literature has to do implicitly with values. It is interesting to observe, however, that the literature that touches children and adults most tends to be directly concerned with moral and ethical values. Leo Tolstoy, who wrote a number of fables and stories for children, said that the distinction between the ethics of high art and of didactic art is that "the bad fable has a moral, while the good fable is a moral." A touching story is told of Tolstoy's older brother, Nicholas. When the boys were playing together, Nicholas said that he had written the secret of the unity of mankind on a green stick, which he had buried by the roadside. It is said that Tolstoy asked in his old age to be buried by the green stick and that the wish was carried out

*I am indebted to Clifton Fadiman for this term; see his "The Hidden Child," pp. 477–483 in the Afterword.

by his family. Presented in the form of high art, Tolstoy's fable "Esarhaddon" (included in "Circles") has to do with an ethical problem—the need to put oneself into the position of one's fellow human being and to understand his point of view.

What one regards as "quality" in literature is a subjective judgment, but an attempt is made here to choose most selections from literature of the highest quality in the sense that it is literature equally worth reading at ten and at fifty, a criterion suggested by C. S. Lewis.

Finally, the selections were made with a view to balance. In order to represent the wide field of children's literature accurately and effectively in the book, it has been necessary to juggle many different kinds of balance simultaneously: that of culture, ethnic group, and sex, as well as genre and period. I have sought to achieve this simultaneous balance insofar as possible, despite my recognition that such a goal is unattainable. Genre types have not been neglected, appearing as subcategories under each theme; they include myth, biblical writing, fable, folk rhymes, folk plays, folktales, fiction, fantasy, biography, poetry, and critical essays.

The emphasis in making the selections, however, is primarily on the thematic approach. To explain why this is so, I must acknowledge that this approach grew out of my own experience in teaching children's literature. I began with the genre approach, but within a few years I found that the method of my teaching had changed—that I was depending largely on mimeographed sheets of my own contriving. These sheets were outline attempts to arrange material in accordance with certain basic themes most deeply felt by all human beings. For several years, the classes were highly experimental. We tried and discarded many themes that, though important, somehow didn't work. Eventually the students and I together worked out a program of themes, many of which are curiously interrelated. At this time and for no other reason (election of the course is on a strictly voluntary basis), classes began to increase in enrollment. One class has now gone from thirty students to three hundred, at which number I have set a ceiling.

But the mimeographing of sheets and assembling of accompanying selections was far too time-consuming, expensive, and cumbersome. One text was needed to demonstrate the critical theory underlying the thematic organization that we used. The idea for such a book evolved naturally, as described above. Selections were made according to specific principles. In any arrangement of material, the meaning of a work of literature had to have first priority, and that meaning had to be reinforced by other works which conveyed the same or a similar meaning. The themes with which these works were concerned had to move emotionally at least some of the students, had to stimulate them to form associations with other works not discussed specifically in class, and had also to be applicable to the newest as well as the oldest material. Further, themes had to show evidence of being important in life. Students had to feel impelled to write stories or plays or articles on some aspect of the themes or to otherwise indicate that the themes were exciting and important to them.

This approach to children's literature is an *active* approach—and that is perhaps its greatest strength. By involving students themselves in the development and amplification of themes, the approach is, I hope, what all approaches to learning should be: a beginning rather than a termination of learning, so that students will continue the lines of research begun in class long after they have left school.

The thematic approach has many values, both psychological and literary. From the psychological standpoint, the themes selected represent eternal verities in which any human being, child or adult, has an immediate and permanent interest. The strength of this natural interest releases the imagination to make numerous connections, linking a given theme with real-life experience and weaving it in with recollections of other literature. This is the active principle of the approach.

When literature is organized in this way, thematically, one's imagination is more readily tempted to draw inferences from totally diverse fields of literature than when one is concerned with only one genre, such as poetry. For this reason, one can plumb the depths of human experience more widely and deeply. With the thematic approach, it is hoped that more children will grow *into* literature instead of out of it.

The hope is to provide a text that "swings free," so that the reader will not feel restricted by traditionalism and obliged to plod faithfully through the material. Anyone should be allowed to dip in wherever he or she wishes and find learning delightful. As Saint Thomas Aquinas said, "Everything lights up everything else." Any approach to the text is practical if it promotes further study.

The element of play is very important in the thematic approach. Since poetry grew out of dance and song, adult readers are encouraged to recapture the dance and song of poetry. They will find that there is nothing evil in having fun and that they can learn best by relaxing their inhibitions and becoming four-year-olds again. (The Explorations at the end of each part suggest some of the ways in which to do this.) One student who had danced out her feeling for poetry while in my class recently wrote me that she had taped music as a background to some of the poetry about Fools, Circles, and other themes, and how the little children she is now teaching did a free-form dance about the classroom in which they interpreted the meanings of such poems as "Moon Folly" and "A Roundabout Turn." Any adult and child can put a record on and do the same together.

Far from divorcing us from our adult roles, a realization of the importance of creative play actually deepens our wisdom and understanding, as some of the greatest minds have discovered. To develop his theory of archetypes, or deeply rooted emotional patterns, Carl Jung played childish games and built sand castles. Einstein played with mechanical wind-up toys.

Although the themes chosen for this book are not intended to be all-inclusive in presenting a world-view to the child, they can be grouped into five broad categories of life experience that are important both for children and adults.

The themes Toys and Games, Fools, Masks and Shadows, and Sex Roles are all concerned with the "serious play" that is the means through which children grow and develop. These sections explore the serious side of play through a look at Toys and Games, those often solemn objects and activities that children use to teach themselves about life and the world; Fools, who are like children in their first clumsy efforts in the adult world; Masks and Shadows, and Sex Roles, both of which involve role playing, a very serious kind of playing indeed—and a kind that literature can help children learn about. The final theme, Circles, enclosing all the others, considers natural cycles such as birth and death and the changing of the seasons. It is also the natural symbol for completion.

These five themes are among a small group of themes with which, in my experience, large numbers of students are deeply concerned. Other literary themes that absorb and sustain both children and adults include Water and the Sea, Birds and Animals, Trees and Hills, Politics, Gratitude, Greed, Work, and Life Problems (which incorporates many other themes, including Death, Growing Up, Competing, Unpredictability, Fear, Coping with Evil, and so on).

This book is meant to suggest how to explore five of the liveliest themes and how to go about exploring other themes that one wants to share with children. One surprise may be how the themes intertwine. For instance, *Pinocchio: The Adventures of a Marionette* might seem to belong exclusively to the Toys section, but Pinocchio can also be regarded as a Fool who learned through experience. His foolish aspect is symbolized when he becomes a donkey. He wears this mask until he earns the right to change his form and he can therefore be discussed very well in connection with Masks and Shadows. His relation to the mother figure, the Blue Fairy, can be considered in connection with Sex Roles. Finally, we find him once again back with his old father, Geppetto, his creator, but now in a higher form: he is no longer a puppet but a real little boy. The story thus belongs in the Circles section as well. These intertwinings may suggest why certain themes seen to have a peculiarly strong appeal both to children and adults. They touch many facets of the whole personality.

In addition to selections from children's literature, each thematic part contains critical essays on the theme or on specific selections, Explorations of material through activities, and a

Suggested Readings list. It is hoped that these additional materials will aid readers in continuing to develop the themes and add ideas of their own. Thematic emphasis is one area in the study of literature in which important growth is only beginning.

A number of creative activities are suggested as Explorations. The themes of this book lend themselves to activities that can be *shared* with children, including storytelling most prominently. One of the best ways to share storytelling is through choral reading. Almost any poem and many stories can be made into choral readings and it's fun to devise ways to make these choral readings dramatic. Plays, pantomime, and puppet shows are other activities in which children and adults can share literature. Rope-skipping to rhymes need not be relegated only to children. It is a heathful and enjoyable experience for children of almost any age. Drawing and painting, clay modeling, and mask making are some of the ways in which deeper emotional responses to the literature can be expressed and shared. Making up games, stories, or poems on the various themes can be very satisfying.

Besides the critical essays bearing directly on the thematic material included in the book, a special section of supplementary essays has been included in the final section. The Afterword, "On Fantasy and the Child," contains essays that are applicable to fantasy in all its literary forms, actually, but that concentrate particularly on the folktale, or fairy tale. Bruno Bettelheim sees folktales as a healing salve to the psyche; G. K. Chesterton is primarily concerned with them as food for the human spirit; Clifton Fadiman sees them as affording an opportunity for the "hidden child" in the adult to share stories with the children he loves; and J. R. R. Tolkien is interested in the aesthetic values of folktales for children and adults. Essentially, however, all four writers see the stories alike, as a wonderful and enriching experience in which all human beings can share.

For editorial assistance, I wish to express appreciation to Carol Boardman, Sheila Gee, Andrea Booth, and Karen Drazen. I also wish to express my gratitude for editorial advice to Professor Irving Baker of the School of Education, University of Connecticut, Professor Mary Field Schwarz of the Department of Curriculum and Teaching, Hunter College, Carol Vassalo, Professor Emeritus of Children's Literature in Education and English at Eastern Connecticut State College, and for her assistance with the bibliographies, Charity Chang, Assistant University Librarian at the University of Connecticut, a specialist in children's literature who is library consultant to the journal *Children's Literature* and reviewer of children's books for the *Hartford Courant.* I am especially aware of my indebtedness to Professor Lee Jacobus and Gordon T. R. Anderson for their encouragement and support, and to Virginia Hans, who was developmental editor for the book.

Contents

I. Toys and Games

A few years ago, I was gazing from an upper window down into the courtyard of a university, where I saw a young man vigorously polishing his sports car. When he finished, he leaned over and gave the car a kiss, right in the middle of the windshield. Like the young man, we all have toys we are fond of that implement the games we play, some of them serious games, such as making a living, and some of them games for fun, such as golf. Subconsciously, like children, many of us combine the development of our personalities with sheer fun in our toys and games. I for one enjoy choosing a good typewriter (my toy) on which to do my writing.

The most elemental toy is the doll, which is often regarded as the projection of the child's fantasy of having children. But this is not the only aspect of the doll, for in an earlier stage of childhood, it is likely to be the object that contains the divinity—the security blanket or teddy bear which has to be in a specific place for the child to sleep safely. Dr. Marie-Louise von Franz of the Jung

Institute, Zurich, suggests that, in this case, the object is not the child's child but the child's god: it is like the soul stones of the Stone Age. That is, the early relationships of the child with the doll may carry the earliest projections of the Self, and the toy becomes the magic object on which the life of the child depends. Later, the toy is used in a game based on the relationship between parent and child. Objects such as dolls and toy animals are also used to carry projections of aspects of the child's personality that are difficult to handle for the child, enabling her or him to work out these problems through play.

The French psychologist and student of child development Jean Piaget has come up with a useful structural classification for children's games: practice games, which are essentially sensory-motor games; symbolic games, "which imply representation of an absent object"; and games with rules. Practice games appear whenever a new skill is acquired, but are identified especially with the first two or three years (the preverbal period and that of early verbal development). Symbolic games of various kinds develop between the ages of four and seven. Games of rules develop from ages seven to eleven and continue as the principal form of play throughout life. (For a more detailed description of the stages in the development of games, see Chapter V, "Classification of Games and Their Evolution after the Beginnings of Language," in Jean Piaget, *Play, Dreams and Imitation in Childhood,* translated by C. Gattegno and F. M. Hodgson [1962].)

All of these stages in game development have their parallels in literature for children. For instance, acting-out folk rhymes like "Patty cake, patty cake, baker's man" are practice games or exercises for very young children. This rhyme has to do with a homely occupation—breadmaking—and gives the young child a feeling of well-being to have a part in the process as the mother helps clap baby's hands and "prepare the loaf." A story like Johnny Gruelle's *Raggedy Ann,* in which children identify with a doll, allows for symbolic play. Skip-rope rhymes are often accompanied by fixed rules which require specified relationships between individuals.

To this third class of children's games would belong the game with punctuation that was played in school in Russia by Kornei Chukovsky (1882–1969), Russia's most popular children's storyteller as well as the distinguished author of many critical and scholarly works. In his charming autobiography (translated in 1976), Chukovsky describes how he tried to help his fellow students with their punctuation problems by tying a string from his shoe to their legs. One yank meant a comma; two, an exclamation mark; three, a question mark; and four, a colon. Unfortunately, he wrote his exercise faster than did his less gifted friends, so that their exercises ended up with commas between syllables, and colons, question marks, and exclamation points in such startling places that the Commission for Verification of Educational Progress flunked all seven of the recipients of Kornei's signals!

Chukovsky is best known to students of children's literature for his work *From Two to Five* (1965),* in which he studies the speech and patterns of learning of children, particularly with respect to their use of poetry. Chukovsky observes that language is a game to the child, who likes to turn things "topsy-turvy." Chukovsky notes that no sooner does a child master an idea than he or she wants to make it a toy. When his two-year-old daughter made an imaginary dog "meow," she was playing a game. Sensing that she knew better about the sound a dog makes but was merely playing, Chukovsky participated by making up other "topsy-turvies," or reversals of reality. He arrived at a theory that a child likes deliberate reversals because they signify for the child "the successful culmination of a certain series of mental efforts which he has made to master his concepts of the world around him."

For this reason, and because of the sheer fun of them for any age, some nonsense verses ("topsy-turvies") are included in this section. Even autograph rhymes often belong in this category. I was noticing in my mother's autograph book, filled in when she was about ten (she was born in 1888), that the following rhyme appears about a woodchuck dying of the whooping cough (it appears again in my childhood collection in the 1920s and in my daughter's book, filled in by classmates in the early 1950s):

Way down yonder not so very far off
A woodchuck died of the whooping cough
He whooped so hard with the whooping cough
That he whooped his head and his tail right off!

And I remember my admiration in 1920 when the big eighth grader who lived next door insisted that he always twisted his words when he acted as usher in church: "Pardon me, Madam, let me sew you to a sheet. Take a chew in the back of the perch."

It should be possible to classify all of the literature in this section according to Piaget's three classes of childhood games. Folk rhymes offer a particularly rich repository of childhood games—riddles, tongue twisters and catches, counting-out rhymes, acting-out rhymes, jump-rope rhymes. From these the reader can make his own extensions into more elaborate circle games, dance games, and so on. From riddles, as Northrop Frye has suggested, more sophisticated forms of literature have emanated, including mystery novels, in which the point is to hold readers in suspense as long as possible, forcing them to guess the ending. Some of the

* Published originally in the Soviet Union in 1925.

folk rhymes possess magical qualities. The chants accompanying rope-skipping, for instance, are in the nature of charms—if the child can get through the ritual of skipping without stumbling and so breaking the magical circle created by the swinging rope, then maybe he/she can get through life, or at least that phase of life with which the chant is concerned.

Most of the emphasis in this section is on folk rhymes (practice games) and on toy stories (symbolic games). Another form of symbolic game can be seen in stories dealing with imaginative play, seen here in the selections by Maurice Sendak and José Maria Sanchez-Silva. When children play-act or create imaginary companions, as in these stories, game-playing is being used in one of its most satisfying ways—to stretch the imagination and encourage the inner life of the child.

The poetry selections are concerned both with toys and games—sailing boats, hopscotch, hide-and-seek, kite flying, swinging, riding stick horses, and various pretend games. Two poems included here—"The Land of Story Books" and "The Land of Counterpane" from Robert Louis Stevenson's *A Child's Garden of Verses*—have shown many sick children that being confined to a bed need not confine their imaginations. Stevenson was himself a sickly little boy whose life was made endurable by his beloved nurse, Alison Cunningham, to whom *A Child's Garden of Verses* was dedicated.

Insight into some of the toys and games that children play is shed by the final essays on Winnie-the-Pooh, Raggedy Ann, and on puppets.

Folk Rhymes

Riddles

Humpty Dumpty sat on a wall,
Humpty Dumpty had a great fall;
Threescore men and threescore more
Cannot place Humpty Dumpty as he
was before.

(An egg)

As round as an apple, as deep as a cup,
And all the king's horses can't fill it up.

(A well)

Two brothers we are,
Great burdens we bear,
All day we are bitterly pressed,
Yet this I must say—
We are full all the day,
And empty when we go to rest.

(A pair of shoes)

Adam and Eve and Pinch-me
Went down to the river to bathe.
Adam and Eve got drowned,
Which one of the three was saved?

(Pinch me)

Old Mother Twitchett has but one eye,
And a long tail which she can let fly,
And every time she goes over a gap,
She leaves a bit of her tail in a trap.

(A needle and thread)

A milk-white bird
Floats down through the air.
And never a tree
But he lights there.

(Snow)

I have a little sister. They call her
Peep-peep;
She wades the waters deep, deep, deep;
She climbs the mountains high, high,
high;
Poor little creature, she has but one eye.

(A star)

Tongue Twisters and Catches

Peter Piper picked a peck of pickled
pepper;
A peck of pickled pepper Peter Piper
picked;
If Peter Piper picked a peck of pickled
pepper,
Where's the peck of pickled pepper
Peter Piper picked?

Swan swam over the sea,
Swim, swan, swim!
Swan swam back again,
Well swum, swan!

Moses supposes his toeses are roses,
But Moses supposes erroneously;
For nobody's toeses are posies of roses
As Moses supposes his toeses to be.

She sells sea shells by the seashore.

1. I am a gold lock.
2. I am a gold key.
1. I am a silver lock.
2. I am a silver key.
1. I am a brass lock.
2. I am a brass key.
1. I am a lead lock.
2. I am a lead key.
1. I am a monk lock.
2. I am a monk key!

1. I one it.
2. I two it.
1. I three it.
2. I four it.
1. I five it.
2. I six it.
1. I seven it.
2. I eight it.
1. Oh, so you *ate* the old dead horse.

Counting-Out Rhymes

One, two, buckle my shoe;
Three, four, open the door;
Five, six, pick up sticks;
Seven, eight, lay them straight;
Nine, ten, a big fat hen;
Eleven, twelve, I hope you're well;
Thirteen, fourteen, draw the curtain;
Fifteen, sixteen, the maid's in the kitchen;
Seventeen, eighteen, she's in waiting;
Nineteen, twenty, my stomach's empty.
Please, Ma'am, to give me some dinner.

As I went up the apple-tree,
All the apples fell on me;
Bake a puddin', bake a pie,
Did you ever tell a lie?
Yes, I did, and many times.
O-U-T, out goes she
Right in the middle of the deep blue sea.

One potato, two potato,
Three potato, four;
Five potato, six potato,
Seven potato, MORE.

ALL TOGETHER*	1—2—3—and a zing zing zing
LEADER	Number one!
NO. 1	Who, me?
LEADER	Yes, you.
NO. 1	Couldn't be.
LEADER	Then who?
NO. 1	Number five!
NO. 5	Who, me?
LEADER	Yes, you.
NO. 5	Couldn't be.
LEADER	Then who?
NO. 5	Number nine!
NO. 9	Who, me?
LEADER	Yes, you.
NO. 9	Couldn't be.
LEADER	Then who?
NO. 9	Number two!
NO. 2	Who, me?
LEADER	Yes, you.
NO. 2	Couldn't be. [Etc.]

* From Harold Courlander, *Negro Folk Music U.S.A.* (New York: Columbia University Press, 1963).

Acting-Out Rhymes

Walking two fingers on the child's arm or leg, the storyteller acts out the spider's adventures.

Incey wincey spider, climbed the water spout,
Down came the rain and washed poor spider out.
Out came the sunshine, dried up all the rain;
Incey wincey spider, climbed the spout again.

Each of the child's toes is gently squeezed as the pigs are counted off. The last line is said in a high pitched voice to imitate the final pig's squeal and then, frequently, the storyteller tickles the child.

This little pig went to market,
This little pig stayed home,
This little pig had roast beef,
This little pig had none,
And this little pig cried, Wee-wee-wee
All the way home.

The sole of the child's foot is treated as the piece of dough on which the baker's activities are mimed.

Patty cake, patty cake,
Baker's man;

That I will master,
As fast as I can;
Prick it and prick it,
And mark it with a T,
And there will be enough
For Jackey and me.

Palms facing the body, the fingers are interlocked so that they too point toward the body. The palms are then brought together to hide the fingers; that's the church. The two index fingers are raised and touch at the tips to represent the steeple. Then, fingers still interlocked, the palms are opened facing upward and the fingers are revealed as people saying their prayers.

Here is the church, and here is the steeple;
Open the door and here are the people.
Here is the parson going upstairs,
And here he is a-saying his prayers.

The child is dandled on the storyteller's knee to the rhythm of a horse trotting.

Ride a cock-horse to Banbury Cross,
To see a fine lady upon a white horse;
Rings on her fingers and bells on her toes,
And she shall have music wherever she goes.

Jump-Rope Rhymes

Lady bird, lady bird, turn around,
Lady bird, lady bird, touch the ground.
Lady bird, lady bird, fly away home.
Lady bird, lady bird, you have gone.
Lady bird, lady bird, go upstairs,
Lady bird, lady bird, say your prayers.
Lady bird, lady bird, turn out the light.
Lady bird, lady bird, say Good night.
Teddy bear, teddy bear, point to the sky.
Teddy bear, teddy bear, show your glass eye.
Teddy bear, teddy bear, pull off your wig.
Teddy bear, teddy bear, dance a jig.

Down in the valley where the green grass grows,
There sat Susie as sweet as a rose.
She sang, she sang, she sang so sweet,
Along came Tommy and kissed her on the cheek.
How many kisses did she receive?
1—2—3—4—till you miss.

In most countries, any "spicy" words, such as salt, vinegar, mustard, *or* pepper, *are signals to turn the rope as rapidly as possible, as in "Mabel, Mabel." In some parts of the deep South,* hot peas *is the signal for fast turning. I've even heard a favorite French rhyme skipped in a Vietnamese orphanage: "O, the lettuce!/ When it grows up, we will eat it/ With oil and with . . . Vinegar!" At the word* vinegar, *thin little legs speeded up.*

Mabel, Mabel, set the table,
Don't forget the salt and PEPPER!

At the word PEPPER the "enders" turn the rope very fast until the skipper misses.

Old Man Daisy,
You're driving me crazy,
Up the ladder, down the ladder,
One, two, three.
Pepper, salt, vinegar.
H, O, T!

SKIP-ROPE RHYMES AS A REFLECTION OF AMERICAN CULTURE

Francelia Butler

The summer before the collapse of South Vietnam, I spent several weeks there collecting folk rhymes at schools and orphanages. One rhyme—sometimes skipped to—was particularly popular on playgrounds:

Let's go sightseeing in Long Thanh,*
Which has in all thirty-six streets:
Basket Street, Silver Street, Hemp-Cloth Street,
Sail Street, Tin Street, Slipper Street, Tray Street,
Horse's Tail Street, Pipe Street, Shoe Street,
Eel Pot Street, Long Bamboo Hurdle Street, Rattan Street,
Musical Instrument Street. . . .

We enjoy what we've seen.
The streets of Long Thanh are prettiest of all.
They stretch in a mesh, like a chessboard.
Back home we miss them greatly,
So we praise them warmly here.

Translated by Doan Quoc Sy, Saigon

Curiously, neither this rhyme nor other foreign folk rhymes used for skipping have the wild juxtapositions often found in American rhymes. Oriental rhymes furnish the clearest contrast. Japanese rhymes, for instance, tend to be more placid, as I discovered in Tokyo, where I arranged to see an exhibition of children skipping rope on the playground of a large school, the elementary division of Toho-Gakuen College. They read and skipped to such old rhymes as this:

One crow sings caw caw caw
Two chickens sing cocicoco cocicoco
Fishes are swimming
Grandfather with white hair.

(On this occasion, incidentally, I was surprised to see that the children each held a bit of paper and were reading the chants. When I asked what the trouble was, the teachers were astonished: "Surely," they said, "in an advanced country like yours, children no longer employ anything so quaint as skip-rope chants!" When I told them that indeed children still chanted, and on almost every playground, they seemed to doubt me. I realized that in trying to imitate Western culture, the Japanese had moved so far, at least in this respect, that they were not imitating us at all.)

In the People's Republic of China, the rhymes often appear to be tests of skill, like this one:

Little ball
Banana swim
Cauliflowers

Given at the Convention on Children's Literature, Piedmont College, Demorest, Georgia, June, 1975.

*Long Thanh is a short reference to Thang Long Thanh, as Hanoi was called during the Ly Dynasty (1009–1225).

one by one
one five six
one five seven
one eight one nine
twenty seven
two five six
two five seven
two eight two nine
thirty seven. . . .

In Malaysia, a number of children's folk rhymes appeared to be in the nature of charms, to help toward self-realization. This one, which I picked up in Penang, is for swinging (skipping is generally done without chants there):

If I swing high
And touch the rooftop
Before my teeth grow
I can read a book.

If I swing high
And touch the treetop
I can buy a new dress
From a Chinese shop.

To be able to buy a dress from the shop of the moneyed people, the Chinese, means, "Someday, with the help of this magic ritual, I will have money."

Proper boys and girls in Thailand can go out to play together by making the excuse that they want to do a kind of skip-rope dance descended from the bamboo dance. A doubled rope is held at each end and shifted unexpectedly. The fun comes in anticipating the movements of the rope holders. One rhyme goes:

Beautiful girls
Beautiful hearts of girls
We dare not go to sleep.
Girls command the sounds of birds
With us, making music
In a land of happiness and gaiety.

The significance of this skip-rope dance lies in the romantic innuendos of the rhyme and in the skill of the performers. Some of this romantic meaning is also found in a rhyme from Laos:

Scattered and gleaming on the hillside
Like the full moon
Are sampots perfect and innumerable,
Sampots of every color,
Some are even yellow.

(Sampots are the squares of cloth men knot about their waists. Yellow is a royal color. The sampots have been washed and spread out on the hillside to dry.) Here is another rhyme from Laos:

Adorned with egrets and with
mother-of-pearl inlaid
The palaces shine like golden stars,
Roofed in with massive gold instead of
thatch.
The queen is named Canda
Graceful as any drawing.

By way of contrast to these gentle rhymes, here is a typical American skip-rope chant, skipped by a disgruntled baby-sitter fearful of future assignments:

Fudge, fudge
Call the judge
Mama's got a baby.
Ain't no girl
Ain't no boy
Just a plain old baby.
Wrap it up in tissue paper
Put it on the elevator
First floor—miss!
Second floor—miss!
Third floor—kick it out the door!

Here we have a statement of the situation, a suggestion of conflict, a carrying or motivating force as the elevator rises, and a violent conclusion. At least some of these elements are found in many American rhymes, which tend to be minidramas:*

Johnnie over the ocean
Johnnie over the sea
Johnnie broke a milk bottle
And blamed it on me.

* The best general collection of American rhymes is *Jump-Rope Rhymes: A Dictionary,* ed. Roger D. Abrahams (Austin and London: published for the American Folklore Society by the University of Texas Press, 1969).

I told Ma
Ma told Pa
Johnnie got a lickin'
Ha! Ha! Ha!

So much for sibling rivalry. Then there are rhymes dealing with unpleasant teachers.

The Devil flew from North to South
With Miss Hooker in his mouth
And when he found she was a fool
He dropped her on the Cherrydale School.

The adult world is satirized:

My mama and your mama lives across the way
Every night they have a fight and this is what they say:
Acca-bacca-soda-cracker
Acca-bacca-boo
Acca-bacca-soda-cracker
Out goes you!

External dangers are dramatized in this old Scottish rhyme turned into something typically American:

Last night, the night before,
A lemon and a pickle come aknockin' at my door.
When I come down to let them in,
They hit me over the head with a roller pin

Authority figures are dealt with:

I won't go to Macy's any more, more, more,
There's a big fat policeman at the door, door, door.
He took me by the collar and made me pay a dollar,
So I won't go to Macy's any more, more, more.

Not infrequently, children go through a stage of petty thievery. Some of them get caught. Similar rhymes have to do with Wanamaker's and Marshall Field's.

The hypocrisy of political figures is considered in this rhyme:

George Washington never told a lie
But he ran around the corner
And stole a cherry pie!

Political chants often contain a note of protest, and protest frequently tends to be bawdy—something that has been so ever since the English rhyme of the Renaissance period, "I had a little nut tree." This skip-rope rhyme is from Harlem:

Abraham Lincoln was a good old soul
He washed his face in the toilet bowl
He jumped out the window with his d— in his hand,
And said, " 'Scuse me, ladies, I'm Superman!"

Children vigorously take up characters in movies, comics, the news, and history and create small "happenings" about them:

Marilyn Monroe
Broke her toe
Riding on a buffalo
On the way to Mexico.

Children understand that something has happened to the great sex symbol, Marilyn Monroe, and equate it with an almost archaic animal: the buffalo.

Sir Charles Chaplin's virility is suggested in this rhyme:

Charlie Chaplin
Went to France
To teach the girlies
How to dance.
Heel, toe, around we go!
Heel, toe, around we go!
And keep the kettle boiling!

Something bad happens to Hitler:

In 1944
Hitler went to war
He lost his socks in the middle of the docks
In 1944.

The prints from the British Museum that illustrate Leslie Daiken's *Children's Games throughout the Year* (London, 1949) suggest that adults skipped rope in early periods of history. But, though scraps of skip-rope rhymes, such as "All in together, girls/No mind the weather, girls" may have classical sources, no skip-rope rhyme has been tracked earlier than the seventeenth century. Under "Ludi," the *Dictionnaire des Antiquités Grecques et Romaines* prints an ancient statue of a Greek maiden swinging a rope of vines over her head. There is no evidence that she chanted as she skipped, and there are countries in Europe and Asia now where children skip without chanting.

The first rhymes chanted by American skippers were lyrical verses descending from English sources. Since children are traditionalists, these rhymes, passed from child to child, still linger alongside their rough, native counterparts. Here is one of the English rhymes with an interesting history:

On the hilltop stands a lady
  Who she is I do not know
All she wears is gold and silver
  And she needs a nice young man.

I first heard this rhyme in 1945 on the playground of a black school at Ball's Hill, Virginia, near Falls Church, where it was preserved by the black culture. The rhyme is from an old English ballad, "O no John," of which there are many versions in Cecil Sharp's collection, *English Folk-Songs from the Southern Appalachians* (1953). Originally, it had to do with seduction involving adultery. The late Arthur Kyle Davis, an eminent folklorist at the University of Virginia, discovered that the colonial patriot John Randolph of Roanoke knew some of the lines in his early childhood, and in 1822, in middle life, Randolph wrote to a friend asking for the rest. It had been taught him, he recalled, "by a mulatto servant girl." The rhyme can be found in New England, the Midwest, and the far West, as well as in the South.

This rhyme, also of English origin, was skipped in the early nineteenth century in Schodack (now Castleton-on-Hudson), New York:

Intry mintry cutry corn,
Appleseed and apple thorn,
Wire, briar, limber lock,
Twelve geese in a flock,
One flew east and one flew west,
And one flew over the cuckoo's nest.

One begins to see the American touch in this mid-nineteenth-century rhyme:

I love my papa, that I do,
And mama says she loves him, too,
But papa says he fears some day
With some bad man I'll run away.

Toward the end of the century, we get this one, recorded by William Wells Newell (*Games and Songs of American Children* [New York, 1883]):

By the old Levitical law
  I marry this Indian to this squaw.
By the point of my jack-knife,
  I pronounce you man and wife.

A variant of this rhyme also was recorded in Virginia. Already we see in it the violence and drama that characterize so many American rhymes. Two children jump together under the rope in a ritualistic marriage. As sexual beings in the inhibited Victorian period, they can ease their consciences by pretending they were forced into marriage at knife-point. Newell himself, collecting in the nineteenth century, suggests a more pious interpretation that seems irrelevant to the rhyme's obvious meaning. Newell explains it as meaning, "If I break this vow, may I perish by the edge of the sword."

Published in 1801, Joseph Strutt's book *Sports and Pastimes of the People of England* indicates that boys were once the jumpers. As everyone knows, rope-skipping now is mainly the province of girls. Various conjectures have been made as to why this is so, the most frequent one being that it is a gentle sport which could be indulged in by young nineteenth-century ladies without even showing the ankles. With diminishing distinctions in sex roles, however, boys are skipping rope again, as scenes on many playgrounds now reveal. In any event, the unique character of American rhymes, their bold confrontations with problems, is a late nineteenth- and early twentieth-century phenomenon. My conjecture is that the nature of the rhymes attests to the American conviction that problems can be solved if one goes about it in a forthright way:

Nine o'clock is striking
Mother, may I go out?
All the boys are calling
Just to take me out.

One will give me coffee
One will give me cake
One will give me fifty cents
To kiss him at the gate.

I don't want your coffee
I don't want your cake.
I don't want your fifty cents
To kiss you at the gate.

I'd rather wash the dishes
I'd rather scrub the floor
I'd rather kiss the iceman
Behind the ice box door.

Of course, if one fails to perform the skipping ritual properly, it can be fatal:

Little Miss Pink
Dressed in blue
Died last night
At quarter past two.
Before she died
She told me this:
When I jump rope
I always miss.

With school integration, rhymes of black and white students are now traded cross-culturally. Black rhymes in America are characterized by their vigor and drama. They often have a choral quality:

O Donna died. O how she die?
Died like this! [gesture] O, she died like this!
Where she live? O, where she live?
Down aroun' the corner in Tennessee.
Hands up! Too chay too chay too chay too
Hands down! Too chay too chay too chay too.

A rhyme, autobiographical in nature, from Southeast Washington, D.C., is dramatic and has black rhythm:

Went downtown to alligator roun'
Sat on the fence and the fence broke down.
Alligator caught me by the seat of the pants
And made me do the hoola dance.

A good cross section of black rhymes may be found in Jean Alexander's *Jump, Clap, and Sing* (1974), a publication of the Children's Area Festival of American Folklife, Washington, D.C.

The rhymes that "catch on" in the States from outside must fit into this dramatic cultural pattern. One rhyme has been given to me by students from the Virgin Islands, Jamaica, and most recently by a student, Donna Andrade, who collected it in the schoolyard of Harding High School, Bridgeport, Connecticut, where, she was told, it had been around since the 1950s. The rhyme comes from black students there. Since it depends for its effect on the double meanings of words in the end rhyme, it recalls similar use of word ambiguities in the Renaissance, such as those employed by Matthew Merrygreek in the mid–sixteenth-century play *Ralph Roister Doister.* The rhyme goes this way:

Miss Lucy had a steamboat, the steamboat had a bell,
Miss Lucy went to heaven, the steamboat went to hel-
Lo operator, give me number nine
If you disconnect me,

I'll kick up your behin-
The refrigerator there's a piece of
glass,
Susie fell upon it and broke her little
as-
Me no more questions, tell me no
more lies.
Boys are in the bathroom, zipping
down flies
Are in the country, bees are in the
park,
Boys and girls are kissing in the dark,
dark, dark!

There seems to be a trend toward making rhymes more openly sexual. When I used to skip the following rhyme in the 1920s, it went:

Cinderella
Dressed in yella
Went downstairs
To meet her fella.

Now on my block I hear it this way:

Cinderella
Dressed in yella
Went downstairs
To kiss her fella.
She made a mistake
And kissed a snake!

Many extremely bawdy skip-rope rhymes can be found, too. Most of them protest sexual inhibitions and seem to stem from the feeling that adults hypocritically deny their sexual existence and demand a standard of sexual conduct from youth that they do not maintain themselves.

In literary accounts of skipping, the magical quality of the ritual has been recognized by Frances Hodgson Burnett in *The Secret Garden* and by the American novelist Ellen Glasgow in her short story "The Shadowy Third." But literary skip-rope rhymes do not show the cultural differences suggested by their oral counterparts. Professor David Sonstroem found a skip-rope rhyme by Alfred Lord Tennyson printed in *Poems in Two Volumes* in 1842, but omitted in all editions after 1850. It depicts a girl of marriageable age skipping rope—and indeed, as indicated earlier, adults once skipped. The rhyme is:

Sure never yet was antelope
Could skip so lightly by.
Stand off, or else my skipping-rope
Will hit you in the eye.
How lightly whirls the skipping-rope!
How fairy-like you fly!
Go, get you gone, you muse and
mope—
I hate that silly sigh.
Nay, dearest, teach me how to hope,
Or tell me how to die.
There, take it, take my skipping-rope,
And hang yourself thereby.

Tennyson's ditty does not have the poignant impact of the following poem by Elias Lieberman, published in *The Saturday Evening Post,* August 23, 1958:

There is a chant that goes with
skipping rope,
A nonsense rhyme as playful as a
breeze
That shakes the rain from trees, a
lilting hope
Designed of fantasies.

All in together
The sheep's in the meadow.

These jingles of her skipping ritual
Are runes to ward off sorrow. They
must hold
When fallen leaves will mold against a
wall
And winter winds grow bold.

The cow's in the clover
All jump over.

The slack rope swings
And through its looping arc
A child who sings
Has leaped beyond the dark.

American commercial firms have

sometimes employed skip-rope rhymes in advertisements. For instance, a pink pig, already conscious of a weight problem, skips rope in *Rexall Nursery Rhymes,* distributed by that drug company in 1905. Entitled "Teaching a Pig How to Skip Rope," the rhyme is:

"This Pig's too stout," said Captain R.
"Her fat is quite distressing;
"But I do hope a Skipping Rope
"To her will be a blessing.

" 'Twill help to shape her shaking
sides
"And make her light and airy—
"An hour a day of such smart play—
"She'll dance like any fairy."

If the maxim is true that the essence of charm is being unconscious of having it, then perhaps it is a mistake to point out that we have a unique culture in our American skipping rhymes. But even up to the present time, Americans have had to undergo so many criticisms for our lack of culture that perhaps a little awareness of our national aptitudes will buoy our spirits. Once when I was speaking on skip-rope rhymes at a folklore convention in Nashville, Tennessee, some young fellow came up to me and drawled, "I declare, I didn't know we had a culture, but I'm mighty glad to hear it." There are other Americans like him who want to think of their country as something more than an amorphous cultural blob somewhere between Europe and the Orient.

Alexis de Tocqueville, who in his *Democracy in America* (1835) showed amazing prophetic perception of the American cultural temper, prophesied that literature in America would evolve to satisfy those who "require strong and rapid emotions, startling passages, truths or errors brilliant enough to rouse them up and plunge them at once, as if by violence, into the midst of the subject." He was a keen observer, interested in the nature of things, who traveled extensively in the United States, sleeping in the huts of pioneers. Possibly he heard some American skip-rope rhymes like "I marry this Indian to this squaw by the point of my jack-knife."

Folk Play

PUNCH AND JUDY

The popular theater of the Italian commedia dell' arte *with its stock characters, Italian puppets with their hero, Pulcinella, and the English clown tradition—all of these were needed to bring "Punchinello" and his wife to the stage of the English puppet theater at the close of the seventeenth century. Punch's distinctive physical attributes—his hunchback and large belly, as well as his hooked nose and chin—developed gradually during the eighteenth century, but his impudence and vitality seem to have appeared almost at once.*

First published in 1854, this text was frequently pirated in children's books during the 1860s and 1870s. In many ways this is the

Engraving by George Cruikshank from *Punch and Judy,* 1828. Photograph of original engraving from George Speaight Collection.

The text was originally published as *The Wonderful Drama of Punch and Judy* (1854) by Papernose Woodensconce Esq. (Robert Brough).

best script of the show ever written. Although it was published as a text for juvenile performers, it is racy and uses vocabulary of the street. Traditionally, the words of Punch and Judy shows are pronounced indistinctly in a garbled form to add to the humor, and also because it is the action rather than the words that carries the show.

Music. The spirited PROPRIETOR *plays* "Pop goes the weasel" *or any other popular melody, as much out of tune as possible. Curtain rises.*

PUNCH *(below):* Root-to-to-to-to-too-o-o-it!

PROPRIETOR: Now, Mister Punch, I 'ope you're ready.

PUNCH: Shan't be a minute; I'm only putting on my boots.

PROP *(perfectly satisfied with the explanation):* Werry good, sir.

He plays with increased vigour.

PUNCH *(pops up):* Root-to-to-to-to-it!

PROP: Well, Mister Punch, 'ow de do?

PUNCH: How de do?

PROP *(affably):* I am pooty well, Mister Punch, I thank you.

PUNCH: Play us up a bit of a dance.

PROP: Cert'ny, Mister Punch.

Music. PUNCH *dances.*

PUNCH: Stop! Did you ever see my wife?

PROP *(with dignity):* I never know'd as 'ow you was married, Mister Punch.

PUNCH: Oh! I've got such a splendid wife! *(Calling below.)* Judy!—Judy, my darling!—Judy, my duck of several diamonds!

Enter JUDY.

PUNCH *(admiring his Wife):* Ain't she a beauty? There's a nose! Give us a kiss. *(They embrace fondly.)* Now play up.

They dance. At the conclusion, PUNCH *hits his* WIFE *on the head with his stick.*

PROP *(severely):* Mister Punch, that's very wrong.

PUNCH: Haven't I a right to do what I like with my own?

JUDY *(taking stick from him):* In course he has. *(Hitting* PUNCH.) Take that!

PUNCH: Oh!

JUDY *(hitting him again):* Oh!

PUNCH: Oh!

JUDY *(hitting him again):* Oh!

PUNCH *(taking stick from her, and knocking her out of sight):* Oh! That was to request her to step downstairs to dress the babby. Such a beautiful babby, you've no idea. I'll go and fetch him.

PUNCH *sinks and rises with* BABY *in his arms.*

PUNCH *(sings):* "Hush-a-bye, baby,
And sleep while you can;
If you live till you're older,
You'll grow up a man."

Did you ever see such a beautiful child? and so good?

THE CHILD *(louder):* Mam-ma-a-a-a!

PUNCH *(thumping him with stick):* Go to sleep, you brat! *(Resumes his song.)* "Hush-a-bye, baby,"—

THE CHILD *(louder):* Mam-ma-a-a-a!

PUNCH *(hitting harder):* Go to sleep!

THE CHILD *(yells):* Ya-a-a-ah-ah!

PUNCH *(hitting him):* Be quiet! Bless him, he's got his father's nose! *(The* CHILD *seizes* PUNCH *by the nose.)* Murder! Let go! There, go to your mother, if you can't be good.

Throws CHILD *out of window.*

PUNCH *(sings, drumming with his legs on the front of the stage):*

"She's all my fancy painted her,
She's lovely, she's divine!"

Enter JUDY *(with maternal anxiety depicted on her countenance).*

JUDY: Where's the boy?
PUNCH: The boy?
JUDY: Yes.
PUNCH: What! didn't you catch him?
JUDY: Catch him?
PUNCH: Yes; I threw him out of window. I thought you might be passing.
JUDY: Oh! my poor child! Oh! my poor child!
PUNCH: Why, he was as much mine as yours.
JUDY: But you shall pay for it; I'll tear your eyes out.
PUNCH: Root-to-to-to-to-oo-it!

Kills her at a blow.

PROP: Mr. Punch, you 'ave committed a barbarous and cruel murder, and you must hanswer for it to the laws of your country.
THE BEADLE *(entering brandishing his staff of office):* Holloa! holloa! holloa! here I am!
PUNCH: Holloa! holloa! holloa! and so am I!

Hits BEADLE.

BEADLE: Do you see my staff, sir?
PUNCH: Do you feel mine?

Hits him again.

BEADLE *(beating time with his truncheon):* I am the Beadle, Churchwarden, Overseer, Street-keeper, Turncock, Stupendiary Magistrate, and Beadle of the parish!
PUNCH: Oh! you are the Beagle, Church-warming-pan, Street-sweeper, Turnip-top, Stupendiary, Magistrate, and Blackbeetle of the parish?
BEADLE: I am the Beadle.
PUNCH: And so am I.
BEADLE: You a Beadle?
PUNCH: Yes.
BEADLE: Where's your authority?
PUNCH: There it is!

Knocks him down.

THE BEADLE *(rising):* Mr. Punch, you are an ugly ill-bred fellow.
PUNCH: And so are you.
BEADLE: Take your nose out of my face, sir.
PUNCH: Take your face out of my nose, sir.
BEADLE: Pooh!
PUNCH: Pooh!

Hits him.

BEADLE *(appealing to the* PROPRIETOR*):* Young man, you are a witness that he has committed an aggravated assault on the majesty of the law.
PUNCH: Oh! he'd swear anything.
PROP *(in a reconciling tone):* Don't take no notice of what he says.
PUNCH: For he'd swear through a brick.
BEADLE: It's a conspiracy; I can see through it.
PROP: Through what?
PUNCH: Through a brick.
BEADLE: This mustn't go on, Mr. Punch; I am under the necessity of taking you up.
PUNCH: And I am under the necessity of knocking you down.

The BEADLE *falls a lifeless corpse.*

PUNCH *(in ecstasies):* Roo-to-to-to-to-it!

Enter a DISTINGUISHED FOREIGNER, *popping up under* PUNCH*'s nose.*

THE DISTINGUISHED FOREIGNER: Shallabala!

PUNCH *aims at and misses him. He disappears, and bobs up on the other side.*

THE ILLUSTRIOUS STRANGER: Shallabala!

PUNCH *makes another failure. The* INTERESTING ALIEN *bobs up in another direction.*

THE NATIVE OF OTHER LANDS: Shallabala!

PUNCH: Why don't you speak English?
THE CONTINENTAL PERSONAGE: Because I can't.
PUNCH: Oh!

He lays the MAN FROM ABROAD *dead at one blow.*

THE EXPIRING IMMIGRANT: Shallabala!

He dies.

PUNCH *(exultingly):* Root-to-to-to-to-it!

PUNCH exults over his successful crimes in a heartless manner, by singing a fragment of a popular melody, and drumming with his heels upon the front of the stage.
Mysterious music, announcing the appearance of the Gho-o-o-o-ost!!! who rises and places its unearthly hands upon the bodies of PUNCH'S victims in an awful and imposing manner. The bodies rise slowly.

PUNCH *(in the same hardened manner, as yet unconscious of the approaching terrors):*
"Rum ti tum ti iddity um.
Pop goes"—
THE GHOST: Boo-o-o-o-oh!
PUNCH *(frightened):* A-a-a-a-ah!

He kicks frantically, and is supposed to turn deadly pale.

GHOST: Boo-o-o-o-oh!!
PUNCH: A-a-a-a-ah!

He trembles like a leaf.

GHOST: Boo-o-o-o-oh!!!

PUNCH faints. The GHOST and bodies disappear. PUNCH, by spasmodic convulsions, expresses that the terrors of a guilty conscience, added to the excesses of an irregular course of life, have brought on an intermittent fever.

PUNCH *(feebly):* I'm very ill: fetch a Doctor.

The DOCTOR rises.

DOCTOR: Somebody called for a Doctor. Why, I declare it's my old friend Punch. What's the matter with him?
THE DOCTOR *(feeling the patient's pulse):* Fourteen—fifteen—nineteen —six. The man is not dead—almost, quite. Punch, *are* you dead?
PUNCH *(starting up and hitting him):* Yes.

He relapses into insensibility.

DOCTOR: Mr. Punch, there's no believing you; I don't believe you are dead.
PUNCH *(hitting him as before):* Yes, I am.
DOCTOR: I tell you what, Punch, I must go and fetch you some physic.

Exit.

PUNCH *(rising):* A pretty Doctor, to come without physic.

Re-enter DOCTOR, with cudgel. PUNCH relapses as before.

DOCTOR: Now, Punch, *are* you dead? No reply! *(Thrashing him.)* Physic! physic! physic!

The mixture as before is repeated each time.

PUNCH *(reviving under the influence of the dose):* What sort of physic do you call that, Doctor?
DOCTOR: Stick-liquorice! stick-liquorice! stick-liquorice!

The mixture as before, repeated each time.

PUNCH: Stop, Doctor! give me the bottle in my own hands. *(Taking stick from him, and thrashing his with it.)* Physic! Physic! physic! physic! *(DOCTOR yells.)* What a simple Doctor! doesn't like his own physic! Stick-liquorice! stick-liquorice! stick-liquorice!
DOCTOR *(calling out):* Punch, pay me my fee, and let me go.
PUNCH: What's your fee?
DOCTOR: A guinea.
PUNCH: Give me change out of a fourpenny-bit.
DOCTOR: But a guinea's twenty-one shillings.
PUNCH: Stop! let me feel for my purse. *(Takes up stick and hits DOCTOR.)* One! two! three! four! Stop! that was a bad

one; I'll give you another. Four! five! six!

Hits DOCTOR twenty-one times. Then looks at him. He is motionless.

PUNCH: Root-to-to-to-to-it! Settled!

PUNCH *(sings):* "I dreamt that I dwelt in marble halls,
With vassals and serfs by my side;
And of all who assembled within those proud walls,
That I was the joy and the"—

JOEY THE CLOWN rises, and takes up the body of the DOCTOR, whose head he bobs in PUNCH'S face.

JOEY: Bob!

PUNCH *(rubbing his nose):* Who said "bob"?

JOEY *(knocking DOCTOR into his face again):* Bob! bob! bob!

PUNCH: Bob! bob! bob! *(Knocks DOCTOR out of sight, and sees JOEY.)* Ah, Joey! was that you?

JOEY: Yes; how's your mother

PUNCH: Well, don't do it again.

JOEY: Why not?

PUNCH: Because I'm nervous! Come and feel how my hand shakes. *(JOEY approaches. PUNCH aims a blow at him, which he dodges.)* Come a little nearer! I won't hurt you.

JOEY *(to PROPRIETOR):* Do you think he will, Mister?

PROP: Well, Joey, I shouldn't think as 'ow he would, if so be as he calls hisself a gentleman.

JOEY: I'll try him.

JOEY, assured of the friendly intentions of PUNCH, approaches him. PUNCH aims a vigorous blow at him, which he again avoids, by dodging to the other side.

PUNCH: There! it didn't hurt, did it?

JOEY: No.

PUNCH *(aims again. JOEY avoids blow as before):* Nor that?

JOEY: No.

PUNCH *(as before):* Nor that?

JOEY: Not a bit.

PUNCH: Then what are you afraid of? Come and shake hands.

JOEY *(to PROPRIETOR):* Do you think I'm safe, Mister?

PROP: Cert'ny Joey; Mr. Punch 'as behaved hisself like a man of his word.

JOEY approaches PUNCH to shake hands. PUNCH aims at him. JOEY avoids blow as before.

PUNCH: Joey, you're a coward.

JOEY: Don't call names.

PUNCH: Then fight fair.

JOEY: Come on.

Music, "Drops brandy". They fight, JOEY avoiding all PUNCH's blows.

PUNCH *(aiming a blow at JOEY on the right side of the stage):* There!

JOEY *(appearing on the left):* No! here!

PUNCH: Oh, very good. There!

Misses again.

JOEY *(popping up his head in front, under the curtains):* Where?

PUNCH *(aims at him):* There!

Misses, and looks over.

JOEY *(putting his head outside curtains, on the right):* Mr. Punch, that was a foul blow.

PUNCH: Then here's a fair one!

Aims again. JOEY disappears. PUNCH looks round the curtains, watching for him.

JOEY *(putting his head out on the other side):* Now, Mr. Punch, I'm ready.

PUNCH: And I'm willing.

Turns quickly round, and hits at him again. JOEY disappears as before. Fight continues, JOEY always vanishing when PUNCH aims a blow, and appearing in an opposite direction. At last PUNCH lays down his stick, and peeps cautiously round the curtains to watch for JOEY.

PUNCH: I've got him now!

JOEY *(rising behind him, and seizing stick):* And how do you like him?

Larrups PUNCH.

PUNCH: Murder! thieves! Toby, come and help your master!

TOBY barks below. JOEY disappears.
TOBY rises, barking. PUNCH embraces him.

PUNCH: There's a beautiful dog! I knew he'd come to help his master; he's so fond of me. Poor little fellow! Toby, ain't you fond of your master?

TOBY snaps.

PUNCH: Oh, my nose!
PROP: Mr. Punch, you don't conciliate the hanimal properly; you should promise him something nice for supper.
PUNCH: Toby, you shall have a pail of water and a broomstick for supper. *(TOBY snaps again.)* I'll knock your brains out.
PROP: Don't go to 'urt the dog, Mr. Punch.
PUNCH: I will.
PROP: Don't!
PUNCH: I'll knock his brains out, and cut his throat!
PROP: How? with your stick?
PUNCH: I will! So here goes. One! two! *(JONES, a respectable tradesman, TOBY's former master, rises, and receives the blow intended for Toby on his head.)* Three!
JONES: Murder!
JONES *(rubbing his head, to PUNCH):* I shall make you pay for my head, sir!
PUNCH: And I shall make you pay for my stick, sir!
JONES: I haven't broken your stick.
PUNCH: And I haven't broken your head.
JONES: You have, sir!
PUNCH: Then it was cracked before.
JONES *(seeing TOBY):* Why, that's my dog Toby! Toby, old friend, how are you?
TOBY: Bow, wow, wow!
PUNCH: He isn't your dog.
JONES: He is!
PUNCH: He isn't!
JONES: He is! A fortnight ago I lost him.
PUNCH: And a fortnight ago I found him.
JONES: We'll see if the dog belongs to you, Mr. Punch. You shall go up to him, and say, "Toby, poor little fellow, how are you?"
PUNCH: Oh! I'm to go up to him, and say, "Toby, poor little fellow, how are you?"
JONES: Yes.
PUNCH: Very good.
PUNCH *(to JONES):* We'll soon see. *(Goes up to TOBY.)* "Toby, poor little fellow, how are you?"

TOBY snaps at PUNCH's nose.

JONES: There! you see!
PUNCH: What?
JONES: That shows the dog's mine.
PUNCH: No; it shows he's mine.
JONES: Then if he's yours, why does he bite you?
PUNCH: Because he likes me.
JONES: Pooh! nonsense! We'll soon settle which of us the dog belongs to, Mr. Punch. We'll fight for him. I'll have the dog to back me up. Toby, I'm going to fight for your liberty. If Punch knocks me down, you pick me up; if Punch wollops me, you wollop him.
PUNCH: But I'm not going to fight three or four of you.
JONES: The dog is only going to back me up.
PUNCH: Then somebody must back me up. *(To PROPRIETOR.)* Will you back me up, sir?
PROP *(always willing to oblige):* Cert'ny, Mr. Punch.

They take places for a fight.

PROP: Now, you don't begin till I say "time." *(PUNCH knocks JONES down.)* Mr. Punch, that wasn't fair.
PUNCH: Why, you said "time."
PROP: I didn't.
PUNCH: What did you say, then?
PROP: I said, "You don't begin till I say 'time.' "
PUNCH: There! you said it again.

Knocks JONES down again.

JONES: Toby, I'm down! back me up.

TOBY flies at PUNCH.

TOBY: G-r-r-r-r-r!

Bites PUNCH.

PUNCH: It isn't fair; he didn't say "time."
JONES: At him again, Toby! Good dog!
TOBY: G-r-r-r-row-wow!

Bites again.

PUNCH: Murder! I say, sir, please to call him off!
PROP: Mr. Punch, you must wait till I say "time."

TOBY attacks PUNCH furiously, defending his former MASTER.

JONES: Perhaps, Mr. Punch, you'll own he's my dog now?
PUNCH: No, I won't.
JONES: Then anything to please you; I'll tell you what we'll do.
PUNCH: What?
JONES: We'll toss up for him.
PUNCH: Very well.
JONES: You cry.

Tosses.

PUNCH: Head!

JONES: Tail! It's a tail. Come along, Toby; you're mine.
PUNCH: He isn't! he's mine.
JONES: I cried tail.
PUNCH: Then take his tail! I cried head; and you shan't have that!
JONES: I'll have my half.
PUNCH: And I'll have mine.

They pull TOBY between them. The struggle lasts for some time, during which TOBY sides with his former MASTER, by whom he is eventually carried off in triumph.

PUNCH *(calling after them):* I wouldn't have him at a gift; he's got the distemper!

A lapse of time is supposed to have occurred. PUNCH is in prison, condemned to death for his numerous crimes.

PUNCH: Oh, dear! I'm in the coal-hole!
PROP: No, Mr. Punch; you are in prison!
PUNCH: What for?
PROP: For having broken the laws of your country.
PUNCH: Why, I never touched 'em.
PROP: At any rate, Mr. Punch, you will be hanged.
PUNCH: Hanged? Oh, dear! oh, dear!
PROP: Yes; and I hope it will be a lesson to you.
PUNCH: Oh, my poor wife and sixteen small children! all of 'em twins! and the oldest only two years and a half old! Br-r-r-r!

Weeps. The HANGMAN rises, and erects the gallows.

HANGMAN: Now, Punch, you are ordered for instant execution.
PUNCH: What's that?
HANGMAN: You are to be hanged by the neck till you are dead! dead! dead!
PUNCH: What! three or four times over?
HANGMAN: No. Place your head in the center of the rope there!
PUNCH *(wringing his hands):* Oh, dear! oh, dear!
HANGMAN: Come, Mr. Punch; Justice can't wait.
PUNCH: Stop a bit; I haven't made my will.
HANGMAN: A good thought. We can't think of letting a man die till he's made his will.
PUNCH: Can't you?
HANGMAN: Certainly not.
PUNCH: Then I won't make mine at all.
HANGMAN: That won't do, Punch. Come, put your head in there.
PUNCH *(putting his head under the noose):* There?
HANGMAN: No; higher up!
PUNCH *(putting his head over):* There?
HANGMAN: No; lower down!
PUNCH: There?
HANGMAN: No, you blockhead; higher!
PUNCH: Well, I never was hanged before; and I don't know how to do it.
HANGMAN: Oh! as you never were hanged before, it's but right I should show you the way. Now, Mr. Punch,

observe me. In the first place, I put my head in the noose—so!

Puts his head in the noose. PUNCH *watches attentively.*

HANGMAN *(with his head in the noose):* Now, Mr. Punch, you see my head?
PUNCH: Yes.
HANGMAN: Well, when I've got your head in, I pull the end of the rope.
PUNCH *(pulling rope a little):* So?
HANGMAN: Yes, only tighter.
PUNCH *(pulling a little more):* So?
HANGMAN: Tighter than that.
PUNCH: Very good; I think I know now.
HANGMAN: Then turn round and bid your friends farewell; and I'll take my head out, and you put yours in.
PUNCH: Stop a minute. *(Pulls the rope tightly.)* Oee! oee! oee! I understand all about it. Now, oee! oee! oee! *(Pulls the rope, and hangs the* HANGMAN.) Here's a man tumbled into a ditch, and hung himself up to dry.

Swings HANGMAN *backwards and forwards.*

PUNCH *(swinging the* HANGMAN*'s rope):* Oee! oee! oee!

A HORRID DREADFUL PERSONAGE *rises behind* PUNCH, *and taps him on the shoulder.*

THE HORRID DREADFUL PERSONAGE: You're come for.
PUNCH *(alarmed):* Who are you?
THE HORRID DREADFUL PERSONAGE *(in a terrible voice):* Bogy!
PUNCH: Oh, dear! what do you want?
BOGY: To carry you off to the land of Bobetty-Shooty, where you will be condemned to the punishment of shaving the monkeys.
PUNCH: Stop! who were you to ask for?
BOGY: Who? why, Punch, the man who was to be hanged.
PUNCH *(pointing to* HANGMAN*):* Then there he is!
BOGY: Oh! is that him? Thank you. Good night!

Carries off HANGMAN.

PUNCH *(knocking them both as they go):* Good night!

Sings.

> Root-to-to-it! Punch is right,—
> All his enemies put to flight;
> Ladies and gentlemen all, good night
> To the freaks of Punch and Judy!

Exit.

THE PROPRIETOR: Ladies hand gentlemen, the drama is concluded; and has you like it, so I hopes you'll recommend it.

Bows gracefully.

Fantasy

THE VELVETEEN RABBIT OR HOW TOYS BECOME REAL

Margery Williams Bianco

The idea that toys can come to life is a frequent theme in children's stories. In some of these stories the toys or dolls have a life seemingly independent of the children to whom they belong, but in others the idea is advanced that toys come to life only if they are loved enough. The Velveteen Rabbit, *stressing the importance of children developing affectionate feelings for their toys, is a gentle and sensitive rendering of this theme.*

Although the sentimentality of this book is distasteful to many adults, one must bear in mind that adults have long been divorced from the simple, creative play-world of stuffed animals and blocks. Roland Barthes, the distinguished French literary critic, points out in an essay, "Toys," that cloth and wooden objects permit the child to creat a "life" (like that created for the Velveteen Rabbit). The child "creates life, not property," according to Barthes.

There was once a velveteen rabbit, and in the beginning he was really splendid. He was fat and bunchy, as a rabbit should be; his coat was spotted brown and white, he had real thread whiskers, and his ears were lined with pink sateen. On Christmas morning, when he sat wedged in the top of the Boy's stocking, with a sprig of holly between his paws, the effect was charming.

There were other things in the stocking, nuts and oranges and a toy engine, and chocolate almonds and a clockwork mouse, but the Rabbit was quite the best of all. For at least two hours the Boy loved him, and then Aunts and Uncles came to dinner, and there was a great rustling of

From Margery Williams Bianco, *The Velveteen Rabbit or How Toys Become Real* (Garden City, N.Y.: Doubleday, 1926), pp. 13–24.

tissue paper and unwrapping of parcels, and in the excitement of looking at all the new presents the Velveteen Rabbit was forgotten.

For a long time he lived in the toy cupboard or on the nursery floor, and no one thought very much about him. He was naturally shy, and being only made of velveteen, some of the more expensive toys quite snubbed him. The mechanical toys were very superior, and looked down upon every one else; they were full of modern ideas, and pretended they were real. The model boat, who had lived through two seasons and lost most of his paint, caught the tone from them and never missed an opportunity of referring to his rigging in technical terms. The Rabbit could not claim to be a model of anything, for he didn't know that real rabbits existed; he thought they were all stuffed with sawdust like himself, and he understood that sawdust was quite out-of-date and should never be mentioned in modern circles. Even Timothy, the jointed wooden lion, who was made by the disabled soldiers, and should have had broader views, put on airs and pretended he was connected with Government. Between them all the poor little Rabbit was made to feel himself very insignificant and commonplace, and the only person who was kind to him at all was the Skin Horse.

The Skin Horse had lived longer in the nursery than any of the others. He was so old that his brown coat was bald in patches and showed the seams underneath, and most of the hairs in his tail had been pulled out to string bead necklaces. He was wise, for he had seen a long succession of mechanical toys arrive to boast and swagger, and by-and-by break their mainsprings and pass away, and he knew that they were only toys, and would never turn into anything else. For nursery magic is very strange and wonderful, and only those playthings that are old and wise and experienced like the Skin Horse understand all about it.

"What is REAL?" asked the Rabbit one day, when they were lying side by side near the nursery fender, before Nana came to tidy the room. "Does it mean having things that buzz inside you and a stick-out handle?"

"Real isn't how you are made," said the Skin Horse. "It's a thing that happens to you. When a child loves you for a long, long time, not just to play with, but REALLY loves you, then you become Real."

"Does it hurt?" asked the Rabbit.

"Sometimes," said the Skin Horse, for he was always truthful. "When you are Real you don't mind being hurt."

"Does it happen all at once, like being wound up," he asked, "or bit by bit?"

"It doesn't happen all at once," said the Skin Horse. "You become. It takes a long time. That's why it doesn't often happen to people who break easily, or have sharp edges, or who have to be carefully kept. Generally, by the time you are Real, most of your hair has been loved off, and your eyes drop out and you get loose in the joints and very shabby. But these things don't matter at all, because once you are Real you can't be ugly, except to people who don't understand."

"I suppose *you* are Real?" said the Rabbit. And then he wished he had not said it, for he thought the Skin Horse might be sensitive. But the Skin Horse only smiled.

"The Boy's Uncle made me Real," he said. "That was a great many years ago; but once you are Real you can't become unreal again. It lasts for always."

The Rabbit sighed. He thought it would be a long time before this magic called Real happened to him. He longed to become Real, to know what it felt like; and yet the idea of growing shabby and losing his eyes and whiskers was rather sad. He wished that he could become it without these uncomfortable things happening to him.

There was a person called Nana who ruled the nursery. Sometimes she took no notice of the playthings lying about, and sometimes, for no reason whatever, she went swooping about like a great wind and hustled them away in cupboards. She called this "tidying up," and the playthings all hated it, especially the tin ones. The Rabbit didn't mind it so much, for wherever he was thrown he came down soft.

One evening, when the Boy was going to bed, he couldn't find the china dog that always slept with him. Nana was in a hurry, and it was too much trouble to hunt for china dogs at bedtime, so she simply looked about her, and seeing that the toy cupboard door stood open, she made a swoop.

"Here," she said, "take your old Bunny! He'll do to sleep with you!" And she dragged the Rabbit out by one ear, and put him into the Boy's arms.

That night, and for many nights after, the Velveteen Rabbit slept in the Boy's bed. At first he found it rather uncomfortable, for the Boy hugged him very tight, and sometimes he rolled over on him, and sometimes he pushed him so far under the pillow that the Rabbit could scarcely breathe. And he missed, too, those long moonlight hours in the nursery, when all the house was silent, and his talks with the Skin Horse. But very soon he grew to like it, for the Boy used to talk to him, and made nice tunnels for him under the bedclothes that he said were like the burrows the real rabbits lived in. And they had splendid games together, in whispers, when Nana had gone away to her supper and left the night-light burning on the mantelpiece. And when the Boy dropped off to sleep, the Rabbit would snuggle down close under his little warm chin and dream, with the Boy's hands clasped close round him all night long.

And so time went on, and the little Rabbit was very happy—so happy that he never noticed how his beautiful velveteen fur was getting shabbier and shabbier, and his tail coming unsewn, and all the pink rubbed off his nose where the Boy had kissed him.

Spring came, and they had long days in the garden, for wherever the Boy went the Rabbit went too. He had rides in the wheelbarrow, and picnics on the grass, and lovely fairy huts built for him under the raspberry canes behind the flower border. And once, when the Boy was called away suddenly to go out to tea, the Rabbit was left out on the lawn until long after dusk, and Nana had to come and look for him with the candle because the Boy couldn't go to sleep unless he was there. He was wet through with the dew and quite earthy from diving into the burrows the Boy had made for him in the flower bed, and Nana grumbled as she rubbed him off with a corner of her apron.

"You must have your old Bunny!" she said. "Fancy all that fuss for a toy!"

The Boy sat up in bed and stretched out his hands.

"Give me my Bunny!" he said. "You mustn't say that. He isn't a toy. He's REAL!"

When the little Rabbit heard that he was happy, for he knew that what the Skin Horse had said was true at last. The nursery magic had happened to him, and he was a toy no longer. He was Real. The Boy himself had said it.

That night he was almost too happy to sleep, and so much love stirred in his little sawdust heart that it almost burst. And into his boot-button eyes, that had long ago lost their polish, there came a look of wisdom and beauty, so that even Nana noticed it next morning when she picked him up, and said, "I declare if that old Bunny hasn't got quite a knowing expression!"

WINNIE-THE-POOH

A. A. Milne

In this immensely popular fantasy for children and grown-up children, the toy animals—Pooh Bear, Owl, Rabbit, Piglet, Eeyore the complaining donkey, Tigger, Kanga and Roo—are brought to life through the power of make-believe. Christopher Robin, wearing the mask of adulthood, enters into adventures with his animal friends in the woods, but at the end of the story is able to move easily out of this "reality" into another, as a small boy on his way to a bath, dragging his teddy bear Pooh up the stairs by one leg—bump, bump, bump.

Not only has Winnie-the-Pooh led to the making of various toy animals, but human beings sometimes turn themselves into toys from the story. I have seen a young man in a Pooh costume bouncing around the toy section of a department store. But the specific children about whom or for whom the Pooh books or the Alice books or the Beatrix Potter books were purportedly written never seemed to get the joy out of the stories that the authors did. One reason might be that though the authors might have thought they were dealing in the particular, actually they were dealing with stories that had taken over and become universal. The authors were the instruments, and the special children for whom the books were written were wise enough to know that the stories were not theirs alone: though Christopher Milne may have thought he angrily smashed the Pooh record into bits because his schoolmates were teasing him with it, possibly something else also triggered his anger—the feeling that he was having to take the responsibility for all childhood.

From A. A. Milne, *Winnie-the-Pooh* (London: Methuen, 1926), Chapter 8. Illustrated by E. H. Shepard.

In which Christopher Robin leads an expotition to the North Pole

One fine day Pooh had stumped up to the top of the Forest to see if his friend Christopher Robin was interested in Bears at all. At breakfast that morning (a simple meal of marmalade spread lightly over a honeycomb or two) he had suddenly thought of a new song. It began like this:

"Sing Ho! for the life of a Bear."

When he had got as far as this, he scratched his head, and thought to himself, "That's a very good start for a song, but what about the second line?" He tried singing "Ho," two or three times, but it didn't seem to help. "Perhaps it would be better," he thought, "if I sang Hi for the life of a Bear." So he sang it . . . but it wasn't. "Very well, then," he said, "I shall sing that first line twice, and perhaps if I sing it very quickly, I shall find myself singing the third and fourth lines before I have time to think of them, and that will be a Good Song. Now then:"

Sing Ho! for the life of a Bear!
Sing Ho! for the life of a Bear!
I don't much mind if it rains or snows,
'Cos I've got a lot of honey on my
nice new nose!
I don't much care if it snows or thaws,
'Cos I've got a lot of honey on my
nice clean paws!
Sing Ho! for a Bear!
Sing Ho! for a Pooh!
And I'll have a little something in an
hour or two!

He was so pleased with this song that he sang it all the way to the top of the Forest, "and if I go on singing it much longer," he thought, "it will be time for the little something, and then the last line won't be true." So he turned it into a hum instead.

Christopher Robin was sitting outside his door, putting on his Big Boots. As soon as he saw the Big Boots, Pooh knew that an Adventure was going to happen, and he brushed the honey off his nose with the back of his paw, and spruced himself up as well as he could, so as to look Ready for Anything.

"Good morning, Christopher Robin," he called out.

"Hallo, Pooh Bear. I can't get this boot on."

"That's bad," said Pooh.

"Do you think you could very kindly lean against me, 'cos I keep pulling so hard that I fall over backwards."

Pooh sat down, dug his feet into the ground, and pushed hard against Christopher Robin's back, and Christopher Robin pushed hard against his, and pulled and pulled at his boot until he had got it on.

"And that's that," said Pooh. "What do we do next?"

"We are all going on an Expedition," said Christopher Robin, as he got up and brushed himself. "Thank you, Pooh."

"Going on an Expotition?" said Pooh eagerly. "I don't think I've ever been on one of those. Where are we going to on this Expotition?"

"Expedition, silly old Bear. It's got an 'x' in it."

"Oh!" said Pooh. "I know." But he didn't really.

"We're going to discover the North Pole."

"Oh!" said Pooh again. "What *is* the North Pole?" he asked.

"It's just a thing you discover," said Christopher Robin carelessly, not being quite sure himself.

"Oh! I see," said Pooh. "Are bears any good at discovering it?"

"Of course they are. And Rabbit and Kanga and all of you. It's an Expedition. That's what an Expedition means. A long line of everybody. You'd better tell the others to get ready, while I see if my gun's all right. And we must all bring Provisions."

"Bring what?"

"Things to eat."

"Oh!" said Pooh happily. "I thought you said Provisions. I'll go and tell them." And he stumped off.

The first person he met was Rabbit.

"Hallo, Rabbit," he said, "is that you?"

"Let's pretend it isn't," said Rabbit, "and see what happens."

"I've got a message for you."

"I'll give it to him."

"We're all going on an Expotition with Christopher Robin!"

"What is it when we're on it?"

"A sort of boat, I think," said Pooh.

"Oh! that sort."

"Yes. And we're going to discover a Pole or something. Or was it a Mole? Anyhow we're going to discover it."

"We are, are we?" said Rabbit.

"Yes. And we've got to bring Prothings to eat with us. In case we want to eat them. Now I'm going down to Piglet's. Tell Kanga, will you?"

He left Rabbit and hurried down to Piglet's house. The Piglet was sitting on the ground at the door of his house blowing happily at a dandelion, and wondering whether it would be this year, next year, sometime, or never. He had just discovered that it would be never, and was trying to remember what *"it"* was, and hoping it wasn't anything nice, when Pooh came up.

"Oh! Piglet," said Pooh excitedly, "we're going on an Expotition, all of us, with things to eat. To discover something."

"To discover what?" said Piglet anxiously.

"Oh! just something."

"Nothing fierce?"

"Christopher Robin didn't say anything about fierce. He just said it had an 'x'."

"It isn't their necks I mind," said Piglet earnestly. "It's their teeth. But if Christopher Robin is coming I don't mind anything."

In a little while they were all ready at the top of the Forest, and the Expotition started. First came Christopher Robin and Rabbit, then Piglet and Pooh; then Kanga, with Roo in her pocket, and Owl; then Eeyore; and, at the end, in a long line, all Rabbit's friends-and-relations.

"I didn't ask them," explained Rabbit carelessly. "They just came. They always do. They can march at the end, after Eeyore."

"What I say," said Eeyore, "is that it's unsettling. I didn't want to come on this Expo—what Pooh said. I only came to oblige. But here I am; and if I am the end of the Expo—what we're talking about—then let me *be* the end. But if, every time I want to sit down for a little rest, I have to brush away half a dozen of Rabbit's smaller friends-and-relations first, then this isn't an Expo—whatever it is—at all, it's simply a Confused Noise. That's what *I* say."

"I see what Eeyore means," said Owl. "If you ask me—"

"I'm not asking anybody," said Eeyore. "I'm just telling everybody. We can look for the North Pole, or we can play 'Here we go gathering Nuts and May' with the end part of an ants' nest. It's all the same to me."

There was a shout from the top of the line.

"Come on!" called Christopher Robin.

"Come on!" called Pooh and Piglet.

"Come on!" called Owl.

"We're starting," said Rabbit. "I must go." And he hurried off to the front of the Expotition with Christopher Robin.

"All right," said Eeyore. "We're going. Only Don't Blame Me."

So off they all went to discover the Pole. And as they walked, they chattered to each other of this and that, all except Pooh, who was making up a song.

"This is the first verse," he said to Piglet, when he was ready with it.

"First verse of what?"

"My song."

"What song?"

"This one."

"Which one?"

"Well, if you listen, Piglet, you'll hear it."

"How do you know I'm not listening?"

Pooh couldn't answer that one, so he began to sing.

They all went off to discover the Pole,
  Owl and Piglet and Rabbit and all;
It's a Thing you Discover, as I've been
    tole
  By Owl and Piglet and Rabbit and
    all.
Eeyore, Christopher Robin and Pooh
And Rabbit's relations all went too—
And where the Pole was none of them
    knew. . . .
  Sing Hey! for Owl and Rabbit and
    all!

"Hush!" said Christopher Robin, turning round to Pooh, "we're just coming to a Dangerous Place."

"Hush!" said Pooh, turning round quickly to Piglet.

"Hush!" said Piglet to Kanga.

"Hush!" said Kanga to Owl, while Roo said "Hush!" several times to himself very quietly.

"Hush!" said Owl to Eeyore.

"Hush!" said Eeyore in a terrible voice to all Rabbit's friends-and-relations, and "Hush!" they said hastily to each other all down the line, until it got to the last one of all. And the last and smallest friend-and-relation was so upset to find that the whole Expotition was saying "Hush!" to *him,* that he buried himself head downwards in a crack in the ground, and stayed there for two days until the danger was over, and then went home in a great hurry, and lived quietly with his Aunt ever-afterwards. His name was Alexander Beetle.

They had come to a stream which twisted and tumbled between high rocky banks, and Christopher Robin saw at once how dangerous it was.

"It's just the place," he explained, "for an Ambush."

"What sort of bush?" whispered Pooh to Piglet. "A gorse-bush?"

"My dear Pooh," said Owl in his superior way, "don't you know what an Ambush is?"

"Owl," said Piglet, looking round at him severely, "Pooh's whisper was a perfectly private whisper, and there was no need—"

"An Ambush," said Owl, "is a sort of Surprise."

"So is a gorse-bush sometimes," said Pooh.

"An Ambush, as I was about to explain to Pooh," said Piglet, "is a sort of Surprise."

"If people jump out at you suddenly, that's an Ambush," said Owl.

"It's an Ambush, Pooh, when people jump at you suddenly," explained Piglet.

Pooh, who now knew what an Ambush was, said that a gorse-bush had sprung at him suddenly one day when he fell off a tree, and he had taken six days to get all the prickles out of himself.

"We are not *talking* about gorse-bushes," said Owl a little crossly.

"I am," said Pooh.

They were climbing very cautiously up the stream now, going from rock to rock, and after they had gone a little way they came to a place where the banks widened out at each side, so that on each side of the water there was a level strip of grass on which they could sit down and rest. As soon as he saw this, Christopher Robin called "Halt!" and they all sat down and rested.

"I think," said Christopher Robin, "that we ought to eat all our Provisions now, so that we shan't have so much to carry."

"Eat all our what?" said Pooh.

"All that we've brought," said Piglet, getting to work.

"That's a good idea," said Pooh, and he got to work too.

"Have you all got something?" asked

Christopher Robin with his mouth full.

"All except me," said Eeyore. "As Usual." He looked round at them in his melancholy way. "I suppose none of you are sitting on a thistle by any chance?"

"I believe I am," said Pooh. "Ow!" He got up, and looked behind him. "Yes, I was. I thought so."

"Thank you, Pooh. If you've quite finished with it." He moved across to Pooh's place, and began to eat.

"It doesn't do them any Good, you know, sitting on them," he went on, as he looked up munching. "Takes all the Life out of them. Remember that another time, all of you. A little Consideration, a little Thought for Others, makes all the difference."

As soon as he had finished his lunch Christopher Robin whispered to Rabbit, and Rabbit said "Yes, yes, of course," and they walked a little way up the stream together.

"I didn't want the others to hear," said Christopher Robin.

"Quite so," said Rabbit, looking important.

"It's—I wondered—It's only—Rabbit, I suppose *you* don't know. What does the North Pole *look* like?"

"Well," said Rabbit, stroking his whiskers, "now you're asking me."

"I did know once, only I've sort of forgotten," said Christopher Robin carelessly.

"It's a funny thing," said Rabbit, "but I've sort of forgotten too, although I did know *once.*"

"I suppose it's just a pole stuck in the ground?"

"Sure to be a pole," said Rabbit, "because of calling it a pole, and if it's a pole, well, I should think it would be sticking in the ground, shouldn't you, because there'd be nowhere else to stick it."

"Yes, that's what I thought."

"The only thing," said Rabbit, "is, *where is it sticking?"*

"That's what we're looking for," said Christopher Robin.

They went back to the others. Piglet was lying on his back, sleeping peacefully. Roo was washing his face and paws in the stream, while Kanga explained to everybody proudly that this was the first time he had ever washed his face himself, and Owl was telling Kanga an Interesting Anecdote full of long words like Encyclopaedia and Rhododendron to which Kanga wasn't listening.

"I don't hold with all this washing," grumbled Eeyore. "This modern Behind-the-ears nonsense. What do *you* think, Pooh?"

"Well," said Pooh, *"I* think—"

But we shall never know what Pooh thought, for there came a sudden squeak from Roo, a splash, and a loud cry of alarm from Kanga.

"So much for *washing,*" said Eeyore.

"Roo's fallen in!" cried Rabbit, and he and Christopher Robin came rushing down to the rescue.

"Look at me swimming!" squeaked Roo from the middle of his pool, and was hurried down a waterfall into the next pool.

"Are you all right, Roo, dear?" called Kanga anxiously.

"Yes!" said Roo. "Look at me sw—" and down he went over the next waterfall into another pool.

Everybody was doing something to help. Piglet, wide awake suddenly, was jumping up and down and making "Oo, I say" noises; Owl was explaining that in a case of Sudden and Temporary Immersion the Important Thing was to keep the Head Above Water; Kanga was jumping along the bank, saying "Are you *sure* you're all right, Roo dear?" to which Roo, from whatever pool he was in at the moment, was answering "Look at me swimming!" Eeyore had turned round and hung his tail over the first pool into which Roo fell, and with his back to the accident was grumbling quietly to himself, and saying, "All this washing; but catch on to my tail, little Roo, and you'll be all right"; and Christopher Robin and Rabbit came hurrying past Eeyore, and were calling out to the others in front of them.

"All right, Roo, I'm coming," called Christopher Robin.

"Get something across the stream lower down, some of you fellows," called Rabbit.

But Pooh was getting something. Two pools below Roo he was standing with a long pole in his paws, and Kanga came up and took one end of it, and between them they held it across the lower part of the pool; and Roo, still bubbling proudly, "Look at me swimming," drifted up against it, and climbed out.

"Did you see me swimming?" squeaked Roo excitedly, while Kanga scolded him and rubbed him down. "Pooh, did you see me swimming? That's called swimming, what I was doing. Rabbit, did you see what I was doing? Swimming. Hallo, Piglet! I say, Piglet! What do you think I was doing! Swimming! Christopher Robin, did you see me—"

But Christopher Robin wasn't listening. He was looking at Pooh.

"Pooh," he said, "where did you find that pole?"

Pooh looked at the pole in his hands.

"I just found it," he said. "I thought it ought to be useful. I just picked it up."

"Pooh," said Christopher Robin solemnly, "the Expedition is over. You have found the North Pole!"

"Oh!" said Pooh.

Eeyore was sitting with his tail in the water when they all got back to him.

"Tell Roo to be quick, somebody," he said. "My tail's getting cold. I don't want to mention it, but I just mention it. I don't want to complain, but there it is. My tail's cold."

"Here I am!" squeaked Roo.

"Oh, there you are."

"Did you see me swimming?"

Eeyore took his tail out of the water, and swished it from side to side.

"As I expected," he said. "Lost all feeling. Numbed it. That's what it's done. Numbed it. Well, as long as nobody minds, I suppose it's all right."

"Poor old Eeyore! I'll dry it for you," said Christopher Robin, and he took out his handkerchief and rubbed it out.

"Thank you, Christopher Robin. You're the only one who seems to understand about tails. They don't think—that's what's the matter with some of these others. They've no imagination. A tail isn't a tail to *them,* it's just a Little Bit Extra at the back."

"Never mind, Eeyore," said Christopher Robin, rubbing his hardest. "Is *that* better?"

"It's feeling more like a tail perhaps. It Belongs again, if you know what I mean."

"Hullo, Eeyore," said Pooh, coming up to them with his pole.

"Hullo, Pooh. Thank you for asking, but I shall be able to use it again in a day or two."

"Use what?" said Pooh.

"What we are talking about."

"I wasn't talking about anything," said Pooh, looking puzzled.

"My mistake again. I thought you were saying how sorry you were about my tail, being all numb, and could you do anything to help?"

"No," said Pooh. "That wasn't me," he said. He thought for a little and then suggested helpfully: "Perhaps it was somebody else."

"Well, thank him for me when you see him."

Pooh looked anxiously at Christopher Robin.

"Pooh's found the North Pole," said Christopher Robin. "Isn't that lovely?"

Pooh looked modestly down.

"Is that it?" said Eeyore.

"Yes," said Christopher Robin.

"Is that what we were looking for?"

"Yes," said Pooh.

"Oh!" said Eeyore. "Well, anyhow—it didn't rain," he said.

They stuck the pole in the ground, and Christopher Robin tied a message on to it:

NorTH PoLE
DICSovERED By
PooH
PooH FouND IT

Then they all went home again. And I think, but I am not quite sure, that Roo had a hot bath and went straight to bed.

But Pooh went back to his own house, and feeling very proud of what he had done, had a little something to revive himself.

IMPUNITY JANE: THE STORY OF A POCKET DOLL

Rumer Godden

Impunity Jane is a tiny, pocket-sized doll who received her name when a clerk in the store where she was on sale told buyers she could be dropped "with impunity." For years she is confined to a boring life in a dollhouse, until shé is stolen by Gideon, who simply wants her to play with. Rumer Godden's descriptions of Impunity Jane's adventures with Gideon capture the joy of play that is so quickly forgotten by adults. Impunity Jane *has much the same message as* William's Doll *(1972) by Charlotte Zolotow. That is, it is fine for boys to like dolls.*

From Rumer Godden, *Impunity Jane: The Story of a Pocket Doll* (New York: Viking, 1954), pp. 18–37. Illustrated by Adrienne Adams.

Then one day Ellen's mother said, "Ellen, you had better get out all your toys. Your cousin Gideon is coming to tea."

Ellen pouted and was cross because she did not like boys, and she had to open the doll's house and dust its furniture and carpets. Everything was thick with dust, even Impunity Jane. She had felt it settling on her, and it made her miserable. The clothes with the big stitches, the lessons, had been better than dust.

"Gideon! Gideon! What a silly name!" said Ellen.

To Impunity Jane it did not sound silly. "G-G-G"—the sound was hard and gay, and she seemed to hear the bugle again, brave and exciting.

Gideon was a boy of seven with brown eyes and curly hair. When he laughed his nose had small wrinkles at the sides, and when he was very pleased—or frightened or ashamed—his cheeks grew red.

From the first moment he came into the nursery he was interested in the doll's house. "Let me play with it," he said, and he bent down and looked into the rooms.

"You can move the furniture about and put out the cups and saucers, as long as you put them all back," said Ellen.

"*That's* not playing!" said Gideon. "Can't we put the doll's house up a tree?"

"A tree? Why the birds might nest in it!" said Ellen.

"Do you think they would?" asked Gideon, and he laughed with pleasure. "Think of robins and wrens sitting on the tables and chairs!"

Impunity Jane laughed too.

"Let's put it on a raft and float it on the river," said Gideon.

"Don't be silly," said Ellen. "It might be swept away and go right out to sea."

"Then fishes could come into it," said Gideon.

"Fishes!"

Impunity Jane became excited, but Ellen still said, "No."

Gideon looked at Impunity Jane on the bead cushion. "Does that little doll just sit there doing nothing?" he asked.

"What could she do?" asked Ellen.

Gideon did not answer, but he looked at Impunity Jane with his bright brown eyes; they twinkled, and suddenly Impunity Jane knew she could make Gideon feel. "Rescue me," wished Impunity Jane as hard as she could. "Gideon, rescue me. Don't leave me here, here where Effie and Elizabeth and Ethel and Ellen have kept me so long. Gideon! *Gideon!*"

But Gideon was tired of Ellen and the nursery. "I think I'll take a ball out into the garden," he said.

"Gideon! Gideon, I shall crack!" cried Impunity Jane. "G-I-D-E-O-N! G-I-D-E-O-N!"

Gideon stopped and looked at Impunity Jane; then he looked round at Ellen. Ellen was eating cherries from a plate her mother had brought in; she ought really to have shared them with Gideon, but she had gobbled most of them up; now she was counting the stones. "Tinker, tailor, soldier, sailor," counted Ellen.

"Gideon, Gideon," wished Impunity Jane.

"Rich man, poor man, beggar man"—and just as Ellen said, "Thief," Gideon, his cheeks red, slid his hand into the doll's house, picked up Impunity Jane, and put her into his pocket.

Ages and ages ago Impunity Jane had been in Grandma's pocket, but Grandma's pocket was nothing to Gideon's. To begin with, Gideon's pockets often had real holes in them, and Impunity Jane could put her head right through them into the world. Sometimes she had to hold onto the edges to avoid falling out altogether, but she was not afraid.

"I'm Imp-imp-impunity," she sang.

Grandma had not run, and oh! the feeling of running, spinning through the air! Grandma had not skated nor ridden on a scooter. "I can skate and I can scoot," said Impunity Jane.

Grandma had not swung; Gideon went on the swings in the park, and Impunity Jane went too, high and higher, high in the air.

Grandma had not climbed trees; Gideon climbed, to the very top, and there he took Impunity Jane out of his pocket and sat her on one of the boughs; she could see far over houses and steeples and trees, and feel the bough moving in the wind.

"I feel the wind. I feel the wind!" cried Impunity Jane.

In Grandma's pocket there had been only Impunity Jane and a folded white handkerchief that smelled of lavender water. In Gideon's pockets were all kinds of things. Impunity Jane never knew what she would find there—string and corks, sweets and sweet-papers, nuts, cigarette cards with beautiful pictures, an important message, a knife with a broken handle, some useful screws and tacks, a bit of pencil, and, for a long time, a little brown snail.

The snail had a polished brown shell with smoke-curl markings. Gideon used to take her out and put her down to eat on the grass; then a head with two horns like a little cow came out one side of the shell and a small curved tail at the other; the tail left a smeary silvery trail like glue; it made the inside of Gideon's pocket beautifully sticky. Gideon called the snail Ann Rushout because of the slow way she put out her horns.

"I once had a chestnut as a pretend snail," said Gideon, "but a real snail's much better."

Impunity Jane thought so too.

But in all this happiness there was a worry. It worried Gideon, and so, of course, it worried Impunity Jane. (If dolls can make you feel, you make them feel as well.)

The worry was this. Gideon was a boy, and boys do not have dolls, not even in their pockets.

"They would call me 'sissy,'" said Gideon, and his cheeks grew red.

On the corner of the street a gang of boys used to meet; they met in the park as well. The leader of the gang was Joe McCallaghan. Joe McCallaghan had brown hair that was stiff as a brush, a turned-up nose, freckles, and gray eyes. He wore a green wolf cub jersey and a belt bristling with knives; he had every kind of knife, and he had bows and arrows, an air gun, a space helmet, and a bicycle with a dual brake control, a lamp, and a bell. He was nine years old and Gideon was only seven but, "He quite likes me," said Gideon.

Once Joe McCallaghan pulled a face at Gideon. "Of course, I couldn't *think* of pulling one at him," said Gideon. "He knows me but I can't know him—yet."

Once Gideon had a new catapult, and Joe McCallaghan took it into his hand to look at it. Gideon trembled while Joe McCallaghan stretched the catapult, twanged it, and handed it back. "Decent weapon," said Joe McCallaghan. Gideon would have said "Jolly wizard!" But how ordinary that sounded now! "Decent weapon, decent weapon," said Gideon over and over again.

Impunity Jane heard him and her china seemed to grow cold. Suppose Joe McCallaghan, or one of the gang, should find out what Gideon had in his pocket?

"I should die," said Gideon.

"But I don't look like a proper doll," Impunity Jane tried to say.

That was true. The white dress with the sprigs had been so smeared by Ann Rushout that Gideon had taken it off and thrown it away. Impunity Jane no longer had dresses with stitches like knives; her dresses had no stitches at all. Gideon dressed her in a leaf, or some feathers, or a piece of rag; sometimes he buttoned the rag with a berry. If you can imagine a dirty little gypsy doll, that is how Impunity Jane looked now.

"I'm not a proper doll," she pleaded, but Gideon did not hear.

"Gideon, will you mail this letter for me?" his mother asked one afternoon.

Gideon took the letter and ran downstairs and out into the street. Ann Rushout lay curled in her shell, but Impunity Jane put her head out through a brand-new hole. Gideon scuffed up the dust with the toes of his new shoes, and Impunity Jane admired the puffs and the rainbow specks of it in the sun (you look at dust in the sun), and so they came to the postbox.

Gideon stood on tiptoe, and had just posted the letter when—"Hands up!" said Joe McCallaghan. He stepped out from behind the postbox, and the gang came from round the corner where they had been hiding.

Gideon was surrounded.

Impunity Jane could feel his heart beating in big jerks. She felt cold and stiff. Even Ann Rushout woke up and put out her two little horns.

"Search him," said Joe McCallaghan to a boy called Puggy.

Impunity Jane slid quickly to the bottom of Gideon's pocket and lay there under Ann Rushout, the cork, the sweets, the pencil, and the string.

Puggy ran his hands over Gideon like a policeman and then searched his pockets. The first thing he found was Ann Rushout. "A snail. Ugh!" said Puggy and nearly dropped her.

"It's a beautiful snail," said Joe McCallaghan, and the gang looked at Gideon with more respect.

Puggy brought out the cork, the sweets—Joe McCallaghan tried one through the paper with his teeth and handed it back—the pencil, a lucky sixpence, the knife—"Broken," said Puggy scornfully, and Gideon grew red. Puggy brought out the string. Then Impunity Jane felt his fingers close round her, and out she came into the light of day.

Gideon's cheeks had been red; now they went dark, dark crimson. Impunity Jane lay stiffly as Puggy handed her to Joe McCallaghan; the berry she had been wearing broke off and rolled in the gutter.

"A doll!" said Joe McCallaghan in disgust.

"Sissy!" said Puggy. "Sissy!"

"Sissy got a dolly," the gang jeered and waited to see what Joe McCallaghan would do.

"You're a sissy," said Joe McCallaghan to Gideon, as if he were disappointed.

Impunity Jane lay stiffly in his hand. "I'm Imp-imp-impunity," she tried to sing, but no words came.

Then Gideon said something he did not know he could say. He did not know how he thought of it; it might have come out of the air, the sky, the pavement, but amazingly it came out of Gideon himself. "I'm not a sissy," said Gideon. "She isn't a doll, she's a model. I use her in my model train."

"A model?" said Joe McCallaghan and looked at Impunity Jane again.

"Will he throw me in the gutter like the berry?" thought Impunity Jane. "Will he put me down and tread on me? Break me with his heel?"

"A model," said Gideon firmly.

"She can be a fireman or a porter or a driver or a sailor," he added.

"A sailor?" said Joe McCallaghan, and he looked at Impunity Jane again. "I wonder if she would go in my model yacht," he said. "I had a lead sailor, but he fell overboard."

"She wouldn't fall overboard," said Gideon.

Joe McCallaghan looked at her again. "Mind if I take her to the pond?" he said over his shoulder to Gideon.

Now began such a life for Impunity Jane. She, a little pocket doll, was one of a gang of boys! Because of her, Gideon, her Gideon, was allowed to be in the gang too. "It's only fair," said Joe McCallaghan, whom we can now call Joe, "it's only fair, if we use her, to let him in."

Can you imagine how it feels, if you are a little doll, to sit on the deck of a yacht and go splashing across a pond? You are sent off with a hard push among ducks as big as icebergs, over ripples as big as waves. Most people would have been afraid and fallen overboard, like the lead sailor, but, "Imp-imp-impunity," sang Impunity Jane and reached the far side wet but perfectly safe.

RAGGEDY ANN AND THE PAPER DRAGON

Johnny Gruelle

As Martin Williams points out in his essay "Some Remarks on Raggedy Ann and Johnny Gruelle" (at the end of this section), Johnny Gruelle was a prolific and gifted hack writer and artist who turned out a "mound of children's stories, illustrated books, comic strips, drawings." Such a vast amount of material has to be sifted carefully in order to find the gold, such as this story of Raggedy Ann and the Paper Dragon. *Williams tells us to notice that Gruelle's Deep Deep Woods, in its innocence, is a very American enchanted place, where the witches and wizards aren't really wicked, just a little mean. The story is an example of the kind in which dolls have a secret life of their own.*

[Meeting the Paper Dragon]

Raggedy Ann and Raggedy Andy and Marggy and her Mama followed the little red magical ball of darning cotton through the woods until they came to a gate made of logs. The little red magical ball rolled through the gate and our friends started to follow it, when a great big Dragon, just like the Dragons you see in Chinese pictures, came right out and opened its mouth and the little red magical ball of darning cotton rolled inside.

"Oh, dear!" cried Marggy's Mama as she sat down on a stone and wiped her eyes with her apron. "Now the little red magical ball is gone and we will never find Daddy."

"Why did you swallow our little red magical ball of darning cotton?" Raggedy Ann asked the great big Dragon.

From *Raggedy Ann and the Paper Dragon*, written and illustrated by Johnny Gruelle (indianapolis, Ind.: The Bobbs-Merrill Company, Inc., 1926).

"Because," the Dragon replied.

"That isn't any reason at all," Raggedy Ann said. "And you ought to be ashamed of yourself! That's what!"

"Well, I'm not," the great big large Dragon replied as it wiggled its long tail. And when Raggedy Ann pointed her rag hand at its nose to make it feel ashamed of itself, the great big large Dragon opened its great large mouth real wide and went, "Gobble! Gobble!"

"Here! You stop that, Mister Dragon!" Raggedy Andy cried, but he was too late for the great big large Dragon had swallowed Raggedy Ann completely.

"Now then, you've gone and done it!" Raggedy Andy cried as he hunted around for a great big stick.

"What are you going to do with that great big stick?" the Dragon asked as he twirled his long tail.

"You just wait and see! That's what!" Raggedy Andy said as he rolled up his sleeves.

"Are we going to have a fight?" the Dragon asked.

Raggedy Andy did not answer the Dragon. Instead, he walked right up to it holding the large stick in front of him. When Raggedy Andy came up to him, the Dragon opened his great big mouth and started to say "Gobble!" Gobble!" just like he had done when he swallowed Raggedy Ann, but Raggedy Andy was too smart for him. Raggedy Andy, just as quick as a wink, put the large stick in the Dragon's mouth and this held the Dragon's mouth wide open.

My! How the Dragon wiggled and wobbled his long tail, but it did no good, for he could not get the stick out of his mouth. And when he wiggled and wobbled his long tail Raggedy Andy and Marggy and her Mama could hear Raggedy Ann and the little red magical ball rattling around way back inside the Dragon. Then they heard a funny scratching sound and here came Raggedy Ann crawling out.

"The Dragon is just made out of paper and thin slats of wood!" Raggedy Ann laughed.

"The reason I did not fight the great big large Dragon was because I saw right away that he was made out of paper," said Raggedy Andy. "And if I had hit him upon the head with the large stick, I would have broken his head in pieces."

"Are you going to take the stick out of his mouth?" Marggy's Mama asked Raggedy Andy, "The great big Dragon might eat someone else up just as he did Raggedy Ann."

Raggedy Ann laughed. "The great big Dragon wouldn't harm anyone even if he

did swallow them," she said. "For he is hollow all the way to the tip of his tail. And if he swallowed anyone, all they would have to do would be to kick real hard and they could kick a large hole right through him."

Raggedy Andy walked up to the large paper Dragon and took the big stick out of its mouth. "There," said Raggedy Andy. "Does that feel better?"

"Yes indeed!" the Dragon replied. "When my mouth was propped open with the stick, it made cold chills run all the way to the tip end of my long tail, and it felt just like someone had left the front door wide open on a cold day."

"Then after this, you mustn't swallow anyone again," said Raggedy Andy.

"I did not swallow Raggedy Ann," the Dragon replied.

"No, he didn't, that's true," Raggedy Ann agreed. "I jumped into his mouth, because I saw right away he was made out of paper and thin slats of wood. I knew someone had to rescue the little red magical ball of darning cotton or we would never find Marggy's Daddy."

"What do you eat, Mister Dragon?" Marggy's Mama asked as she walked up and thumped the Dragon's head to see if he really and truly was paper.

"I never eat anything," the Dragon replied, "But lots of times when I yawn the wind blows pieces of paper right in my mouth and dry leaves and I do not know how to get them out again! I'm afraid maybe if mice find out I have pieces of paper and nice dry leaves in me, they might build nests in my paper body. And you know how mice are, sometimes they chew holes in things."

"I tell you what let's do! Let's pull him up into a tree by the tip end of his tail and shake all the leaves and pieces of paper out." Raggedy Andy said.

Marggy and her Mama couldn't climb trees like Raggedy Ann and Raggedy Andy, so they stayed upon the ground and boosted the paper Dragon's tail up to Raggedy Ann and Andy. Then Raggedy Ann and Raggedy Andy shook the paper Dragon's tail until all the leaves and pieces of paper rattled down to his mouth. Then Marggy and her Mama cleaned all the leaves and paper out of the paper Dragon's mouth and he felt very, very much better.

Then Raggedy Ann and Raggedy Andy and Marggy and her Mama told the paper Dragon good-bye and followed the little red magical ball of darning cotton through the woods.

[Hiding from Mr. Doodle]

Raggedy Ann and Raggedy Andy and Marggy and her Mama had gone only a short way when they heard a loud noise in back of them.

"Land sakes!" cried Raggedy Ann. "What can be making all that racket?" But because the others did not know, of course they could not tell, so they just had to wait until whatever made the racket reached them.

The noise grew louder and louder until they saw the paper Dragon coming through the woods as fast as he could wiggle. The paper Dragon wiggled and twisted along so fast his long tail bumped against the trees blumpity smack, crash, blump!

"Dear me! Something must be wrong with the paper Dragon!" Raggedy Ann said. "He will tear a lot of holes in his sides if he isn't careful the way he smacks into the trees and stones!"

The paper Dragon was so out of breath when he reached Raggedy Ann all he could say was "Run!" And he said it with such a wheeze no one could understand what he said.

"Whatever made you wiggle so fast through the woods, Mister Dragon?" Raggedy Andy asked. "You've snagged a lot of holes in your tail, and while you rest we will mend them with paper and glue."

"But we haven't any glue!" Marggy's Mama said.

"Maybe we can use the cream out of a cream puff!" Raggedy Ann suggested.

And as there were lots of pieces of paper blowing about through the woods Raggedy Ann and Raggedy Andy soon stuck patches on every hole in the paper Dragon's body.

"Ah! That feels ever so much better," the paper Dragon said. "I guess the reason I got out of breath was because I had so many holes in my long body, and the air leaked out of the holes."

"Maybe you ran with your mouth open," Marggy said.

"Yes, that's true," the Dragon replied. "Let's see now, what was I going to tell you? I guess it slipped out of the holes, for I have completely forgotten what it was."

"Try to think real hard," suggested Raggedy Andy. "Raggedy Ann and I often think so hard we rip stitches out of our heads."

"But I have no stitches in my head," the Dragon replied.

"Then we'll just sit here and wait until you think without ripping any stitches," said Raggedy Ann.

So the Raggedys and Marggy and her Mama sat down and waited for the Dragon to remember.

"Can't you remember what it was?" Raggedy Andy asked after they had sat there awhile.

"I haven't the least idea," the paper Dragon replied. "I can't seem to think very well."

"Maybe if you would scratch your head, it would help," said Raggedy Ann.

"Oh, he can't scratch his head," Raggedy Andy laughed. "He hasn't any hands to scratch with."

"Of course not," Raggedy Ann laughed. "It was silly of me to suggest it!"

"But we could take sticks and scratch his head for him," Marggy said.

"Maybe that will help," the paper Dragon said.

So Raggedy Ann and Raggedy Andy and Marggy and her Mama each got a stick and scratched the Dragon's head.

After they had scratched awhile, the paper Dragon said, "That's enough! I remember what it was now! You must run and run fast!"

"But why should we run?" Raggedy Ann asked. "If we run, we will get ahead of the little magical red ball of darning cotton and you know, the little red ball rolls through the woods and is leading us to where Marggy's Daddy is."

"Well, you had better run anyway!" the Dragon said. "For there's a queer man running after you, and the only reason he isn't here now is because I wiggled through the woods so much faster than he can run."

"Who is it?" Raggedy Ann asked of the others.

"I'll tell you who it is," the Dragon said. "It's Mr. Doodle!"

"Oh dear!" Marggy cried. "He wants to take me back to his house to chop wood for him!"

"Well, he will never do that," Raggedy Andy said. "We will hide some place and wait until he runs by, then we will go another way."

"Here's a dandy place to hide," said Raggedy Ann. "Quick! Everyone get in this great big hollow tree. Afterwards we will catch up with the magic ball."

So they all squeezed into the great big hollow tree. Even the Dragon, and waited for Mr. Doodle to run by them.

"Here he comes now, I can hear him!" the Dragon said to Raggedy Ann and Raggedy Andy and Marggy and her Mama. The Dragon was the last to crawl into the great big hollow tree so he could hear better than the others.

"He's coming lickety split through the woods," the Dragon whispered.

"Goody! Now he's going by! It's stuffy in here all crowded together and I will be glad when Mr. Doodle runs past," said Raggedy Ann.

"Oh shucks!" the Dragon cried out loud.

"Be quiet!" Raggedy Ann said. "He will hear you sure!"

"That's just it!" the Dragon said. "He has heard us and he is pulling and yanking my tail now!"

"He's pulling me out of the tree!" the Dragon wailed.

Indeed, this was true, for the others

soon felt the Dragon slipping and slipping until suddenly he was yanked right out of the great big hollow tree.

"Ha! Ha! Ha!" laughed Mr. Doodle. "You thought you could fool me did you?"

"How did you know where we were?" Raggedy Andy asked as he and the others came out.

"Why, who wouldn't know where you were when the foolish Dragon had ten or fifteen feet of his tail sticking out of the tree!"

"I knew I would spoil it all, if I hid in the tree with you! I'm so sorry!" the Dragon cried.

"Don't you care," Raggedy Andy whispered. "You did the best you knew how and we are glad of that."

"Now," said Mr. Doodle. "I've come to take Marggy home with me to chop the wood."

"Dear me," Raggedy Ann exclaimed. "If you worked as hard chopping your wood as you have chasing us, you would have the wood all chopped!"

"I'm too tired to chop wood, I tell you," Mr. Doodle shouted as he gave Marggy's arm a pull.

"Now see here," the Dragon cried. "I guess we will have to fight!" So Mr. Doodle took off his coat and rolled up his sleeves. "The rest of you had better keep back out of the way," he said.

So Raggedy Ann passed the doughnuts and cream puffs. "For," she said as they took seats back out of the way. "We might as well have lunch while we wait for the Dragon to fight Mr. Doodle."

The fight between Mr. Doodle and the Dragon was a great sight to see. The Dragon could growl very loud when he wanted to and he growled louder than usual. But Mr. Doodle, even if he was so lazy that he wanted Marggy to chop his wood for him, was very brave and every time the Dragon growled, Mr. Doodle stuck out his tongue at the Dragon.

This made the Dragon growl louder than ever and Raggedy Andy grew so excited he put a cream puff into his eye instead of his mouth and the cream puff covered his shoe button eye so that he could only watch the fight with one eye until Raggedy Ann wiped the cream puff off with her pocket hanky. The little white one with blue flowers on it.

Each time the Dragon rushed at Mr. Doodle and growled, Mr. Doodle jumped back. And each time Mr. Doodle rushed at the Dragon, the Dragon jumped back. And the fight lasted until both Mr. Doodle and the Dragon grew so excited, they forgot what they were doing, and both rushed at each other at the same time. This surprised the Dragon so much, he stopped suddenly and opened his mouth and he had no sooner done this than Mr. Doodle, who was as much surprised as the

Dragon, lost his balance and fell right into the Dragon's mouth.

"Hm!" the Dragon said. "The great fight is over!"

"I'm glad that you swallowed Mr. Doodle instead of Mr. Doodle swallowing you!" Raggedy Andy told the Dragon as he patted him upon the head.

"Silly!" Raggedy Ann laughed at Raggedy Andy. "How could Mr. Doodle swallow the Dragon when the Dragon is so much larger?"

"I never thought of that," Raggedy Andy giggled. He knew when the joke was on him.

But suddenly the Dragon looked worried and it only took Raggedy Andy a moment to find out why. Mr. Doodle, inside the paper Dragon, had started stomping around.

"If you don't let me out, I'll kick out all your slats!" Mr. Doodle shouted from inside the paper Dragon.

"I believe I had better let him out," the Dragon said. "I think he has nails in his shoes!"

So the Dragon opened his mouth and Mr. Doodle walked out. Mr. Doodle was so tired though, he had to sit down and rest. "We'll have another fight as soon as I rest up a bit."

And because they did not believe in being stingy, Raggedy Ann and Raggedy Andy gave Mr. Doodle three cream puffs and six doughnuts to help him rest.

After resting and eating three cream puffs and six doughnuts, Mr. Doodle jumped to his feet. "Now we must continue our fight!" he cried to the Dragon.

"I won't fight you if you fall inside my mouth again and kick around like you did before. Your shoes have nails in them!" the Dragon said.

"I guess I'll take off my shoes then," Mr. Doodle agreed. "That will make it a fair fight, don't you think?"

When Mr. Doodle had taken off his shoes with the nails in the bottom the Dragon said, "I will never permit you to take Marggy home with you to chop your wood."

And Mr. Doodle replied, "And I will never permit you to not permit me to take Marggy home with me to chop my wood." And with this, Mr. Doodle stuck out his tongue at the Dragon and the Dragon growled very loud at Mr. Doodle. Then Mr. Doodle pushed upon the Dragon and the Dragon pushed upon Mr. Doodle and back and forth they tussled until finally the Dragon pushed the hardest and pushed Mr. Doodle over on his back.

Of course you have guessed by this time that Mr. Doodle was losing the fight with the Dragon, and it made him so angry he lost his temper, and before anyone could say, "Scat!" Mr. Doodle picked up a stone and threw it right smack dab through the kind Dragon's paper side.

"Aren't you ashamed of yourself, Mr. Doodle?" Raggedy Ann cried.

"I don't care," Mr. Doodle replied. "He shouldn't have pushed me over on my back, that's what!"

Marggy's Mama, before she stopped to think that Mr. Doodle did not belong to her, caught Mr. Doodle and turned him over her knee. And I wish that you could have heard the paddywhacks she gave him with her slipper. When Marggy's Mama had finished paddywacking Mr. Doodle, Mr. Doodle ran home as fast as he could.

"Ha! Ha! Ha!" the Dragon laughed in spite of the hole in his side, "Marggy's Mama is the one who really won the great fight!"

Raggedy Andy hunted around through the woods until he found a Sunday newspaper and with this and some of the cream from the cream puffs, Raggedy Andy and Raggedy Ann covered the hole in the paper Dragon's side. The Sunday newspaper was printed in colors and it made the paper Dragon much prettier than he had been and everyone told him so. And after they had thanked the kindly paper Dragon for rescuing Marggy from Mr. Doodle, they left the Dragon trying to wiggle around so that he could see the beautiful Sunday newspaper patch they had pasted on his side.

THE STEADFAST TIN-SOLDIER

Hans Christian Andersen

This story of the one-legged tin-soldier who remains steadfast despite his misadventures—falling out a window, sailing through the gutter in a paper boat, being swallowed by a big fish which miraculously ends up in the very house the tin-soldier started out from—exhibits the poignancy characteristic of many of Andersen's tales. When Andersen was a boy, his father made him a puppet theater, and Hans made the costumes for the puppets himself. The skill with which he brings the toys in this story to life reveals the love he must have had for his puppets.

There were once five and twenty tin-soldiers: they were all brothers, because they had all been born from one old tin spoon. They carried rifles on their shoulders, and they held their heads up and looked straight in front of them. Their uniform was red and blue and very fine indeed. The very first thing they heard in this world, when the lid of the box in which they lay was taken off, was the word "Tin-soldiers!" shouted by a small boy as he clapped his hands. He had been given them because it was his birthday, and he now set them out on the table. One soldier looked exactly like another—only a single one of them was a little different: he had one leg because he had been cast the last, and there wasn't enough tin left. Yet he stood just as firm on his one leg as the others did on their two, and he's the one the story is really about.

On the table where they were set out were many other toys, but the one that caught the eye most was a fine cardboard castle. Through the little windows you could see right into the rooms. Outside stood little trees round a little mirror which was meant to look like a lake. Wax swans swam on it and were reflected there. It was altogether charming, but the most charming thing about it was undoubtedly a little young lady who stood in the middle of the open castle door: she was cut out of cardboard, too, but she wore a skirt of the finest linen and a narrow blue ribbon draped round her shoulders. This was fastened in the middle by a shining spangle, as big as the whole of her face. This little lady stretched both her arms out, for she was a dancer, and raised one leg so high in the air that the tin-soldier could not find it at all, and believed that she had only one leg like himself.

"She'd be the wife for me!" he thought. "But she's of very high birth: she lives in a castle, and I have only a box—besides, there are five and twenty of us, and there isn't room for her! But I can try

Translated by L.W. Kingsland.

to make her acquaintance!" And so he lay down full-length behind a snuff-box which stood on the table, and from there he had a good view of the fine little lady, who continued to stand on one leg without losing her balance.

When it was late in the evening, all the tin-soldiers were put in their box and the people of the house went to bed. And now the toys began to play—they played at visiting and soldiers and going to fine balls. The tin-soldiers rattled in their box, for they wanted to join in, but they couldn't get the lid off. The nut-crackers jumped head-over-heels, and the slate-pencil made a dreadful noise on the slate: there was such a row that the canary woke up and began to chat with them—in verse, too! There were only two who didn't move from their places, and they were the tin-soldier and the little dancer: she held herself so upright upon the tip of her toes, with both arms stretched out; he stood just as firmly on his one leg, and his eyes didn't leave her for one second.

Now the clock struck twelve, and with a clatter the lid sprang off the snuff-box: there was no snuff in it, no, but a little black goblin popped up—it was a sort of trick.

"Tin-soldier!" said the goblin. "Will you keep your eyes to yourself!"

But the tin-soldier pretended he hadn't heard.

"Just you wait till tomorrow!" said the goblin.

When morning came and the children were up, the tin-soldier was put over on the window-ledge, and whether it was the goblin or a draught that did it, the window suddenly swung open and out fell the tin-soldier head-first from the third story. He fell at a dreadful pace, his leg in the air, and ended up upon his head, with his bayonet stuck between the paving-stones.

The maid and the small boy went down at once to look for him, but although they came very near to treading on him, they still couldn't see him. If the tin-soldier had shouted, "Here I am!" they would have found him right enough, but he considered it wasn't done to cry out when he was in uniform.

Now it began to rain, and the drops fell thicker and thicker until it was a regular shower. When it was over a couple of street-urchins came by.

"Look!" said one of them. "There's a tin-soldier! He must go for a sail!"

And so they made a boat from a newspaper, put the tin-soldier in the middle, and away he sailed down the gutter. Both the boys ran along by his side, clapping their hands. Heavens above, what waves there were in the gutter, and what a current there was! It had been a real downpour. The paper boat tossed up and down, and every now and then whirled round so quickly that the tin-soldier became quite giddy. But he remained steadfast, and without moving a muscle, he looked straight in front of him and kept his rifle on his shoulder.

All at once the boat was driven into a long stretch of gutter that was boarded over, and here it was quite as dark as it was in his box at home.

"I wonder where I shall get to now," he thought. "Yes, yes, it's all the goblin's fault! Ah, if only the young lady were here in the boat, it might be twice as dark for all I'd care!"

At that very moment there appeared a great water-rat that lived under the gutter-boarding.

"Have you got your passport?" asked the rat. "This way with your passport!"

But the tin-soldier said nothing, and held his rifle even more tightly. The boat was carried along and the rat followed. Ooh, how it ground its teeth, and shouted to sticks and straws, "Stop him! Stop him! He's not paid his toll! He's not shown his passport!"

But the current grew stronger and stronger. The tin-soldier could already catch a glimpse of daylight ahead where the boarding left off, but he also heard a roaring which was quite enough to terrify a bolder man than he: just imagine, where the boarding ended, the gutter emptied straight out into a big canal! It would be just as dangerous for him to be swept into that, as it would be for us to go sailing over a great waterfall.

He was already so close to it now that he could not stop himself. The boat swept out. The poor tin-soldier held himself as stiffly as he could—no one should say of him that he as much as blinked an eyelid. The boat spun round three or four times and filled with water right to the brim, so that nothing could stop it from sinking. The tin-soldier stood up to the neck in water, and the boat sank deeper and deeper. The paper became looser and looser, and now the water flowed over the soldier's head. Then he thought of the pretty little dancer whom he would never see again, and these words rang in the tin-soldier's ears:

Onward, onward, warrior!
Death's what you must suffer!

Now the paper parted, and the tin-soldier fell through—and he was at once swallowed by a big fish.

Oh, how dark it was inside! It was even worse than it was under the gutter-boarding, and it was so cramped, too! But the tin-soldier remained steadfast, and lay full-length with his rifle on his shoulder.

The fish twisted and turned about in the most frightening manner. At last it became quite still, and a flash of lightning seemed to pass right through it. Daylight shone quite brightly, and someone cried out, "The tin-soldier!" The fish had been caught, taken to market, sold and brought up to the kitchen, where the maid had cut it open with a big knife. She picked the soldier up by the waist with two fingers and took him into the living-room, where they all wanted to see the remarkable man who had travelled about in the inside of a fish: but the tin-soldier's head was not a bit turned by their admiration. They stood him up on the table, and there—well, what wonderful things can happen in the world!—the tin-soldier was in the very same room he had been in before, he saw the very same children, and the toys were standing on the table—there was the fine castle with the lovely little dancer: she was still standing on one leg with the other raised high in the air—she, too, was steadfast. The tin-soldier was deeply moved—he was ready to weep tin tears, but that was hardly the thing to do. He looked at her and she looked at him, but they said nothing.

At that very moment one of the small boys took the tin-soldier and threw him right into the stove—he gave no reason at all for doing it: the goblin in the box must have been to blame.

The tin-soldier stood in a blaze of light and felt terribly hot, but whether it was really the heat of the fire or the heat of love, he didn't know. His bright colours had completely gone—no one could say whether this had happened on his travels or whether it was the result of his sorrow. He looked at the little dancer, and she looked at him: he felt himself melting, but he still stood steadfast with his rifle on his shoulder. A door opened and the wind caught the dancer: she flew like a sylph right into the stove to the tin-soldier, burst into flame and vanished. Then the soldier melted to a blob of tin, and the next day, when the maid cleared the ashes out, she found him in the shape of a little heart. Nothing remained of the dancer but her spangle, and that was burnt coal-black.

PINOCCHIO: THE ADVENTURES OF A MARIONETTE

Carlo Collodi

To summarize the story from which this selection is taken, Geppetto, an old Italian, carves a puppet out of a piece of wood. In so doing, like all creative artists, he repeats on a minute scale the act of world creation. Almost immediately, however, the mischievous but lovable puppet, Pinocchio, begins to cause the old man trouble, even landing him in jail. In an attempt to avoid work and school, Pinocchio goes off on a series of adventures in which he falls in with bad companions, though from time to time a Blue Fairy has a beneficent influence on him. During one period he has behaved so much like an ass that he quite appropriately turns into a donkey. Very slowly his character improves, so that by the time he is swallowed by a Dogfish, he has become quite good. In the Fish, he discovers his father, old Geppetto, whom he rescues. At the end of the story, the two are united and Pinocchio has become a human being.

One of the masterpieces of fantasy, Pinocchio *is open to many levels of understanding. Here the familiar theme of a wooden doll or puppet coming to life has been given an important new twist: Pinocchio, the living puppet, becomes a real boy when he himself learns to love. The Blue Fairy, a sort of idealized mother and guide, helps the unregenerate puppet who is constantly misbehaving and breaking promises, through the healing power of love. She becomes his*

From Carlo Collodi, *Pinocchio: The Adventures of a Marionette* (Boston: Ginn, 1904), Chapter 3 (pp. 9–14), Chapter 34 (pp. 185–193), Chapter 35 (pp. 194–199), Chapter 36 (pp. 201–212). Translated by Walter S. Cramp, with editorial revision by Sara E. H. Lockwood. Illustrated by Charles Copeland.

inspiration, and he yearns to be with her and to please her. On one level, then, this is a story of growth and self-development—Pinocchio progresses from wood to living wood to human. On another level, Pinocchio *is a very human and humorous presentation of well-intentioned waywardness and unconscious misbehavior—a set of contradictions with which children of all ages eagerly identify.*

[The Making of Pinocchio]

Geppetto's home consisted of one room on the ground floor. It received light from a window under a staircase. The furniture could not have been more simple,—a broken chair, a hard bed, and a dilapidated table. On one side of the room there was a fireplace with wood burning; but the fire was painted, and above it there was also painted a boiling pot with clouds of steam all around it that made it quite real.

As soon as he entered Geppetto began to make a marionette. "What name shall I give him?" he said to himself. "I think I will call him Pinocchio. That name will bring with it good fortune. I have known a whole family called Pinocchio. Pinocchio was the father, Pinocchio was the mother, and the children were called little Pinocchios, and everybody lived well. It was a happy family."

When he had found the name for the marionette he began to work with a will. He quickly made the forehead, then the hair, and then the eyes. After he had made the eyes, just imagine how surprised he was to see them look around, and finally gaze at him fixedly! Geppetto, seeing himself looked at by two eyes of wood, said to the head, "Why do you look at me so, eyes of wood?"

No response.

After he had made the eyes he made the nose; but the nose began to grow, and it grew, grew, grew, until it became a great big nose, and Geppetto thought it would never stop. He tried hard to stop it, but the more he cut at it the longer that impertinent nose became.

After the nose he made the mouth. The mouth was hardly finished when it commenced to sing and laugh. "Stop laughing," said Geppetto, vexed; but it was like talking to the wall. "Stop laughing, I tell you," he said again in a loud tone. Then the features began to make grimaces.

Geppetto feigned not to see this impertinence and continued to work. After the mouth he made the chin, then the neck, then the shoulders, then the body, then the arms and hands.

Hardly had he finished the hands when Geppetto felt his wig pulled off. He turned quickly, and what do you think he saw?—his yellow wig in the hands of the marionette! "Pinocchio! give me back my wig immediately," said the old man. But Pinocchio, instead of giving back the wig, put it on his own head, making himself look half smothered.

At this disobedience Geppetto looked very sad, a thing he had never done before in all his life. Turning to Pinocchio, he said: "Bad little boy! You are not yet finished and already lack respect to your father. Bad, bad boy!" And he dried a tear.

There were now only the legs and feet to make. Scarcely were they finished when they began to kick poor Geppetto. "It is my fault," he said to himself; "I ought to have thought of this at first! Now it is too late!" Then he took the marionette in his arms and placed him on the ground to make him walk. Pinocchio behaved at first as if his legs were asleep and he could not move them. Geppetto led him around the room for some time, showing him how to put one foot in front of the other. When his legs were stretched Pinocchio began to walk and then to run around the room. When he saw the door open he jumped into the street and ran away.

Poor Geppetto ran as fast as he could, but he was not able to catch him; Pinocchio jumped like a rabbit. He made a noise with his wooden feet on the hard road like twenty pairs of little wooden shoes.

"Stop him! stop him!" cried Geppetto; but the people in the street, seeing the wooden marionette running as fast as a rabbit, stopped to look at it, and laughed, and laughed, and laughed, so that it is really hard to describe how they enjoyed it all.

Finally, through good fortune, a soldier appeared, who, hearing all the noise, thought that some colt had escaped from its master. He planted himself in the middle of the road and with a fixed look determined to catch the runaway. Pinocchio, when he saw the soldier in the road, tried to pass between his legs, but he could not do it. The soldier, scarcely moving his body, seized the marionette by the nose (which was a very ridiculous one, just the size to be seized by a soldier) and consigned him to the hands of Geppetto, who tried to correct him by pulling his ears. But just imagine—when he searched for the ears he could not find them! Do you know why? Because, in the haste of making Pinocchio, he did not finish carving them.

Taking him by the neck, Geppetto led him back, saying as he did so, "When we get home I must punish you."

Pinocchio, at this threat, threw himself on the ground and refused to walk farther. Meanwhile the curious people and the loungers began to stop and surround them. First one said something, then another. "Poor marionette!" said one of them, "he is right not to want to go back to his home. Who knows how hard Geppetto beats him?" And others added maliciously: "That Geppetto appears to be a kind man, but he is a tyrant with boys. If he gets that poor marionette in his hands, he will break him in pieces."

Altogether they made so much noise that the soldier gave Pinocchio back his liberty and took to prison instead the poor old man, who, not finding words at first with which to defend himself, wept bitterly, and on approaching the prison stammered out: "Wicked son! and to think I tried so hard to make a good marionette! I ought to have thought of all this at first."

What happened afterward is a story so strange that you will hardly believe it. However, I will tell it to you in the following chapters.

* * *

[Pinocchio Is Swallowed by the Dogfish]

When the donkey had been under water about an hour, the buyer, talking to himself, said: "Now my nice-looking lame donkey ought to be dead by this time. I will pull him up and then set to work to make a drum." And he began to pull the rope with which he had bound the donkey. He pulled and pulled and pulled, until he saw coming out of the water—what do you think? Instead of a dead donkey he saw a marionette, alive and kicking, struggling and twisting like an eel.

Seeing the wooden marionette, the buyer thought that he was dreaming; and he stood there astonished, with his mouth open and his eyes nearly out of his head. When he found words he said, "Where is the little donkey that I threw overboard?"

"I am that little donkey," replied the marionette, laughing.

"You?"

"I."

"Ah! You cheat! Do you think that you can make fun of me?"

"Make fun of you? On the contrary, I speak to you seriously."

"But how is it that a little while ago you were a donkey and now, after you have been in the water for an hour, you are a wooden marionette?"

"It is the effect of the sea water. The sea never tells its secrets, and this is one of its little tricks."

"Take care, marionette, take care! Do not think that you can pull wool over my eyes. Woe to you if I lose my patience!"

"Very well. Do you wish to know the true story? Untie my legs and I will tell you."

The buyer, curious to know the true story, untied the knots that bound the marionette; and then Pinocchio, finding himself as free as a bird in the air, said: "Know, then, that I was at first a wooden marionette as I am to-day. But I was on the point of becoming a boy, just like other boys, when I listened to the advice of a bad companion, and one morning I awoke and found myself turned into a donkey with big ears and a beautiful tail. What shame I felt when I saw that I had a tail! I was then led to a square where a master bought me and taught me to do tricks and dance. One night, when I was performing, I fell and sprained my leg so badly that I could hardly stand on it. Then the master, who did not know what to do with a lame donkey, sold me to you."

"Yes; I paid twenty-five cents for you. But who will give me my money back?"

"Yes; you bought me and planned to beat me by placing my skin over a drum."

"Where shall I find another skin?"

"That is not for me to say."

"Tell me, then, if you please, is your story finished?"

"No," replied the marionette; "there are a few more words, and then I shall be through. After you bought me you led me here to kill me; but then, being a humane man, you decided to drown me. This delicate attention on your part is most honorable and I shall always remember your goodness. You would have succeeded if it had not been for the good Fairy."

"Who is the Fairy?"

"She is my mamma, who is like all other mammas in this world. She liked me and tried to make me a good and studious boy. As soon as the good Fairy saw me in danger of drowning she sent a school of fishes, which, believing that I was really dead, began to eat me. And what mouthfuls they took! Some ate my ears; some my neck and mane; some the skin on my legs; some the hair on my back; and among them there was one big fish that ate my tail at one bite. When the fish had eaten everything they finally came to the bones,—or rather, they came to the wood. Finding that too hard for their teeth, they went away and did not even look back to say good-by."

"I do not believe your silly story," said the buyer, now very angry. "I know I have spent twenty-five cents and I want my money again. Do you know what I will do? I will carry you back to the square and sell you for a piece of kindling wood."

"All right!" said Pinocchio. Thus saying, he jumped into the water and, swimming lightly, drew away from the coast, calling to the poor buyer: "Good-by, dear sir! If you want a drumhead, don't forget me." And then he laughed and kept on swimming.

After a little time he turned around and shouted: "Good-by, dear sir! If you want a piece of kindling wood, don't forget me."

Almost in the twinkling of an eye he was so far away that he could hardly be seen; that is, one could see only a little black point on the water, splashing around just like a jolly dolphin.

Meanwhile, as Pinocchio swam around, he saw not very far away a rock which looked like white marble. On the top of the rock there was a beautiful Goat that bleated and made a sign to him to come nearer. The most singular thing about this goat was the color of its wool. It was not white or black or any color that other goats have. It was blue, just like the hair of the beautiful Fairy.

I will leave you to imagine how the heart of Pinocchio began to beat. He redoubled his efforts to reach the rock. Already he was halfway there when he saw coming out of the water the horrible head of a sea monster, with mouth opened wide like an abyss and three rows of teeth that would frighten you, even to see them painted in a picture book.

Can you guess who that monster was? It was no other than the huge Dogfish described several times in this story. On account of his destructive and bloodthirsty nature he was called "The Attila of fishes and fishermen."

Imagine the fright of poor Pinocchio at the sight of the monster! He sought to avoid him,—to change his road. He tried to escape; but that immense open mouth came always toward him with the velocity of an arrow.

"Hurry, Pinocchio!" cried the Goat, bleating loudly. And Pinocchio swam desperately with his arms, with his chest, with his legs, and with his feet.

"Hurry, Pinocchio, for the monster approaches you!" And Pinocchio, gathering his force, redoubled his strokes.

"Take care! take care! He is gaining! Hurry! Oh, hurry, or you are lost!" Pinocchio swam faster than ever, and away they both raced, going as fast as bullet balls. As they approached the rock the Goat held out its two front paws to aid Pinocchio to land. But—

It was too late! The monster had been too quick. Drawing in a quantity of water, he drank Pinocchio just as if he were sucking an egg. He swallowed him with such violence that the marionette arrived in the stomach of the Dogfish with such force that he was stunned for a quarter of an hour.

When he regained consciousness after being swallowed he did not know where he was. All around him was darkness so intense that he thought he had put his head into the top of an ink bottle. He listened but he heard nothing. From time to time he felt a great gust of wind striking his face. At first he did not know whence the wind came, but afterward he thought it was from the lungs of the monster; for you must know, my little readers, that the Dogfish was a great sufferer from asthma, and when he breathed it sounded like the north wind.

At first Pinocchio tried to be brave; but when he had tried and then tried again to find an exit and found himself still enclosed in the body of the monster, he began to cry and to scream: "Help! help! Oh, dear me! Is there no one who can save me?"

"Who wishes to be saved?" asked a voice that sounded in the darkness like a guitar out of tune.

"Who is it that speaks like that?" asked Pinocchio, feeling himself nearly frozen with fear.

"It is I. I am a poor Tunny fish, who was swallowed at the same time you were. What kind of fish are you?"

"I have nothing to do with fishes. I am a marionette."

"Then, if you are not a fish, why were you swallowed by the monster?"

"It is all your fault. If you had not been there, I surely should have escaped. And now what can we do in this dark place?"

"We must resign ourselves to our fate, and wait until we are digested."

"But I do not wish to be digested," said Pinocchio, beginning to cry.

"Neither do I wish to be digested," added the Tunny; "but I am philosopher enough to console myself by thinking that it is more dignified to die under water than to be soaking in vinegar and oil."

"Nonsense!" cried Pinocchio.

"It is my opinion," replied the Tunny; "and the opinion of fishes should be respected."

"As for me," said Pinocchio, "I wish to go away from here; I want to escape."

"Escape if you can."

"Is the Dogfish very large?" asked the marionette.

"Why, his body is a mile long without counting his tail."

In the meantime Pinocchio thought he saw in the distance a little glimmer of light.

"What can that be?" he asked.

"Some poor unfortunate that is probably being digested."

"Well, I am going to see. It may be some old fish that can tell me the way to walk around here."

"I wish you good luck, my poor marionette."

"Good-by, Tunny."

"Good-by, marionette, and good fortune go with you."

"When shall we meet again?"

"Who knows? It is better not to think of that."

[Pinocchio Finds Geppetto]

As soon as Pinocchio had said good-by to his friend the Tunny, he moved around, groping in the darkness. Walking inside the Dogfish, he advanced toward the little light that shone so far away.

As he groped along he felt his feet wading in a puddle of greasy, slippery water. The water had such a pungent odor of fried fish that he thought it must be Lent.

The more he walked, the clearer and more distinct became the light, until finally he arrived at the end of the passage. What did he find? I will let you guess a thousand times. He found a little table all nicely set, and lighted by a candle stuck into a green bottle. Seated behind the table he saw an old man with snow-white beard and hair, who was slowly eating some little live fish.

At the sight of the poor old man Pinocchio became so overjoyed that he nearly lost his senses. He wished to laugh; he wished to cry. He did not know what to do. He finally murmured some joyous sounds, for words stuck in his throat. Giving a cry of pleasure, he rushed to the old man, threw his arms around his neck, and cried: "Oh, my dear father! At last I have found you! Now I will never leave you again, never, never, never!"

"Do my eyes tell me truly?" asked the old man, rubbing them. "Do I really see my dear Pinocchio?"

"Yes, yes; it is I, truly, Pinocchio! And you have already forgiven me, have you not? Oh, my papa! How good you are! And to think that I— Oh, but if you only knew how many things have happened to me,—how many troubles and trials! Just imagine, the day you sold your coat for my A B C card I ran away from school and met some marionettes, and the manager wished to put me on the fire so that I could cook some mutton that he wanted to eat. He gave me some pieces of gold for you; but when I went toward home I met a Fox and a Cat, who led me to an inn called the Red Lobster, where they ate like wolves. I left the inn at night and met assassins who began to run after me and finally caught me and hanged me to a large oak. Then a beautiful Fairy with Blue Hair sent a carriage to take me to her house, where there were doctors who said if I was not dead it was a sign that I was alive. Then I told a lie and my nose commenced to grow so that I could not pass through the door of the room. After that I met the Fox and the Cat, who advised me to put the money in the ground and watch it grow. I lost it all, for I believed their story. When I told the judge of the town he put me in prison for being so foolish. After I was set free I walked along a road and, feeling hungry, I looked for a bunch of grapes; but I was caught in a trap and a farmer took me to his house and made me play dog. After I had caught the thieves that robbed his hencoop, he set me free; and I met a Serpent with a smoking tail, and it laughed so hard that it died. Then I hurried to the house of the beautiful Fairy, but she was gone. Oh, how unhappy I was! Then a Dove, seeing me cry, said to me, "I have seen your papa making a ship to go and look for you"; and I said, "Oh! if I had wings I would fly to him!" And the Dove said, "Get on my back"; and away we flew all night. The next day, when we arrived at the shore, the fishermen, looking toward the sea, said to me, "There in that boat is a poor old man who will sink"; for the water was so rough. And I ran to a rock and recognized you, because my heart told me that you were there; and I made a sign for you to come back to the shore—"

"I recognized you also," said Geppetto, "and I would willingly have come back; but how could I?—the sea was so rough and my boat was so frail. Then a horrible Dogfish that was near me put out its tongue and swallowed me like a pill."

"And how long have you been shut up here?" asked Pinocchio.

"Two years, Pinocchio, that seemed like two centuries."

"And how have you lived? And where did you find the candle and the matches to light it?"

"I will tell you all. Fortunately, when the Dogfish swallowed me he swallowed also the provisions I had on board the ship —"

"What? He swallowed all in a mouthful?" asked Pinocchio, surprised.

"All in a mouthful. But he did not like the mast of the boat; for that stuck in his teeth like a toothpick and he spat that out. As the boat was loaded with preserved meat, figs, biscuits, wine, raisins, coffee, sugar, candles, and matches, I was well supplied. To-day, however, I am burning my last candle—"

"And after that?"

"Why, my dear boy, we shall both be left in the dark."

"Then, Papa," said Pinocchio, "there is no time to lose. We must hurry and escape."

"How?"

"Why, we must escape from the mouth of the Dogfish and throw ourselves into the sea."

"But I do not know how to swim."

"That does not matter. You can get on my back and I will take you to the shore."

"You are dreaming, my boy," said Geppetto, shaking his head.

"Try it and see. Anyway, we shall have the consolation of dying together."

And without saying any more Pinocchio took the candle and started to walk toward the mouth of the Dogfish. "Come along, and do not be afraid, Papa," said Pinocchio.

And thus they walked along for a little while, traversing the whole length of the Dogfish's stomach. When they arrived at the end they stopped so as to look carefully before trying to escape.

Now, my little readers, you must know that the Dogfish, being very old and suffering from asthma and palpitation of the heart, was obliged to sleep with his mouth open. Pinocchio, therefore, looking up through the throat, saw the starry heavens and the light of the moon.

"This is truly the time to escape," whispered Pinocchio; "the Dogfish sleeps and the sea is very smooth. Come, then, Papa. Follow me and we shall soon be outside."

No sooner said than done. They mounted the throat of the huge sea monster and, arriving in the immense mouth, began to walk on the tips of their toes along the tongue. Suddenly the Dogfish sneezed. The candle was blown out, and both Geppetto and Pinocchio were given a violent shake and found themselves back once more in the Dogfish's stomach.

"Now we are truly lost," said Geppetto.

"Give me your hand, and be careful not to slip."

"Where are you leading me?"

"Come along and do not be afraid."

Thus saying, Pinocchio took his papa's hand and again they mounted the throat of the monster, always going on tiptoe. Then passing along the tongue and the three rows of teeth, they found themselves out in the air.

"Get on my back," said Pinocchio, "and hold on tight."

Scarcely had Geppetto placed his arms around Pinocchio's neck when the brave marionette began to swim. The sea was as smooth as oil, the moon was resplendent, and the Dogfish continued to sleep so soundly that not even a cannon shot would have awakened him.

[Pinocchio Becomes a Real Boy]

While Pinocchio swam fast so as to reach the beach quickly, he perceived that his papa, who sat on his back, trembled just as if he had a high fever. Did he tremble from cold or fear? Who knows? Perhaps a little of both. But Pinocchio, believing that he trembled from fear, said to him in a comforting tone: "Courage, Papa! In a little while we shall arrive on the shore safe and sound."

"But where is the shore?" asked the old man, becoming more and more uneasy and straining his eyes to see it, just as tailors do when they thread a needle. "Here we are, swimming all night; and I see only sky and sea."

"But I see the shore," said the marionette. "Through your skill in making me, I can see in the night as well as a cat."

Poor Pinocchio pretended to be in good humor; but he was really beginning to lose heart. His strength was giving out and his breath growing shorter. In fact, he could not swim much longer and the shore could not be seen.

He swam until he had no more breath. Then he turned his head toward Geppetto and said in broken tones, "Help me, Papa, or I shall die."

The father and the boy were nearly drowned when they heard a voice, like a guitar out of tune, saying, "Who is going to die?"

"My papa and I."

"I recognize that voice. You are Pinocchio."

"Exactly; and who are you?"

"I am Tunny, your companion in the Dogfish's stomach."

"How did you escape?"

"I followed your example. You taught me the way; and after I saw you go, I went also."

"Oh, my friend, you have come just in time! I pray you, for the love you bear your little tunny fishes, to help us, or we are lost."

"With all my heart! Get on my back and in a few minutes we shall reach land."

As you may easily imagine, Geppetto and Pinocchio quickly accepted the invitation.

"Are we too heavy?" asked Pinocchio.

"Heavy? Why, you are like two shadows. It seems to me that I have two small shells on my back."

When they arrived at the shore Pinocchio was the first to jump down, and he helped his papa. Then he turned to the Tunny and, with a voice that trembled with emotion, said: "My friend, you have saved my papa and me. I do not know how to thank you. Permit me to kiss you as a sign of eternal friendship."

The Tunny put his nose out of the water, and Pinocchio, kneeling on the ground, gave the fish an affectionate kiss. At this sign of tenderness the poor Tunny, who was not accustomed to such kindness, felt himself so moved that he began to cry like a baby, and quickly sank into the water to hide his tears.

In the meantime the sun arose. Then Pinocchio, offering his arm to his papa, who was very weak, said: "Lean on my arm, dear Papa, and let us go. We will walk just as slowly as ants, and when we are tired we will rest ourselves."

"And where shall we go?" asked Geppetto.

"In search of a house where we can get a bit to eat and some straw to lie upon."

But they had not gone a hundred steps when they saw two ugly faces asking for money. They were the faces of the Fox and the Cat; but one would not have recognized them. Just think! the Cat who feigned to be blind had really become so, and the Fox's hair was all shaggy and he had lost his tail.

"Oh, Pinocchio," cried the Fox, "give a little charity to two old people."

"Two old people," repeated the Cat.

"Good-by, masqueraders," replied Pinocchio; "you deceived me once and now you are paying for it."

"Believe us, Pinocchio, we are to-day truly poor and starving."

"Truly," repeated the Cat.

"If you are poor, you deserve it. Remember the proverb that says, "Stolen money will never bear fruit." Good-by, deceivers!"

"Have compassion on us."

"On us," said the Cat.

"Good-by. Remember the proverb that says, "Stolen wheat always makes poor bread." "

"Do not abandon us."

"Good-by. Remember the proverb, "Whoever steals the cloak of his neighbor usually dies without a shirt." "

Geppetto and Pinocchio continued their walk until they saw a small farmhouse with a straw roof.

"That house is inhabited by some one," said Pinocchio. "Let us go and knock at the door."

"Who is there?" said a voice inside, when they had reached the house.

"We are a poor papa and his son, without bread or a home," replied the marionette.

"Turn the key and the door will open," said the same voice.

Pinocchio turned the key and the door opened. As soon as they entered the house they looked around, but saw no one. "Where is the master of this house?" asked Pinocchio, greatly surprised.

"Here I am, up here."

Papa and son turned quickly and saw on a rafter the Talking Cricket.

"Oh, my dear Cricket!" said Pinocchio, saluting him politely.

"Now you call me your dear Cricket, do you not? Do you remember the time when you struck me with a hammer?"

"Yes, you were right, Cricket. Take a hammer and hit me, but spare my poor papa."

"I will have pity on you both; but I wished to remind you of your ugly manners."

"Yes, Cricket, you were right to tell me what you did. You were right, and I will bear in mind the lessons you have taught me. But tell me, how did you build such a nice large house?"

"This little house was given me yesterday by a beautiful Goat that had blue wool?"

"And where has the Goat gone?" asked Pinocchio, with lively curiosity.

"I do not know."

"And when will it return?"

"Never. Yesterday it went away bleating. I thought I heard it say, 'Poor Pinocchio! I shall never see him again. The Dogfish has swallowed him.' "

"It said that? Then it was she. It was the beautiful Fairy," said Pinocchio, and he began to cry.

When he had cried a long time he dried his eyes and prepared a nice bed of straw for his papa. Then he said to the Talking Cricket, "Tell me, Cricket, where I can find a glass of milk for my poor papa."

"Three fields from here you will see a farmer who has cows. Go to him and you will find the milk you seek."

Pinocchio ran toward the farmer and said to him, "Will you please give me some milk?"

"How much do you want?"

"I want a glassful."

"A glass of milk costs one cent. Where is the money?"

"I have nothing," cried Pinocchio, mortified.

"If you have no money, I have no milk."

"I am so sorry!" said Pinocchio.

"Wait a minute," said the farmer; "I think we can arrange it. Do you know how to draw water from a well?"

"I can try."

"Well, draw me one hundred bucketfuls and I will give you a glass of milk."

"All right!"

Pinocchio worked so hard that when he had finished he was wet with perspiration from head to foot. He had never felt so tired in all his life.

"I have a little donkey that draws water for me; but to-day he is sick, poor thing!"

"May I see him?" asked Pinocchio.

"Certainly."

As soon as Pinocchio saw the donkey he recognized him. "I think I know that donkey," said he. Speaking to it in the donkey language, he asked, "Who are you?" At the question the donkey opened his eyes and replied in the same language, "I am Lamp Wick"; then he closed his eyes again.

"Oh, my poor Lamp Wick," said Pinocchio in an undertone; and then he took a little hay and gave it to him.

"Why do you take so much interest in a donkey that is not worth a cent?" asked the farmer.

"I will tell you. He was a friend of mine."

"Your friend?"

"Yes; a school companion."

"How is that?" asked the farmer, bursting into laughter. "You had donkeys for school companions?"

The marionette felt so mortified at these words that he took the glass of milk and returned to his papa.

From that day, for five months afterward, Pinocchio continued to get up in the morning at daybreak to draw water for the farmer; and he gained only a little milk for his trouble. He was not contented with simply doing that; he learned to make straw mats and sold them to buy food for his daily wants. Among other things, he made a little cart so that he could take his papa out and give him a little fresh air.

In the evenings he practiced reading and writing. In fact, he behaved so nicely that his papa was overjoyed. One morning he said to Geppetto: "I am going to market to buy a jacket, a cap, and a pair of shoes. When I come back I shall be dressed like a real gentleman."

Outside the house he began to run, because he was so happy. Suddenly he heard himself called by name, and, turning, he saw a beautiful Snail.

"Do you not know me?" asked the Snail.

"It seems to me— It seems to me—"

"Don't you remember the Snail that lived with the beautiful Fairy with the Blue Hair?"

"I remember all," cried Pinocchio. "Tell me quickly, where is the beautiful Fairy now?"

At these words the Snail replied with his usual slowness, "The beautiful Fairy lies ill in a hospital."

"In a hospital?"

"Yes. Wounded by so many misfortunes, she is very sick and so poor that she eats only a mouthful of bread each day."

"Truly? Oh, what a blow you have given me! Oh, my poor Fairy, my poor Fairy! If I had a million, I would give it all to you, but I have only forty cents, which I was going to use to buy some clothes. Take my money, Snail, and carry it quickly to the good Fairy."

"And what about your clothes?"

"What does that matter? I would sell these rags in order to help her. Go, Snail, and in two days come back, and I will have some more money for her."

The Snail began to get excited and ran as if a bird were after him.

When Pinocchio returned home his papa asked him, "Where are your new clothes?"

"I heard from the Snail that my good Fairy was ill in the hospital and so poor that she had no food, so I sent her the forty cents."

That night, instead of going to bed, Pinocchio worked until midnight. Afterward he went to bed and slept. And while he slept he thought he saw the good Fairy, all beautiful and happy and smiling, who, after giving him a kiss, said: "Good Pinocchio! For your good heart I pardon all your misdeeds. Boys that help their parents lovingly in their troubles always deserve praise and affection." Just here Pinocchio's dream ended and he awoke with his eyes opened wide.

Now imagine, little readers, the great surprise of Pinocchio, upon waking, to find that he was no longer a wooden marionette, but that he had become a boy like all the others! He gave a glance around him and, instead of a bed of straw, he saw a room beautifully furnished. Jumping down from his bed, he found prepared for him a nice new suit, a new cap, and a pair of new shoes.

He had scarcely dressed himself

when, like all boys who have a new suit, he put his hands into his pockets; and just imagine his surprise when he pulled out a small pocketbook of mother-of-pearl, on which were written these words: "The Fairy with the Blue Hair returns the forty cents to her dear Pinocchio and thanks him with all her heart." Opening the pocketbook, he found, instead of forty pennies, forty pieces of gold.

Afterward he went to look in the looking-glass and he did not know himself. He saw no longer the reflection of a wooden marionette, but the image of a bright and intelligent boy with chestnut hair and large bright eyes. Pinocchio was greatly surprised. In the midst of these marvels that happened one after another he did not know whether it was all real or whether it was a dream.

"Where is my papa?" he cried suddenly. Then, entering the next room, he found Geppetto well and as young as when he first began his profession of carving.

"What does it all mean, dear Papa?" asked Pinocchio.

"It means that you must try to deserve all this beautiful house," said Geppetto.

"I *will* try," said Pinocchio. "And why is it that you look so well and young?"

"Because when bad boys become good, they cause everything to change for the better and make the whole family happy."

"And the old wooden Pinocchio—where is it hidden?"

"There it is," replied Geppetto, pointing to a wooden marionette leaning on a chair with its head limp, its arms hanging down, and its legs crossed, so that it was a wonder that it could stand at all.

Pinocchio turned to look at his old self; and after he had regarded it a little while, he said with great satisfaction: "How naughty I was when I was a marionette! and how happy I am now that I have become a real live boy!"

Fiction

THE SIGN ON ROSIE'S DOOR

Maurice Sendak

Maurice Sendak has been widely praised as an illustrator and, increasingly, as a writer of fantasy. Where the Wild Things Are *(1963),* Higglety Pigglety Pop! *(1967), and* Night Kitchen *(1970), especially, show the boldness of imagination and oneness with the child that are characteristic of Sendak. In 1970, he was awarded the Hans Christian Andersen Medal, the first time an American artist had received this award.*

The Sign on Rosie's Door *is a hilarious and accurate representation of children at play. The selection that follows is the first chapter of the book.*

From Maurice Sendak, *The Sign on Rosie's Door* (New York: Harper and Row, 1960), Chapter 1. Illustrated by the author.

There was a sign on Rosie's door.

It read, "If you want to know a secret, knock three times."

Kathy knocked three times and Rosie opened the door.

"Hello, Kathy."

"Hello, Rosie. What's the secret?"

"I'm not Rosie any more," said Rosie. "That's the secret."

"Then who are you?" asked Kathy.

"I'm Alinda, the lovely lady singer."

"Oh," said Kathy.

"And someday," said Rosie, "I'll sing in a great musical show."

"When?" Kathy asked.

"Now, in my back yard. Want to come?"

"Can I be somebody too?" asked Kathy.

Rosie had to think for a minute.

"I suppose," she said finally, "you can be Cha-Charoo, my Arabian dancing girl."

"All right," said Kathy. "I'll come."

And everybody came. Dolly and Pudgy and Sal.

"Now sit down everybody," Rosie said.

They all sat down on folding chairs.

"Now keep quiet everybody," said Rosie. "The show is going to begin."

They all sat quietly. Rosie and Kathy disappeared behind the cellar door.

"This is a good show," Pudgy whispered.

"It is," said Dolly.

BAM, BAM, BAM! came the sound of a drum from behind the cellar door.

"Ladies and gentlemen!" cried a faraway voice. "We have for your pleasure Cha-Charoo, the Arabian dancing girl. Clap and shout hooray!"

Everybody shouted and clapped. The cellar door opened and Kathy stepped out. She wore a nightgown and had a towel over her head. She waved her arms and took three little steps.

"Cha-Charoo-roo-roo," she sang softly.

"That's enough," cried the voice from behind the cellar door.

"Clap, everybody, and shout hooray!"

Clap. Clap. Clap!

"Hooray. Hooray. Hooray!"

"Now comes the best part of the show," the voice continued. "Me, Alinda, the lovely lady singer, who will sing for your pleasure "On the Sunny Side of the Street." Everybody say Oh and Ah!"

"Oh!"

"Ah!"

"Oh, ah!"

The cellar door opened and out came Alinda. She wore a hat with feathers sticking out, a lady's dress, and high-heeled shoes.

"Hello, everybody!" someone said.

Everybody turned and saw Lenny wearing a fireman's hat.

"Can I play too?" he asked.

"We're not playing," Alinda shouted. "It's a real show and you can't."

"Why?"

"Because."

"Anyway," said Lenny, "I have to go put out a fire. Everybody want to come?"

They all shook their heads no.

Lenny ran out of the yard.

"Now I'll sing," Alinda said.

She closed her eyes. "On the sun—"

"Want to know something?" asked Lenny.

He was back again.

"What?" asked Alinda.

"I know a trick," said Lenny.

"What trick?"

"First," Lenny explained, "I throw my fireman's hat up in the air and then the one who catches it can keep it. Everybody want to play?"

They all shook their heads yes.

"All right," said Alinda.

Lenny threw the hat high into the air and it landed on Rosie's window ledge.

"How will we catch it now?" Kathy asked.

"We'll have to climb up for it," said Alinda.

So they did. Sal climbed on top of Pudgy. Dolly climbed on top of Sal. Kathy on top of Dolly. Lenny on top of Kathy, and Alinda on top of everybody. She took the fireman's hat off the window ledge and put it on her head.

"I caught it, it's mine," she shouted. "Hooray for me!"

They all climbed down.

"Come on, Pudgy," he called. "Come on, Sal, help me put the fire out!"

"We better help him," said Pudgy.

"He needs us," said Sal.

"But—" Alinda began.

But they were already gone.

"I better go too," said Dolly.

"I didn't sing my song yet," said Alinda.

"I'm hungry," Dolly answered. And she went home.

"Now I'll sing," Alinda said.

She stretched out her arms. "On the sun—"

"Give me back my hat," said Lenny. "I have to go put out another fire."

"No," said Alinda. "You said for keeps."

"It was only a game," said Lenny, "and my mother says I shouldn't give anything away any more."

He pulled the hat off Alinda's head and ran out of the yard.

They were all gone. Two of the folding chairs lay on their sides.

"It's getting late," said Kathy. "I have to go home."

"Wasn't it a wonderful show?" asked Rosie.

"It was the best I ever saw," Kathy answered. "Let's have another one soon."

"Same time, same place," said Rosie.

"Good-by, Cha-Charoo."

"Good-by, Alinda."

Rosie was all alone. She climbed on top of a folding chair and said very quietly, "Ladies and gentlemen, Alinda will now sing 'On the Sunny Side of the Street.' "

And she sang the song all the way to the end.

THE BOY AND THE WHALE

José Maria Sanchez-Silva

The Boy's best friend was the Whale. They were seldom apart—sometimes he kept her in a glass of water, sometimes just loose in his pocket, and together they had many adventures. However, although the Boy loved the Whale better than anyone in the world, he had to keep her a secret, for she was an imaginary whale. As the Boy grew older he started to forget about the Whale, allowing her to go when she announced that she was going to the Arctic Circle to visit her Grandmother. When she came to say good-bye it was for the last time. Santiago was no longer a Boy—he had grown up.

This gentle story of a child's imaginary companion captures one of the most common of children's play experiences. The selection that follows is from the first chapter of the book.

The Boy was a boy like most other boys. He lived in Madrid with his family, and he had a Grandmother, a Father, a Mother, a Sister and a Whale.

His Grandmother was old and wise. She had very good hearing, so good that sometimes she could even hear what the Boy was thinking.

The Boy rarely saw his Father, because his Father was still asleep when he got up. Later, when the Boy came home from school for lunch, his Father was still at the office, and when he came home in the afternoon his Father had gone back to the office. When his Father came home at last, tired out, the Boy had gone to bed.

His Mother was a special person; she was someone with whom he was always safe, especially when he was frightened or hurt. The Boy loved her very much when she was there, but sometimes he would forget her and when he realized it, he used to run and find her and give her a kiss. "What an affectionate child he is!" said his Grandmother.

The Boy's Sister was hardly anything at all, she was so small. When she was born and they had shown her to him, all red and covered with down, the Boy thought, "I'd rather have my whale."

Indeed, the Whale was not quite as ordinary as the rest of the family. There was something rather mysterious about her. She was like all other whales, as whales go, except for one detail—she

From José Maria Sanchez-Silva, *The Boy and the Whale* (New York: McGraw-Hill, 1964), Chapter 1 (pp. 7–26). Translated by Michael Heron.

could make herself large or small as the Boy wanted. At her biggest she weighed a million tons and was almost a mile long; at her smallest she fitted into his pocket. But if he wanted she could also be the size of a dog, a horse or an elephant.

The Whale was the Boy's very own. He could not remember how long he had had her, she had always been with him. Perhaps she had been born at the same time as he was?

One of the Boy's favorite places for playing with his Whale was under the table in the sewing room. But he kept her with him all the time and at night he left her in a glass of water on his bedside table. It was very simple. When the Boy went to bed he opened his hand above the glass and said, "Goodnight, Whale."

When he got up in the morning he closed his hand above the glass and said, "Time to get up, Whale."

On some nights he was so sleepy that he didn't have time to leave his Whale in the water and he went to sleep with her clasped in his hand. When this happened he had nice dreams.

The Boy had never been very interested in toys, but when he did play with them his Whale played, too. The Boy wasn't very old, but for several years now he had been seen, both at home and in the street, trailing a piece of string. And *he* knew perfectly well that at the other end of the string was—the Whale.

Sometimes when he said his prayers he prayed for his Whale as well. It was so wonderful to have a Whale!

While the Boy's Sister was still a baby the Whale and he used to play with her very gently, although once she fell out of the Boy's arms and if it hadn't been for the Whale who got underneath at once and caught her, heaven only knows what would have happened.

Later, between them, they made her laugh. You should have seen the funny positions the Whale could get into. She could stand on her tail, she could stand on her head and she could walk along on her tail and both fins, looking like a lobster. That made his Sister laugh most of all because of the clumsy hops the Whale had to make. And little by little the Boy and his Whale showed her how to walk, on those rare occasions when there was no one else in the house except the Grandmother, who kept dropping off to sleep. Then the Boy and his Whale used to play with the Sister, but very, very quietly.

If the Sister laughed they could go on, but when she stopped it was better to run away quickly, because a flood of tears, like a storm, was very close.

And when the storm came the Grandmother would wake up and wonder what was the matter.

"What's wrong with my darling? She was sleeping so peacefully and I was sitting here watching her all the time. Let's see, let's see."

And she changed the baby's diapers, but that didn't help. She shook up the pillow in the cot, but that didn't help either. And in desperation she had to pick her up.

A few years later, quite suddenly, the Boy realized that his Sister was no longer a baby and he tried to share his games with her. For a long time he had been finding it hard to keep the Whale a secret, and finally his will power gave way and he told her. She pulled a very odd face.

"Where is she?" she asked.

"Well, no one can see her," said the Boy.

"What's her name?"

The Boy remembered that his Whale didn't have a name. She was simply called the Whale. But perhaps that was not fair, he thought, so he said the first name that came into his head.

"She's called Josefina."

That seemed to impress his Sister. It was quite different if the Whale was called Josefina.

The Boy told himself that he would only call the Whale Josefina when he was talking to his Sister; on his own he would go on calling her just the Whale.

But he had forgotten what chatterboxes little girls are. On Sunday at lunch time, in front of everybody, she pointed at him with her spoon and shouted, "He's got a whale!"

His Father thought she was talking

about some sort of insect and asked in alarm, "Where?"

His Grandmother chuckled and when his Father realized that no one could carry a whale around he merely said: "What nonsense!" And he took a sip of soda water.

Meanwhile the Boy flashed a look at his Sister which said, "You'd better watch out."

But he had forgotten that the Whale might have an opinion about her new name. When lunch was over and he was searching for his Sister to carry out his threat, he joined the Whale under the table in the sewing room and this is what he heard: "Do you know something? I quite like the name Josefina."

Although she didn't say much the Whale did talk on important occasions. The first time the Boy heard her was when he wondered out loud if whales could jump.

"Yes, we can jump," said the Whale.

"Do you speak Spanish?" asked the Boy after a long pause.

And the Whale, who was as old and wise as the Boy's Grandmother, replied very good-temperedly, "No."

From that day the Whale used to tell him stories, although they were always shorter than the Boy would have liked. In the very first story she tried to explain something about how whales lived.

While the Boy was busy talking to the Whale under the table, his Sister came into the sewing room and settled down to play with her dolls. The Boy got up very quietly, jumped out at her and smacked her for telling tales. Then he pulled her hair for luck. The little girl screamed and yelled, and the Grandmother appeared quickly to make peace. His Sister was carried out in her Grandmother's arms, but quite suddenly she jumped down, ran back to the sewing room and, crimson with rage, shouted from the door, "Josefina isn't real, Josefina isn't real!"

"Don't take any notice," said the Whale.

The Boy was still very small when he learned that whales really live in the sea, but the Boy had never been to the seaside. Although the Whale explained it all very carefully, he could hardly believe that the sea had more water in it than a thousand million bathrooms with the bathtubs overflowing.

The Boy had never seen the sea because he lived in Madrid (in the middle of Spain) and his family also had a house in Torrelodones, a place nearby which is cool in summer. But the Whale took him to the sea one night.

In the sea the Whale made herself enormous without being asked, and the Boy rode on her back, which was as firm and comfortable as a mattress. After that they went to sea when he wanted to be alone with the Whale, because what the Boy liked best of all in the world was to be an island. With the Boy perched on top, the two of them, surrounded by the water in the darkness, used to talk, play and think, without anyone bothering them. Except his Grandmother who sometimes spied his head among the waves and said, "Supper time," or "Time to go to bed."

If it was raining heavily the Boy climbed into the Whale's mouth. Then, on the high seas, with the Whale her real size, the boy could shelter safely. He thought—and it was perfectly true—that her mouth was as big, if not bigger, than the living room at home. It would even have held the two pianos (his and his Grandmother's) which had to be left outside in the passage.

His Mother and Father knew nothing about the Whale. Once, and once only, the Boy had told his Mother, "Mummy, I've got a whale in my glass."

But luckily for him he said it when he was ill in bed and his Mother called his Grandmother saying, "Fetch the thermometer, quickly!"

It was a different matter with his Grandmother. I've already told you that the Boy's Grandmother sometimes heard his thoughts. She also heard everything that was said in the house and the house next door, and in the house at Torrelodones and the house next door to that as well. He had no need to tell her that he had a whale.

Almost before he knew how to read, his Grandmother had given him a book about animals with pictures and photographs of whales showing their fins looking like ears. The Boy was fascinated by it and often used to ask her, "Grandmother, tell me more about whales."

First of all she told him that they spouted up great jets of water.

"Steam," corrected the Whale when the Boy told her what he knew.

And it was this remark which was to blame for what happened next day in the shower. The bathroom was another of the Boy's favorite places for playing with the Whale, for it is a place you can have to yourself for a while. Once he had ordered her to make herself big in there and he had had to squash himself against the wall to let her grow. Suddenly he was frightened and had to shout quickly, "Make yourself small!"

But worse was to come, for on this day he did not dare to ask her to make herself big, and he decided to play by himself. He climbed up on two chairs and arranged them so that he could swivel the shower head upwards; then he turned on the water. It did not much look like a whale blowing, but it made a mess of the bathroom and cost him a smacking from his Father and a day without his favorite pudding.

It was not that his Grandmother knew such a lot about whales, but she did her very best because she really loved her grandson.

"Did Grandfather know much more about whales than you?" asked the Boy.

"Well, not really. What your Grandfather was really interested in was partridges."

And so his poor Grandmother racked her brains to find things to tell him about whales and, between what she remembered from her childhood and what she found out secretly from her friends and relations, she always had some piece of information. She also had a whole collection of whale stories to tell him.

One story was about Saint Brendan and the island which later turned out to be a whale. This story made a great impression on the Boy. But the first story was the one about the prophet Jonah who was carried off by a whale to take a message from God to the city of Nineveh. He liked that one, too.

The story of Sinbad the Sailor, which she also told him, was rather like the one about the island of Saint Brendan but he did not like it as much. He liked some of her other stories though.

One afternoon his Grandmother asked, "You're very fond of whales, aren't you?"

The Boy's eyes shone and he said very slowly, "Yes, I've got one."

"Have you?"

The light died out of his eyes. "But you can't see her." His Grandmother understood perfectly: she was at the age when people understand.

"Of course I can't," she said, "because I'm grown up."

The Boy looked doubtful.

"Yes. That's the only reason," and she sighed. "If only I could turn myself into a little girl again!"

"What would happen?"

"I'd be able to see her."

"And what would you do?"

"I would ask her to take good care of you."

"Can I tell her that?"

"Yes. And give her my kind regards."

At that moment the Whale said, "Wish her the same from me."

But his Grandmother did not hear and the Boy had fallen alseep.

* * *

Poetry

THE DUEL
Eugene Field

The gingham dog and the calico cat
Side by side on the table sat;
'Twas half past twelve, and (what do
you think!)
Nor one nor t'other had slept a wink!
The old Dutch clock and the Chinese
plate
Appeared to know as sure as fate
There was going to be a terrible spat.
(I wasn't there; I simply state
What was told to me by the Chinese
plate.)

The gingham dog went,
"Bow-wow-wow!"
And the calico cat replied, "Mee-ow!"
The air was littered, an hour or so,
With bits of gingham and calico,
While the old Dutch clock in the
chimney place
Up with its hands before its face,
For it always dreaded a family row.
(Now mind, I'm only telling you
What the old Dutch clock declares is
true.)

The Chinese plate looked very blue,
And wailed, "Oh, dear! What shall we
do?"
But the gingham dog and the calico cat
Wallowed this way and tumbled that,
Employing every tooth and claw
In the awfullest way you ever saw—
And, oh, how the gingham and calico
flew!
(Don't fancy I exaggerate;
I got my news from the Chinese
plate.)

Next morning, where the two had sat
They found no trace of dog or cat;
And some folks think unto this day
That burglars stole that pair away.
But the truth about the cat and pup
Is this: they ate each other up!
Now what do you really think of that!
(The old Dutch clock, it told me so,
And that is how I came to know.)

THE LAND OF STORY BOOKS
Robert Louis Stevenson

At evening when the lamp is lit,
Around the fire my parents sit;
They sit at home and talk and sing,
And do not play at anything.

Now, with my little gun, I crawl
All in the dark along the wall,
And follow round the forest track
Away behind the sofa back.

There, in the night, where none can
spy,
All in my hunter's camp I lie,
And play at books that I have read
Till it is time to go to bed.

These are the hills, these are the woods,
These are my starry solitudes;
And there the river by whose brink
The roaring lions come to drink.

I see the others far away
As if in firelit camp they lay,
And I, like to an Indian scout,
Around their party prowled about.

So, when my nurse comes in for me,
Home I return across the sea,
And go to bed with backward looks
At my dear Land of Story Books.

US TWO

A. A. Milne

Wherever I am, there's always Pooh,
There's always Pooh and Me.
Whatever I do, he wants to do.
"Where are you going to-day?" says
Pooh:
"Well, that's very odd 'cos I was too.
Let's go together," says Pooh, says he.
"Let's go together," says Pooh.

"What's twice eleven?" I said to Pooh.
("Twice what?" said Pooh to Me.)
"I *think* it ought to be twenty-two."
"Just what I think myself," said Pooh.
"It wasn't an easy sum to do,
But that's what it is," said Pooh, said he.
"That's what it is," said Pooh.

"Let's look for dragons," I said to Pooh.
"Yes, let's," said Pooh to Me.
We crossed the river and found a few—
"Yes, those are dragons all right," said
Pooh.
"As soon as I saw their beaks I knew.
That's what they are," said Pooh, said
he.
"That's what they are," said Pooh.

"Let's frighten the dragons," I said to
Pooh.
"That's right," said Pooh to Me.
"*I'm* not afraid," I said to Pooh,
And I held his paw and I shouted "Shoo!
Silly old dragons!"—and off they flew.
"I wasn't afraid," said Pooh, said he,
"I'm *never* afraid with you."

So wherever I am, there's always Pooh,
There's always Pooh and Me.
"What would I do?" I said to Pooh,
"If it wasn't for you," and Pooh said:
"True,
It isn't much fun for One, but Two
Can stick together," says Pooh, says he.
"That's how it is," says Pooh.

BLOCK CITY

Robert Louis Stevenson

What are you able to build with your
blocks?
Castles and palaces, temples and docks.
Rain may keep raining, and others go
roam,
But I can be happy and building at
home.

Let the sofa be mountains, the carpet be
sea,
There I'll establish a city for me:
A kirk and a mill and a palace beside,
And a harbour as well where my vessels
may ride.

Great is the palace with pillar and wall,
A sort of a tower on the top of it all,
And steps coming down in an orderly
way
To where my toy vessels lie safe in the
bay.

This one is sailing and that one is
moored:
Hark to the song of the sailors on board!
And see, on the steps of my palace, the
kings
Coming and going with presents and
things!

Now I have done with it, down let it go!
All in a moment the town is laid low.
Block upon block lying scattered and
free,
What is there left of my town by the
sea?

Yet as I saw it, I see it again,
The kirk and the palace, the ships and
the men,
And as long as I live and where'er I
may be,
I'll always remember my town by the
sea.

PAPER BOATS

Rabindranath Tagore

Day by day I float my paper boats one
by one,
Down the running stream,
In big black letters I write my name on
them and the name of the village
where I live.
I hope that someone in some strange
land will find them and know who I
am.
I load my little boats with shiuli flowers
from our garden, and hope that
these blooms of dawn will be
carried safely to land in the night.
I launch my paper boats and look up
into the sky and see the little clouds
setting their white bulging sails.
I know not what playmate of mine in
the sky sends them down the air to
race with my boats!
When night comes I bury my face in my
arms and dream that my paper
boats float on and on under the
midnight stars.
The fairies of sleep are sailing in them,
and the lading is their baskets full of
dreams.

A SWING SONG

William Allingham

Swing, swing,
Sing, sing,
Here! my throne and I am a king!
Swing, sing,
Swing, sing,
Farewell, earth, for I'm on the wing!

Low, high,
Here I fly,
Like a bird through sunny sky;
Free, free,
Over the lea,
Over the mountain, over the sea!

Up, down,
Up and down,
Which is the way to London Town?
Where? Where?
Up in the air,
Close your eyes and now you are there!

Soon, soon,
Afternoon,
Over the sunset, over the moon;
Far, far,
Over all bar,
Sweeping on from star to star!

No, no,
Low, low,
Sweeping daisies with my toe.
Slow, slow,
To and fro,
Slow—slow—slow—slow.

THE LAND OF COUNTERPANE

Robert Louis Stevenson

When I was sick and lay a-bed,
I had two pillows at my head,
And all my toys beside me lay
To keep me happy all the day.

And sometimes for an hour or so
I watched my leaden soldiers go,
With different uniforms and drills,
Among the bed-clothes, through the
hills;

And sometimes sent my ships in fleets
All up and down among the sheets;
Or brought my trees and houses out,
And planted cities all about.

I was the giant great and still
That sits upon the pillow-hill,
And sees before him, dale and plain,
The pleasant land of counterpane.

LINES AND SQUARES

A. A. Milne

Whenever I walk in a London street,
I'm ever so careful to watch my feet;
And I keep in the squares,
And the masses of bears,
Who wait at the corners all ready to eat
The sillies who tread on the lines of the street,
Go back to their lairs,
And I say to them, "Bears,
Just look how I'm walking in all the squares!"

And the little bears growl to each other, "He's mine,
As soon as he's silly and steps on a line."
And some of the bigger bears try to pretend
That they came round the corner to look for a friend;
And they try to pretend that nobody cares
Whether you walk on the lines or squares.
But only the sillies believe their talk;
It's ever so portant how you walk.
And it's ever so jolly to call out, "Bears,
Just watch me walking in all the squares!"

THE KITE

Harry Behn

How bright on the blue
Is a kite when it's new!

With a dive and a dip
It snaps its tail

Then soars like a ship
With only a sail

As over tides
Of wind it rides,

Climbs to the crest
Of a gust and pulls,

Then seems to rest
As wind falls.

When string goes slack
You wind it back

And run until
A new breeze blows

And its wings fill
And up it goes!

How bright on the blue
Is a kite when it's new!

But a raggeder thing
You never will see

When it flaps on a string
In the top of a tree.

THE PICKETY FENCE

David McCord

The pickety fence
The pickety fence
Give it a lick it's
The pickety fence
Give it a lick it's
A clickety fence
Give it a lick it's
A lickety fence
Give it a lick
Give it a lick
Give it a lick
With a rickety stick
Pickety
Pickety
Pickety
Pick

HIDING
Dorothy Aldis

I'm hiding, I'm hiding,
And no one knows where;
For all they can see is my
Toes and my hair.

And I just heard my father
Say to my mother—
"But, darling, he must be
Somewhere or other;

"Have you looked in the inkwell?"
And Mother said, "Where?"
"In the *inkwell,"* said Father. But
I was not there.

Then "Wait!" cried my mother—
"I think that I see
Him under the carpet." But
It was not me.

"Inside the mirror's
A pretty good place,"
Said Father and looked, but saw
Only his face.

"We've hunted," sighed Mother,
"As hard as we could
And I *am* so afraid that we've
Lost him for good."

Then I laughed out aloud
And I wiggled my toes
And Father said—"Look, dear,
I wonder if those

"Toes could be Benny's?
There are ten of them, see?"
And they *were* so surprised to find
Out it was me!

BLUM
Dorothy Aldis

Dog means dog,
And cat means cat;
And there are lots
Of words like that.

A cart's a cart
To pull or shove,
A plate's a plate,
To eat off of.

But there are other
Words I say
When I am left
Alone to play.

Blum is one.
Blum is a word
That very few
Have ever heard.

I like to say it,
"Blum, Blum, Blum"—
I do it loud
Or in a hum.

All by itself
It's nice to sing:
It does not mean
A single thing.

TIPTOE

Karla Kuskin

Yesterday I skipped all day,
The day before I ran,
Today I'm going to tiptoe
Everywhere I can.
I'll tiptoe down the stairway.
I'll tiptoe through the door.
I'll tiptoe to the living room
And give an awful roar
And my father, who is reading,
Will jump up from his chair
And mumble something silly like
"I didn't see you there."
I'll tiptoe to my mother
And give a little cough
And when she spins to see me
Why, I'll softly tiptoe off.
I'll tiptoe through the meadows,
Over hills and yellow sands
And when my toes get tired
Then I'll tiptoe on my hands.

MY PLAN

Marchette Chute

When I'm a little older
  I plan to buy a boat,
And up and down the river
  The two of us will float.

I'll have a little cabin
  All painted white and red
With shutters for the window
  And curtains for the bed.

I'll have a little cookstove
  On which to fry my fishes,
And all the Hudson River
  In which to wash my dishes.

CHANSON INNOCENTE

e. e. cummings

in Just-
spring   when the world is mud-
luscious the little
lame balloonman

whistles   far   and wee

and eddieandbill come
running from marbles and
piracies and it's
spring

when   the   world   is puddle-wonderful

the queer
old balloonman whistles
far   and   wee
and bettyandisbel come dancing

from hop-scotch and jump-rope and

it's
spring
and
  the

          goat-footed

balloonMan   whistles
far
and
wee

THE CENTAUR

May Swenson

The summer that I was ten—
Can it be there was only one
summer that I was ten? It must

have been a long one then—
each day I'd go out to choose
a fresh horse from my stable

which was a willow grove
down by the old canal.
I'd go on my two bare feet.

But when, with my brother's jack-knife,
I had cut me a long limber horse
with a good thick knob for a head,

and peeled him slick and clean
except a few leaves for the tail,
and cinched my brother's belt

around his head for a rein,
I'd straddle and canter him fast
up the grass bank to the path,

trot along in the lovely dust
that talcumed over his hoofs,
hiding my toes, and turning

his feet to swift half-moons.
The willow knob with the strap
jouncing between my thighs

was the pommel and yet the poll
of my nickering pony's head.
My head and my neck were mine,

yet they were shaped like a horse.
My hair flopped to the side
like the mane of a horse in the wind.

My forelock swung in my eyes,
my neck arched and I snorted.
I shied and skittered and reared,

stopped and raised my knees,
pawed at the ground and quivered.
My teeth bared as we wheeled

and swished through the dust again.
I was the horse and the rider,
and the leather I slapped to his rump

spanked my own behind.
Doubled, my two hoofs beat
a gallop along the bank,

the wind twanged in my mane,
my mouth squared to the bit.
And yet I sat on my steed

quiet, negligent riding,
my toes standing the stirrups,
my thighs hugging his ribs.

At a walk we drew up to the porch.
I tethered him to a paling.
Dismounting, I smoothed my skirt

and entered the dusky hall.
My feet on the clean linoleum
left ghostly toes in the hall.

Where have you been? said my mother.
Been riding, I said from the sink,
and filled me a glass of water.

What's that in your pocket? she said.
Just my knife. It weighted my pocket
and stretched my dress awry.

Go tie back your hair, said my mother,
and *Why is your mouth all green?*
Rob Roy, he pulled some clover
as we crossed the field, I told her.

Essays

SOME REMARKS ON RAGGEDY ANN AND JOHNNY GRUELLE

Martin Williams

Martin Williams, Director of the Jazz and Popular Culture Programs at the Smithsonian Institution, is currently working on some long-forgotten Gruelle magazine stories as additions to the Raggedy Ann chronicle.

Raggedy Ann is found everywhere: in card shops, doll shops, dime stores, bookstores. There are some twenty books in print, from the original Raggedy Ann series. Yet, if you look in any standard reference volume, you will find no entry on her or her author, Johnny Gruelle, dead since 1938. He was not even in *Who's Who.*

Johnny Gruelle was a hack. Or, to put it more politely, he was a prolific author and illustrator. He turned out a mound of children's stories, illustrated books, comic strips, drawings. He even illustrated an ambitious edition of the Grimm Brothers, very handsome stuff considering it was done by a self-taught illustrator.

Now if a man is that prolific, if he writes so many books in a series, and other material as well, one is apt to view his work with suspicion. His writing couldn't be very good if there's that much of it. And generally speaking, much of Gruelle's writing isn't good. But the interesting thing to me is that the best of Gruelle is very good indeed, and unique, as far as I know, in children's literature.

Probably I do not need to say that some hacks write well on occasion. Robert Greene, the Elizabethan playwright, might be considered a hack, but he is still read, and some of his plays are very good. Daniel Defoe is the standard example of a hack whose best work is still read. Here in America, we have the example of another children's author, the man who wrote *The Wizard of Oz.* L. Frank Baum wrote an incredible amount of material, under various pseudonyms, some male and some female, in addition to some fourteen books about Oz. We are only beginning to acknowledge that Baum was a very good writer and that some of his books are really excellent—say, *The Patchwork Girl of Oz,* or *Tik Tok of Oz,* or even better, a non-Oz book called *Queen Zixi of Ix,* which I sometimes think is the best American children's story ever written.

The problem with people who are prolific is that one has to read all in order to find any real good works. One has to sift, examine, and look at all, and that's not necessarily easy. I don't mean to say that I've done something terribly hard in reading Gruelle, but I have read a great deal of him, including all the Raggedy Ann books, and I have come to certain conclusions about him.

Biographically, from what I can discover from talking to a few people, and from looking Gruelle up in the few places where one can look him up, this very talented, very prolific man was a born innocent. It seems that he went through most

An edited transcription of a tape-recorded talk delivered at the University of Connecticut, October 25, 1973.

of his life, almost until the end, without a moral problem to his name. He was kind to everybody simply because it didn't occur to him to be any other way. He was never tempted to be rude or mean. And it is that kind of moral innocence which is both the virtue and the limitation of his writing.

Johnny Gruelle was born in Arcalo, Illinois, in 1880, but he was raised in Indianapolis. His father, Richard B. Gruelle, was a self-taught painter, well-known in the Middlewest for his landscapes. I think the American Middlewest, its ways, and its language are very much present in the Raggedy Ann books. If you want to find out attitudes and speech patterns of people of that time, I think you'll discover a lot of them in Raggedy Ann.

Gruelle and his brother Justin and sister Prudence apparently had healthy, somewhat casual upbringings. The father seemed to have let his children come and go pretty much as they wanted to, within reason. But they were all brought up with the idea of the importance of art with a little "a," rather than of a refined, somewhat snobbish thing called Art, with a capital "A." If one drew and painted, one produced art—whether it was editorial cartoons, comic strips, portraits of the wealthy or landscapes or whatever. Quality wasn't what made it art or not art. One did his best and didn't worry about Art.

While still in his late teens, Johnny Gruelle had become the cartoonist on *The Indianapolis Star,* and then a few years later, on *The Cleveland Press.* He did every kind of drawing that a newspaper might require of a staff cartoonist. He drew weather cartoons, political cartoons, and he illustrated stories for which there weren't photographs. He got through his work so fast and so well that he had time on his hands. He used that time writing and illustrating original children's tales. It turned out that the editor liked these, so he published them in the paper too.

Then in 1910, Johnny went to visit his father, who had by then moved to Norwalk, Connecticut. While he was there, the New York paper which was then called the *Herald* held a contest to see who could come up with the best idea for a Sunday comic feature. Johnny Gruelle entered the contest twice, under two different names, and he won the first prize and the second prize. The first prize went to the adventures of an imaginary little elf named Mr. Twee Deedle, which continued for several years in the *Tribune* and the *Herald Tribune,* and was syndicated to other papers as well.

Johnny, married by then, had moved his family up to a town in Connecticut near Norwalk, called Silvermine, an artists' colony. In Silvermine, he began turning out an incredible quantity of material for everything from *Physical Culture* magazine to joke magazines like *Judge,* and he wrote and illustrated children's stories for *Good Housekeeping* and *Woman's World.*

Gruelle was a not uncommon combination of laziness and industry. Behind a man like that there is often a driving woman. Gruelle's wife Myrtle was apparently just that. She used to stop him if he felt like going fishing or like playing with the neighborhood children. She might drag him in to his studio and sit him down and say, "You've got some drawing to finish for *Life* magazine." And while he drew—this man-child Johnny Gruelle—she would sit and read him fairy tales.

The Gruelles had a daughter named Marcella whom they loved much. (At that point they had no other children; there were subsequently two sons, Worth and John Junior). Marcella died unexpectedly when she was fourteen years old. She had had a rag doll that had belonged to Prudence, Johnny's sister, her aunt. It was called Raggedy Ann, and in memory of Marcella, Gruelle wrote and illustrated a series of stories about the doll, and Marcella's other dolls, little short tales of imaginary about-the-house adventures. These became *Raggedy Ann Stories,* published in 1914. They were so popular that they were followed by sequels. Indeed, there was a sequel almost every year, and sometimes two a year, until 1937, the year before Gruelle died.

In the meantime, of course, the popularity of the Raggedy Ann books had meant other uses of the character. In the mid-1930's, for instance, Gruelle used to do a single newspaper panel drawing each day for a small distributing syndicate. Daily, there was a little drawing of Raggedy Ann with a verse, or a bit of advice, always very cheerful and happy and sunshiny, as the stories usually are. Also in the '30's, partly for reasons of health and perhaps other reasons that I'm not quite sure of yet, Gruelle moved his family (the two small boys by then) to Miami. There this adult innocent met his first real temptations and, it seems, succumbed to them. Unexpectedly, he evidently gave up his former way of life. People in Silvermine tell me that when he would return north for a visit, he would be overweight, bloated, puffy-eyed, and talking away about the fact that he was busy every afternoon attending cocktail parties. Within a few years, Gruelle was dead. It was a combination of his illness plus the suddenly fast life he had begun to live in Florida, it seems. And as I have said, there was very little attention paid to his death, although his books were still selling then, as they still are now.

The first group of *Raggedy Ann Stories* is based on the idea, not a new one, that dolls have a secret life. They come to life when people are asleep or when people go away on a trip. They can walk and talk and have all kinds of adventures on their own. The dolls find a puppy and adopt it and have to make arrangements for the puppy when "the real-for-sure folks," as Gruelle calls them, return. Or, Raggedy Ann falls in a bucket of paint and has to be scraped and washed and have another face painted on. There one gets a double perspective of the way the real people are thinking about all this—the way Marcella particularly is thinking about it—and the way Raggedy Ann (without ever admitting it to the real people, of course) is thinking about it herself.

These first stories were followed almost immediately by a collection of *Raggedy Andy Stories.* Raggedy Andy is of course the brother doll to Raggedy Ann. Some of these tales, I think, are charming. One of them tells how all the dolls sneak down into the kitchen one evening while the real-for-sure people are away and have a wild taffy pull. There's a last-minute escape, when the dolls get everything cleaned up and everything exactly the way it was. Before the adults come through the front door, they all scatter up to the nursery and back into bed and get back in the same position as they were when they had been left.

Many of the stories in these early books are trivial. But children often like them. They like the premise of the secret life of the dolls and they don't mind the repetitiousness. There are other, later, collections of short Raggedy Ann tales. One is called *Marcella Stories,* and another is called *Beloved Belindy.* Now, Beloved Belindy was a black "Mammy" doll of a kind that would never be written about now. I don't think she's really patronized. I think she's just a nice matriarchal being in the midst of the other dolls, who happens to be black. I do think that some of the black servants in Gruelle's book are patronized but I don't think Belindy was. Anyway, *Beloved Belindy* was the fourth collection of short domestic tales about the dolls.

To go back a little bit, however, the third Raggedy Ann book, meanwhile, had been of a different sort. It is not a collection of short stories but a long tale called *Raggedy Ann and Andy and the Camel with the Wrinkled Knees.* (Long titles, and long phrases like that, charmed Johnny Gruelle, and he used them all the time.) In this story, Gruelle took us into his own version of fairyland, which he called the Deep Deep Woods.

It is supposedly a wooded area behind Marcella's backyard. But Gruelle's Deep Deep Woods is a very American enchanted place, by which I mean it is a singular combination of European elements and ones that he made up himself, using a very American imagination. There are witches but they aren't really very evil; they're unkind maybe, but that's the worst you could say about them. And there are wizards and magicians, some of whom are a little mean, and some of whom put spells on you but they aren't really very bad spells. And sometimes they hide people away. But that's about it.

Then there are princesses and princes: they are all very handsome or beautiful and sometimes they're disguised as other people or other things, and reveal themselves in the end. And there are kings, some of whom are grouches of course. Along with this there are little magical beings with names like Sniznoddle, Snarleyboodle, Little Weekie the Goblin, the Bollivar, the Snoopwiggy, and his friend, the Wiggysnoop, and Mr. Hokus, who of course is a magician. And there are magic spells that can be broken with riddles like "why does a snickersnaper snap snickers?" That's not very European, is it?

The Deep Deep Woods is—again like Gruelle himself—an innocent kind of world, mostly full of niceness and kindliness and some naughtiness. Raggedy Ann herself early acquires a heart that is sewn inside her, a candy heart on which is written, "I love you." Well, if you've got "I love you" written all over your heart, you don't have many moral decisions to make. They come easy.

There is one device in these stories that comes up over and over again, one which is typical of the popular children's writing of the time—it also shows up in British children's literature—and that is the almost endless feast of sweets: donuts, creampuffs, ice cream sodas, ice cream. Book after book has mud puddles which turn out to be chocolate ice cream rather than mud, or fountains in the middle of the woods, enchanted fountains, which put out sodas, or bushes on which grow cookies or cream puffs or donuts. Everyone stops and eats his head off. It's enough to make a diet-conscious adult sick to his stomach.

There's another aspect of Raggedy Ann's kindliness that I find a little disturbing. On occasion, Raggedy Ann behaves like a real busybody in the Deep Deep Woods. She finds out that owls eat mice and she doesn't like that, so she converts the owls to cream puffs. You know, she has a wonderfully uncomplicated idea of what's best for everybody else. (Sometimes it reminds me of American foreign policy.)

But then there are marvelous small touches. For instance, in the book called *Raggedy Ann in the Deep Deep Woods,* the two dolls are wandering along, looking at the sights and saying hello to the animals, and they run into two owls who live in a tree top. Mama Owl, who's old, and Papa Owl, who's also old and tired from having worked for years in a buttonhole factory. It's typical of Gruelle's inventiveness to make up that kind of thing.

But in reading these books, one may decide that this man is just pouring out words, and pouring out plots and ideas and incidents, and one may wonder: does he have any writing *style?* Does he have any sense of how to put words together gracefully? Or is he just pushing the plot along?

I think he did have a writing style, and I think it too was distinctly American. The hint comes from those words like the Snarlyboodle, and the Snoopwiggy, and Little Weekie. That's the kind of word-making that little children indulge in, making words and names out of bits and pieces of other words and sounds they've heard adults use. And I think Johnny Gruelle succeeded in several ways in writing stories by using the methods of a child, not an adult. For another example, there are the little repetitions he uses. Hookey the Goblin is always Hookey the Goblin. He's never the Goblin and he's almost never Hookey. That's his name, the whole thing:

> "Mary Jane Adams lives down the street."
> "Oh, Mary Jane?"
> "No! Mary Jane Adams."

We've all heard children do this kind of thing, particularly small children. They're just learning to talk, perhaps, and just learning names, just learning the fact that most of us have three names, (and some of us four and five) and they like to say it all.

It's a verbal game with them, and Gruelle used it in his books.

In *Raggedy Ann and Andy and the Camel with the Wrinkled Knees,* there's a character named the Tired Old Horse, but sometimes he's the Old Tired Horse, sometimes he might be the Tired Horse and sometimes he might be the Old Horse but usually he's the Tired Old Horse or the Old Tired Horse, and he is never, never just the Horse. Elves and gnomes and fairies, or fairies and gnomes and elves, or gnomes and elves and fairies, and so forth —any order in which you can put the three together will show up eventually, but hardly ever two of the three and certainly never just one of the three.

In *The Camel with the Wrinkled Knees* there are princesses and princes, and there is a Loony King and there is a witch, and there is the Old Tired Horse. But soon we meet a group of pirates who have a ship, a great big pirate ship that navigates on the land by virtue of the fact that it has four wooden legs which walk the ship along like a great horse. These pirates run around doing pirate things to the dolls and the people. But very early, Gruelle's charming drawings begin to reveal something to us: the great big red nose on the pirate leader is a false nose, and the bandanna on the mean-looking pirate covers up the curly hair of a little girl. Gruelle's drawings reveal to us that this assemblage is really a group of Marcella's friends who are playing a game, pretending they are pirates. Soon we realize that the whole story is a game being played by the children about the dolls, and that they're making it up as they go along. We have all done that as children, surely. We start making up a story and acting it out with a group of our playmates. And it rambles and rambles; it goes in this direction and that. It goes in every direction it can go in until mother calls us for lunch or supper.

Johnny Gruelle put these tales together with the same kind of easy whimsy, the same kind of casualness, which children use when improvising a story-game for themselves. and he's the only writer that I've ever read (I may be ignorant of others) who consciously uses an imitation of the way children make up stories in writing a book for children.

Raggedy Ann and the Camel with the Wrinkled Knees is a very good example of it, and there are several other very good ones. For instance, *Raggedy Ann and the Magic Wishing Pebble.* (Now a magic wishing pebble is a wonderful thing if you find one. Look for one: it is absolutely white and absolutely round. If you find an absolutely white and absolutely round pebble, it will give you all the magic wishes that you want.) As I say, it's a good book, but the characters do spend some time in the opening pages sitting around a cookie bush, gorging on soda and donuts.

Did Gruelle write any *great* books? I think he did write one great book: the book which was originally called *The Paper Dragon: A Raggedy Ann Adventure,* and is now published as *Raggedy Ann and the Paper Dragon.* It's about a little girl named Marggy who has lost her father. Well, he's sort of misplaced actually; it isn't a very bad situation. Nobody is anguished about the old boy. He's probably all right, but, you know, somebody's sort of misplaced him somewhere so we ought to find him. There's a naughty magician involved, and there's Marggy's mother in the story. And Raggedy Ann and Raggedy Andy are typically helping them in finding Marggy's father, or Marggy's Daddy as Gruelle would put it, in the Deep Deep Woods. The dragon of the title is a very Oriental dragon until it gets a hole punched in his side and is patched with a Sunday comic section stuck on with some filling from a cream puff. That Americanizes him.

The dragon is completely hollow inside and at one point the bad guy of the story props his mouth open with a stick because he wants to use him for a chicken coop. But that doesn't work very well because if the chickens can run in easily, they can also run out easily. The dragon is also full of dry leaves; it seems that a lot of fallen leaves blew in while he was yawning. Raggedy Andy gets put inside him at one point. He wanders around for a little while, and, as I remember, he can't find anything or anybody. All he finds are these dry leaves which have the dragon coughing from time to time, and eventually have him coughing Raggedy Andy out. It's that kind of rambling, meandering narrative which Gruelle does very charmingly, and particularly in this book.

The book also has good characterizations. Of course they are brief, almost blunt. Characterizations generally are brief and blunt in children's books, and very much so in this book, particularly of Raggedy Andy. He loves to get into boxing and wrestling matches. They never really amount to much, but he likes to box and wrestle. The villains and the bad magicians are always irascible and usually rather foolish—propping the dragon's mouth open so that the chickens could get in, but also get out. At one point, the villain says something like, "If you want to find Marggy's Daddy, you must do something for me first. That's the way it always is in fairy tales." And Raggedy Ann says, "But this isn't a fairy tale." "Of course it's a fairy tale!" he answers. "How else could you two rag dolls be walking around and talking if it wasn't a fairy tale?" That's blunt, and that's probably a child's way of looking at it.

There is one other Gruelle book which I'd like to recommend especially. As I said earlier, there's a whole collection of dolls in Marcella's doll nursery, and one of them is Uncle Clem the Scotch Doll. There's a book built around him called *Wooden Willie,* in which the Scotch Doll and the doll called Beloved Belindy have an adventure. Incidentally, this story originally appeared as a newspaper serial in 1922, and in that version it is a Raggedy Ann and Andy adventure.

I haven't said very much about Gruelle's illustrations, but anyone who has ever seen Gruelle's drawings, in that soft line of his, knows he has seen something special. To know how good they are, simply compare them to those in the books published after Johnny's death that have illustrations done by others, chiefly by Justin Gruelle, his brother, or by Worth Gruelle, his son.

I think there's no question that Johnny Gruelle's reputation would be much higher, and that he would be in the histories of children's literature, if he hadn't written so much. But he did write some very good books. And he had his own way of depicting a child's mind and a child's outlook. So I would like to think that before my life is over, we can read about Johnny Gruelle in volumes on American writers and in volumes on American artists.

THE PUPPET IMMORTALS OF CHILDREN'S LITERATURE

Michael Michanczyk

Michael Michanczyk is a professional puppeteer from Plantsville, Connecticut.

An art form without a muse, puppetry, not unlike the Greek drama, is rooted in the religious tradition and folk literature of western and eastern cultures. From the medieval miracle plays to the English Punch and Judy show, to the other side of the globe and the epic tales of the Mahabharata and the Ramayana, puppet characters have portrayed man's anthropomorphic struggle with the restive questions of death, resurrection, and immortality. In this respect puppetry is like the great body of folk literature that we customarily classify as children's literature. But puppetry has the distinction of vividly enacting those curiously significant stories.

Puppetry in children's literature is of two types: (1) literature written about, or containing, a puppet character or characters; and (2) literature written, or in the oral tradition, performed by puppets. In the former category there is only one classic of its kind, namely *Pinocchio,* while in the later category there are numerous examples. I shall restrict myself to a brief discussion of the significance of the puppet portrayal in the first, and in the second to a discussion of the religious overtones and philosophical implications of puppetry and children's literature.

While today in America puppetry is relegated to the category of mere children's entertainment, the puppet dramas of the past were an instructive and entertaining form of art, with religious and philosophical ideas conveyed through the symbolic stylizations of hand, rod, shadow, and string puppets. In fact, in at least India, Java, and Japan, these dramas antedated the theater of actors and actually determined the style of production in the later human theater. For example, the Japanese puppet theater, *ningyo shibai* ("doll theater"), or *ayatsuri shibai* ("manipulation theater"), today referred to as Bunraku, after the nineteenth-century puppeteer Bunrakuen, were responsible for the growth of the Kabuki "song-dance-skill" theater of people.[1] Human actors learned and improved their art from the puppet actors they imitated. Why the puppet theater preceded the human theater will be discussed later with respect to the shadow puppet dramas.

The puppeteer, too, like the plays and puppets, has been associated with the religious drama—with the early Greek priests and their automatic mechanisms to inspire wonder, no less than with the *dalangs* of Java, who are initiated into their vocation by a priest "who writes the mystic syllable 'Ongg' on the *dalang's* tongue with the stem of a flower dipped in honey."[2] Whether they are accorded as illustrious a birth as the first puppeteer of India, Adi Nat, who sprang from the lips of Brahma the Creator, or whether theirs is a more humble beginning among a troupe of itinerant Italian performers of the commedia dell' arte, puppeteers have entertained in the sacred tradition of their art, inspiring laughter, tears, and awe. Theirs was, and still is, not just a miniature theater for children. The motto printed on the proscenium of the nineteenth-century toy theater of Benjamin West then read *Quibus minus facimus multum* ("We make much out of less").[3]

The industrial revolution produced a diminished interest in the puppet, and substituted for it the automated figure, or robot, and subsequently the refined figures of the Disney audio-animatronics. What was once a popular theater of the people has, generally speaking, been trounced by technology and forced to stare into the corner as an immature form of "children's theater," usually with insipid scripts, shoddy or unimaginative staging, and less than expert manipulation. However, where there is still a tradition of the art, puppetry remains and grows despite condescension; that is reason enough for speculation and experimentation, and for puppetry to define its own artistic veracities, names, "abstraction, motion, and synthesis."[4]

1. Faubion Bowers, *Japanese Theatre* (New York: Hill and Wang, 1959), pp. 31–35.

2. Bil Baird, *The Art of the Puppet* (New York: Macmillan, 1965), p. 56.

3. George Speaight, *The History of the English Toy Theater* (London: Studio Vista, 1969), p. 174. First published as Juvenile Drama (1946).

4. Basil Milovsoroff, "Toward a Better Puppet Theatre," *The Puppetry Journal* 3 (January-February 1971): 7.

Carl Jung's description of the term *individuation* might well serve to explain the vicissitudes and vacillations of character and attitude that lead to the transformation of the puppet Pinocchio into a boy after his initiation from dream into the reality of life. "Individuation means becoming a single, homogeneous being, and, in so far as individuality embraces our innermost, last, and incomparable uniqueness, it also implies being one's own self. We could therefore translate individuation as 'coming to selfhood' or 'self-realization.'"[5]

Pinocchio's willfulness leads the puppet through many misadventures; tricked, cheated, exploited, and burlesqued, he is climactically devoured by the mammoth Dogfish. This same monster has ingested the vessel upon which the puppet's "little papa" has been searching for his prodigal creation. Geppetto and Pinocchio, reunited in the belly of the Dogfish, are contritely reconciled, and the puppet's cleverness is finally put to good use in the first act of manly heroism of his wayward career; the puppet plots their escape through the mouth of the sleeping gargantuan. The Dogfish snores as the escape marks the puppet's first step initiation into adulthood, and soon thereafter the puppet becomes a boy.

In his article about the marionette, "Das Übermarinetten," (obviously, Pinocchio is a string puppet), the set designer Gordon Craig advocates the puppet as the subliminal superior to the human actor. He credits this natural superiority to the fact that the puppets are "egoless," and because they impersonate no one; they are what they were created to be, and no more. As a puppet then, Pinocchio is the dupe of the strings of determinism. It is only after his initiation into manhood that he transcends his manipulation, and realizes the divine providence that has pulled the strings of self-realization. To quote again from Jung:

> But again and again I note that the individuation process is confused with coming of the ego into consciousness and that the ego is in consequence identified with the self, which naturally produces a hopeless conceptual muddle. Individuation is then nothing but egocentricness and autoeroticism. But the self comprises infinitely more than a mere ego. It is as much one's self, and all other selves, as the ego. Individuation does not shut one out from the world, but gathers the world to oneself.[6]

A parallel to the swallowing of the puppet by the Dogfish is the Old Testament story of Jonah and the Whale, always a popular show for puppeteers. Jonah, through his faith in the omnipotence and omniscience of God, is delivered safely from the bowel of the whale. Both the prophet and the puppet undergo a period of trial, or initiation, and both survive the cosmic trauma of inevitable death, being swallowed whole by the macrocosm, and find rebirth in the discovery of the self or microcosm. For Jonah, the event reaffirmed God's will; the puppet's dream ends in his conversion to boyhood and consequently to humanity.

This puppet classic exemplifies many of man's quintessential emotions about puppets, dolls, and masks, namely that they are filled with "mana," possessed by psychic energy or even a "soul." The puppet probably stimulates this feeling more than the others because movement, the criterion which defines puppetry, particularly inspires the notion of animism. In India, for example, there is a quaint custom among the Rajasthani *bhats,* or puppeteers, that when a puppet has died (outlived its usefulness) it is sailed down a holy river. *Kathputli,* or puppets, were regarded as little celestial creatures sent to the earth by the gods for man's amusement. "The longer the figure floats, the

5. Carl Jung, "Two Essays on Analytical Psychology," in *Collected Works,* ed. R.F.C. Hull (Princeton: Princeton University Press, 1926), VII, 171.

6. Carl Jung, "The Structure and Dynamics of the Psyche," *Works,* VIII, 226.

more kindly are the gods in judging its actions and experiences on earth."[7]

To give another kind of historical example, Heinrich von Kleist, in his famous essay on the puppet theater, "Über das Marionetten theater," states that "only God and the marionette can be perfect." In what sense he means that these entities of antithetical planes of existence are both the epitome of perfection is not always expressly clear; however, it does indicate the author's notion of the almost subliminal life of the puppet.

Among the myths of puppetry, the creation of the string puppet is sometimes counted among the miracles of St. Francis of Assisi. Another story has it that the name "marionette," applied to the string puppet, derives from the fact that in the Middle Ages the Nativity was performed by puppets, or "little Marys," hence the name "marionette." However obscure the derivation of the term, puppet plays were an integral part of the church service in medieval times, beginning about the tenth century with moving puppets accompanying biblical recitations. These illustrated Bible lessons were an early attempt to educate the common people, adults and children alike, with a visual aid.

The Bible was the source of inspiration to the puppeteers, and they drew as well upon the most dramatic stories of the miracles of the Church of Rome. One production in the Church of St. James at Dieppe in 1443 celebrated the Assumption of the Blessed Virgin Mary. As Bil Baird relates in his history of the puppet theater,

> Four life-size angels beat their wings in time to the music of the organ and the voices of the choir. Two smaller ones sounded an Ave Maria on little bells to signal the end of each office, accompanied by two huge angels blowing trumpets. Below and at either side were angels holding large chandeliers ablaze with wax candles to light the scene. When the service was over and priests came to snuff the candles, these angels would quickly dodge from side to side to prevent it, and bring a laugh from the congregation.[8]

Such a lively burlesque, during such a solemn feast day of the Church, while not inconsistent with the talents of the puppet, did not sit square with the priests and Pope, and eventually led to the puppet's expulsion from the churches. What had begun as an educational tool for manifesting the literature proved too delightful, distracting, ribald, risqué, and sacrilegious an entertainment.

Today in Poland there survives the remnant of these Miracle plays, the Polish *szopka,* or manger. At Christmas time, these cathedral-like theaters are set up in front of the churches. First made by the brickmakers' guild, they are still made by peasant brickmakers during the winter as a pastime while unemployed. Tiny figures are moved on the several levels of the theater (three levels might denote heaven, earth, and hell) through slots in the stage. Thus the religious connection between the puppet and the Church has survived to form a lasting impression, dramatizing with childlike simplicity the narratives of the Bible.

In the high Middle Ages, the friars took the puppets to the town square. Their scripts were likely improvised, perhaps loosely based on familiar stories, but more often than not with added local appeal and topical allusions. One such puppet play, modified and passed down from generation to generation among the folk, was the familiar English Punch and Judy show.

In 1828 Payne Collier, dramatist and puppet enthusiast, along with George Cruikshank, the artist-illustrator, witnessed a Punch show performed at the King's Arm Tavern by the Italian showman Giovanni Piccini, recognized as the best puppeteer of his kind. Collier copied the script as performed, and Cruikshank supplied the illustrations. Their book was published that same year.

7. Baird, p. 47.

8. Ibid, p. 64.

Punch has numerous cousins throughout Europe and Asia—Karaghioz in Turkey, Karaguez in Greece, Punchinello in Italy, Polichinelle in France, Hanswurst to Kasperle in Germany, Kasparck in Czechoslovakia, Vitez Laszlo in Hungary, and Petrouchka in Russia. But it is the English Punch that has become the archetype of all antiheroes, delighting children and adults with his antics. It is Punch's final outrage that is of particular interest to our discussion. The events leading to this culminating act are the successive murders of his neighbor Scaramouche, his wife Judy, the baby, the constable and officer, the hangman Jack Ketch, and finally the duel with and defeat of the arch fiend.

Punch defiantly takes the name of the devil in vain, taunting,

> They're out! They're out! I've done the trick.
> Jack Ketch is dead—I'm free;
> I do not care, now, if old Nick
> Himself should come for me.[9]

Sure enough the devil pops up his horns at the mention of his name and after a few preliminary bouts of fisticuffs, Punch screams out in his squeaky voice,

> Oh, my head! What is that for?
> Pray, Mr. Devil let us be friends.

The Devil hits him again and Punch begins to grow angry.

> Why you must be one very stupid Devil not to know your best friend when you see him. Well, if you won't, we must try which is the best man, Punch, or the Devil.[10]

A life-and-death struggle ensues; Punch and the Devil score wins over each other with successive blows on the opponent's head. Punch deals the *coup de grâce.* Hoisting the devil upon his "physic stick," he exclaims,

> Hurrah! Hurrah! The Devil's dead[11]

9. Diana John, *St. George and the Dragon, Punch and Judy* (Baltimore: Penguin, 1966), p. 83.
10. Ibid. p. 85.
11. Ibid. p. 86.

More eloquent times have echoed this cock's crow of the cuckolded common man against the motions of the devil, symbol of all evil in the world, author of death. As John Donne, addressing Death, had said before Punch, but might have said with more bathos if he were Punch confronted by a mere puppet-devil,[12]

> Why swell'st thou then?
> One short sleep past, we wake eternally
> And Death shall be no more; Death thou shalt die!

Although Donne's poem is certainly an affirmation of the faith of man and the power of the Deity, Punch's story, too, is an affirmation of earthly stubbornness in the face of the unconquerable. The declaration is the same, the immortality of man, and by inference, the spirit of the puppet. What started as a marionette show turned into the fierce battle between hand puppets wielding clubs, violently fighting, amusing the crowds that gathered in front of the castelet. Brutal as the show they watched is the earnest struggle of life against death that the Punch show personifies.

Shadow puppetry was popular in the eastern countries of China, India, Java, and Siam, and later in Egypt, Turkey, and Greece. But it is in India and Java that the great religious epics of the Ramayana and the Mahabharata are still performed much in the same way they were hundreds of years ago.

The effect of seeing gods which one can never truly see except in the mind's eye because of their spiritual effluvium is conjured up upon the lighted screen of the *dalang.* Rama, the god-man, and his espoused wife Sita, the mythic ancestors of the Javanese, moral exemplars of male and female archetypes, appear in silhouette. Princess Sita remains pure when threatened by the ravaging Ravana; the flames of immolation refuse to touch this sacred woman. And Rama, the hero of the race of the gods, rescues his queen and honors his

12. Speaight, pp. 8–10.

father's promise to his stepmother. Such are the puppets of the shadow world.

It is significant that Plato alludes to shadow puppets in his image of the "cave" in Book VII of the *Republic,* because it demonstrates that puppets existed and were well enough known to inspire such a metaphor. Yet the implied attitude toward the shadow world is very different:

> Imagine mankind as dwelling in an underground cave with a long entrance open to the light across the whole width of the cave; in this they have been from childhood, with necks and legs fettered, so they have to stay where they are. They cannot move their heads round because of the fetters, and they can only look forward, but light comes to them from fire burning behind them higher up at a distance. Between the fire and prisoners is a road above their level, and along it imagine a low wall has been built, as puppet showmen have screens in front of their people over which they work their puppets.[13]

Imagine the reality of a shadow world upon a mind unable to identify the true forms casting shadows in passing. A parable of ignorance needing enlightenment, the shadow puppet world is an illusion created in the viewer's mind. The myth of the Chinese emperor (shadow puppets in China go back to the seventh and ninth centuries A.D.) offers a revealing contrast. Unable to bear the grief of his wife's death, he offers a reward to anyone able to produce her likeness once again. Moving silhouettes stir his memory of things past and return his wife to him once more.

The Javanese shadow puppets, the *wayang kulit,* as far back as the eleventh century A.D., inspired a reflection akin to Plato's. The *Meditation of Ardjuna—Ardjuna Wiwaka,* composed by the court poet of King Airlangga (1035–1049), says: "There are people who weep, are sad and aroused watching the puppets, though they know they are merely carved pieces of leather manipulated and made to speak. These people are like men who, thirsting for sensuous pleasures, live in a world of illusion; they do not realize the magic hallucinations they see are not real."[14]

A combination of puppet theater, folk literature, and religion produced the puppet immortals of children's literature. It is interesting to note, in conclusion, that when Michel Fokine staged Igor Stravinsky's "Petrouchka," the body of the murdered puppet lies upon the stage. The showman tugs at the poor dead puppet when suddenly the ghost of Petrouchka appears over the tent shaking his fist, frightening the showman offstage, and reminding the audience of his immortality.

13. Rex Warner, *The Greek Philosophers* (New York: New American Library, 1966), p. 78.

14. James R. Brandon, *On Thrones of Gold: Three Javanese Shadow Plays* (Cambridge, Mass.: Harvard University Press, 1970), p. 3.

TOYS AND LITERATURE

Leonard R. Mendelsohn

Leonard R. Mendelsohn teaches English at Concordia University, Montreal. He has written on Renaissance drama, Milton, Kafka, and other subjects including children's literature.

In the Disney version of *Pinocchio,* Geppetto's fashioning of the marionette which is to become his son touches off a marvelously harmonious response among the myriads of the old toymaker's creations. Wooden soldiers, cuckoo clocks, figurines atop music boxes, innumerable puppets, and intricate curios awake to perform in a symphonic scenario, one which calls forth participation from Geppetto himself, his cat, Figaro, and Cleo the goldfish. The dance of toys celebrates a triumphal union —the heart of man has become inseparably linked to his creation. Until this moment, whatever consummate skill Geppetto had infused into his works, there had remained a gap, small but chasmic, between him and his toys. Now the gap was spanned, and all creation, human animal and inanimate alike, unite in celebration.

From this point on, throughout the tale of *Pinocchio,* only the fuzziest of distinctions remain among man, spirit, and animal, as well as between toy and human. The interplay is full and free. Pinocchio mingles with Geppetto, school companions, the Blue Fairy, the fox and the cat, the laughing serpent, and a troup of marionettes. He even succeeds, though quite unwillingly, in merging completely with a donkey; and for a time it appears that he might remain among beasts and carvings, never to become a real boy. Since boys can become jackasses in fact and feature, with only an imperceptible abuse of logic it might follow that a toy could indeed wander into the realm of man or animal, assuming as it did a complex of their traits. Relationships are notoriously contagious. A child conversing with his teddy bear is changed. Could not the teddy bear become modified as well?

This festivity of toys in *Pinocchio* is also an example of Disney's manhandling of yet another classic. Collodi's Geppetto is not Disney's beloved artisan, but a none too successful carpenter with a hankering to make a marionette. The latter's spare living quarters—the underside of a staircase, pitifully adorned by a facade of a fireplace with only a picture of fire and kettle—have been transformed by fairy godfather Walt into a quite charming cottage crowded by an overplus of imaginative toys. But Walt's alterations notwithstanding, his vision of a joyous festival in which artist and creation—animate and inanimate, spirited and silent—awake and sing is a satisfying fulfillment of the creative ideal. To dance with one's own masterpiece represents the ultimate transference of creative energy, the penetrating of that narrow and frustratingly difficult barrier between life and art.

The dance of toys of course considerably predates Disney. The ageless dream of the witching hour when playthings come to life has sustained countless plots and episodes in children's stories, as well as occasional musical compositions, including Haydn's *Toy Symphony,* Tchaikovsky's *Nutcracker Suite,* and Victor Herbert's *The Chocolate Soldier.* Toys have supplied literary motifs and characters in exhausting abundance. Some authors have exploited this treasure trove, relying on an audience's willing suspension of disbelief, to produce little more than a toy shelf infested with dialogue. Their plots and activities are familiarly bland, accomplishing only that tediously comic imitation of life of the prodigious doll who sucks, sips, sobs, sprinkles, and speaks anything from pabulum to parables. Such a doll remains hopelessly distant from humankind, while becoming despoiled of the inscrutably compelling qualities that her ragged cousin possesses. More than a few writers have requested that their readers dream life into a teddy bear, rocking horse, or jumping jack only to discover for their now expectant readers a world as mundane as the one they had given over. Enid Blyton's endless Noddy series typifies such stillborn toy traumas. While the illustrations for the Noddy books parade colorful snatches of the toy kingdom before enchanted eyes, the text itself provides but a spiceless concoction of birthday parties, temper tantrums, and kiddy car escapades. The toys behave like junior G-men and other little people who play at some sort of grown-up games. But their notion of the adult world is disappointingly dull. Deprived of its own innate charm, the toy becomes no more than an inert replica of the world we live in.

While it is undeniably true that toys have no life independent of the mind of man, it by no means follows that toys are merely models of the human world. They are, more accurately, extensions of the so-termed real world, and as such they extend to horizons that could never have been approached without them. The sugarplum fairies behave like a liberated idea, and their suggestive motions are so airy that it is probable that only music and dance could trace their antics. As such, they are untampered-with denizens of the toy world. It is no less the task of the writer as of the composer to provide a disciplined and systematic exploration of the toy realm without excavating it out of existence.

On a plane more concrete than that of the sugarplum fairies is L. Frank Baum's sawhorse in *Jack Pumpkinhead and the Sawhorse* (1914), a workaday object wished into life by Necessity—the mother whose tireless womb has spawned endless improbables. True to his real-world counterpart the sawhorse is inflexible, indefatigable, and invulnerable. In personality he is irascible as well, perhaps a consistent outgrowth of his static composition. Baum permits his sawhorse to retain qualities of his familiar life as he remains unjointed and stiff, while in virtual contradiction to these qualities he can sprint almost as swift as thought, conveying stick figures, doll-like creatures, and real-life boys through a succession of excruciating episodes.

While, strictly speaking, the sawhorse is not a toylike literary plaything, he is initially inanimate, is summoned into life by an intense relationship, and behaves consistently like the more successful toy figures in literature. For all his magically acquired attributes, he yet behaves like a sawhorse. He cannot, for example, obey commands until ears are pasted on his makeshift head. The reason for his remaining a recognizable carpentry appliance seems sensible enough. If all Tip required was transportation, he could with the same pen and ink have been supplied with a Palomino, a Pegasus, or even a flying carpet. But Tip and Jack Pumpkinhead need a special kind of mobility, one that could figuratively speaking maintain its balance while implanting its feet squarely in four different realms. One foot was settled in the ordinary, a second in the marvelous, a third in the static, and a fourth in the eventful. Each of the four is dependent upon the others.

Our fascination with the sawhorse surely does not derive from his coming alive, a commonly dull design, but from coordination of the four realms. He is a wooden creature and thus static, but he is given qualities of speed and unhampered directness. Even so, he remains basically a silent carpentry device whose marvelous powers produce actions sometimes quite beyond the control of his masters.

The point at which these four—the ordinary, the marvelous, the static, and the eventful—intersect contains the key to the toy's secret life as well as to its literary potential. On the one hand we are never to forget that a toy is a toy, while on the other hand we cannot overlook the profound influence exerted by members of this inanimate and thus presumably lifeless kingdom. Fortunate literary endeavors involving toys—including E. Nesbit's *The Magic City,* A. A. Milne's Pooh books, Lewis Carroll's *Alice in Wonderland,* any number of nursery rhymes, and some of Robert Louis Stevenson's verses—preserve the toy world intact and at the same time probe the mystery that underlies its silence.

To overstate the fact of any toy's actual lifelessness is to disregard the warm, creative, and responsive relationship into which it inevitably enters. The intensity of the relationship of a toy with its maker, an enthralled child, or a curious sentimental adult can so overwhelm all existing notions of reality that a genuine dialogue, or at least the convincing appearance of one, does in fact emerge. The interaction of child and toy not infrequently invokes situations in which the distinction between ventriloquist and dummy permanently fades, its disappearance revealing the toy's capacity for active participation in a relationship. The rag doll and rocking horse alike demonstrate ability to expand upon a situation, thereby sustaining the intriguing suggestion that the toy's role is more than that of a dumb presence.

The manner in which a toy arises from the status of passive respondent to full and provocative partnership is conveyed with humorous efficiency in the opening chapter of Milne's *Winnie-the-Pooh.* On the first page we encounter Edward Bear, who is being unceremoniously bounced head-end down the stairs as he trails the daily descent of Christopher Robin. This scene, now a virtual archetypal portrait of young boy with stuffed companion, focuses not upon the lad but upon the teddy bear. Is it not, after all, the presence of the bear that contributes the distinctive shape to the situation?

Accordingly, the narrative begins with the perspective of the bear, and even as the perspective shifts to that of the boy or the narrator, the teddy bear remains the focal point. Pooh's pivotal significance is so acute that ultimately he leaves off being mute and enters the dialogue. Christopher Robin as spokesman requests a story for the benefit of a presumably attentive Pooh. Pooh, an innate egoist, at least according to his companion, naturally prefers tales about himself. The narration begins, only to be interrupted by a query posed by the boy, a question immediately qualified by the explanation that he is merely a mouthpiece. Christopher Robin asks what it means to "live under the name of."

> "It means he had the name over the door in gold letters, and he lived under it."
> "Winnie-the-Pooh wasn't quite sure," said Christopher Robin.
> "Now I am," said a growly voice.
> "Then I will go on," said I.

The relationship of the three—Pooh, Christopher Robin, and narrator—is so emphatically centered upon the teddy bear Pooh that Milne, who discreetly retreats behind the name of "I," and Christopher Robin, an acknowledged spokesman for a cause but obliquely his own, become distinctly subordinate roles. With Pooh's preeminence unchallenged, need anyone blink as a growly voice enters the discussion? Pooh has prompted the situation, dominated its content and perspective, and usurped the key role for himself. To permit him speech as well is but a small concession to reality and a realistic assessment of his role. Perhaps in life as well as in fiction the toy is a force that dominates and determines those who come under its spell, acting as a creator in no less a fashion than the individual who formed it into existence.

But speech, implied, intended, or real, is by no means a necessary factor in a toy's sphere of influence. Speech—like other of the effigy-type features of dolls, puppets, and stuffed animals—is not at all essential in permitting a toy an active rather than a passive role. Such potential for active influence is inherent also in a number of toys that share no homologous qualities with man, as for example the mouthless, unhuman shapes of blocks, balls, marbles, and tops. In each of these the relationship with child, or with adult for that matter, can be of an intensity and degree of responsiveness quite equal to that evoked by the effigy toys.

Blocks, for all their apparent simplicity, are the most flexible and thus the most creative and evocative medium in the toy kingdom. The analogy of the child with blocks to the engineer or architect actually obscures rather than suggests the creative essence of building blocks, a creativity it would be no exaggeration to assert quite exceeds the imagination generally exhibited in architecture or in engineering. Playroom building blocks are a medium far more appropriate to art and literature than is the work of the architect, whose efforts must cater to a pragmatic world in which functional demands inevitably overshadow the aesthetic impulse. The nursery builder, on the other hand, need consider only his own dreams and the potential of his materials, while all other concerns yield to the overriding creative enterprise. It is quite possible, even probable, that the structure being raised by young hands is inspired by or somehow linked to some incipient narrative, or that its construction will inspire involvement in an ensuing epic that swells to the limits of the imagination. At the very least, the edifice need not subscribe to the demands of skyline or office space. Its very existence is dependent upon a narrative or an aesthetic mode.

The very frailty of the block kingdom is in fact one of its chief virtues. In the mundane world an edifice is as permanent as a scar, intrusively gripping its place upon the landscape, yielding to alteration only through expensive and laborious effort. Such inflexibility is in sharp contrast to the structure comprised of building blocks, which are not only facile and flexible but also accommodate changes of mood and intention. Once more, these playroom fixtures prove more sufficient factors of literary creativity than forms of engineering enterprise. Many modern toys, however, are molded in the engineering tradition rather than in the conventional mode of the playroom, and with their ever more sophisticated properties they forfeit creative elasticity. As they join ranks with mechanical marvels, they shed the suggestiveness and inventiveness that is the basic heritage of the realm of toys. A child occupied with blocks is constructing a realm more fragile, yet one perhaps more fraught with possibility, than even the composition of the writer. The child composes a plot and a setting simultaneously, neither of which is ever fixed. Both are rearranged in a moment, or are held in easy abeyance. The child builds, revises, strikes down, or starts anew—working on a setting to suit an image, to meet a challenge, or simply to try out a new form. Castles or skyscrapers, bridges, temples, tunnels, and experimental designs arise in the imagination and then furnish its creator with a stage on which to declaim, withdraw, respond, or expand.

The nursery rhyme "Humpty Dumpty," although it does not specifically mention building blocks, functions on a principle similar to the playroom activity. There is the predominant image of Humpty poised on a structure, followed by an event that prompts a synthesis of the imaginative and creative resources to reconstruct the initial image. The brief stanza comprises construction, destruction, artistic challenge, and narrative. The block kingdom likewise pursues an image, perhaps one that will conform to a hastily composed plot line. The image that inspired the activity endures even in the face of imminent collapse, for it is in the nature of blocks, just as it is Humpty's memorable destiny, to scatter. Yet the image survives the ruins. Perhaps the original moment can never be reconstructed, but the busy involvement continues, enlisting all resources. The image, the challenge, the imaginative pursuit, and the narrative coherence are qualities shared by the nursery lyric and the child with building blocks.

Though the toy, like a poem, is created in a certain period of time, it is the moment of impact, with participant or with reader, that is the essential reality of its creative life. The rich variety of the toy's impact parallels other dimensions of poetry as well. The experience of toys is less rigorous, less structured, and thus less likely to be recorded than poetry. In order to deal with this elusive quality, many writers simply translate the experience of toys into the idiom of the familiar world. Such an idiom fails pitifully in dealing with the uniquely imaginative elements of the toy kingdom. There are writers, however, like Milne, Baum, and Carroll, who focus upon the impact and in the process have captured revealing portraits of this provocative world. Collodi and Stevenson among others have demonstrated that the area of impact is as wide as it is suggestive. The soul of the toy realm is, like any spiritual quality, difficult to define, trace, or describe, but the difficult is by no means the impossible. The behavior of the toy realm comprises much more than its static exterior, and the dynamic properties beneath are temptingly close to the endeavors of art.

Explorations

STORYTELLING AND ACTING OUT

1. *(Counting-Out Rhymes)* "Number one!" is a choral chant that you can do with several children or just two. Get some rock 'n' roll into the rhythm as you chant it.
2. *(Punch and Judy)* Buy or make some puppets. One good way is simply to attach small dot figures to the ends of stout, foot-long wires or sticks and use them to manipulate the puppets through the open top of a cardboard theater. Try putting on a simplified version of a Punch and Judy show. From the beginning, people have made up their own lines—just improvised—in such shows, so do it whatever way you like.
3. *(The Velveteen Rabbit)* Storytelling is one of the best ways in which an adult can share with a child. It is a difficult art, however, one that needs preparation. Learning to read well aloud is an important first step, for it prepares one for an eventual departure from the text. This departure should take place only when the material is familiar and a good rapport with children has been established. Read aloud the selection from *The Velveteen Rabbit.* If this is one of your early ventures into storytelling, practice reading the story as expressively as you can. Remember that you are trying to communicate the story through sharing it—and yourself—with your audience of children. Since you have only part of the story here, you and the children might try to imagine an ending for it.
4. Make up your own "Expotition to the North Pole" with a group of children. This kind of acting out encourages expressiveness and imagination.

"Let's go toward the North Pole."

"Get on your furs. Don't forget your mukluks." (gesture of putting them on)

"We must be getting near it. My, it's cold! (shudders)

"Down we go. (whrr of plane) Walk down the ramp." (steps)

"There are no trees! Feel the gritty tundra under your feet!" (wiggle feet)

"Look out! Here comes a polar bear!"(dodge)

"Crawl in that igloo!" (bend down)

"Whoo! (sigh) That was a close escape!"

"It's smoky in here!" (cough)

"I'm hungry! Let's cook a caribou steak."

"My, that's good." (chewing and rubbing stomachs)

"Time to go home! Step carefully over those ice cakes." (picky steps)

"Look! There's Santa Claus and he's heading down South!" (look up)

"And there's Rudolf, the Red-Nosed Reindeer! Let's sing to him!" (sing "Rudolf")

"Let's have a snow fight!" (mime fight)

"I got some down my neck!" (writhe and grimace)
"Time to go home. Put on your skis." (mime skiing)
"Get up on the plane again." (mime walking up steps)
"Whrr! We're off!" (mime taking off in airplane)
"Look, there's our house!" (wave)
"We've made it. Down the steps!" (mime walking down)
"That was fun but I'm tired. Let's go to bed." (lean head on hands)

This kind of imaginary journey can be adapted to any country.

5. *(Impunity Jane)* Try acting out the story of Impunity Jane in a puppet theater. You can each play several roles.
6. *(Raggedy Ann)* Read this story out loud (see suggestions in Exploration 3, above). Then have a child tell the story back to you.
   Make a Raggedy Ann, a Raggedy Andy, and a Paper Dragon, and try acting out the show in your puppet theater. Add some other adventures of these three, making them up out of your head.
7. *(Tin Soldier)* Read the story to yourself. Then tell it to a child, remembering to share yourself as well as the story (see suggestions in Exploration 3). When telling the story, as opposed to reading it aloud, you have the advantage of being able to adjust the words to the age and comprehension of the child—that is, you can be even more aware of your audience. You will want to keep certain choice phrases exactly as they appear in the original story, however.
8. *(Rosie's Door)* Read the selection to a group of children. Then have a sing-in, with each of the children contributing a solo. Have them dress up in costumes to suit their roles.
9. *(Us Two)* This poem makes a good choral reading for children. Tell them to say, "Said Pooh," whenever you pause. Read the poem with lots of expression.
10. *(Duel)* This poem also lends itself well to choral reading. Read it through to the children first and then let them say, "Bow wow wow" and "Mee-ow" in stanza two; wail, "Oh, dear, what shall we do?" in stanza three; and give the triumphant line, "They ate each other up!" when you pause in stanza four.
11. *(Pickety Fence)* Read this poem to a child so often that both of you can chant it from memory. Then each of you speak alternate lines in a staccato, "picky" way.
12. *(Swing Song)* This poem can be read so gracefully that it goes well with a soft musical accompaniment. Pick one that suits you, and then you and your favorite child can dance to it.

PARTICIPATING IN OTHER WAYS

1. *(Riddles)* Read the riddles to a child. Let the child guess the answers and tell the riddles in turn to other children. (The riddles are easy to learn.) Children particularly enjoy "Adam and Eve and Pinch Me."
2. *(Riddles)* Try making up a riddle yourself. A child may respond by making one up voluntarily.
3. *(Tongue Twisters)* Have a contest with a child or children to see who can say these tongue twisters correctly first.
4. (Punch and Judy) Not only is *Punch and Judy* great fun for adults and children to perform with new variations on the old lines, but it also

suggests the possibility of restoring the nineteenth-century art of playing on an even smaller stage—that of the Toy Theater, which was a stage for living-room-sized audiences, mainly in England. Robert Louis Stevenson wrote an essay on the art of the Toy Theater, and many famous Englishmen, including Charles Dickens and Winston Churchill, played with such theaters as boys. They began with people cutting sketches of actors and actresses out of theater programs, mounting them on cardboard, and putting on simplified versions of popular plays at home in the parlor. Characters were moved on and off stage with long wires having tiny clips attached to the end. A whole stage convention grew up around these tiny figures—moving them up and down might suggest the emotion of excitement, shaking them back and forth might suggest grief or fear. There is no reason why such simple stories as Cinderella, Bluebeard, Aladdin, or plays of one's own contriving might not be produced in this way for contemporary children and adults.

5. *(Paper Boats)* After reading this poem aloud to a group of children, make some paper boats by folding paper. You might make some other paper toys, too, using the Japanese art of origami. Books on the subject (and paper) are available from Charles Tuttle Publishing Company, Rutland, Vermont, and from other places.

   After reading this poem, discuss with a child some of the places that things might go which move on water—bottles and boats and shells.
6. Iris Vinton's *The Folkways Omnibus of Children's Games* (1970) contains descriptions and histories of dozens of games from around the world. Choose a game from another culture and learn to play it. Does it bring alive any skills or feelings that you weren't in touch with before?
7. Locate any tapes or musical recordings that have to do with toys and play snatches to children. Note the role of the toys in these musical stories. Three recordings that could be used are Tchaikovsky's *Nutcracker Suite,* Herbert's *The Chocolate Soldier,* or Haydn's *Toy Symphony.* Encourage the children to dance and move like toys in response to this music.
8. Convert any story in this book into an indoor or outdoor game.

Selected Readings

READINGS FOR CHILDREN

Andersen, Hans Christian. *The Emperor and the Nightingale.* Retold and illustrated by Bill Sokol. New York: Pantheon, 1959. Fantasy (picture book).

———. *The Nightingale.* Translated by Eva Le Gallienne. Illustrated by Nancy Ekholm Burkert. New York: Harper, 1965. Fantasy (picture book).

Bailey, Carolyn Sherwin. *Miss Hickory.* Illustrated by Ruth Gannett. New York: Viking, 1962. Fantasy.

Bianco, Margery Williams. *The Little Wooden Doll.* Illustrated by Pamela Bianco. New York: Macmillan, 1925. Fantasy.

Bond, Michael. *A Bear Called Paddington.* Illustrated by Peggy Fortnum. Boston: Houghton Mifflin, 1960; first published in 1958. Fantasy.

Boston, Lucy Maria. *The Castle of Yew.* Illustrated by Margery Gill. New York: Harcourt, 1965. Fantasy (imaginative play).

Clarke, Pauline. *The Return of the Twelves.* Illustrated by Bernarda Bryson. New York: Coward, McCann, 1963. Fantasy.

Craig, M. Jean. *The Dragon in the Clock Box.* Illustrated by Kelly Oechsli. New York: Norton, 1961. Fantasy (imaginative play—picture book).

De Angeli, Marguerite. *The Book of Nursery and Mother Goose Rhymes.* Garden City, N.Y.: Doubleday, 1954. Nursery rhymes (picture book).

Dolbier, Maurice. *Torten's Christmas Secret.* Illustrated by Robert Henneberger. Boston: Little, Brown, 1951. Fantasy (picture book).

Du Bois, William Pène. *William's Doll.* New York: Harper, 1972. Fiction (picture book).

Field, Rachel. *Hitty: Her First Hundred Years.* Illustrated by Dorothy P. Lathrop. New York: Macmillan, 1929. Fantasy.

Freeman, Don. *Corduroy.* New York: Viking, 1968. Fantasy (picture book).

Godden, Rumer. *Candy Floss.* Illustrated by Adrienne Adams. New York: Viking, 1960. Fantasy.

———. *The Doll's House.* Illustrated by Tasha Tudor. New York: Viking, 1962. Fantasy.

———. *The Fairy Doll.* Illustrated by Adrienne Adams. New York: Viking, 1956. Fantasy.

———. *Home Is the Sailor.* Illustrated by Jean Primrose. New York: Viking, 1964. Fantasy.

———. *The Story of Holly and Ivy.* Illustrated by Adrienne Adams. New York: Viking, 1958. Fantasy.

Goffstein, M. B. *Goldie the Dollmaker.* New York: Farrar, 1969. Fantasy (picture book).

Gray, Genevieve. *A Kite for Bennie.* Illustrated by Floyd Sowell. New York: McGraw, 1972. Fiction.

Greenaway, Kate. *Kate Greenaway's Book of Games.* Illustrated by the author. New York: Viking, 1976. 19th-century game book.

Jones, Elizabeth Orton. *Big Susan.* Illustrated by the author. New York: Macmillan, 1967. Fantasy.

Konigsburg, E. L. *Jennifer, Hecate, MacBeth, William McKinley and Me, Elizabeth.* Illustrated by the author. New York: Atheneum, 1967. Fiction (imaginative play).

Leisk, David [Crockett Johnson]. *Ellen's Lion.* Illustrated by the author. New York: Harper, 1959. Fantasy.

Linde, Gunnel. *The White Stone.* Translated by Richard and Clara Winston. Illustrated by Imero Gobbato. New York: Harcourt, 1966. Fantasy (imaginative play).

Lindgren, Astrid. *Pippi Longstocking.* Illustrated by Louis S. Glanzman. New York: Viking, 1950. Fantasy (imaginative play).

Lionni, Leo. *Alexander and the Wind-Up Mouse.* New York: Pantheon, 1969. Fantasy (picture book).

Mendoza, George. *And I Must Hurry for the Sea Is Coming In.* Illustrated by DeWayne Dalrymple. Englewood Cliffs, N.J.: Prentice-Hall, 1971. Fantasy (imaginative play).

Parrish, Anne. *Floating Island.* Illustrated by the author. New York: Harper, 1930. Fantasy.

Piper, Watty. *The Little Engine That Could.* Illustrated by George and Doris Hauman. Bronx, N.Y.: Platt & Munk, 1954. Fantasy (picture book).

Rockwell, Anne. *Games (And How to Play Them).* New York: Thomas Crowell, 1973. Informational book (picture book).

Sandburg, Carl. *The Wedding Procession of the Rag Doll and the Broom Handle and Who Was in It.* Illustrated by Harriet Pincus. New York: Harcourt, 1967. Fantasy.

Shulevitz, Uri. *One Monday Morning.* Illustrated by the author. New York: Scribner, 1967. Fantasy (imaginative play—picture book).

Snyder, Zilpha. *The Changeling.* Illustrated by Alton Raible. New York: Atheneum, 1970. Fiction (imaginative play).

———. *The Egypt Game.* Illustrated by Alton Raible. New York: Atheneum, 1970. Fiction (imaginative play).

Stevenson, Robert Louis. *A Child's Garden of Verses.* Illustrated by Florence Edith Storer. New York: Scribner, 1909. Poetry.

Thomas, Ianthe. *Walk Home Tired, Billy Jenkins.* Illustrated by Thomas di Grazia. New York: Harper, 1974. Fiction (imaginative play).

Wildsmith, Brian, illus. *Brian Wildsmith's Mother Goose.* New York: Franklin Watts, 1963. Mother Goose rhymes (picture book).

Williams, Ursula Moray. *The Toymaker's Daughter.* Illustrated by Shirley Hughes. Des Moines: Meredith, 1968. Fantasy.

Yates, Elizabeth. *Carolina's Courage.* Illustrated by Nora S. Unwin. New York: Dutton, 1964. Historical fiction.

REFERENCES FOR ADULTS

Abrahams, Roger D., ed. *Jump-Rope Rhymes: A Dictionary.* Published for the American Folklore Society. Austin, Tex.: University of Texas Press, 1969.

Baird, Bil. *The Art of the Puppet.* New York: Macmillan, 1965.

Baring-Gould, William S. and Cecil. *The Annotated Mother Goose.* New York: Clarkson N. Potter, 1962.

Cambon, Glauco. "Pinocchio and the Problem of Children's Literature." *Children's Literature* 2 (1973): 50–60

Chase, Richard, ed. *Old Songs and Singing Games.* New York: Dover, 1972.

———. *Singing Games and Playparty Games.* Illustrated by Joshua Tolford. New York: Dover, 1967.

Chukovsky, Kornei. *The Silver Crest: My Russian Boyhood.* Translated by Beatrice Stillman. New York: Holt, 1976.

———. *From Two to Five.* Berkeley, Calif.: University of California Press, 1965: first published in the Soviet Union in 1925.

Crews, Frederick C. *The Pooh Perplex.* New York: E. P. Dutton, 1963.

Culff, Robert. *The World of Toys.* London: Hamlyn Group, 1969.

Fraser, Lady Antonia (Parkenham). *A History of Toys.* New York: Delacorte Press, 1966.

Heisig, James W. "Pinocchio: Archetype of the Motherless Child." *Children's Literature* 3 (1974): 23–35.

Lurie, Alison. "Back to Pooh Corner." *Children's Literature* 2 (1973): 11–17.

Milne, Christopher. *The Enchanted Places: A Memoir of the Real Christopher Robin and Winnie-the-Pooh.* New York: Dutton, 1975. Autobiography.

Murray, Patrick. *Toys.* London: Studio Vista Limited, 1968.

Piaget, Jean. Chapter 5, "Classification of Games and Their Evolution after the Beginnings of Language. In *Play, Dreams and Imitation in Childhood.* Translated by C. Gattegno and F. M. Hodgson. New York: Norton, 1962.

Singer, Dorothy G. "Piglet, Pooh, and Piaget." *Psychology Today,* June 1972, pp. 71–74, 96.

Singer, Jerome L. *The Child's World of Make-Believe: Experimental Studies of Imaginative Play . . .* with chapters by Ephriam Biblow et al. New York: Academic Press, 1973.

Speaight, George. *The History of the English Toy Theatre.* London: Studio Vista, 1969; first published in 1946 under the title *Juvenile Drama: The History of the English Toy Theatre.*

———. *Punch and Judy: A History.* London: Studio Vista, 1970.

Stevens, Martin. *The Toy Maker.* A beautiful puppet show on film, about the unity of all human beings through the creator—"The Toy Maker." The film can be obtained through most state libraries, as well as through Boy Scout and Girl Scout organizations. It can also be rented from Picture Films Distribution, Alfred Wallace, 420 Riverside Drive, New York, N.Y. 10025.

Vinton, Iris. *The Folkways Omnibus of Children's Games.* Illustrated by Alex D'Amato. Harrisburg, Pa.: Stackpole, 1970.

II. Fools

All kinds of fools exist and, at times, each of us acts out all kinds of foolishness. Because we can identify with the protagonists, literature about fools has a special appeal. In his *Type and Motif-Index of the Folktales of England and North America* (Indiana University Folklore Series No. 20, The Hague, Netherlands, 1960), Ernest W. Baughman lists various categories of foolishness found in folktales, some of which are: absurd ignorance, misunderstandings, disregard of facts, absentmindedness, short-sightedness, lack of logic, absurd scientific theories, gullibility, talkativeness, foolish imitation, literal-mindedness, foolish extremes, making easy problems hard, and irrational cowardice.

Some fools, like the fool in Shakespeare's *King Lear,* use the mask of foolishness to protect themselves from the consequences they might otherwise suffer for daring to tell the truth, or simply as a way of saying profound things palatably. They are fools in the sense that by earthly, materialistic standards their behavior is stupid, but by spiritual standards it is wise—they have what the Old Testament calls "wisdom of heart."

In his *Punch and Judy: A History* (London, 1970), George Speaight writes: "The first fool was the village idiot, whose drivelling inanities sometimes seemed to conceal wisdom and prophecy, and it is a pleasing mark of primitive societies that the lunatic has sometimes been revered and cared for as one 'possessed by God.' " Speaight also draws a distinction between the "natural" and the "artificial" fool. Shakespeare's fool is not a natural fool, the lunatic or simpleton, but an artificial or professional fool, an intimate of kings. Often such fools wore special parti-colored costumes and carried a mock scepter with a fool's head at the end, a costume descending at least from Roman times. That is, they were clowns, the dramatic aspect of the fool.

Whether an artificial fool or a natural fool, whether in a town, a puppet show, or a king's court, the figure of the fool has always had a certain mystery attached to it, as evidenced in the Tarot card pack—those ancient playing cards in which every card has a number except that of the fool. "The significance of this," J. E. Cirlot points out in *A Dictionary of Symbols* (New York, 1962), "is that the Fool is to be found on the fringe of all orders and systems. . . . This very fact is in itself a pointer to the mystic symbolism of the Fool."

In the folklore of almost every culture, stories can be found about simpletons who win out in the end. "The Sea of Gold," "The Golden Goose," and "Jack and the Beanstalk," in this section, are three excellent examples of this type of story. Because children often feel stupid when they are confronted by the confusing mysteries of the adult world, they can easily identify with these simpleton heroes. As the headnote to "The Golden Goose" suggests, Bruno Bettelheim has observed that such tales of simpletons "offer the child the consolation and hope for the future he needs most." *Rufus M.* by Eleanor Estes is a good modern story about a child who seems foolish in his first excursion into the adult world, but persists until his efforts succeed.

The ability to accept life without reflection, comparison, analysis, or possession is what is so endearing about such clowns as Charlie Chaplin or Simple Simon. They can savor even the pain of life with something of a sad smile. At the same time we recognize with a satisfied chuckle that often simplicity can defeat those so materialistic that they are blinded to true reality. So did the Madman of Naranath in the Indian tale defeat the greedy villagers. This story, by the way, has a close parallel in a delightful Jewish story told here by Isaac Bashevis Singer about "Shrewd Todie and Lyzer the Miser." (Singer has also written about the fools of Chelm, Chelm being a Russian town supposedly inhabited by fools, like the English town of Gotham. Actually, many countries have a town or area in which the people are regarded as fools, sometimes because at one time or another they have been poorer or less educated than their neighbors.)

Such droll stories of fools as Padraic Colum's literary folktale about the twelve silly sisters and Isaac Bashevis Singer's tale of "The Mixed-Up Feet and the Silly Bridegroom" might serve as an example of several of Baughman's categories, notably, making easy problems hard.

People are fools who judge a situation in terms of their own limited knowledge of it. In John Saxe's poem "The Blind Men and the Elephant," blindness is a metaphor for intellectual blindness; for physically blind people would be more careful in their conclusions. (Like the prophet Tiresias, in fact, many of them "see" better than those with eyes.) More complex, psychologically, are Edward Lear's rhymes, particularly his limericks. Bounded by the strictures of the inhibited Victorian period in which he lived, Lear sometimes encased in his rhymes and accompanying drawings a large number of foolish characters, who appear in boxes, barrels, teapots, tents, and other objects.

The literature about fools, finally, is appealing because fools are, above all, human—and therefore tales about fools bring with them always a certain joy and delight in the human condition. This brief tale from an eighteenth-century pamphlet or chapbook about the Wise Men of Gotham captures the feeling.

Chap book cover page

Once upon a time the people of Gotham wanted to capture a pretty cuckoo bird so that it would sing for them all year. Finally, they located a bird in a tree. They thought and thought about how they could catch it and finally came up with an idea—of course, they would simply build a fence around it!

So they worked quietly, night and day, building a fence to close in a meadow in which the bird could be happy. Finally, the last stakes were placed and they all gathered about to see how the bird would react to this pleasant surprise. Surely this was a day to make merry with ale and cheese and bread, to rest after the sweating labor.

Just as the company gathered, the bird, conscious of the stir, looked up from his nest. "Cuckoo!" he chirped. "Cuckoo!" And flew away.

"Ah," sighed the people of Gotham, shaking their heads. "Next time, we must make the fence higher."

Myth

THE GOLDEN TOUCH
Retold by Nathaniel Hawthorne

The stupidity of those who yearn for gold above all else is a popular theme in folklore, which, for all its earthiness, is usually inclined to place spiritual values higher on the scale than earthly ones. Hawthorne's retelling of the Greek myth of King Midas is much longer and more elaborate than the original, and it is deeply affecting as it shows the wretchedness of the foolish King, whose beloved daughter is turned to gold because of his avarice.

Once upon a time, there lived a very rich king whose name was Midas; and he had a little daughter, whom nobody but myself ever heard of, and whose name was Marygold.

This King Midas was fonder of gold than of anything else in the world. He valued his royal crown chiefly because it was composed of that precious metal. If he loved anything better, or half so well, it was the one little maiden who played so merrily around her father's footstool. But the more Midas loved his daughter, the more did he desire and seek for wealth. He thought, foolish man! that the best thing he could possibly do for this dear child would be to bequeath her the immensest pile of yellow, glistening coin that had ever been heaped together since the world was made. Thus, he gave all his thoughts and all his time to this one purpose. If ever he happened to gaze for an instant at the gold-tinted clouds of sunset, he wished that they were real gold, and that they could be squeezed safely into his strong box. When little Marygold ran to meet him, with a bunch of buttercups and dandelions, he used to say, "Poh, poh, child! If these flowers were as golden as they look, they would be worth the plucking!"

And yet, in his earlier days, before he was so entirely possessed of this insane desire for riches, King Midas had shown a great taste for flowers. He had planted a garden, in which grew the biggest and beautifullest and sweetest roses that any mortal ever saw or smelt. These roses were still growing in the garden, as large, as lovely, and as fragrant, as when Midas used to pass whole hours in gazing at them, and inhaling their perfume. But now, if he looked at them at all, it was only to calculate how much the garden would be worth if each of the innumerable rose-petals were a thin plate of gold. And though he once was fond of music the only music for poor Midas, now, was the chink of one coin against another.

At length Midas had got to be so exceedingly unreasonable that he could scarcely bear to see or touch any object that was not gold. He made it his custom, therefore, to pass a large portion of every day in a dark and dreary apartment, under ground, at the basement of his palace. It was here that he kept his wealth. To this dismal hole—for it was little better than a dungeon—Midas betook himself, whenever he wanted to be particularly happy. Here, after carefully locking the door, he would take a bag of gold coin, or a gold cup as big as a washbowl, or a heavy golden bar or a peck-measure of gold-dust, and bring them from the obscure corners of the room into the one bright and narrow sunbeam that fell from the dungeon-like window. He valued the sunbeam for no other reason but that his treasure would not shine without its help. And then would he reckon over the coins in the bag, toss up the bar, and catch it as it came down; sift the gold-dust through his fingers; look at the funny image of his own face, as reflected in the burnished circumference of the cup; and whisper to himself, "O Midas, rich King Midas, what a happy man art thou!"

Midas was enjoying himself in his treasure-room, one day, as usual, when he perceived a shadow fall over the heaps of gold; and, looking suddenly up, what should he behold but the figure of a stranger, standing in the bright and narrow sunbeam! It was a young man, with a cheerful and ruddy face. Whether it was that the imagination of King Midas threw a yellow tinge over everything, or whatever the cause might be, he could not help fancying that the smile with which the stranger regarded him had a kind of golden radiance in it. Certainly, although his figure intercepted the sunshine, there was now a brighter gleam upon all the piled-up treasure than before. Even the remotest corners had their share of it, and were lighted up, when the stranger smiled, as with tips of flame and sparkles of fire.

As Midas knew that he had carefully turned the key in the lock, and that no mortal strength could possibly break into his treasure-room, he, of course, concluded that his visitor must be something more than mortal. Midas had met such beings before now, and was not sorry to meet one of them again.

The stranger gazed about the room; and when his lustrous smile had glistened upon all the golden objects that were there, he turned again to Midas.

"You are a wealthy man, friend Midas!" he observed. "I doubt whether any other four walls, on earth, contain so much gold as you have contrived to pile up in this room."

"I have done pretty well—pretty well," answered Midas, in a discontented tone. "But, after all, it is but a trifle, when you consider that it has taken me my whole life to get it together. If one could live a thousand years, he might have time to grow rich!"

"What!" exclaimed the stranger. "Then you are not satisfied?"

Midas shook his head.

"And pray what would satisfy you?" asked the stranger. "Merely for the curiosity of the thing, I should be glad to know."

Midas paused and meditated. He felt a presentiment that this stranger, with such a golden lustre in his good-humored smile, had come hither with both the power and the purpose of gratifying his utmost wishes. Now, therefore, was the fortunate moment, when he had but to speak, and obtain whatever possible, or seemingly impossible thing, it might come into his head to ask. So he thought, and thought, and thought, and heaped up one golden mountain upon another, in his imagination, without being able to imagine them big enough. At last, a bright idea occurred to King Midas. It seemed really as bright as the glistening metal which he loved so much.

Raising his head, he looked the lustrous stranger in the face.

"Well, Midas," observed his visitor, "I see that you have at length hit upon something that will satisfy you. Tell me your wish."

"It is only this," replied Midas. "I am weary of collecting my treasures with so much trouble, and beholding the heap so diminutive, after I have done my best. I wish everything that I touch be changed to gold!"

The stranger's smile grew so very broad that it seemed to fill the room like an outburst of the sun, gleaming into a shadowy dell, where the yellow autumnal leaves—for so looked the lumps and particles of gold—lie strewn in the glow of light.

"The Golden Touch!" exclaimed he. "You certainly deserve credit, friend Midas, for striking out so brilliant a conception. But are you quite sure that this will satisfy you?"

"How could it fail?" said Midas.

"And will you never regret the possession of it?"

"What could induce me?" asked Midas. "I ask nothing else, to render me perfectly happy."

"Be it as you wish, then," replied the stranger, waving his hand in token of farewell. "Tomorrow, at sunrise, you will find yourself gifted with the Golden Touch."

The figure of the stranger then became exceedingly bright, and Midas involuntarily closed his eyes. On opening them again, he beheld only one yellow sunbeam in the room, and all around him, the glistening of the precious metal which he had spent his life in hoarding up.

Whether Midas slept as usual that night, the story does not say. At any rate, day had hardly peeped over the hills, when King Midas was broad awake, and stretching his arms out of bed, began to touch the objects that were within reach. He was anxious to prove whether the Golden Touch had really come, according to the stranger's promise. So he laid his finger on a chair by the bedside, and on various other things, but was grievously disappointed to perceive that they remained of exactly the same substance as before. Indeed, he felt very much afraid that he had only dreamed about the lustrous stranger, or else that the latter had been making game of him. And what a miserable affair would it be, if after all his hopes, Midas must content himself with what little gold he could scrape together by ordinary means, instead of creating it by a touch!

All this while, it was only the gray of the morning, with but a streak of brightness along the edge of the sky, where Midas could not see it. He lay in a very disconsolate mood, regretting the downfall of his hopes, and kept growing sadder and sadder, until the earliest sunbeam shone through the window, and gilded the ceiling over his head. It seemed to Midas that this bright yellow sunbeam was reflected in rather a singular way on the white covering of the bed. Looking more closely, what was his astonishment and delight, when he found that this linen fabric had been transmuted to what seemed a woven texture of the purest and brightest gold! The Golden Touch had come to him with the first sunbeam!

Midas started up, in a kind of joyful frenzy, and ran about the room, grasping at everything that happened to be in his way. He seized one of the bed-posts, and it became immediately a fluted golden pillar. He pulled aside a window-curtain, in order to admit a clear spectacle of the wonders which he was performing; and the tassel grew heavy in his hand—a mass of gold. He took up a book from the table. At his first touch, it assumed the appearance of such a splendidly bound and giltedged volume as one often meets with, nowadays; but, on running his fingers through the leaves, behold! It was a bundle of thin golden plates, in which all the wisdom of the book had grown illegible. He hurriedly put on his clothes, and was enraptured to see himself in a magnificent suit of gold cloth, which retained its flexibility and softness, although it burdened him a little with its weight. He drew out his handkerchief, which little Marygold had hemmed for him. That was likewise gold, with the dear child's neat and pretty stiches running all along the border, in gold thread!

Somehow or other, this last transformation did not quite please King Midas. He would rather that his little daughter's handiwork should have remained just the same as when she climbed his knee and put it into his hand.

But it was not worth while to vex himself about a trifle. Midas now took his spectacles from his pocket, and put them on his nose, in order that he might see more distinctly what he was about. In those days, spectacles for common people had not been invented, but were already worn by kings; else, how could Midas have had any? To his great perplexity, however, excellent as the glasses were, he discovered that he could not possibly see through them. But this was the most natural thing in the world; for, on taking them off, the transparent crystals turned out to be plates of yellow metal, and, of course, were worthless as spectacles, though valuable as gold. It struck Midas as rather inconvenient that, with all his wealth, he could never again be rich enough to own a pair of serviceable spectacles.

"It is no great matter, nevertheless," said he to himself, very philosophically. "We cannot expect any great good, without its being accompanied with some small inconvenience. The Golden Touch is worth the sacrifice of a pair of spectacles, at least, if not of one's very eyesight. My own eyes will serve for ordinary purposes, and little Marygold will soon be old enough to read to me."

King Midas went down stairs, and smiled, on observing that the balustrade of the staircase became a bar of burnished gold, as his hand passed over it, in his descent. He lifted the door-latch (it was brass only a moment ago, but golden when his fingers quitted it), and emerged into the garden. Here, as it happened, he found a great number of beautiful roses in full bloom, and others in all the stages of lovely bud and blossom. Very delicious was their fragrance in the morning breeze. Their delicate blush was one of the fairest sights in the world; so gentle, so modest, and so full of sweet tranquillity, did these roses seem to be.

But Midas knew a way to make them far more precious, according to his way of thinking, than roses had ever been before. So he took great pains in going from bush to bush, and exercised his magic touch most indefatigably; until every individual flower and bud, and even the worms at the heart of some of them, were changed to gold. By the time this good work was completed, King Midas was summoned to breakfast; and as the morning air had given him an excellent appetite, he made haste back to the palace.

On this particular morning, the breakfast consisted of hot cakes, some nice little brook-trout, roasted potatoes, fresh boiled eggs, and coffee, for King Midas himself, and a bowl of bread and milk for his daughter Marygold.

Little Marygold had not yet made her appearance. Her father ordered her to be called, and, seating himself at table, awaited the child's coming, in order to begin his own breakfast. To do Midas justice, he really loved his daughter, and loved her so much the more this morning, on account of the good fortune which had befallen him. It was not a great while before he heard her coming along the passageway crying bitterly. This circumstance surprised him, because Marygold was one of the cheerfullest little people whom you would see in a summer's day, and hardly shed a thimbleful of tears in a twelvemonth. When Midas heard her sobs, he determined to put little Marygold in better spirits, by an agreeable surprise; so, leaning across the table, he touched his daughter's bowl (which was a China one, with pretty figures all around it), and transmuted it to gleaming gold.

Meanwhile, Marygold slowly and disconsolately opened the door, and showed herself with her apron at her eyes, still sobbing as if her heart would break.

"How now, my little lady!" cried Midas. "Pray what is the matter with you, this bright morning?"

Marygold, without taking the apron from her eyes, held out her hand, in which was one of the roses which Midas had so recently transmuted.

"Beautiful!" exclaimed her father. "And what is there in this magnificent golden rose to make you cry?"

"Ah, dear father!" answered the child,

as well as her sobs would let her; "it is not beautiful, but the ugliest flower that ever grew! As soon as I was dressed I ran into the garden to gather some roses for you; because I know you like them. But, oh dear, dear me! What do you think has happened? Such a misfortune! All the beautiful roses, that smelled so sweetly and had so many lovely blushes, are blighted and spoilt! They are grown quite yellow, as you see this one, and have no longer any fragrance! What can have been the matter with them?"

"Poh, my dear little girl,—pray don't cry about it!" said Midas, who was ashamed to confess that he himself had wrought the change which so greatly afflicted her. "Sit down and eat your bread and milk! You will find it easy enough to exchange a golden rose like that (which will last hundreds of years) for an ordinary one which would wither in a day."

"I don't care for such roses as this!" cried Marygold, tossing it contemptuously away. "It has no smell, and the hard petals prick my nose!"

The child now sat down to table, but was so occupied with her grief for the blighted roses that she did not even notice the wonderful transmutation of her China bowl. Perhaps this was all the better; for Marygold was accustomed to take pleasure in looking at the queer figures, and strange trees and houses, that were painted on the circumference of the bowl; and these ornaments were now entirely lost in the yellow hue of the metal.

Midas, meanwhile, had poured out a cup of coffee, and, as a matter of course, the coffee-pot, whatever metal it may have been when he took it up, was gold when he set it down. He thought to himself, that it was rather an extravagant style of splendor, in a king of his simple habits, to breakfast off a service of gold, and began to be puzzled with the difficulty of keeping his treasures safe. The cupboard and the kitchen would no longer be a secure place of deposit for articles so valuable as golden bowls and coffee-pots.

Amid these thoughts, he lifted a spoonful of coffee to his lips, and, sipping it, was astonished to perceive that, the instant his lips touched the liquid, it became molten gold, and, the next moment, hardened into a lump!

"Ha!" exclaimed Midas, rather aghast.

"What is the matter, father?" asked little Marygold, gazing at him, with the tears still standing in her eyes.

"Nothing, child, nothing!" said Midas. "Eat your milk, before it gets quite cold."

He took one of the nice little trouts on his plate, and, by way of experiment, touched its tail with his finger. To his horror, it was immediately transmuted from an admirably fried brook-trout into a goldfish. A very pretty piece of work, as you may suppose; only King Midas, just at that moment, would much rather have had a real trout in his dish than this elaborate and valuable imitation of one.

"I don't quite see," thought he to himself, "how I am to get any breakfast!"

He took one of the smoking-hot cakes, and had scarcely broken it, when, to his cruel mortification, though, a moment before, it had been of the whitest wheat, it assumed the yellow hue of Indian meal. Almost in despair, he helped himself to a boiled egg, which immediately underwent a change similar to those of the trout and the cake. The egg, indeed, might have been mistaken for one of those which the famous goose, in the story-book, was in the habit of laying; but King Midas was the only goose that had had anything to do with the matter.

"Well, this is a quandary!" thought he, leaning back in his chair, and looking quite enviously at little Marygold, who was now eating her bread and milk with great satisfaction. "Such a costly breakfast before me, and nothing that can be eaten."

Hoping that, by dint of great dispatch, he might avoid what he now felt to be a considerable inconvenience, King Midas next snatched a hot potato, and attempted to cram it into his mouth, and swallow it in a hurry. But the Golden Touch was too nimble for him. He found his mouth full, not of mealy potato, but of solid metal, which so burnt his tongue that he roared aloud, and, jumping up from the table, began to dance and stamp about the room, both with pain and affright.

"Father, dear father!" cried little Marygold, who was a very affectionate child, "pray what is the matter? Have you burnt your mouth?"

"Ah, dear child," groaned Midas, dolefully, "I don't know what is to become of your poor father!"

Already, at breakfast, Midas was excessively hungry. Would he be less so by dinner-time? And how ravenous would be his appetite for supper, which must undoubtedly consist of the same sort of indigestible dishes as those now before him.

These reflections so troubled wise King Midas that he began to doubt whether, after all, riches are the one desirable thing in the world. But this was only a passing thought. So fascinated was Midas with the glitter of the yellow metal that he would still have refused to give up the Golden Touch for so paltry a consideration as a breakfast.

Nevertheless, so great was his hunger, and the perplexity of his situation, that he again groaned aloud, and very grievously too. Our pretty Marygold could endure it no longer. She sat, a moment, gazing at her father, and trying, with all the might of her little wits, to find out what was the matter with him. Then, with a sweet and sorrowful impulse to comfort him, she started from her chair, and, running to Midas, threw her arms affectionately about his knees. He bent down and kissed her. He felt that his little daughter's love was worth a thousand times more than he had gained by the Golden Touch.

"My precious, precious Marygold!" cried he.

But Marygold made no answer.

Alas, what had he done? The moment the lips of Midas touched Marygold's forehead, a change had taken place. Her sweet, rosy face, so full of affection as it had been, assumed a glittering yellow color, with yellow tear-drops, congealing on her cheeks. Her beautiful brown ringlets took the same tint. Her soft and tender little form grew hard and inflexible within her father's encircling arms. Oh, terrible misfortune! The victim of his insatiable desire for wealth, little Marygold was a human child no longer, but a golden statue!

Yes, there she was, with the questioning look of love, grief, and pity, hardened into her face. It was the prettiest and most woeful sight that ever mortal saw. All the features and tokens of Marygold were there; even the beloved little dimple remained in her golden chin. But, the more perfect was the resemblance, the greater was the father's agony at beholding this golden image, which was all that was left him of a daughter. It had been a favorite phrase of Midas, whenever he felt particularly fond of the child, to say that she was worth her weight in gold. And now the phrase had become literally true. And now, at last, when it was too late, he felt how infinitely a warm and tender heart, that loved him, exceeded in value all the wealth that could be piled up betwixt the earth and sky!

Midas, in the fulness of all his gratified desires, began to wring his hands and bemoan himself; and now he could neither bear to look at Marygold, nor yet to look away from her. Except when his eyes were fixed on the image, he could not possibly believe that she was changed to gold. But, stealing another glance, there was the precious little figure, with a yellow tear-drop on its yellow cheek, and a look so piteous and tender, that it seemed as if that very expression must needs soften the gold, and make it flesh again. This, however, could not be.

While Midas was in this tumult of despair, he suddenly beheld a stranger standing near the door. Midas bent down his head, without speaking; for he recognized the same figure which had appeared to him, the day before, in the treasure-room, and had bestowed on him this disastrous faculty of the Golden Touch. The stranger's countenance still wore a smile, which seemed to shed a yellow lustre all about the room, and gleamed on little Marygold's image, and on the other objects that had been transmuted by the touch of Midas.

"Well, friend Midas," said the stranger, "pray how do you succeed with the Golden Touch?"

Midas shook his head.

"I am very miserable," said he.

"Very miserable, indeed!" exclaimed the stranger. "And how happens that? Have I not faithfully kept my promise with you? Have you not everything that your heart desired?"

"Gold is not everything," answered Midas. "And I have lost all that my heart really cared for."

"Ah! So you have made a discovery, since yesterday?" observed the stranger. "Let us see, then. Which of these two things do you think is really worth the most—the gift of the Golden Touch, or one cup of clear cold water?"

"O blessed water!" exclaimed Midas. "It will never moisten my parched throat again!"

"The Golden Touch," continued the stranger, "or a crust of bread?"

"A piece of bread," answered Midas, "is worth all the gold on earth!"

"The Golden Touch," asked the stranger, "or your own little Marygold, warm, soft, and loving as she was an hour ago?"

"Oh, my child, my dear child!" cried poor Midas, wringing his hands. "I would not have given that one small dimple in her chin for the power of changing this whole big earth into a solid lump of gold!"

"You are wiser than you were, King Midas!" said the stranger, looking seriously at him. "Your own heart, I perceive, has not been entirely changed from flesh to gold. Were it so, your case would indeed be desperate. But you appear to be still capable of understanding that the commonest things, such as lie within everybody's grasp, are more valuable than the riches which so many mortals sigh and struggle after. Tell me, now, do you sincerely desire to rid yourself of this Golden Touch?"

"It is hateful to me!" replied Midas.

A fly settled on his nose, but immediately fell to the floor; for it, too, had become gold. Midas shuddered.

"Go, then," said the stranger, "and plunge into the river that glides past the bottom of your garden. Take likewise a vase of the same water, and sprinkle it over any object that you may desire to change back again from gold into its former substance. If you do this in earnestness and sincerity, it may possibly repair the mischief which your avarice has occasioned."

King Midas bowed low; and when he lifted his head, the lustrous stranger had vanished.

You will easily believe that Midas lost no time in snatching up a great earthen pitcher (but, alas me! it was no longer earthen after he touched it), and hastening to the river-side. As he scampered along, and forced his way through the shrubbery, it was positively marvellous to see how the foliage turned yellow behind him, as if the autumn had been there, and nowhere else. On reaching the river's brink, he plunged headlong in, without waiting so much as to pull off his shoes.

"Poof! poof! poof!" snorted King Midas, as his head emerged out of the water. "Well, this is really a refreshing bath, and I think it must have quite washed away the Golden Touch. And now for filling my pitcher!"

As he dipped the pitcher into the water, it gladdened his very heart to see it change from gold into the same good, honest earthen vessel which it had been before he touched it. He was conscious, also, of a change within himself. A cold, hard, and heavy weight seemed to have gone out of his bosom. Perceiving a violet, that grew on the bank of the river, Midas touched it with his finger, and was overjoyed to find that the delicate flower retained its purple hue, instead of undergoing a yellow blight. The curse of the Golden Touch had, therefore, really been removed from him.

King Midas hastened back to the palace; and, I suppose, the servants knew not what to make of it when they saw their royal master so carefully bringing home an earthen pitcher of water. But that water, which was to undo all the mischief that his folly had wrought, was more precious to Midas than an ocean of molten gold could have been. The first thing he did, as you need hardly be told, was to sprinkle it by handfuls over the golden figure of little Marygold.

No sooner did it fall on her than you would have laughed to see how the rosy color came back to the dear child's cheek! And how she began to sneeze and sputter! —and how astonished she was to find herself dripping wet, and her father still throwing more water over her!

"Pray do not, dear father!" cried she. "See how you have wet my nice frock, which I put on only this morning!"

For Marygold did not know that she had been a little golden statue; nor could she remember anything that had happened since the moment when she ran with outstretched arms to comfort poor King Midas.

Her father did not think it necessary to tell his beloved child how very foolish he had been, but contented himself with showing how much wiser he had now grown. For this purpose, he led little Marygold into the garden, where he sprinkled all the remainder of the water over the rosebushes, and with such good effect that above five thousand roses recovered their beautiful bloom. There were two circumstances, however, which as long as he lived, used to put King Midas in mind of the Golden Touch. One was, that the sands of the river sparkled like gold; the other, that little Marygold's hair had now a golden tinge, which he had never observed in it before she had been transmuted by the effect of his kiss.

When King Midas had grown quite an old man, and used to trot Marygold's children on his knee, he was fond of telling them this marvellous story, pretty much as I have now told it to you. And then would he stroke their glossy ringlets, and tell them that their hair, likewise, had a rich shade of gold, which they had inherited from their mother.

"And to tell you the truth, my precious little folks," quoth King Midas, diligently trotting the children all the while, "ever since that morning, I have hated the very sight of all other gold, save this!"

Fable

THE MAN, THE BOY, AND THE DONKEY

Aesop

Aesop, a slave who became ambassador from Lydia to Greece, is considered to be the originator of the fable form. His name is possibly derived from the Greek adjective aithops, *or "dark," or the noun* Aithiops, *or Ethiopian. One version of the life of Aesop describes him as black and Ethiopian (Maximus Planudes,* Provenium vitae Aesopi*). He is said to have lived sometime in the sixth century* B.C. *Aesop's fables typically embody a moral message and consist of simple situations, concretely conceived and presented. Like the foolish people of Gotham, or like such cinema clowns as Laurel and Hardy, the father and son of this fable are lost in their own private fog of foolishness.*

A man and his son were once going with their Donkey to market. As they were walking along by its side a countryman passed them and said: "You fools, what is a Donkey for but to ride upon?"

So the Man put the Boy on the Donkey and they went on their way. But soon they passed a group of men, one of whom said: "See that lazy youngster, he lets his father walk while he rides."

So the Man ordered his Boy to get off, and got on himself. But they hadn't gone far when they passed two women, one of whom said to the other: "Shame on that lazy lout to let his poor little son trudge along."

Well, the Man didn't know what to do, but at last he took his Boy up before him on the Donkey. By this time they had come to the town, and the passers-by began to jeer and point at them. The Man stopped and asked what they were scoffing at. The men said: "Aren't you ashamed of yourself for overloading that poor Donkey of yours—you and your hulking son?"

The Man and Boy got off and tried to think what to do. They thought and they thought, till at last they cut down a pole, tied the Donkey's feet to it, and raised the pole and the Donkey to their shoulders. They went along amid the laughter of all who met them till they came to Market Bridge, when the Donkey, getting one of his feet loose, kicked out and caused the

Boy to drop his end of the pole. In the struggle the Donkey fell over the bridge, and his fore-feet being tied together he was drowned.

"That will teach you," said an old man who had followed them:

"Please all, and you will please none."

Folk Rhymes

In the Oxford English Dictionary, *Simple Simon is listed under the category of "Lacking in ordinary sense or intelligence; more or less foolish, silly, or stupid." References to previous dictionaries are quoted in which Simple Simon is described as "a natural, a silly fellow," or "a credulous gullible person." That is, Simon qualifies as a natural fool, prey to all the tragic mishaps that this condition entails.*

Simple Simon met a pieman,
  Going to the fair;
Says Simple Simon to the pieman,
  Let me taste your ware.

Says the pieman to Simple Simon,
  Show me first your penny;
Says Simple Simon to the pieman,
  Indeed I have not any.

Simple Simon went a-fishing,
  For to catch a whale;
All the water he had got
  Was in his mother's pail.

Simple Simon went to look
  If plums grew on a thistle;
He pricked his finger very much,
  Which made poor Simon whistle.

The first recorded appearance of this mournful little fool's song was in 1684.

When I was a little boy
  I had but little wit,
'Tis a long time ago,
  And I have no more yet;
Nor ever, ever shall,
  Until that I die,
For the longer I live,
  The more fool am I.

It bears a resemblance to the sad song of the clown at the end of Shakespeare's Twelfth Night.

> *When that I was and a little tiny boy,*
> *With hey, ho, the wind and the rain;*
> *A foolish thing was but a toy,*
> *For the rain it raineth every day. . . .*

The Fool sings a similar song in act III, scene 2, of King Lear.

Because fools and clowns often have the power to be able to recover magically from accidents—as this "wise" man does when he scratches his eyes out and in again—people can laugh at them safely. Our human impulse to laugh at disaster may be related to a need to develop equanimity in the face of misfortune.

The "quickest hedge" in the next-to-last line is a hedge composed of living shrubs or trees, especially hawthorn.

There was a man so wise,
He jumped into
A bramble bush,
And scratched out both his eyes.
And when he saw,
His eyes were out,
And reason to complain,
He jumped into a quickset hedge,
And scratched them in again.

Gotham is a village near Nottingham which traditionally has been considered a town of fools. The source of its reputation may have been when King John (1340-1399) expressed the wish to travel through town. The townspeople were reluctant, for in those days any road traveled by the king thereafter became a public road or highway. All villagers played the fool in order to convince the king's outriders that they were mad and the king should therefore travel another way.

This rhyme has often been used to discourage children who beg, "Tell me a story."

Three wise men of Gotham
They went to sea in a bowl,
And if the bowl had been stronger
My song had been longer.

Folktales

THE SEA OF GOLD

(Japanese)

Retold by Yoshiko Uchida

The fool in this story is Hikoichi the cook, who is mocked by the fishermen of the boat on which he works for talking to and feeding the fish of the sea as if they were his best friends. But the laughter of the fishermen at his foolishness is stopped when, one magical night, the King of the Sea rewards Hikoichi's kindness a hundredfold. The motif of the fool who is rewarded for the "foolishness" of kindness, gentleness, and goodness is found in folktales of many cultures.

On a small island, where almost every able-bodied man was a fisherman, there once lived a young man named Hikoichi. He was gentle and kind, but he was not very bright, and there was no one on the whole island who was willing to teach him how to become a fisherman.

"How could we ever make a fisherman out of you?" people would say to him. "You are much too slow to learn anything!"

But Hikoichi wanted very badly to go to work, and he tried hard to find a job. He looked and looked for many months until finally he found work as cook on one of the fishing boats. He got the job, however, only because no one else wanted it. No one wanted to work in a hot steaming galley, cooking rice and chopping vegetables, while the boat pitched and rolled in the middle of the sea. No one wanted to be the cook who always got the smallest share of the boat's catch. But Hikoichi didn't mind at all. He was happy to have any kind of job at last.

Illustrated by Marianne Yamaguchi.

The fishermen on his boat liked to tease him and they would often call him Slowpoke or Stupid. "Get busy and make us something decent to eat, Stupid!" they would shout to him. Or, "The rice is only half-cooked, Slowpoke!" they would complain.

But no matter how they shouted or what they called him, Hikoichi never grew angry. He only answered, "Yes sir," or "I'm sorry, sir," and that was all.

Hikoichi was very careful with the food he cooked, and he tried not to waste even a single grain of rice. In fact, he hated to throw away any of the leftovers, and he stored them carefully in the galley cupboards. On the small, crowded fishing vessel, however, there was no room for keeping useless things. Every bit of extra space was needed to store the catch, for the more fish they took back to the island, the more money they would all make. When the men discovered that Hikoichi was saving the leftovers, they scolded him harshly.

"Stupid fool!" they shouted. "Don't use our valuable space for storing garbage. Throw it into the sea!"

"What a terrible waste of good food," Hikoichi thought, but he had to do as he was told. He gathered up all the leftovers he had stored and took them up on deck.

"If I must throw this into the sea," he said to himself, "I will make sure the fish have a good feast. After all, if it were not for the fish, we wouldn't be able to make a living." And so, as he threw the leftovers into the water, he called out, "Here fish, here, good fish, have yourselves a splendid dinner!"

From that day, Hikoichi always called to the fish before he threw his leftovers into the sea. "*Sah sah,* come along," he would call. "Enjoy some rice from my galley!" And he continued talking to them until they had devoured every morsel he tossed overboard.

The fishermen laughed when they heard him. "Listen to the young fool talking to the fish," they jeered. And to Hikoichi they said, "Maybe someday they will answer you and tell you how much they enjoyed your dinner."

But Hikoichi didn't pay any attention to the fishermen. He silently gathered all the scraps from the table and continued to toss them out to the fish at the end of the day. Each time he did, he called to the fish as though they were his best friends, and his gentle voice echoed far out over the dancing waves of the sea.

In such a fashion, many years went by until Hikoichi was no longer a young man. He continued to cook for the men on his fishing boat, however, and he still fed and talked to the fish every evening.

One day, the fishing boat put far out to sea in search of bigger fish. It sailed for three days and three nights, going farther and farther away from the small island. On the third night, they were still far out at sea when they dropped anchor. It was a quiet star-filled night with a full moon glowing high in the sky. The men were tired from the day's work and not long after dinner, they were all sound asleep.

Hikoichi, however, still had much to do. He scrubbed the pots, cleaned up his galley and washed the rice for breakfast. When he had finished, he gathered all the leftovers in a basket and went up on deck.

"Gather around, good fish," he called as always. "Enjoy your dinner."

He emptied his basket and stayed to watch the fish eat up his food. Then, he went to his bunk to prepare for bed, but somehow the boat felt very peculiar. It had stopped rolling. In fact, it was not moving at all and felt as though it were standing on dry land.

"That's odd," Hikoichi thought, and he ran up on deck to see what had happened. He leaned over the rail and looked out.

"What!" he shouted. "The ocean is gone!"

And indeed it had disappeared. There was not a single drop of water anywhere. As far as Hikoichi could see, there was nothing but miles and miles of sand. It was as though the boat were standing in the middle of a vast desert of shimmering sand.

"What has happened?" Hikoichi wondered. "Have we suddenly beached ourselves on an unknown island? Did the ocean dry up? But no, that is impossible. I must be dreaming!"

Hikoichi blinked hard and shook his head. Then he pinched himself on the cheek, but he was not dreaming. Hikoichi was alarmed. He wanted to go below to wake the others, but he knew they would be very angry to be awakened in the middle of the night. They would shout at him and call him a stupid fool and tell him he was out of his mind. Hikoichi decided he wouldn't awaken them after all. If the boat was still on land in the morning, the men

would see for themselves.

Hikoichi could not believe his eyes. He simply had to get off the boat to see if they really were standing on dry land. Slowly, he lowered himself down a rope ladder and reached the sand below. Carefully, he took a step and felt his foot crunch on something solid. No, it wasn't water. It really was sand after all. Hikoichi blinked as he looked around, for under the light of the moon, the sand glittered and sparkled like a beach of gold. He scooped up a handful and watched it glisten as it slid through his fingers.

"Why, this is beautiful," Hikoichi thought, and his heart sang with joy at the splendor of the sight. "I must save some of this sand so I can remember this wonderful night forever." He hurried back onto the boat for a bucket, filled it with the sparkling sand and then carried it aboard and hid it carefully beneath his bunk. He looked around at the other men, but they were all sound asleep. Not one seemed to have noticed that the boat was standing still. Hikoichi slipped quietly into his narrow, dark bunk, and soon he too was sound asleep.

The next morning Hikoichi was the first to wake up. He remembered the remarkable happening of the night before, and he leaped out of bed, ready to call the other men to see the strange sight. But as he got dressed, he felt the familiar rocking of the boat. He hurried up on deck and he saw that once again they were out in the middle of the ocean with waves all about them. Hikoichi shook his head, but now he could no longer keep it all to himself. As soon as the other men came up on deck, he told his story.

"It's true," he cried as he saw wide grins appear on the men's faces. "The ocean was gone and for miles and miles there was nothing but sand. It glittered and sparkled under the full moon and it was as though we were sailing on a sea of golden sand!"

The men roared with laughter. "Hikoichi, you were surely drunk," they said. "Now put away your daydreams and fix us some breakfast."

"No, no, I wasn't drunk and I wasn't dreaming," Hikoichi insisted. "I climbed down the ladder and I walked on the sand. I picked it up and felt it slip through my fingers. It wasn't a dream. It really wasn't."

"Poor old Slowpoke," the men sneered. "Your brain has finally become addled. We will have to send you home."

It was then that Hikoichi remembered his bucket. "Wait! Come with me and I can prove it," he said, and he led the men down to his bunk. Then, getting down on his hands and knees, he carefully pulled out his bucket of sand.

"There!" he said proudly. "I scooped this up when I went down and walked on the sand. Now do you believe me?"

The men suddenly stopped laughing. "This isn't sand," they said, reaching out to feel it. "It's gold! It's a bucket full of pure gold!"

"Why didn't you get more, you poor fool?" one of the men shouted.

"You've got to give some of it to us," another added.

"We share our fish with you. You must share your gold with us," said still another.

Soon all the men were yelling and shouting and pushing to get their hands on Hikoichi's bucket of gold.

Then the oldest of the fishermen spoke up. "Stop it! Stop it!" he called out. "This gold doesn't belong to any of you. It belongs to Hikoichi."

He reminded the men how Hikoichi had fed the fish of the sea for so many years as though they were his own children.

"Now the King of the Sea has given Hikoichi a reward for his kindness to the fish," he explained. And turning to Hikoichi, he added, "You are not stupid or a fool or a slowpoke, my friend. You are gentle and kind and good. This gift from the Kingdom of the Sea is your reward. Take all the gold and keep it, for it belongs only to you."

The shouting, pushing fishermen suddenly became silent and thoughtful, for they knew the old fisherman was right. They were ashamed of having laughed at Hikoichi year after year, and they knew that he truly deserved this fine reward.

Without another word the men went back to work. They completed their catch that day and the heavily laden boat returned once more to the little island.

The next time the boat put out to sea, Hikoichi was no longer aboard, for now he had enough gold to leave his job as cook forever. He built himself a beautiful new house, and he even had a small boat of his own so he could still sail out to sea and feed the fish. He used his treasure from the sea wisely and well, and he lived a long and happy life on the little island where no one ever called him Stupid or Slowpoke again.

THE GOLDEN GOOSE

(German)

The simpleton hero of this story collected by the Brothers Grimm is the youngest of three sons. Some psychologists believe that the youngest son actually represents the intuitive part of the personality and that his victory over his brothers is the result of being in tune with the unconscious. Children find it very easy to identify with Dummling, who is despised by his parents and brothers, because they are often in the position of feeling small, stupid, and inadequate in the world. Thus, stories of simpletons who triumph in the world are good ones to share with children. As Bruno Bettelheim suggests in The Uses of Enchantment *(1976), "On the simplest and most direct level, fairy tales in which the hero is the youngest and most inept offer the child the consolation and hope for the future he needs most. Though the child thinks little of himself—a view he projects onto others' views of him—and fears he will never amount to anything, the story shows that he is already started on the process of realizing his potentials."*

There was a man who had three sons. The youngest was called Dummling, and was on all occasions despised and ill-treated by the whole family. It happened that the eldest took it into his head one day to go into the wood to cut fuel; and his mother gave him a delicious pasty and a bottle of wine to take with him, that he might re-

Translated by Edgar Taylor.

fresh himself at his work. As he went into the wood, a little old man bid him good day, and said, "Give me a little piece of meat from your plate, and a little wine out of your bottle; I am very hungry and thirsty." But this clever young man said, "Give you my meat and wine! No, I thank you; I should not have enough left for myself": and away he went. He soon began to cut down a tree; but he had not worked long before he missed his stroke, and cut himself, and was obliged to go home to have the wound dressed. Now it was the little old man that caused him this mischief.

Next went out the second son to work; and his mother gave him too a pasty and a bottle of wine. And the same little old man met him also, and asked him for something to eat and drink. But he too thought himself vastly clever, and said, "Whatever you get, I shall lose; so go your way!" The little man took care that he should have his reward; and the second stroke that he aimed against a tree hit him on the leg; so that he too was forced to go home.

Then Dummling said, "Father, I should like to go and cut wood too." But his father answered, "Your brothers have both lamed themselves; you had better stay at home, for you know nothing of the business." But Dummling was very pressing; and at last his father said, "Go your way; you will be wiser when you have suffered for your folly." And his mother gave him only some dry bread, and a bottle of sour beer; but when he went into the wood, he met the little old man, who said, "Give me some meat and drink, for I am very hungry and thirsty." Dummling said, "I have only dry bread and sour beer; if that will suit you, we will sit down and eat it together." So they sat down; and when the lad pulled out his bread, behold it was turned into a capital pasty, and his sour beer became delightful wine. They ate and drank heartily; and when they had done, the little man said, "As you have a kind heart, and have been willing to share every thing with me, I will send a blessing upon you. There stands an old tree; cut it down, and you will find something at the root." Then he took his leave, and went his way.

Dummling set to work, and cut down the tree; and when it fell, he found in a hollow under the roots a goose with feathers of pure gold. He took it up, and went on to an inn, where he proposed to sleep for the night. The landlord had three daughters; and when they saw the goose, they were very curious to examine what this wonderful bird could be, and wished very much to pluck one of the feathers out of its tail. At last the eldest said, "I must and will have a feather." So she waited till his back was turned, and then seized the goose by the wing; but to her great surprise there she stuck, for neither hand nor finger could she get away again. Presently in came the second sister, and thought to have a feather too; but the moment she touched her sister, there she too hung fast. At last came the third, and wanted a feather; but the other two cried out, "Keep away! for heaven's sake, keep away!" However, she did not understand what they meant. "If they are there," thought she, "I may as well be there too." So she went up to them; but the moment she touched her sisters she stuck fast, and hung to the goose as they did. And so they kept company with the goose all night.

The next morning Dummling carried off the goose under his arm; and took no notice of the three girls, but went out with them sticking fast behind; and wherever he travelled, they too were obliged to follow, whether they would or no, as fast as their legs could carry them.

In the middle of a field the parson met them; and when he saw the train, he said, "Are you not ashamed of yourselves, you bold girls, to run after the young man in that way over the fields? is that proper behaviour?" Then he took the youngest by the hand to lead her away; but the moment he touched her he too hung fast, and followed in the train. Presently up came the clerk; and when he saw his master the parson running after the three girls, he wondered greatly, and said, "Hollo! hollo! your reverence! whither so fast? there is a christening to-day." Then he ran up, and took him by the gown, and in a moment he was fast too. As the five were thus trudging along, one behind another, they met two labourers with their mattocks coming from work; and the parson cried out to them to set him free. But scarcely had they touched him, when they too fell into the ranks, and so made seven, all running after Dummling and his goose.

At last they arrived at a city, where reigned a king who had an only daughter. The princess was of so thoughtful and serious a turn of mind that no one could make her laugh; and the king had proclaimed to all the world, that whoever could make her laugh should have her for his wife. When the young man heard this, he went to her with his goose and all its train; and as soon as she saw the seven all hanging together, and running about, treading on each other's heels, she could not help bursting into a long and loud laugh. Then Dummling claimed her for his wife; the wedding was celebrated, and he was heir to the kingdom, and lived long and happily with his wife.

JACK AND THE BEANSTALK

Retold by James Reeves

This is a story about growing up, maturing. One of the interpretations of the story is that the child, who considers himself stupid—selling the cow for beans—turns out not to be stupid at all as his intuitions prove valid and he succeeds in a series of tests that bring him to full maturity. The first thing Jack grasps for is gold, but this money is not enough; on his second trip, he discovers the golden goose, or the art of producing as well as spending money; still this is not enough, and on the third trip, he obtains a golden harp—the musical, artistic part of life which greatly enriches his existence. The terror of the giant—that forbidding figure which represents the way adults look to the child—is overcome. This classic English folktale has been in print in various versions since the eighteenth century and undoubtedly dates much earlier. The chant "Fie, foh, and fum, I smell the blood of a British man" is found in act III, scene 4, of King Lear *(1607).*

1

Once upon a time there was a poor widow who lived in a cottage with her only son Jack. Jack was a clever boy, strong, good-natured, and ready with his hands; but he did not go out and work for a living, staying at home instead and helping his mother about the house and garden. He chopped wood to make the fire, dug and weeded the little vegetable patch, and milked their one cow, Milky White. The widow cooked and cleaned and mended, so that the two of them, though they were poor, lived in contentment and had enough to eat and drink.

Now one year, after a hard, cold spring, there was a dry summer, and the grass in the meadow withered; so that Milky White gave no milk. Jack and his mother were soon without butter, nor had they milk to drink and to sell. Their vegetables did not grow because of the dry weather, and they were forced to spend the little money they had saved.

"Jack," said his mother, "I think we had better sell Milky White. She will soon die if she can get no grass, and we must have money for food and drink."

"Very well, mother," said Jack. "I will take her to market, and with the money I get we will buy goods to start a shop. We can get dishes and mugs, and laces and thread, and penny books and things of that sort that our neighbours need; and soon we shall be rich. You shall see. Tomorrow is market-day, and I shall set off first thing in the morning."

"I shall be sorry to lose Milky White," sighed the widow, "but go she must. Get a good price for her, mind you—not less than ten pounds, or twelve perhaps."

"Not a penny less than fifteen," said Jack, "and don't be surprised if I come back with twenty."

So next morning, when he had what little breakfast his mother could provide, Jack drove Milky White out of the field and down the lane which used to be full of puddles and mud but was now baked dry and hard as a biscuit. He broke himself a switch from the hedge and gave the cow a touch on her side every now and then to keep her moving. Presently they reached the high road, and off they went towards the market town.

They had not been going long when they met a queer old man bent nearly double and tapping his way along with a stick. He looked up as Jack drew near, and Jack saw that he had very bright and twinkling eyes.

"Good day," he said, for he was always a friendly boy.

"Good day, young man," said the traveller, "and where are you off to this bright day?"

"I am off to market to sell my cow," Jack told him.

"Oh, indeed," said the old man. "I wonder what sort of a bargain you'll make. Let's see if you're as smart as you look. Can you tell me how many beans make five?"

"Why, that's not hard," laughed Jack, thinking the old man was a bit simple. "Two in my left hand, two in my right hand, and one in my mouth."

"Right you are. Now just come here, young man."

So Jack went closer to the bright-eyed fellow, who put his hand in his wallet and drew out five beans.

"And there they are," he said. "How would you like them in exchange for the cow?"

"What! Five beans in exchange for Milky White?" asked Jack. "What sort of a bargain do you call that?"

"Ah!" said the old man. "These are no common beans. Just plant them, and they'll grow right up to the sky. You look the sort of young fellow that has a mind for marvels and mysteries and such like. Have you ever heard of such a marvel as that, now?"

Well, Jack said he hadn't; but how was he to know whether the beans were truly magical, as the old man had said?

"I'll tell you what," said the man. "Just you take the beans and give me the cow; and if the beans aren't as I say, meet me here tomorrow at the same time, and you shall have the cow back again, and no harm done."

Jack thought this was a fair offer, so without more argument he took the beans and handed Milky White's halter over to the bright-eyed man. He had forgotten all about the fifteen or twenty golden pounds he was to take home to his mother, and thought of nothing but the wonderful beans that were going to grow up to the sky. So off went the old man with Milky White, and back home went Jack with the five beans safely in the pocket of his trousers.

Jack's mother was surprised to see him home so early.

"Well," she said, "bless me! I see you've sold Milky White—and a good price you must have got for her or you wouldn't be back so soon. How much? Ten? Fifteen? Don't say it was twenty! A good cow she was to be sure, but—"

"Mother," interrupted Jack, "I got no money for her at all. After all, mother, anybody can get *money*—but just you wait till you see what I did get."

"No money!" said the widow. "No money? You let Milky White go for nothing, then, you foolish boy?"

"Not for nothing," said Jack. "Just you look here. This is what I got for her."

So saying, he pulled the five beans out of his pocket and put them into his mother's hand.

"Is that all?" she said, hardly able to believe her eyes. "Beans? You take my only cow to market, and all you bring home is a few dried-up miserable good-for-nothing—"

"They're not ordinary beans, mother," said Jack. "They're magic beans!"

Jack's mother was a good-tempered woman, but this time she was really angry.

"Magic fiddlesticks!" she cried. "Why, you poor foolish, ignorant vagabond, you've been cheated, that's what! Now we are ruined, and I shan't live to see the end of your disgrace. Why, these aren't even fit to make soup of! Get to bed, you blockhead, this instant. There's no supper for such a dolt, nor ever likely to be from this day on."

So without giving Jack a chance to speak up for himself, she threw the beans out of the window and fairly pushed the boy upstairs to his little room and slammed the door after him.

Poor Jack lay down on his bed and began to think how foolish he had been. He was sorry, too, to think how greatly he had disappointed his old mother, and what a useless good-for-nothing she must think him! Hungry as he was, he hardly missed his supper, and in a little while, without bothering to undress, he fell asleep.

2

In the morning Jack was amazed to find the room filled with a pale-green light, and at first he thought he must be dreaming. Then he heard the well-known sound of the neighbour's cock crowing and the barking of the old sheep-dog from the farmyard over the way. Looking towards the window, he saw that it was covered with a pattern of broad green leaves growing from strong, twisting stems. They looked like—yes, they *were*—bean leaves! The magic beans! What had happened to them?

He jumped up from the bed and ran to the window. Of course! His mother had tossed them into the garden the evening before, and they must have sprouted in the night. Then they were magic! He threw open the window and looked down. There, sprouting from the ground below, was a strong ladder of beanstalks, twisting and twining together, with strong green leaves growing out all round. Then he looked up. Yes, the beanstalk grew right up—up and up to the very sky. The top was lost in the clouds.

Without stopping to think, Jack climbed on to the window-sill and tested his weight on the beanstalk. It bore him easily. At once he started to climb up. He was a good climber, and not in the least afraid of heights. Up and up he went, climbing, climbing, climbing—climbing, climbing, climbing, till he could look down and see his mother's cottage far away below, with a wisp of blue smoke rising lazily from the chimney and some dish-cloths drying on the garden hedge. Soon he was lost in the clouds.

On top of the clouds the sun shone brilliantly; stretching away out of sight there was a broad, white road. Jack stepped off the beanstalk-ladder and began to walk along the road. Not a man, not a beast, not a house was in sight. Now and again a strange bird flew past. Otherwise there was no sign of life.

Just when Jack was beginning to think the road would go on for ever, he saw in the distance a tall, tall house; and when he got closer, a tall, tall woman came out of the door with a pail in her hand. Jack hurried up to the house and asked the woman, as bold as brass, if she could give him some breakfast.

"Run away from here, little boy!" she cried. "For it's no breakfast you'll get, but it's breakfast you'll *be*! My man is an ogre—a great big tremendous ogre, as fierce as ten tigers, and it's mighty fond he is of a boy like yourself, grilled on toast with a piece of butter on top to make him tender!"

"Well, ma'am," said Jack. "I'm starving with hunger, and there's no food for me at home. If you can spare me a bite of breakfast, I don't care if I'm eaten myself afterwards."

Well, the ogre's wife was not a bad sort, though she had been hardened by having an ogre for a husband. So she looked round to see if the ogre was in sight, then pushed Jack in at the door, sat him down in the kitchen, and gave him some bread and cheese and a mug of new milk.

Just as Jack was finishing his breakfast, there came a terrible noise, and the house began to shake. Thump, thump, thumpety thump! It was the ogre coming home.

"Quick!" said the woman. "Into the oven with you! He won't look there. If he catches sight of you, he'll make no more than three mouthfuls of you, or maybe two."

So into the great oven jumped Jack, and the ogre's wife slammed the door after him, just as the ogre came into the kitchen. He was carrying three dead calves on his belt, and he flung them down on the table and told his wife to cook them for his breakfast. Then he looked round and sniffed. Snuff, snuff, sniff! Jack could hear him through the oven door, though it was made of cast iron with solid brass knobs. And then he heard the ogre's great voice shouting:

"Fee, fi, foh, fum!
I smell the blood of a British man.
Be he alive, or be he dead,
I'll grind his bones to make my
bread!"

Ogres have very sharp noses, and he must have smelt the smell of Jack. But his wife said:

"Nonsense, now! It's nothing but the smell of the boy you had last night for supper. Sit you down and take your boots off, and I'll have your breakfast ready in two shakes."

Well, the ogre took his boots off, and his wife cooked the three calves for his breakfast; and after breakfast the ogre went to an iron-bound chest that stood against the wall and took out three bags of gold. He emptied them on the table and began to count them. When he had counted the gold, he put it back into the bags; but he was sleepy with going out all night in search of his breakfast, and presently he started to doze. After a bit he began snoring, and Jack heard his snores through the door of the oven, even though it was of cast iron with knobs of solid brass. The ogre's snores were like ten thunderstorms in the mountains during the hot, hot days of August when the land is covered with drought and all the river-beds are dusty and parched. Then the ogre's wife opened the door of the oven and let Jack out.

"You'd best get along as quick as you can," she whispered. "It's asleep he is, and Heaven help you if he wakes before you're away."

Jack's sharp eyes had caught sight of the three money-bags on the table, and while the woman's back was turned, he grabbed one of them and ran out of the door as fast as he could go. With the bag of gold clutched in his hand, he sped back along the broad white road till he came to the beanstalk. He looked back and saw that he was not being followed; then he stepped on to the beanstalk and climbed down as fast as he could. As he did so, he dropped the bag of gold, and of course it fell right into his mother's garden.

"Lord-a-mercy!" she cried as the bag burst asunder at her feet. "'Tis a long time I've lived, and a many things I've seen, but never before has it rained gold pieces on a fine summer morning. *And* boys!" she added, as Jack came flying down the beanstalk just as she was beginning to pick up the gold.

"Well, mother," said he, clasping her in his arms and dancing round with her all over the onion bed, "what do you think of your idle, good-for-nothing, dunder-headed, ignorant, stupid son *now*? I hope these little bits of gold I've brought down from the sky will help to keep the wolf from the door."

The old woman admitted that her son was smarter than she had thought, though, of course, she had known all along that he was smarter than most sons. The beans had turned out to be not such a bad bargain after all—though, of course, if *she* hadn't had the sense to drop them out of the window right on a patch of good soil, they might never have sprouted at all.

Well, off they went to the town and bought Jack's mother a new black dress, and a couple of fine hams to eat, and a pony and trap to go home in, and a set of new dishes, and a brand new axe and a pocket-knife and a few more things such as a boy needs. And for a long time they lived in comfort and happiness on the gold pieces that Jack had brought home from the ogre's house. They never lacked meat and drink; and all their time was taken up with using the fine, new things they had wanted so long and were now able to buy.

3

Even a bag of gold does not last for ever, and the time came when Jack and his mother had no more money. Jack did not want to sell the pony and trap and the other things they had bought with the ogre's money; sooner than do that, he decided to pay a second visit to the tall house to see what he might find there. Of course, it would be dangerous, because no doubt the ogre's wife remembered his first visit and the lost bag of gold. Still, Jack was not the boy to mind a little danger. Indeed, he rather liked it, for life in his mother's cottage did not bring many adventures.

So stepping once more from the window one fine morning, he climbed the beanstalk ladder, up, up, and up, till he came to the broad white road on the far side of the clouds. Striding briskly along, he soon reached the ogre's house, and there was the tall woman at the door shaking out a mop.

"Good day to you, ma'am," said Jack, "and how are you this morning?"

"I was middling well till I seen you, young fellow-me-lad," said the ogre's wife.

"Well, how about a bite of breakfast?"

"Last time I gave you a bite of breakfast," said she, "there was a bag of gold vanished from under my very nose."

"You don't say so!" said Jack in a tone of great surprise. "Now how could that have been?"

"Maybe you know more about it than I do," said the ogre's wife.

"Well, maybe I do," said Jack. "And if you give me a bite of breakfast, I'll tell you all I know."

The ogre's wife was very curious about the bag of gold, so she agreed to give Jack breakfast, and led the way into the kitchen. There she set before him some bread and cheese and a mug of milk.

When he had nearly finished it, there was a tremendous noise and the whole house shook. Thump, thump, thumpety thump! It was the ogre coming home for his breakfast.

"Into the oven with you," said the ogre's wife, bundling Jack in and shutting the door after him. The door flew open with a bang, and the ogre came in. Two great oxen were hanging at his belt.

"Here, wife," he said, throwing them down on the table. "Cook me those for breakfast. But what's this I smell?

"Fee, fi, foh, fum!
I smell the blood of a British man.
Be he alive or be he dead,
I'll grind his bones to make my bread!"

"Stuff and nonsense!" said his wife. "It's last night's supper you're smelling—them two fat boys you had grilled on toast. Now sit down and rest yourself while I make your breakfast."

After breakfast the ogre said to his wife:

"Bring me my hen that lays the golden eggs."

So the woman went out and brought in a fine grey-and-white speckled hen, and the ogre put it on the table and said, "Lay!" Instantly the hen laid an egg of pure gold. It dropped on the table and rolled towards the edge, and the ogre caught it and put it in his pocket. Then he said "Lay!" once more, and once more the hen dropped a golden egg on the kitchen-table. But this time the ogre did not pocket it, for all of a sudden he felt sleepy after his night's work; his head fell forward and he began to snore. The noise was like the noise of twenty thunderstorms—so loud was it that it terrified Jack, even though he was inside the oven with a door of cast iron with knobs of solid brass.

As soon as her husband was asleep, the woman let Jack out of the oven, for she wanted to hear what he had to say about the stolen money-bag. Jack noticed the hen standing on the table with the golden egg beside it, and he thought it would be a useful hen to have. So he said to the ogre's wife:

"Just step outside and fetch me a mug of water from the pump, for being in the oven has made me mighty thirsty, and I can't tell you my tale with a dry throat."

She did as she was bid, and instantly Jack took hold of the hen, tucked it under one arm, and ran out of doors. This alarmed the hen, which instantly set up a cackling.

The ogre jumped up from his sleep, seized his great holly club, and sprang out of doors after Jack. The ogre's wife, who was in the back yard, rushed in to see what had happened, but by this time Jack, the hen, and the ogre had all disappeared.

Jack tore down the road like the wind, with the ogre after him. The ogre had longer legs, but he was scarcely awake, and the breakfast he had eaten was still heavy inside him. Besides, Jack was nimble, and made the best of what start he had. Down the white road he ran, dodging and turning, with the grey hen under his arm flapping its wings and cackling as if to awaken the dead. The ogre pelted after him, swinging his great knobbly club and calling out in the most terrible language imaginable. The wind of his words seemed to drive Jack faster and faster forward, but the ogre was gaining on him. He was only a few yards behind. A terrible swing of his club nearly caught Jack full on the top of his head, but Jack dodged and flew on. Then something happened which saved him. A great cloud, bigger than all the others, rolled up from the side of the road and covered everything in a thick white mist. With a mighty effort Jack rushed forward and buried himself in the mist. He could only see the road for a few yards ahead. Plunging into a ditch by the roadside and lying there unseen, Jack waited till the ogre went thundering past, laying about him with the club and swearing horribly. A few minutes later he came stumping back again, and Jack heard him mutter something about going home, for he had no luck that day. As soon as the ogre was out of earshot, Jack climbed out of the ditch and went on. In a few minutes he had reached the beanstalk and was clambering down, the hen tucked safely under his arm. Down and down he went, until he came out of the cloud and could see his mother pottering about in the garden below.

"There!" he said, landing breathless at her feet and clutching the speckled hen. "What do you think of this?"

"Lord-a-mercy!" said his mother. "What will the boy be up to next?"

She followed the boy into the cottage, and he closed the door carefully behind her to make sure the hen did not escape. Then he set it down on the floor and told it to lay. The hen squatted down and in a few moments laid another perfect golden egg. The widow was full of amazement at the cleverness of her wonderful son. No sooner was the hen shut up securely in a wooden hutch than she put her shawl round her head and set off to town to buy the food they so sadly needed. And after that, whenever they wanted anything, they just told the speckled hen to lay an egg; and soon they were once more prosperous and happy.

4

At last Jack began to hanker after a little excitement. He decided to visit the ogre's house once more. Of course, he knew it would be dangerous, because now both the ogre and his wife would try to kill him. But he was not afraid, and one fine morning he stepped outside on to the beanstalk and began his upward climb. He climbed and he climbed and he climbed till he came to the broad white road. The sun was shining, and he felt light-hearted and careless. Nevertheless, when he got near the tall house, he advanced with care. There, sure enough, was the ogre's wife at the door. He waited till she disappeared, then he crept up to the door and looked cautiously inside. There was no one to be seen. The woman must be out in the back yard, or perhaps upstairs.

Jack slipped into the kitchen and looked round for somewhere to hide. The woman would be sure to look in the oven; besides, a sizzling noise came out of it and it was very hot. Evidently there was something baking. So instead, Jack lifted the lid of the copper and looked inside. There was plenty of room. He climbed carefully in and lowered the lid.

He was not a moment too soon, for just then the ogre's wife came in, and in a few minutes there was a thump, thump, thumpety thump! and the ogre himself stalked in, shaking the whole house and calling for his breakfast. All at once he stopped and sniffed the air, very suspiciously.

"Fee, fi, foh, fum!"

he said in threatening tones,

"I smell the blood of a British man.
Be he alive or be he dead,
I'll grind his bones to make my
bread!"

This time his wife did not say "Nonsense!" She said, "Now maybe you are right, husband, for I think I smell something myself."

She went to the oven and opened it. Inside were three whole sheep roasting for the ogre's breakfast. And of course Jack was not there. She took out the sheep and set them on the table, and the ogre began his breakfast. Then she began looking round the room, under the chairs, in the cupboards, and even in the great chest where the ogre kept his money-bags.

"I can smell boy," said the ogre.

"Depend upon it," said his wife, "it's that dratted child who stole the hen, and it's dearly I'd like to get my hands on the throat of him, so I would."

And she went on searching, but she never thought of looking in the copper.

"There's not a sign of him," said the ogre's wife at last.

"Well, I could have sworn I smelt boy," said the ogre.

Then he finished his breakfast and began to feel sleepy, so he settled down in the rocking chair and called for his magic harp. The woman brought out a little golden harp and put it on the table.

"Sing, harp," said she, and at once the harp began to play and sing all by itself. Very strange and very beautiful were the songs it sang, until after a while the ogre fell asleep and the rumble of his snores reached Jack in the copper. Jack peeped out and saw that the ogre's wife had gone out of the room. He crept quietly out of the copper and seized the magic harp. No sooner had he done this than the harp made a great crashing chord and sang out loud and clear, "Help, master! Help, master!" Jack ran out of the door clutching the harp, and the ogre sprang up, seized his holly club, and followed.

Down the broad white road ran Jack, and fortunately the ogre tripped on the doorstep in his haste to get out of the house. Cursing and swearing, he got up, rubbed his bruises, picked up his club, which had fallen from his hand, and began pounding along after Jack.

This time no kindly cloud rolled up to hide the boy, and although he twisted and turned to avoid his pursuer, the ogre gained on him steadily. And all the time the harp sounded its agonized cry, "Master, master, help me!"

Jack reached the beanstalk not a moment too soon. He began to climb down it like lightning, hardly stopping to put his feet on the steps made by the leaves. He almost slid down. When he was half-way to the ground, the whole beanstalk shook as if it had been hit by a hurricane. Jack looked up for a moment and saw that the ogre had jumped on to the beanstalk and was climbing down after him. Madly the beanstalk tottered and swayed under the ogre's weight, and every second brought him closer.

As he neared the ground Jack shouted:

"Mother, mother, where are you? The axe! Fetch the axe!"

Just as Jack bumped to the ground, his mother came running out of the cottage with the new axe in her hand. There was a sudden shadow over the whole garden as the huge ogre came nearer and nearer. Jack swung the axe and brought it down with all his force on the twisted stem of the beanstalk. The whole mighty plant shook and swayed. One more blow and the stem was cut right through. With a horrible cry the ogre lost his hold and fell to the ground. He broke his neck and died instantly, and there was a great hole in the ground where he fell, which it took Jack three days to fill up again afterwards.

Well, that was the end of the magic beanstalk, and that was the end of the ogre too. As for his wife and the tall house, they were never heard of again, though I daresay they are still there at the end of the broad road above the clouds. Whenever the wind was fierce and strong, Jack used to tell his mother that it must be the ogre's wife moaning for the loss of her husband. But I daresay he was wrong, for it is well known that ogres' wives lose little time in getting themselves new husbands when anything happens to the old one.

Jack and his mother went on living happily in the little cottage. Whenever they wanted money, they told the speckled hen to lay; and whenever they were dull, they told the magic harp to sing. Very strange and very wonderful were the songs it sang, so that they were never without company, for people came from near and far to listen.

THE MADMAN OF NARANATH

(Indian)

Retold by Shankar

People often make fools of themselves because of greed, creating a classic human situation. The Madman of Naranath in this story and Shrewd Todie in the next are both tricksters who well understand this human weakness.

K. Shankar Pillai, known as "Shankar," has been an important figure in the history of children's culture in India. As executive trustee of the Children's Book Trust, located in New Delhi, he was instrumental in establishing a large children's library, an international doll museum, and an international competition known as Shankar's Children's Competition. Shankar has also contributed to children's literature through his editorship of the journal Children's World, *which is published at Nehru House, New Delhi.*

People believe that the Madman of Naranath was someone who lived in Kerala hundreds of years ago.

He once wanted to give a feast to his friends because it was his birthday, so he invited a large number of people. He bought a lot of rice and vegetables and all the other things necessary for the feast. He also engaged several cooks.

He found, however, that he did not have all the specially large pots and pans that would be required to cook the various dishes for so many people. He went to all the neighbouring houses and borrowed whatever pots and pans he could get. With great difficulty he was able to get all he needed. At last the food was cooked and the feast was served. It was a grand feast and the guests were happy.

After the feast was over, although many days passed, the Madman was not in a mood to return the pots and pans he had borrowed. Some of the neighbours went to him and asked for their pots. He assured them that all were safe and they would be returned without further delay.

After two days he began to return the pots and pans. Along with each one he gave a smaller one of the same kind. Everyone asked him why he did this.

"I put all these pots and pans in my underground cellar," he explained, "and the cellar has some magic power. It can give life to whatever is put there. One day when I looked into the cellar I found all the pots and pans singing and dancing. I did not want to disturb them, so I shut the door again and left them to themselves. That is why there was so much delay in returning them.

"Then, when I finally went to bring them up from the cellar, I found that each one of them now had a baby. Since the pots do not belong to me, their children cannot belong to me either, so I am only giving you what belongs to you."

The Madman's friends were all very happy to receive an extra pot or pan with their own.

Months passed. The Madman of Naranath decided to observe the death anniversary of his father. He wanted to do it in a big way, so he invited a thousand people to a feast.

This time also he had to borrow large cooking pots and now he needed many more than he had borrowed before.

The people were only too willing to lend him all the pots and pans they had. They carried them to his house themselves.

In the end he collected such a large

number of cooking pots that he had more than he needed, but he accepted them all with gratitude.

As soon as the feast was over, the Madman secretly hired two large country-boats. He loaded all the pots and pans onto them, and sent them off to the town, which was a busy port. There he sold them for a large sum of money. He returned home and lived happily.

Days passed. The people who had lent him their pots and pans asked him to return them.

"Return your pots and pans?" he asked. "But I don't think I have any of them with me."

"How dare you say that?" they shouted. "We lent you all our cooking utensils for your feast, and now you deny having received them."

"Now please don't shout at me," he said, "it disturbs me. I do not deny that I borrowed your pots and pans, but you see I put them all in my cellar, and now I don't think they are there."

"Then where are they?" asked the angry people.

"I do not know," said the Madman.

When the people found that the Madman was not going to return their cooking pots, they took the matter to court.

The Madman of Naranath appeared before the magistrate.

"You are charged with cheating all these people," the magistrate said. "I order you to return all their cooking pots."

"Sir," replied the Madman, "I am not guilty. My cellar has a magic power. It gives life to everything kept there. I once put a number of cooking pots in my cellar, and each one of them had a baby pot. All these people who are accusing me now were very happy when their pots had babies. When I returned the pots, each one of these people accepted the baby pot with the mother pot. Each one of them was quite convinced that both belonged to him."

"Well?" asked the magistrate.

"Sir, the second time I stored the cooking pots in the cellar a sad thing happened. I found that all the pots and pans had died—there was not even one left. If you admit birth, sir, you must admit death as well."

The magistrate saw the logic of what the Madman said, and he dismissed the case.

SHREWD TODIE AND LYZER THE MISER

(Jewish)

Retold by Isaac Bashevis Singer

Isaac Bashevis Singer's stories for children are remarkable for their warmth and humor and for their simple directness. He is a master storyteller who is able to tell stories to children without talking down to them. Fools are one of Singer's favorite subjects, and he has even written a book for children on them, The Fools of Chelm and Their History *(1973). Chelm in Russia, like its English counterpart Gotham, was an entire town occupied by fools. This story should be read together with the preceding one, "The Madman of Naranath," because they treat an identical theme in different cultural settings.*

In a village somewhere in the Ukraine there lived a poor man called Todie. Todie had a wife, Shaindel, and seven children, but he could never earn enough to feed them properly. He tried many trades and failed in all of them. It was said of Todie that if he decided to deal in candles the sun would never set. He was nicknamed Shrewd Todie because whenever he managed to make some money, it was always by trickery.

This winter was an especially cold one. The snowfall was heavy and Todie had no money to buy wood for the stove. His seven children stayed in bed all day to keep warm. When the frost burns outside, hunger is stronger than ever, but Shaindel's larder was empty. She reproached Todie bitterly, wailing, "If you can't feed your wife and children, I will go to the rabbi and get a divorce."

"And what will you do with it, eat it?" Todie retorted.

In the same village there lived a rich man called Lyzer. Because of his stinginess he was known as Lyzer the Miser. He permitted his wife to bake bread only once in four weeks because he had discovered that fresh bread is eaten up more quickly than stale.

Todie had more than once gone to Lyzer for a loan of a few gulden, but Lyzer had always replied: "I sleep better when the money lies in my strongbox rather than in your pocket."

Lyzer had a goat, but he never fed her. The goat had learned to visit the houses of the neighbors, who pitied her and gave her potato peelings. Sometimes, when there were not enough peelings, she would gnaw on the old straw of the thatched roofs. She also had a liking for tree bark. Nevertheless, each year the goat gave birth to a kid. Lyzer milked her but, miser that he was, did not drink the milk himself. Instead he sold it to others.

Todie decided that he would take revenge on Lyzer and at the same time make some much-needed money for himself.

One day, as Lyzer was sitting on a box eating borscht and dry bread (he used his chairs only on holidays so that the upholstery would not wear out), the door opened and Todie came in.

"Reb Lyzer," he said, "I would like to ask you a favor. My oldest daughter, Basha, is already fifteen and she's about to become engaged. A young man is coming from Janev to look her over. My cutlery is tin, and my wife is ashamed to ask the young man to eat soup with a tin spoon. Would you lend me one of your silver spoons? I give you my holy word that I will return it to you tomorrow."

Lyzer knew that Todie would not dare to break a holy oath and he lent him the spoon.

No young man came to see Basha that evening. As usual, the girl walked around barefoot and in rags, and the silver spoon lay hidden under Todie's shirt. In the early years of his marriage Todie had possessed a set of silver tableware himself. He had, however, long since sold it all, with the exception of three silver teaspoons that were used only on Passover.

The following day, as Lyzer, his feet bare (in order to save his shoes), sat on his box eating borscht and dry bread, Todie returned.

"Here is the spoon I borrowed yesterday," he said, placing it on the table together with one of his own teaspoons.

"What is the teaspoon for?" Lyzer asked.

And Todie said: "Your tablespoon

Translated by the author and Elizabeth Shub. Illustrated by Margot Zemach.

gave birth to a teaspoon. It is her child. Since I am an honest man, I'm returning both mother and child to you."

Lyzer looked at Todie in astonishment. He had never heard of a silver spoon giving birth to another. Nevertheless, his greed overcame his doubt and he happily accepted both spoons. Such an unexpected piece of good fortune! He was overjoyed that he had loaned Todie the spoon.

A few days later, as Lyzer (without his coat, to save it) was again sitting on his box eating borscht with dry bread, the door opened and Todie appeared.

"The young man from Janev did not please Basha because he had donkey ears, but this evening another young man is coming to look her over. Shaindel is cooking soup for him, but she's ashamed to serve him with a tin spoon. Would you lend me . . . "

Even before Todie could finish the sentence, Lyzer interrupted. "You want to borrow a silver spoon? Take it with pleasure."

The following day Todie once more returned the spoon and with it one of his own silver teaspoons. He again explained that during the night the large spoon had given birth to a small one and in all good conscience he was bringing back the mother and newborn baby. As for the young man who had come to look Basha over, she hadn't liked him either, because his nose was so long that it reached to his chin. Needless to say that Lyzer the Miser was overjoyed.

Exactly the same thing happened a third time. Todie related that this time his daughter had rejected her suitor because he stammered. He also reported that Lyzer's silver spoon had again given birth to a baby spoon.

"Does it ever happen that a spoon has twins?" Lyzer inquired.

Todie thought it over for a moment. "Why not? I've even heard of a case where a spoon had triplets."

Almost a week passed by and Todie did not go to see Lyzer. But on Friday morning, as Lyzer (in his underdrawers to save his pants) sat on his box eating borscht and dry bread, Todie came in and said, "Good day to you, Reb Lyzer."

"A good morning and many more to you," Lyzer replied in his friendliest manner. "What good fortune brings you here? Did you perhaps come to borrow a silver spoon? If so, help yourself."

"Today I have a very special favor to ask. This evening a young man from the big city of Lublin is coming to look Basha over. He is the son of a rich man and I'm told he is clever and handsome as well. Not only do I need a silver spoon, but since he will remain with us over the Sabbath I need a pair of silver candlesticks, because mine are brass and my wife is ashamed to place them on the Sabbath table. Would you lend me your candlesticks? Immediately after the Sabbath, I will return them to you."

Silver candlesticks are of great value and Lyzer the Miser hesitated, but only for a moment.

Remembering his good fortune with the spoons, he said: "I have eight silver candlesticks in my house. Take them all. I know you will return them to me just as you say. And if it should happen that any of them give birth, I have no doubt that you will be as honest as you have been in the past."

"Certainly," Todie said. "Let's hope for the best."

The silver spoon, Todie hid beneath his shirt as usual. But taking the candlesticks, he went directly to a merchant, sold them for a considerable sum, and brought the money to Shaindel. When Shaindel saw so much money, she demanded to know where he had gotten such a treasure.

"When I went out, a cow flew over our roof and dropped a dozen silver eggs," Todie replied. "I sold them and here is the money."

"I have never heard of a cow flying over a roof and laying silver eggs," Shaindel said doubtingly.

"There is always a first time," Todie answered. "If you don't want the money, give it back to me."

"There'll be no talk about giving it back," Shaindel said. She knew that her husband was full of cunning and tricks—but when the children are hungry and the larder is empty, it is better not to ask too many questions. Shaindel went to the marketplace and bought meat, fish, white flour, and even some nuts and raisins for a pudding. And since a lot of money still remained, she bought shoes and clothes for the children.

It was a very gay Sabbath in Todie's house. The boys sang and the girls danced. When the children asked their father where he had gotten the money, he replied: "It is forbidden to mention money during the Sabbath."

Sunday, as Lyzer (barefoot and almost naked to save his clothes) sat on his box finishing up a dry crust of bread with borscht, Todie arrived and, handing him his silver spoon, said: "It's too bad. This time your spoon did not give birth to a baby."

"What about the candlesticks?" Lyzer inquired anxiously.

Todie sighed deeply. "The candlesticks died."

Lyzer got up from his box so hastily that he overturned his plate of borscht.

"You fool! How can candlesticks die?" he screamed.

"If spoons can give birth, candlesticks can die."

Lyzer raised a great hue and cry and had Todie called before the rabbi. When the rabbi heard both sides of the story, he burst out laughing. "It serves you right," he said to Lyzer. "If you hadn't chosen to believe that spoons give birth, now you would not be forced to believe that your candlesticks died."

"But it's all nonsense," Lyzer objected.

"Did you not expect the candlesticks to give birth to other candlesticks?" the rabbi said admonishingly. "If you accept nonsense when it brings you profit, you must also accept nonsense when it brings you loss." And he dismissed the case.

The following day, when Lyzer the Miser's wife brought him his borscht and dry bread, Lyzer said to her, "I will eat only the bread. Borscht is too expensive a food, even without sour cream."

The story of the silver spoons that gave birth and the candlesticks that died spread quickly through the town. All the people enjoyed Todie's victory and Lyzer the Miser's defeat. The shoemaker's and tailor's apprentices, as was their custom whenever there was an important happening, made up a song about it:

Lyzer, put your grief aside.
What if your candlesticks have died?
You're the richest man on earth
With silver spoons that can give birth
And silver eggs as living proof
Of flying cows above your roof.
Don't sit there eating crusts of
bread—
To silver grandsons look ahead.

However, time passed and Lyzer's silver spoons never gave birth again.

Literary Folktales

THE TWELVE SILLY SISTERS

Padraic Colum

Another gifted storyteller in a folk tradition is Padraic Colum, who brings back to life in his stories not only the characters, but also the lilting sound of Irish folktales. The "fair and considerate" Nabla, unruffled by what other women would consider catastrophes, is presented in stark contrast to the ninny Gibbie O'Flaherty and her eleven silly sisters. The exaggeration is characteristic of Irish storytelling, as is the strong hint of fairyland epitomized by "the Pooka," who takes the shape of a great black horse and goes galloping through the countryside on Hallowe'en.

The Lord of Omey went to visit his cousin, the fair and considerate Nabla, one evening, and he found her molding candles, which was the right and proper thing for a young woman to be doing when the dark nights of winter were coming on. "My jewel you are," said the Lord of Omey to his cousin, "and it's not you that the Pooka will want to carry off to-night." He said that because it was Hallowe'en, and on Hallowe'en the Pooka goes through the country and he carries off whoever he meets that night who has no business being abroad.

The Pooka has the shape of a horse—the shape of a great black horse. On Hallowe'en, as I have said, he goes galloping through the countryside, and he gives the Pooka's jaunt to this or that person that he meets going home late. Sometimes what the Pooka does in this regard is good, but more often it is bad. It would be a bad thing if he carried off the little girl who has gone down the road to fetch the fiddler in to play for us. And it would be a bad thing, the Lord of Omey thought, if the Pooka would carry off any one who had any relation to him. But he knew that whoever the Pooka might carry off it would not be his cousin, the fair and considerate Nabla, who, as I have said, was molding candles against the dark nights that were coming on, and who had no intention of being abroad without having any business being abroad, on any night, letting alone the night of Hallowe'en. "My jewel you are," said the Lord of Omey to her, "and to-morrow we will go to the Abbey, and I will wed you there and give you the keys of my castle, upstairs and downstairs, the attic and the cellar." She gave him her word that she would go with him, because, as I have told you, Nabla was wise and considerate, and besides she loved O'Tool, the Lord of Omey, every bit as much as he loved her.

Now the Lord of Omey and Nabla, the lady he was to marry, were inside the Abbey church. The Lord of Omey was standing before the altar with the ring between his fingers, when a tall, fiery-headed fighting man appeared at the church door. With the fright he got at seeing him there, O'Tool dropped the ring upon the flagstones.

"My master sent me to tell you, O'Tool," said the red-headed fighting man, "that you are not to get married."

"Not to get married!" said the Lord of Omey.

"At least, not to get married to the woman that's before you," said the red-headed fellow. "But my master isn't one to keep you from having a spouse; he's sending you one of his own daughters. The priest needn't go."

Now, although the O'Tools were Lords of Omey, they had lords over them, and the lords that were over them were the O'Flaherties, and the O'Flaherties were all terrible fighting men. Their battle shout was enough to make every one else leave the battlefield. The sight of their fiery red heads coming across the country was enough to make the people put a bar on the gate of the town and a bolt on every house inside of it. And the O'Tools were the mildest clan in the whole of Connacht. Not a man of them would say "boo" to a goose belonging to one of the O'Flaherties, let alone to one of their fighting men.

"My master says he's sending you one of his own daughters," said the red-headed fighting man. "The priest needn't go."

And the priest did not go. The messenger did not go, either. Indeed, the only one who went out of the Abbey church was the fair and considerate Nabla. She went to the castle of Omey, and got there before any of the rest of them. Did I tell you that she had got the keys of the castle before she came up to the altar? She had, then. She opened the attic and went in, and her mother went along with her, and there the two of them stayed in O'Tool's castle.

The Abbey church was filled with redheads, for all the O'Flaherties came in. And with them came the first of O'Flaherty's daughters, the one that was to be bride to the O'Tool.

There was nothing for the Lord of Omey to do but to pick up the ring he had let fall upon the flagstones, take the lady's finger out of her mouth, and put the ring on her finger. And so they were married, the Lord of Omey and Gibbie, the daughter of O'Flaherty.

And when they went back to O'Tool's castle the bride did everything that a silly person would do. That day she gave wine to the tax-gatherers and water to the poets. She left honey beside a boy and expected him not to eat it. She left milk beside a child and expected it not to drink it. She left food beside a generous man and expected him not to give it away to the hungry ones who came to the door. I could spend the whole of Hallowe'en night (and it's not the shortest night of the year) telling you of all the silly things Gibbie did when she came into the castle of Omey.

She gave orders that O'Tool's horses were to have their shoes taken off before they came into the castle yard. This was to prevent their tramping and stamping while her kinsfolk ate around O'Tool's tables. And when the Lord of Omey heard that order given, he cried tears down. His gallant horses to be lamed by coming without shoes over the sharp cobbles of the castle yard! But he could do nothing about it, for the order was given to one of the redheads who had come out of her father's country. O'Tool cried for his horses that night, as he sat at his wedding supper.

But Nabla, his wise and considerate cousin, was above in the attic. The order that was given was told her, and she came down the backstairs of the castle in the blackness of the night. She went out into the castle yard, and she took the straw from under the cows in the byres, and she strewed the stones of the castle yard with the straw. And no one knew what she did but Pincher, the watchdog that had but one tooth. The horses came in, and they went silently upon the straw, and their hoofs were not hurt by the sharp cobblestones, and so they came safe.

The next morning, before she would get up, Gibbie had the servants go out into the garden and bring her in the sundial, so that she should know what time it was.

She was silly, and her sisters were silly, too. The eleven of them came to spend a while with her. So that they might not be lonely in O'Tool's castle, Gibbie had a bed made that would hold all the eleven of them. But she forgot to have a blanket made that would go across that bed. What she gave them covered this one and that one, but never all of them. They pulled the cover from one to the other of them, but they were cold sleeping and cold waking up every night they were in O'Tool's castle.

The eleven sisters got tired of having so little sleep and so much perishing in the bed that was made for them, and they made up their minds to go back to their father's castle in Ballinakill. Gibbie, their sister, knew what was due to ladies of their rank and degree, and she would not let them go unattended. And first she called on Nabla, thinking that she was the goose girl, to go with them. But then she decided that she herself was the best company that her sisters could have, and she made up her mind to go halfway with them.

When they were a little way outside the castle they sat down by the edge of a pool to bathe their feet. They were still sitting there when the one they took to be the goose girl came up to them. "Why are you sitting there so still, ladies?" said she when she came up to them, "when the day is so fair for your journey."

"Fair it is," said Gibbie, "but what can we do? Our legs in the pool are all mixed up together and none of us can recognize our own legs, and how can we go off walking when we don't know what legs to pull up?"

"What will you give me," said the one they took to be the goose girl, "if I make each of you know your own legs?"

"I'll give you the only shiny thing I have about me," said Gibbie, "the ring off my finger."

What did she do but pull off a piece of a bramble bush. She went back to the pool and drew the brambles along the legs of each of the sisters. They pulled their legs out of the pool immediately. "Though our legs are scratched," said they, "we know them now, and it is better we should be going on our way with scratched legs than be sitting here the whole of the day with our legs in the cold water."

"But give me my reward."

Gibbie took the ring off her finger and gave it to her. The goose girl, who was really the wise and considerate Nabla, went back to the castle, and the sisters started off again, the twelve of them.

And when they were halfway Gibbie would have left them to go back to the castle, but her sisters would not let her go without company, and so they went halfway back to the castle with her. And she went halfway back with them. And they went halfway back with her. And they were going and coming, and coming and going, until the black night came down upon the ground.

And it was the night of Hallowe'en, the night when the Pooka goes abroad. He came upon the sisters as they were going backward and forward and forward and backward on the road between Omey and Ballinakill. He was a horse so black that you could see yourself in his skin. He came galloping up, with fire in his eyes and froth on his jaws. He took the twelve sisters on his back and away with him, through bushes and briers, over hills and through hollows, until he brought them to a certain place that I know of.

It is called the Townland of Mischance. Where that place is is written down, but then, as they say, An rud e scribheann an Puca leigheann se fein e. "What the Pooka writes, only he himself can read." In the Townland of Mischance the twelve sisters stayed, and every one in it was like themselves. They gave wine to the tax-gatherers and water to the poets. They left food near a generous man and expected him not to give it to the hungry ones who came to the door. And I think I was in that place myself a day or two ago.

But the place I was in then and the place I'm in now aren't alike. Here we're wise enough not to go abroad on Hallowe'en night unless we have business to bring us abroad. We're not the sort would ever be given the Pooka's jaunt. Well, there Gibbie and her eleven sisters stayed, and the O'Flaherties, for all their chasing up and down the country, were never able to find them. The sisters were in their right place there, and they were well enough off.

And the Lord of Omey met his cousin, the fair and considerate Nabla, some time after his wife and her sisters went away from him. He was walking near the Abbey church and she was walking near the same place. They went in together. And there he married her. And he didn't have to look for a second ring, either—Nabla had in her hand the ring he was ready to put upon her finger the time before.

THE MIXED-UP FEET AND THE SILLY BRIDEGROOM

Isaac Bashevis Singer

The four foolish daughters in this story who get their feet mixed up in bed are apparently related to the twelve silly sisters in the preceding story who get their legs mixed up when they are bathing their feet in a pool. But the mixed-up feet are only an introduction to some more serious foolishness, that carried out by Lemel the silly bridegroom.

Near the village of Chelm there was a hamlet called East Chelm, where there lived a tenant farmer called Shmelka and his wife, Shmelkicha. They had four daughters, all of whom slept in the same broad bed. Their names were Yenta, Pesha, Trina, Yachna.

As a rule the girls got up early in the morning to milk the cows and help their mother with the household chores. But one winter morning they stayed in bed later than usual. When their mother came to see what was keeping them, she found all four struggling and screaming in the bed. Shmelkicha demanded to know what all the commotion was about and why they were pulling each other's hair. The girls replied that in their sleep they had gotten their feet mixed up, and now they didn't know whose feet belonged to whom, and so of course they couldn't get up.

As soon as she learned about her daughters' mixed-up feet, Shmelkicha, who was from Chelm proper, became ex-

Translated by the author and Elizabeth Shub. Illustrated by Maurice Sendak.

ceedingly frightened. She remembered that a similar event had taken place in Chelm many years before and, oh, how much trouble there had been. She ran at once to a neighbor and begged her to milk the cows, and she herself set off for Chelm to ask the town's Elder what to do. Before she left, she said to the girls, "You stay in bed and don't budge until I return. Because once you get up with the wrong feet, it will be very difficult to set things right."

When Shmelkicha arrived in Chelm and told the Elder about what had happened to her daughters, he clutched his white beard with one hand, placed the other on his forehead, and was immediately lost in thought. As he pondered he hummed a Chelm melody.

After a while he said, "There is no perfect solution for a case of mixed-up feet. But there is something that sometimes helps."

He told Shmelkicha to take a long stick, walk into the girls' room, and unexpectedly whack the blanket where their feet were. "It is possible," explained the wise Elder, "that in surprise and pain each girl will grab at her own feet and jump out of bed." A similar remedy had once been used in such a case, and it had worked.

Many townspeople were present when the Elder made his pronouncement, and as always they admired his great wisdom. The Elder stated further that in order to prevent such an accident in the future, it would be advisable to gradually marry off the girls. Once each girl was married and had her own house and her own husband, there would be no danger that they would get their feet mixed up again.

Shmelkicha returned to East Chelm, picked up a stick, walked into her daughters' room, and whacked the quilt with all her might. The girls were completely taken aback, but before a moment had passed, they were out of bed, screaming in pain and fright, each jumping on her own feet. Shmelka, their father, and a number of neighbors who had followed Shmelkicha into the house and witnessed what had happened, again came to the conclusion that the wisdom of the Elder of Chelm knew no bounds.

Shmelka and Shmelkicha immediately decided to carry out the rest of the Elder's advice and started looking for a husband for their eldest daughter. They soon found a young man of Chelm called Lemel. His father was a coachman, and Lemel himself already owned a horse and wagon. It was clear that Yenta's future husband would be a good provider.

When they brought the couple together to sign the marriage agreement, Yenta began to cry bitterly. Asked why she was crying, she replied, "Lemel is a stranger, and I don't want to marry a stranger."

"Didn't I marry a stranger?" her mother asked.

"You married Father," Yenta answered, "and I have to marry a total stranger." And her face became wet with tears.

The match would have come to nothing, but luckily they had invited the Elder of Chelm to be present. And, after some pondering, he again found the way out. He said to Yenta, "Sign the marriage contract. The moment you sign it, Lemel becomes your betrothed. And when you marry, you will not be marrying a stranger, you will be marrying your betrothed."

When Yenta heard these words, she was overjoyed. Lemel kissed the Elder three times on his huge forehead, and the rest of the company praised the wisdom of the Elder of Chelm, which was even greater than that of wise King Solomon.

But now a new problem arose. Neither Lemel nor Yenta had learned to sign their names.

Again the Elder came to the rescue: "Let Yenta make three small circles on the paper, and Lemel three dashes. These will serve as their signatures and seal the contract."

Yenta and Lemel did as the Elder ordered, and everybody was gay and happy. Shmelkicha treated all the witnesses to cheese blintzes and borscht, and the first plate naturally went to the Elder of

Chelm, whose appetite was particularly good that day.

Before Lemel returned to Chelm proper, from where he had driven in his own horse and wagon, Shmelka gave him as a gift a small penknife with a mother-of-pearl handle. It happened to be the first day of Hanukkah, and the penknife was both an engagement gift and a Hanukkah present.

Since Lemel often came to East Chelm to buy from the peasants the milk, butter, hay, oats, and flax which he sold to the townspeople of Chelm, he soon came to visit Yenta again. Shmelka asked Lemel whether his friends in Chelm had liked his penknife, and Lemel replied that they had never seen it.

"Why not?" Shmelka asked.

"Because I lost it."

"How did you lose it?"

"I put the penknife into the wagon and it got lost in the hay."

Shmelka was not a native of Chelm but came from another nearby town, and he said to Lemel, "You don't put a penknife into a wagon full of straw and hay and with cracks and holes in the bottom to boot. A penknife you place in your pocket, and then it does not get lost."

"Future Father-in-law, you are right," Lemel answered. "Next time I will know what to do."

Since the first gift had been lost, Shmelka gave Lemel a jar of freshly fried chicken fat to replace it. Lemel thanked him and returned to Chelm.

Several days later, when business again brought Lemel to East Chelm, Yenta's parents noticed that his coat pocket was torn, and the entire left side of his coat was covered with grease stains.

"What happened to your coat?" Shmelkicha asked.

Lemel replied, "I put the jar of chicken fat in my pocket, but the road is full of holes and ditches and I could not help bumping against the side of the wagon. The jar broke, and it tore my pocket and the fat ran out all over my clothes."

"Why did you put the jar of chicken fat into your pocket?" Shmelka asked.

"Didn't you tell me to?"

"A penknife you put into your pocket. A jar of chicken fat you wrap in paper and place in the hay so that it will not break."

Lemel replied, "Next time I will know what to do."

Since Lemel had had little use out of the first two gifts, Yenta herself gave him a silver gulden, which her father had given her as a Hanukkah gift.

When Lemel came to the hamlet again, he was asked how he had spent the money.

"I lost it," he replied.

"How did you lose it?"

"I wrapped it in paper and placed it in the hay. But when I arrived in Chelm and unloaded my merchandise, the gulden was gone."

"A gulden is not a jar of chicken fat," Shmelka informed him. "A gulden you put into your purse."

"Next time I will know what to do."

Before Lemel returned to Chelm, Yenta gave her fiancé some newly laid eggs, still warm from the chickens.

On his next visit he was asked how he had enjoyed the eggs, and he replied that they had all been broken.

"How did they break?"

"I put them into my purse, but when I tried to close it, the eggs broke."

"Nobody puts eggs into a purse," Shmelka said. "Eggs you put into a basket bedded with straw and covered with a rag so that they will not break."

"Next time I will know what to do."

Since Lemel had not been able to enjoy the gifts he had received, Yenta decided to present him with a live duck.

When he returned, he was asked how the duck was faring, and he said she had died on the way to Chelm.

"How did she die?"

"I placed her in a basket with straw and covered it well with rags, just as you had told me to. When I arrived home, the duck was dead."

"A duck has to breathe," Shmelkicha said. "If you cover her with rags, she will suffocate. A duck you put in a cage, with some corn to eat, and then she will arrive safely."

"Next time I will know what to do."

Since Lemel had gained neither use nor pleasure from any of his gifts, Yenta decided to give him her goldfish, a pet she had had for several years.

And again on his return, when asked about the goldfish, he replied that it was dead.

"Why is it dead?"

"I placed it in a cage and gave it some corn, but when I arrived it was dead."

Since Lemel was still without a gift, Yenta decided to give him her canary, which she loved dearly. But Shmelka told her that it seemed pointless to give Lemel any more gifts, because whatever you gave him either died or got lost. Instead Shmelka and Shmelkicha decided to get the advice of the Elder of Chelm.

The Elder listened to the whole story, and as usual clutched his long white beard with one hand and placed the other on his high forehead.

After much pondering and humming he proclaimed, "The road between East Chelm and Chelm is fraught with all kinds of dangers, and that is why such misfortunes occur. The best thing to do is to have a quick marriage. Then Lemel and Yenta will be together, and Lemel will not have to drag his gifts from one place to another, and no misfortunes will befall them."

This advice pleased everyone, and the marriage was soon celebrated. All the peasants of the hamlet of East Chelm and half of the townspeople of Chelm danced and rejoiced at the wedding. Before the year was out, Yenta gave birth to a baby girl and Lemel went to tell the Elder of Chelm the good tidings that a child had been born to them.

"Is the child a boy?" the Elder asked.

"No."

"Is it a girl?"

"How did you guess?" Lemel asked in amazement.

And the Elder of Chelm replied, "For the wise men of Chelm there are no secrets."

Fiction

RUFUS M.
Eleanor Estes

This modern story treats directly the theme of the young child who feels small and inadequate in relation to those who are older than he is, in this case his older brother and sisters. Rufus wants to do everything that they do, even sewing and taking books out from the library when he can't read. His persistent efforts to get a library card are both funny and moving as they express the powerful desire in a young child to prove self-worth. The Moffats, who appear in this story and in The Moffats *(1941) and* The Middle Moffat *(1942), are among the most natural and likable of book families.*

Rufus M. That's the way Rufus wrote his name on his heavy arithmetic paper and on his blue-lined spelling paper. Rufus M. went on one side of the paper. His age, seven, went on the other. Rufus had not learned to write his name in school, though that is one place for learning to write. He had not learned to write his name at home either, though that is another place for learning to write. The place where he had learned to write his name was the library, long ago before he ever went to school at all. This is the way it happened.

One day when Rufus had been riding his scooter up and down the street, being the motorman, the conductor, the passengers, the steam, and the whistle of a locomotive, he came home and found Joey, Jane, and Sylvie, all reading in the front yard. Joey and Jane were sitting on the steps of the porch and Sylvie was sprawled in the hammock, a book in one hand, a chocolate-covered peppermint in the other.

Rufus stood with one bare foot on his scooter and one on the grass and watched them. Sylvie read the fastest. This was natural since she was the oldest. But Joey turned the pages almost as fast and Jane went lickety-cut on the good parts. They were all reading books and he couldn't even read yet. These books they were reading were library books. The library must be open today. It wasn't open every day, just a few days a week.

"I want to go to the library," said Rufus. "And get a book," he added.

"We all just came home from there," said Jane, while Joey and Sylvie merely

From Eleanor Estes, *Rufus M.* (New York: Harcourt, Brace and World, 1943), Chapter 1.

went on reading as though Rufus had said nothing. "Besides," she added, "why do you want a book anyway? You can't even read yet."

This was true and it made Rufus mad. He liked to do everything that they did. He even liked to sew if they were sewing. He never thought whether sewng was for girls only or not. When he saw Jane sewing, he asked Mama to let him sew too. So Mama tied a thread to the head of a pin and Rufus poked that in and out of a piece of goods. That's the way he sewed. It looked like what Jane was doing and Rufus was convinced that he was sewing too, though he could not see much sense in it.

Now here were the other Moffats, all with books from the library. And there were three more books stacked up on the porch that looked like big people's books without pictures. They were for Mama no doubt. This meant that he was the only one here who did not have a book.

"I want a book from the library," said Rufus. A flick of the page as Sylvie turned it over was all the answer he got. It seemed to Rufus as though even Catherine-the-cat gave him a scornful glance because he could not read yet and did not have a book.

Rufus turned his scooter around and went out of the yard. Just wait! Read? Why, soon he'd read as fast if not faster than they did. Reading looked easy. It was just flipping pages. Who couldn't do that?

Rufus thought that it was not hard to get a book out of the library. All you did was go in, look for a book that you liked, give it to the lady to punch, and come home with it. He knew where the library was for he had often gone there with Jane and some of the others. While Jane went off to the shelves to find a book, he and Joey played the game of Find the Duke in the Palmer Cox Brownie books. This was a game that the two boys had made up. They would turn the pages of one of the Brownie books, any of them, and try to be the first to spot the duke, the brownie in the tall hat. The library lady thought that this was a noisy game, and said she wished they would not play it there. Rufus hoped to bring a Brownie book home now.

"Toot-toot!" he sang to clear the way. Straight down Elm Street was the way to the library; the same way that led to Sunday School, and Rufus knew it well. He liked sidewalks that were white the best for he could go the fastest on these.

"Toot-toot!" Rufus hurried down the street. When he arrived at the library, he hid his scooter in the pine trees that grew under the windows beside the steps. Christmas trees, Rufus called them. The ground was covered with brown pine needles and they were soft to walk upon. Rufus always went into the library the same way. He climbed the stairs, encircled the light on the granite arm of the steps, and marched into the library.

Rufus stepped carefully on the strips of rubber matting that led to the desk. This matting looked like dirty licorice. But it wasn't licorice. He knew because once when Sylvie had brought him here when he was scarcely more than three he had tasted a torn corner of it. It was not good to eat.

The library lady was sitting at the desk playing with some cards. Rufus stepped off the matting. The cool, shiny floor felt good to his bare feet. He went over to the shelves and luckily did find one of the big Palmer Cox Brownie books there. It would be fun to play the game of Find the Duke at home. Until now he had played it only in the library. Maybe Jane or Joe would play it with him right now. He laughed out loud at the thought.

"Sh-sh-sh, quiet," said the lady at the desk.

Rufus clapped his chubby fist over his mouth. Goodness! He had forgotten where he was. Do not laugh or talk out loud in the library. He knew these rules. Well, he didn't want to stay here any longer today anyway. He wanted to read at home with the others. He took the book to the lady to punch.

She didn't punch it though. She took it and she put it on the table behind her and then she started to play cards again.

"That's my book," said Rufus.

"Do you have a card?" the lady asked.

Rufus felt in his pockets. Sometimes he carried around an old playing card or two. Today he didn't have one.

"No," he said.

"You'll have to have a card to get a book."

"I'll go and get one," said Rufus.

The lady put down her cards. "I mean a library card," she explained kindly. "It looks to me as though you are too little to have a library card. Do you have one?"

"No," said Rufus. "I'd like to though."

"I'm afraid you're too little," said the lady. "You have to write your name to get one. Can you do that?"

Rufus nodded his head confidently. Writing. Lines up and down. He'd seen that done. And the letters that Mama had tied in bundles in the closet under the stairs were covered with writing. Of course he could write.

"Well, let's see your hands," said the lady.

Rufus obligingly showed this lady his hands, but she did not like the look of them. She cringed and clasped her head as though the sight hurt her.

"Oh," she gasped. "You'll just have to go home and wash them before we can even think about joining the library and borrowing books."

This was a complication upon which Rufus had not reckoned. However, all it meant was a slight delay. He'd wash his hands and then he'd get the book. He turned and went out of the library, found his scooter safe among the Christmas trees, and pushed it home. He surprised Mama by asking to have his hands washed. When this was done, he mounted his scooter again and returned all the long way to the library. It was not just a little trip to the library. It was a long one. A long one and a hot one on a day like this. But he didn't notice that. All he was bent on was getting his book and taking it home and reading with the others on the front porch. They were all still there, brushing flies away and reading.

Again Rufus hid his scooter in the pine trees, encircled the light, and went in.

"Hello," he said.

"Well," said the lady. "How are they now?"

Rufus had forgotten he had had to wash his hands. He thought she was referring to the other Moffats. "Fine," he said.

"Let me see them," she said, and she held up her hands.

Oh! His hands! Well, they were all right, thought Rufus, for Mama had just washed them. He showed them to the lady. There was a silence while she studied them. Then she shook her head. She still did not like them.

"Ts, ts, ts!" she said. "They'll have to be cleaner than that."

Rufus looked at his hands. Supposing he went all the way home and washed them again, she still might not like them. However, if that is what she wanted, he would have to do that before he could get the Brownie book . . . and he started for the door.

"Well now, let's see what we can do," said the lady. "I know what," she said. "It's against the rules but perhaps we can wash them in here." And she led Rufus into a little room that smelled of paste where lots of new books and old books were stacked up. In one corner was a little round sink and Rufus washed his hands again. Then they returned to the desk. The lady got a chair and put a newspaper on it. She made Rufus stand on this because he was not big enough to write at the desk otherwise.

Then the lady put a piece of paper covered with a lot of printing in front of Rufus, dipped a pen in the ink well and gave it to him.

"All right," she said. "Here's your application. Write your name here."

All the writing Rufus had ever done before had been on big pieces of brown wrapping paper with lots of room on them. Rufus had often covered those great sheets of paper with his own kind of writing at home. Lines up and down.

But on this paper there wasn't much space. It was already covered with writing. However, there was a tiny little empty space and that was where Rufus must write his name, the lady said. So, little space or not, Rufus confidently grasped the pen with his left hand and dug it into the paper. He was not accustomed to pens, having always worked with pencils until now, and he made a great many holes and blots and scratches.

"Gracious," said the lady. "Don't bear down so hard! And why don't you hold it in your right hand?" she asked, moving the pen back into his right hand.

Rufus started again scraping his lines up and down and all over the page, this time using his right hand. Wherever there was an empty space he wrote. He even wrote over some of the print for good measure. Then he waited for the lady, who had gone off to get a book for some man, to come back and look.

"Oh," she said as she settled herself in her swivel chair, "is that the way you write? Well . . . it's nice, but what does it say?"

"Says Rufus Moffat. My name."

Apparently these lines up and down did not spell Rufus Moffat to this lady. She shook her head.

"It's nice," she repeated. "Very nice. But nobody but you knows what it says. You have to learn to write your name better than that before you can join the library."

Rufus was silent. He had come to the library all by himself, gone back home to wash his hands, and come back because he wanted to take books home and read them the way the others did. He had worked hard. He did not like to think he might have to go home without a book.

The library lady looked at him a moment and then she said quickly before he could get himself all the way off the big chair, "Maybe you can *print* your name."

Rufus looked at her hopefully. He thought he could write better than he could print, for his writing certainly looked to him exactly like all grown people's writing. Still he'd try to print if that was what she wanted.

The lady printed some letters on the top of a piece of paper. "There," she said. "That's your name. Copy it ten times and then we'll try it on another application."

Rufus worked hard. He worked so hard the knuckles showed white on his brown fist. He worked for a long, long time, now with his right hand and now with his left. Sometimes a boy or a girl came in, looked over his shoulder and watched, but he paid no attention. From time to time the lady studied his work and she said, "That's fine. That's fine." At last she said, "Well, maybe now we can try." And she gave him another application.

All Rufus could get, with his large generous letters, in that tiny little space where he was supposed to print his name, was R-U-F. The other letters he scattered here and there on the card. The lady did not like this either. She gave him still another blank. Rufus tried to print smaller and this time he got RUFUS in the space, and also he crowded an M at the end. Since he was doing so well now the lady herself printed the *offat* part of Moffat on the next line.

"This will have to do," she said. "Now take this home and ask your mother to sign it on the other side. Bring it back on Thursday and you'll get your card."

Rufus's face was shiny and streaked with dirt where he had rubbed it. He never knew there was all this work to getting a book. The other Moffats just came in and got books. Well, maybe they had had to do this once too.

Rufus held his hard-earned application in one hand and steered his scooter with the other. When he reached home Joey, Jane and Sylvie were not around any longer. Mama signed his card for him, saying, "My! So you've learned how to write!"

"Print," corrected Rufus.

Mama kissed Rufus and he went back out. The lady had said to come back on Thursday, but he wanted a book today. When the other Moffats came home, he'd be sitting on the top step of the porch, reading. That would surprise them. He smiled to himself as he made his way to the library for the third time.

Once his application blew away. Fortunately it landed in a thistle bush and did not get very torn. The rest of the way Rufus clutched it carefully. He climbed the granite steps to the library again only to find that the big round dark brown doors were closed. Rufus tried to open them but he couldn't. He knocked at the door, even kicked it with his foot, but there was no answer. He pounded on the door but nobody came.

A big boy strode past with his newspapers. "Hey, kid," he said to Rufus. "Library's closed!" And off he went, whistling.

Rufus looked after him. The fellow said the library was closed. How could it have closed so fast? He had been here such a little while ago. The lady must still be here. He did want his Brownie book. If only he could see in, he might see the lady and get his book. The windows were high up but they had very wide sills. Rufus was a wonderful climber. He could shinny up trees and poles faster than anybody on the block. Faster than Joey. Now, helping himself up by means of one of the pine trees that grew close to the building, and by sticking his toes in the ivy and rough places in the bricks, he scrambled up the wall. He hoisted himself up on one of the sills and sat there. He peered in. It was dark inside, for the shades had been drawn almost all the way down.

"Library lady!" he called, and he knocked on the windowpane. There was no answer. He put his hands on each side of his face to shield his eyes, and he looked in for a long, long time. He could not believe that she had left. Rufus was resolved to get a book. He had lost track of the number of times he had been back and forth from home to the library, and the library home. Maybe the lady was in the cellar. He climbed down, stubbing his big toe on the bricks as he did so. He stooped down beside one of the low dirt-spattered cellar windows. He couldn't see in. He lay flat on the ground, wiped one spot clean on the window, picked up a few pieces of coal from the sill and put them in his pocket for Mama.

"Hey, lady," he called.

He gave the cellar window a little push. It wasn't locked so he opened it a little and looked in. All he could see was a high pile of coal reaching up to this window. Of course he didn't put any of that coal in his pocket for that would be stealing.

"Hey, lady," he yelled again. His voice echoed in the cellar but the library lady did not answer. He called out, "Hey lady," every few seconds, but all that answered him was an echo. He pushed the window open a little wider. All of a sudden it swung wide open and Rufus slid in, right on top of the coal pile, and crash, clatter, bang! He slid to the bottom, making a great racket.

A little light shone through the dusty windows, but on the whole it was very dark and spooky down here and Rufus really wished that he was back on the outside looking in. However, since he was in the library, why not go upstairs quick, get the Brownie book, and go home? The window had banged shut, but he thought he could climb up the coal pile, pull the window up, and get out. He certainly hoped he could anyway. Supposing he couldn't and he had to stay in this cellar! Well, that he would not think about. He looked around in the dusky light and saw a staircase across the cellar. Luckily his application was still good. It was torn and dirty but it still had his name on it, RUFUS M, and that was the important part. He'd leave this on the desk in exchange for the Brownie book.

Rufus cautiously made his way over to the steps but he stopped halfway across the cellar. Somebody had opened the door at the top of the stairs. He couldn't see who it was, but he did see the light reflected and that's how he knew that somebody had opened the door. It must be the lady. He was just going to say, "Hey, lady," when he thought, "Gee, maybe it isn't the lady. Maybe it's a spooky thing."

Then the light went away, the door was closed, and Rufus was left in the dark again. He didn't like it down here. He started to go back to the coal pile to get out of this place. Then he felt for his application. What a lot of work he had done to get a book and now that he was this near to getting one, should he give up? No. Anyway, if it was the lady up there, he knew her and she knew him and neither one of them was scared of the other. And Mama always said there's no such thing as a spooky thing.

So Rufus bravely made his way again to the stairs. He tiptoed up them. The door at the head was not closed tightly. He pushed it open and found himself right in the library. But goodness! There in the little sink room right opposite him was the library lady!

Rufus stared at her in silence. The library lady was eating. Rufus had never seen her do anything before but play cards, punch books, and carry great piles of them around. Now she was eating. Mama said not to stare at anybody while they were eating. Still Rufus didn't know the library lady ate, so it was hard for him not to look at her.

She had a little gas stove in there. She could cook there. She was reading a book at the same time that she was eating. Sylvie could do that too. This lady did not see him.

"Hey, lady," said Rufus.

The librarian jumped up out of her seat. "Was that you in the cellar? I thought I heard somebody. Goodness, young man! I thought you had gone home long ago."

Rufus didn't say anything. He just stood there. He had gone home and he had come back lots of times. He had the whole thing in his mind; the coming and going, and going and coming, and sliding down the coal pile, but he did not know where to begin, how to tell it.

"Didn't you know the library is closed now?" she demanded, coming across the floor with firm steps.

Rufus remained silent. No, he hadn't known it. The fellow had told him but he hadn't believed him. Now he could see for himself that the library was closed so the library lady could eat. If the lady would let him take his book, he'd go home and stay there. He'd play the game of Find the Duke with Jane. He hopefully held out his card with his name on it.

"Here this is," he said.

But the lady acted as though she didn't even see it. She led Rufus over to the door.

"All right now," she said. "Out with you!" But just as she opened the door the sound of water boiling over on the stove struck their ears, and back she raced to her little room.

"Gracious!" she exclaimed. "What a day!"

Before the door could close on him, Rufus followed her in and sat down on the edge of a chair. The lady thought he had gone and started to sip her tea. Rufus watched her quietly, waiting for her to finish.

After a while the lady brushed the crumbs off her lap. And then she washed her hands and the dishes in the little sink where Rufus had washed his hands. In a library a lady could eat and could wash. Maybe she slept here too. Maybe she lived here.

"Do you live here?" Rufus asked her.

"Mercy on us!" exclaimed the lady. "Where'd you come from? Didn't I send you home? No, I don't live here and neither do you. Come now, out with you, young man. I mean it." The lady called all boys "young man" and all girls "Susie." She came out of the little room and she opened the big brown door again. "There," she said. "Come back on Thursday."

Rufus's eyes filled up with tears.

"Here's this," he said again, holding up his application in a last desperate attempt. But the lady shook her head. Rufus went slowly down the steps, felt around in the bushes for his scooter, and with drooping spirits he mounted it. Then for the second time that day, the library lady changed her mind.

"Oh, well," she said, "come back here, young man. I'm not supposed to do business when the library's closed, but I see we'll have to make an exception."

So Rufus rubbed his sooty hands over his face, hid his scooter in the bushes again, climbed the granite steps and, without circling the light, he went back in and gave the lady his application.

The lady took it gingerly. "My, it's dirty," she said. "You really ought to sign another one."

"And go home with it?" asked Rufus.

He really didn't believe this was possible. He wiped his hot face on his sleeve and looked up at the lady in exhaustion. What he was thinking was: All right. If he had to sign another one, all right. But would she just please stay open until he got back?

However, this was not necessary. The lady said, "Well now, I'll try to clean this old one up. But remember, young man, always have everything clean—your hands, your book, everything, when you come to the library."

Rufus nodded solemnly. "My feet too," he assured her.

Then the lady made Rufus wash his hands again. They really were very bad this time, for he had been in a coal pile, and now at last she gave Rufus the book he wanted—one of the Palmer Cox Brownie books. This one was "The Brownies in the Philippines."

And Rufus went home.

When he reached home, he showed Mama his book. She smiled at him, and gave his cheek a pat. She thought it was fine that he had gone to the library and joined all by himself and taken out a book. And she thought it was fine when Rufus sat down at the kitchen table, was busy and quiet for a long, long time, and then showed her what he had done.

He had printed RUFUS M. That was what he had done. And that's the way he learned to sign his name. And that's the way he always did sign his name for a long, long time.

But, of course, that was before he ever went to school at all, when the Moffats still lived in the old house, the yellow house on New Dollar Street; before this country had gone into the war; and before Mr. Abbot, the curate, started leaving his overshoes on the Moffats' front porch.

Drama

BUSU
(Japanese)

Japanese kyogen, *or comic interludes in longer plays, seem to have developed gradually out of the entertainment of court jesters or clowns. By the fourteenth century, their style was somewhat set by Zen principles of taste: extreme restraint and reliance on suggestion, so that the audience can bring knowledge and imagination to the performance.* Kyogen *means "mad words"—that is, there is supposed to be a tinge of unreality in the reality in these plays. In some respects they resemble the Western theater of the absurd in their restraint and their concern with social comment. They are still performed as interludes in tragedies and comedies. The broad humor and brevity of the following interlude make it a good choice for acting by or for children.*

Characters: THE LORD OF THE HOUSE, TARO *and* JIRO, *his attendants.*

LORD: I am the master of this household. I wish to summon my houseboys and give them some important instructions today. Taro boy, are you there?

TARO: *Ha!*

LORD: Call Jiro boy too.

TARO: Indeed I will. Jiro boy, Master is calling.

JIRO: Very well.

TARO AND JIRO: Here we are.

LORD: It is nothing very special that I want you for. I am going out for a jaunt, so take good care of the house.

TARO AND JIRO: Very well, sir. We will take good care of the house.

LORD: I have something very important to entrust to you. Wait there!

TARO AND JIRO: *Ha!*

LORD: *Yai, Yai!* I am going to entrust this to your care. Guard it well!

TARO AND JIRO: What is that, may we ask?

LORD: This is *busu.*

TARO: Oh, if that is *rusu,* a watchman, then I can go with you.

JIRO: I, too, would like to go with you.

LORD: What? What did you think I said?

TARO: I thought you said that was *rusu.* That is the reason I suggested accompanying you.

LORD: You are mistaken. I said this is a *busu,* a deadly poison. Be careful, for even if the wind from that direction

Translated by Shio Sakanish.

touches you, you will be killed. Never under any circumstances go near it, but guard it well.

TARO: If it is as dangerous as that, why does my master keep it in the house?

LORD: That is indeed a very reasonable question. I will tell you. The *busu* belongs to the lord of the house, and handled by him, it is not only harmless but also very useful. But should anyone else touch it, he dies instantly. So do not go near it, but guard it well from a distance.

TARO: If that is the case . . .

JIRO: We will be careful.

LORD: I shall not be very long.

TARO AND JIRO: We will be waiting for your return. (*THE LORD goes out.*)

TARO: That is that! Very good. Now we can visit with each other without any interference.

JIRO: We have never been left by ourselves so nicely as this.

TARO: Wherever Master went, he has always taken one of us with him. This is most extraordinary. That *busu* must be exceedingly valuable.

JIRO: As you say, since he has left us to guard it, it must be something very valuable.

TARO: Oh, mercy!

JIRO: What is the matter?

TARO: A gust of wind came from the direction of the *busu,* and I thought that was the last of me.

JIRO: That was not wind.

TARO: Lucky it wasn't. Well, I have a notion to look at that *busu.*

JIRO: I dare say! You are indeed a reckless fellow. Master told us that he can handle it, but if anyone else touches it, he will be killed instantly. Don't be silly!

TARO: What you say is true enough. But suppose by chance someone asks us: "I hear your master has a thing called *busu,* but what is it like?" We cannot very well say we have no idea what it is, can we? I will have just a peek.

JIRO: What you say is reasonable enough, but if the wind kills us, what will happen if we have a peek? Let it alone.

TARO: That is the point. If the wind from that direction kills us, we must not get in the wind. You fan while I take a look.

JIRO: Take a look while fanning? That is a good idea.

TARO: Then I will fan while you untie the cord.

JIRO: All right. Fan hard, please, while I am about it.

TARO: All right.

JIRO: Fan hard, hard!

TARO: I am. I am fanning.

JIRO: Coming! Coming!

TARO: Go on! Go on!

JIRO: It's untied.

TARO: Good! Now you take the cover off.

JIRO: Since I untied the cord, you take the cover off.

TARO: All right. You fan as hard as you can.

JIRO: I certainly will.

TARO: Coming! Fan hard! It is off. Anyway it is not a monster, I see.

JIRO: How do you know?

TARO: If it were, it would fly at us. I know now it is not.

JIRO: Right you are.

TARO: Now I am going to have a look. Fan hard, hard. Hee-hee, I have seen it.

JIRO: How does it look?

TARO: Something whitish.

JIRO: Let me have a look. I can't see. Oh, I call that a bit grayish.

TARO: *Yum, yum!* It looks good. I want to taste it.

JIRO: Don't be a fool! You will die this instant. Let it alone. If the wind kills us, what would happen when you eat it?

TARO: I am bewitched by that *busu.* I cannot help it even if I am killed! I am going to taste it.

JIRO: Master entrusted it to us. You can't have it while there is any breath in me.

TARO: Let go of my sleeve.

JIRO: I cannot, while I am here.

TARO: Let go now.

JIRO: I cannot.

TARO: Let go, I say.

JIRO: Never, never.

TARO *(chanting):* Tearing away from detaining hands, I approach this strange thing, *busu.*

JIRO: How awful! My companion will be killed this instant.

TARO: Oh, oh! I cannot resist it. I cannot.

JIRO: Come, come! What is the matter?

TARO: *Yum, yum!* My tongue is melting in my mouth! Wonderful!

JIRO: What is it? What is it?

TARO: It's sugar!

JIRO: Let me taste it, too. Sure, it is.

TARO: Master fooled us. Delicious! I cannot leave it alone. Give it to me.

JIRO: Don't eat it all up by yourself. Let me have a little of it.

TARO: You have some too. But, look! You have eaten it all up. That is a pretty thing, indeed. I will tell Master as soon as he comes back.

JIRO: Now look here. You first opened it even when I told you not to. I will tell him that.

TARO: That's a joke, but this is terrible. What had we better do?

JIRO: Indeed, what can we do?

TARO: I have a scheme. Tear that precious scroll which Master is so fond of.

JIRO: What a reckless fellow you are! Tear the scroll on top of eating the *busu?* I can't.

TARO: I have an idea; so go ahead.

JIRO: *Sara, sara!* There I have done it.

TARO: Well done. I will tell him when he comes back.

JIRO: Now look here! You told me to do it, and that is unfair.

TARO: *Ha, ha!* That was a joke. Now you smash the big bowl and the stand.

JIRO: You must be out of your mind. They are Master's pet treasures. I can't.

TARO: Go on! They all help to get us out of the difficulty.

JIRO: All right, then. *Garan, chin, gara-rin!*

TARO: Very good! Set up a big howl when you hear Master coming.

JIRO: Will howling help us?

TARO: Sure! I hear him coming. Come this way.

LORD: I have taken a stroll very leisurely. My boys must be waiting for me. I must hasten home.

Yai, yai! Taro boy and Jiro boy! I have come home.

TARO: He is here. Howl hard.

TARO AND JIRO: *Wa-wo-wa, boo-waa!*

LORD: What is this all about? Instead of coming out to welcome me, they start weeping bitterly. What is the matter?

TARO: Jiro boy, you speak up.

JIRO: No, you tell him, please.

LORD: One of you, tell me quickly.

TARO: Then I will tell my master. After you went out, we became a little lonesome, and Jiro suggested that we wrestle together. I told him that I had never wrestled before, but as he insisted, we began. But Jiro was so good that he tripped me up several times. In order to protect myself, I clutched at that scroll, and as—you—see—it—got—that—

JIRO: As you see, it got . . . *(Both weep.)*

LORD: Good gracious! The most precious scroll, and you tore it to pieces. Unpardonable! What else did you do?

TARO: And he caught me by the waist and threw me over that bowl and the stand, and they broke . . .

JIRO: To pieces . . .

LORD: This is an inexcusable outrage. What shall I do to you? Is there anything else?

TARO: We were so mortified that we decided to kill ourselves at once, and since you told us that the *busu* in the box would kill us instantly, we opened the box and ate it. But unfortunately we are not dead yet.

JIRO: Alas, not yet.

TARO: As death came not with a mouthful, I took another mouthful. Yet, no death.

JIRO: Three mouthfuls and four mouthfuls! Alas, I could not die.

TARO: Even five and six! Alas, no!

TARO AND JIRO: Though we have taken ten mouthfuls, nay all that there was of the *busu,* yet are we alive. Our lives are charmed. They have not come to their appointed close.

LORD: You confounded scoundrels!

TARO AND JIRO: Pardon us! Pardon us!

LORD: Never, never! Running away? Catch them, catch them!

Poetry

MOON FOLLY

(The Song of Conn the Fool)

Fannie Stearns Gifford

The fool in the poem "Moon Folly" is an idealist. The tree represents his poetic imagination.

I will go up the mountain after the
Moon:
She is caught in a dead fir-tree.
Like a great pale apple of silver and
pearl,
Like a great pale apple is she.

I will leap and will catch her with quick
cold hands
And carry her home in my sack.
I will set her down safe on the oaken
bench
That stands at the chimney-back.

And then I will sit by the fire all night,
And sit by the fire all day.
I will gnaw at the Moon to my heart's
delight
Till I gnaw her slowly away.

And while I grow mad with the Moon's
cold taste
The World will beat at my door,
Crying "Come out!" and crying "Make
haste,
And give us the Moon once more!"

But I shall not answer them ever at all.
I shall laugh, as I count and hide
The great black beautiful Seeds of the
Moon
In a flower-pot deep and wide.

Then I shall lie down and go fast asleep,
Drunken with flame and aswoon.
But the seeds will sprout and the seeds
will leap,
The subtle swift seeds of the Moon.

And some day, all of the World that
cries
And beats at my door shall see
A thousand moon-leaves spring from my
thatch
On a wonderful white Moon-tree!

Then each shall have Moons to his
heart's desire:
Apples of silver and pearl;
Apples of orange and copper fire
Setting his five wits aswirl!

And then they will thank me, who mock
me now,
"Wanting the Moon is he,"—
Oh, I'm off to the mountain after the
Moon,
Ere she falls from the dead fir-tree!

THE PURPLE COW

Gelett Burgess

I never saw a Purple Cow,
I never hope to see one;
But I can tell you, anyhow,
I'd rather see than be one.

JABBERWOCKY

Lewis Carroll

This brilliant nonsense poem, which has been analyzed by linguists, logicians, and philosophers, as well as literary critics, made its first appearance in 1855 (first stanza only) as a parody of Anglo-Saxon poetry, and reappeared in Through the Looking-Glass *(1871) as a longer poem. Alice describes it as well as anyone: "It seems very pretty," she said when she had finished it, "but it's* rather *hard to understand! . . . Somehow it seems to fill my head with ideas—only I don't exactly know what they are! However,* somebody *killed* something: *that's clear, at any rate—"*

'Twas brillig, and the slithy toves
Did gyre and gimble in the wabe:
All mimsy were the borogoves,
And the mome raths outgrabe.

"Beware the Jabberwock, my son!
The jaws that bite, the claws that catch!
Beware the Jubjub bird, and shun
The frumious Bandersnatch!"

He took his vorpal sword in hand:
Long time the manxome foe he sought—
So rested he by the Tumtum tree,
And stood awhile in thought.

And, as in uffish thought he stood,
The Jabberwock, with eyes of flame,
Came whiffling through the tulgey wood,
And burbled as it came!

One, two! One, two! And through and through
The vorpal blade went snicker-snack!
He left it dead, and with its head
He went galumphing back.

"And hast thou slain the Jabberwock?
Come to my arms, my beamish boy!
O frabjous day! Callooh! Callay!"
He chortled in his joy.

'Twas brillig, and the slithy toves
Did gyre and gimble in the wabe:
All mimsy were the borogoves,
And the mome raths outgrabe.

THE FOOL'S SONG

William Carlos Williams

This poetry sings. Children could dance to it.

I tried to put a bird in a cage.
O fool that I am!
For the bird was Truth.
Sing merrily, Truth: I tried to put
Truth in a cage!

And when I had the bird in the cage,
O fool that I am!
Why, it broke my pretty cage.
Sing merrily, Truth: I tried to put
Truth in a cage!

And when the bird was flown from the cage,
O fool that I am!
Why, I had nor bird nor cage.
Sing merrily, Truth: I tried to put
Truth in a cage!
Heigh-ho! Truth in a cage.

THE BLIND MEN AND THE ELEPHANT

John G. Saxe

It was six men of Indostan
  To learning much inclined,
Who went to see the Elephant
  (Though all of them were blind),
That each by observation
  Might satisfy his mind.

The First approached the Elephant,
  And happening to fall
Against his broad and sturdy side,
  At once began to bawl:
"God bless me! but the Elephant
  Is very like a wall!"

The Second, feeling of the tusk,
  Cried, "Ho! what have we here
So very round and smooth and sharp?
  To me 'tis mighty clear
This wonder of an Elephant
  Is very like a spear!"

The Third approached the animal,
  And happening to take
The squirming trunk within his hands,
  Thus boldly up and spake:
"I see," quoth he, "the Elephant
  Is very like a snake!"

The Fourth reached out his eager hand,
  And felt about the knee.
"What most this wondrous beast is like
  Is mighty plain," quoth he;
"'Tis clear enough the Elephant
  Is very like a tree!"

The Fifth, who chanced to touch the ear
  Said, "E'en the blindest man
Can tell what this resembles most;
  Deny the fact who can,
This marvel of an Elephant
  Is very like a fan!"

The Sixth no sooner had begun
  About the beast to grope,
Than, seizing on the swinging tail
  That fell within his scope,
"I see," quoth he, "the Elephant
  Is very like a rope!"

And so these men of Indostan
  Disputed loud and long,
Each in his own opinion
  Exceeding stiff and strong.
Though each was partly in the right,
  And all were in the wrong!

THE OSTRICH IS A SILLY BIRD

Mary E. Wilkins Freeman

The ostrich is a silly bird,
  With scarcely any mind.
He often runs so very fast,
  He leaves himself behind.

And when he gets there, has to stand
  And hang about till night,
Without a blessed thing to do
  Until he comes in sight.

DINKY

Theodore Roethke

O what's the weather in a Beard?
It's windy there, and rather weird,
And when you think the sky has cleared
  —Why, there is Dirty Dinky.

Suppose you walk out in a Storm,
With nothing on to keep you warm,
And then step barefoot on a Worm
—Of course, it's Dirty Dinky.

As I was crossing a hot hot Plain,
I saw a sight that caused me pain,
You asked me before,
I'll tell you again:
—It *looked* like Dirty Dinky.

Last night you lay a-sleeping?
No! The room was thirty-five below;
The sheets and blankets turned to snow.
—He'd got in: Dirty Dinky.

You'd better watch the things you do,
You'd better watch the things you do.
You're part of him; he's part of you
—*You* may be Dirty Dinky.

Rhyme and Limericks

THE AKOND OF SWAT

Edward Lear

This rhyme is fun for a choral reading. Have someone with a strong voice read the couplets and let the crowd shout the capitalized letters at the end of alternate lines.

Who, or why, or which, or *what,*
Is the Akond of SWAT?
Is he tall or short, or dark or fair?
Does he sit on a stool or a sofa or chair,
or SQUAT,
The Akond of Swat?
Is he wise or foolish, young or old?
Does he drink his soup and his coffee cold,
or HOT,
The Akond of Swat?
Does he sing or whistle, jabber or talk,
And when riding abroad does he gallop or walk,
or TROT,
The Akond of Swat?
Does he wear a turban, a fez, or a hat?
Does he sleep on a mattress, a bed, or a mat,
or a COT,
The Akond of Swat?
When he writes a copy in round-hand size,
Does he cross his T's and finish his I's
with a DOT,
The Akond of Swat?
Can he write a letter concisely clear
Without a speck or a smudge or smear
or BLOT,
The Akond of Swat?
Do his people like him extremely well?
Or do they, whenever they can, rebel,
or PLOT,
At the Akond of Swat?
If he catches them then, either old or young,
Does he have them chopped in pieces or hung,
or SHOT,
The Akond of Swat?
Do his people prig in the lanes or park?
Or even at times, when days are dark,
GAROTTE?
O the Akond of Swat!
Does he study the wants of his own dominion?
Or doesn't he care for public opinion
a JOT,
The Akond of Swat?
To amuse his mind do his people show him
Pictures, or any one's last new poem,
or WHAT,
For the Akond of Swat?
At night if he suddenly screams and wakes,
Do they bring him only a few small cakes,
or a LOT,
For the Akond of Swat?
Does he live on turnips, tea, or tripe?
Does he like his shawl to be marked with a stripe,
or a DOT,
The Akond of Swat?
Does he like to lie on his back in a boat
Like the lady who lived in that isle remote,
SHALLOTT,
The Akond of Swat?
Is he quiet, or always making a fuss?
Is his steward a Swiss or a Swede or a Russ,
or a SCOT,
The Akond of Swat?
Does he like to sit by the calm blue wave?

Or to sleep and snore in a dark green
cave,
or a GROTT,
The Akond of Swat?
Does he drink small beer from a silver
jug?
Or a bowl? or a glass? or a cup? or a
mug?
or a POT,
The Akond of Swat?
Does he beat his wife with a
gold-topped pipe,
When she lets the gooseberries grow too
ripe,
or ROT,
The Akond of Swat?
Does he wear a white tie when he dines
with friends,
And tie it neat in a bow with ends,
or a KNOT,
The Akond of Swat?

Edward Lear

There was a Young Lady of Dorking,
Who bought a large bonnet for walking;
But its colour and size, so bedazzled her
eyes,
That she very soon went back to
Dorking.

All illustrations for the limericks by Edward Lear are by the author.

There was an Old Man on some rocks,
Who shut his wife up in a box,
When she said, "Let me out," he
exclaimed, "Without doubt,
You will pass all your life in that box."

There was an old man, who when little
Fell casually into a kettle;
But, growing too stout, He could never
get out,
So he passed all his life in that kettle.

There was an old person of Bar,
Who passed all her life in a jar,
Which she painted pea-green, to appear
more serene,
That placid old person of Bar.

The Absolutely Abstemious Ass,
who resided in a Barrel, and only lived
on
Soda Water and Pickled Cucumbers.

Anthony Euwer

There was a young lady from Woosester
Who ussessed to crow like a roosester.
She ussessed to climb
Seven trees at a time—
But her sisester ussessed to boosester.

A diner while dining at Crewe,
Found quite a large mouse in his stew.
Said the waiter, "Don't shout,
And wave it about,
Or the rest will be wanting one, too."

Gelett Burgess

I wish that my room had a floor;
I don't care so much for a floor.
But this walking around
Without touching the ground
Is getting to be quite a bore.

G. T. Johnson

There was a young farmer of Leeds,
Who swallowed six packets of seeds.
It soon came to pass
He was covered with grass,
And he couldn't sit down for the weeds.

There was a young man of Herne Bay,
Who was making explosives one day;
But he dropped his cigar
In the gunpowder jar.
There *was* a young man of Herne Bay.

One day I went out to the zoo,
For I wanted to see the old gnu,
But the old gnu was dead.
They had a new gnu instead,
And that gnu, well, he knew he was
new.

Essays

THE FOOL AND THE CHILD

Jerome Griswold

Jerome Griswold teaches English at Northeastern University, Boston.

A fool needs friends when he is Out in Public because he is likely to "act natural." He is likely to start laughing hysterically, for instance, if a waitress in a steak restaurant appears to take his order dressed as a cowperson. He'll insist on reading, perhaps out loud, all the signs at a fried chicken emporium ("50 pieces or more 20% off." "100 drumsticks 35% off." "The Blimp Box—$4.85."). In other words, a fool needs friends because he is a social misfit. He needs someone to touch the side of the head and say something like "absentminded" to explain his behavior. In this way, the fool is like the child—he too is dependent on others, he too is given room in which "to act up." I think this is why the fool appeals to children and why he appears so frequently in children's literature. The fool, like the child, is protected. Both can get away with a lot more than other people are allowed, because their society doesn't take them seriously. And, for their part, fools and children don't take seriously what their society takes seriously.

Think of the opportunity. By being a little "touched" you can get away with much more. You can be a critic with impunity. You can be a prankster. You can be comically wise. You can say and do what you like without fear. And sometimes you can even get paid for it. There are a good number of cultures that pay fools to be around. They feel it is important that there be someone who can say what he wants to anybody. In Moslem, Anglo-Saxon, and Irish cultures the fool had a place inside the castle. He could speak against the king when others might be afraid to. This seems to be the role of the fool in Shakespeare's *King Lear.* When the mad Lear will listen only to what he wants to hear, the fool is the only one who will tell him the truth. The fool in that play is the wise man.

The fool is wise because he sees things clearly. He does not depend on others' opinions, and often he does not depend on his head. He sees things with his heart. At one point the fool in *King Lear* sees the dishonesty in society and asks us to look at a judge trying a thief. If you exchanged them, he asks, could you tell the difference between them? A problem with seeing things so clearly, however, is that they may then be seen literally. Isn't that the point of most moron jokes? Take the one about the moron who saw a man installing a fire alarm in his house. "I've seen those things," says the moron, "and they don't work." "Why is that?" enquires the man. "Oh, they ring all right," replies the moron, "but the fire burns on just the same." The fool who sees things literally is not a member of society's family of good sense.

But sometimes not having good sense can work to the fool's advantage. There is a story about the Sufi fool-figure, Nasrudin, who would stand in the marketplace and, when people offered him a handful of coins, would always choose the smallest. One day a helpful old man counseled Nasrudin to take the largest of the coins. Nasrudin replied that if he did that, people would no longer feel so smugly that he was a fool, and he would be penniless.

As adults we seem to grow unable to simply let things happen but must build or do things so they work to our advantage. As a result we come close to losing our sense of play. We are seldom tempted to do silly things for their own sake, though often our society seems to suggest we do such things for the most grave of reasons. We are asked, for example, in a television commercial to test the strength of a particular denture cleanser by cooking a pair of false teeth in a blueberry pie. Every once in awhile society just becomes too serious and we have to let off steam. Recognizing this human need, some religions, such as Tibetan Buddhism and Indian Hinduism, have developed special ceremonies and occasions when the religious can simply let off steam. One day out of the year the masters at a Zen monastery disappear and the students drink and act shamelessly. Christians have their Carnival or Mardi Gras to have a bit of fun before the Lenten season of severe earnestness.

The fool is the year-round antidote to strained seriousness. He is a revolutionary, but in a unique way. The conventional revolutionary is deadly serious. He matches his earnestness to the earnestness he is fighting. But the fool goes about it in a different way. The fool doesn't fight earnestness, he dissolves it. He throws a cream pie at the policeman. He cracks everyone up.

In our own time the figure of the fool has been associated with the counterculture. The zany days of day-glo costumes and love-in antics in the sixties have been written about in Tom Wolfe's book about Ken Kesey and the Pranksters, *Electric Kool-Aid Acid Test.* In the seventies the cult of the child comes close to the foolishness of the sixties. Why, for instance, has the child guru Maharaj Ji been so popular? One answer is that people seem attracted to him because of his use of *lila,* or the sense of play. Rennie Davis, who in the sixties was a political activist and one of the Chicago Seven, reports he had a mystical experience when he saw the child guru drive his motorcycle through the ranks of his followers splashing mud on them. People seem to want to go backward to a time before they were serious, to a time when they were foolish.

The fool *is* countercultural. He is on the side of the stage making comments. He is an outsider. Societies often choose outsiders to play as fools. For this reason fools have been albinos, dwarfs, pygmies, those with physical deformities, and the insane. In societies like those of Renaissance France and Italy, which were particularly male, the female fool notably appears. In militaristic societies, like those of post-Renaissance Germany and Russia, the fool is often the professor. In fact, Peter the Great frequently turned unemployed graduate students, whom he had helped with the equivalent of our fellowships, into fools to amuse him.

The fool emancipates us from unnecessary seriousness by giving us his outside view. He shows us when we are muddled with bogus problems. He tells us, in short, that life is too important a thing to be taken seriously. I think this is the reason gurus throughout all times have told youths to try on the role of the fool. Youths are sometimes too pompously serious and yet too inexperienced. The true fools of the gods, Oscar Wilde tells us, are those who do not know themselves but pretend that they do. This affected surety closes the door to more experience. Sometimes, in the role of the fool, a youth can have that arrogance eroded by frequent humiliations, and when that arrogance is gone he can begin to learn again.

St. Paul calls Christians "fools for Christ" and says, "Make no mistake about it: if any one of you think himself wise, in the ordinary sense of the word, then he must learn to be a fool before he can become wise." Tolstoy may have remembered these words when, in his later years of Christian pietism, he wrote *Ivan the Fool.* Tolstoy's Ivan is not wise in the ways of the world. He is a fool whose "immature" mind preserves his innocence. On the other hand, Ivan's brothers, Semyon the Soldier and Taras the Merchant, *are* wise in the ways of the world. Far from foolish, they are deadly earnest about what they want: wealth and power. As a result, they are conniving, full of guile and deceit, always plotting to satisfy their selfish worldly desires. Ivan, because he is a fool, cannot detect this in his brothers. He answers each of their requests with "why not?" Ivan helps others selflessly without any desire for reciprocal favors. But his brothers, because they help only themselves and no one else, become all the more vulnerable to attack.

Ivan is indifferent to the attractions of power and wealth. Because he does not care what happens to his own fortunes, he can be clear-sighted. He may not be privy to the ways of the world but he has, nonetheless, an instinctive and elementary rectitude that comes from his foolish literalmindedness: he refuses one brother more soldiers because providing soldiers resulted in a neighbor's death; he refuses to give more gold to the other brother because providing gold caused Mixlova to lose her cow. It is because Ivan and his subjects are not wise in the ways of the world that, in their kingdom, military conscription is impossible and gold is used only for trinkets.

Ivan does not use his head. He speaks from the heart and his actions are completely natural. In this he is far different from his brothers. Where his brothers operate by worldly wisdom and deify themselves and their interests, Ivan lives in a world that humbles him. It is a world where, despite what the devil might suggest, a man cannot cheat his fate through intellectual labors but must necessarily be humble and work. It is a world where a fool has a place because man is not its creator or controller. It is a world of folk magic where Ivan's God is transcendent and man is a little less in control, a little more foolish, than we might like to believe.

INTERVIEW WITH ISAAC BASHEVIS SINGER

Isaac Bashevis Singer was born in Poland in 1904 and grew up in Warsaw, where he was educated by his father, a rabbi, and at a rabbinical seminary. Generally regarded as the greatest contemporary Yiddish writer, he has been highly praised for his rich novels of Jewish life—novels such as The Family Moskat, Satan in Goray, *and* The Magician of Lublin*—and for his collections of short stories, including* Gimpel the

This interview was conducted in the children's literature class, University of Connecticut, Storrs, April 1976. All of the questions asked in the interview came from the students in the class.

Fool. *His writings for children include* Zlateh the Goat, When Shlemiel Went to Warsaw, *and* The Fools of Chelm and Their History.

Q. Do you feel that it is necessary for people to be able to identify with a particular tradition of folktale in order to be able to respond and to understand your novels? children's stories?

A. No. I don't think so. My novels are translated into many languages. The Japanese translate everything I write almost immediately, and I don't think the Japanese really have studied enough European culture or Jewish culture or whatever you call it to understand. I think that if a writer writes clearly and has a story to tell, everybody will understand. In other words, you don't need any preparations and any commentary and footnotes to understand me.

Q. Do you have any particular favorites from your own work in your children's stories?

A. Well, this question I am asked wherever I go, both about my children's stories and the stories for the adults, and I always have the same answer. I say to the man or to the woman, "Do you have children and which is your favorite child?" They always refuse to answer me. Some people say that their youngest child they think they love best, but it is only imagination. I have sometimes this idea—that the latest story I love best—but I really cannot judge. We don't know. Once I publish something, I have a feeling that this is my child and I am not going to discriminate between one child and another.

Q. What values do you believe should be stressed in today's children's literature?

A. I would say that we are living now in a time where people, I don't know who they are, would like to bring in a lot of corruption in our lives thinking that this is good for us. And lately I have seen that they even try, these powers whoever they are, to corrupt children. I have seen books for children where they teach the children to disobey their parents, to spit on authority, to use bad language. I think this is a real danger because if we bring up a generation with false ideas, we are going to have a society which will be completely corrupted. Although I don't believe a writer should sit down and write a story with a moral, just the same, in an exceptional time like this, we should see to it that our children should get from what they read the right kind of ideas, at least not the wrong ones. I would say that the Ten Commandments, or most of the Ten Commandments, are as valid for children as they are for adult people, and they should be really stressed in our writing. We should tell our children, not directly, but through our stories, that the commandments are as valid today as they were four thousand years ago. We should honor father and mother, and we are not allowed to steal and murder and do many of the other things which some false liberals think that today they are permitted in the name of one or of another idea. All I can say is that we should be more careful from a moral point of view when we write for children than when we write for adults. Just the same I am against preaching. I don't like it when a writer writes a sermon instead of a story. Let him write a good story and if the story is good the moral will be implicit.

Q. This is sort of an extension of this last question. Do you do or think anything differently when you approach a children's story than when you write for adults?

A. I would say that the laws of writing are the same when you write for an adult or when you write for a child. In my case I need three conditions to write a story. The first condition is that I must have a plot. I don't believe in writers who say that they are writing a slice of life, that they will sit down to write and let their pen do what it is in the mood of doing. In most of the cases the pen is not in the mood to write a good story. So this is the first condition. The second condition is that I must have a desire or a passion to write a story. Sometimes I have a story, but the desire or the passion to write it is lacking and then I will not write. But there is a third condition, and most important. I must have the conviction or the illusion that I am the only one who is able to write this particular story. Without this conviction or without this illusion, I will not write this story. When I wrote *Zlateh the Goat,* I felt that I could write this story. Other people may write other stories, better stories, but this particular story I can write. If I am convinced that it is *my* story, I write it. With all these three conditions fulfilled, I don't worry too much about the message. At least I didn't worry about it until now. Lately I begin to worry a little bit about the message, but just the same I say that we don't need new messages. If all the messages were to disappear and we would be left with the Ten Commandments, we would have enough messages for the next ten thousand years.

Q. What do you read in your leisure time? Do any particular authors or books have a strong influence on your work?

A. Well, I read all kinds of books, but I would say when I really want to enjoy reading I go back to the masters of the 19th century. It is true I was born in the 20th century, but very near to the 19th. In addition, these masters were storytellers. They were not sociologists or psychologists or psychoanalysts. Men like Tolstoy and Balzac and Dostoevsky and Dickens—I go back to them. I think that too much psychology and sociology and too much commentary do a lot of damage to literature. They have done a lot of damage in this century where people thought that by writing a story or a novel they were going to save the world.

Q. Of what importance are folktales in American society?

A. I think that folktales or folklore are very important to literature. All great writers, like Pushkin and all the others, made use of folklore, because actually a man does not have enough imagination to create folklore himself. He must take from the people. When literature divorces itself from folklore it becomes rationalistic, pragmatic, too positivistic, and it loses its charm. Emile Zola dreamed about writing a rationalistic, a scientific novel. He never succeeded. Neither did his disciples. Literature must be in one way or another connected with folklore because literature must have roots, and roots and folklore are almost synonyms.

Q. Are any of the characters in your children's stories related to real people or are they purely fictional?

A. Before I sit down to write I always take as a model a real person. I don't think that a writer should invent character. He should invent action, but he should take a ready-made character because nature has provided us with so many real characters, and so many different characters, and so many rich characters that we really are not in need to invent them. Everyone of us knows people with different kinds of characters, and they can be used easily in literature. Of course sometimes I will combine characters. I will take two characters whom I know, and make from them one character. But I always have to use material which God and nature have already prepared for me, and I think this is true with almost all writers. You can always find out whom Tolstoy meant by this hero and that hero. It was always either his father or his uncle or some neighbor or acquaintance.

Q. Where do you get your ideas for such stories as *Alone in the Wild Forest*?

A. First of all, I get them from folklore and then from imagination—and if you ask where I got my imagination, I would really be embarrassed. I don't know. Maybe the genes. There must be some source where we all get it because not only writers have imagination, so have engineers and businessmen and lawyers and doctors. It is a quality almost every human being has, more or less.

Q. How would you say that you put a part of yourself into your folktales?

A. Well, it has been said many times that all literature is autobiographical. Sooner or later no matter about whom you write, you write about yourself. Even if you write about someone whom you hate, you express yourself by hating this person, because if the reader knows whom you hate, he can learn from this whom you love. It is always autobiographical. Actually we see everything through our own eyes, our spirit, our way of thinking, our categories of thinking.

Q. What was your motivation for going into children's literature?

A. No motivation at all. I could have told you it was my love for children—I really love children—but I never actually believed that I am a writer for children. I wrote always about demons and sometimes sex, and I didn't think that this was really the material for children. But I had a friend who was an editor at Harper's, and she bothered me for years asking, why don't you write for children? Until one day I went to my publisher, Farrar, Straus and Giroux, and said that Harper's was interested in a book for children. Would you allow me to write a book for Harper's? They thought it over and they said, "What! You are going to write for children? You will never succeed. It's not your field. But if they want to lose their heads and their money, let them have it." And they gave me their permission, and I wrote the first book, which was called *Zlateh the Goat.* And then I wrote another for Scribner's. Then suddenly my publishers decided that I am a writer for children and they forbade me to write for other publishers. Well, I admit that I approached this field without too many ideals and too many messages. I just wanted to satisfy a friend of mine who was after me for a long time. The net result was that she translated many of my stories from English into Yiddish, and now whenever I get a check, she gets a check. Which proves to you that altruism sometimes pays.

Q. What were the most influential books on your own work that you read when you were young?

A. When I was young almost every writer influenced me. The moment I read a book I decided that I can do it too, and I tried to imitate the writer. It took me long years before I convinced myself that imitation will not do, that I have to find myself, my own environment, my own way of living, and my own way of thinking. But now in my old age I feel that no one really influences me to a high degree. Naturally, life itself influences you. Whatever you do, whatever you think, whomever you meet, has some little influence on your life, but I could really not point out and say this writer has influenced me more. If I must do it I would say that Gogol did. I loved very much Gogol's writings, his humanness, his mysticism. As a matter of fact, a few years ago I was asked by an editor of a magazine to write a review about a collection of Gogol's stories, and when I read these stories I said to myself, "Although this man lived a hundred years before me, he managed to steal some of my style and my ideas."

Q. What particular difficulties have you encountered in having your work translated from Yiddish into English?

A. Translation is a very difficult business, and I say not only is it a difficult business, but it is also a bad business, because the translator is really never well paid, and good translation is very rare. In my younger days when I came to this country, before I knew English, whenever people found some fault in my writing, I had one excuse: it's the fault of the translator. But lately I have begun to translate myself, and I have acquired some compassion for the translators. I see now how difficult it is really to convey an idiom from one language into another.

Q. Your brother was a great rationalist; how did you get along with him?

A. My brother was a rationalist and I was a mystic, but I loved him very much. I think that there has never yet been a war between mystics and rationalists or realists, because a mystic is also a realist. He thinks that mysticism is a real thing. We had many discussions at some times, but it never came to a bloody war, and I still today consider my brother my teacher and master. He has given me many rules about writing. One of these rules is that events never get dated, they never get obsolete, but commentary becomes obsolete very soon. Sometimes it is obsolete at the very beginning. So the best thing for a writer is to tell the story and to leave the commentary to the critics.

Q. You say you are a mystic in your work. I wonder how much of that mysticism you draw from the Cabala—if it is part of your integral being or if it is something you have used as a source of folklore?

A. No man becomes a mystic because he reads books. First he is a mystic and then he looks for books about mysticism. By just reading books he may know a lot about mysticism and still not be a mystic. There is a professor who is a great expert in the Cabala, but I would not call him a Cabalist. My impression is that he really does not believe in these things, but he knows about them. In my case it is the opposite. I am a Cabalist but I know little about the Cabala. I know enough to be able to write about it. Fiction, not science.

Q. How do you feel about the use of symbolism in children's books?

A. My feelings are that one should write for children first of all with clarity. I don't think that books should be written so that children cannot understand them. Symbolism may be good for adults, not even too good for adults if it is too much, but certainly symbolism is not good for children. The same thing is true about illustration. If you draw a lion, he should look like a lion and not like a locomotive. Many of the so-called modernist illustrators think that they can do with a child the same thing as they do with the adults to create this kind of super-modernism. I think that it is not good for the child. Because although the child is by nature a mystic, he is also by nature a realist. He wants people and animals and things to look as he sees them with his own eyes. If a book is clear and there is a story in it and it makes sense, and if the illustrations are clear, the child will like it. Naturally we cannot avoid controversy. People will always look for excuses to fight, and many critics will tear down a book for no reason whatsoever just because they are in a mood to do so. I have no axe to grind. The critics were all nice to me. However, I know that some of them may be very dangerous.

Q. You mentioned that you don't necessarily have to invent characters. You can draw from the ones that you know. But you also mentioned "God" or "nature-created," and I wondered if Spinoza was a particularly important philosopher for you?

A. Well, when I was a boy I was really delighted when I read for the first time Spinoza's *Ethics.* I was fascinated with the idea that nature is God and God is nature. If nature is God, this means that I am part of God. And to see myself suddenly the little boy there on Krochmalna Street being a part of the Almighty pleased me very much. Until today I feel that there is a great deal of truth in Pantheism. The only thing I don't agree on with Spinoza is that he saw in God only two attributes, which were extension and thinking, and I feel, like the Cabalist, that God has many other attributes like wisdom, beauty, and so on. I think that Spinoza has limited God by giving him only these two attributes, which are more or less matter and logic, while God being so great can have millions of other attributes, especially good ones.

Q. How can critics be dangerous?

A. Well, if critics will tear down a good writer again and again, they will discourage the writer. It doesn't happen too often, but it did happen in history. When I read about all the bad criticism which Lord Byron got in his time and Edgar Allan Poe and some like him, I ask myself how is this possible that these critics could not see the brilliance of these great writers. And some people say this could have happened only one hundred years ago; it could never happen today. And I say to myself, since people are the same it can happen today, and as a matter of fact, it happens all the time. But I would say that a good writer never takes it too much to heart, is not too much discouraged. He knows that people are people, and he keeps on doing his work, and I say to all real and potential writers, don't take opinions too seriously. If you think that the critic is right and he gives you good advice, take it. If you think that he gives you bad advice, just ignore it. Let's finish this talk on this happy note: ignore the critics!

Explorations

STORYTELLING AND ACTING OUT

1. *(Golden Touch)* Since Nathaniel Hawthorne is a gifted storyteller, you might read this story until you can repeat it in your own words, inserting a few of Hawthorne's expressions from time to time to get the flavor of his style. Don't attempt to do it, though, unless you really want to, because much of the success of telling a story depends upon the desire to tell it.
2. *(Sea of Gold)* Read over this story so often that you can tell it to a child. Remember that children don't have the false values of Hikoichi's companions. Hikoichi is childlike in his nonattachment to things valued by adults. Ask a child why Hikoichi is rewarded.
3. *(Golden Goose)* The message about greed and attachment to things that don't matter is so important that it is reiterated again and again in old tales. Here is a chance to improve your art of oral narration with a giggly story that carries the same message as "The Golden Touch" and "The Sea of Gold." Tell the story as a group of children act it out by touching one another and marching in a train about a room.
4. *(Jack and the Beanstalk)* Read the story often enough so that a child is impelled to come in with "Fee, fi, fo, fum!" at the proper times.

   Act the story out in a puppet theater or a Toy Theater (see Explorations in "Toys and Games" for suggestions). Climbing up and down a beanstalk is an entertaining action for a puppet to perform, especially with a giant puppet in hot pursuit.
5. *(Madman of Naranath/Shrewd Todie)* Which version of this old tale do you prefer? If you like, read it often enough to tell it in your own words but in the style of the original—that is, inject some characteristic expressions and phrases. It's usually fatal to try to talk in dialect—too hard to imitate effectively and to understand—so, in general, stick to a straight rendition, allowing a few expressions from the original to convey the cultural flavor of the version you have chosen.
6. *(Busu)* Choose a cast of three, and act or mime the Japanese interlude "Busu." The humor in the interlude should be played broadly, especially the fanning of the *busu,* the tearing of the scroll, the howling and weeping when the master comes home, and the running away at the end.

   Make up a brief play or "happening" of your own, like "Busu," basing it on some foolishness that children can appreciate.
7. *(Moon Folly)* This poem is easy to memorize. It sings itself into the mind. Repeat it frequently enough to "sing it" into a child's memory. The tree in the poem has to do with the poetic imagination. A tree with a similar meaning appears in Hans Christian Andersen's story "The Goblin and the Grocer" and in William Butler Yeats' poem "The Song of Wandering

Aengus." You might want to reinforce the image by reading the Andersen story or the Yeats poem, both of which are readily available.

8. *(Dirty Dinky)* This poem has a real lilt to it that delights almost everybody. It's one of those rhymes that tends to run in one's head. Say it over aloud with a group of children so it runs in everybody's head.
9. *(Akond of Swat)* Chant this nonsense poem with some children. Tell them what to shout at the ends of couplets, which are easy to learn by heart.
10. *(Lear's Limericks)* Many of Lear's characters are enclosed in boxes or other objects. Think of the boxes that enclose you. Your house? Your job? Your fears? Ask a child for suggestions.
11. Discuss with a child the foolish things you both have done. Make up a little story about them together.
12. If you know older children, you might want to mime Henry Miller's beautiful story "The Smile at the Foot of the Ladder." All you need is somebody who can dance and clown, a clown suit, a stepladder, and a cardboard moon covered with silver paper. The story should be drastically cut for narration, and there should be an effective narrator. Though this story has to do with a deep subject—various ways of approaching life—a child can enjoy it as much as an adult, provided that it is well presented.
13. Find a story of drolls or simpletons or fools outside this book and tell it to a group of children. The story of "The Three Sillies" from Joseph Jacobs' *English Fairy Tales* (1892) might appeal to you, or one of Carl Sandburg's *Rootabaga Stories* (1922), such as the one about "The Huckabuck Family and How They Raised Pop Corn in Nebraska and Quit and Came Back." Practice the storytelling skills you have learned so far: making sure you really want to tell the story, sharing yourself as well as the story with the children, using your voice expressively, adjusting your choice of words to the age and comprehension of the children, staying aware of your audience, and keeping certain choice phrases and expressions from the wording of the original story.

PARTICIPATING IN OTHER WAYS

1. *(Golden Touch)* After reading Nathaniel Hawthorne's retelling of this Greek myth, consider how people who are too imbued with material things—"thingisme," the French novelist Alain Robbe-Grillet calls it—do become inanimate statues, at least in a figurative sense. Others are affected by them, too, are frozen by the evil about them. The Greeks had a superb way of projecting philosophical truth in the form of stories. Now play the game of "Statues"—remember it? You twirl somebody, who then is "frozen" in whatever position he or she is left in when you let go. Only the magic of your touch can revive them.
2. *(Simple Simon)* Think of other silly things Simple Simon could do. Ask a child for suggestions.
3. *(Golden Goose)* Draw a picture of all the people attached to one another in this story, with the princess laughing at the sight.
4. *(Madman of Naranath)* Get a travel book from the library with pictures of India (a travel agency might have a brochure) and draw a picture of how you think the Madman of Naranath might look.
5. *(Rufus M.)* This story about a child's library experience can trigger a

useful work for you and a group of children. First, you write a publishing house and try to obtain some discarded dummies, paste-ups, color separations, prints, galleys, page proofs, and signatures—as well as a plastic plate—in short, some of the steps in book publication. Then arrange a display in a classroom or local library. (If adults and children know how much work goes into making a book, they are likely to be more careful of them.) An excellent book on stages in publishing a children's book is Joanna Foster's *Pages, Pictures, and Print* (1958).

6. *(Fool's Song)* Make up a tune to go with this poem. If you're shy, confine it to the shower at first, and then try it with an audience of one or two children. You can make it a musical contest and they can sing one back to you.
7. *(Blind Men and the Elephant)* People with eyes who cannot see are proverbial. Often blind people have clearer vision, as they see with an inner eye. This poem has to do with people capable of seeing only one aspect of a situation. Can you draw a picture of the men and the elephant?
8. *(Jabberwocky)* Read this poem aloud. Often nonsense is used to express the inexpressible. Think of something you don't dare say out loud and make up a nonsense poem about it which you share with a child. Have the child share her or his own nonsense poem with you.
9. *(Purple Cow)* Conduct a purple cow drawing contest with a group of children. Have them choose the winner and tell you why they chose it.
10. Make up a limerick like one of Lear's, but on some subject of your own choosing. Have a child help you with it.

Selected Readings

READINGS FOR CHILDREN

Brewton, Sara and John E., eds. *Laughable Limericks.* Illustrated by Ingrid Fetz. New York: Thomas Crowell, 1965. Poetry.

Carrick, Malcolm. *The Wise Men of Gotham.* Adapted and illustrated by Malcolm Carrick. New York: Viking, 1975. (Fiction stories first appeared in 1450).

Ciardi, John. *The Man Who Sang the Sillies.* Illustrated by Edward Gorey. Philadelphia: Lippincott, 1961. Poetry.

Clouston, William Alexander. *The Book of Noodles: Stories of Simpletons; or Fools and Their Follies.* Detroit: Gale Research Company, 1969; first published in London by Elliott Stock, 1888. Fiction.

Cole, William, ed. *Humorous Poetry for Children.* Illustrated by Ervine Metzl. Cleveland: World, 1955. Poetry.

———. *Oh, How Silly!* Illustrated by Tomi Ungerer. New York: Viking, 1970. Poetry.

———. *Oh, That's Ridiculous!* Illustrated by Tomi Ungerer. New York: Viking, 1972. Poetry.

———. *Oh, What Nonsense!* Illustrated by Tomi Ungerer. New York: Viking, 1966. Poetry.

Daniels, Guy, trans. *Foma the Terrible.* Illustrated by Imero Gobbato. New York: Delacorte, 1970. Folktale (picture book).

Domanska, Janina. *Marilka.* Illustrated by the author. New York: Macmillan, 1970. Fantasy (picture book).

Du Bois, William Pène. *Bear Party.* Illustrated by the author. New York: Viking, 1969. Fantasy (picture book).

Duvoisin, Roger. *Petunia.* Illustrated by the author. New York: Knopf, 1950. Fantasy (picture book).

Elkin, Benjamin. *Six Foolish Fishermen.* Illustrated by Katherine Evans. Chicago: Children's Press, 1957. Folktale (picture book).

Felt, Sue. *Rosa-Too-Little.* Garden City, N.Y.: Doubleday, 1950. Fiction (picture book).

Gág, Wanda, trans. and illus. *Tales from Grimm.* New York: Coward, McCann, 1936. Folktales. See especially "Clever Elsie" and "Goose Hans."

Ginsburg, Mirra. *Three Rolls and One Doughnut: Fables from Russia.* Illustrated by Anita Lobel. New York: Dial, 1970. Folktales. See especially title story and "Hatchet Gruel."

Grahame, Kenneth. *The Reluctant Dragon.* Illustrated by Ernest K. Shepard. New York: Holiday House, 1953; first published in 1938. Fantasy.

Hutchins, Pat. *Titch.* Illustrated by the author. New York: Macmillan, 1969. Fiction (picture book).

Kelen, Emery. *Mr. Nonsense: A Life of Edward Lear.* New York: Norton, 1973. Biography.

Kipling, Rudyard. *The Elephant's Child.* Illustrated by Leonard Weisgard. New York: Walker, 1970. Fantasy (from the *Just So Stories,* originally published in 1902).

Krauss, Ruth. *The Carrot Seed.* Illustrated by Crockett Johnson. New York: Harper, 1945. Fiction (picture book).

Leaf, Munro. *The Story of Ferdinand.* Illustrated by Robert Lawson. New York: Viking, 1936. Fantasy (picture book).

Lear, Edward. *The Complete Nonsense of Edward Lear.* Edited and Introduced by Holbrook Jackson. New York: Dover, 1951; first published in 1846. Nonsense poetry.

Levin, Meyer. *Classic Hassidic Tales: Marvellous Tales of Rabbi Baal Shem and of His Great Grandson, Rabbi Nachman.* Retold from Hebrew, Yiddish, and German Sources by Meyer Levin. Illustrated by Marek Szwarc. New York: Penguin, 1975; first published in 1932 under the title *The Golden Mountain.*

Lionni, Leo. *Frederick.* New York: Pantheon, 1967. Fantasy (picture book).

Nash, Ogden, ed. *The Moon Is Shining Bright as Day.* Philadelphia: Lippincott, 1953. Poetry.

Ransome, Arthur. *The Fool of the World and the Flying Ship.* Illustrated by Uri Shulevitz. New York: Farrar, 1968. Folktale (picture book).

Richards, Laura E. *Tirra Lirra.* Illustrated by Marguerite Davis. Boston: Little, Brown, 1955. Poetry.

Rieu, E. V. *The Flattered Flying Fish and Other Poems.* Illustrated by E. H. Shepard. New York: Dutton, 1962. Poetry.

Sandburg, Carl. *Rootabaga Stories.* Illustrated by Maud and Miska Petersham. New York: Harcourt, 1936. Folktales. See especially "The Huckabuck Family & How They Raised Popcorn in Nebraska & Quit & Came Back."

Shulevitz, Uri, illus. *Soldier and Tsar in the Forest: A Russian Tale.* Translated by Richard Lourie. New York: Farrar, 1972. Folktale (picture book).

Singer, Isaac Bashevis. *The Fools of Chelm and Their History.* Illustrated by Uri Shulevitz. Translated by the author and Elizabeth Shub. New York: Farrar, 1973. Folktales.

______. *When Schlemiel Went to Warsaw and Other Stories.* Illustrated by Margot Zemach. Translated by the author and Elizabeth Shub. New York: Farrar, 1968. Folktales.

Smith, William Jay. *Boy Blue's Book of Beasts.* Illustrated by Juliet Kepes. Boston: Little, Brown, 1956. Poetry.

______. *Laughing Time.* Illustrated by Juliet Kepes. Boston: Little, Brown, 1953. Poetry.

______. *Mister Smith and Other Nonsense.* Illustrated by Don Bologuese. New York: Delacorte, 1968. Poetry.

______. *Typewriter Town.* New York: Dutton, 1960. Poetry.

Steel, Flora Annie. *English Fairy Tales.* Illustrated by Arthur Rackham. New York: Macmillan, 1962. Folktales. See especially "Mr. and Mrs. Vinegar," "Lazy Jack," "The Wise Men of Gotham," and "Of Drowning Eels."

Wyndham, Lee. "How the Sons Filled the Hut." In *Tales the People Tell in Russia.* Illustrated by Andrew Antal. New York: Messner, 1970. Folktale.

Zemach, Harve. *Salt: A Russian Tale.* Illustrated by Margot Zemach. Chicago: Follett, 1965. Folktale (picture book).

Zemach, Margot. *The Three Sillies.* New York: Holt, 1963. Folktale (picture book).

REFERENCES FOR ADULTS

Ashton, John. *Chap-Books of the Eighteenth Century.* Illustrated. New York: Benjamin Blom, 1966; first published in 1882.

Blake, Kathleen. *Play, Games, and Sport: The Literary Works of Lewis Carroll.* Cornell University Press, 1974.

Miller, Henry. *The Smile at the Foot of the Ladder.* In *About Henry Miller* by Edwin Corle. New York: Duell, 1948. Paperback edition by New Directions, 1974.

Noakes, Vivian. *Edward Lear: The Life of a Wanderer.* Boston: Houghton Mifflin, 1968. Biography.

Peers, Edgar A. *Elizabethan Drama and Its Mad Folk.* Cambridge, England: W. Heffer, 1914.

Singer, Isaac Bashevis. *A Day of Pleasure: Stories of a Boy Growing Up in Warsaw.* Illustrated with photos by Roman Vishniac. New York: Farrar, 1969. Autobiography.

Tolstoy, Leo. *The Tale of Ivan the Fool and His Two Brothers, Semyon the Soldier and Taras the Big-Belly, and of His Sister, Malyana the Mute, and of the Old Devil and the Three Imps.* In *Fables and Fairy Tales* by Leo Tolstoy, translated by Ann Dunnigan. New York: New American Library, 1962. Folktales.

Welsford, Enid. *The Fool: His Social and Literary History.* Garden City, N.Y.: Doubleday, 1961.

Wright, Louis B. "Elizabethan Strolling Players." *Journal of English and Germanic Philology* 26 (1927): 294–303.

———. "Madmen as Vaudeville Performers on the Elizabethan Stage." *Journal of English and Germanic Philology* 30 (1931): 48–54.

III. Masks and Shadows

The person we call "I" presents a far from simple unity. In addition to the inner "I," or ego, Jung believes that we possess at least two other aspects of personality: a *mask,* or persona, which forms the outer personality seen by the world, and a *shadow,* or hidden personality, which we usually suppress (see M. Esther Harding's essay "The Shadow," at the end of the section, for a more detailed analysis of these two aspects of personality). Because masks and shadows are integral aspects of personality, they are frequently encountered as themes in children's literature.

Each of us wears a mask (a metaphorical one, at least), which we put on when we go out each day. The mask is the social role we have decided to assume, and if our mask is artificial, we run the risk of being called "phonies." We should comfort ourselves, however, in the knowledge that phonies are actually idealists who want to be something they aren't and that ultimately many of them become their mask. In this way, they resemble Puss in

Boots's poor master, who assumes the clothes of a rich gentleman and eventually becomes one. But the role playing goes beyond superficial appearances of beauty or wealth. Sometimes it is the fate of human beings to look like monsters or toads, and this appearance masks their spiritual beauty. In "Beauty and the Beast," a good man who has been bewitched is masked in the body of a monster. The diminutive body of the brave little tailor masks a courageous heart. The scarred and ugly face of Little Burnt-Face masks a beautiful soul, and the invisibility of the Great Chief masks a god.

In real life and in literature, masks are sometimes worn for protection or to accomplish certain ends. In the Greek myth, Perseus wears a mask—a cap of darkness—to hide his identity. In the amusing story "The Emperor's New Clothes," the absence of a mask—his clothes—bares the emperor's vanity to the world. People from primitive cultures have often disguised their faces and bodies with actual masks in order to protect themselves from the spirits or to gain magical power through identification with the spirit portrayed by a particular mask. So that the mask will be imbued with the tree spirit, sometimes the mask is carved on the living wood of the tree itself and then separated from the tree. The Mah-Meri people, an aboriginal tribe living off the west coast of Malaysia, were haunted long ago by the spirit of a huge Siamang (large black gibbon) which one of their hunters had killed. In desperation, the tribe decided to create an effigy of the Siamang, to honor its spirit. The effigy came to life, so the story goes, and the people were protected forever from other Siamangs. To this day, the lifelike, carved Siamang mask is worn at ceremonial dances by the Mah-Meri.

According to Jungian psychology, the shadow consists of the unacceptable, suppressed parts of our personalities. For instance, we like to think of ourselves as honest, straightforward, and generous—but we are not always that way in actuality. Because we cannot bear to confront our shadows, few of us have insight into our own personalities. Therefore, we project our faults onto others. In coming to grips with the shadow, in recognizing it as an aspect of our personalities, we must accept the relativity of good and evil, and see that the shadow can be used positively and creatively. We can identify the shadow in ourselves by looking closely at what we hate in others—greed, jealousy, ambition, sneakiness.

Not recognizing one's own shadow creates an inauthentic person. At least, this is the theory; and it seems to account for the presence of the shadow in some stories, such as the negative shadow traits of the twin personality in the biblical tale of Cain and Abel, the hideous nature of Mr. Hyde, the double of Dr. Jekyll in Robert Louis Stevenson's classic, the dissolute character of the protagonist's double reflected in Oscar Wilde's *The Picture of Dorian Gray,* or the eerie, shadowlike character who mimics the narrator in Hans Christian Andersen's "The Shadow," a story that is included here.

In these stories, the shadow always remains apart, never fusing with other personality aspects to reinforce the whole personality. Another frequently encountered type of shadow story presents two children—one good and one bad—with the bad child eventually becoming good. If we apply a Jungian interpretation and regard this bad-child–good-child as a single child, then it is possible to say that the dynamic shadow and the good mask have successfully come together. Thomas Day's *Sandford and Merton* is an eighteenth-century book about a good boy and a bad boy whose extremes are brought closer together by education through life experience, an idea borrowed from Rousseau. Maria Edgeworth (1767–1849) wrote several children's stories of this type for didactic purposes. Horatio Alger, in the early twentieth century, also used the good-boy–bad-boy pattern as part of his fictional formula. Frances Hodgson Burnett's *The Secret Garden* (1909), in which a bad-tempered, sickly boy of wealthy background is influenced positively by a lively, good-natured Yorkshire boy, is one of the most famous examples of this type of story. A danger here is that this type of story can be used to force a child into adopting a socially approved mask, rather than being used for genuine integration of the mask and shadow into a more complete and balanced personality.

The process of recognizing the shadow and using it constructively is an interesting one. In Aesop's fable "The Dog and the Shadow," the "shadow" or reflection that the dog is snapping at is his own greed, but he fails to recognize it. On the other hand, Tolstoy's King Esarhaddon (in "Circles") sees his shadow—the cruel side to his personality—when his head is forcibly stuck under water and he fears that he will drown. The shock causes a deep change in his attitude toward others.

Shadows are collective as well as personal. An entire culture can have a shadow and can be brought to recognize it, as the American people have been painfully realizing with respect to their treatment of minorities. A book like Ronald Syme's biography of Geronimo is an attempt to deal with this type of collective shadow.

The relationship of the human being to the personal shadow is a complex one, as depicted in Andersen's story "The Shadow." This story reveals that it is essential to guard the well-being of one's shadow at all times, that the shadow is a vital part of the person—an idea expressed also in "Fox Boy and His Shadow" by Jaime de Angulo. This idea appears as well in Robert Louis Stevenson's poem "My Shadow" and in Sir James M. Barrie's *Peter Pan,* in which Peter Pan loses his shadow and Wendy sews it on him.

The shadow seems to be rooted in an archaic, amoral kind of

second personality ("the Trickster"), which occasionally bursts forth and surprises the modern person to whom it belongs. The American Winnebago Indians have a famous cycle of Trickster tales (from which "The Elk's Head" is included here), which shows this amoral character in many outlandish situations. The impulsive trickster, driven by his passions, is related to the theme of Fools as well as to Shadows, as we have already seen in such characters as the Madman of Naranath and Shrewd Todie.

There are many "shadows" besides the psychological one. The *Oxford English Dictionary* lists at least six additional meanings to be discovered in the literature in this section: darkness itself ("How Jahdu Ran Through the Darkness in No Time at All"), the physical shadow or dark figure cast by the body on a surface ("Fox Boy and His Shadow"), a reflected image ("The Dog and the Shadow"), phantom or shade ("The Flute" and "How Jahdu Ran Through the Darkness in No Time at All"), a vain and insubstantial object of pursuit ("The Dog and the Shadow"), and a prefiguration or foreshadowing (the Platonic shadow, seen in *The Last Battle,* in which human beings and the whole Narnian civilization are seen as imperfect shadows of their perfect counterparts in heaven).

Whatever its meaning, the dark shadow is usually neglected. Only when we begin to understand that without awareness of shadow there can be no awareness of light, will we come to appreciate the value of this mysterious darkness that follows us everywhere.

Masks

Myth

PERSEUS
(Greek)
Retold by Edith Hamilton

The mask worn in this myth is a "cap of darkness," which makes the wearer invisible. It is given to Perseus along with two other magical gifts, winged sandals and a wallet that is always the right size for anything carried in it. Aided by these gifts and by the gods Hermes and Athena, Perseus is able to cut off the head of Medusa, one of the three Gorgons, terrible golden-scaled creatures with great wings and snake-hair. Edith Hamilton has pointed out that this is the only myth in which magic is featured prominently.

The petrifying gaze of Medusa belongs to the realm of death, and Medusa herself is an aspect of the Terrible Great Goddess, which many cultures associate with death (in her positive aspect, of course, the Mother Goddess is associated with life).

King Acrisius of Argos had only one child, a daughter, Danaë. She was beautiful above all the other women of the land, but this was small comfort to the King for not having a son. He journeyed to Delphi to ask the god if there was any hope that some day he would be the father of a boy. The priestess told him no, and added what was far worse: that his daughter would have a son who would kill him.

The only sure way to escape that fate was for the King to have Danaë instantly put to death—taking no chances, but seeing to it himself. This Acrisius would not do. His fatherly affection was not strong, as events proved, but his fear of the gods was. They visited with terrible punishment those who shed the blood of kindred. Acrisius did not dare slay his daughter. Instead, he had a house built all of bronze and sunk underground, but with part of the roof open to the sky so that light and air could come through. Here he shut her up and guarded her.

Illustrated by Steele Savage.

So Danaë endured, the beautiful,
To change the glad daylight for
brass-bound walls,
And in that chamber secret as the
grave
She lived a prisoner. Yet to her came
Zeus in the golden rain.

As she sat there through the long days and hours with nothing to do, nothing to see except the clouds moving by overhead, a mysterious thing happened, a shower of gold fell from the sky and filled her chamber. How it was revealed to her that it was Zeus who had visited her in this shape we are not told, but she knew that the child she bore was his son.

For a time she kept his birth secret from her father, but it became increasingly difficult to do so in the narrow limits of that bronze house and finally one day the little boy—his name was Perseus—was discovered by his grandfather. "Your child!" Acrisius cried in great anger. "Who is his father?" But when Danaë answered proudly, "Zeus," he would not believe her. One thing only he was sure of, that the boy's life was a terrible danger to his own. He was afraid to kill him for the same reason that had kept him from killing her, fear of Zeus and the Furies who pursue such murderers. But if he could not kill them outright, he could put them in the way of tolerably certain death. He had a great chest made, and the two placed in it. Then it was taken out to sea and cast into the water.

In that strange boat Danaë sat with her little son. The daylight faded and she was alone on the sea.

When in the carven chest the winds
and waves
Struck fear into her heart she put her
arms,
Not without tears, round Perseus
tenderly
She said, "O son, what grief is mine.
But you sleep softly, little child,
Sunk deep in rest within your
cheerless home,
Only a box, brass-bound. The night,
this darkness visible,
The scudding waves so near to your
soft curls,
The shrill voice of the wind, you do
not heed,
Nestled in your red cloak, fair little
face."

Through the night in the tossing chest she listened to the waters that seemed always about to wash over them. The dawn came, but with no comfort to her for she could not see it. Neither could she see that around them there were islands rising high above the sea, many islands. All she knew was that presently a wave seemed to lift them and carry them swiftly on and then, retreating, leave them on something solid and motionless. They had made land; they were safe from the sea, but they were still in the chest with no way to get out.

Fate willed it—or perhaps Zeus, who up to now had done little for his love and his child—that they should be discovered by a good man, a fisherman named Dictys. He came upon the great box and broke it open and took the pitiful cargo home to his wife who was as kind as he. They had no children and they cared for Danaë and Perseus as if they were their own. The two lived there many years, Danaë content to let her son follow the fisherman's humble trade, out of harm's way. But in the end more trouble came. Polydectes, the ruler of the little island, was the brother of Dictys, but he was a cruel and ruthless man. He seems to have taken no notice of the mother and son for a long time, but at last Danaë attracted his attention. She was still radiantly beautiful even though Perseus by now was full grown, and Polydectes fell in love with her. He wanted her, but he did not want her son, and he set himself to think out a way of getting rid of him.

There were some fearsome monsters called Gorgons who lived on an island and were known far and wide because of their deadly power. Polydectes evidently talked to Perseus about them; he probably told him that he would rather have the head of one of them than anything else in the world. This seems practically certain from the plan he devised for killing Perseus. He announced that he was about to be married and he called his friends together for a celebration, including Perseus in the invitation. Each guest, as was customary, brought a gift for the bride-to-be, except Perseus alone. He had nothing he could give. He was young and proud and keenly mortified. He stood up before them all and did exactly what the King had hoped he would do, declared that he would give him a present better than any there. He would go off and kill Medusa and bring back her head as his gift. Nothing could have suited the King better. No one in his senses would have made such a proposal. Medusa was one of the Gorgons,

> And they are three, the Gorgons, each
> with wings
> And snaky hair, most horrible to
> mortals.
> Whom no man shall behold and draw
> again
> The breath of life,

for the reason that whoever looked at them was turned instantly into stone. It seemed that Perseus had been led by his angry pride into making an empty boast. No man unaided could kill Medusa.

But Perseus was saved from his folly. Two great gods were watching over him. He took ship as soon as he left the King's hall, not daring to see his mother first and tell her what he intended, and he sailed to Greece to learn where the three monsters were to be found. He went to Delphi, but all the priestess would say was to bid him seek the land where men eat not Demeter's golden grain, but only acorns. So he went to Dodona, in the land of oak trees, where the talking oaks were which declared Zeus's will and where the Selli lived who made their bread from acorns. They could tell him, however, no more than this, that he was under the protection of the gods. They did not know where the Gorgons lived.

When and how Hermes and Athena came to his help is not told in any story, but he must have known despair before they did so. At last, however, as he wandered on, he met a strange and beautiful person. We know what he looked like from many a poem, a young man with the first down upon his cheek when youth is loveliest, carrying, as no other young man ever did, a wand of gold with wings at one end, wearing a winged hat, too, and winged sandals. At sight of him hope must have entered Perseus' heart, for he would know that this could be none other than Hermes, the guide and the giver of good.

This radiant personage told him that before he attacked Medusa he must first be properly equipped, and that what he needed was in the possession of the nymphs of the North. To find the nymphs' abode, they must go to the Gray Women who alone could tell them the way. These women dwelt in a land where all was dim and shrouded in twilight. No ray of sun looked ever on that country, nor the moon by night. In that gray place the three women lived, all gray themselves and withered as in extreme old age. They were strange creatures, indeed, most of all because they had but one eye for the three, which it was their custom to take turns with, each removing it from her forehead when she had had it for a time and handing it to another.

All this Hermes told Perseus and then he unfolded his plan. He would himself guide Perseus to them. Once there Perseus must keep hidden until he saw one of them take the eye out of her forehead to pass it on. At that moment, when none of the three could see, he must rush forward and seize the eye and refuse to give it back until they told him how to reach the nymphs of the North.

He himself, Hermes said, would give him a sword to attack Medusa with—which could not be bent or broken by the Gorgon's scales, no matter how hard they were. This was a wonderful gift, no doubt, and yet of what use was a sword when the creature to be struck by it could turn the swordsman into stone before he was within striking distance? But another great deity was at hand to help. Pallas Athena stood beside Perseus. She took off the shield of polished bronze which covered her breast and held it out to him. "Look into this when you attack the Gorgon," she said. "You will be able to see her in it as in a mirror, and so avoid her deadly power."

Now, indeed, Perseus had good reason to hope. The journey to the twilight land was long, over the stream of Ocean and on to the very border of the black country where the Cimmerians dwell, but Hermes was his guide and he could not go astray. They found the Gray Women at last, looking in the wavering light like gray birds, for they had the shape of swans. But their heads were human and beneath their wings they had arms and hands. Perseus did just as Hermes had said, he held back until he saw one of them take the eye out of her forehead. Then before she could give it to her sister, he snatched it out of her hand. It was a moment or two before the three realized they had lost it. Each thought one of the others had it. But Perseus spoke out and told them he had taken it and that it would be theirs again only when they showed him how to find the nymphs of the North. They gave him full directions at once; they would have done anything to get their eye back. He returned it to them and went on the way they had pointed out to him. He was bound, although he did not know it, to the blessed country of the Hyperboreans, at the back of the North Wind, of which it is said: "Neither by ship nor yet by land shall one find the wondrous road to the gathering place of the Hyperboreans." But Perseus had Hermes with him, so that the road lay open to him, and he reached that host of happy people who are always banqueting and holding joyful revelry. They showed him great kindness: they welcomed him to their feast, and the maidens dancing to the sound of flute and lyre paused to get for him the gifts he sought. These were three: winged sandals, a magic wallet which would always become the right size for whatever was to be carried in it, and, most important of all, a cap which made the wearer invisible. With these and Athena's shield and Hermes' sword Perseus was ready for the Gorgons. Hermes knew where they lived, and leaving the happy land the two flew back across Ocean and over the sea to the Terrible Sisters' island.

By great good fortune they were all asleep when Perseus found them. In the mirror of the bright shield he could see them clearly, creatures with great wings and bodies covered with golden scales and hair a mass of twisting snakes. Athena was beside him now as well as Hermes. They told him which one was Medusa and that was important, for she alone of the three could be killed; the other two were immortal. Perseus on his winged sandals hovered above them, looking, however, only at the shield. Then he aimed a stroke down at Medusa's throat and Athena guided his hand. With a single sweep of his sword he cut through her neck and, his eyes still fixed on the shield with never a glance at her, he swooped low enough to seize the head. He dropped it into the wallet which closed around it. He had nothing to fear from it now. But the two other Gorgons had awakened and, horrified at

the sight of their sister slain, tried to pursue the slayer. Perseus was safe; he had on the cap of darkness and they could not find him.

So over the sea rich-haired Danaë's
 son,
Perseus, on his winged sandals sped,
Flying swift as thought.
In a wallet of silver,
A wonder to behold,
He bore the head of the monster,
While Hermes, the son of Maia,
The messenger of Zeus,
Kept ever at his side.

On his way back he came to Ethiopia and alighted there. By this time Hermes had left him. Perseus found, as Hercules was later to find, that a lovely maiden had been given up to be devoured by a horrible sea serpent. Her name was Andromeda and she was the daughter of a silly vain woman,

That starred Ethiop queen who strove
To set her beauty's praise above
The sea-nymphs, and their power
 offended.

She had boasted that she was more beautiful than the daughters of Nereus, the Sea-god. An absolutely certain way in those days to draw down on one a wretched fate was to claim superiority in anything over any deity; nevertheless people were perpetually doing so. In this case the punishment for the arrogance the gods detested fell not on Queen Cassiopeia, Andromeda's mother, but on her daughter. The Ethiopians were being devoured in numbers by the serpent; and, learning from the oracle that they could be freed from the pest only if Andromeda were offered up to it, they forced Cepheus, her father, to consent. When Perseus arrived the maiden was on a rocky ledge by the sea, chained there to wait for the coming of the monster. Perseus saw her and on the instant loved her. He waited beside her until the great snake came for its prey; then he cut its head off just as he had the Gorgon's. The headless body dropped back into the water; Perseus took Andromeda to her parents and asked for her hand, which they gladly gave him.

With her he sailed back to the island and his mother, but in the house where he had lived so long he found no one. The fisherman Dictys' wife was long since dead, and the two others, Danaë and the man who had been like a father to Perseus, had had to fly and hide themselves from Polydectes, who was furious at Danaë's refusal to marry him. They had taken refuge in a temple, Perseus was told. He learned also that the King was holding a banquet in the palace and all the men who favored him were gathered there. Perseus instantly saw his opportunity. He went straight to the palace and entered the hall. As he stood at the entrance, Athena's shining buckler on his breast, the silver wallet at his side, he drew the eyes of every man there. Then before any could look away he held up the Gorgon's head; and at the sight one and all, the cruel King and his servile courtiers, were turned into stone. There they sat, a row of statues, each, as it were, frozen stiff in the attitude he had struck when he first saw Perseus.

When the islanders knew themselves freed from the tyrant it was easy for Perseus to find Danaë and Dictys. He made Dictys king of the island, but he and his mother decided that they would go back with Andromeda to Greece and try to be reconciled to Acrisius, to see if the many years that had passed since he had put them in the chest had not softened him so that he would be glad to receive his daughter and grandson. When they reached Argos, however, they found that Acrisius had been driven away from the city, and where he was no one could say. It happened that soon after their arrival Perseus heard that the King of Larissa, in the North, was holding a great athletic contest, and he journeyed there to take part. In the discus-throwing when his turn came and he hurled the heavy missile, it swerved and fell among the spectators.

Acrisius was there on a visit to the King, and the discus struck him. The blow was fatal and he died at once.

So Apollo's oracle was again proved true. If Perseus felt any grief, at least he knew that his grandfather had done his best to kill him and his mother. With his death their troubles came to an end. Perseus and Andromeda lived happily ever after. Their son, Electryon, was the grandfather of Hercules.

Medusa's head was given to Athena, who bore it always upon the aegis, Zeus's shield, which she carried for him.

Folktales

WHY NO ONE LENDS HIS BEAUTY

(Nigerian)

Retold by Harold Courlander

Once upon a time, according to this folktale, a person was able to masquerade in another person's actual physical appearance, not merely in another person's clothes. The story seems to be commenting on the old idea that beauty is only skin-deep, and that one must take care not to confuse inner and outer beauty.

Before, before, in the beginning of things, people wore their beauty as they wore clothes. It is said that there was a girl named Shoye who possessed beauty that was the pride of her village. Wherever she went, people said: "When before has anyone seen such beauty?"

There was another girl in the village named Tinuke. She did not have such beauty to wear. She envied Shoye. She went to her one day and said: "I must go on a journey for my family. I have no beauty. Lend me your good looks until I return." Shoye did not hesitate. She gave her good looks to Tinuke. Tinuke took the beauty. Her face shone with it. She walked gracefully. She left the village and went on her journey.

People who saw her said: "Whenever has such a beautiful girl been seen?" She went to the town where a chief lived. His friends told him: "There is a girl in the town. She comes from another place. She has great beauty." The chief sent for Tinuke. He saw her beauty. He took her as a wife. She did not return to her own village.

Shoye waited. She was very ugly. When she went to the market, people said: "When before has anyone seen such ugliness?"

Tinuke did not return. Shoye's friends said: "Tinuke has surely stolen your beauty. You must find her." So Shoye went in search of Tinuke. She came to the town of the chief.

People said: "What ugliness! She has a hideous face! It will bring bad luck on us. Send her away!" But Shoye would not go away. She heard that Tinuke now lived in the house of the chief. She went there. She asked for Tinuke. Tinuke would not come. She hid behind the walls of the chief's compound.

When the chief passed through his gate, he saw Shoye there. He said: "Who is the girl with the ugly face crouching before my estate?"

His guards said: "She asks for Tinuke. Tinuke will not see her."

The chief spoke to Shoye. He said: "Why do you wait here?"

Shoye answered: "I have a friend in my village. She borrowed my beauty. She came here. She now lives in your house. She does not return to her village. She does not return what she borrowed."

The chief said: "You mean that beautiful girl that I have taken as my wife? How could such beauty not belong to the one who wears it?" He sent for Tinuke. She came. She saw Shoye. She was ashamed. She gave Shoye's beauty back to her. Shoye took it. Her face shone. She walked gracefully. Tinuke was now ugly.

People said: "Whenever has a chief had so ugly a wife?"

The chief said: "Beauty and good character are not the same thing. Because a woman wears beauty does not mean that she behaves well. This girl Tinuke came to me wearing beauty, but her character was faulty. Shoye, who was ugly because someone else borrowed her beauty, her behavior was good. One may borrow beauty but not good character. Thus, beauty deceives. And, therefore, I order that henceforth one may not lend his beauty to another. Each person shall wear what is his own."

Thereafter, it was this way. One could neither lend nor borrow beauty. Each person wore what was his own. And there came to be a saying:

"Beauty is only worn; it is not the same as character."

LITTLE BURNT-FACE

(American Indian—Micmac)

Retold by Frances J. Olcott

This folktale is an Indian version of Cinderella, but it is also a fascinating study of masks, or appearances. The Great Chief, who is a god, wears the mask of invisibility to everyone but Little Burnt-Face, who is pure of heart. Scarred and beaten by her envious sisters, she wears the mask of ugliness. When the god becomes visible to her, she is restored to her original beauty. It has been suggested that Little Burnt-Face represents the scorched desert; the Great Chief, the rainfall that makes the desert beautiful again. In one version of this story the girl is called Little Scar-Face. Through the healing power of love, she is so transformed that she becomes known as Little Star-Face.

Once upon a time, in a large Indian village on the border of a lake, there lived an old man who was a widower. He had three daughters. The eldest was jealous, cruel, and ugly; the second was vain; but the youngest of all was very gentle and lovely.

Now, when the father was out hunting in the forest, the eldest daughter used to beat the youngest girl, and burn her face with hot coals; yes, and even scar her pretty body. So the people called her "Little Burnt-Face."

When the father came home from hunting he would ask why she was so scarred, and the eldest would answer quickly: "She is a good-for-nothing! She was forbidden to go near the fire, and she disobeyed and fell in." Then the father would scold Little Burnt-Face and she would creep away crying to bed.

By the lake, at the end of the village, there was a beautiful wigwam. And in that wigwam lived a Great Chief and his sister. The Great Chief was invisible; no one had ever seen him but his sister. He brought her many deer and supplied her with good things to eat from the forest and lake, and with the finest blankets and garments. And when visitors came all they ever saw of the Chief were his moccasins; for when he took them off they became visible, and his sister hung them up.

Now, one Spring, his sister made known that her brother, the Great Chief, would marry any girl who could see him.

Then all the girls from the village—except Little Burnt-Face and her sisters—and all the girls for miles around hastened to the wigwam, and walked along the shore of the lake with his sister.

And his sister asked the girls, "Do you see my brother?"

And some of them said, "No"; but most of them answered, "Yes."

Then his sister asked, "Of what is his shoulder-strap made?"

And the girls said, "Of a strip of rawhide."

"And with what does he draw his sled?" asked his sister.

And they replied, "With a green withe."

Then she knew that they had not seen him at all, and said quietly, "Let us go to the wigwam."

So to the wigwam they went, and when they entered, his sister told them not to take the seat next the door, for that was where her brother sat.

Then they helped his sister to cook the supper, for they were very curious to see the Great Chief eat. When all was ready, the food disappeared, and the brother took off his moccasins, and his sister hung them up. But they never saw the Chief, though many of them stayed all night.

One day Little Burnt-Face's two sisters put on their finest blankets and brightest strings of beads, and plaited their hair beautifully, and slipped embroidered moccasins on their feet. Then they started out to see the Great Chief.

As soon as they were gone, Little Burnt-Face made herself a dress of white birch-bark, and a cap and leggings of the same. She threw off her ragged garments, and dressed herself in her birch-bark clothes. She put her father's moccasins on her bare feet; and the moccasins were so big that they came up to her knees. Then she, too, started out to visit the beautiful wigwam at the end of the village.

Poor Little Burnt-Face! She was a sorry sight! For her hair was singed off, and her little face was as full of burns and scars as a sieve is full of holes; and she shuffled along in her birch-bark clothes and big moccasins. And as she passed through the village the boys and girls hissed, yelled, and hooted.

And when she reached the lake, her sisters saw her coming, and they tried to shame her, and told her to go home. But the Great Chief's sister received her kindly, and bade her stay, for she saw how sweet and gentle Little Burnt-Face really was.

Then as evening was coming on, the Great Chief's sister took all three girls walking beside the lake, and the sky grew dark, and they knew the Great Chief had come.

And his sister asked the two elder girls, "Do you see my brother?"

And they said, "Yes."

"Of what is his shoulder-strap made?" asked his sister.

"Of a strip of rawhide," they replied.

"And with what does he draw his

sled?" asked she.

And they said, "With a green withe."

Then his sister turned to Little Burnt-Face and asked, "Do you see him?"

"I do! I do!" said Little Burnt-Face with awe. "And he is wonderful!"

"And of what is his sled-string made?" asked his sister gently.

"It is a beautiful Rainbow!" cried Little Burnt-Face.

"But, my sister," said the other, "of what is his bow-string made?"

"His bow-string," replied Little Burnt-Face, "is the Milky Way!"

Then the Great Chief's sister smiled with delight, and taking Little Burnt-Face by the hand, she said, "You have surely seen him."

She led the little girl to the wigwam, and bathed her with dew until the burns and scars all disappeared from her body and face. Her skin became soft and lovely again. Her hair grew long and dark like the Blackbird's wing. Her eyes were like stars. Then his sister brought from her treasures a wedding-garment, and she dressed Little Burnt-Face in it. And she was most beautiful to behold.

After all this was done, his sister led the little girl to the seat next the door, saying, "This is the Bride's seat," and made her sit down.

And then the Great Chief, no longer invisible, entered, terrible and beautiful. And when he saw Little Burnt-Face, he smiled and said gently, "So we have found each other!"

And she answered, "Yes."

Then Little Burnt-Face was married to the Great Chief, and the wedding-feast lasted for days, and to it came all the people of the village. As for the two bad sisters, they went back to their wigwam in disgrace, weeping with shame.

THE BRAVE LITTLE TAILOR

(German)

The tailor in this famous folktale not only wears a mask himself—pretending to be a bold, giant-killing hero—but belongs to a profession associated with creation of the mask, or persona. Someone who makes clothes for people is a magical character, for he is able to suggest a great deal about the wearer through the clothes he creates. Traditionally, the tailor in folktales is small and lives by his wits. He is therefore a character with whom small children can identify. This story suggests that creating a bold persona for oneself—and having the quick wits to capitalize on it—is a good way to succeed in a world full of giants, wild beasts, and mean-hearted people.

From *The Blue Fairy Book,* edited by Andrew Lang (London, 1889).

One summer's day a little tailor sat on his table by the window in the best of spirits, and sewed for dear life. As he was sitting thus a peasant woman came down the street, calling out: "Good jam to sell, good jam to sell." This sounded sweetly in the tailor's ears; he put his frail little head out of the window, and shouted: "Up here, my good woman, and you'll find a willing customer." The woman climbed up the three flights of stairs with her heavy basket to the tailor's room, and he made her spread out all the pots in a row before him. He examined them all, lifted them up and smelt them, and said at last: "This jam seems good, weigh me four ounces of it, my good woman; and even if it's a quarter of a pound I won't stick at it." The woman, who had hoped to find a good market, gave him what he wanted, but went away grumbling wrathfully. "Now heaven shall bless this jam for my use," cried the little tailor, "and it shall sustain and strengthen me." He fetched some bread out of a cupboard, cut a round off the loaf, and spread the jam on it. "That won't taste amiss," he said; "but I'll finish that waistcoat first before I take a bite." He placed the bread beside him, went on sewing, and out of the lightness of his heart kept on making his stitches bigger and bigger. In the meantime the smell of the sweet jam rose to the ceiling, where heaps of flies were sitting, and attracted them to such an extent that they swarmed on to it in masses. "Ha! who invited you?" said the tailor, and chased the unwelcome guests away. But the flies, who didn't understand English, refused to let themselves be warned off, and returned again in even greater numbers. At last the little tailor, losing all patience, reached out of his chimney corner for a duster, and exclaiming: "Wait, and I'll give it to you," he beat them mercilessly with it. When he left off he counted the slain, and no fewer than seven lay dead before him with outstretched legs. "What a desperate fellow I am!" said he, and was filled with admiration at his own courage. "The whole town must know about this;" and in great haste the little tailor cut out a girdle, hemmed it, and embroidered on it in big letters, "Seven at a blow." "What did I say, the town? no, the whole world shall hear of it," he said; and his heart beat for joy as a lamb wags his tail.

The tailor strapped the girdle round his waist and set out into the wide world, for he considered his workroom too small a field for his prowess. Before he set forth he looked round about him, to see if there was anything in the house he could take with him on his journey; but he found nothing except an old cheese, which he took possession of. In front of the house he observed a bird that had been caught in some bushes, and this he put into his wallet beside the cheese. Then he went on his way merrily, and being light and agile he never felt tired. His way led up a hill, on the top of which sat a powerful giant, who was calmly surveying the landscape. The little tailor went up to him, and greeting him cheerfully said: "Good-day, friend; there you sit at your ease viewing the whole wide world. I'm just on my way there. What do you say to accompanying me?" The giant looked contemptuously at the tailor, and said: "What a poor wretched little creature you are!" "That's a good joke," answered the little tailor, and unbuttoning his coat he showed the giant the girdle. "There now, you can read what sort of a fellow I am." The giant read: "Seven at a blow"; and thinking they were human beings the tailor had slain, he conceived a certain respect for the little man. But first he thought he'd test him, so taking up a stone in his hand, he squeezed it till some drops of water ran out. "Now you do the same," said the giant, "if you really wish to be thought strong." "Is that all?" said the little tailor; "that's child's play to me," so he dived into his wallet, brought out the cheese, and pressed it till the whey ran out. "My squeeze was in sooth better than yours," said he. The giant didn't know what to say, for he couldn't have believed it of the little fellow. To prove him again, the giant lifted a stone and threw it so high that the eye could hardly follow it. "Now, my little pigmy, let me see you do that." "Well thrown," said the tailor; "but, after all, your stone fell to the ground; I'll throw one that won't come down at all." He dived into his wallet again, and grasping the bird in his hand, he threw it up into the air. The bird, enchanted to be free, soared up into the sky, and flew away never to return. "Well, what do you think of that little piece of business, friend?" asked the tailor. "You can certainly throw," said the giant; "but now let's see if you can carry a proper weight." With these words he led the tailor to a huge oak tree which had been felled to the ground, and said: "If you are strong enough, help me to carry the tree out of the wood." "Most certainly," said the little tailor: "just you take the trunk on your shoulder; I'll bear the top and branches, which is certainly the heaviest part." The giant laid the trunk on his shoulder, but the tailor sat at his ease among the branches; and the giant, who couldn't see what was going on behind him, had to carry the whole tree, and the little tailor into the bargain. There he sat behind in the best of spirits, lustily whistling a tune, as if carrying the tree were mere sport. The giant, after dragging the heavy weight for some time, could get on no further, and shouted out: "Hi! I must let the tree fall." The tailor sprang nimbly down, seized the tree with both hands as if he had carried it the whole way, and said to the giant: "Fancy a big lout like you not being able to carry a tree!"

They continued to go on their way together, and as they passed by a cherry tree the giant grasped the top of it, where the ripest fruit hung, gave the branches into the tailor's hand, and bade him eat. But the little tailor was far too weak to hold the tree down, and when the giant let go the tree swung back into the air, bearing the little tailor with it. When he had fallen to the ground again without hurting himself, the giant said: "What! do you mean to tell me you haven't the strength to hold down a feeble twig?" "It wasn't strength that was wanting," replied the tailor; "do you think that would have been anything for a man who has killed seven at a blow? I jumped over the tree because the hunstmen are shooting among the branches near us. Do you do the like if you dare." The giant made an attempt, but couldn't get over the tree, and stuck fast in the branches, so that here too the little tailor had the better of him.

"Well, you're a fine fellow, after all," said the giant; "come and spend the night with us in our cave." The little tailor willingly consented to do this, and following his friend they went on till they reached a cave where several other giants were sitting round a fire, each holding a roast sheep in his hand, of which he was eating. The little tailor looked about him, and thought: "Yes, there's certainly more room to turn round in here than in my workshop." The giant showed him a bed, and bade him lie down and have a good sleep. But the bed was too big for the little tailor, so he didn't get into it, but crept away into the corner. At midnight, when the giant thought the little tailor was fast asleep, he rose up, and taking his big iron walking-stick, he broke the bed in two with a blow, and thought he had made an end of the little grasshopper. At early dawn the giants went off to the wood, and quite forgot about the little tailor, till all of a sudden they met him trudging along in the most cheerful manner. The giants were terrified at the apparition, and, fearful lest he should slay them, they all took to their heels as fast as they could.

The little tailor continued to follow his nose, and after he had wandered about for a long time he came to the courtyard of a royal palace, and feeling tired he lay down on the grass and fell asleep. While he lay there the people came, and looking him all over read on his girdle: "Seven at a blow." "Oh!" they said, "what can this great hero of a hundred fights want in our peaceful land? He must indeed be a mighty man of valour." They went and told the King about him, and said what a weighty and useful man he'd be in time of war, and that it would be well to secure him at any price. This counsel pleased the King, and he sent one of his courtiers down to the little tailor, to offer him, when he awoke, a commission in their army. The messenger remained standing by the sleeper, and waited till he stretched his limbs and opened his eyes, when he tendered his proposal. "That's the very thing I came here for," he answered; "I am quite ready to enter the King's service." So he was received with all honour, and given a special house of his own to live in.

But the other officers resented the success of the little tailor, and wished him a thousand miles away. "What's to come of it all?" they asked each other; "if we quarrel with him, he'll let out at us, and at every blow seven will fall. There'll soon be an end of us." So they resolved to go in a body to the King, and all to send in their papers. "We are not made," they said, "to hold out against a man who kills seven at a blow." The King was grieved at the thought of losing all his faithful servants for the sake of one man, and he wished heartily that he had never set eyes on him, or that he could get rid of him. But he didn't dare to send him away, for he feared he might kill him along with his people, and place himself on the throne. He pondered long and deeply over the matter, and finally came to a conclusion. He sent to the tailor and told him that, seeing what a great and warlike hero he was, he was about to make him an offer. In a certain wood of his kingdom there dwelt two giants who did much harm; by the way they robbed, murdered, burnt, and plundered everything about them; "no one could approach them without endangering his life. But if he could overcome and kill these two giants he should have his only daughter for a wife, and half his kingdom into the bargain; he might have a hundred horsemen, too, to back him up." "That's the very thing for a man like me," thought the little tailor; "one doesn't get the offer of a beautiful princess and half a kingdom every day." "Done with you," he answered; "I'll soon put an end to the giants. But I haven't the smallest need of your hundred horsemen; a fellow who can slay seven men at a blow need not be afraid of two."

The little tailor set out, and the hundred horsemen followed him. When he came to the outskirts of the wood he said to his followers: "You wait here, I'll manage the giants by myself;" and he went on into the wood, casting his sharp little eyes right and left about him. After a while he spied the two giants lying asleep under a tree, and snoring till the very boughs bent with the breeze. The little tailor lost no time in filling his wallet with stones, and then climbed up the tree under which they lay. When he got to about the middle of it he slipped along a branch till he sat just above the sleepers, when he threw down one stone after the other on the nearest giant. The giant felt nothing for a long time, but at last he woke up, and pinching his companion said: "What did you strike me for?" "I didn't strike you," said the other "you must be dreaming." They both lay down to sleep again, and the tailor threw down a stone on the second giant, who sprang up and cried: "What's that for? Why did you throw something at me?" "I didn't throw anything," growled the first one. They wrangled on for a time, till, as both were tired, they made up the matter and fell asleep again. The little tailor began his game once more, and flung the largest stone he could find in his wallet with all his force, and hit the first giant on the chest. "This is too much of a good thing!" he yelled, and springing up like a madman, he knocked his companion against the tree till he trembled. He gave, however, as good as he got, and they became so enraged that they tore up trees and beat each other with them, till they both fell dead at once on the ground. Then the little tailor jumped down. "It's a mercy," he said, "that they didn't root up the tree on which I was perched, or I should have had to jump like a squirrel on to another, which, nimble though I am, would have been no easy job." He drew his sword and gave each of the giants a very fine thrust or two on the breast, and then went to the horsemen and said: "The deed is done, I've put an end to the two of them; but I assure you it has been no easy matter, for they even tore up trees in their struggle to defend themselves; but all that's of no use against one who slays seven men at a blow." "Weren't you wounded?"

asked the horsemen. "No fear," answered the tailor; "they haven't touched a hair of my head." But the horsemen wouldn't believe him till they rode into the wood and found the giants weltering in their blood, and the trees lying around, torn up by the roots.

The little tailor now demanded the promised reward from the King, but he repented his promise, and pondered once more how he could rid himself of the hero. "Before you obtain the hand of my daughter and half my kingdom," he said to him, "you must do another deed of valour. A unicorn is running about loose in the wood, and doing much mischief; you must first catch it." "I'm even less afraid of one unicorn than of two giants; seven at a blow, that's my motto." He took a piece of cord and an axe with him, went out to the wood, and again told the men who had been sent with him to remain outside. He hadn't to search long, for the unicorn soon passed by, and, on perceiving the tailor, dashed straight at him as though it were going to spike him on the spot. "Gently, gently," said he, "not so fast, my friend;" and standing still he waited till the beast was quite near, when he sprang lightly behind a tree; the unicorn ran with all its force against the tree, and rammed its horn so firmly into the trunk that it had no strength left to pull it out again, and was thus successfully captured. "Now I've caught my bird," said the tailor, and he came out from behind the tree, placed the cord round its neck first, then struck the horn out of the tree with his axe, and when everything was in order led the beast before the King.

Still the King didn't want to give him the promised reward, and made a third demand. The tailor was to catch a wild boar for him that did a great deal of harm in the wood; and he might have the huntsmen to help him. "Willingly," said the tailor; "that's mere child's play." But he didn't take the huntsmen into the wood with him, and they were well enough pleased to remain behind, for the wild boar had often received them in a manner which did not make them desire its further acquaintance. As soon as the boar perceived the tailor it ran at him with foaming mouth and gleaming teeth, and tried to knock him down; but our alert little friend ran into a chapel that stood near, and got out of the window again with a jump. The boar pursued him into the church, but the tailor skipped round to the door, and closed it securely. So the raging beast was caught, for it was far too heavy and unwieldy to spring out of the window. The little tailor summoned the huntsmen together, that they might see the prisoner with their own eyes. Then the hero betook himself to the King, who was obliged now, whether he liked it or not, to keep his promise, and hand him over his daughter and half his kingdom. Had he known that no hero-warrior, but only a little tailor stood before him, it would have gone even more to his heart. So the wedding was celebrated with much splendour and little joy, and the tailor became a king.

After a time the Queen heard her husband saying one night in his sleep: "My lad, make that waistcoat and patch these trousers, or I'll box your ears." Thus she learnt in what rank the young gentleman had been born, and next day she poured forth her woes to her father, and begged him to help her to get rid of a husband who was nothing more nor less than a tailor. The King comforted her, and said: "Leave your bedroom door open to-night, my servants shall stand outside, and when your husband is fast asleep they shall enter, bind him fast, and carry him on to a ship, which shall sail away out into the wide ocean." The Queen was well satisfied with the idea, but the armour-bearer, who had overheard everything, being much attached to his young master, went straight to him and revealed the whole plot. "I'll soon put a stop to the business," said the tailor. That night he and his wife went to bed at the usual time; and when she thought he had fallen asleep she got up, opened the door, and then lay down again. The little tailor, who had only pretended to be asleep, began to call out in a clear voice: "My lad, make that waistcoat and patch those trousers, or I'll box your ears.

I have killed seven at a blow, slain two giants, led a unicorn captive, and caught a wild boar, then why should I be afraid of those men standing outside my door?" The men, when they heard the tailor saying these words, were so terrified that they fled as if pursued by a wild army, and didn't dare go near him again. So the little tailor was and remained a king all the days of his life.

THE MASTER CAT; OR, PUSS IN BOOTS

(French)

Derived from Charles Perrault

The clever tricks of Puss in Boots succeed in creating an entirely new persona for his poor young master. Through one sharp maneuver after another, the poor young fellow is transformed into the rich, handsomely dressed owner of a castle and vast estate. Puss, the creator of this illusion, is the real hero of the story, which has a great deal to say about the value of appearances in a materialistic world.

There was a miller who left no more estate to the three sons he had than his mill, his ass, and his cat. The partition was soon made. Neither the scrivener nor attorney was sent for. They would soon have eaten up all the poor patrimony. The eldest had the mill, the second the ass, and the youngest nothing but the cat.

The poor young fellow was quite comfortless at having so poor a lot.

"My brothers," said he, "may get their living handsomely enough by joining their stocks together; but, for my part, when I have eaten up my cat, and made me a muff of his skin, I must die of hunger."

The Cat, who heard all this, but made as if he did not, said to him with a grave and serious air:

From an old English version of the eighteenth century (1729), as reproduced in *The Blue Fairy Book*, edited by Andrew Lang (London, 1889). Illustrated by G. P. Jacomb Hood.

"Do not thus afflict yourself, my good master; you have nothing else to do but to give me a bag, and get a pair of boots made for me, that I may scamper through the dirt and the brambles, and you shall see that you have not so bad a portion of me as you imagine."

The Cat's master did not build very much upon what he said; he had, however, often seen him play a great many cunning tricks to catch rats and mice; as when he used to hang by the heels, or hide himself in the meal, and make as if he were dead; so that he did not altogether despair of his affording him some help in his miserable condition. When the Cat had what he asked for, he booted himself very gallantly, and, putting his bag about his neck, he held the strings of it in his two fore paws, and went into a warren where was great abundance of rabbits. He put bran and sow-thistle into his bag, and, stretching out at length, as if he had been dead, he waited for some young rabbits, not yet acquainted with the deceits of the world, to come and rummage his bag for what he had put into it.

Scarce was he lain down but he had what he wanted: a rash and foolish young rabbit jumped into his bag, and Monsieur Puss, immediately drawing close the strings, took and killed him without pity. Proud of his prey, he went with it to the palace, and asked to speak with his Majesty. He was shown upstairs into the King's apartment, and, making a low reverence, said to him:

"I have brought you, sir, a rabbit of the warren, which my noble Lord, the Master of Carabas" (for that was the title which Puss was pleased to give his master) "has commanded me to present to your Majesty from him."

"Tell thy master," said the King, "that I thank him, and that he does me a great deal of pleasure."

Another time he went and hid himself among some standing corn, holding still his bag open; and, when a brace of partridges ran into it, he drew the strings, and so caught them both. He went and made a present of these to the King, as he had done before of the rabbit which he took in the warren. The King, in like manner, received the partridges with great pleasure, and ordered him some money, to drink.

The Cat continued for two or three months thus to carry his Majesty, from time to time, game of his master's taking. One day in particular, when he knew for certain that he was to take the air along the river-side, with his daughter, the most beautiful princess in the world, he said to his master:

"If you will follow my advice your fortune is made. You have nothing else to do but go and wash yourself in the river, in that part I shall show you, and leave the rest to me."

The Marquis of Carabas did what the Cat advised him to, without knowing why or wherefore. While he was washing the King passed by, and the Cat began to cry out:

"Help! help! My Lord Marquis of

Carabas is going to be drowned."

At this noise the King put his head out of the coach-window, and, finding it was the Cat who had so often brought him such good game, he commanded his guards to run immediately to the assistance of his Lordship the Marquis of Carabas. While they were drawing the poor Marquis out of the river, the Cat came up to the coach and told the King that, while his master was washing, there came by some rogues, who went off with his clothes, though he had cried out: "Thieves! thieves!" several times, as loud as he could.

This cunning Cat had hidden them under a great stone. The King immediately commanded the officers of his wardrobe to run and fetch one of his best suits for the Lord Marquis of Carabas.

The King caressed him after a very extraordinary manner, and as the fine clothes he had given him extremely set off his good mien (for he was well made and very handsome in his person), the King's daughter took a secret inclination to him, and the Marquis of Carabas had no sooner cast two or three respectful and somewhat tender glances but she fell in love with him to distraction. The King would needs have him come into the coach and take part of the airing. The Cat, quite overjoyed to see his project begin to succeed, marched on before, and, meeting with some countrymen, who were mowing a meadow, he said to them:

"Good people, you who are mowing, if you do not tell the King that the meadow you mow belongs to my Lord Marquis of Carabas, you shall be chopped as small as herbs for the pot."

The King did not fail asking of the mowers to whom the meadow they were mowing belonged.

"To my Lord Marquis of Carabas," answered they altogether, for the Cat's threats had made them terribly afraid.

"You see, sir," said the Marquis, "this is a meadow which never fails to yield a plentiful harvest every year."

The Master Cat, who went still on before, met with some reapers, and said to them:

"Good people, you who are reaping, if you do not tell the King that all this corn belongs to the Marquis of Carabas, you shall be chopped as small as herbs for the pot."

The King, who passed by a moment after, would needs know to whom all that corn, which he then saw, did belong.

"To my Lord Marquis of Carabas," replied the reapers, and the King was very well pleased with it, as well as the Marquis, whom he congratulated thereupon. The Master Cat, who went always before, said the same words to all he met, and the King was astonished at the vast estates of my Lord Marquis of Carabas.

Monsieur Puss came at last to a stately castle, the master of which was an ogre, the richest that had ever been known; for all the lands which the King had then gone over belonged to this castle. The Cat, who had taken care to inform himself who this ogre was and what he could do, asked to speak with him, saying he could not pass so near his castle without having the honour of paying his respects to him.

The ogre received him as civilly as an ogre could do, and made him sit down.

"I have been assured," said the Cat, "that you have the gift of being able to change youself into all sorts of creatures you have a mind to; you can, for example, transform yourself into a lion, or elephant, and the like."

"That is true," answered the ogre very briskly; "and to convince you, you shall see me now become a lion."

Puss was so sadly terrified at the sight of a lion so near him that he immediately got into the gutter, not without abundance of trouble and danger, because of his boots, which were of no use at all to him in walking upon the tiles. A little while after, when Puss saw that the ogre had resumed his natural form, he came down, and owned he had been very much frightened.

"I have been moreover informed," said the Cat, "but I know not how to believe it, that you have also the power to take on you the shape of the smallest animals; for example, to change yourself into a rat or a mouse; but I must own to you I take this to be impossible."

"Impossible!" cried the ogre; "you shall see that presently."

And at the same time he changed himself into a mouse, and began to run about the floor. Puss no sooner perceived this but he fell upon him and ate him up.

Meanwhile the King, who saw, as he passed, this fine castle of the ogre's, had a mind to go into it. Puss, who heard the noise of his Majesty's coach running over the draw-bridge, ran out, and said to the King:

"Your Majesty is welcome to this castle of my Lord Marquis of Carabas."

"What! my Lord Marquis," cried the King, "and does this castle also belong to you? There can be nothing finer than this court and all the stately buildings which surround it; let us go into it, if you please."

The Marquis gave his hand to the Princess, and followed the King, who went first. They passed into a spacious hall, where they found a magnificent collation, which the ogre had prepared for his friends, who were that very day to visit him, but dared not to enter, knowing the King was there. His Majesty was perfectly charmed with the good qualities of my Lord Marquis of Carabas, as was his daughter, who had fallen violently in love with him, and, seeing the vast estate he possessed, said to him, after having drunk five or six glasses:

"It will be owing to yourself only, my Lord Marquis, if you are not my son-in-law."

The Marquis, making several low bows, accepted the honour which his Majesty conferred upon him, and forthwith, that very same day, married the Princess.

Puss became a great lord, and never ran after mice any more but only for his diversion.

Fantasy

THE EMPEROR'S NEW CLOTHES

Hans Christian Andersen

The saying "Clothes make the man" refers to the idea of clothing as a mask. This idea can be extended to include manners and possessions, as well as clothing—all the outer trappings that are used to impress people with the importance of a personage, such as the vain Emperor of this story, and to create what we today would call his "image." Andersen, from the bitterness of personal experience, is mocking fools in high places and the stupidity of people who do not see them as they really are.

Many years ago there lived an Emperor who was so exceedingly fond of fine new clothes that he spent all his money on rich dresses. He did not care for his soldiers, nor for the theatre, nor for driving about, except for the purpose of showing his new clothes.

He had a dress for every hour of the day, and just as they say of a king, "He is in Council," they always said of him, "The Emperor is in his Wardrobe."

Well, the great town in which he lived was very busy. Every day a number of strangers arrived.

One day two rogues came along, saying they were weavers, and that they knew how to weave the finest stuff one could imagine. Not only, said they, were the colours and designs exceedingly beautiful, but the clothes that were made of their material had the wonderful quality of being invisible to everybody who was either unfit for his position, or was extraordinarily stupid.

"They must be splendid clothes," thought the Emperor; "by wearing them I could easily discover what persons in my kingdom are unfit for their posts. I could distinguish the wise from the stupid. I must have that stuff woven for me at once!" So he gave the two rogues a large sum of money, in order that they might begin their work without delay.

The rogues put up two looms, and pretended to be working, but they had nothing at all in the frames. Again and again they demanded the finest silks and the most magnificent gold thread, but they put it all in their own pockets, and worked at their empty looms late into the night.

"Now, I should like to know how far they have got on with that stuff," thought the Emperor; but he felt quite uncomfort-

Translated by W. Angeldorff.

able when he remembered that those who were stupid or unfit for their positions could not see it. He did not think for a moment that he had anything to fear for himself; but nevertheless, he would rather send somebody else first to see how the stuff was getting on.

Everybody in the town knew what a remarkable quality the stuff possessed, and each was anxious to see how bad or how stupid his neighbours were.

"I will send my honest old minister to the weavers," thought the Emperor; "he can judge best how the stuff looks, for he is intelligent, and no one is better fit for his office than he."

So the clever old minister went out into the hall, where the two rogues were sitting at work on their empty looms.

"Goodness me!" he thought, and opened his eyes wide; "I cannot see anything," but he did not say so. Both of the rogues begged him to be so kind as to step nearer, and asked him was it not a pretty design, and were not the colours beautiful, and they pointed to the empty looms.

But the poor old minister kept on opening his eyes wider and wider: he could not see anything, for there was nothing there.

"Goodness me!" he thought; "am I really stupid? I never thought so, and nobody must know it. Am I really unfit for my office? No; I must certainly not tell anybody that I cannot see the stuff."

"Well, what do you think of it?" asked the one who was weaving.

"Oh, it is beautiful! most magnificent!" replied the old minister, and looked through his spectacles. "What a pattern! and what colours! Yes, I must tell the Emperor that I like it very much indeed."

"Ah! we are very glad of that," said both weavers, and then they described the colours, and explained the strange patterns.

The old minister listened attentively, so as to be able to repeat it all when he returned to the Emperor, and this he did.

The rogues now asked for more money, and for more silk and gold thread, which they required for weaving. They put everything into their pockets, and not a thread went on the frames, but nevertheless they continued to work at the empty looms.

Soon afterwards the Emperor sent another clever statesman to see how the weaving was getting on, and whether the stuff was nearly ready. The same thing happened to him as to the minister; he looked and looked, but as there was nothing on the empty frames, he could not see anything.

"Now, is not that a beautiful piece of stuff?" said both rogues, and described the beauty of the pattern, which did not exist at all.

"I am not stupid," thought the statesman, "so it must be that I am unfit for the high position I hold; that is very strange, but I must not let anybody notice it." So he praised the piece of stuff which he could not see, and said how pleased he was with the beautiful colours and the pretty pattern.

"Oh! it is really magnificent!" he said to the Emperor.

All the people in the town were talking about the beautiful stuff, and the Emperor himself wished to see it while it was still on the loom. With a whole suite of chosen courtiers, among whom were the two honest old statesmen who had been there before, the Emperor went to the two cunning rogues, who were now weaving as fast as they could, but without thread or shuttle.

"Well! is it not magnificent?" cried the two clever statesmen; "does your majesty recognise how beautiful is the pattern, how charming the colours?" and they pointed to the empty looms, for they thought that the others could see the stuff.

"What?" thought the Emperor; "I cannot see anything; this is terrible! Am I stupid; or am I not fit to be Emperor? This would be the most dreadful thing that could happen to me! Yes, it is very beautiful," he said at last; "we give our highest approbation"; and he nodded as if he were quite satisfied, and gazed at the empty looms.

He would not say that he saw nothing,

and the whole of his suite looked and looked; but, like the others, they were unable to see anything. So they said, just like the Emperor, "Yes, it is very pretty," and they advised him to have some clothes made from this magnificent stuff, and to wear them for the first time at the great procession that was about to take place. "It is magnificent! beautiful! excellent!" they said one to another, and they were all so exceedingly pleased with it that the Emperor gave the two rogues a decoration to be worn in the button-hole, and the title "Imperial Weavers."

The rogues worked throughout the whole of the night preceding the day of the procession, and had over sixteen candles alight, so that people should see how busy they were in preparing the Emperor's new clothes.

They pretended to take the stuff off the looms, cut it in the air with great scissors, and sewed with needles without thread, and at last they said—

"See! now the clothes are ready!"

The Emperor, followed by his most distinguished courtiers, came in person, and the rogues lifted their arms up in the air, just as if they held something, and said, "See! here are the trousers, here is the coat, here is the cloak," and so forth. "It is all as light as a cobweb; one might imagine one had nothing on, but that is just the beauty of it!"

"Yes," said all the courtiers; but they could not see anything, because there was nothing.

"Will your imperial highness condescend to undress?" said the rogues; "we will then attire your majesty in the new clothes, here, in front of the mirror."

"Oh! how well they look! how beautifully they fit!" said everyone; "what a pattern! what colours! It is indeed a magnificent dress."

"They are standing outside with the canopy which is to be carried over your majesty in the procession," announced the Master of the Ceremonies.

"Well, I am ready," said the Emperor. "Does it not fit me well!" and he turned again to the mirror, for he wanted it to appear that he was admiring his rich costume.

The chamberlains who were to carry the train fumbled with their hands on the floor just as if they were holding the train up; they raised their hands in the air, but dared not let anybody notice that they saw nothing: and so the Emperor went in procession beneath the magnificent canopy, and all the people in the street and at the windows said: "Oh! how beautiful the Emperor's new clothes are; what a splendid train, and how well everything fits!"

No one would admit that he could see nothing, for that would have shown that he was either unfit for his post or very stupid. None of the Emperor's dresses had ever been so much admired.

"But he has nothing on at all!" said a little child.

"Just hear the voice of the innocent," said his father, and one whispered to the other what the child had said. " 'He has nothing on,' says a little child; 'he has nothing on!' "

"But he has nothing on," cried the whole of the people at last; and the Emperor shivered, for it seemed to him that they were right.

But he thought to himself, "I must go through with the procession," and he walked with even greater dignity than before; and the chamberlains followed, carrying the train which did not exist at all.

Shadows

Fable

THE DOG AND THE SHADOW

Aesop

In this fable the word "shadow" is used in two ways: to mean a reflected image and a vain and unsubstantial object of pursuit, contrasted with the tangible reality that substance possesses.

It happened that a Dog had got a piece of meat and was carrying it home in his mouth to eat it in peace. Now on his way home he had to cross a plank lying across a running brook. As he crossed, he looked down and saw his own shadow reflected in the water beneath. Thinking it was another dog with another piece of meat, he made up his mind to have that also. So he made a snap at the shadow in the water, but as he opened his mouth the piece of meat fell out, dropped into the water and was never seen more.

Beware lest you lose the substance by grasping at the shadow.

From *The Fables of Aesop,* edited by Joseph Jacobs (1894). Illustrated by Richard Heighway.

Folk Rhymes

In psychological terms, one of the definitions of the "shadow" is "that which is kept hidden away because it is unacceptable to the world" (see Esther Harding's essay "The Shadow" at the end of this section for further discussion of this idea). But in such an all-inclusive, unself-conscious form of literature as folk rhymes, we find the shadow displayed for all to see.

* * *

The smugness of Jack Horner may hide an act that suggests a serious character flaw, certainly one that belongs to the "shadow" side. Traditionally, Jack is supposed to have stolen a deed to a rich Catholic manor. That is, he "pulled out a plum" from a pie of such deeds which he was to present to Henry VIII. This in itself is simple theft, but according to the story, to ensure his hold on the land, he sat in judgment of the abbot responsible for the land and voted to have him hanged, drawn, and quartered.

Little Jack Horner sat in the corner
  Eating his Christmas pie.
He put in his thumb and pulled out a
    plum,
  And said "What a good boy am I!"

Thieves are common in folk rhymes. Two other famous ones are Tom, the piper's son, and the Knave of Hearts (see following rhyme). The "pig" referred to in line two is not a real pig, but a pastry one. In the eighteenth century, pigs made of paste, with currant filling and two currant eyes, were hawked in the streets of English towns.

Tom, Tom, the piper's son,
Stole a pig and away did run.
The pig was eat, and Tom was beat,
And Tom went roaring down the street.

The following rhyme is known today because of its inclusion by Lewis Carroll in Alice in Wonderland. *The version he used is briefer (first six lines only) and is used to build a chapter around (Chapter XI, "Who Stole the Tarts?").*

  The Queen of Hearts
  She made some tarts,
All on a summer's day;
  The Knave of Hearts
  He stole the tarts,
And took them clean away.
  The King of Hearts
  Called for the tarts,
And beat the Knave full sore;
  The Knave of Hearts
  Brought back the tarts,
And vow'd he'd steal no more.

The ringing of the bell serves as an alarm in this rhyme, but it also carries the feeling of a perverse delight and excitement at the cat's being put in the well. In rhymes like this, children have the satisfaction of hearing a wicked thought expressed, but having it safely contained again almost at once (in the last six lines).

The refrain "Ding dong bell" is very old. Shakespeare uses it in songs in both The Merchant of Venice *and* The Tempest, *and it goes back at least to the sixteenth century.*

Ding dong bell,
The cat is in the well,
Who put her in?
Little Johnny Green,
Who pulled her out?
Little Tommy Stout.
What a naughty boy was that,
To try to drown poor pussy cat,
Who never did him any harm,
And kill'd the mice in his father's barn.

In the world of the imagination, the child can respond violently when inner imps ("blackbirds") are accusing.

As I went over the water,
The water went over me,
I saw two little blackbirds sitting on a
tree:
The one called me rascal,
The other called me thief;
I took my little black stick,
And knocked out all their teeth!

Bad acts in a nursery rhyme are often magically reversed: stolen tarts are brought back again; the cat is retrieved from the well; the spider thrown to the bottom of the stairs is thrown up again. This allows the child to identify safely with the naughtiness described in the verse, and the shadow can be released in a healthy way.

Old Father Long-Legs
Can't say his prayers:
Take him by the left leg,
And throw him down stairs.
And when he's at the bottom,
Before he long has lain,
Take him by the right leg,
And throw him up again.

The frightening feeling of being scared by a strange creature like a spider can be less frightening when nursery rhyme tells children this reaction is natural.

Little Miss Muffet
Sat on a tuffet,
Eating her curds and whey;
There came a big spider,
Who sat down beside her
And frightened Miss Muffet away.

Crookedness belongs to the shadow, and is therefore avoided. There is a natural relief, then, as an entire rhyme lets everything be crooked.

William and Ceil Baring-Gould, editors of The Annotated Mother Goose *(1962), suggest that the crooked man of this rhyme may have been General Sir Alexander Leslie of Scotland; the "crooked sixpence," his antagonist Charles I; the "crooked stile," the border between England and Scotland; and the "crooked house," the understanding the two reached at last. Whether this is true or not, there are political implications in many children's rhymes.*

There was a crooked man, and he
walked a crooked mile,
He found a crooked sixpence against a
crooked stile;
He bought a crooked cat, which caught
a crooked mouse,
And they all lived together in a little
crooked house.

Folktales

THE ELK'S HEAD

(American Indian—Winnebago)

Retold by Paul Radin

Trickster stories appear in many cultures, and the story-cycle of the Winnebago Indians, from which the following tale is taken, is believed to be the most archaic one dealing with this strange, clownish figure. Because the amoral trickster represents a stage of primitive consciousness, people who listen to stories about him can look at him humorously—and feel superior because they are no longer so stupid, greedy, or foolish as he is. The Winnebago story that follows is full of laughter and irony, and we can imagine the hilarity of the tribe as the tale was recounted.

We have encountered the trickster earlier in this anthology, in the rough jesting of Punch and Judy *("Toys and Games") and in such characters as the Madman of Naranath and Shrewd Todie ("Fools"). C. G. Jung has pointed out that the trickster can appear in a modern person, as a kind of second, inferior personality—childish and full of mischief—and has identified this component as the "shadow."*

As he was running along, he came to a valley. There he heard someone beating a drum, the drumming followed by many war whoops. Somebody there was making a great noise. So loud was this noise that it seemed to reach the skies. "Well, I wonder what these people are up to? I guess I will go over and see for I have not had any fun for a long time. Whatever they are doing, I will join them. If they are going to dance, why I will dance too. I used to be a fine dancer." Thus Trickster spoke. Then, as he walked across the valley, again and again he heard that noise. Everyone was shouting with joy. It was wonderful! "Ah! There must be many people over there," he was thinking to himself. Again he heard them shout and, once again, when the drum was beaten, it seemed as if the heavens would burst asunder. Then again the people gave a tremendous shout. Now he became so anxious to join them that he began to run. The shouting was now quite close to him. Yet he could see no one anywhere. Again he heard the shouting. It was very loud. It sounded as if the sky would burst asunder.

To him it seemed as if, even at that moment, he was walking in the midst of people shouting. Yet he did not see anything. Not far away, however, he saw, lying around, the bones of an animal and, farther still, he saw an object that turned out, on closer inspection, to be an elk's skull. It had many horns branching in every direction. He watched this head quite carefully and then he saw where the noise had come from and where the celebration was taking place. It was in the elk's skull. The head was filled with many flies. They would go inside and then, when they rushed out, they made the noise that he had heard and which he had taken to be shouting. He looked at the flies and he saw that they were enjoying themselves greatly and he envied them.

"Well, I said that I would join in whatever they were doing and I am going to. I wonder what I would have to do in order to join them?" Thus pondered Trickster. Then he said, "Younger brothers, you are certainly having a lot of fun. You surely are doing an important thing. I would very much like to be like one of you. How can I do it? Do show me how I can do it so that I, too, can join you." Thus he spoke. Then they answered him, "Well, there is no difficulty involved. We enter through the neck as you must have seen by this time." Thus they spoke. Then Trickster tried to enter but failed. He wanted very much to enter but he was unable. "How do you manage to get in, my younger brothers?" he asked. Great man that he was, he could not accomplish it, much as he wished to! Then they said to him, "If you wish to come in just say, 'Neck, become large!' and it will become large. In that way you can enter. That is the way we do it." Thus they told him.

So he sat down and said, "Neck, become large!" and the hole in the neck became large. Then he put his head in and entered. He put his head in up to his neck. All the flies ran away and the opening into which he had thrust his head became small again. Thus he was held fast. He tried to free himself exerting all his power but it was of no avail. He could do absolutely nothing. He was unable to free his head from the skull of the elk. When he realized that nothing could be done, he went down to the stream wearing the skull. He had long branching antlers, for he was wearing an elk's skull. When he came to the river he walked along the edge, and as he went along he came to a place inhabited by human beings. There he waited until night. The next morning he did the following. As soon as the people came to get water from the river, he stretched himself out and lay there with his raccoon-skin blanket, quite a fear-inspiring object to look upon. His whole body was covered with the raccoon-skin blanket and he had long branching horns on his head.

Early in the morning a woman came for water and saw him. She started to run back but he said to her, "Turn back; I will bless you!" So she turned back and when she got there, he said to her, "Now, go home. Get an axe and bring it over here. Then use all the offerings that are customary, of which your relations will tell you. If you strike the top of my head with the axe, you will be able to use what you find therein as medicine and obtain anything that you wish. I am an elk-spirit. I am blessing this village." Thus he spoke to her. Then he continued, "I am one of the great spirits living in these waters."

So the woman went home and when she got there she told all the people what had happened. "There is a waterspirit at the place where we dip for water who blessed me. He told me that he had a 'medicine-chest' in the box that he carried and that if we brought an axe and suitable offerings, placed them there and then split his head open, what we found within his skull we could use for making various medicines." Thus she spoke.

Thereupon the people went to the river with their various offerings and, sure enough, there they found him, quite fear-inspiring to look upon. The offerings—red feathers, white deer skin, and red-yarn belts—they brought in great quantities. After they had placed all these things before him, they selected a man who was to take the axe. He struck the skull and split it open and behold! there they found Trickster laughing at them. He arose and said, "A nice head-dress I have been wearing but now you have spoiled it!" Then he laughed uproariously. When he got up the people said, "It is Trickster!" However, he spoke to them and said, "Inasmuch as you have made these offerings to me they will not be lost. For whatsoever be the purpose for which you use this head, that purpose will be accomplished." So then they made themselves various medicinal instruments and afterwards found that they were efficacious. Then Trickster left and continued wandering.

FOX BOY AND HIS SHADOW

(American Indian—California)

Retold by Jaime de Angulo

Jaime de Angulo, a professional linguist, worked and lived among the California Indians. Drawing on his experience and the tales he heard, he wrote these stories for his own children. In them he trapped the Indian spirit so effectively that poets like William Carlos Williams and Ezra Pound praised his work. In the spirit of very primitive tales, all process is seen as action; and man, animals, inanimate objects such as shadows—all of nature—are depicted as an indistinguishable whole.

The next morning Bear woke up early, long before the sun was up. It was the very beginning of the break of dawn when Bear sat up and started to sing. He was singing softly to himself, sort of humming. Then he got up and stretched himself and went to the spring to wash his face. He started a campfire while it was yet all dark. Then he started to cook breakfast. He was heating stones, small round stones.

Illustrated by the author.

"Mother, what was he singing? Who is that man he said was coming over the mountains from the east singing with the daylight?"

"Oh, he was singing about his shadow. That song is what the shadow sings. Your shadow, also. You must make him sing that way in the morning. Everybody's shadow comes home in the dawn, singing like that."

"But what do you mean, 'comes home'?"

"Sure, he comes home to you, your shadow does. You are his home."

"But where has he been?"

"Oh, he's been going around during the night, visiting, going places, and in the morning he comes home to you."

"Does he always come?"

"No, sometimes he gets lost. That's why your father was singing. We are in a strange place; his shadow might be wandering around, looking for him. But if the shadow hears him singing, he says to himself, 'Oh, that's me over there. That's where I belong.' "

"And if he gets lost, what happens then?"

"Then you get sick and you die. You can't keep on living without your shadow."

Fox Boy thought a moment, then he said, "But Father is not going to die because he's singing and his shadow must have heard him. I'd better sing too, so my shadow will hear me."

"Do you think you can remember the song? Listen, we'll sing it together.

I'm coming, I'm coming. Over the mountains I come home.
I'm coming, I'm coming. With the daylight I come home.
I'm coming, I'm coming. From the east I come home.

Now, look, we'd better get up and help Bear cook breakfast."

So they got up and washed their faces at the spring. Then Antelope took some acorn flour and made a mush. Then she picked some hot stones from the fire with a couple of sticks and dropped them into the mush which was in a small basket. The hot stones made a hissing sound, *hwishshshshhh, hwishshshshsh, hwish.* Pretty soon the mush was bubbling and boiling. Little Fox Boy couldn't wait. He put his two fingers in the mush.

"Ouch!" he yelled, jumping up and down and shaking his fingers.

"Well, why don't you wait and let it cool a little? Nobody is going to take it away from you. Take your time, take your time. It never was that people couldn't wait a minute. Watch me. Watch how I do it."

Now Antelope deftly scooped some mush with her two fingers and she licked them off, quickly, just like that!

"That's the way to do it," she said.

"Oh, I can do that, myself," said Fox. He was so quick that he smeared his nose with the mush, and they all laughed.

Breakfast over, they rolled up their things, shouldered their packs and started traveling again, *tras* . . . *tras* . . . *tras* . . . up the trail, *tras* . . . *tras* . . . *tras* . . . down the trail, *tras* . . . *tras* . . . *tras* . . . along the level trail. They traveled all day, and that night they made their camp by a little stream. And Little Fox Boy crawled in between Bear and Antelope under the rabbitskin blanket and was soon fast asleep.

THE TWO TRAVELERS

(German)

This story collected by the Brothers Grimm is a typical shadow story of a good-hearted tailor and a mean-spirited shoemaker. These two are clear-cut opposites in several ways: the tailor is optimistic, cheerful, extroverted, by profession concerned with appearances; the shoemaker is pessimistic, gloomy, introverted, and by profession concerned with the humblest, most grounded article of clothing—shoes. These characters can be said to represent the dual nature of humanity. In this story the struggle is not resolved in unifying the two sides, but in simply getting rid of the more unpleasant one.

Hill and vale do not meet, but the children of men do, good and bad. In this way a shoemaker and a tailor once met on their travels. The tailor was a handsome little fellow who was always merry and full of enjoyment. He saw the shoemaker coming towards him from the other side, and as he observed by his bag what kind of a trade he plied, he sang a little mocking song to him:

"Sew me the seam,
Draw me the thread,
Spread it over with pitch,
Knock the nail on the head."

The shoemaker, however, could not bear a joke; he pulled a face as if he had drunk vinegar, and made a gesture as if he were about to seize the tailor by the throat. But the little fellow began to laugh, reached him his bottle, and said: "No harm was meant, take a drink, and swallow your anger down." The shoemaker took a very hearty drink, and the storm on his face began to clear away. He gave the bottle back to the tailor, and said: "I took a hearty gulp; they say it comes from much drinking, but not from great thirst. Shall we travel together?" "All right," answered the tailor, "if only it suits you to go into a big town where there is no lack of work." "That is just where I want to go," answered the shoemaker. "In a small hamlet there is nothing to earn, and in the country, people like to go barefoot." They trav-

Translated by Margaret Hunt and James Stern.

eled therefore onwards together, and always set one foot before the other like a weasel in the snow.

Both of them had time enough, but little to bite and to break. When they reached a town they went about and paid their respects to the tradesmen, and because the tailor looked so lively and merry, and had such fine red cheeks, every one gave him work willingly, and when luck was good the master's daughters gave him a kiss beneath the porch, as well. When he again fell in with the shoemaker, the tailor had always the most in his bundle. The ill-tempered shoemaker made a wry face, and thought: "The greater the rascal the more the luck," but the tailor began to laugh and to sing, and shared all he got with his comrade. If a couple of pence jingled in his pockets, he ordered good cheer, and thumped the table in his joy till the glasses danced, and it was lightly come, lightly go, with him.

When they had traveled for some time, they came to a great forest through which passed the road to the capital. Two foot-paths, however, led through it, one of which was a seven days' journey, and the other only two, but neither of the travelers knew which way was the short one. They seated themselves beneath an oak-tree, and took counsel together how they should forecast, and for how many days they should provide themselves with bread. The shoemaker said: "One must look before one leaps, I will take with me bread for a week." "What!" said the tailor, "drag bread for seven days on one's back like a beast of burden, and not be able to look about. I shall trust in God, and not trouble myself about anything! The money I have in my pocket is as good in summer as in winter, but in hot weather bread gets dry, and moldy into the bargain; even my coat does not last as far as it might. Besides, why should we not find the right way? Bread for two days, and that's enough." Each, therefore, bought his own bread, and then they tried their luck in the forest.

It was as quiet there as in a church. No wind stirred, no brook murmured, no bird sang, and through the thickly leaved branches no sunbeam forced its way. The shoemaker spoke never a word, the bread weighed so heavily on his back that the sweat streamed down his cross and gloomy face. The tailor, however, was quite merry, he jumped about, whistled on a leaf, or sang a song, and thought to himself: "God in Heaven must be pleased to see me so happy."

This lasted two days, but on the third the forest would not come to an end, and the tailor had eaten up all his bread, so after all his heart sank down a yard deeper. Nevertheless, he did not lose courage, but relied on God and on his luck. On the evening of the third day he lay down hungry under a tree, and rose again next morning hungry still; so also passed the fourth day, and when the shoemaker seated himself on a fallen tree and devoured his dinner, the tailor was only a spectator. If he begged for a little piece of bread, the other laughed mockingly, and said: "You have always been so merry, now you can see for once what it is to be sad: the birds which sing too early in the morning are struck by the hawk in the evening." In short, he was pitiless. But on the fifth morning the poor tailor could no longer stand up, and was hardly able to utter one word for weakness; his cheeks were white, and his eyes red. Then the shoemaker said to him: "I will give you a bit of bread today, but in return for it, I will put out your right eye. The unhappy tailor, who still wished to save his life, had to submit; he wept once more with both eyes, and then held them out, and the shoemaker, who had a heart of stone, put out his right eye with a sharp knife. The tailor called to remembrance what his mother had formerly said to him when he had been eating secretly in the pantry. "Eat what one can, and suffer what one must." When he had consumed his dearly bought bread, he got on his legs again, forgot his misery and comforted himself with the thought that he could always see enough with one eye. But on the sixth day, hunger made itself felt again, and gnawed him almost to the heart. In the evening he fell down by a tree, and on the seventh morning he could not raise himself up for faintness, and death was close at hand. Then said the shoemaker: "I will show mercy and give you bread once more, but you shall not have it for nothing, I shall put out your other eye for it." And now the tailor felt how thoughtless his life had been, prayed to God for forgiveness, and said: "Do what you will, I will bear what I must, but remember that our Lord God does not always look on passively, and that an hour will come when the evil deed which you have done to me, and which I have not deserved of you, will be requited. When times were good with me, I shared what I had with you. My trade is of that kind that each stitch must always be exactly like the other. If I no longer have my eyes and can sew no more I must go abegging. At any rate do not leave me here alone when I am blind, or I shall die of hunger." The shoemaker, however, who had driven God out of his heart, took the knife and put out his left eye. Then he gave him a bit of bread to eat, held out a stick to him, and drew him on behind him.

When the sun went down, they got out of the forest, and before them in the open country stood the gallows. Thither the shoemaker guided the blind tailor, and then left him alone and went his way. Weariness, pain, and hunger made the wretched man fall asleep, and he slept the whole night. When day dawned he awoke, but knew not where he lay. Two poor sinners were hanging on the gallows, and a crow sat on the head of each of them. Then one of the men who had been hanged began to speak, and said: "Brother, are you awake?" "Yes, I am awake," answered the second. "Then I will tell you something," said the first; "the dew which this night has fallen down over us from the gallows, gives every one who washes himself with it his eyes again. If blind people did but know this, how many would regain their sight who do not believe that to be possible."

When the tailor heard that, he took his pocket-handkerchief, pressed it on the grass, and when it was moist with dew, washed the sockets of his eyes with it. Immediately was fulfilled what the man on the gallows had said, and a couple of healthy new eyes filled the sockets. It was not long before the tailor saw the sun rise behind the mountains; in the plain before him lay the great royal city with its magnificent gates and hundred towers, and the golden balls and crosses which were on the spires began to shine. He could distinguish every leaf on the trees, saw the birds which flew past, and the midges which danced in the air. He took a needle out of his pocket, and as he could thread it as well as ever he had done, his heart danced with delight. He threw himself on his knees, thanked God for the mercy he had shown him, and said his morning prayer. Nor did he forget to pray for the poor sinners who were hanging there swinging against each other in the wind like the pendulums of clocks. Then he took his bundle on his back and soon forgot the pain of heart he had endured, and went on his way singing and whistling.

The first thing he met was a brown foal running about the fields at large. He caught it by the mane, and wanted to spring on it and ride into the town. The foal, however, begged to be set free. "I am still too young," it said, "even a light tailor such as you are would break my back in two—let me go till I have grown strong. A time may perhaps come when I may reward you for it."

"Run off," said the tailor, "I see you are still a giddy thing." He gave it a touch with a switch over its back, whereupon it kicked up its hind legs for joy, leapt over hedges and ditches, and galloped away into the open country.

But the little tailor had eaten nothing since the day before. "The sun to be sure fills my eyes," said he, "but the bread does not fill my mouth. The first thing that comes my way and is even half edible will have to suffer for it." In the meantime a stork stepped solemnly over the meadow towards him. "Halt, halt!" cried the tailor, and seized him by the leg: "I don't know if you are good to eat or not, but my hunger leaves me no great choice. I must cut your head off, and roast you." "Don't do that," replied the stork; "I am a sacred bird which brings mankind great profit, and no one does me an injury. Leave me my life, and I may do you good in some other way." "Well, be off, Cousin Longlegs," said the tailor. The stork rose up, let its long legs hang down, and flew gently away.

"What's to be the end of this?" said the tailor to himself at last, "my hunger grows greater and greater, and my stomach more and more empty. Whatsoever comes in my way now is lost." At this moment he saw a couple of young ducks which were on a pond come swimming towards him. "You come just at the right moment," said he, and laid hold of one of them and was about to wring its neck. On this an old duck, which was hidden among the reeds, began to scream loudly, and swam to him with open beak, and begged him urgently to spare her dear children. "Can you not imagine," said she, "how your mother would mourn if any one wanted to carry you off, and give you your finishing stroke?" "Just be quiet," said the good-tempered tailor, "you shall keep your children," and put the prisoner back into the water.

When he turned round, he was standing in front of an old tree which was partly hollow, and saw some wild bees flying in and out of it. "There I shall at once find the reward of my good deed," said the tailor, "the honey will refresh me." But the Queen-bee came out, threatened him and said: "If you touch my people, and destroy my nest, our stings shall pierce your skin like ten thousand red-hot needles. But if you will leave us in peace and go your way, we will do you a service for it another time."

The little tailor saw that here also nothing was to be done. "Three dishes empty and nothing on the fourth is a bad dinner!" He dragged himself therefore with his starved-out stomach into the town, and as it was just striking twelve, all was ready-cooked for him in the inn, and he was able to sit down at once to dinner. When he was satisfied he said: "Now I will get to work." He went round the town, sought a master, and soon found a good situation. And as he had thoroughly learnt his trade, it was not long before he became famous, and every one wanted to have his new coat made by the little tailor, whose importance increased daily. "I can go no further in skill," said he, "and yet things improve every day." At last the King appointed him court-tailor.

But what odd things do happen in the world! On the very same day his former comrade the shoemaker also became court-shoemaker. When the latter caught sight of the tailor, and saw that he had once more two healthy eyes, his conscience troubled him. "Before he takes revenge on me," thought he to himself, "I must dig a pit for him." He, however, who digs a pit for another, falls into it himself. In the evening when work was over and it had grown dusk, he stole to the King and said: "Lord King, the tailor is an arrogant fellow and has boasted that he will get the gold crown back again which was lost in ancient times." "That would please me very much," said the King, and he caused the tailor to be brought before him next morning, and ordered him to get the crown back again, or to leave the town for ever. "Oho!" thought the tailor, "a rogue gives more than he has got. If the surly King wants me to do what can be done by no one, I will not wait till morning, but will go out of the town at once, to-day." He packed up his bundle, therefore, but when he was without the gate he could not help being sorry to give up his good fortune, and turn his back on the town in which all had gone so well with him. He came to the pond where he had made the acquaintance of the ducks; at that very moment the old one, whose young ones he had spared, was sitting there by the shore, pluming herself with her beak. She knew him again instantly, and asked why he was hanging his head so. "You will not be surprised when you hear what has befallen me," replied the tailor, and told her his fate. "If that be all," said the duck, "we can help you. The crown fell into the water, and lies down below at the bottom; we will soon bring it up again for you. In the meantime just spread out your handkerchief on the bank." She dived down with her twelve young ones, and in five minutes she was up again and sat with the crown resting on her wings, and the twelve young ones were swimming round about and had put their beaks under it, and were helping to carry it. They swam to the shore and put the crown on the handkerchief. No one can imagine how magnificent the crown was; when the sun shone on it, it gleamed like a hundred thousand carbuncles. The tailor tied his handkerchief together by the four corners, and carried it to the King, who was full of joy, and put a gold chain round the tailor's neck.

When the shoemaker saw that one blow had failed, he contrived a second, and went to the King and said: "Lord King, the tailor has become insolent again; he boasts that he will copy in wax the whole of the royal palace, with everything that pertains to it, loose or fast, inside and out." The King sent for the tailor and ordered him to copy in wax the whole of the royal palace, with everything that pertained to it, movable or immovable, within and without, and if he did not succeed in doing this, or if so much as one nail on the wall were wanting, he should be imprisoned for his whole life underground.

The tailor thought: "It gets worse and worse! No one can endure that!" and threw his bundle on his back, and went forth. When he came to the hollow tree, he sat down and hung his head. The bees came flying out, and the Queen-bee asked him if he had a stiff neck, since he hung his head so. "Alas, no," answered the tailor, "something quite different weighs me down," and he told her what the King had demanded of him. The bees began to buzz and hum amongst themselves, and the Queen-bee said: "Just go home again, but come back to-morrow at this time, and bring a large sheet with you, and then all will be well." So he turned back again, but the bees flew to the royal palace and straight into it through the open windows, crept round about into every corner, and inspected everything most carefully. Then they hurried back and modelled the palace in wax with such rapidity that any one looking on would have thought it was growing before his eyes. By the evening all was ready, and when the tailor came next morning, the whole of the splendid building was there, and not one nail in the wall or tile of the roof was wanting, and it was delicate withal, and white as snow, and smelt sweet as honey. The tailor wrapped it carefully in his cloth and took it to the King, who could not admire it enough, placed it in his largest hall, and in return for it presented the tailor with a large stone house.

The shoemaker, however, did not give up, but went for the third time to the King and said: "Lord King, it has come to the tailor's ears that no water will spring up in the court-yard of the castle, and he has boasted that it shall rise up in the midst of the court-yard to a man's height and be clear as crystal." Then the King ordered the tailor to be brought before him and said: "If a stream of water does not rise in my court-yard by to-morrow as you have promised, the executioner shall in that very place make you shorter by a head." The poor tailor did not take long to think about it, but hurried out to the gate, and because this time it was a matter of life and death to him, tears rolled down his face. Whilst he was thus going forth full of sorrow, the foal to which he had formerly given its liberty, and which had now become a beautiful chestnut horse, came leaping towards him. "The time has come," it said to the tailor, "when I can repay you for your good deed. I know already what is needful to you, but you shall soon have help; get on me, my back can carry two such as you." The tailor's courage came back to him; he jumped up in one bound, and the horse went full speed into the town, and right up to the court-yard of the castle. It galloped as quick as lightning thrice round it, and at the third time it fell violently down. At the same instant, however, there was a terrific clap of thunder, a fragment of earth in the middle of the court-yard sprang like a cannonball into the air, and over the castle, and directly after it a jet of water rose as high as a man on horseback, and the water was as pure as crystal, and the sunbeams began to dance on it. When the King saw this, he arose in amazement, and went and embraced the tailor in the sight of all men.

But good fortune did not last long. The King had daughters in plenty, one still prettier than the other, but he had no son. So the malicious shoemaker betook himself for the fourth time to the King, and said: "Lord King, the tailor has not given up his arrogance. He has now boasted that if he liked, he could cause a son to be brought to the Lord King through the air." The King commanded the tailor to be summoned, and said: "If you cause a son to be brought to me within nine days, you shall have my eldest daughter to wife." "The reward is indeed great," thought the little tailor; "one would willingly do something for it, but the cherries grow too high for me, if I climb for them, the bough will break beneath me, and I shall fall."

He went home, seated himself cross-legged on his work-table, and thought over what was to be done. "It can't be managed," cried he at last, "I will go away; after all, I can't live in peace here." He tied up his bundle and hurried away to the gate. When he got to the meadow, he perceived his old friend the stork, who was walking backwards and forwards like a philosopher. Sometimes he stood still, took a frog into close consideration, and at length swallowed it down. The stork came to him and greeted him. "I see," he began, "that you have your pack on your back. Why are you leaving the town?" The tailor told him what the King had required of him, and how he could not perform it, and lamented his misfortune. "Don't let that turn your hair grey," said the stork, "I will help you out of your difficulty. For a long time now, I have carried the children in swaddling-clothes into the town, so for once in a way I can fetch a little prince out of the well. Go home and be easy. In nine days from this time repair to the royal palace, and there will I come." The little tailor went home, and at the appointed time was at the castle. It was not long before the stork came flying thither and tapped at the window. The tailor opened it, and Cousin Longlegs came carefully in, and walked with solemn steps over the smooth marble pavement. He had, moreover, a baby in his beak that was as lovely as an angel, and stretched out its little hands to the Queen. The stork laid it in her lap, and she caressed it and kissed it, and was beside herself with delight. Before the stork flew away, he took his traveling bag off his back and handed it over to the Queen. In it there were little paper parcels with colored sweetmeats, and they were divided amongst the little princesses. The eldest, however, received none of them, but instead got the merry tailor for a husband. "It seems to me," said he, "just as if I had won the highest prize. My mother was right after all, she always said that whoever trusts in God and only has good luck, can never fail."

The shoemaker had to make the shoes in which the little tailor danced at the wedding festival, after which he was commanded to quit the town for ever. The road to the forest led him to the gallows. Worn out with anger, rage, and the heat of the day, he threw himself down. When he had closed his eyes and was about to sleep, the two crows flew down from the heads of the men who were hanging there, and pecked his eyes out. In his madness he ran into the forest and must have died there of hunger, for no one has ever either seen him or heard of him again.

THE FLUTE

(Nigerian)

Retold by Chinua Achebe

One of the meanings of "shadow" is phantom, or ghostly spirit. In this folktale the boundary between the land of people and the land of spirits is explored. The message of the story is quite clear—one must respect the spirits or face the prospect of bringing down terrible trouble on oneself. Chinua Achebe is Africa's best-known writer and has been highly praised as a gifted spokesman for his country and its problems.

Long, long ago there was a man who had two wives. The senior wife had many children but the other had only one son. One day, as the season of the rains drew near, the man and his family went to work on their farm. They set out at the first light of dawn because they had a long journey ahead of them. Their farm was at the boundary between the land of men and of spirits.

They worked hard and long planting their yams. But as evening approached the man looked up constantly to watch the sun's position in the sky. He looked up one last time and called out to his family to get their things quickly together and ready for home. They gathered their hoes and machetes and baskets together and hurried away because they knew that soon darkness would descend and the spirits would come to work on their own yam fields.

They passed seven forests and crossed seven rivers and returned to their home. It was then that the only son of the man's younger wife discovered that he had forgotten his flute in the farm. This flute was the only thing he could call his own; he had made it himself from a bamboo stalk. He rose up with great sadness and said he was going back to the farm in search of his flute. His mother begged him in tears not to go; his father pleaded with him at first gently and then in anger for his stubbornness. When they found they could not move him, they let him go.

He crossed the seven rivers and the seven wilds and came at last to the farm. And surely the spirits were there bent over their work planting ghost-yams. At the boy's approach they all straightened up and regarded him with anger in their eyes. Fear froze the boy where he stood; everywhere was silence. And then the leader of the spirits spoke. His voice was like the dry bark of thunder through a throat of iron: *Taa! Human Boy! Who sent you here? What are you looking for? Foolish fly that follows the corpse into the ground, did nobody tell you that we are abroad at this time? Answer me at once!*

I have only one flute in the world, said the boy boldly, *and I forgot it under that dead tree over there. I did not mean to offend you but only to take back my flute.*

Flute? Hmm. Tell me, will you recognize this flute of yours if you see it, human boy?

The boy said yes. Then the spirit reached down into his goatskin bag and brought out a flute shining like the yellow metal. *Is this it?* The boy shook his head. *Now, is it this?* He held up another flute shining white like the kernel of the water of heaven. The boy said no and shook his head. Finally he brought out a miserable-looking bamboo flute and before he could ask the boy jumped up and down with joy and said it was his. *Take it and blow for us,* said the spirit. And this was the song the boy blew on his flute:

Awful Spirit, undisputed
Lord by night of this estate!
Father told me death awaited
All who ventured here so late.
"Please, my son, please wait till
morning,"
Cried my mother. But her warning
Fell unheeded. How could you
Contain yourself and sleep till dawn
When your flute in damp and dew
Lay forsaken and forlorn.

The spirits were delighted with the boy's playing and they laughed haw-haw-haw through their noses. *We like your playing,* said their leader to the boy, *and we like your manners. And we are going to make you a present.* He made a sign with his left hand and two youngster spirits brought forward two pots, one large and the other small and both firmly sealed. *Take one of these,* he said to the boy; and he took the smaller pot. The spirits nodded to one another in satisfaction.

Go well, said their leader to the boy. *When you reach home call your mother and your father and break the pot before them.* The boy thanked him and set out for home.

If you hear doom-doom on your way, the spirit called out to him, *run into the bush; but if you hear jam-jam, come back to the road.*

On his way the boy heard *doom-doom* and hid in the bush. Then he heard *jam-jam* and came out again and continued his journey. He passed the seven rivers and the seven forests and reached his father's compound. He called his parents together as the spirit had told him and broke the pot in front of them. Immediately the compound was filled with every good thing: yellow and white metals, cloths and velvets, foods of all kinds, sheep and goats and cows and many other things of value.

The boy's mother filled two baskets with gifts and offered them to the senior wife. But she was blind with envy and rejected the gift. That night she did not sleep.

At the first crow of the cock in the morning the senior wife roused her first son from sleep. *Go and get your flute; we are going to the farm,* she ordered. When they got to the farm there was no work for them to do because all the work had been done on the previous day. But they hung around until sunset. Then she said: *Let us go home.* They picked up their baskets and the boy picked up his flute. *Foolish boy!* said the woman boxing his ears, *don't you know how to forget your flute?* So the boy dropped his flute and they set out for home. As soon as they entered their hut the woman said to her son: *Now, go back for your flute.* He cried and protested but she pushed him out of the hut and told him not to come back without his flute and a pot of presents.

He passed the seven streams and seven forests and arrived at the farm where the spirits were bent in work. *Mpf! Mpf,* he sniffed in disgust. *I choke with the stench of spirits!*

The king of spirits asked him what he came for and he replied: *My mother sent me to bring my flute and a pot of presents. Mpf! Mpf!*

Will you recognize the flute if you see it?

What sort of question is that? It is my flute, isn't it?

The spirit reached into his bag and brought out a flute of shining precious metal and the boy promptly claimed it as his own. All the spirits growled in displeasure.

Take it and blow for us, said their

leader to the boy. *I hope you have not been spitting into it,* said the boy, wiping the mouth of the flute against his flank. Then he blew this song:

King of Spirits he stinks
Mpf! Mpf!
Old Spirit he stinks
Mpf! Mpf!
Young Spirit he stinks
Mpf! Mpf!
Mother Spirit she stinks
Mpf! Mpf!
Father Spirit he stinks
Mpf! Mpf!
They have seven rivers in their town
Mpf! Mpf!
But none knows how to wash
Mpf! Mpf!

When he finished all the spirits were silent. Then their leader ordered two pots brought forward and the boy grabbed the bigger one without waiting to hear anything about them.

When you get home, said the spirit, *call your father and your mother and break the pot before them.*

I know that, said the boy.

On your way, if you hear doom-doom, go into the bush; but if you hear jam-jam, come out again.

Without stopping to thank the spirits the boy lifted the pot on to his head and walked away. He came to a certain place and heard doom-doom and stayed on the road looking this way and that to see what it was. Later he heard jam-jam and went into the bush.

He reached home at last, having crossed the seven rivers and traversed seven wilds. His mother, who had been waiting outside the compound gate all evening, was happy to see him carrying such a big pot.

They said I should break it before my father and yourself, he said. *What does your father know about it?* she said, and steered him to her hut. She shut the doors and then filled in every crack in the wall so that nothing might escape to the other huts in the compound. When everything was ready she broke the pot. Leprosy, small-pox, yaws and worse diseases without names and every abomination filled the hut and killed the woman and all her children.

In the morning, as there was no sign of life in her hut her husband forced open the door and peeped in. That peep was more than enough. He struggled with the hideous things fighting to come out and luckily managed to shut and secure the door again. But a few of the diseases and abominations had escaped and spread through the world. But the worst of them —those without a name—remained in that hut.

Literary Folktale

HOW JAHDU RAN THROUGH DARKNESS IN NO TIME AT ALL

Virginia Hamilton

Jahdu is a magical character who seems to be a version of the trickster. He is the central character of a set of stories told to Lee Edward, a young black boy, by his baby-sitter, Mama Luka. The shadow theme is used imaginatively in several ways in this story: in the trickster nature of Jahdu, in the darkness through which Jahdu runs, and in the strange figure of the shadow fisherman.

Mama Luka sat in her tight little room in a fine, good place called Harlem. She sat facing the window with her chin resting in the palm of her hand. Yes, she did. The window blinds were raised high to let in the rays of the sun. But there was no sunlight this day, for rain poured down the window in a steady stream.

Mama Luka watched over Lee Edward while his mother worked and while his father found work whenever he could. Lee Edward came to her house as soon as his school was out for the day. He came, smiling and laughing, because he loved the Jahdu stories Mama Luka would tell. He loved the way she would reach into the air to catch a Jahdu story going by. He loved Mama Luka almost as much as he loved his own mama. Mama Luka sometimes called him Little Brother the way his own mama did. But this day, Mama Luka had been quiet more than once.

Illustrated by Ray Prather.

"If this rain won't stop its crying," she told Lee Edward, "I'm going to bed for a month of Sundays."

Lee Edward sat close to Mama Luka where he liked to be. He could see the way she smiled and hear every word she said. But Mama Luka wouldn't smile. She wouldn't talk much and Lee Edward didn't know how to make her feel good again. He didn't know how to shut off the rain. Now claps of thunder rolled around the sky, filling Mama Luka's room with loudness, like anger.

Mama Luka had a letter beside her. Once and again she read the letter and then placed it next to her on the chair. Every time she did that, Lee Edward tried hard to find something to say.

"Mama Luka, I like your hair like that," he told her. "It's the best beautiful hair I ever did see."

"Little Brother, thank you so much," she said. She had to smile. "Do you really like my hair like this?"

"I like the way it is long and the way it is black," Lee Edward said.

"So do I," said Mama Luka. "I never will cut it."

"No, never do," said Lee Edward.

"I never will sell it to the people who make wigs, either," Mama Luka said.

"Never do," Lee Edward said again.

Mama Luka had black skin and a nose as curved as the beak of a parrot. She could wear her hair in one long pigtail down her back and she could sit on it. But now she had unbraided her hair so it fell over her shoulders. It hung down her back in waves of dark.

There was a rumble of thunder. The rain hit Mama Luka's window harder, like it meant to come straight through.

Lee Edward shivered. "Look's like the sun's never coming out again," he said. "Wouldn't it be something if it never did?"

"Be something I surely wouldn't like," Mama Luka told him, "but you know, once it did rain forty days and forty nights."

Lee Edward grinned. "That was in Noah's time," he said, "but the sun did come out again after the flood."

"And that's the truth," said Mama Luka. "Yet, I remember me a time . . . a Jahdu time. . . . "

Lee Edward stared at Mama Luka. She had reached into the air to grab something Lee Edward couldn't see. Whatever Mama Luka had taken out of the air must have been dark and wiggly. She had to open her eyes wide to see it. And she had a time keeping it quiet in her lap.

Lee Edward was happy. Even with the thunder rolling around and banging against the sky, and even with the rain hitting the window in a steady fall, and even with the letter which had first made Mama Luka feel blue, she was still going to tell a Jahdu tale.

"Goody for me!" Lee Edward yelled. "Mama Luka, what one is it?"

"Slow down there, you darkness thing," Mama Luka said to what Lee Edward couldn't see. She cupped her hands over her mouth and swallowed what had been in her hands.

"A darkness thing?" said Lee Edward. "How does it taste?"

But Mama Luka wouldn't say. She never would tell anything before she was ready. She knew a roomful of Jahdu stories. She knew what Jahdu looked like, but that was her secret. She always knew where he had been and where he was going. She told every Jahdu story slow and easy, just the way she was about to tell one now.

"Lee Edward," she began, "I can't find me one taste in this story that lasts long enough for me to tell you about it."

"Well, tell me *something,*" Lee Edward said.

"I can tell you this," Mama Luka said. "We have here a Jahdu story of a time-ago lost."

"A what kind of time?" Lee Edward wanted to know.

Mama Luka looked closely at Lee Edward. "Little Brother, are you going to be scared?" she asked him.

"Maybe a little," he said. "I don't like darkness things so much."

"You still want me to tell you about it?" asked Mama Luka.

"I don't care if it is scary!" Lee Edward finally said.

"Darkness won't have to mean scary," said Mama Luka.

"So tell it," Lee Edward said.

"I'm getting myself ready," said Mama Luka.

THIS IS THE JAHDU STORY SO DARK AND WIGGLY,
ABOUT A TIME-AGO LOST,
THAT MAMA LUKA TOLD TO LEE EDWARD.

Jahdu came running along. He was heading east to the place where he had been born, for he thought he had better be born again. Yes, he did. He was running out of his Jahdu dust that put things to sleep and woke them up. And he would have to be reborn in order to get enough Jahdu dust.

Jahdu had been to the good place called Harlem. He had been a strong black boy who owned a dog named Rufus. But Jahdu never stayed one kind of person for very long. He had learned how to change himself into whomever he wished from his friend Chameleon. Now he was his own Jahdu self again.

"Woogily!" said Jahdu after a long time of running. "The East surely is far and far. It has been night longer than any night I can remember. I wish it would end and morning would come."

Jahdu kept running on. He couldn't see a thing on either side of him. He couldn't see where he had been or where he was going through the darkness. Jahdu should have walked instead of running but he had not been in the world forever. Even though he could turn himself into whatever he wished, and even though he had magic enough to put things to sleep and wake them up again, he was still very young. And he was only three and one-half feet tall.

All at once, Jahdu tripped over something and fell, sprawled on the ground.

"Now what was that lying right in the middle of the dark?" Jahdu said.

"A-heh, a-heh-heh," a voice went, laughing.

"Who in the world is that?" Jahdu said to the darkness.

"How you was, Jahdu?" said the voice. "A-heh, a-heh-heh."

Jahdu felt around on the ground. He felt a short tuft of something, like a feathery tail. He felt some flat toes grown together and another something the same, like a pair of webbed feet. Jahdu caught hold of a large, feathered body lying on its back. He touched a queer bird's head with a bill pointing straight up in the darkness. From head to foot, the big crazy bird smelled like fish.

"Phew!" said Jahdu.

"Loon-a-tic," said the bird, "loon-a-tock. Wind my fish and eat my clock."

"You crazy, Loon," Jahdu said. "What are you doing lying on the ground?" He knew his old friend Loon, even in the dark. But never before had he heard of Loon lying on his back.

Lazily, Loon said, "How you doing, Jahdu?"

"I'm doing fine," said Jahdu, "but why aren't you flying over some ocean searching for your supper?"

"I haven't got the time," Loon said, very carefully. "Have you got the time, Jahdu?"

"Now why would I want to go flying over water in search of my supper?" asked Jahdu.

"Have you . . . " Loon began, sounding nervous, "got the time?"

"What's the matter with you?" Jahdu said. "And no, I haven't got the time. All I know is that it's night and it's been the longest night I've ever run through."

"That's what I thinking," Loon said excitedly.

"You're not making much sense," Jahdu told him. "Here, let me help you up."

"I staying right laying low," said Loon. "A-heh, a-heh-heh."

Lying out here in the dark, Jahdu thought, I bet old Loon caught himself some kind of head cold.

"Loon," he said, "how long have you been stretched out on your back?"

"A-heh," Loon said, shaking all over. "Go ask time, I haven't got the anybody."

"What are you trying to say?" Jahdu asked.

"Just going right, keep on," said crazy Loon. "Light gets until it."

"What in the world!" Jahdu said, holding onto Loon as tightly as he could.

"Light way all the not," said Loon. And then, shouting, "GRAY BUT SOMEWHAT!"

"Poor Loon," said Jahdu. "You were always silly. But now you are really scared and I can't make head nor tail out of what you're saying." Jahdu smoothed out Loon's long feathers. "You were my friend," he said. "Remember the time I used my magic to put you to sleep? Then I woke you up and you took off flying over the ocean looking for me. It wasn't until you spotted me and were about to land that you found out your feet were tied together. Remember that trick I played, Loon?"

"A-heh, yeah," Loon said, calmer now.

"You had to crash-land," Jahdu went on. "Your head was buried a foot deep in the sand when I found you—you're not still mad at me, are you, Loon?"

Loon was quiet a moment. "A-heh, no, Jahdu," he said at last. "Just find me some light."

"Find your own light," said Jahdu. "I just remembered, I have to be running along."

"But it gone," Loon said. "All light gone and I lost in the dark."

Loon sounded so pitiful that Jahdu couldn't very well leave him.

"Oh, all right, you can ride with me," Jahdu told him. "Here, climb up and hold on tight."

Jahdu strained under Loon's weight, then steadied himself. "Now you lead the way," he told Loon. "Just sniff for fish wherever there might be fish. Once you smell fish, we have found water and you can eat. I wouldn't mind having a few fish myself to help me along to the East."

So Jahdu and Loon went running on. That is, Jahdu went running and Loon went on riding. After a long time of riding and running, in which darkness stayed dark and light was nowhere to be seen, Loon moved his bill to the right of Jahdu.

"You want me to go south?" Jahdu asked him.

"A-heh, yes," Loon said.

Jahdu veered to the right for what seemed nights. Then, with another nudge from the bill of Loon, he went east again. After a long panting silence of running, Jahdu yelled out through the dark: "I can smell it! Loon, there is salt in the air!"

Jahdu smelled the salt of seawater but Loon was smelling fish of seawater. He was smelling fish and more fish and so much fish, he tried to fly away from Jahdu right then and there.

"Stay where you are," Jahdu told him. "We'll be there pretty soon. But looky here, have you noticed something? I can almost see in front of me. I mean, I think I can almost see. It's getting lighter, or at least, not quite so dark. Doesn't that make you feel better, Loon? Loon . . . ?"

Loon was still swooning over the smell of fish. He was numb and deaf because of the sweet smell of fish.

"It's all right, poor old Loon. We're almost there now," Jahdu told him. "I can hear water lapping at the seashore."

All at once Jahdu bumped into something and bounced away from it. Jahdu lost his balance and he and Loon rolled down what felt like a low, sandy hill. With a great splash, he and Loon tumbled into chilly water full of the most juicy fish Loon ever did gobble up as fast as he could.

Jahdu had never eaten raw fish. But he swallowed them now so that he could run that much faster to the East.

"Woogily!" he said. "That was the most sudden surprise I've had in this darkness." Jahdu sat still and looked around as hard as he could. "I can see things," he said. "I can almost see shadow. There's almost a shadow up there on the sand bank. And the shadow is . . . almost . . . fishing!"

The almost shadow sat comfortably, as if he were sitting in the sun.

"Well, for goodness sake," said Jahdu, going closer to the almost shadow, "good evening, friend Fisherman, I think Loon and I must have tripped over you."

Fisherman didn't say anything. He kept right on doing what he had been doing, which was almost fishing. When Jahdu peered through the dark and gazed at the shadow, he saw that Fisherman wasn't fishing at all.

"Friend Fisherman," Jahdu said, "you've got your fishhook stuck in the sand."

Fisherman went on reeling in his line with a few grains of sand covering his fishhook and emptying the bit of sand into his fish box. Yes, he did.

"Something is awfully wrong with this fisherman," Jahdu said to himself. "If I could just light up this place a little."

"Pardon me," Jahdu said to Fisherman. "Would you happen to have a match on you? That's too bad," Jahdu added when Fisherman didn't answer.

Jahdu peered into Fisherman's face. He couldn't see much, even up close. Far off in the water he could hear Loon still busy catching fish.

"Fisherman," said Jahdu, "you could catch fish just like Loon out there. All you have to do is ease yourself toward the water's edge. Then you could cast your rod into the water and catch all kinds of fish. Well, Fisherman, did you hear me? Fisherman!"

"Haven't got the time," Fisherman finally said, very sadly. He reeled in his line and emptied the few grains of sand into his fish box.

"You're as crazy as Loon," Jahdu told him, "but *you* make me angry!" With that, Jahdu began running around Fisherman as fast as he could. Faster and faster he ran as only Jahdu knew how.

As soon as the Jahdu dust fell, Fisherman should have fallen asleep. But he didn't, for Jahdu's dust was not as strong as it used to be.

"Woogily!" said Jahdu. "I'd better give Fisherman some more of my dust." He ran around Fisherman a second time. More Jahdu dust rose out of Jahdu and fell over Fisherman. And this time Fisherman fell fast asleep.

"There!" said Jahdu. "I still have my magic but I'd better get to the East and be reborn before it's all gone."

Just then old Loon came waddling out of the water. His bill bulged with the fish he'd already eaten.

"How can you be so piggish?" Jahdu said to him. "I think you'd better empty your bill of fish into Fisherman's fish box."

In the shadowy dark, Loon shook his head.

"I put that fisherman to sleep for fishing in the sand," said Jahdu. "If you're not careful, I'll put you to sleep as well. And you'll stay asleep until I decide to wake you up again."

Suddenly Loon took a flying leap straight up in the air. But try as he might for a quick take-off, he'd eaten too many fish. He couldn't get his fat belly off the ground.

"Serves you right," Jahdu told him. "You'd better not try a stunt like that again."

Jahdu led Loon over to the fisherman's fish box. He tickled Loon under his right wing where he was most ticklish. Loon laughed so hard, fish flew out of his bill into Fisherman's fish box.

"A-heh! Whoo-hoo! Ahhhh-a-haaa!" Loon sighed.

"Well, of course you feel better," Jahdu told him. "No Loon could even swallow with that many fish in his bill. Now. You listen to me. I want you to stay right here with Fisherman until I . . . "

Jahdu never had a chance to finish what he had started to say. For all at once Loon ran to the water. Whistling like Loons will do and flapping his wings in a fury, he made clouds of sand-dust darkness. Yes, he did. He skimmed over the water, skating along on his webbed toes. But his wings tired out and he sank like a stone, straight to the bottom.

Jahdu had to dive in and haul him out. "Loon, you dumb bird!" Jahdu said. "I ought to . . . I really ought—I think I will." He hurled big, soggy Loon onto the sand and began running around him fast and faster. A tiny bit of Jahdu dust rose out of Jahdu and fell over Loon. It was only enough dust to make Loon yawn twice.

"Oh, my goodness," said Jahdu. He had to run around Loon three times. Loon tried to get away each time.

"Stand still, Loon," Jahdu yelled.

"Won't," said Loon, and he didn't.

But finally, Jahdu was able to run around Loon in circles. When all that was left of the Jahdu dust settled, Loon was deeply asleep and snoring his loonful tune.

Jahdu stayed close by Fisherman and the snoring Loon. During one long period of quiet snoring Loon commenced talking in his sleep and Fisherman began walking.

"What a silly pair," Jahdu said. "I should let them sleep for a whole night year. I would, too, if I didn't have to be hurrying on."

Jahdu started running around Loon and Fisherman slowly and slower. What little Jahdu dust there was rose out of Fisherman and Loon and settled back into Jahdu. Very quickly, Loon and Fisherman gave every sign of waking. When they were sleepily sitting, Jahdu spoke to them.

"I've got to be going," he said to both of them. "Loon here can catch you some fish," he told Fisherman.

"Jahdu, don't leave me here in the dark," Loon said, sounding ready to cry.

"I have to," Jahdu said. "You saw how little dust I have left. I've got to get to the East as fast as I can to get me some more dust."

"Take me with you," Loon said mournfully.

"I can't carry you all that way, Loon, I'm sorry," Jahdu told him.

"But it dark!" Loon cried. "I lost. I scared."

"I know!" said Jahdu, patting Loon's feathers. "And it's a strange, long kind of dark. Do you remember when it started?"

"No," said Loon. "I only afraid. I only out of food. I only could think of being scared and hungry."

"Well, I didn't pay much attention to the dark either," said Jahdu. "When you have magic the way I do, you don't bother about the length of a night."

Jahdu and Loon were silent. After a while, they thought to move Fisherman close to the water's edge so he could catch his own fish.

"See?" Loon said. "He be all right. Take me with you."

"Loon, I told you, I've got to travel fast to the East. You're too slow to walk and you can't see to fly, which means I'd have to carry you. But listen, I'll help you out if I can."

"How, Jahdu?" asked Loon.

"Just for you," Jahdu said grandly, "I'll find out what's happened to the light."

"Just for me?" said Loon.

"You're my friend, aren't you?" said Jahdu.

"And will be ever, Jahdu," said Loon.

"Then it's settled," Jahdu told him. "You stay right here where you have as much fish as you want."

Loon began to look doubtful, and Jahdu said quickly, "A little while ago when you were sleeping, I heard this lion roaring in the dark. He sure did sound hungry!"

"A-heh-heh," Loon said, "I guess I stay put. No telling what going to wander out there in darkness."

"So good-by, old Loon," Jahdu said. Already, he was running away. "Good-by, Fisherman," he called. "I hope to see you both after I've found the East . . . and what's happened to the light, too."

"Good-by, a-heh, Jahdu," Loon called sadly.

Jahdu went running on. He had what was left of his Jahdu magic back within him. He was alone again in darkness and he was glad to be on his way. The darkness did have some shadow now. Jahdu followed the shadow dark toward the East.

"Woogily!" Jahdu said. "I'm so glad to be running along again. I'm going to be reborn. It can just stay dark forever, I don't care!"

THIS IS THE END OF THE JAHDU STORY SO WIGGLY AND DARK,
OF A TIME-AGO LOST,
THAT MAMA LUKA TOLD ONE DAY TO LEE EDWARD.

Fantasy

THE SHADOW
Hans Christian Andersen

Andersen's story "The Shadow" is one of many written in the nineteenth century on the popular shadow theme. As K. Narayan Kutty points out in his essay on this story (included at the end of the section), it is also "an intensely autobiographical story." It is of interest, therefore, not only in itself, as a treatment of the shadow theme, but also as a fascinating glimpse into the psychology of one of the greatest writers for children.

In the hot countries the sun can burn properly. People become as brown as mahogany all over—but it was only to the hot countries that a learned man from the cold ones had come. He imagined he would be able to run about as he did at home, but he soon got out of the habit of doing that. He and all sensible people had to stop indoors. The window-shutters and the doors were kept shut all day, and it looked as if the whole house were asleep or else nobody was at home. The narrow street with the tall houses, where he lived, was so built that from morning to night the sunshine lay on it; really it was unbearable. This learned man from the cold countries—he was a young man and a clever one—he felt as if he was living in a fiery furnace. It exhausted him, and he grew quite thin, and even his shadow contracted and got much smaller than it was at home; the sun exhausted it, too. Not until evening, when the sun was down, did they begin to revive.

Translated by M. R. James.

That, now, was really a pleasure to see. As soon as lights were brought into the room the Shadow stretched itself all up the wall—yes, up to the ceiling, too, so long did it make itself, for it had to stretch itself to get its strength back. The learned man went out on the balcony, to stretch himself there, and as the stars came out in the lovely clear sky he seemed to himself to be coming to life again.

On all the balconies in the street—and in the hot countries every window has a balcony—people came out, for air one must have, even if one's accustomed to be the colour of mahogany. Very lively it became—upstairs and downstairs. Shoemakers and tailors and everybody else moved out into the street; tables and chairs were brought out and lamps lit—thousands of them—and some talked and others sang; and the people took walks, and the carriages drove out, and the donkeys with bells on them went by—"Kling-a-ling-a-ling!" There were funerals, with singing of psalms; the street-boys fired off throw-downs; the church bells rang out, and altogether it was very lively down in the street. Only in one house, straight opposite to that in which the foreign learned man lived, was there complete stillness. And yet somebody lived in it, for there were flowers on the balcony, that grew splendidly in the hot sun, which they couldn't have done without being watered, and there must be somebody to water them; so there must be people there. The door of it, too, was opened at night, but inside it was quite dark; at any rate in the front room. But from further in there was a sound of music. To the foreign scholar it seemed incomparably beautiful, but it might easily be that he fancied it so, for in the hot countries everything seemed to him matchless, but for the heat. The landlord said he didn't know who had taken the house opposite, for you couldn't see any people, and as for the music, he thought it horribly tiresome. "It's like someone sitting practising a piece he can't get on with—always the same piece. No doubt he's saying, 'I shall get it right in time', but he won't get it right, however long he goes on playing."

One night the foreign scholar woke up. The door to the balcony stood open where he slept and the curtain before it was lifted by the breeze, and he thought there was a marvellous light coming from the balcony opposite. All the flowers were shining like flames of the most lovely colours, and among the flowers stood a slender, graceful maiden; herself, too, shining, as it seemed. It positively dazzled his eyes, and he shut them as tight as ever he could, and woke up completely. With a single jump he was on the floor, and very quietly he stole behind the curtain, but the maiden was gone, the light was gone, the flowers shone no longer, though they stood there as fair as ever. The door was ajar, and from far within the music was sounding, soft and beautiful; such as would entrance one into delicious thought. It really was like magic—and who was it that lived there? Where was the proper entrance? The whole ground floor was a succession of shops, and people couldn't always be passing through them.

One evening the foreign scholar was sitting out on his balcony, and a lamp was hung in the room behind him, and so it very naturally happened that his shadow passed across to the wall opposite, and there it stayed, right opposite among the flowers on the balcony, and when the learned man moved the shadow moved, too—it always does.

"I think my Shadow is the only living thing to be seen over there," said the learned man. "Look how snug it's sitting among the flowers, and the door's standing ajar. Now if only the Shadow was sharp enough to go in and look about and then come and tell me what it saw! Yes, you'd be some use then," he said in joke. "Do, please, go in there! Do! Are you going?" With that he nodded to the Shadow, and the Shadow nodded back. "Well, go then, but don't stay away!" The learned man got up and his Shadow, on the balcony opposite, got up too. The learned man turned, and the Shadow turned too, and if anyone had been observing carefully, they would have seen, quite plain, that the Shadow went in by the half-open door of the balcony over the way, at the moment when the learned man went into his own room and let fall the long curtain behind him.

Next morning the learned man went out to take his coffee and read the papers. "What's this?" he said, when he came out into the sunshine. "I haven't got any shadow! Why, then it really did go away last night and has not come back; that's rather tiresome, that is."

It did annoy him, but not so much because his shadow was gone, as because he knew that there was a story about a man without a shadow which everyone at home in the cold countries knew; and if the learned man went there and told them his own story they would say he was merely imitating the other, and that he had no business to do. So he determined to say nothing at all about it, which was very sensible of him.

In the evening he went out on to his balcony again; he had put the lamp behind him, very properly, for he knew that a shadow always needs its master for a screen, but he couldn't entice it back. He made himself little and he made himself big, but no shadow came, nobody came. He coughed loudly, but it was no good.

It was amazing, to be sure; but in those hot countries everything grows very fast, and after a week had passed he saw, to his great delight, that a new shadow was growing out of his feet when he went into the sunlight: the root must have been left behind. In three weeks' time he had a very tolerable shadow, which, when he betook himself home to the northern country, grew more and more on the way, so that at last it was so long and so big that he would have been contented with half as much.

So the learned man came home and wrote books about what there was of truth and goodness and beauty in the world; and days passed by, and years—many years.

He was sitting in his room one evening, and there came a very gentle knock at the door. "Come in!" said he; but nobody came in, so he opened the door, and there standing before him was an extraordinarily thin man, so thin as to be quite remarkable. This person was, for the rest, extremely well dressed, and evidently a man of distinction.

"Whom have I the honour of addressing?" asked the learned man.

"Ah, I thought very likely you wouldn't recognize me," said the well-dressed man. "I've become so much of a body that I've actually got flesh and clothes; you never expected to see me in such fine condition. Don't you recognize your old shadow? To be sure, you certainly never thought I should ever come back. Things have gone wonderfully well with me since I was with you last, and I have become very well-to-do in every respect. If I wish to buy myself out of service, I have the means." And he rattled a large bunch of valuable seals that hung to his watch, and put his hand to the heavy gold chain that was round his neck: and how his fingers did glitter with diamond rings, and all real too!

"Well, well! I can't get over it," said the learned man. "What does it all mean?"

"I admit, it's by no means an ordinary affair," said the Shadow. "But, then, you yourself are not an ordinary man; and I, as you very well know, have trod in your footsteps from a child. As soon as you found that I was ripe to go out into the world by myself, I went my own way. I am now in the most brilliant circumstances, but there came a sort of longing over me to see you once more before you die, as die you must. I wanted, too, to see this part of the world again, for one has always a fondness for one's Fatherland. I am aware that you have got another shadow in my place; if I have anything to pay, either to it or to you, I hope you will be so good as to let me know."

"Well, and is it really you?" said the scholar. "It is indeed most remarkable! I could never have believed that my old shadow could come back to me as a man."

"Do tell me what I have to pay," said the Shadow; "I don't at all like to be in debt of any kind."

"How can you talk so?" said the learned man. "What debt is there to talk of? Be as free as the next man; I am extraordinarily pleased at your good fortune. Do sit down, old friend, and just tell me a little about how it all came about, and what you saw at the house over the way, out there in the hot country."

"I will tell you," said the Shadow, seating himself; "but you must promise me that you won't tell anyone here in the town, wherever you may meet me, that I was once your Shadow. I have some thoughts of becoming engaged. I could support more families than one."

"Be quite easy," said the scholar; "I won't tell anyone who you really are. Here's my hand on it. I promise it, and one man, one word, you know." "One word, one shadow," said the Shadow; he was obliged to phrase it so.

It was indeed most remarkable to see how much of a man the Shadow was: all dressed out in the finest possible black broadcloth, with varnished boots and a hat that would shut up so that it was only crown and brim, not to speak of what we know already, the seals, the gold chain, and the diamond rings. The Shadow was, in fact, extraordinarily well dressed, and this was just what made him a complete man.

"Now I'll tell you my story," said the Shadow, planting his feet, in the varnished boots, as firmly as he could on the arm of the learned man's new shadow, which lay at his feet like a poodle dog: and this was either out of pride or perhaps in hopes of getting it to stick to him; while the prostrate shadow kept very quiet in order to listen, for it wanted to know how a shadow could get free as this one had done, and work up to be its own master.

"Do you know who it was that lived in the house over the way?" said the Shadow. "It was the most beautiful thing there is: it was Poetry. I was there for three weeks, and the effect was the same as if one had spent three thousand years in reading everything that has been sung and written. I say it, and it is the truth. I have seen everything, and I know everything."

"Poetry!" cried the learned man. "Yes! Yes! She often dwells, a hermit, in great cities. Poetry! I saw her for one single brief moment, but my eyes were full of sleep. She was standing on the balcony and shining as the Northern Lights shine. Tell me, tell me of her. Thou wast on the balcony, thou wentest through the door, then—" "Then I was in the ante-room," said the Shadow. "You were always sitting looking across at the ante-room. There was no light there at all; there was a sort of twilight, but one door stood open, leading straight to a second, and into a long row of rooms and halls. There was light there. I should have been killed outright by the light, had I gone in to where the maiden was, but I was careful, I gave myself time—as indeed one must."

"And what sawest thou then?" asked the scholar.

"I saw everything, and I will tell you about it. But—it isn't that I'm in the least proud—but considering I'm a free man, and what accomplishments I possess, not to mention my good position and my very easy circumstances—I should very much prefer you to address me as 'you.' "

"I beg your pardon," said the scholar; "it's merely old habit which sticks by me. You're perfectly right, and I shall keep it in mind. But now, do tell me everything you saw."

"Everything!" said the Shadow. "For I saw everything and I know everything."

"What was it like in the innermost hall?" asked the scholar. "Was it like being in the green wood? Was it like a solemn temple? Were the halls like the starlit sky seen from the top of the high mountains?" "Everything was there," said the Shadow; "I didn't go absolutely in, I stayed in the room next to it in the twilight, but I was admirably placed, and saw everything and know everything. I have been in the court of Poetry, in the ante-chamber."

"But what did you see? Did all the gods of ancient days pass through the vast halls? Did the heroes of old times fight their battles there? Were there lovely children playing and telling of their dreams?"

"I tell you I was there, and you may imagine I saw everything there was to be seen. Had you been over there you would not have turned into a man, but I did; and, moreover, I learned to know my innermost nature, all that was inborn in me, the kinship I had with Poetry. When I was with you I never thought about it, but, as you know, every time the sun rose or set I used to become amazingly large. In the moonlight, indeed, I was almost plainer to be seen than you yourself. At that time I did not comprehend my own nature, but in that ante-room it became clear to me; I became a man. When I came out I was matured, but you were no longer in the hot countries. I was ashamed, as a man, to go about as I was. I needed boots and clothes and all the human paraphernalia that make a man recognizable. I made my way (I tell you this, you won't put it in a book), I made my way to the cake-woman's skirt, and hid myself under it. Little did the woman think how great a thing she had in hiding, and not till the evening did I come out. I ran along the street in the moonlight. I stretched myself right up the wall (it tickles one in the back deliciously). I ran up, I ran down; I peeped through the topmost windows, into the rooms, on to the roof. I peeped where no one else could, and saw what nobody else saw, and what nobody was meant to see. Take it all round, the world's a mean place. I wouldn't have become a man if it hadn't been generally assumed that it's a good thing to be one. I saw the most incredible things, among wives, among husbands, among parents and among those darling admirable children. I saw," said the Shadow, "what no human being was allowed to know, but what everybody very much wants to know, that is their neighbours' wrongdoings. If I'd written a newspaper it would have been read, I tell you! But I wrote direct to the people concerned, and there was a panic in every town I visited. They were terribly afraid of me, and they became amazingly fond of me. The professors made me a professor, the tailors gave me new clothes. I'm admirably fitted out. The master of the mint coined money for me, and the women said I was very good-looking. In this way I became the man I am. And now I must bid you good-bye. Here's my card; I live on the sunny side, and I'm always at home when it rains." And off went the Shadow.

"That is a most remarkable affair," said the learned man.

A year and a day passed, and the Shadow came again. "How goes it?" he asked.

"Alas!" said the learned man. "I write about the true and the good and the beautiful. But nobody cares to hear about such things, and I'm quite in despair. I feel it very keenly."

"But I don't," said the Shadow; "I'm getting fat and that's what everybody ought to try to be. You don't understand the way of the world, you know; you'll get quite ill like this, you ought to travel. I'm going to travel this summer; will you come with me? I should like to have a companion; will you go with me as my shadow? It'll be a real pleasure to have you with me, and I'll pay expenses."

"That's going a bit too far," said the learned man.

"Why, that's as you take it," said the Shadow. "It'll do you all the good in the world to travel. If you'll be my shadow you shan't have a penny to pay for the trip."

"That's absolute madness!" said the learned man.

"But after all, the world's like that," said the Shadow, "and so it always will be." And off he went.

The learned man was in a bad way: sorrow and trouble were on him, and as for his talk about the true and the beautiful and the good, most people appreciated it as a cow does roses. At last he became quite ill. "You really look like a shadow," people said to him; and the learned man shivered, for it was exactly what he was thinking.

"You ought to take some baths," said the Shadow, who paid him a visit. "There's nothing else for it. I'll take you with me for old acquaintance sake. I'll pay expenses, and you shall write a description and amuse me with it on the journey. I'm going to the baths, for my beard won't grow as it should, and that is an ailment; one must have a beard. Now do be reasonable and accept my invitation; we'll travel as friends."

So they set off. The Shadow was the master and the master was the shadow. They drove together, they rode and walked together side by side or in front or behind, according as the sun shone. The Shadow was always careful to keep in the master's place, and the learned man didn't really think much about that; he was a very good soul, extremely kind and friendly. And so one day said he to the Shadow: "As we've become travelling companions (as we are) and as we've grown up together from childhood, wouldn't it be nice to drink brotherhood, and call each other 'thou'? It's more sociable, isn't it?"

"Now you're talking," said the Shadow (who was in fact the master). "What you say is very frank and very well meant. I'll be equally frank and well meaning. You as a scholar know very well what an odd thing Nature is. Some people can't bear to touch brown paper, it makes them sick; others feel it all over their body when someone scratches a pane of glass with a nail. Now I get just that sensation when I hear you say 'thou' to me. I feel absolutely as if I were crushed down on the ground, as I was in my first situation with you. You understand, it's merely a sensation, not pride at all. I can't bear you saying 'thou' to me, but I'll gladly say 'thou' to you; and that's meeting you halfway."

So the Shadow addressed his former master as "thou."

"Upon my word, it's rather much," thought the learned man, "that I should have to say 'you' and he should say 'thou.' " But he had to put up with it.

Eventually they came to a watering-place where there were a number of visitors, and among them a beautiful Princess, who was suffering from the complaint of seeing too well; which is, of course, very distressing.

She noticed at once that the newcomer was a very different sort of person from all the rest. "People say he has come here to get his beard to grow, but I can see the real reason. He can't cast a shadow."

Her curiosity was roused, and very soon she got into conversation with the strange gentleman, on the promenade. Being a Princess, she did not need to beat about the bush, so she said: "What's the matter with you is that you can't cast a shadow."

"Your Royal Highness must be considerably better," said the Shadow. "I am aware that your complaint is that you see too well; but it has yielded, and you are cured. I have, in fact, a quite unusual shadow. Do you see the person who always goes about with me? Other people have an ordinary shadow, but I don't care about what is ordinary. You give your servant finer clothes for his livery than you wear yourself, and just so I have had my shadow smartened up into a man. What's more, you can see that I have even given him a shadow. It costs money, but I do like to have something peculiar to myself."

"What!" thought the Princess. "Can I really have recovered? These baths are the best that exist! Waters certainly have an amazing power in these days. Still, I shan't go away; it's becoming lively here. I have an extraordinary liking for that stranger. I only hope his beard won't grow, for he'll go away if it does."

In the evening the Princess and the Shadow danced together in the great ballroom. She was light, but he was lighter, and such a partner she had never had. She told him what country she came from, and he knew it; he had been there, but at a time when she was not at home. He had peeped in at windows, upstairs and downstairs, and seen one thing and another, and so he could answer the Princess's questions and give her information that quite astounded her. He must be the wisest man on earth, she thought, and she conceived the greatest respect for his knowledge; and when they danced together a second time she fell in love with him. Of this the Shadow was well aware, for she gazed at him as if she would see through him. Yet once again they danced together, and she was on the point of speaking out. But she was careful. She thought of her country and realm and the many people she had to govern. "Wise he is," she thought to herself; "and that is a good point. He dances beautifully, and that's another. But is his knowledge thorough? That's equally important; that must be sifted." So she began very gradually to put to him some of the very most difficult questions, things she couldn't have answered herself, and the Shadow pulled a very odd face.

"Can't you answer me that?" asked the Princess.

"That was part of my nursery lessons," said the Shadow. "I really believe my shadow there behind the door can answer that."

"Your shadow?" said the Princess. "That would be most remarkable."

"Well, I don't say for certain that he can," said the Shadow, "but I think it, seeing he has been following me and listening to me all these years—I do think it. But your Royal Highness will permit me to call your attention to the fact that he takes such pride in passing for a man, that if he's to be in the right temper (as he must be to answer properly), he must be treated exactly like a man." "I'm perfectly agreeable to that," said the Princess. So she went across to the learned man at the door and talked to him about the sun and the moon, and about human nature, both outward and inward, and he answered her most wisely and well.

"What a man must he be who has so wise a shadow!" thought she. "It would be a real blessing for my people and my realm if I chose him for my consort. I will!"

And very soon they were agreed, the Princess and the Shadow, but no one was to know of it till she got back to her own kingdom.

"No one, not even my shadow," said the Shadow, who had his own thoughts about the matter.

And now they were in the country over which the Princess ruled when she was at home.

"Listen, my good friend," said the Shadow to the learned man. "I am now become as fortunate and as powerful as anyone can be, and now I will do something special for you. You shall always live with me in the palace, and drive out with me in my royal coach, and you shall have a hundred thousand rix-dollars a year. But you must allow yourself to be called a shadow by everyone, you must never say that you were at one time a man, and once a year, when I sit on the balcony in the sunshine and allow myself to be looked at, you must lie at my feet as a shadow ought to do. I may as well tell you that I am going to marry the Princess. The wedding is to take place this evening."

"No, no! That is really too much," said the learned man. "I won't allow it. I won't do it! It's deceiving the whole country and the Princess too. I shall tell the whole story—that I am the man and you are the shadow; you're only dressed up."

"Nobody will believe it," said the Shadow. "Do be reasonable, or I shall call the guard."

"I shall go straight to the Princess," said the learned man. "But I shall go first," said the Shadow, "and you'll go to prison." And there he had to go, for the sentries obeyed the one whom they knew the Princess was to marry.

"You are all in a tremble," said the Princess, when the Shadow came into her room. "Has anything happened? You mustn't be ill to-night; we're going to be married."

"I have had the most terrible experience that can occur to anyone," said the Shadow. "Only think of it—to be sure, a poor shadow's brain isn't equal to the strain—only think, my shadow has gone mad! He believes that he is the man and that I—just think of it—am his shadow!"

"That is awful," said the Princess; "I hope he is shut up?"

"Indeed he is. I'm afraid he'll never get the better of it."

"Poor shadow," said the Princess; "it's most unfortunate for him. It would really be a kindness to rid him of his little bit of life: indeed, when I come to think of it, I do believe it is essential that he should be quite quietly put out of the way."

"It's really very hard!" said the Shadow. "He was a faithful servant to me," and with that he seemed to sigh.

"You are a noble character," said the Princess.

That evening the whole town was illuminated, and the cannons went off "Boom!" And the soldiers presented arms. It *was* a wedding, to be sure! The Princess and the Shadow went out on the balcony to show themselves and receive one last "Hurrah!"

The learned man heard nothing of all this, for he had already been executed.

DORP DEAD

Julia Cunningham

In this century, generally, books and stories for children whose effect depends on a frightening, sinister atmosphere, menacing characters, and violent events—in other words, stories about the shadow side of things—have often been suppressed by well-intentioned adults. The following contemporary story is an exception (although it has caused some controversy). Dorp Dead *is a fantasy allegory about understanding love (the Hunter) and its compulsive, demanding opposite, or shadow (Mr. Kobalt, the eccentric ladder maker). Gilly Ground, suspicious of all adults, is the young orphan who is caught between these two warring aspects of adult nature.*

While I am setting out the soup bowls, the wedge of supper cheese, and the bread, I am just as busy rubbing a mental smudge, as I used to do on my arithmetic papers, all over my meeting with the Hunter. I don't want any permanent design left in my memory of his face, his words, or even the tower, so lovely and lonely, blued by the dusk.

I lift up the lid of the pot and inhale the odor of the thick soup that is our daily dinner and this helps me to meld back into my frame of Kobalt's routine. Then I realize something is missing. The dog. He is always at full length under the kitchen table when I come in at six: Maybe he got shut out by mistake, though this would be almost impossibly unlikely.

I call, "Mash! Here, Mash!" but no click, click of his ungainly paws across the slick floor. And as I involuntarily look at their absence I see something that sends me cold with shock: a trail of dark drops streak the surface of the stone.

I lower the fire under the soup, straighten the spoons that have been joggled sideways by my colliding with the table as I spy the stains, and then, with a half-hour to go before Kobalt will leave his work for the day, I follow the scarlet track. My alarm mounts as the droplets become blobs and then splashes, but at last they cease in front of the tool shed in the corner of the rose garden. I rip open the door and then I am down on my knees beside the shuddering, no longer mud-colored heap of dog. I grab up a sack from the corner, gather him into my arms, and stagger back to the kitchen. I drop the burlap on the floor, nudge it flat with one toe, and lay him as gently as I can on top of it. I reach for the dish towel but my hand stops in

From Julia Cunningham, *Dorp Dead* (New York: Pantheon, 1965), Chapters 6-7.

midair as though controlled by an invisible force. It digs into my pocket and draws out a handkerchief. I am talking in a whisper to Mash while I drench the cloth in running water and then begin to wipe him clean of clots and dried stripes of blood. The dog never whimpers or moves as time after time I squeeze out the handkerchief and return to bathe his wounds. I don't know what I am saying to him, I just let any old thing rise into my mouth and come out, but somewhere I think I tell him a piece of a fairy tale about a prince who was changed into a beast. It is the first story I remember being told by someone who must have been my grandmother. I am hurrying to get done before Kobalt's entrance but I keep on pretending my fingers are really feathers so I won't hurt the dog. I see that the slashes are not deep and that there will be no scars. The bleeding has stopped. He must have been whipped early, maybe before I left my room for the mountains. I remind myself like a litany behind my murmuring to Mash that he is Kobalt's dog, not mine, and the "not mine, not mine" musics itself into a tune that sounds like the moans of wind around the broken window-hole of my tower. Now he has raised his head and is staring at me with the same muddy eyes I think I saw so long ago this morning in my own mirror. I have finished wiping the last injured inch of him when I hear the pounding tread of Kobalt coming through the hall. I stuff the handkerchief into my pants pocket, prop Mash on his feet and whisk the sacking out of sight into a bottom cupboard, and just as I come out of my stoop, I feel something wet and velvety swipe across the back of my left hand. Only once, one single caress of a lick, from an animal who never before showed any caring. Somehow this injects me with enough strength to show myself as calm as a boulder in a blizzard as Master Kobalt strides in and takes his seat at the table.

I am resolved to do what I do, small as it is, so after I have ladled out the soup and Kobalt is already eating I simply sit there and do not pick up my spoon. It is six mouthfuls before the man notices my stillness. Between dipping in a seventh time and carrying the load of meat chunks and vegetables to his lips he says, "Well? You are sick?"

I try to look into his eyes but they are directed at my bowl. "No," I answer, my voice thready but clear. "Mash is."

The short, giant-muscled carpenter permits what seems like two minutes to be ticked off by the five kitchen clocks. Then he points with his spoon toward the floor. "You have some scrubbing up to do after supper."

The dog is behind my chair. I can hear his breathing. I want to let the whole thing drop into yesterday right then and there but that tiny, tired whuffling of breath keeps me bold.

"Why?" I ask. "Why did you beat him?"

Kobalt's shoulders hoist in what might or what might not be a shrug. "He is getting old. I will soon need another dog and Mash must learn to die."

The words are like a blow on the back of my neck, stunning my body into paralysis. As though the scene were a hundred miles away, I sit there and watch this man finish his soup to the last cube of potato, wipe his broad mouth carefully with his napkin, get up and go into the living room. I go on sitting until I am aware that my stomach juices are slowly rising into my throat. Quickly I get up, the soup bowl clutched in one hand, and place it before Mash. My legs and arms are so weighted I nearly drop the cheese plate as I mechanically replace it in the cooler and the bread I can't swallow seems baked of lead as I put it into its special box. But at last the room is as it was. I feel something warm bump the back of my knees. It is the dog, leaning against me as if to tell me it is okay with him—a "don't worry" kind of pressure. I kneel down beside him and rub my cheek against one of his limp ears.

Am I, too, a dog, a human dog, to be trained and used until I am no longer young or willing enough to co-operate? Am I, too, learning to die? The Hunter's words strike back at me: "Are you bewitched, boy?" and now there is no anger in me but something much worse—fear.

I tiptoe into the hall and see Kobalt in his chair by the fire, reading his book on time patterns, his body as stiffly correct as if he were carved in wood, fastened with concealed glue forever to the silk cushion at his back. I stand, ghostlike, in the dimness as the pages of his book turn to ten, fifteen, twenty—his daily portion of print—and the apprehension seeps out of me. What is there to be afraid of? He is a man, however eccentric, like any other. He sleeps, rises in the morning, eats, works, and draws breath just as I do. If he is also cruel—and I do not forgive the injuries to Mash—then perhaps I, too, have dished out my share of meanness during my less long lifetime, in forms not quite so obvious.

But when he finally resets his book at exact right-angles to the edges of the table beside him, gets up, and goes to his locked room with only a nodded good-night toward me, I'm not so certain why I'm trying to forget the cool horror of his words, "Mash must learn to die."

I squat by the fire and leaf through my memories of my grandmother. She was old, she knew that she had to die, and she never faced anything sideways but lived right up to the last minute and maybe beyond because when they put her in the ground she wasn't in the box. She was behind me where the real things are, like trees and grass and birds in their nests. I never turned to prove her visibility. I didn't have to. Just feeling her presence was enough and I had no tears for the ceremony going on in front of me.

I hang around thinking so long that Mash finally finds sleep in a corner of the hearth without our usual conversation. I am more at home inside myself somehow. Maybe it is the covering warmth of the fire, maybe because my grandmother came close again. But I do know I have to take some kind of action, and what I do is very peculiar. I sneak into the carpenter shop, change the position of five completed ladders from one wall to another, crisscross them into a rigid tangle, and then mount quietly to my room. The round, blank moon seems to center my window as though pasted onto the outside of the glass, and I wonder as I take to my bed if my dreams will be sweet or sour.

As I am slicing the breakfast bread the next morning I have no chance to rummage through my head to review what my dreaming really was, because suddenly a thundery clatter like nightmare comes from the carpenter shop. It's as though an enormous bird with a wingspread of six feet has got trapped in that large room and is smashing itself against the walls. No such noise—not even a miniature of it—has ever been permitted before in the contrived silence of this house.

I snake through the hall and what I see stops me as short as a wall. Kobalt, his arms flailing, is pushing and shoving the ladders and lumber into a jumble of giant jackstraws. His lips are drawn back over his stained teeth and his face is as white as glacial snow. Now he begins to kick at the fallen spars of wood as though, at any instant, they might loom upward and strike him down. He seizes a neat stack of finished rungs and hurls them, one by one, at the ceiling. They fall around him like hail, bouncing off his shoulders. What stops this dervish of destruction is the sight of me.

I think he is going to pick me up like a length of wood and smash me against a wall, but instead he freezes into a stillness like the core of a cyclone. His voice is so crowded with growls I have trouble sorting out the words: "It was you! You who moved those ladders! To enrage me. You know what I am and what I wish. Yet you did it, you deliberately did it! You shall be punished, now and—" There he breaks off and a casing of calmness so absolute falls over him I feel the first twinge of real fright. "First you will restore this room to order. Then you are to climb up the tallest ladder and sit there until I tell you to come down. Start now. I am watching."

It takes me what seems a very long time to pick up and restack the havoc of lumber because my hands are awkward with iciness and my arms lack half their power, but at last all is as it was and I obey his final command by humping myself to the summit of the highest jointed ladder in the room and sitting on the top rung. I clench my fingers like clamps to each side of my perch. Is he going to topple it over? Which bones will splinter when I hit the floor?

But he does not approach an inch nearer. Instead he steps into the hall and I hear the lock in the door click it finally shut.

I am not dizzy but I close my eyes. I am attempting to understand. But maybe I really did understand last night when I moved the five ladders from their places. I half-knew what it would do to this strange, time-controlled person who, for some reason I can't discover, gives me good shelter, clothes, food, an opportunity to learn, and a refuge from the disjointed, bonging world of the orphanage. And now I know for sure why I did it. To avenge the whiplashes on the hide of his spiritless dog. And it worked. It bombed him out of his eerie peace. But what happens when the dam cracks or the tree-trunk is sawn through? I wish I could start yesterday over, return to the moment I take the first step up the pathway to the tower and turn about-face, and never go, never meet the Hunter, never be stabbed by the rightness of his question: "Are you bewitched, boy?" If I could magic the fifteen clocks in this house and all the others across the surface of the earth, I would do it.

But I recover no shadow of ease or release from this daydream. It is too fragile. It wisps off the ground glass of what really is, like the cover of morning's first mist. I am a prisoner just as certainly as Kobalt is a prisoner, but the terrible difference is that he chose his dungeon and he has become the jailer of mine.

I shift my weight just enough so as not to shake the ladder. My backbone is aching a little. I force my thoughts to walk forward even if they lead me to a gallows. To him I am a clock to be wound, or a front door to be opened only three times a day, or a creature to make soup and keep the plates clean, or—I halt before the next image but break through its thorns as I used to the thickets on the way to the tower—or a dog. I am no more alive to Kobalt than Mash. And from Mash he drew blood.

I am at the end, the last point of land before drowning, and I clang a steel shutter down over my mind and concentrate on nothingness—a desolate country that shows no green.

I never know the duration of that trancelike session on the ladder and I don't leave the barrenness of the nothing-landscape until I begin to smell the meat for lunch mixing its scent with that of the shaved wood. I open my eyes on Kobalt who fills the threshold with solid sternness. He beckons me down but it is several minutes before I can loosen the tension in my leg and arm joints enough to descend, flat-footed and unsteady.

I think, as I scoop my chair up under the kitchen table and cut into the chunk of beef, that Kobalt will have something to say. If ever, now. But he treats today like all the others with his deep and ordinary habit of silence. I stuff the food into me the way I used to when I was first put into the orphanage, as though the next meal might not show up. Kobalt finishes before me and disappears into his shop. With the torpor of a slug I stack the dishes, wash them, and give them back to their cupboards. I go upstairs, pull out my history book, and fasten myself to the sentence where I left off yesterday. I believe I am reading but I'm not. The page might as well be wiped free of any words at all. I am not in revolutionary France where the book is, but at the window, wondering what is in the locked room neighboring mine, Kobalt's room. I've never really cared before but I do now. It seems important or maybe my newborn curiosity is just an escape from myself. I unlatch the middle frame of the window and push it up. I look down. The high distance from the ground reminds me of those hours on the ladder, though this drop is three times longer, so I twist my head to the right and stare at the protruding window sill of the other room. I note—I have never investigated before—that there is a very narrow ledge running from the base of my sill to his. It would just about support half of my foot if I Indian-walked it.

Suddenly I am invaded by action. I straddle the sill, one leg in, one leg out, shift my weight and, my palms flat against the smooth outer stone, I inch my body across the three feet separating the two windows. I grab hold of the small jut in the center of Kobalt's window frame, crooking my fingers as tight as I can along the tiny hold, and peer in. I think I get just one blink, one flash of that interior, for in the next instant I am teetering wildly, one foot in midair, and then I fall crashingly downward and land in a crumple on the dirt-packed, grassless ground.

I draw in a couple of breaths to test my ribs. Then I untangle myself and lie spread-eagled, cautiously lifting first my arms, then my legs. Everything works except my left ankle. It seems to be invaded by a porcupine, so full of stings and jabs I stuff my knuckles into my mouth. I force myself into a sitting position. I must get up. After what I saw in that room I know that if I am disabled I am licked, done for. I raise my back upwards with my good leg, using my arms as props, and turn to stand. I make it but even this lightest of pressures on my ankle makes my lunch surge into my throat. I swallow down the bitterness again and again until I can control the convulsions in my stomach. I set my teeth and somehow drag myself into the kitchen. I go down on my knees, crawl to the closet where the cleaning things are stowed, and yank out a long dustcloth. I tear it into three strips and bind them, one after the other, around my ankle which now hurts so piercingly part of me wishes the foot would just drop off.

I use the table to hoist myself erect. I must get back to my room. Kobalt mustn't guess that I am crippled. I hobble as far as the stairs, then seat myself on the first step and with my good leg as a lever begin the tortured, backward journey up that endless flight. I bruise my back each time I slide myself onto the next ledge but I don't care. All that counts is my final arrival in my own room.

At last there are no more steps. Once more I go on all fours and, covering the brief space of hall, collapse into my room, pushing the door closed with my left arm.

I think I lie prone on the floor for a while, because it is not so difficult later to get onto my chair. Now I am once again where I was, facing my history book, but what has gone between, what I have seen, is so bursting with dread I have to fight my own will to make my hand pick up a pencil and draw on a square of paper what I glimpsed in that locked room. I have to redesign it this very instant or I will never believe it exists. My hand jerks and the lines wobble but I keep going, and when I am done I stare at the crude unreality of the sketch until I am certain it is true. It shows a cage made of discarded ladder rungs and side rails. A large cage but not large enough for Kobalt. It is just my size!

I snatch up the sheet of paper, scrabble it into a ball, and then tear it into such minute bits it snows itself all over my blotter.

THE TALE OF TWO BAD MICE

Beatrix Potter

The temper tantrums of the "bad mice," Tom Thumb and Hunca Munca, are violent and spontaneous, just like those of small children when they are disappointed. The determined naughtiness of the mice makes this a very satisfying story for children to project their own anger onto.

Beatrix Potter (1866-1943) is one of many examples of great writers whose work is appreciated both by children and by adults. Like many of these writers she also had a traumatic growing-up period and never had children of her own. She had to battle her family over her first engagement when she was thirty-nine (to Norman Warne of the publishing house which published her books) and the quarrel was only solved when her fiancé died. She again had to battle her parents over her engagement to a country lawyer, William Heelis, in 1913, when she was forty-seven. This battle she won. She became a happy farm woman in Sawrey in the Lake Country in England and did very little writing thereafter. In 1970 in Sawrey, I talked to an old man who knew her well. He said she was regarded by some of the villagers as a bit of an eccentric, for she liked to tramp about her property in the rain "like an old waller" or builder of stone fences, with a gunny sack in front and another in back, knotted at the shoulders to keep off the rain. Her deep understanding of animals was manifest in her farm life as it had been previously in her drawings—one can almost get inside her animals and sense the warm animal fragrance and the beating heart.

Once upon a time there was a very beautiful doll's-house; it was red brick with white windows, and it had real muslin curtains and a front door and a chimney.

It belonged to two Dolls called Lucinda and Jane, at least it belonged to Lucinda, but she never ordered meals.

Jane was the Cook; but she never did any cooking, because the dinner had been bought ready-made, in a box full of shavings.

There were two red lobsters and a ham, a fish, a pudding, and some pears and oranges.

They would not come off the plates, but they were extremely beautiful.

One morning Lucinda and Jane had gone out for a drive in the doll's perambulator. There was no one in the nursery, and it was very quiet. Presently there was a little scuffling, scratching noise in a corner near the fireplace, where there was a hole under the skirting-board.

Tom Thumb put out his head for a moment, and then popped it in again.

Tom Thumb was a mouse.

A minute afterwards, Hunca Munca, his wife, put her head out, too; and when she saw that there was no one in the nursery, she ventured out on the oil cloth under the coal-box.

The doll's-house stood at the other

side of the fire-place. Tom Thumb and Hunca Munca went cautiously across the hearth rug. They pushed the front door—it was not fast.

Tom Thumb and Hunca Munca went upstairs and peeped into the dining-room. Then they squeaked with joy!

Such a lovely dinner was laid out upon the table! There were tin spoons, and lead knives and forks, and two dolly-chairs—all *so* convenient!

Tom Thumb set to work at once to carve the ham. It was a beautiful shiny yellow, streaked with red.

The knife crumpled up and hurt him; he put his finger in his mouth.

"It is not boiled enough; it is hard. You have a try, Hunca Munca."

Hunca Munca stood up in her chair, and chopped at the ham with another lead knife.

"It's as hard as the hams at the cheesemonger's," said Hunca Munca.

The ham broke off the plate with a jerk, and rolled under the table.

"Let it alone," said Tom Thumb; "give me some fish, Hunca Munca!"

Hunca Munca tried every tin spoon in turn; the fish was glued to the dish.

Then Tom Thumb lost his temper. He put the ham in the middle of the floor, and hit it with the tongs and with the shovel—bang, bang, smash, smash!

The ham flew all into pieces, for underneath the shiny paint it was made of nothing but plaster!

Then there was no end to the rage and disappointment of Tom Thumb and Hunca Munca. They broke up the pudding, the lobsters, the pears and the oranges.

As the fish would not come off the plate, they put it into the red-hot crinkly paper fire in the kitchen; but it would not burn either.

Tom Thumb went up the kitchen chimney and looked out at the top—there was no soot.

While Tom Thumb was up the chimney, Hunca Munca had another disappointment. She found some tiny canisters upon the dresser, labelled—Rice—Coffee—Sago—but when she turned them upside down, there was nothing inside except red and blue beads.

Then those mice set to work to do all the mischief they could—especially Tom Thumb! He took Jane's clothes out of the chest of drawers in her bedroom, and he threw them out of the top floor window.

But Hunca Munca had a frugal mind. After pulling half the feathers out of Lucinda's bolster, she remembered that she herself was in want of a feather bed.

With Tom Thumb's assistance she carried the bolster downstairs, and across the hearth rug. It was difficult to squeeze the bolster into the mouse-hole; but they managed it somehow.

Then Hunca Munca went back and fetched a chair, a book-case, a bird-cage, and several small odds and ends. The book-case and the bird-cage refused to go into the mouse-hole.

Hunca Munca left them behind the coal-box, and went to fetch a candle.

Hunca Munca was just returning with another chair, when suddenly there was a noise of talking outside upon the landing. The mice rushed back to their hole, and the dolls came into the nursery.

What a sight met the eyes of Jane and Lucinda! Lucinda sat upon the upset kitchen stove and stared; and Jane leant against the kitchen dresser and smiled—but neither of them made any remark.

The book-case and the bird-cage were rescued from under the coal-box—but Hunca Munca has got the cradle, and some of Lucinda's clothes.

She also has some useful pots and pans, and several other things.

The little girl that the doll's-house belonged to, said—"I will get a doll dressed like a policeman!"

But the nurse said—"I will set a mouse-trap!"

So that is the story of the two Bad Mice—but they were not so very naughty after all, because Tom Thumb paid for everything he broke.

He found a crooked sixpence under the hearth rug; and upon Christmas Eve, he and Hunca Munca stuffed it into one of the stockings of Lucinda and Jane.

And very early every morning—before anybody is awake—Hunca Munca comes with her dust-pan and her broom to sweep the Dollies' house!

The End

THE LAST BATTLE

C. S. Lewis

This is the next-to-last chapter of The Last Battle, *after the struggle has been resolved between King Tirian and the forces of evil, represented by Shift the Ape and his dupe, Puzzle the Donkey. The children who help in the battle are Jill, Lucy, Eustace, Edmund, and Peter. The king, the children, and the remaining Narnians are killed in the battle or make their way into Aslan's country by way of the stable. Aslan's country is both a representation of the Christian heaven and Plato's ideal reality, of which our earthly reality is only a shadow, or imperfect representation.*

Farther Up and Farther In

"Know, O Warlike Kings," said Emeth, "and you, O Ladies whose beauty illuminates the universe, that I am Emeth the seventh son of Harpha Tarkaan of the city of Tehishbaan, Westward beyond the desert. I came lately into Narnia with nine and twenty others under the command of Rishda Tarkaan. Now when I first heard that we should march upon Narnia I rejoiced; for I had heard many things of your Land and desired greatly to meet you in battle. But when I found that we were to go in disguised as merchants (which is a shameful dress for a warrior and the son of a Tarkaan) and to work by lies and trickery, then my joy departed from me. And most of all when I found we must wait upon a monkey, and when it began to be said that Tash and Aslan were one, then the world became dark in my eyes. For always since I was a boy I have served Tash and my great desire was to know more of him and, if it might be, to look upon his face. But the name of Aslan was hateful to me.

"And, as you have seen, we were called together outside the straw-roofed hovel, night after night, and the fire was kindled, and the Ape brought forth out of the hovel something upon four legs that I could not well see. And the people and the Beasts bowed down and did honour to it. But I thought, The Tarkaan is deceived by the Ape: for this thing that comes out of

From C. S. Lewis, *The Last Battle* (New York: Macmillan, 1956), Chapter 15.

the stable is neither Tash nor any other god. But when I watched the Tarkaan's face, and marked every word that he said to the Monkey, then I changed my mind: for I saw that the Tarkaan did not believe in it himself. And then I understood that he did not believe in Tash at all: for if he had, how could he dare to mock him?

"When I understood this, a great rage fell upon me and I wondered that the true Tash did not strike down both the Monkey and the Tarkaan with fire from heaven. Nevertheless I hid my anger and held my tongue and waited to see how it would end. But last night, as some of you know, the Monkey brought not forth the yellow thing but said that all who desired to look upon Tashlan—for so they mixed the two words to pretend that they were all one—must pass one by one into the hovel. And I said to myself, Doubtless this is some other deception. But when the Cat had gone in and had come out again in a madness of terror, then I said to myself, Surely the true Tash, whom they called on without knowledge or belief, has now come among us, and will avenge himself. And though my heart was turned into water inside me because of the greatness and terror of Tash, yet my desire was stronger than my fear, and I put force upon my knees to stay them from trembling, and on my teeth that they should not chatter, and resolved to look upon the face of Tash though he should slay me. So I offered myself to go into the hovel; and the Tarkaan, though unwillingly, let me go.

"As soon as I had gone in at the door, the first wonder was that I found myself in this great sunlight (as we all are now) though the inside of the hovel had looked dark from outside. But I had no time to marvel at this, for immediately I was forced to fight for my head against one of our own men. As soon as I saw him I understood that the Monkey and the Tarkaan had set him there to slay any who came in if he were not in their secrets: so that this man also was a liar and a mocker and no true servant of Tash. I had the better will to fight him; and having slain the villain, I cast him out behind me through the door.

"Then I looked about me and saw the sky and the wide lands and smelled the sweetness. And I said, By the Gods, this is a pleasant place: it may be that I am come into the country of Tash. And I began to journey into the strange country and to seek him.

"So I went over much grass and many flowers and among all kinds of wholesome and delectable trees till lo! in a narrow place between two rocks there came to meet me a great Lion. The speed of him was like the ostrich, and his size was an elephant's; his hair was like pure gold and the brightness of his eyes like gold that is liquid in the furnace. He was more terrible than the Flaming Mountain of Lagour, and in beauty he surpassed all that is in the world even as the rose in bloom surpasses the dust of the desert. Then I fell at his feet and thought, Surely this is the hour of death, for the Lion (who is worthy of all honour) will know that I have served Tash all my days and not him. Nevertheless, it is better to see the Lion and die than to be Tisroc of the world and live and not to have seen him. But the Glorious One bent down his golden head and touched my forehead with his tongue and said, Son, thou art welcome. But I said, Alas, Lord, I am no son of thine but the servant of Tash. He answered, Child, all the service thou hast done to Tash, I account as service done to me. Then by reason of my great desire for wisdom and understanding, I overcame my fear and questioned the Glorious One and said, Lord, is it then true, as the Ape said, that thou and Tash are one? The Lion growled so that the earth shook (but his wrath was not against me) and said, It is false. Not because he and I are one, but because we are opposites, I take to me the services which thou hast done to him. For I and he are of such different kinds that no service which is vile can be done to me, and none which is not vile can be done to him. Therefore if any man swear by Tash and keep his oath for the oath's sake, it is by me that he has truly sworn, though he know it not, and it is I who reward him. And if any man do a cruelty in my name, then, though he says the name Aslan, it is Tash whom he serves and by Tash his deed is accepted. Dost thou understand, Child? I said, Lord, thou knowest how much I understand. But I said also (for the truth constrained me), Yet I have been seeking Tash all my days. Beloved, said the Glorious One, unless thy desire had been for me thou wouldst not have sought so long and so truly. For all find what they truly seek.

"Then he breathed upon me and took away the trembling from my limbs and caused me to stand upon my feet. And after that, he said not much but that we should meet again, and I must go Farther up and Farther in. Then he turned him about in a storm and flurry of gold and was gone suddenly.

"And since then, O Kings and Ladies, I have been wandering to find him and my happiness is so great that it even weakens me like a wound. And this is the marvel of marvels, that he called me Beloved, me who am but as a dog—"

"Eh? What's that?" said one of the Dogs.

"Sir," said Emeth. "It is but a fashion of speech which we have in Calormen."

"Well, I can't say it's one I like very much," said the Dog.

"He doesn't mean any harm," said an older Dog. "After all, *we* call our puppies *Boys* when they don't behave properly."

"So we do," said the first Dog. "Or *girls*."

"S-s-sh!" said the Old Dog. "That's not a nice word to use. Remember where you are."

"Look!" said Jill suddenly. Someone was coming, rather timidly, to meet them; a graceful creature on four feet, all silvery-grey. And they stared at him for a whole ten seconds before five or six voices said all at once, "Why, it's old Puzzle!" They had never seen him by daylight with the lion-skin off, and it made an extraordinary difference. He was himself now: a beautiful donkey with such a soft, grey coat and such a gentle, honest face that if you had seen him you would have done just what Jill and Lucy did—rushed forward and put your arms round his neck and kissed his nose and stroked his ears.

When they asked him where he had been he said he had come in at the door along with all the other creatures but he had—well, to tell the truth, he had been keeping out of their way as much as he could; and out of Aslan's way. For the sight of the real Lion had made him so ashamed of all that nonsense about dressing up in a lion-skin that he did not know how to look anyone in the face. But when he saw that all his friends were going away westward, and after he had had a mouthful or so of grass ("And I've never tasted such good grass in my life," said Puzzle) he plucked up his courage and followed. "But what I'll do if I really have to meet Aslan, I'm sure I don't know," he added.

"You'll find it will be all right when you really do," said Queen Lucy.

Then they all went forward together, always westward, for that seemed to be the direction Aslan had meant when he cried out "Farther up and farther in." Many other creatures were slowly moving the same way, but that grassy country was very wide and there was no crowding.

It still seemed to be early and the morning freshness was in the air. They kept on stopping to look round and to look behind them, partly because it was so beautiful but partly also because there was something about it which they could not understand.

"Peter," said Lucy, "where is this, do you suppose?"

"I don't know," said the High King. "It reminds me of somewhere but I can't give it a name. Could it be somewhere we once stayed for a holiday when we were very, very small?"

"It would have to have been a jolly good holiday," said Eustace. "I bet there isn't a country like this anywhere in *our* world. Look at the colours? You couldn't get a blue like the blue on those mountains in our world."

"Is it not Aslan's country?" said Tirian.

"Not like Aslan's country on top of that mountain beyond the eastern end of the world," said Jill. "I've been there."

"If you ask me," said Edmund, "it's like somewhere in the Narnian world. Look at those mountains ahead—and the big ice-mountains beyond them. Surely they're rather like the mountains we used to see from Narnia, the ones up Westward beyond the Waterfall?"

"Yes, so they are," said Peter. "Only these are bigger."

"I don't think *those* ones are so very like anything in Narnia," said Lucy. "But look there." She pointed southwards to their left, and everyone stopped and turned to look. "Those hills," said Lucy, "the nice woody ones and the blue ones behind—aren't they very like the southern border of Narnia?"

"Like," cried Edmund after a moment's silence. "Why, they're exactly like. Look, there's Mount Pire with his forked head, and there's the pass into Archenland and everything!"

"And yet they're not like," said Lucy. "They're different. They have more colours on them and they look farther away than I remembered and they're more . . . more . . . oh, I don't know. . . . "

"More like the real thing," said the Lord Digory softly.

Suddenly Farsight the Eagle spread his wings, soared thirty or forty feet up into the air, circled round and then alighted on the ground.

"Kings and Queens," he cried, "we have all been blind. We are only beginning to see where we are. From up there I have seen it all—Ettinsmuir, Beaversdam, the Great River, and Cair Paravel still shining on the edge of the Eastern Sea. Narnia is not dead. This is Narnia."

"But how can it be?" said Peter. "For Aslan told us older ones that we should never return to Narnia, and here we are."

"Yes," said Eustace. "And we saw it all destroyed and the sun put out."

"And it's all so different," said Lucy.

"The Eagle is right," said the Lord Digory. "Listen, Peter. When Aslan said you could never go back to Narnia, he meant the Narnia you were thinking of. But that was not the real Narnia. That had a beginning and an end. It was only a shadow or a copy of the real Narnia which has always been here and always will be here: just as our own world, England and all, is only a shadow or copy of something in Aslan's real world. You need not mourn over Narnia, Lucy. All of the old Narnia that mattered, all the dear creatures, have been drawn into the real Narnia through the Door. And of course it is different; as different as a real thing is from a shadow or as waking life is from a dream." His voice stirred everyone like a trumpet as he spoke these words: but when he added under his breath "It's all in Plato, all in Plato: bless me, what *do* they teach them at these schools!" the older ones laughed. It was so exactly like the sort of thing they had heard him say long ago in that other world where his beard was grey instead of golden. He knew why they were laughing and joined in the laugh himself. But very quickly they all became grave again: for, as you know, there is a kind of happiness and wonder that makes you serious. It is too good to waste on jokes.

It is as hard to explain how this sunlit land was different from the old Narnia as it would be to tell you how the fruits of that country taste. Perhaps you will get some idea of it if you think like this. You may have been in a room in which there was a window that looked out on a lovely bay of the sea or a green valley that wound away among mountains. And in the wall of that room opposite to the window there may have been a looking-glass. And as you turned away from the window you suddenly caught sight of that sea or that valley, all over again, in the looking-glass. And the sea in the mirror, or the valley in the mirror, were in one sense just the same as the real one: yet at the same time they were somehow different—deeper, more wonderful, more like places in a story: in a story you have never heard but very much want to know. The difference between the old Narnia and the new Narnia was like that. The new one was a deeper country: every rock and flower and blade of grass looked as if it meant more. I can't describe it any better than that: if you ever get there you will know what I mean.

It was the Unicorn who summed up what everyone was feeling. He stamped his right fore-hoof on the ground and neighed and then cried:

"I have come home at last! This is my real country! I belong here. This is the land I have been looking for all my life, though I never knew it till now. The reason why we loved the old Narnia is that it sometimes looked a little like this. Bree-hee-hee! Come farther up, come farther in!"

He shook his mane and sprang forward into a great gallop—a Unicorn's gallop which, in our world, would have carried him out of sight in a few moments. But now a most strange thing happened. Everyone else began to run, and they found, to their astonishment, that they could keep up with him: not only the Dogs and the humans but even fat little Puzzle and short-legged Poggin the Dwarf. The air flew in their faces as if they were driving fast in a car without a windscreen. The country flew past as if they were seeing it from the windows of an express train. Faster and faster they raced, but no one got hot or tired or out of breath.

Biography

GERONIMO: THE FIGHTING APACHE

Ronald Syme

Cultures have shadows too—one of the prominent shadows cast by the American people is that of its poor treatment of minority groups, including the American Indians. Long repressed, this shadow is now coming into the open, even in children's books like this excellent biography of the great Apache leader, Geronimo. The selection takes up his story in 1879, when fifty-year-old Geromino and his exhausted band of followers have finally decided in favor of making a peace treaty.

If the political leaders in Washington had been humane and possessed any integrity, Arizona and the neighboring states might have forgotten the name of Geronimo. But because those politicians were corrupt and greedy, this relatively peaceful time proved to be only temporary.

Throughout 1879, Geronimo and his 300 to 400 Chiricahua lived in the comparative freedom of their own mountains. Game of all kinds was plentiful, and none of the White Eyes interfered with them. And then the blow fell.

The news came from Washington. The Warm Springs reservation and the Chiricahua reservation were to be taken away from the Apache nation. No compensation was to be paid for this confiscation of land, which had been given to the Indians with the solemn promise that it would remain theirs "for as long as the mountains shall stand." As of today it has still not been returned to the Apache people.

Worst of all, however, was the news that from then on all Apaches were to be taken to the San Carlos reservation. There they were to be herded together and abandoned to a miserable, aimless existence with scanty rations, inadequate clothing and blankets, no medical supervision, and little hope of being able to provide extra food for themselves.

The prospect was too much for Geronimo and his undying, brooding hatred of all the White Eyes. Instead, as he later described, he went off on his own:

> We separated, each leader taking his own band. Some of them went to San Carlos and some to Old Mexico, but I took my own people back to Warm

From Ronald Syme, *Geronimo: The Fighting Apache* (New York: William Morrow, 1975), pp. 39-61.

Springs and rejoined Victorio's band.

Victorio knew that the Government had decided to seize the Warm Springs reservation. But the area had always belonged to his tribe, and they loved it greatly. The land was rich and fertile, the surrounding hills and forests and mountains were plentiful with game. The Warm Springs Indians with Victorio were still hoping that by some miracle they would be overlooked by the soldiers. They were living peacefully and interfering with no one in the hope of avoiding official attention. In order to remain in their favorite area, they were prepared to run the risk of being shot on sight by soldiers or armed civilians, the penalty decreed by the Government for any Indians found off a reservation. They preferred their present way of life to that of some of the Chiricahua who, under Taza and Naiche (Natchez), the sons of Cochise, had plodded off to San Carlos.

General Crook was still sympathetic toward the Apaches, but he had his orders to fulfill. The last of the tribe must be rounded up. His men appeared at the Warm Springs reservation, and Geronimo surrendered voluntarily to them. He described the scene later in these words:

> Two companies of [Indian] scouts were sent from San Carlos. When they came to Warm Springs they sent word for me and Victorio to come to town. As soon as we arrived, soldiers met us, disarmed us, and took us both to headquarters. Victorio was released and I was sentenced to the guardhouse and put in chains. When I asked them why they did this, they said it was because I had left Apache Pass.
>
> I do not think that I ever belonged to those soldiers at Apache Pass, or that I should have asked them where I might go.
>
> I was kept prisoner for four months, during which time I was transferred to San Carlos. Then I think I had another trial, although I was not present. In fact, I do not know that I had another trial, but I was told that I had, and at any rate, I was released.

If the American authorities had deliberately tried to make Geronimo an even more dangerous enemy, they could scarcely have done better. He was a warrior and proud of his standing in the tribe. To be loaded into a mule cart and taken in chains to San Carlos, where many hundreds of Apaches saw his humiliation, was a terrible disgrace. To be confined for months in a small prison cell under constant guard was a terrible punishment to a man like Geronimo to whom freedom was part of his natural heritage.

Victorio and 400 of his followers had also been brought under armed guard to San Carlos. There were now more than 5000 silent, moody, and depressed Apaches—men, women and children—living on that dreary reservation.

They were in a mood of bitter resentment. The President had sent them word through his official representatives that under their chief, Victorio, they would be free to remain permanently within their territory at Ojo Caliente. Yet only two years after that promise had been made, they were removed by armed soldiers and brought to the reservation at San Carlos. They told each other bitterly that perhaps the reason was that White Eyes might have suspected the presence of gold in the surrounding mountains. Gold, declared the Apaches, apparently counted for more than the solemn word of the Great White Chief, who had ordered them to be brought to the worst place in all Apache country.

Camp Goodwin on the Gila River was the local headquarters for these Indians. Built as a cavalry barracks in 1864, it had been abandoned within a few years owing to the dangerous prevalence of malaria fever, carried by mosquitoes that bred in the nearby swamps.

Much of Arizona had a reasonably temperate climate, but in the level, sandy country around Camp Goodwin the heat was intolerable. United States politicians expected the wretched Apaches to inhabit this area rather than to seek relief in the higher surrounding country, even though they would still be within the limits of the reservation. It was a harsh restriction on the tribe.

Lieutenant Britton Davis, a twenty-two-year-old Texan, arrived to undertake military duties at Camp Goodwin in 1882. He was a fair-minded young officer, the son of a judge. Before long the Apaches recognized him as possessing the qualities that they themselves most admired—honesty, courage, and justice. During the next four years, Davis came to understand and respect the Apache Indians. Long years after he resigned his commission in 1886, he wrote an excellent book about Geronimo and this period of Arizona history. To this day, *The Truth About Geronimo* remains a most valuable reference work.

Of the site chosen by the Government as suitable territory for the Apache Indians, Davis wrote:

> A gravelly flat, it was dotted here and there by the drab adobe buildings of the Agency. Scrawny, dejected lines of scattered cottonwoods, shrunken almost lifeless, marked the course of the streams. Rain was so infrequent that it seemed like a phenomenon when it came at all. Almost continuously dry, hot, dust- and gravel-laden winds swept the plain, denuding it of every vestige of vegetation. In summer a temperature of 110 degrees in the shade was cool weather. At all other times of the year flies, gnats, unnameable bugs swarmed in millions. Everywhere the naked, hungry, dirty, frightened little Indian children, darting behind bushes or into wikiups [low, crudely thatched huts] at sight of you. Everywhere the sullen, stolid, hopeless, suspicious faces of the older Indians challenging you. San Carlos was our idea of "Hell's Forty Acres."

Davis might have added that conditions on the reservation were sometimes made worse by the often dishonest or apathetic Indian Agents who came and went. Those obscure officials were assisted in their authority and duties by a number of white scouts, most of whom were hard-faced gunslingers with no time for any live Indian. They saw no reason why the Apaches should be treated as human beings and seldom troubled to do so themselves.

The Government had devised a number of hazy ideas about encouraging the Apaches to take up agriculture. But during the early days on the San Carlos reservation, the lack of irrigation, tools, and seeds made the scheme impossible. Not even a promised herd of cattle appeared. The Apaches refused to raise hogs, an animal they despised because it ate snakes. Day after day the Indians were left idle, ill-fed, and with nothing to occupy their minds or bodies.

Geronimo was one of the worst affected by this miserable existence. His naturally surly and suspicious nature heightened his resentment and hatred. He became morose, ill-tempered, and, according to Davis, began to drink too much of the tiswin beer, which the Indian women brewed from corn. Before long he earned a reputation among the white officials as a deceitful man whose word was not to be trusted. Geronimo held the same views regarding the White Eyes. The wretched existence his people were leading at San Carlos was final proof to him that no white Americans could ever be trusted.

Victorio and Geronimo abandoned the reservation in the fall of 1881. With them went 310 followers—men, women, and children. Among them was the great young woman warrior, Lozen. She was so honored and respected by the men that they granted her a place in their tribal councils. Juh and his son, Delshinne, and a splendid old veteran chief named Nana also rode with the fugitives. How Geronimo's band procured rifles and horses remains a mystery. They were, however, well armed and well mounted.

News of the outbreak reached the camp police while the party was still moving out. Police Chief Sterling rode after them and ordered the Apaches to return. When they refused to do so, he swung up his rifle to shoot the subchief, Loco. Another Indian, moving more swiftly, shot Sterling dead.

While frantically clicking telegraph keys warned settlements throughout the southwest, Geronimo, Juh, and the other leaders guided their people along Indian trails that led south. Geronimo says:

> We went on toward Old Mexico, but on the second day after this United States soldiers [cavalry] overtook us about three o'clock in the afternoon and we fought until dark. The ground where we were attacked was very rough, which was to our advantage, for the troops were compelled to dismount in order to fight us. I do not know how many soldiers were killed, but we lost only one warrior and three children. We had plenty of guns and ammunition we had accumulated while living on the reservation and the remainder we had obtained from the White Mountain Apaches when we left the reservation.

Another Apache, a young boy named Kaywaykla who took part in this flight, lived until 1963. In later years he published an account of his tragic experiences. He wrote of this incident, in which three soldiers died:

> They spent two nights at that place. Ussen [the Apache God] had delivered them from bondage and they were obligated to render thanks to Him according to their custom—with song and dance. Once in the mountains they could rest and rejoice, a free people again. In the land of Juh [a spacious and fertile sanctuary high up in the Sierra Madre] there would be no pursuit. Security and abundance would come in a short time. The horrors of San Carlos would fade.

Almost as soon as they reached the border they were located and attacked again, this time by Mexican cavalry. Once more those heroic Apaches, men and women alike, beat off one attack after another with accurate rifle fire. The older boys joined in whenever they could find a spare rifle, even though the recoil of a heavy Springfield bruised their shoulders and sometimes knocked them down.

Kaywaykla wrote:

> Lozen, her head concealed by a screen of cactus, dropped a man with every shot. Three times the Mexicans charged before deciding that the Apaches were not to be dislodged by that means.

Skirmishing and fighting almost every day, the Apaches finally reached comparative safety in the mountains.

The Sierra Madre range rose in places to a height of 12,000 feet. On its western side, in the state of Sonora, the mountains resembled a giant comb, high ridges of rock forming the teeth. Between them were deep valleys, usually choked with undergrowth. From high in these sierras the Apaches were able to descend by secret paths to obtain necessary supplies from nearby Mexican villages. Pursuing troops were unable to follow them into the mountains.

Juh, in spite of his great size and formidable prowess as a warrior, had a more amiable nature than Geronimo. During an earlier stay in the Sierra Madre, he had established a reasonably friendly relationship with the Mexicans of the settlements. He used it to trade with them now. Probably there was not much honesty on either side. If the Apaches stole a herd of cattle or horses in Sonora, they took the animals through the passes and sold them in Chihuahua, the state that lay east of the mountains. At other times they reversed the process. The Mexican traders drove hard bargains, but they were happy to exchange rifles, ammunition, clothing, needles, knives, and a potent spirit called mescal for animals that they were buying very cheaply. They were not able to rely on their own troops for protection, so they preferred to remain on more or less friendly terms with the Apaches.

In Arizona, a first-class political row built up as a result of the Apaches' flight. The settlers in lonely areas were alarmed and outraged. Officials began to take a closer look at the San Carlos reservation. What they discovered was too much even for their smug consciences.

In October, 1882, a Federal grand jury charged that Agent Tiffany of San Carlos "had kept eleven men in confinement for fourteen months without charges or any attempt to accuse them, knowing them to be innocent."

The shocking indictment of reservation conditions continued:

> The present investigations of the grand jury have laid bare the infamy of Agent Tiffany and a proper idea can be formed of the fraud and villainy which are constantly practised in open violation of the law and in defiance of public justice. Frauds, speculation, conspiracy, larceny, plots, and counterplots seem to be the rule of action upon the reservation.

Agent Tiffany was properly punished, but his imprisonment did not bring Geronimo and his Apaches back to the reservation.

Poetry

THE MEWLIPS

J. R. R. Tolkien

The shadows where the Mewlips
 dwell
 Are dark and wet as ink,
And slow and softly rings their bell,
 As in the slime you sink.

You sink into the slime, who dare
 To knock upon their door,
While down the grinning gargoyles
 stare
 And noisome waters pour.

Beside the rotting river-strand
 The drooping willows weep,
And gloomily the gorcrows stand
 Croaking in their sleep.

Over the Merlock Mountains a long and
 weary way,
 In a mouldy valley where the trees
 are grey,
By a dark pool's borders without wind
 or tide,
 Moonless and sunless, the Mewlips
 hide.

The cellars where the Mewlips sit
 Are deep and dank and cold
With single sickly candle lit;
 And there they count their gold.

Their walls are wet, their ceilings
 drip;
 Their feet upon the floor
Go softly with a squish-flap-flip,
 As they sidle to the door.

They peep out slyly; through a crack
 Their feeling fingers creep,
And when they've finished, in a sack
 Your bones they take to keep.

Beyond the Merlock Mountains, a long
 and lonely road,
 Through the spider-shadows and the
 marsh of Tode,
And through the wood of hanging trees
 and the gallows-weed,
 You go to find the Mewlips—and the
 Mewlips feed.

THE GARDEN SEAT

Thomas Hardy

Its former green is blue and thin,
And its once firm legs sink in and in;
Soon it will break down unaware,
Soon it will break down unaware.

At night when reddest flowers are black
Those who once sat thereon come back;
Quite a row of them sitting there,
Quite a row of them sitting there.

With them the seat does not break
 down,
Nor winter freeze them, nor floods
 drown,
For they are as light as upper air,
They are as light as upper air!

SOMETIMES I FEEL THIS WAY

John Ciardi

I have one head that wants to be good,
And one that wants to be bad.
And always, as soon as I get up,
One of my heads is sad.

"Be bad," says one head. "Don't you know
It's fun to be bad. Be as bad as you like.
Put sand in your brother's shoe—that's fun.
Put gum on the seat of your sister's bike."

"What fun is that?" says my other head.
"Why not go down before the rest
And set things out for breakfast? My,
That would please Mother. Be good—that's best."

"What! Better than putting frogs in the sink?
Or salt in the tea-pot? Have some fun.
Be bad, be bad, be good and bad.
You know it is good to be bad," says One.

"Is it good to make Sister and Brother sad?
And Mother and Daddy? And when you do,
Is it good to get spanked? Is it good to cry?
No, no. Be good—that's best," says Two.

So one by one they say what they say,
And what they say is "Be Good—Be Bad."
And if One is happy that makes Two cry.
And if Two is happy that makes One sad.

Someday maybe, when I grow up,
I shall wake and find I have just one—
The happy head. But which will it be?
I wish I knew. They are both *some* fun.

WILD WEST

Robert Boylan

Now let us speak of cowboys who on swift
White horses over blue-black deserts sped,
Their pistols blazing and their proud blood shed
In paint-flecked shanties on the haunted cliffs
Or in the bars of ghost-towns. Let us tell
The legends of fierce heroes motherless,
Not Indians, not Easterners, whose quests
And daring deeds inscribed their names in hell.
Bravely they shot it out, did Wyatt Earp,
Billy the Kid, Bill Hickok, Jesse James.
Now what remains but moving-picture dreams
Of all that fury and fast villainy?
Lone cactuses where bullets spit and ripped
The courage of the eyelid from the eye?
A rusting stirrup and a rowel thrust
Up from the calcifying sun-baked dust
Where some unknown avenger fell to sleep?
A wind-blown piece of buckskin that looked grand
When it was stretched upon the living hip
Of him who lies now six feet under ground?
Cowboys were not immortal. All they did,
Guzzling and gunning, ended when they died.

MY AUNT

Ted Hughes

You've heard how a green thumb
Makes flowers come
Quite without toil
Out of any old soil.

Well, my Aunt's thumbs were green.
At a touch, she had blooms

Of prize Chrysanthemums—
The grandest ever seen.

People from miles around
Came to see those flowers
And were truly astounded
By her unusual powers.

One day a little weed
Pushed up to drink and feed
Among the pampered flowers
At her water-can showers.

Day by day it grew
With ragged leaves and bristles
Till it was tall as me or you—
It was a King of Thistles.

"Prizes for flowers are easy,"
My Aunt said in her pride.
"But was there ever such a weed
The whole world wide?"

She watered it, she tended it,
It grew alarmingly.
As if I had offended it,
It bristled over me.

"Oh Aunt!" I cried. "Beware of that!
I saw it eat a bird."
She went on polishing its points
As if she hadn't heard.

"Oh Aunt!" I cried. "It has a flower
Like a lion's beard—"
Too late! It was devouring her
Just as I had feared!

Her feet were waving in the air—
But I shall not proceed.
Here ends the story of my Aunt
And her ungrateful weed.

WINDY NIGHTS

Robert Louis Stevenson

Whenever the moon and stars are set,
  Whenever the wind is high,
All night long in the dark and wet,
  A man goes riding by.
Late in the night when the fires are out,
Why does he gallop and gallop about?

Whenever the trees are crying aloud,
  And ships are tossed at sea,
By, on the highway, low and loud,
  By at the gallop goes he:
By at the gallop he goes, and then
By he comes back at the gallop again.

MY INSIDE-SELF

Rachel Field

My Inside-Self and my Outside-Self
  Are different as can be.
My Outside-Self wears gingham smocks,
  And very round is she,
With freckles sprinkled on her nose,
  And smoothly parted hair,
And clumsy feet that cannot dance
  In heavy shoes and square.

But, oh, my little Inside-Self—
  In gown of misty rose
She dances lighter than a leaf
  On blithe and twinkling toes;
Her hair is blowing gold, and if
  You chanced her face to see,
You would not think she could belong
  To staid and sober me!

THE OLD WIFE AND THE GHOST

James Reeves

There was an old wife and she lived all alone
In a cottage not far from Hitchin:
And one bright night, by the full moon light,
Comes a ghost right into her kitchen.

About that kitchen neat and clean
The ghost goes pottering round.
But the poor old wife is deaf as a boot
And so hears never a sound.

The ghost blows up the kitchen fire,
As bold as bold can be;
He helps himself from the larder shelf,
But never a sound hears she.

He blows on his hands to make them warm,
And whistles aloud "Whee-hee!"
But still as a sack the old soul lies
And never a sound hears she.

From corner to corner he runs about,
And into the cupboard he peeps;
He rattles the door and bumps on the floor,
But still the old wife sleeps.

Jangle and bang go the pots and pans,
As he throws them all around;
And the plates and mugs and dishes and jugs,
He flings them all to the ground.

Madly the ghost tears up and down
And screams like a storm at sea;
And at last the old wife stirs in her bed—
And it's "Drat those mice," says she.

Then the first cock crows and morning shows
And the troublesome ghost's away.
But oh! what a pickle the poor wife sees
When she gets up next day.

"Them's tidy big mice," the old wife thinks.
And off she goes to Hitchin,
And a tidy big cat she fetches back
To keep the mice from her kitchen.

MY SHADOW

Robert Louis Stevenson

I have a little shadow that goes in and out with me,
And what can be the use of him is more than I can see.
He is very, very like me from the heels up to the head;
And I see him jump before me, when I jump into my bed.

The funniest thing about him is the way he likes to grow—
Not at all like proper children, which is always very slow;
For he sometimes shoots up taller like an india-rubber ball,
And he sometimes gets so little that there's none of him at all.

He hasn't got a notion of how children ought to play,
And can only make a fool of me in every sort of way.
He stays so close beside me, he's a coward, you can see;
I'd think shame to stick to nursie as that shadow sticks to me!

One morning, very early, before the sun was up,
I rose and found the shining dew on every buttercup;
But my lazy little shadow, like an arrant sleepy-head,
Had stayed at home behind me and was fast asleep in bed.

THE LISTENERS

Walter de la Mare

"Is there anybody there?" said the
Traveller,
Knocking on the moonlit door;
And his horse in the silence champed
the grasses
Of the forest's ferny floor:
And a bird flew up out of the turret,
Above the Traveller's head:
And he smote upon the door a second
time;
"Is there anybody there?" he said.
But no one descended to the Traveller;
No head from the leaf-fringed sill
Leaned over and looked into his grey
eyes,
Where he stood perplexed and still.
But only a host of phantom listeners
That dwelt in the lone house then
Stood listening in the quiet of the
moonlight
To that voice from the world of men:
Stood thronging the faint moonbeams
on the dark stair,
That goes down to the empty hall,
Hearkening in an air stirred and shaken
By the lonely Traveller's call.
And he felt in his heart their
strangeness,
Their stillness answering his cry,
While his horse moved, cropping the
dark turf,
'Neath the starred and leafy sky;
For he suddenly smote on the door,
even
Louder, and lifted his head:—
"Tell them I came, and no one
answered,
That I kept my word," he said.
Never the least stir made the listeners,
Though every word he spake
Fell echoing through the shadowiness of
the still house
From the one man left awake:
Ay, they heard his foot upon the stirrup,
And the sound of iron on stone,
And how the silence surged softly
backward,
When the plunging hoofs were gone.

FORGOTTEN

Child's Poem from Terezín Concentration Camp (1942–44)

You wanton, quiet memory that haunts
me all
the while
In order to remind me of her whom
love I send.

Perhaps when you caress me sweetly, I
will smile,
You are my confidante today, my very
dearest friend.

You sweet remembrance, tell a fairy tale
About my girl who's lost and gone, you
see.
Tell, tell the one about the golden grail
And call the swallow, bring her back to
me.

Fly somewhere back to her and ask her,
soft and low,
If she thinks of me sometimes with love,
If she is well and ask her too before you
go
If I am still her dearest, precious dove.
And hurry back, don't lose your way,
So I can think of other things,
But you were too lovely, perhaps, to
stay.
I loved you once. Goodbye, my love!

MOLLY MEANS

Margaret Walker

The familiar shadow figure of the hag can be attributed to the dominance of male values in our society (see "Sex Roles"). As a result, the female dominant has fallen into the unconscious, to reappear in distorted form in our consciousness as the frightening hag or witch, who possesses great power.

Old Molly Means was a hag and a witch;
Chile of the devil, the dark, and sitch.
Her heavy hair hung thick in ropes
And her blazing eyes was black as pitch.
Imp at three and wench at 'leben
She counted her husbands to the number seben.
O Molly, Molly, Molly Means
There goes the ghost of Molly Means.

Some say she was born with a veil on her face
So she could look through unnatchal space
Through the future and through the past
And charm a body or an evil place
And every man could well despise
The evil look in her coal black eyes.
Old Molly, Molly, Molly Means
Dark is the ghost of Molly Means.

And when the tale begun to spread
Of evil and of holy dread:
Her black-hand arts and her evil powers
How she cast her spells and called the dead,
The younguns was afraid at night
And the farmers feared their crops would blight.
Old Molly, Molly, Molly Means
Cold is the ghost of Molly Means.

Then one dark day she put a spell
On a young gal-bride just come to dwell
In the lane just down from Molly's shack
And when her husband come riding back
His wife was barking like a dog
And on all fours like a common hog.
O Molly, Molly, Molly Means
Where is the ghost of Molly Means?

The neighbors come and they went away
And said she'd die before break of day
But her husband held her in his arms
And swore he'd break the wicked charms;
He'd search all up and down the land
And turn the spell on Molly's hand.
O Molly, Molly, Molly Means
Sharp is the ghost of Molly Means.

So he rode all day and he rode all night
And at the dawn he come in sight
Of a man who said he could move the spell
And cause the awful thing to dwell
On Molly Means, to bark and bleed
Till she died at the hands of her evil deed.
Old Molly, Molly, Molly Means
This is the ghost of Molly Means.

Sometimes at night through the shadowy trees
She rides along on a winter breeze.
You can hear her holler and whine and cry.
Her voice is thin and her moan is high,
And her cackling laugh or her barking cold
Bring terror to the young and old.
O Molly, Molly, Molly Means
Lean is the ghost of Molly Means.

Essays

THE SHADOW

M. Esther Harding

A psychoanalyst and writer, M. Esther Harding, M.D., worked with C. G. Jung at Zurich in 1922 and in subsequent years. Her other works are The Way of All Women, Women's Mysteries, Journey into Self *(on* Pilgrim's Progress), *and* Psychic Energy. *She died in 1971.*

. . . When the "I," the *autos,* has been born, the child at first expresses himself with all his needs, reactions, and desires untrammeled by any thought of appropriateness or of consequences. But immediately he is subjected to a process of training—a training that has been imposed upon him before he even had an "I" that could protest, a training whose object is to teach him how to adapt to society, what is permissible or not, what will produce love and acceptance and what will be frowned upon or punished. At this very early stage in his development, a child begins to develop a *persona,* a mask of good and adapted behavior. For instance, a mother says, "Now you must be a good boy," meaning, "You must behave *like* a good boy." For it is obvious that no one can become good simply because he is told to do so; one's being is not to be changed by admonition. When as children we had been naughty, our nurse used to say, "Now you must sit on that chair until you say you are sorry." We were not in the least sorry and we knew it and refused to say we were. But the minutes stretched on interminably—we couldn't sit there all day, or so it seemed. So eventually we mumbled the required words and were released. But we knew we had lied, for we were not sorry at all. And so a child learns to repress, to thrust down into unconsciousness the unacceptable parts of his personality. As a result the personal part of the psyche becomes more or less clearly divided into three parts. There is the "I," the ego, that represents what I call *myself;* then there is the *persona,* the mask that I wear to show to the world; and there is still another part that I know, or partly know, exists, but which I prefer to keep hidden because it is unacceptable to the world—this is called the *shadow,* and it is usually almost entirely forgotten—that is, it becomes unconscious to myself, although it may be quite obvious to others.

When the "I," the ego, comes into being and becomes the focus for consciousness, it is as if a light were lighted in the room of the psyche that had formerly

From M. Esther Harding, "Projections to Persons of the Same Sex: The Shadow," in *The I and the Not I: A Study in the Development of Consciousness* (Princeton, N.J.: Princeton University Press, 1965), Bollingen Series LXXIX, pp. 72-73, 77-84.

been completely dark. As the light is small, it illuminates only a small part of the room. The rest is in shadow; its contents are invisible. But they are not nonexistent, and they may be perceived in projection. . . .

If an individual is unaware of his shadow, being completely identified with his conscious personality, he will be entirely convinced of his own rectitude. The elements in his own nature which cannot be accommodated in this shining personality will be projected to someone in his immediate environment, a brother, son, friend, or, more often, a *bête noire,* the associate whom he particularly dislikes, whose faults he cannot avoid seeing and criticizing on every occasion, in season and out. And here we often see a very strange effect of unconsciousness. For the one on whom the shadow has fallen is unavoidably influenced in an unconscious way by the projection, and if the two people are closely connected, the recipient of the projection may be constrained to live the negative role projected upon him. We see this sometimes in a group where there is someone who is "completely right," who never, never raises his voice, never says an unkind thing about anybody. He seems to have no shadow, no natural human weakness. But then his shadow falls on the others in the group, and they are compelled to express his negative and all-too-human reactions. They find themselves making critical remarks that are really more incisive and destructive than would be warranted by their own feelings. For there is something peculiarly exasperating about someone who has no shadow. We find ourselves obliged to disagree with him whether we want to or not.

The compulsion to live another's shadow is most apt to occur within a family relationship, where the interaction of the members of the group is so profoundly influenced by unconscious factors. It can be the cause of neurosis or of delinquent behavior in the children of parents who have refused to accept the responsibility for their own shadows: the children have to live the shadow side.

The effects resulting from unconsciousness of the shadow are so numerous, so prevalent, and so far-reaching that I am at a loss where to begin to discuss them. In individual relationships projection of the shadow, or of parts of it, can produce misunderstandings, quarrels, endless bickerings. An attitude based on *unconscious* inferiorities may result in suspicion of everyone. For instance, a groceryman whom I once asked to review his bill immediately became defensive and even rude because he assumed that I was suspicious of him and was accusing him of shortchanging me, whereas the fact was that I thought he had shortchanged himself. But it took quite a bit of soothing talk to assure him of my good intentions. Unconscious inferiority may make us act in a domineering and demanding way in order to fend off the suspected or anticipated depreciation. Or we may project to others virtues they do not possess as a compensation for our own feelings of inferiority: this occurs when we are not living up to our real potential.

If we do not live up to our own potential, the positive qualities will be repressed into the shadow, and we will have what I have sometimes called a bright shadow instead of a dark one. When we project this bright shadow onto someone else, the person who carries the projection will seem to us to be "always right," able to do easily and well things that are difficult for us, and so on. We burden him with our expectations of his abilities instead of acquiring for ourselves the possibilities of achievement which are potentially present in us. A person who is content to take an inferior position, who prefers to have an easy job rather than to buckle down and develop himself and his work, and who then admires, and overadmires, someone else who does things well has projected his bright shadow onto his neighbor.

* * *

And so it becomes evident that the shadow poses a moral problem, and that to become conscious of it requires a moral effort. How can we, without undertaking a psychological analysis, become aware of our shadow? We have already noted that where we are unduly concerned with another person's shortcomings we should suspect a psychological involvement on our own part, and that we are projecting some part of our own unacceptable qualities to that person. Typical examples are the overvirtuous lady who concerns herself with "fallen girls" or the man who goes around with a chip on his shoulder, suspecting everyone else of lacking that particular virtue on which he prides himself.

There is another area in which we can observe the working of the shadow. When, for instance, we become aware that we have not produced the effect we intended, it may be that the shadow spoke louder than the ego. Perhaps, in talking to an acquaintance, we meant to be kind or sympathetic, only to find that he was hurt or offended by what we said, and still more by the way in which we said it, although we had thought our manner irreproachable. "It isn't what you said. It's the *way* you said it that hurt me so," is the complaint the shadow evokes. Now the *way* we said it comes from the unconscious. We intend to say something that is rather neutral or pleasant, and we say it in such a way, or with such an intonation, that it produces the opposite effect from the one we intended. That is, our unconscious has spoken through us. This is the shadow. When someone complains, "It's the way you said it," look out for the shadow! You were not completely sincere in what you said—consciously you were sincere, but unconsciously someone else in you was contradicting what you said.

The shadow, too, takes a part in situations where we blunder over some task we would expect to be able to perform correctly. Here the one who acts, who does, is not the conscious ego but the shadow. We exclaim with considerable irritation, "How silly of me! Why, I *never* do that!" And the strange thing is we can go on exclaiming, "I never do that!" without ever stopping to take note of the frequency of these supposed exceptions to the invariable rule of our correct behavior. If we did pause to take stock, we would be in for a very unpleasant surprise and would probably suffer a severe shock to our self-esteem. But usually we prefer not to become conscious of these shadow contents, and then they fall upon someone in the environment where they become glaringly evident. This is a case of a projected shadow.

But what is the value of becoming aware of the shadow? Why should we take steps to unearth all this unpleasant stuff? What function does the shadow perform in the psyche? Since the shadow consists of all the elements of the natural personality that have been discarded and overcome as a result of training and in accordance with the demands of society, if we repress them, the conscious personality is obviously diminished. We have doubtless seen them at times and have prayed that we be not led into evil, but may walk in the good. But still the shadow persists, which is just as well, for if we could actually dispose of our shadow in this way, there would be nothing left but a well-disciplined ego, a robot, with its prescribed adaptation via the persona, and we would be able to function only in accordance with the rules and expectations of society.

But man is a natural living being, and the life spirit in him is maimed by such rigid restrictions if it is not entirely broken. It is essential for life that at some point the laws of society must be broken; the living spirit insists on transgressing the law. And here is the beginning of consciousness. So long as consciousness is nonexistent, to follow the natural way produces no conflict. An infant wets his diaper without any conflict, until the law of the nursery begins to be impressed on him, and even then for a long while this natural act causes no conflict or sense of guilt. It is only when a dawning awareness arises that the child feels fear or shame when scolded, and not until a good deal later does he begin to develop any inner sense of responsibility for self-control. I remember the child of a friend of mine, who was something under two. He would sit on the floor playing with his toys. One day he discovered that in the kitchen there was a whole row of little taps on the gas stove that were just within reach. Although he had been scolded a number of times for turning on the little taps, he could not refrain from playing with them. Finally his mother, feeling she must do something about this, slapped the child's hands and said, "No, no!" The child sat down on the floor once more with his toys and was quiet for a while. Suddenly a gleam came into his eyes, and he began to scramble up, but he paused and, touching the hand that had been slapped, exclaimed, "Oh, no! Oh, my, no! No, no, no!"

At some point in the child's life there is likely to be a more or less deliberate breach of the law, a transgression, perhaps committed without conscious intent, which is followed by a spontaneous sense of guilt. The child either runs to his mother and confesses (and the value of the happening may so easily be destroyed by her attitude), *or,* as with Adam and Eve, the child is obliged to take upon himself the guilt of his act, and so makes a most important step toward greater self-consciousness. This explains, perhaps, some part of the mystery of the presence of evil in God's world. For consciousness is not possible without freedom, and freedom involves the ability to deviate. But how do we know whether we are free to deviate if we always follow the law? And so we come back to the necessity of keeping the shadow in view, for to lose our shadow is a serious psychological mishap. As a result of the loss of the shadow, we lose at the same time our substance, our reality, and consequently are unable to make any impression on real objects which have substance. . . .

ACHEBE'S "THE FLUTE"

Marianne Whelchel

Marianne Whelchel is visiting assistant professor at Trinity College, Hartford, Connecticut.

Chinua Achebe (1930–), the internationally known Nigerian author of *Things Fall Apart, Arrow of God,* and other novels and books of poetry, writes for children as well as for adults. His children's fiction includes *Chike and the River,* an adventure story, and *How the Leopard Got Its Claws,* a contemporary animal fable. In the late sixties he helped found a press (later destroyed in the Biafran war) for the publication of Nigerian children's books. Returning to Nigeria in the summer of 1976 after four years as visiting professor and writer in the United States, Achebe plans to continue writing for children and to support Nwamife Publishers, a press with goals similar to those of the press he cofounded. He is particularly interested now in recording Nigerian folktales.

"The Flute" is Achebe's retelling of a folktale that occurs in many variations throughout Nigeria, other parts of Africa, and the rest of the world. Folktale collectors Barbara K. and Warren S. Walker include another version of this tale in *Nigerian Folk Tales.* In their version, titled "Envy Can Kill," the two children are girls instead of boys, but the plot and theme are essentially the same. In a recent

All quotations from Achebe come from my own interview with him conducted on April 30, 1976.

interview Achebe himself commented on this widespread recurrence of variants of a given folktale:

> Such variations on themes are quite common around the world. Certainly in Africa you will find stories occurring again and again over a wide area and also in various forms, in many variations. And my theory is that this really proves that these stories were designed by our ancestors to tell us something. It's as if they're repeating it, you know, for a purpose; drumming it into you and saying: "Listen, listen, listen; this is important, this is valuable, this is to be avoided . . . you know, pride is wrong, or dangerous; appearances are deceptive." And they go on and change it slightly here; and simply by doing that draw your attention to the various possibilities of exploiting the underlying ideas of the story and also make it more memorable. And I visualize the transmission of culture in the same way—as the ancients who saw the world in the making, passing on this experience in the form of myths and stories, and emphasizing again and again what in their view is important.

Because Achebe believes in the relevance to contemporary experience of the wisdom carried in the folktales, he is particularly interested in recording them before they are lost. Tales such as "The Flute" are part of Nigeria's rich oral tradition, a tradition now threatened by Nigeria's move toward universal literacy. As a culture becomes literate, the oral tradition is lost unless definite steps are taken to preserve it. Achebe believes those steps must be taken by serious artists and writers. He is not satisfied with word-for-word transcription of the tales as told by village storytellers, for each storyteller has his own version and unless one finds an outstanding storyteller, it is probably better for a writer like himself to re-create the original tale, which he may have heard in childhood from his mother or older sister or brother. According to Achebe, the recording of the oral tradition is "not a mechanical thing":

> The story has to be retold, has to be re-created for this age, and this is the work of people who make stories, not people who just stumble on things in the course of their other work, whether they're anthropologists, or district officers, or missionaries, or what have you.

Achebe envisions two steps in the recording of folktales: the first is recording the tale in the original Nigerian language and the second, translating it into English. Much of the original folktale experience is lost when one first encounters the tale in a book. For instance, if "The Flute" were told in an Igbo village gathering or within a family, visual and sound effects would play an important part. The two boys' flute songs would be sung by the storyteller and on certain lines the audience would join in. The song is so important a part of the folktale in its original form that there are very few stories that do not have songs. Thus, when recording the tales in the original Igbo, Achebe wants to involve Nigerian artists and musicians. Musical tapes might supplement the written tales. In the English version the song is lost, for, Achebe explains, the song really cannot be translated so as to retain both content and singability. This is true of translations from many languages but is particularly true of translations from Igbo, a tonal language in which part of the song's music comes from the tonality of the language itself.

Interestingly, Achebe uses this same folktale, "The Flute," in one of his adult novels, *Arrow of God.* Though the version included here has been changed somewhat, that the same tale can be told to both children and adults illustrates what Achebe believes to be an important quality of good children's literature. Speaking of his use of this particular story for both adults and children, Achebe talks of the various levels of interpretation a story may have:

> . . . a story is a story, but its interpretation is something else. You don't tell interpretation, you tell a

> story, and if it's a good story it will have these various levels of interpretation, and an adult will get a lot more out of it—not a lot more, but something different from it than a child. A child will see a story, will see dramatic situations and so on but would not be in a position to relate this to the scheme of the universe. This is something that an adult can do and this is what tells you that those who made children's stories were not second-rate storymakers. That's what we tend to do today, to leave it to second-rate storymakers. It's only good storytellers who can create stories that have these various levels, you know, like *Alice in Wonderland.* A child can read it and it's just a nice, pleasant story, and an adult will read it and see the whole politics of society displayed there, and this is what makes a good story. So you can tell a story to children and tell the same story to adults for different reasons.

In *Arrow of God* the story is introduced when the second wife of the protagonist tells it to her children. The situation there suggests the multiple uses of the tale, for the children in the novel clearly respond to it as a good tale, while the adult readers of the novel see the story commenting on what has been taking place in the novel itself. The wife telling the tale is suffering from the unreasonable jealousy of her husband's first wife. Thus, the adult reader of the novel sees the tale both as tale and as the second wife's (and possibly the author's) indirect censuring of the senior wife's jealous behavior.

The child who reads or hears "The Flute" as presented in this anthology will find in the story both entertainment and instruction. On one level the story is a fine adventure tale, for the boy who owns the bamboo flute takes great risks to recover it and he succeeds better than he had dreamed. It is also a story of personal values pitted against social and cultural ones. In going to search for the flute at night, the boy defies a cultural taboo that requires him to respect the spirits' right to the fields after dark and he disobeys his parents. On the face of it, then, his defiance should evoke disapproval and punishment. We know, however, that the quest for the flute is not merely an act of defiance for its own sake—the boy is very afraid of the spirits but undertakes the trip anyway. The tale makes a point of the boy's fear; when he sees the spirits, fear freezes him, and when he sings to the spirits he reveals that he knows death may be the penalty for disrespecting them. Because he undertakes the search despite his great fear, we understand how much the simple bamboo flute means to him. In his song he explains to the spirits his devotion to the flute in terms that suggest it is almost human:

> How could you
> Contain yourself and sleep till dawn
> When your flute in damp and dew
> Lay forsaken and forlorn.

Thus, we know the trip is not made for selfish reasons. In going after the flute the boy asserts personal values that take priority over his parents' and the spirits' right to respect. And he is approved of for doing so. His devotion to his own simple flute when he has the opportunity to replace it with a seemingly more valuable gold or white one, his obvious fear of the spirits, and his scrupulous respect of them in everything except his coming to the fields by night make it clear that his motives are pure and that his action is not a question of mere defiance but of values held with conviction and courage. Impressed by the boy's courage and devotion, the spirits reward him grandly. Thus, one moral of the story is that the individual is sometimes right to place his own values above society's and that he is even to be admired for doing so.

In discussing his children's adventure story *Chike and the River,* Achebe points out that the teaching and entertainment aspects of stories are not necessarily separable. In that story the young boy Chike moves from a small bush village to a city where his curiosity and adventurous spirit lead him to capture some robbers. Achebe believes that many of his countrymen in

Nigeria are generally in need of a more adventurous spirit, as there is less a premium on adventure there than in many Western cultures. Thus, the element of adventure in that story is itself a teaching aspect. The same might be said for "The Flute," which approves an adventure taken on behalf of personal values.

There is, however, a delicate balance in "The Flute" between individual and social or cultural values. As a common function of folktales is to legitimize and to teach a society's values, we would not expect a tale from a culture that places high value on the family and respect for ancestors and spirits to treat lightly a child's defiance of these values. And this tale does not. Except for breaking the taboo against entering the fields at night when the spirits inhabit them, the boy respects the spirits. He even apologizes to them: " 'I did not mean to offend you but only to take back my flute.' " Further, his reward depends upon scrupulous obedience to their instructions about his return home and his opening of the pot. His reward also depends upon a display of respect for his parents.

The second boy's experience obviously underlines the moral points already made. Encouraged by his mother, he disregards for purely selfish reasons the taboo of visiting the fields at night, and he does not hesitate to insult and disobey the spirits and to show his greed in claiming the flute "of shining precious metal" and in choosing the larger pot. Further encouraging him in his greed and defiance of the spirits' instructions upon his arrival home, his mother seals her hut and opens the pot without inviting her husband. The boy and his mother are, of course, rewarded for their greed and defiance by death. The tale, then, manages to uphold the important cultural values of respect for family and for spirits, while at the same time it presents an instance in which personal values may rightly take precedence over social ones. And the second boy's story makes it clear that the values which may acceptably and temporarily replace social ones may not be rooted in the desire for mere selfish gain. The tale censures greed, envy, and self-seeking defiance of social taboos and affirms adventure, courage, and unselfishness.

A LOOK AT ANDERSEN'S "THE SHADOW"

K. Narayan Kutty

K. Narayan Kutty teaches children's literature at Eastern Connecticut State College, Willimantic, Connecticut.

"And a word is a shadow."*

"The Shadow" is one of Hans Christian Andersen's many original compositions. There is no evidence that it is based on a fairy tale or folktale that Andersen read or

*The original of this sentence in Danish has been translated in various ways into English. M. R. James, on whose translation this essay is based, translates it as "One word, one shadow." See Hans Christian Andersen, *Forty-Two Stories,* tr. by M. R. James (London: Faber and Faber, 1968), p. 238. I think, however, that Erik Christian Haugaard's version of the sentence as "And a word is a shadow" is more in keeping with the spirit of Andersen's story as I understand it. See *The Complete Fairy Tales and Stories of Hans Christian Andersen,* tr. by E. C. Haugaard (New York: Doubleday, 1974), p. 338.

heard. The originality of Andersen's treatment of the shadow theme in this story is felt strikingly, even after one has compared it with Adalbert von Chamisso's famous literary fairy tale in German, "Peter Schlemihl" (1814), the central theme of which is Peter Schlemihl's selling of his shadow to the devil in return for material possessions and the tragic consequences of that Faustian act. Andersen met with Chamisso during his visit to Germany in 1831. In his autobiography, *The Fairy Tale of my Life,* Andersen speaks warmly of the mutual admiration in which he and Chamisso held each other.* Undoubtedly, Andersen had read "Peter Schlemihl" before his visit with Chamisso. Andersen knew German, and it is quite possible that he was aware of the popularity of the shadow theme in German folklore and literature. Therefore, the influence on Andersen of Chamisso's tale, Goethe's *Märchen* (1795), and E. T. A. Hoffmann's "The Story of the Lost Reflection" (1815) and his other tales, in which the shadow theme figures prominently, is unmistakable. In fact, the narrator in "The Shadow," in what appears to be a pointed allusion to "Peter Schlemihl," says of its scholar hero:

> It [the loss of the shadow] did annoy him, but not so much because his shadow was gone, as because he knew that there was a story about a man without a shadow which everyone at home in the cold countries knew; and if the learned man went there and told them his own story they would say that he was merely imitating the other, and that he had no business to do. So he determined to do nothing at all about it, which was very sensible of him.†

Influence does not necessarily lead to imitation; that is what Andersen is telling the reader through the passage above. The scholar's fear of unfair criticism by his own people of a unique experience of his echoes Andersen's fear of what his detractors—and there were many of them in Denmark—would say about his own original story, "The Shadow." The allusion to "Peter Schlemihl" may be taken as Andersen's thinly veiled suggestion to the reader to consider how different his treatment of the shadow theme is from Chamisso's. Andersen's hostile critics took a long time to realize that he never touched any literary material which he did not make his own. Besides, Andersen was too conscientious and dedicated a writer to be ever guilty of plagiarism. The simple truth about him is that he did not have to plagiarize; he never lacked material for his stories. In sum, what his reading of tales with the shadow theme did to Andersen was to awaken in him new perceptions about the reality of the self and about the artistic possibilities of those perceptions.

Andersen's autobiography and biographies; his diaries, letters, and journals; and those who knew him intimately inform us how tormented, frustrated, depressed, and self-conscious a person he was. Like many other writers of his time, he possessed a romantic imagination and temperament. His stories, such as "The Travelling Companion," "The Snow Queen," "The Nightingale," "The Ugly Duckling," and "The Shadow," to mention only a few, demonstrate that his perceptions of himself and of the world were complex. He was aware of mysterious and shadowy forces working within him. But what is remarkable about Andersen is that he never wanted to abandon himself to the complexities and mysteries of human existence. His romantic yearnings were always tempered by an ordering and controlling classical and Christian vision. "The Shadow" is a unique story, not only because it is built on the conflict between opposing forces within Andersen, but also because it allows the romantic ego in him to dominate his classical spirit completely. What Andersen accomplishes by this will

*Hans Christian Andersen, *The Fairy Tale of My Life* (New York: British Book Center, 1954), p. 71.

† M. R. James, p. 236. All subsequent references to "The Shadow" are to James's translation.

be discussed toward the end of this essay.

"The Shadow" is totally free from Gothic elements; it never resorts to magic for surprise and suspense; and its use of fantasy is limited to the personification of the hero's shadow which is necessary for the dramatic externalization of the destructive inner self's total domination over the weak, but morally and creatively superior, conscious self. "The Shadow" has nothing to do with God or the devil. It is essentially a limited but sustained and unified exploration of the sundered consciousness of an artist who is estranged from himself, who is fascinated with what he dreads within himself. The subtleties and suggestivity of Andersen's style and imagery, even in translation, make "The Shadow" so complex and meaningful a story that one feels that Erik Christian Haugaard's description of it as a "brilliant Kafkaesque tale"* is justified.

The claims made above in behalf of "The Shadow" may appear to put it outside the field of children's literature. But, actually, they do not. Imaginative young readers will find "The Shadow" an excitingly inventive and dramatic story refreshingly different from the mindless stories they are treated to in the children's literature bazaar. They will find Andersen's deft handling of the hero's shadow a whole new experience in the realm of the fanciful. They will be grateful to Andersen for not burdening this haunting and intellectually puzzling story with tiresome moralizing; but they will not fail to respond to the unobtrusive moral vision in the story which, on their level, is the tragedy of the scholar's inability to assert the truth he possesses against falsehood that masquerades as truth. Let us now see what Andersen has to offer his adult readers.

The first thing we are told about the young scholar is that he has come to a hot Southern country from a cold Northern country. (M. R. James reports that Andersen began writing "The Shadow" in Naples, and I presume it was in the year 1831, when he first visited Naples.†) Why does Andersen choose this setting? He does so to set the stage for the emergence of the hero's shadow. In the cold countries of the North, the visible features of life fade into darkness at sunset; in the South, on the contrary, life begins only after nightfall. The Southern sun keeps people indoors. The young scholar's pattern of life changes radically as a result of his arrival in the South. His consciousness of time, space, and of reality changes as he stays passive during the day and becomes active at night. The shadow figure, in all literature dealing with it, is usually a figure of the night.

The story does not suggest that the scholar was preoccupied with his shadow before he came to the South. The strange and alien South seems to activate the repressed subterranean forces that the scholar harbors within him. Among the factors contributing to the scholar's increased awareness of his self is his freedom in the South from the usual restraints of his ascetic pursuit of the true, the good, and the beautiful—and from the inhibitions resulting from the restrictions imposed on him by his critical countrymen in the North. Life in the South is chaotic. Reality is not ordered here. There is excitement in the manner in which the repressed energies of the day explode at night. Unfamiliar sights and sounds greet the young scholar in the streets of the city where he lives. In the streets, light and darkness, death and life, children and adults, noise and music all mingle together. Life in the South has a vitality all its own, so much so that the scholar finds it "matchless." This joyous response of the scholar reveals that the scholar's shadow, who represents the unlived life of his master, is beginning to assert itself. It is significant that when life revives at night the scholar notices that his shadow is much taller than himself.

As his awareness of his self expands, which is shown by the emergence of the shadow as taller than its owner, the

* Erik Christian Haugaard, p. xxiii.

† M. R. James, p. 13.

scholar's grip on his conscious self weakens. He begins to mistake illusions for reality. His mind becomes a prey to chimeras. He becomes inquisitive about the house opposite his and about the unknown occupant of it. Although no one seems to be living in the house, the scholar sees the house mysteriously lit at night. He sees "flaming" flowers in the balcony of the house. From the brightly lit rooms inside he hears mesmerizing music. One night, he sees a lovely maiden standing inside the house.

It does not require much interpretive skill to learn that Andersen is clearly using the house opposite the scholar's as an externalization of the world of the shadow inside the scholar. Note that the house seems to be uninhabited during the day. Also note that the house is illuminated only when the passive consciousness of the scholar becomes active at night. Add to this, first, the presence of the scholar's formidable shadow in the scholar's room and, second, the scholar's yearning to find out the entrance to the house, so that he can be with the lovely apparition there—and his inability to do so. What it all comes to is this: the scholar is about to unleash the shadow that he has been holding captive within him all along. If more evidence for this is needed, all that one has to do is to read what the scholar says when he comes out of his room into the balcony prompted by the vision of romantic splendor in the house opposite. Says the scholar:

> I think my Shadow is the only living thing to be seen over there. . . . Look how snug it's sitting among the flowers, and the door is standing ajar. Now if only the Shadow was sharp enough to go in and look about and then come and tell me what it saw! Yes, you'd be some use then. . . . (236)

The literal shadow that the scholar sees himself casting on the house opposite, Andersen suggests, is also his metaphorical Shadow. On the metaphorical level, the scholar's unleashing of his Shadow should be construed as his romantic yearning to experience beauty and sexuality on the physical level, a yearning that his classical temperament will not approve of. It seems as though the scholar is no longer content to contemplate and create beauty; he craves for the physical possession of what he contemplates. He wants to emancipate a certain part of his being that he has been repressing in obligation to a moral duty, the disinterested pursuit of truth, goodness, and beauty. He seems to be willing to forget the claims of the truthful and good in preference for beauty.

Willingness, as we know, is not readiness. Andersen's scholar is unable to deal with the newly surfaced reality about his self. He is unable to go all the way in his attempt to possess that which he contemplates; he is not quite ready to manifest himself in his totality. He seems to recoil from the very energies that he wants to unleash. He is confused and perplexed. His perplexity leads him to create another shadow in the place of the old one which refuses to return. He resumes his former existence. In the words of the narrator:

> So the learned man came home and wrote books about what was left of truth and goodness and beauty in the world, and days passed by, and years—many years. (237)

There is no suggestion in this passage or in any following it that the scholar returns to his former existence with any renewed faith in it. There seems to be no passion or joy in the life he resumes. He merely endures it, cynically. At the same time he is unable to give it up. Helplessly, he is torn between what he does and what he would like to do. What he does is dull, and what he would like to do will bring chaos into his existence. He is not strong enough to take on the life that the shadowy being within him prompts him to, nor is he able to dedicate himself to the pursuit of the true, the good, and the beautiful, committedly. This petrification of being in the scholar appears irresolvable. These truths about the scholar are only reinforced by the return of his Shadow. The Shadow's return to his master shows that the scholar has not banished him from his consciousness, even after developing a new shadow. Perhaps old shadows die hard or not at all.

When the Shadow returns to his master, he is a man. Andersen transforms the shadow of the scholar into his *doppelgänger* or double. The reason for this is not hard to guess. Andersen wants to depict the shadow of the scholar as his antiself, the opposite of the hero in everything. The Shadow on his return appears as the personification of the scholar's invisible other half. The Shadow is secretive, apprehensive of his role as a man in society, arrogant, irreverent, defiant of authority, proud, cynical about art, and totally absorbed in the things that belong to the world of appearance—clothes, boots, trinkets, money, etc. He does everything that his master's morality and values won't permit him to do. His egotism is sublime; he reiterates time and again the implausible claim that he knows everything. As the scholar's shadow, he has access to places where the scholar cannot go. He has personal experience of the evil that exists in the deepest recesses of the human heart; but, instead of writing about it, so that men may see themselves reflected in it, the Shadow uses it to blackmail people who, out of fear of him, fill his pockets with gold and cover his person with expensive clothes. His desire is to become visible, so that he is recognized, a privilege denied to the humble and self-effacing scholar. Words that are sacred to the scholar are mere shadows to the Shadow. For him, everything is permissible. He is amoral. He can lie and deceive. What he wants is power and self-gratification.

What is remarkable about the story is that, even after witnessing the emergence of his shadow as a diabolically destructive being, the scholar is unable to break himself free from him. He is unable to reject him because he is secretly fascinated with the power and confidence that exude from his Shadow who, after all, is a being that the scholar has stealthily nurtured within him. This fascination is deepened by the fact that ever since his return from the South the scholar has been living a meaningless life. He has become spiritually and physically weak. People remark that he has become so thin as to look like his shadow. But the scholar is also fearful of his Shadow, as the Shadow's strength lies in his total rejection of the values the scholar stands for. There seems to be no way for the scholar to come to terms with the ambivalent attitude toward his Shadow that ties him to it in an inextricable symbiosis.

Meekly, the scholar allows his Shadow to address him "thou," and later, although under protest, he agrees to call the Shadow "you," as though the Shadow were his master. As further proof of his degradation into masochistic servitude, the scholar agrees to go to the sunny South, reversing roles with his Shadow. This indicates his willingness to undermine his conscious self and its values, so as to enable his antiself to become more visible to the outside world. He loses his vision so completely that he does not see the machinations of his Shadow, designed to bring about his destruction by slow degrees. The Shadow deceives the scholar into thinking that the baths in the South and the carefree life he will have will make a new man of him. In the following passage the narrator describes the scholar's mental and physical condition, as the Shadow's stranglehold on the scholar becomes tighter and tighter:

> The learned man was in a bad way; sorrow and trouble were on him, and as for his talk about the true and the beautiful and the good, most people appreciated it as a cow does roses. At last he became quite ill. (241)

It is not then his work that the scholar cares for, but for the world's opinion of it. The dazzling success of the Shadow in the world is clearly behind the scholar's self-abnegation, which is what leads him to his final destruction at the hands of his Shadow.

The scholar does try to tell the truth about his Shadow, that he is only a shadow and not the master of the shadow that he claims to be. But this happens at a time when the Shadow has succeeded in blinding even those who have the capacity to see truth clearly. Andersen introduces a Princess in the climactic scenes of "The Shadow." The problem with the Princess is that she sees everything too clearly. At the health spot, where the Shadow goes accompanied by the scholar with the intention of growing a beard (he wants complete visibility), the Princess notices that the Shadow has no shadow. But the Shadow convinces her that the scholar is *his* shadow—and thus the one who sees too clearly is easily deceived.

The Princess is obviously a personification of the lovely apparition that the scholar saw in the house opposite his in the South. The scholar does not remember that he had sent his Shadow into her house to find out more about her. The muse of poetry that the scholar asks about in his conversations with his Shadow is also the same lovely maiden that he once saw in a vision. But in her physical manifestation as a Princess, the muse of poetry has none of the spiritual wisdom and purity that the abstract muse has. And that is precisely why the scholar does not see her as anything more than a princess. The Shadow, on the contrary, is bewitched by her beauty and wants to possess her, which is precisely what the scholar in his disturbed condition in the South wanted to do. When the scholar realizes that his Shadow intends to marry the Princess by deceiving her about his true identity, he is appalled. He wants to tell the Princess the truth; but by that time the Shadow convinces the Princess that the scholar has gone mad and that he should be disposed of. The scholar is executed before the marriage of the deceiver and the deceived takes place.

Why does Andersen make his negative Shadow successful and the scholar a failure? "The Shadow" is a story about the dangers of romantic individualism untempered by classical and Christian humility. The scholar is a victim of bad faith; he is destroyed by his vacillating spirit. The scholar is punished for self-betrayal and for lack of self-knowledge. The question still remains: why make the Shadow so powerful as to make it possible for him to destroy his master and assume his role? The answer lies in the fact that the Shadow is only seemingly successful. He stands for the illusory self of the scholar. He has no substantial existence without his master, no matter how hard he tries to become the master. Andersen cannot destroy the Shadow without bringing about the destruction of the Shadow's master in the story. Nothing is real in the story; and no one in it has any real substance. And so must they be. "The Shadow" is about shadowy things, about dreams and phantoms. The truth of the story is behind it, not in it.

"The Shadow" is an intensely autobiographical story. Those who know Andersen's life well will notice that the reality embodied in the scholar's ambivalent attitude toward his Shadow is one that Andersen experienced most powerfully in his own life. He craved for wealth, power, and recognition. He wanted to be as visible as the scholar's Shadow. He knew the demon that he harbored within him. But as a Christian and as an artist in the classical mold, he also knew how to control the demon that stalked within him. He created the scholar in his own image, but an image that did not tell the whole truth about him. And it is for this reason also that he rejects the scholar; for Andersen, in actuality, was much more than the scholar—he never allowed the demon within him to destroy him or his art.

Explorations

STORYTELLING AND ACTING OUT

1. *(Brave Little Tailor/Puss in Boots)* The need to get along in a materialistic world lies behind these two stories. Pretension is used to outwit pretension. Children like to put these stories on as puppet shows—not as finished performances, but in their own way. Let them show you how. There is at least one mask in each one.
2. *(Emperor's New Clothes)* This story is fun to mime in a variety of ways. Tell it in your own words while three or four children act out what you are saying. As they get to know the story well, they can say the words themselves in their own way. (When the emperor prepares to don his imaginary clothes, he can stand behind a screen and toss over it almost—but not quite—all his clothes.)

   Have ten children stand in a row and tell the story in turn. Try having each child say just one word, so that the story progresses in a fast round, word by word.
3. *(Dog and His Shadow)* Act out this fable in a tableau or "living picture" of silent and motionless participants. Action can be portrayed by a series of separate tableaux. Try staging tableaux for other fables you know. (If you prefer, act out the fables in pantomime).
4. *(Little Jack Horner/Tom, Tom)* These are two folk rhymes that are easy to present in tableaux. They can also be performed as choral plays, with you saying one line with exaggerated gestures and voice, and a child saying the next.
5. *(Old Father Long-Legs/Little Miss Muffet/There was a crooked man)* are other rhymes that lend themselves well to tableaux or choral plays, with each person taking an alternate line and acting it out (or saying it) vigorously. Two or many can play at this.
6. *(Elk's Head)* This story is a good one for a larger group of children to pantomime. There are many parts to be assigned besides that of Trickster: several children can play the insects that fly in and out of the elk's skull; several others can play the members of the tribe who discover Trickster when his head is stuck in the skull. This is a funny story—the Winnebago Indians considered Trickster an object of fun—so be sure to encourage the children to exaggerate its humor in their pantomime.
7. *(Two Travelers)* This story is told objectively in the original, favoring neither the tailor or the shoemaker. After telling or reading the story to a group of children, discuss the two characters fully, asking for verbal descriptions and physical impersonations of the tailor and the shoemaker. When you think the children have clear pictures of these two characters, ask a child to retell the story from the point of view of the character she or he prefers. Discuss that version with the children, then ask anoth-

er child to retell the story from the point of view of the opposite character. Discuss this version. Which version do the children prefer?

8. *(Flute)* Read the story so many times to yourself that you can imagine chanting its refrains beside an African campfire. Then read it aloud to a group of children, leading them in chanting the refrains "Awful spirit . . . " and "King of Spirits" with you.

   The theme of Masks and Shadows leads naturally to ghost stories and stories of the supernatural. These stories can be wonderfully gripping if the storyteller is able to employ available resources of personal expression. Here are the key ones: a voice that can rise and fall at appropriate points in the action, change in vocal character, pause at the right moments and pace itself; a face that is mobile and alive; gestures that are natural and free. Practice telling "The Flute" until you feel you are using your own resources of personal expression as fully as you can (without overdoing it—remember, naturalness is essential in the storyteller's art). Then tell the story to a group of children. If they enter into the mood of the story, have them tell their own ghost stories. You should be able to see your own expressiveness reflected in their storytelling style.

9. *(Jahdu)* Read this story aloud to some children. Can one of the children tell it back to you?

   Present *Jahdu* as a shadow puppet story. Books on how to do this are available in the children's section of a library (one such book is listed in the Selected Readings for this section), or you can figure out how to do it yourself. Cut figures out of cardboard; attach them to stout wires or sticks. Put up a white sheet and put a light behind it. Stand behind the sheet, at the side, and manipulate the figures in such a way that those in front of the sheet can see the story. More elaborate figures can be made by cutting out separate arms and legs and head, and joining them to the trunk with brads. Attach separate wires to each appendage. Jahdu running through the darkness and the shadow fisherman should both be effective in silhouette.

10. *(Geronimo)* Read the selection from this biography aloud to a group of older children and discuss it with them thoroughly afterward. When you are sure that the problems posed in the selection as well understood, have the children choose someone to play the part of Geronimo and someone else to play the part of an interviewer. Have the children write down questions they would like the interviewer to ask Geronimo. Change parts after awhile so that several sets of children can participate.

11. *(My Shadow/My Inside-Self)* In these two poems Robert Louis Stevenson sees his physical shadow, mostly, and Rachel Field sees her inside shadow. Both shadows are happy ones. Is your inside shadow happy? Have a group of children tell you about their inside shadows. Maybe the shadows can be persuaded to tell their stories to the group.

12. *(Windy Nights)* Read this poem aloud to a group of children, along with Alfred Noyes's "The Highwayman" and Washington Irving's story "The Headless Horsemen" (the last two selections should be readily available at a library). Compare the images of the horsemen in the three pieces. Can the shadow of the horsemen be our own restless dreams? Ask the children, in turn, what this image means to them.

PARTICIPATING IN OTHER WAYS

1. Think about the masks that are worn by characters in this section—Perseus' cap of darkness; Shoye's ugly mask, worn after her beauty was borrowed; Little Burnt-Face's scarred face and body; the brave little tailor's boldness; Puss in Boots's confidence—and then try to render them in actual masks. Cut the masks out from cardboard, and color or paint them boldly to illustrate the face that each character shows to the world.
2. *(Elk's Head)* With some children, draw a group picture of Trickster wearing an elk's head. If the children don't know what an elk's head looks like, find one in a picture book of animals.
3. *(Fox Boy)* Sing the song that Mother and Fox Boy sing together in this story. Make up your own tune.
4. *(Dorp Dead)* This story is for older children. A child who is interested in the story might draw the cage that Gilly drew. Ask the child to consider whether the cage was really in Kobalt's room or did Gilly imagine it? Does it matter?
5. *(Two Bad Mice)* With a child's help, make a stuffed mouse. You might call it "Hunca Munca" after the mouse in Beatrix Potter's story. Let it be a bad mouse, doing naughty things.
6. *(Mewlips)* With the help of a child, make up your own song about "The Mewlips." You don't need to write it down, but a child might like to dance to it.
7. Make up a shadow game and play it with a group of children. One child should lead the way; the other should follow as his shadow. Encourage the child playing the shadow role to give vent to imagination. How do the children think the nonshadow should behave? Let several pairs of children play this game.
8. (*The Flute*) This story can be very effectively mimed. Have a clear-voiced narrator tell the story while children act out the parts.

Selected Readings

READINGS FOR CHILDREN

Masks

Alexander, Lloyd. *The Cat Who Wished to Be a Man.* New York: Dutton, 1973. Fantasy.

Andersen, Hans Christian. *The Ugly Duckling.* Illustrated by Adrienne Adams. New York: Scribner, 1965. Fantasy (picture book).

Clark, Ann Nolan. *Secret of the Andes.* Illustrated by Jean Charlot. New York: Viking, 1952. Fiction.

Farmer, Penelope. *The Summer Birds.* Illustrated by James Spanfeller. New York: Harcourt, 1962. Fantasy.

Fox, Paula. *The Stone-Faced Boy.* Illustrated by Donald A. Mackay. Scarsdale, N.Y.: Bradbury, 1968. Fiction.

Gard, Joyce. *Talargain.* New York: Holt, 1965. Fantasy.

Hauff, Wilhelm. *Dwarf Long-Nose.* Translated by Doris Orgel. Illustrated by Maurice Sendak. New York: Random House, 1960. Fantasy.

Heady, Eleanor B. "Little Crow." In *When the Stones Were Soft: East African Fireside Tales.* Illustrated by Tom Feelings. New York: Funk & Wagnalls, 1968. Folktale.

Massie, Diane Redfield. *Dazzle.* Illustrated by the author. New York: Parents', 1969. Fantasy (picture book).

Musick, Ruth Ann. *Telltale Lilac Bush and Other West Virginia Ghost Tales.* Lexington, Ky.: University of Kentucky Press, 1965. Folktales.

Picard, Barbara Leonie. *One Is One.* New York: Holt, 1966. Historical fiction.

Shulevitz, Uri. *The Magician.* Adapted from the Yiddish of I. L. Peretz. Illustrated by the author. New York: Macmillan, 1973. Folk legend (picture book).

Sutcliff, Rosemary. *The Witch's Brat.* Illustrated by Richard Lebenson. New York: Walck, 1970. Historical fiction.

Taylor, Mark. *The Fisherman and the Goblet.* Illustrated by Taro Yashima. Los Angeles: Golden Gate, 1971. Folktale (picture book).

Zemach, Harve. *The Tricks of Master Dabble.* Illustrated by Margot Zemach. New York: Holt, 1965. Fantasy.

Shadows

Aldis, Dorothy. *Nothing Is Impossible: The Story of Beatrix Potter.* Illustrated by Richard Cuffari. New York: Atheneum, 1969. Biography.

Alger, Leclaire [Nic Leodhas, Sorche]. *Gaelic Ghosts.* Illustrated by Nonny Hogrogian. New York: Holt, 1963. Folktales.

———. *Ghosts Go Haunting.* Illustrated by Nonny Hogrogian. New York: Holt, 1965. Folktales.

______. *Twelve Great Black Cats and Other Eerie Scottish Tales.* Illustrated by Vera Bock. New York: Dutton, 1971. Folktales.

Arkhurst, Joyce Cooper. *The Adventures of Spider: West African Folk Tales.* Boston: Little, Brown, 1964. Folktales (trickster).

Boston, L. M. *The Children of Green Knowe.* Illustrated by Peter Boston. New York: Harcourt, 1955. Fantasy.

______. *The Enemy at Green Knowe.* Illustrated by Peter Boston. New York: Harcourt, 1964. Fantasy.

Brewton, Sara and John E., eds. *Shrieks at Midnight: Macabre Poems, Eerie and Humorous.* Illustrated by Ellen Raskin. New York: Thomas Crowell, 1969. Poetry.

Chauncy, Nan. *The Secret Friends.* Illustrated by Brian Wildsmith. New York: Franklin Watts, 1962. Fantasy.

Chekhov, Anton Pavlovich. *Shadow and Light: Nine Stories.* Illustrated by Ann Grifalconi. Translated by Miriam Morton. New York: Doubleday, 1968. Fiction.

Cleaver, Vera and Bill. *Me Too.* Philadelphia: Lippincott, 1973. Fiction.

Clifford, Eth. *The Year of the Three-Legged Deer.* Illustrated by Richard Cuffari. Boston: Houghton Mifflin, 1971. Historical fiction.

Clymer, Eleanor. *My Brother Stevie.* New York: Holt, 1967. Fiction.

Cole, William, ed. *Beastly Boys and Ghastly Girls.* Illustrated by Tomi Ungerer. Cleveland: World, 1964. Poetry.

Corcoran, Barbara. *A Trick of Light.* Illustrated by Lydia Dabcovich. New York: Atheneum, 1973. Fiction.

Cooper, Susan. *The Dark Is Rising.* Illustrated by Alan E. Cober. New York: Atheneum, 1973. Fantasy.

Estes, Eleanor. *The Hundred Dresses.* Illustrated by Louis Slobodkin. New York: Harcourt, 1944. Fiction.

Farmer, Penelope. *Emma in Winter.* Illustrated by James Spanfeller. New York: Harcourt, 1966. Fantasy.

Fisher, Aileen. *In the Middle of the Night.* Illustrated by Adrienne Adams. New York: Thomas Crowell, 1965. Poetic fiction (picture book).

Fox, Paula. *The Slave Dancer.* Illustrated by Eros Keith. Scarsdale, N.Y.: Bradbury, 1973. Historical fiction.

Garfield, Leon. *The Restless Ghost: Three Stories.* Illustrated by Saul Lambert. New York: Pantheon, 1969. Fantasy.

Garner, Alan. *Elidor.* New York: Walck, 1967. Fantasy.

Ginsburg, Mirra. *The Proud Maiden, Tungak, and the Sun: A Russian Eskimo Tale.* Illustrated by Igor Galanin. New York: Macmillan, 1975. Folktale.

Hickman, Janet. *The Valley of the Shadow.* New York: Macmillan, 1974. Historical fiction.

. . . *I Never Saw Another Butterfly.* Children's Drawings and Poems from Terezín Concentration Camp 1942-1944. New York: McGraw, 1964. Poetry.

Ish-Kishor, Sulamith. *A Boy of Old Prague.* Illustrated by Ben Shahn. New York: Pantheon, 1963. Historical fiction.

Jones, Hettie. *Coyote Tales.* Illustrated by Louis Mofsie. New York: Holt, 1974. Folktales (trickster).

LeGuin, Ursula. *A Wizard of Earthsea.* Illustrated by Ruth Robbins. Berkeley, Calif.: Parnassus, 1968. Fantasy.

Lindgren, Astrid. *The Tomten.* Adapted from a poem by Viktor Rydberg. Illustrated by Harald Wiberg. New York: Coward, McCann, 1961. Fantasy (picture book).

Little, Jean. *Home from Far.* Illustrated by Jerry Lazare. Boston: Little, Brown, 1965. Fiction.

Mahy, Margaret. *The Boy with Two Shadows.* Illustrated by Jenny Williams. New York: Franklin Watts, 1971. Fantasy (picture book).

Moore, Lilian, and Webster, Lawrence, eds. *Catch Your Breath: A Book of Shivery Poems.* Illustrated by Gahan Wilson. Champaign, Ill.: Garrard, 1973. Poetry.

Neville, Emily C. *Berries Goodman.* New York: Harper, 1965. Fiction.

Pearce, Philippa. *Tom's Midnight Garden.* Illustrated by Susan Einzig. Philadelphia: Lippincott, 1959. Fantasy.

Rinkoff, Barbara. *The Watchers.* New York: Knopf, 1972. Fiction.

Robinson, Joan G. *When Marnie Was There.* New York: Coward, McCann, 1968. Fantasy.

Ryan, Cheli Duran. *Hildilid's Night.* Illustrated by Arnold Lobel. New York: Macmillan, 1971. Fantasy (picture book).

Sauer, Julia. *Fog Magic.* Illustrated by Lynd Ward. New York: Viking, 1943. Fantasy.

Schwebell, Gertrude C. *The Man Who Lost His Shadow and Nine Other German Fairy Tales.* Illustrated by Max Barsis. New York: Dover, 1974; first published in 1957 under the title *Where Magic Reigns: German Fairy Tales since Grimm.* Folktales.

Sendak, Maurice. *In the Night Kitchen.* Illustrated by the author. New York: Harper, 1970. Fantasy (picture book).

______. *Where the Wild Things Are.* Illustrated by the author. New York: Harper, 1963. Fantasy (picture book).

Sherlock, Philip M. *Anansi the Spider Man: Jamaican Folk Tales.* Illustrated by Marcia Brown. New York: Thomas Crowell, 1954. Folktales (trickster).

Smith, Mary and R.A. *Long Ago Elf.* Chicago: Follett, 1968. Fantasy (picture book).

Snyder, Zilpha. *The Changeling.* Illustrated by Alton Raible. New York: Atheneum, 1970. Fiction.

Sturton, Hugh. *Zomo the Rabbit.* Illustrated by Peter Warner. New York: Atheneum, 1966. Folktales (trickster).

Sutcliff, Rosemary. *Knight's Fee.* Illustrated by Charles Keeping. New York: Walck, 1960. Historical fiction.

Ullman, James Ramsey. *Banner in the Sky.* Philadelphia: Lippincott, 1954. Fiction.

Viorst, Judith. *Alexander and the Terrible, Horrible, No Good, Very Bad Day.* Illustrated by Ray Cruz. New York: Atheneum, 1972. Fiction (picture book).

Wojciechowska, Maia. *Shadow of a Bull.* Illustrated by Alvin Smith. New York: Atheneum, 1970. Fiction.

REFERENCES FOR ADULTS

Andersen, Hans Christian. *The Fairy Tale of My Life.* Illustrated by Niels Larsen Stevns. Copenhagen, Denmark: Nyt Nordisk Forlag, 1943.

Beck, Robert E., ed. *Literature of the Supernatural.* New York: Lothrop, 1975.

Bursill, Henry. *Hand Shadows to Be Thrown upon the Wall: A Series of Novel and Amusing Figures Formed by the Hand.* New York: Dover, 1967; first published in 1859.

Franz, Marie-Luise von. *Shadow and Evil in Fairy Tales.* Zurich, Switzerland: Spring Publications, 1964.

Jung, C. G. *Man and His Symbols.* Garden City, N.Y.: Doubleday, 1964. See discussions of both "masks" and "shadows."

Larsen, Svend. *Hans Christian Andersen.* Odense, Denmark: Flensted, 1971.

LeGuin, Ursula. "The Child and the Shadow." *Quarterly Journal of the Library of Congress* 32, no. 2 (April 1975): 139-48.

Lommel, Andreas. *Masks: Their Meaning and Function.* New York: McGraw, 1972.

MacGowan, Kenneth, and Rosse, Herman. *Masks and Demons.* New York: Harcourt, 1923.

McCaslin, Nellie. *Creative Dramatics in the Classroom.* 2d. ed. New York: David McKay, 1974.

Radin, Paul. *The Trickster. A Study in American Indian Mythology.* Westport, Conn.: Greenwood, 1956.

Rogers, Robert. *A Psychoanalytic Study of The Double in Literature.* Detroit: Wayne State University Press, 1970.

Shalleck, Jamie. *Masks.* New York: Viking, 1973.

Sorell, *The Other Face: The Mask in the Arts.* Indianapolis and New York: Bobbs-Merrill, 1973.

IV. Sex Roles

A variety of views about sex roles appear in folktales and also fiction for children. In addition to the traditional socialized female-male roles that predominate in most of the folk literature (see "Feminists and Fairytales: A Controversy," at the end of this section, for a detailed discussion of this point and its implications), some folktales show merging sex roles. That is, by the standards of twentieth-century sex-role conditioning (not feminist ideology), they show men acting as women and women acting as men. Other tales suggest role reversal. Still other tales deal with unisex or androgyny. A greater range with respect to treatment of sex roles is beginning to be found also in contemporary fiction for children. As a result of the resurgence of the feminist movement in the 1960s, a few books of quality are beginning to appear in which children are simply human beings who happen to be male or female. That is, a strong attempt is being made to eliminate sex-role conditioning through fiction.

In certain parts of the world, in various periods in history, sex roles have not been sharply separated. The Greeks, for example, portray the intermingling of these roles in their plays, philosophy, and myths. The idea that man and woman were once one, but became separated into two parts—each looking for its mate; the idea of the cleaving together of Hermaphroditus and Salmacis in one body; the goddesses with "masculine" assignments and gods with "feminine" assignments (Artemis, goddess of the hunt, and Apollo, god of the arts)—these are all symbols of the mingled roles of men and women. In the Greek myth of Atalanta, retold here in a contemporary version, an abandoned girl-child takes on many of the attributes of a man in order to survive—and retains them later because she likes the independence they bring.

Folktales abound in which men act as women or women act as men. In the Nigerian tale "Nana Miriam," a woman surpasses her own father in magic and in hunting. The Japanese tall tale "Three Strong Women" shows a daughter, mother, and even a "feeble" grandmother besting a mighty male wrestling champion. In the Swedish tale "The Master Maid" and the English tale "Mollie Whipple," women play the heroic role and bring the stories to a successful conclusion.

Role reversal carried to the point where one sex dresses, as well as behaves, like the other is suggested by some myths, folktales, plays, and stories. Most notable in Greek myth is the great Hercules, who when dominated by Omphale, Queen of Lydia, dressed as a woman and did women's chores. Shakespeare's plays and other plays of the Elizabethan and Jacobean periods often have to do with girls masquerading as boys. Viola, masquerading as Sebastian in *Twelfth Night,* appeals as Sebastian both to Orsino and to Olivia. In *As You Like It,* Rosalind, as played on the stage in Shakespeare's time, was a boy playing the part of a girl masquerading as a boy.

As society sharpened sex-role differentiation in the Victorian period, an urge for reversals seemed to take place, which surfaced through fantasy. Maggie Browne (pseudonym for Margaret Andrewes) wrote a children's fantasy entitled *Wanted—A King, or How Merle Set the Nursery Rhymes to Rights* (1890). In this story, a girl goes about in a boy's body (which she never loses):

> "But you got it (your body) back, I suppose?" said Merle.
>
> "No, I didn't," said the boy, indignantly, "not my own body. This one doesn't belong to me. I really am a girl, and I was ten years old when I came to Endom, and when I wanted to go out again Grunter Grim said he had given my own body away, and this was the best he could do for me. That's what he does—gives back the wrong bodies, and then down in that stupid world, every one is astonished because big people are often cowards and little people brave, some girls more like boys, and some

> boys more like girls. It is easy enough to explain it if they only knew the reason why."

The author assumes that there are such things as male and female roles.

Despite the range of sex-role behavior in the literature just described, when one looks over the field of old tales and of fiction for children written during the nineteenth or first half of the twentieth century, one discovers that there are very few stories indeed which do not have strong sex-role differentiation. The advantage of seeking out exceptions to this rule is that, through them, children can learn that human beings are not so simple as they seem to be in the myriad of books designed for children—and that one cannot make fixed rules about human nature.

A significant point about the changing sex roles in modern fiction for children is that, generally, the emphasis has been on girls developing the so-called masculine qualities and capabilities, and not on boys developing "feminine" ones. In other words, in our society, it appears that "masculine" attributes are still assigned a higher value. Though having all the "feminine" attributes of warmth, charm, and sensibility, "Jo" in Louisa M. Alcott's nineteenth-century classic *Little Women* also is "the man of the family" when her father is away and shows "masculine" ingenuity and self-reliance. Some feminists regard it as a very sexist book, condescending to women. Less objectionable to them is the poignant story of the fate of the girl in the Canadian classic, L. M. Montgomery's *Anne of Green Gables* (1908). Anne's foster parents are disappointed to find the boy they thought they were adopting is actually a girl. Ultimately, they realize they have the best of all human traits in one freckled, red-headed girl. Through the years, stories about girls have tended to show less sex-role conditioning, but still not completely so. Enid Bagnold's "Velvet" (*National Velvet,* 1935) is a girl jockey whom none can equal. Meg and Mrs. Murry display their strong capabilities in Madeleine L'Engle's *A Wrinkle in Time* (1962). Louise Fitzhugh's *Harriet the Spy* (1964) is a tomboyish child detective-reporter. Jean George's *Julie of the Wolves* (1972) is a capable and intelligent Eskimo girl who is able to survive alone in the wilderness.

Modern stories and books about boys have shown far less change in sex-role conditioning, perhaps because of our cultural terror of effeminacy. *Free to Be . . . You and Me,* a Ms. Foundation Project (1974), is an outstanding exception. This anthology for children contains music, poetry, and stories that reveal the changing attitudes toward sex roles in society with respect to both boys and girls. The book contains the song "William's Doll"*—William wants a doll so that when he has a child of his own, he will know how to take proper care of it. The

* Based on Charlotte Zolotow's book *William's Doll* (1972).

selection from *Impunity Jane* by Rumer Godden (in "Toys and Games") takes up the same theme. *It's Like This, Cat* by Emily Neville and *A Taste of Blackberries* by Doris Buchanan Smith are examples in this section of contemporary realistic fiction that show the changing sex roles of boys.

Literature symbolically or openly can reveal that the dichotomy between the traits of the sexes is not so rigid as society sometimes conceives it. Boys can have "feminine" warmth and sensitivity, and girls can have "masculine" traits of courage and strength. In the whole person, these traits can fuse. However, the problem of good and at the same time wholesome reading for children that frees them from the boundaries of sex-role conditioning is still with us. Anne Devereaux Jordan's essay "Sugar 'n Spice 'n Snips 'n Snails" (included at the end of the section) suggests some books for children that have broken away from the rigidity of strictly dichotomized sex roles.

The problem of what constitutes "masculine" and "feminine" traits and of whether such differentiated traits exist at all in the psychological sense is one that will be puzzled and argued over for years to come. Even among feminists, attitudes have changed since the days of the pioneers of the National Woman Suffrage Association. As a child, I was a friend of Harriet Taylor Upton, a woman who was for many years treasurer of that group. She also held the first important political post open to women, that of vice chairman of the Republican National Committee. She played an active role in several states, particularly in Tennessee, in bringing about the ratification of the Federal Suffrage Amendment. She was very interested in children's literature, and for many years while in Washington, D.C., she cut out the Thornton Burgess stories from the *Washington Evening Star* and (after reading them herself) sent them on to me with her comments. I vividly remember how she explained to my parents that girls should have a chance to enter whatever occupation appealed to them. Yet in spite of all this, she was by no means a feminist in a later sense of the word, for she still thought in terms of "feminine" traits and "masculine" traits and seemed unaware that these might be the result of conditioning. I recall that when I was seven, she told me: "You can do any job a man can do, but never forget that you are a woman. Always keep your shirtwaist and skirt pinned together so that the safety pin doesn't show."

Myth

ATALANTA

(Greek)

Retold by Betty Miles

In the classical Greek version of this myth Atalanta's father left her on a mountainside to die because he was disappointed that she was not a son. She survived and became a swift-footed young maiden skilled in the hunt. Although she was determined never to marry, she had many suitors. Finally, she announced that she would marry whoever could beat her in a footrace (believing that no man could do so). A clever young man named Melanion (or Hippomenes) tricked her into losing the race by distracting her with three tempting gold apples, thrown in her path one by one. Her freedom was lost forever.

This is a contemporary retelling of the myth in which both a fair race and friendship are possible between the two sexes.

Once upon a time, not long ago, there lived a princess named Atalanta, who could run as fast as the wind.

She was so bright, and so clever, and could build things and fix things so wonderfully, that many young men wished to marry her.

"What shall I do?" said Atalanta's father, who was a powerful king. "So many young men want to marry you, and I don't know how to choose."

"You don't have to choose, Father," Atalanta said. "I will choose, and I'm not sure that I will choose to marry anyone at all."

Illustrated by Barbara Bascove.

"Of course you will," said the king. "Everybody gets married. It is what people do."

"But," Atalanta told him, with a toss of her head, "I intend to go out and see the world. When I come home, perhaps I will marry and perhaps I will not."

The king did not like this at all. He was a very ordinary king; that is, he was powerful and used to having his own way. So he did not answer Atalanta, but simply told her, "I have decided how to choose the young man you will marry. I will hold a great race, and the winner—the swiftest, fleetest young man of all—will win the right to marry you."

Now Atalanta was a clever girl as well as a swift runner. She saw that she might win both the argument and the race—provided that she herself could run in the race, too. "Very well," she said. "But you must let me race along with the others. If I am not the winner, I will accept the wishes of the young man who is."

The king agreed to this. He was pleased; he would have his way, marry off his daughter, and enjoy a fine day of racing as well. So he directed his messengers to travel throughout the kingdom announcing the race with its wonderful prize: the chance to marry the bright Atalanta.

As the day of the race drew near, flags

were raised in the streets of the town, and banners were hung near the grassy field where the race would be run. Baskets of ripe plums and peaches, wheels of cheese, ropes of sausages and onions, and loaves of crusty bread were gathered for the crowds.

Meanwhile, Atalanta herself was preparing for the race. Each day at dawn, dressed in soft green trousers and a shirt of yellow silk, she went to the field in secret and ran across it—slowly at first, then fast and faster, until she could run the course more quickly than anyone had ever run it before.

As the day of the race grew nearer, young men began to crowd into the town. Each was sure he could win the prize, except for one; that was Young John, who lived in the town. He saw Atalanta day by day as she bought nails and wood to make a pigeon house, or chose parts for her telescope, or laughed with her friends. Young John saw the princess only from a distance, but near enough to know how bright and clever she was. He wished very much to race with her, to win, and to earn the right to talk with her and become her friend.

"For surely," he said to himself, "it is not right for Atalanta's father to give her away to the winner of the race. Atalanta herself must choose the person she wants to marry, or whether she wishes to marry at all. Still, if I could only win the race, I would be free to speak to her, and to ask for her friendship."

Each evening, after his studies of the stars and the seas, Young John went to the field in secret and practiced running across it. Night after night, he ran fast as the wind across the twilight field, until he could cross it more quickly than anyone had ever crossed it before.

At last, the day of the race arrived.

Trumpets sounded in the early morning, and the young men gathered at the edge of the field, along with Atalanta herself, the prize they sought. The king and his friends sat in soft chairs, and the townspeople stood along the course.

The king rose to address them all. "Good day," he said to the crowds. "Good luck," he said to the young men. To Atalanta he said, "Good-bye. I must tell you farewell, for tomorrow you will be married."

"I am not so sure of that, Father," Atalanta answered. She was dressed for the race in trousers of crimson and a shirt of silk as blue as the sky, and she laughed as she looked up and down the line of young men.

"Not one of them," she said to herself, "can win the race, for I will run fast as the wind and leave them all behind."

And now a bugle sounded, a flag was dropped, and the runners were off!

The crowds cheered as the young men and Atalanta began to race across the field. At first they ran as a group, but Atalanta soon pulled ahead, with three of the young men close after her. As they neared the halfway point, one young man put on a great burst of speed and seemed to pull ahead for an instant, but then he gasped and fell back. Atalanta shot on.

Soon another young man, tense with the effort, drew near to Atalanta. He reached out as though to touch her sleeve, stumbled for an instant, and lost speed. Atalanta smiled as she ran on. I have almost won, she thought.

But then another young man came near. This was Young John, running like the wind, as steadily and as swiftly as Atalanta herself. Atalanta felt his closeness, and in a sudden burst she dashed ahead.

Young John might have given up at this, but he never stopped running. Nothing at all, thought he, will keep me from winning the chance to speak with Atalanta. And on he ran, swift as the wind, until he ran as her equal, side by side with her, toward the golden ribbon that marked the race's end. Atalanta raced even faster to pull ahead, but Young John was a strong match for her. Smiling with the pleasure of the race, Atalanta and Young John reached the finish line together, and together they broke through the golden ribbon.

Trumpets blew. The crowd shouted and leaped about. The king rose. "Who is that young man?" he asked.

"It is Young John from the town," the people told him.

"Very well. Young John," said the king, as John and Atalanta stood before him, exhausted and jubilant from their efforts. "You have not won the race, but you have come closer to winning than any man here. And so I give you the prize that was promised—the right to marry my daughter."

Young John smiled at Atalanta, and she smiled back. "Thank you, sir," said John to the king, "but I could not possibly marry your daughter unless she wished to marry me. I have run this race for the chance to talk with Atalanta, and, if she is willing, I am ready to claim my prize."

Atalanta laughed with pleasure. "And I," she said to John, "could not possibly marry before I have seen the world. But I would like nothing better than to spend the afternoon with you."

Then the two of them sat and talked on the grassy field, as the crowds went away. They ate bread and cheese and purple plums. Atalanta told John about her telescopes and her pigeons, and John told Atalanta about his globes and his studies of geography. At the end of the day, they were friends.

On the next day, John sailed off to discover new lands. And Atalanta set off to visit the great cities.

By this time, each of them has had wonderful adventures, and seen marvelous sights. Perhaps some day they will be married, and perhaps they will not. In any case, they are friends. And it is certain that they are both living happily ever after.

Folktales

NANA MIRIAM

(Nigerian)

Retold by Hans Baumann

This folktale opens with a description of the two sexes existing in harmony and balance in abilities and powers. The father, Fara Maka, instructs his tall, strong, and beautiful daughter, Nana Miriam, in nature lore and magic. But Nana Miriam possesses within her additional magic powers that no one suspects. Through these, she is able to defeat a devouring hippopotamus and restore prosperity to her people. Even though she has outshone him, her father is proud of her. The story thus remains faithful to its original positive portrayal of a man and his daughter.

Fara Maka was a man of the Songai tribe, who lived by the River Niger. He was taller than the other men and he was also stronger. Only he was very ugly. However, no one thought that important, because Fara Maka had a daughter who was very beautiful. Her name was Nana Miriam and she too was tall and strong. Her father instructed her in all kinds of things. He went with her to the sandbank and said, "Watch the fish!" And he told her the names of all the various kinds. Everything there is to know about fish he taught her. Then he asked her, "What kind is the one swimming here, and the other one over there?"

"This is a so-and-so," replied Nana Miriam. "And that is a such-and-such."

"Male or female?" asked Fara Maka.

"I don't know," said Nana Miriam.

"This one is a female, and so is the other one," explained Fara Maka. "But the third one over there is a male." And each time he pointed to a different fish.

That was how Nana Miriam came to learn so much. And in addition she had magic powers within her, which no one suspected. And because her father also taught her many magic spells, she grew stronger than anyone else in the Land of the Songai.

Beside the great river, the Niger, there lived a monster that took the form of a hippopotamus. This monster was insatiable. It broke into the rice fields and devoured the crops, bringing famine to the

Translated by Stella Humphries.

Songai people. No one could tackle this hippopotamus, because it could change its shape. So the hunters had all their trouble for nothing and they returned to their villages in helpless despair. Times were so bad that many died of hunger.

One day, Fara Maka picked up all his lances and set out to kill the monster. When he saw it, he recoiled in fear, for huge pots of fire were hung around the animal's neck. Fara Maka hurled lance after lance, but each one was swallowed by the flames. The hippopotamus monster looked at Fara Maka with scorn. Then it turned its back on him and trotted away.

Fara Maka returned home furious, wondering whom he could summon to help him. Now there was a man of the Tomma tribe who was a great hunter. His name was Kara-Digi-Mao-Fosi-Fasi, and Fara Maka asked him if he would hunt the hippopotamus with his one hundred and twenty dogs. "That I will," said Kara-Digi-Mao-Fosi-Fasi.

So Fara Maka invited him and his one hundred and twenty dogs to a great banquet. Before every dog, which had an iron chain around its neck, was placed a small mound of rice and meat. For the hunter, however, there was a huge mound of rice. None of the dogs left a single grain of rice uneaten, and neither did Kara-Digi-Mao-Fosi-Fasi. Well fortified, they set out for the place where the monster lived.

As soon as the dogs picked up the scent, Kara-Digi-Mao-Fosi-Fasi unchained the first one. The chain rattled as the dog leaped forward towards its quarry. One chain rattled after the other, as dog after dog sprang forward to attack the hippopotamus. But the hippopotamus took them on one by one, and it gobbled them all up. The great hunter Kara-Digi-Mao-Fosi-Fasi took to his heels in terror. The hippopotamus charged into a rice field and ate that too.

When Fara Maka heard from the great hunter what had happened, he sat down in the shadow of a large tree and hung his head.

"Haven't you been able to kill the hippopotamus?" Nana Miriam asked him.

"No," said Fara Maka.

"And Kara-Digi-Mao-Fosi-Fasi couldn't drive it away either?"

"No."

"So there is no one who can get the better of it?"

"No," said Fara Maka.

"Then I'll not delay any longer," said Nana Miriam. "I'll go to its haunts and see what I can see."

"Yes, do," said her father.

Nana Miriam walked along the banks of the Niger, and she soon found the hippopotamus eating its way through a rice field. As soon as it saw the girl it stopped eating, raised its head and greeted her.

"Good morning," replied Nana Miriam.

"I know why you have come," said the hippopotamus. "You want to kill me. But no one can do that. Your father tried, and he lost all his lances. The great hunter Kara-Digi-Mao-Fosi-Fasi tried, and all his dogs paid with their lives for his presumption. And you are only a girl."

"We'll soon see," answered Nana Miriam. "Prepare to fight with me. Only one of us will be left to tell the tale."

"Right you are!" shouted the hippopotamus and with its breath it set the rice field afire. There it stood in a ring of flame through which no mortal could pass.

But Nana Miriam threw magic powder into the fire, and the flames turned to water.

"Right!" shouted the hippopotamus, and a wall of iron sprang up making a ring around the monster. But Nana Miriam plucked a magic hammer from the air, and shattered the iron wall into fragments.

Now for the first time the hippopotamus felt afraid, and it turned itself into a river that flowed into the Niger.

Again Nana Miriam sprinkled her magic powder. At once the river dried up and the water changed back into a hippopotamus. It grew more and more afraid and when Fara Maka came up to see what was happening, the monster charged him blindly. Nana Miriam ran after it, and when it was only ten bounds away from her father, she seized it by its left hind foot and flung it across the Niger. As it crashed against the opposite bank, its skull was split and it was dead. Then Fara Maka, who had seen the mighty throw, exclaimed, "What a daughter I have!"

Very soon, the whole tribe heard what had happened, and the Dialli, the minstrel folk, sang the song of Nana Miriam's adventure with the hippopotamus, which used to devastate the rice fields. And in the years that followed, no one in the Land of the Songai starved any more.

THREE STRONG WOMEN

(A Tall Tale from Japan)

Retold by Claus Stamm

Like many tall tales, this one begs to be told or read aloud. The three jolly superwomen of the story—mother, daughter, and grandmother—are patient and affectionate with the conceited wrestler Forever-Mountain. From them he learns modesty, as well as to become the best wrestler in the kingdom. As in the two preceding stories, the relationship between strong women and men is presented positively.

Long ago, in Japan, there lived a famous wrestler, and he was on his way to the capital city to wrestle before the Emperor.

He strode down the road on legs thick as the trunks of small trees. He had been walking for seven hours and could, and probably would, walk for seven more without getting tired.

The time was autumn, the sky was a cold, watery blue, the air chilly. In the small bright sun, the trees along the roadside glowed red and orange.

The wrestler hummed to himself, "Zun-zun-zun," in time with the long swing of his legs. Wind blew through his thin brown robe, and he wore no sword at his side. He felt proud that he needed no sword, even in the darkest and loneliest places. The icy air on his body only reminded him that few tailors would have been able to make expensive warm clothes for a man so broad and tall. He felt much as a wrestler should—strong, healthy, and rather conceited.

A soft roar of fast-moving water beyond the trees told him that he was passing above a river bank. He "zun-zunned" louder; he loved the sound of his voice and wanted it to sound clearly above the rushing water.

He thought: They call me Forever-Mountain because I am such a good strong wrestler—big, too. I'm a fine, brave man and far too modest ever to say so . . .

Just then he saw a girl who must have come up from the river, for she steadied a bucket on her head.

Her hands on the bucket were small, and there was a dimple on each thumb, just below the knuckle. She was a round little girl with red cheeks and a nose like a friendly button. Her eyes looked as though she were thinking of ten thousand funny stories at once. She clambered up onto the road and walked ahead of the wrestler, jolly and bounceful.

"If I don't tickle that fat girl, I shall regret it all my life," said the wrestler under his breath. "She's sure to go 'squeak' and I shall laugh and laugh. If she drops her bucket, that will be ever funnier—and I can always run and fill it again and even carry it home for her."

He tiptoed up and poked her lightly in the ribs with one huge finger.

"Kochokochokocho!" he said, a fine, ticklish sound in Japanese.

The girl gave a satisfying squeal, giggled, and brought one arm down so that the wrestler's hand was caught between it and her body.

"Ho-ho-ho! You've caught me! I can't move at all!" said the wrestler, laughing.

"I know," said the jolly girl.

He felt that it was very good-tempered of her to take a joke so well, and started to pull his hand free.

Somehow, he could not.

He tried again, using a little more strength.

"Now, now—let me go, little girl," he said. "I am a very powerful man. If I pull too hard I might hurt you."

"Pull," said the girl. "I admire powerful men."

She began to walk, and though the wrestler tugged and pulled until his feet dug great furrows in the ground, he had to follow. She couldn't have paid him less attention if he had been a puppy—a small one.

Ten minutes later, still tugging while trudging helplessly after her, he was glad that the road was lonely and no one was there to see.

"Please let me go," he pleaded. "I am the famous wrestler Forever-Mountain. I must go and show my strength before the Emperor"—he burst out weeping from shame and confusion—"and you're hurting my hand!"

The girl steadied the bucket on her head with her free hand and dimpled sympathetically over her shoulder. "You poor, sweet little Forever-Mountain," she said. "Are you tired? Shall I carry you? I can leave the water here and come back for it later."

"I do not want you to carry me. I want you to let me go, and then I want to forget I ever saw you. What do you want with me?" moaned the pitiful wrestler.

"I only want to help you," said the girl, now pulling him steadily up and up a narrow mountain path. "Oh, I am sure you'll have no more trouble than anyone else when you come up against the other wrestlers. You'll win, or else you'll lose, and you won't be too badly hurt either way. But aren't you afraid you might meet a really *strong* man someday?"

Forever-Mountain turned white. He stumbled. He was imagining being laughed at throughout Japan as "Hardly-Ever-Mountain."

She glanced back.

"You see? Tired already," she said. "I'll walk more slowly. Why don't you come along to my mother's house and let us make a strong man of you? The wrestling in the capital isn't due to begin for three months. I know, because Grandmother thought she'd go. You'd be spending all that time in bad company and wasting what little power you have."

"All right. Three months. I'll come along," said the wrestler. He felt he had nothing more to lose. Also, he feared that the girl might become angry if he refused, and place him in the top of a tree until he changed his mind.

"Fine," she said happily. "We are almost there."

She freed his hand. It had become red and a little swollen. "But if you break your promise and run off, I shall have to chase you and carry you back."

Soon they arrived in a small valley. A simple farmhouse with a thatched roof stood in the middle.

"Grandmother is at home, but she is an old lady and she's probably sleeping." The girl shaded her eyes with one hand. "But Mother should be bringing our cow back from the field—oh, there's Mother now!"

She waved. The woman coming around the corner of the house put down the cow she was carrying and waved back.

She smiled and came across the grass, walking with a lively bounce like her daughter's. Well, maybe her bounce was a little more solid, thought the wrestler.

"Excuse me," she said, brushing some cow hair from her dress and dimpling, also like her daughter. "These mountain paths are full of stones. They hurt the cow's feet. And who is the nice young man you've brought, Maru-me?"

The girl explained. "And we have only three months!" she finished anxiously.

"Well, it's not long enough to do much, but it's not so short a time that we can't do something," said her mother, looking thoughtful. "But he does look terribly feeble. He'll need a lot of good things to eat. Maybe when he gets stronger he can help Grandmother with some of the easy work about the house."

"That will be fine!" said the girl, and she called her grandmother—loudly, for the old lady was a little deaf.

"I'm coming!" came a creaky voice from inside the house, and a little old woman leaning on a stick and looking very sleepy tottered out of the door. As she came toward them she stumbled over the roots of a great oak tree.

"Heh! My eyes aren't what they used to be. That's the fourth time this month I've stumbled over that tree," she complained and, wrapping her skinny arms about its trunk, pulled it out of the ground.

"Oh, Grandmother! You should have let me pull it up for you," said Maru-me.

"Hm. I hope I didn't hurt my poor old back," muttered the old lady. She called out, "Daughter! Throw that tree away like a good girl, so no one will fall over it. But make sure it doesn't hit anybody."

"You can help Mother with the tree," Maru-me said to Forever-Mountain. "On second thought, you'd better not help. Just watch."

Her mother went to the tree, picked it up in her two hands, and threw it—clumsily and with a little gasp, the way a woman throws. Up went the tree, sailing end over end, growing smaller and smaller as it flew. It landed with a faint crash far up the mountainside.

"Ah, how clumsy," she said. "I meant to throw it *over* the mountain. It's probably blocking the path now, and I'll have to get up early tomorrow to move it."

The wrestler was not listening. He had very quietly fainted.

"Oh! We must put him to bed," said Maru-me.

"Poor, feeble young man," said her mother.

"I hope we can do something for him. Here, let me carry him, he's light," said the grandmother. She slung him over her shoulder and carried him into the house, creaking along with her cane.

The next day they began the work of making Forever-Mountain over into what they thought a strong man should be. They gave him the simplest food to eat, and the toughest. Day by day they prepared his rice with less and less water, until no ordinary man could have chewed or digested it.

Every day he was made to do the work of five men, and every evening he wrestled with Grandmother. Maru-me and her mother agreed that Grandmother, being old and feeble, was the least likely to injure him accidentally. They hoped the exercise might be good for the old lady's rheumatism.

He grew stronger and stronger but was hardly aware of it. Grandmother could still throw him easily into the air—and catch him again—without ever changing her sweet old smile.

He quite forgot that outside this valley he was one of the greatest wrestlers in Japan and was called Forever-Mountain. His legs had been like logs; now they were like pillars. His big hands were hard as stones, and when he cracked his knuckles the sound was like trees splitting on a cold night.

Sometimes he did an exercise that wrestlers do in Japan—raising one foot high above the ground and bringing it down with a crash. Then people in nearby villages looked up at the winter sky and told one another that it was very late in the year for thunder.

Soon he could pull up a tree as well as the grandmother. He could even throw one—but only a small distance. One evening, near the end of his third month, he wrestled with Grandmother and held her down for half a minute.

"Heh-heh!" She chortled and got up, smiling with every wrinkle. "I would never have believed it!"

Maru-me squealed with joy and threw her arms around him—gently, for she was afraid of cracking his ribs.

"Very good, very good! What a strong man," said her mother, who had just come home from the fields, carrying, as usual, the cow. She put the cow down and patted the wrestler on the back.

They agreed that he was now ready to show some *real* strength before the Emperor.

"Take the cow along with you tomorrow when you go," said the mother. "Sell her and buy yourself a belt—a silken belt. Buy the fattest and heaviest one you can find. Wear it when you appear before the Emperor, as a souvenir from us."

"I wouldn't think of taking your only cow. You've already done too much for me. And you'll need her to plow the fields, won't you?"

They burst out laughing, Maru-me squealed, her mother roared. The grandmother cackled so hard and long that she choked and had to be pounded on the back.

"Oh, dear," said the mother, still laughing. "You didn't think we used our cow for anything like *work!* Why, Grandmother here is stronger than five cows!"

"The cow is our pet." Maru-me giggled. "She has lovely brown eyes."

"But it really gets tiresome having to carry her back and forth each day so that she has enough grass to eat," said her mother.

"Then you must let me give you all the prize money that I win," said Forever-Mountain.

"Oh, no! We wouldn't think of it!" said Maru-me. "Because we all like you too much to sell you anything. And it is not proper to accept gifts of money from strangers."

"True," said Forever-Mountain. "I will now ask your mother's and grandmother's permission to marry you. I want to be one of the family."

"Oh! I'll get a wedding dress ready!" said Maru-me.

The mother and grandmother pretended to consider very seriously, but they quickly agreed.

Next morning Forever-Mountain tied his hair up in the topknot that all Japanese wrestlers wear, and got ready to leave. He thanked Maru-me and her mother and bowed very low to the grandmother, since she was the oldest and had been a fine wrestling partner.

Then he picked up the cow in his arms and trudged up the mountain. When he reached the top, he slung the cow over one shoulder and waved good-by to Maru-me.

At the first town he came to, Forever-Mountain sold the cow. She brought a good price because she was unusually fat from never having worked in her life. With the money, he bought the heaviest silken belt he could find.

When he reached the palace grounds, many of the other wrestlers were already there, sitting about, eating enormous bowls of rice, comparing one another's weight and telling stories. They paid little attention to Forever-Mountain, except to wonder why he had arrived so late this year. Some of them noticed that he had grown very quiet and took no part at all in their boasting.

All the ladies and gentlemen of the court were waiting in a special courtyard for the wrestling to begin. They wore many robes, one on top of another, heavy with embroidery and gold cloth, and sweat ran down their faces and froze in the winter afternoon. The gentlemen had long swords so weighted with gold and precious stones that they could never have used them, even if they had known how. The court ladies, with their long black hair hanging down behind, had their faces painted dead white, which made them look frightened. They had pulled out their real eyebrows and painted new ones high above the place where eyebrows are supposed to be, and this made them all look as though they were very surprised at something.

Behind a screen sat the Emperor—by himself, because he was too noble for ordinary people to look at. He was a lonely old man with a kind, tired face. He hoped the wrestling would end quickly so that he could go to his room and write poems.

The first two wrestlers chosen to fight were Forever-Mountain and a wrestler who was said to have the biggest stomach in the country. He and Forever-Mountain both threw some salt into the ring. It was understood that this drove away evil spirits.

Then the other wrestler, moving his stomach somewhat out of the way, raised his foot and brought it down with a fearful stamp. He glared fiercely at Forever-Mountain as if to say, "Now stamp, you poor frightened man!"

Forever-Mountain raised his foot. He brought it down.

There was a sound like thunder, the earth shook, and the other wrestler bounced into the air and out of the ring, as gracefully as any soap bubble.

He picked himself up and bowed to the Emperor's screen.

"The earth-god is angry. Possibly there is something the matter with the salt," he said. "I do not think I shall wrestle this season." And he walked out, looking very suspiciously over one shoulder at Forever-Mountain.

Five other wrestlers then and there decided that they were not wrestling this season, either. They all looked annoyed with Forever-Mountain.

From then on, Forever-Mountain brought his foot down lightly. As each wrestler came into the ring, he picked him up very gently, carried him out, and placed him before the Emperor's screen, bowing most courteously every time.

The court ladies' eyebrows went up even higher. The gentlemen looked disturbed and a little afraid. They loved to see fierce, strong men tugging and grunting at each other, but Forever-Mountain was a little too much for them. Only the Emperor was happy behind his screen, for now, with the wrestling over so quickly, he would have that much more time to write his poems. He ordered all the prize money handed over to Forever-Mountain.

"But," he said, "you had better not wrestle any more." He stuck a finger through his screen and waggled it at the other wrestlers, who were sitting on the ground weeping with disappointment like great fat babies.

Forever-Mountain promised not to wrestle any more. Everybody looked relieved. The wrestlers sitting on the ground almost smiled.

"I think I shall become a farmer," Forever-Mountain said, and left at once to go back to Maru-me.

Maru-me was waiting for him. When she saw him coming, she ran down the mountain, picked him up, together with the heavy bags of prize money, and carried him halfway up the mountainside. Then she giggled and put him down. The rest of the way she let him carry her.

Forever-Mountain kept his promise to the Emperor and never fought in public again. His name was forgotten in the capital. But up in the mountains, sometimes, the earth shakes and rumbles, and they say that is Forever-Mountain and Maru-me's grandmother practicing wrestling in the hidden valley.

THE MASTER-MAID
(Swedish)

Compared with many European folktales, this one (collected by Asbjornsen and Möe) has very little sex-role stereotyping. Marcia Lieberman protests even this story, however, in her feminist critique of fairy tales for children (reprinted at the end of this section), pointing out that although the Master-Maid is clever, she is passive and always acts through another.

Once upon a time there was a king who had many sons. I do not exactly know how many there were, but the youngest of them could not stay quietly at home, and was determined to go out into the world and try his luck, and after a long time the King was forced to give him leave to go. When he had travelled about for several days, he came to a giant's house, and hired himself to the giant as a servant. In the morning the giant had to go out to pasture his goats, and as he was leaving the house he told the King's son that he must clean out the stable. "And after you have done that," he said, "you need not do any more work to-day, for you have come to a kind master, and that you shall find. But what I set you to do must be done both well and thoroughly, and you must on no account go into any of the rooms which lead out of the room in which you slept last night. If you do, I will take your life."

"Well to be sure, he is an easy master!" said the Prince to himself as he walked up and down the room humming and singing, for he thought there would be plenty of time left to clean out the stable; "but it would be amusing to steal a glance into his other rooms as well," thought the Prince, "for there must be something that he is afraid of my seeing, as I am not allowed to enter them." So he went into the first room. A cauldron was hanging from the walls; it was boiling, but the Prince could see no fire under it. "I wonder what is inside it," he thought, and dipped a lock of his hair in, and the hair became just as if it were all made of copper. "That's a nice kind of soup. If anyone were to taste that his throat would be gilded," said the youth, and then he went into the next chamber. There, too, a cauldron was hanging from the wall, bubbling and boiling, but there was no fire under this either. "I will just try what this is like too," said the Prince, thrusting another lock of his hair into it, and it came out silvered over. "Such costly soup is not to be had in my father's palace," said the Prince; "but everything depends on how it tastes," and then he went into the third room. There, too, a cauldron was hanging from the wall, boiling, exactly the same as in the two other rooms, and the Prince took pleasure in trying this also, so he dipped a lock of hair in, and it came out so brightly gilded that

Translated by Mrs. Alfred Hunt.

it shone again. "Some talk about going from bad to worse," said the Prince; "but this is better and better. If he boils gold here, what can he boil in there?" He was determined to see, and went through the door into the fourth room. No cauldron was to be seen there, but on a bench someone was seated who was like a king's daughter, but, whosoever she was, she was so beautiful that never in the Prince's life had he seen her equal.

"Oh! in heaven's name what are you doing here?" said she who sat upon the bench.

"I took the place of servant here yesterday," said the Prince.

"May you soon have a better place, if you have come to serve here!" said she.

"Oh! but I think I have got a kind master," said the Prince. "He has not given me hard work to do to-day. When I have cleaned out the stable I shall be done."

"Yes, but how will you be able to do that?" she asked again. "If you clean it out as other people do, ten pitchforksful will come in for every one you throw out. But I will teach you how to do it: you must turn your pitchfork upside down, and work with the handle, and then all will fly out of its own accord."

"Yes, I will attend to that," said the Prince, and stayed sitting where he was the whole day, for it was soon settled between them that they would marry each other, he and the King's daughter; so the first day of his service with the giant did not seem long to him. But when evening was drawing near she said that it would now be better for him to clean out the stable before the giant came home. When he got there he had a fancy to try if what she had said were true, so he began to work in the same way that he had seen the stable-boys doing in his father's stables, but he soon saw that he must give up that, for when he had worked a very short time he had scarcely room left to stand. So he did what the Princess had taught him, turned the pitchfork round, and worked with the handle, and in the twinkling of an eye the stable was as clean as if it had been scoured. When he had done that, he went back again into the room in which the giant had given him leave to stay, and there he walked backwards and forwards on the floor, and began to hum and to sing.

Then came the giant home with the goats. "Have you cleaned the stable?" asked the giant.

"Yes, now it is clean and sweet, master," said the King's son.

"I shall see about that," said the giant, and went round to the stable, but it was just as the Prince had said.

"You have certainly been talking to my Master-maid, for you never got that out of your own head," said the giant.

"Master-maid! What kind of a thing is that, master?" said the Prince, making himself look as stupid as an ass; "I should like to see that."

"Well, you will see her quite soon enough," said the giant.

On the second morning the giant had again to go out with his goats, so he told the Prince that on that day he was to fetch home his horse, which was out on the mountain-side, and when he had done that he might rest himself for the remainder of the day, "for you have come to a kind master, and that you shall find," said the giant once more. "But do not go into any of the rooms that I spoke of yesterday, or I will wring your head off," said he, and then went away with his flock of goats.

"Yes, indeed, you are a kind master," said the Prince; "but I will go in and talk to the Master-maid again; perhaps before long she may like better to be mine than yours."

So he went to her. Then she asked him what he had to do that day.

"Oh! not very dangerous work, I fancy," said the King's son. "I have only to go up the mountain-side after his horse."

"Well, how do you mean to set about it?" asked the Master-maid.

"Oh! there is no great art in riding a horse home," said the King's son. "I think I must have ridden friskier horses before now."

"Yes, but it is not so easy a thing as you think to ride the horse home," said the

Master-maid; "but I will teach you what to do. When you go near it, fire will burst out of its nostrils like flames from a pine torch: but be very careful, and take the bridle which is hanging by the door there, and fling the bit straight into its jaws, and then it will become so tame that you will be able to do what you like with it." He said he would bear this in mind, and then he again sat in there the whole day by the Master-maid, and they chatted and talked of one thing and another, but the first thing and the last now was, how happy and delightful it would be if they could but marry each other, and get safely away from the giant; and the Prince would have forgotten both the mountain-side and the horse if the Master-maid had not reminded him of them as evening drew near, and said that now it would be better if he went to fetch the horse before the giant came. So he did this, and took the bridle which was hanging on a crook, and strode up the mountain-side, and it was not long before he met with the horse, and fire and red flames streamed forth out of its nostrils. But the youth carefully watched his opportunity, and just as it was rushing at him with open jaws he threw the bit straight into its mouth, and the horse stood as quiet as a young lamb, and there was no difficulty at all in getting it home to the stable. Then the Prince went back into his room again, and began to hum and to sing.

Towards evening the giant came home. "Have you fetched the horse back from the mountain-side?" he asked.

"That I have, master; it was an amusing horse to ride, but I rode him straight home, and put him in the stable too," said the Prince.

"I will see about that," said the giant, and went out to the stable, but the horse was standing there just as the Prince had said. "You have certainly been talking with my Master-maid, for you never got that out of your own head," said the giant again.

"Yesterday, master, you talked about this Master-maid, and to-day you are talking about her; ah! heaven bless you, master, why will you not show me the thing? for it would be a real pleasure to me to see it," said the Prince, who again pretended to be silly and stupid.

"Oh! you will see her quite soon enough," said the giant.

On the morning of the third day the giant again had to go into the wood with the goats. "To-day you must go underground and fetch my taxes," he said to the Prince. "When you have done this, you may rest for the remainder of the day, for you shall see what an easy master you have come to," and then he went away.

"Well, however easy a master you may be, you set me very hard work to do," thought the Prince; "but I will see if I cannot find your Master-maid; you say she is yours, but for all that she may be able to tell me what to do now," and he went to her. So, when the Master-maid asked him what the giant had set him to do that day, he told her that he was to go underground and get the taxes.

"And how will you set about that?" said the Master-maid.

"Oh! you must tell me how to do it," said the Prince, "for I have never yet been underground, and even if I knew the way I do not know how much I am to demand."

"Oh! yes, I will soon tell you that; you must go to the rock there under the mountain-ridge, and take the club that is there, and knock on the rocky wall," said the Master-maid. "Then someone will come out who will sparkle with fire: you shall tell him your errand, and when he asks you how much you want to have you are to say: 'As much as I can carry.' "

"Yes, I will keep that in mind," said he, and then he sat there with the Master-maid the whole day, until night drew near, and he would gladly have stayed there till now if the Master-maid had not reminded him that it was time to be off to fetch the taxes before the giant came.

So he set out on his way, and did exactly what the Master-maid had told him. He went to the rocky wall, and took the club, and knocked on it. Then came one so full of sparks that they flew both out of his eyes and his nose. "What do you want?" said he.

"I was to come here for the giant, and demand the tax for him," said the King's son.

"How much are you to have then?" said the other.

"I ask for no more than I am able to carry with me," said the Prince.

"It is well for you that you have not asked for a horse-load," said he who had come out of the rock. "But now come in with me."

This the Prince did, and what a quantity of gold and silver he saw! It was lying inside the mountain like heaps of stones in a waste place, and he got a load that was as large as he was able to carry, and with that he went his way. So in the evening, when the giant came home with the goats, the Prince went into the chamber and hummed and sang again as he had done on the other two evenings.

"Have you been for the tax?" said the giant.

"Yes, that I have, master," said the Prince.

"Where have you put it then?" said the giant again.

"The bag of gold is standing there on the bench," said the Prince.

"I will see about that," said the giant, and went away to the bench, but the bag was standing there, and it was so full that gold and silver dropped out when the giant untied the string.

"You have certainly been talking with my Master-maid!" said the giant, "and if you have I will wring your neck."

"Master-maid?" said the Prince; "yesterday my master talked about this Master-maid, and to-day he is talking about her again, and the first day of all it was talk of the same kind. I do wish I could see the thing myself," said he.

"Yes, yes, wait till to-morrow," said the giant, "and then I myself will take you to her."

"Ah! master, I thank you—but you are only mocking me," said the King's son.

Next day the giant took him to the Master-maid. "Now you shall kill him, and boil him in the great big cauldron you know of, and when you have got the broth ready give me a call," said the giant; then he lay down on the bench to sleep, and almost immediately began to snore so that it sounded like thunder among the hills.

So the Master-maid took a knife, and cut the Prince's little fingers, and dropped three drops of blood upon a wooden stool; then she took all the old rags, and shoe-soles, and all the rubbish she could lay hands on, and put them in the cauldron; and then she filled a chest with gold dust, and a lump of salt, and a water-flask which was hanging by the door, and she also took with her a golden apple, and two gold chickens; and then she and the Prince went away with all the speed they could, and when they had gone a little way they came to the sea, and then they sailed, but where they got the ship from I have never been able to learn.

Now, when the giant had slept a good long time, he began to stretch himself on the bench on which he was lying. "Will it soon boil?" said he.

"It is just beginning," said the first drop of blood on the stool.

So the giant lay down to sleep again, and slept for a long, long time. Then he began to move about a little again. "Will it soon be ready now?" said he, but he did not look up this time any more than he had one the first time, for he was still half asleep.

"Half done!" said the second drop of blood, and the giant believed it was the Master-maid again, and turned himself on the bench, and lay down to sleep once more. When he had slept again for many hours, he began to move and stretch himself. "Is it not done yet?" said he.

"It is quite ready," said the third drop of blood. Then the giant began to sit up, and rub his eyes, but he could not see who it was who had spoken to him, so he asked for the Master-maid, and called her. But there was no one to give him an answer.

"Ah! well, she has just stolen out for a little," thought the giant, and he took a spoon, and went off to the cauldron to have a taste; but there was nothing in it but shoe-soles, and rags, and such trumpery as that, and all was boiled up together, so that he could not tell whether it was porridge or milk pottage. When he saw this, he understood what had happened, and fell into such a rage that he hardly knew what he was doing. Away he went after the Prince and the Master-maid, so fast that the wind whistled behind him, and it was not long before he came to the water, but he could not get over it. "Well, well, I will soon find a cure for that: I have only to call my river-sucker," said the giant, and he did call him. So his river-sucker came and lay down, and drank one, two, three draughts, and with that the water in the sea fell so low that the giant saw the Master-maid and the Prince out on the sea in their ship. "Now you must throw out the lump of salt," said the Master-maid, and the Prince did so, and it grew up into such a great high mountain right across the sea that the giant could not come over it, and the river-sucker could not drink any more water. "Well, well, I will soon find a cure for that," said the giant, so he called to his hill-borer to come and bore through the mountain so that the river-sucker might be able to drink up the water again. But just as the hole was made, and the river-sucker was beginning to drink, the Master-maid told the Prince to throw one or two drops out of the flask, and when he did this the sea instantly became full of water again, and before the river-sucker could take one drink they reached the land and were in safety. So they determined to go home to the Prince's father, but the Prince would on no account permit the Master-maid to walk there, for he thought that it was unbecoming either for her or for him to go on foot.

"Wait here the least little bit of time, while I go home for the seven horses which stand in my father's stable," said he; "it is not far off, and I shall not be long away, but I will not let my betrothed bride go on foot to the palace."

"Oh! no, do not go, for if you go home to the King's palace you will forget me, I foresee that."

"How could I forget you? We have suffered so much evil together, and love each other so much," said the Prince; and he insisted on going home for the coach with the seven horses, and she was to wait for him there, by the sea-shore. So at last the Master-maid had to yield, for he was so absolutely determined to do it. "But when you get there you must not even give yourself time to greet anyone, but go straight into the stable, and take the horses, and put them in the coach, and drive back as quickly as you can. For they will all come round about you; but you must behave just as if you did not see them, and on no account must you taste anything, for if you do it will cause great misery both to you and to me," said she; and this he promised.

But when he got home to the King's palace one of his brothers was just going to be married, and the bride and all her kith and kin had come to the palace; so they all thronged round him, and questioned him about this and that, and wanted him to go in with them; but he behaved as if he did not see them, and went straight to the stable, and got out the horses and began to harness them. When they saw that they could not by any means prevail on him to go in with them, they came out to him with meat and drink, and the best of everything that they had prepared for the wedding; but the Prince refused to touch anything, and would do nothing but put the horses in as quickly as he could. At last, however, the bride's sister rolled an apple across the yard to him, and said: "As you won't eat anything else, you may like to take a bite of that, for you must be both hungry and thirsty after your long journey." And he took up the apple and bit a piece out of it. But no sooner had he got the piece of apple in his mouth than he forgot the Master-maid and that he was to go back in the coach to fetch her.

"I think I must be mad! what do I want with this coach and horses?" said he; and then he put the horses back into the stable, and went into the King's palace, and there it was settled that he should marry the bride's sister, who had rolled the apple to him.

The Master-maid sat by the sea-shore for a long, long time, waiting for the Prince, but no Prince came. So she went away, and when she had walked a short distance she came to a little hut which stood all alone in a small wood, hard by the King's palace. She entered it and asked if she might be allowed to stay there. The hut belonged to an old crone, who was also an ill-tempered and malicious troll. At first she would not let the Master-maid remain with her; but at last, after a long time, by means of good words and good payment, she obtained leave. But the hut was as dirty and black inside as a pigstye, so the Master-maid said that she would smarten it up a little, that it might look a little more like what other people's houses looked inside. The old crone did not like this either. She scowled, and was very cross, but the Master-maid did not trouble herself about that. She took out her chest of gold, and flung a handful of it or so into the fire, and the gold boiled up and poured out over the whole of the hut, until every part of it both inside and out was gilded. But when the gold began to bubble up the old hag grew so terrified that she fled away as if the Evil One himself were pursuing her, and she did not remember to stoop down as she went through the doorway, and so she split her head and died. Next morning the sheriff came travelling by there. He was greatly astonished when he saw the gold hut shining and glittering there in the copse, and he was still more astonished when he went in and caught sight of the beautiful young maiden who was sitting there; he fell in love with her at once, and straightway on the spot he begged her, both prettily and kindly, to marry him.

"Well, but have you a great deal of money?" said the Master-maid.

"Oh! yes; so far as that is concerned, I am not ill off," said the sheriff. So now he had to go home to get the money, and in the evening he came back, bringing with him a bag with two bushels in it, which he set down on the bench. Well, as he had such a fine lot of money, the Master-maid said she would have him, so they sat down to talk.

But scarcely had they sat down together before the Master-maid wanted to jump up again. "I have forgotten to see to the fire," she said.

"Why should you jump up to do that?" said the sheriff; "I will do that!" So he jumped up, and went to the chimney in one bound.

"Just tell me when you have got hold of the shovel," said the Master-maid.

"Well, I have hold of it now," said the sheriff.

"Then may you hold the shovel, and the shovel you, and pour red-hot coals over you, till day dawns," said the Master-maid. So the sheriff had to stand there the whole night and pour red-hot coals over himself, and, no matter how much he cried and begged and entreated, the red-hot coals did not grow the colder for that. When the day began to dawn, and he had power to throw down the shovel, he did not stay long where he was, but ran away as fast as he possibly could; and everyone who met him stared and looked after him, for he was flying as if he were mad, and he could not have looked worse if he had been both flayed and tanned, and everyone wondered where he had been, but for very shame he would tell nothing.

The next day the attorney came riding by the place where the Master-maid dwelt. He saw how brightly the hut shone and gleamed through the wood, and he too went into it to see who lived there, and when he entered and saw the beautiful young maiden he fell even more in love with her than the sheriff had done, and began to woo her at once. So the Master-maid asked him, as she had asked the sheriff, if he had a great deal of money, and the attorney said he was not ill off for that, and would at once go home to get it; and at night he came with a great big sack of money—this time it was a four-bushel sack—and set it on the bench by the Master-maid. So she promised to have him, and he sat down on the bench by her to arrange about it, but suddenly she said that she had forgotten to lock the door of the porch that night, and must do it.

"Why should you do that?" said the attorney; "sit still, I will do it."

So he was on his feet in a moment, and out in the porch.

"Tell me when you have got hold of the door-latch," said the Master-maid.

"I have hold of it now," cried the attorney.

"Then may you hold the door, and the door you, and may you go between wall and wall till day dawns."

What a dance the attorney had that night! He had never had such a waltz before, and he never wished to have such a dance again. Sometimes he was in front of the door, and sometimes the door was in front of him, and it went from one side of the porch to the other, till the attorney was well-nigh beaten to death. At first he began to abuse the Master-maid, and then to beg and pray, but the door did not care for anything but keeping him where he was till break of day.

As soon as the door let go its hold of him, off went the attorney. He forgot who ought to be paid off for what he had suffered, he forgot both his sack of money and his wooing, for he was so afraid lest the house-door should come dancing after him. Everyone who met him stared and looked after him, for he was flying like a madman, and he could not have looked worse if a herd of rams had been butting at him all night long.

On the third day the bailiff came by, and he too saw the gold house in the little wood, and he too felt that he must go and see who lived there; and when he caught sight of the Master-maid he became so much in love with her that he wooed her almost before he greeted her.

The Master-maid answered him as she had answered the other two, that if he had a great deal of money she would have him. "So far as that is concerned, I am not ill off," said the bailiff; so he was at once told to go home and fetch it, and this he did. At night he came back, and he had a still larger sack of money with him than the attorney had brought; it must have been at least six bushels, and he set it down on the bench. So it was settled that he was to have the Master-maid. But hardly had they sat down together before she said that she had forgotten to bring in the calf, and must go out to put it in the byre.

"No, indeed, you shall not do that," said the bailiff; "I am the one to do that." And, big and fat as he was, he went out as briskly as a boy,

"Tell me when you have got hold of the calf's tail," said the Master-maid.

"I have hold of it now," cried the bailiff.

"Then may you hold the calf's tail, and the calf's tail hold you, and may you go round the world together till day dawns!" said the Master-maid. So the bailiff had to bestir himself, for the calf went over rough and smooth, over hill and dale, and, the more the bailiff cried and screamed, the faster the calf went. When daylight began to appear, the bailiff was half dead; and so glad was he to leave loose of the calf's tail that he forgot the sack of money and all else. He walked now slowly—more slowly than the sheriff and the attorney had done, but, the slower he went, the more time had everyone to stare and look at him; and they used it too, and no one can imagine how tired out and ragged he looked after his dance with the calf.

On the following day the wedding was to take place in the King's palace, and the elder brother was to drive to church with his bride, and the brother who had been with the giant with her sister. But when they had seated themselves in the coach and were about to drive off from the palace one of the trace-pins broke, and, though they made one, two, and three to put in its place, that did not help them, for each broke in turn, no matter what kind of wood they used to make them of. This went on for a long time, and they could not get away from the palace, so they were all in great trouble. Then the sheriff said (for he too had been bidden to the wedding at Court): "Yonder away in the thicket dwells a maiden, and if you can but get her to lend you the handle of the shovel that she uses to make up her fire I know very well that it will hold fast." So they sent off a messenger to the thicket, and begged so prettily that they might have the loan of her shovel-handle of which the sheriff had spoken that they were not refused; so now they had a trace-pin which would not snap in two.

But all at once, just as they were starting, the bottom of the coach fell in pieces. They made a new bottom as fast as they could, but, no matter how they nailed it together, or what kind of wood they used, no sooner had they got the new bottom into the coach and were about to drive off than it broke again, so that they were still worse off than when they had broken the trace-pin. Then the attorney said, for he too was at the wedding in the palace: "Away there in the thicket dwells a maiden, and if you could but get her to lend you one-half of her porch-door I am certain that it will hold together." So they again sent a messenger to the thicket, and begged so prettily for the loan of the gilded porch-door of which the attorney had told them that they got it at once. They were just setting out again, but now the horses were not able to draw the coach. They had six horses already, and now they put in eight, and then ten, and then twelve, but the more they put in, and the more the coachman whipped them, the less good it did; and the coach never stirred from the spot. It was already beginning to be late in the day, and to church they must and would go, so everyone who was in the palace was in a state of great distress. Then the bailiff spoke up and said: "Out there in the gilded cottage in the thicket dwells a girl, and if you could but get her to lend you her calf I know it could draw the coach, even if it were as heavy as a mountain." They all thought that it was ridiculous to be drawn to church by a calf, but there was nothing else for it but to send a messenger once more, and beg as prettily as they could, on behalf of the King, that she would let them have the loan of the calf that the bailiff had told them about. The Master-maid let them have it immediately—this time also she would not say "no."

Then they harnessed the calf to see if the coach would move; and away it went, over rough and smooth, over stock and stone, so that they could scarcely breathe, and sometimes they were on the ground, and sometimes up in the air; and when they came to the church the coach began to go round and round like a spinning-wheel, and it was with the utmost difficulty and danger that they were able to get out of the coach and into the church. And when they went back again the coach went quicker still, so that most of them did not know how they got back to the palace at all.

When they had seated themselves at the table the Prince who had been in service with the giant said that he thought they ought to have invited the maiden who had lent them the shovel-handle, and the porch-door, and the calf up to the palace, "for," said he, "if we had not got these three things, we should never have got away from the palace."

The King also thought that this was both just and proper, so he sent five of his best men down to the gilded hut, to greet the maiden courteously from the King, and to beg her to be so good as to come up to the palace to dinner at mid-day.

"Greet the King, and tell him that, if he is too good to come to me, I am too good to come to him," replied the Master-maid.

So the King had to go himself, and the Master-maid went with him immediately, and, as the King believed that she was more than she appeared to be, he seated her in the place of honour by the youngest bridegroom. When they had sat at table for a short time, the Master-maid took out the cock, and the hen, and the golden apple which she had brought away with her from the giant's house, and set them on the table in front of her, and instantly the cock and the hen began to fight with each other for the golden apple.

"Oh! look how those two there are fighting for the golden apple," said the King's son.

"Yes, and so did we two fight to get out that time when we were in the mountain," said the Master-maid.

So the Prince knew her again, and you may imagine how delighted he was. He ordered the troll-witch who had rolled the apple to him to be torn in pieces between four-and-twenty horses, so that not a bit of her was left, and then for the first time they began really to keep the wedding, and, weary as they were, the sheriff, the attorney, and the bailiff kept it up too.

MOLLY WHIPPLE

Retold by James Reeves

In this story, one is not so much aware of Molly as a girl as of Molly as a courageous and clever human being. Molly and her two sisters are left in the woods by their parents, who can no longer afford to keep them. Their situation becomes desperate when they are taken in by a murderous giant and his wife. Not only does Molly succeed in saving her sisters and herself through her daring, but she cleverly outwits the giant three more times in order to take his magic sword, his purse, and his ring from him (compare "Jack and the Beanstalk," in "Fools").

There was once a poor couple who lived in a little house with their sons and daughters. They had so many children that they were at their wits' end to know how to feed and clothe them. Every day they seemed to be in need of more and more money, but the man could not work hard enough to earn more; as for his wife, she was at it from morning till night, cooking and sewing, cleaning and mending. At last there was only one thing to do. They went off into the woods with their three youngest children and left them there. The hearts of the poor couple were heavy, for they did not want to part with the three girls, but they feared that if they did not do so, the others might starve.

The three little girls walked on and on in search of food and shelter, and at last they came to a house at the edge of the wood. Darkness was beginning to fall, and there was a light in the window. They knocked at the door, and a woman opened it.

"Can you give us some supper?" they asked. "We have lost our home and are hungry."

"I can't do that, my dears," said the woman. "My husband is a great giant, and if he comes home and finds you, he'll kill you, and perhaps eat you whole for his supper."

"Oh, please," said the eldest of the three girls in a very small voice, "we're not afraid. Don't you think you could give us just a little supper? We're *so* tired and hungry."

And she began to cry.

Then the giant's wife thought to herself that after all it might not be a bad idea to keep the three girls for the night—perhaps her husband would be glad of a change from his usual mutton and beef and pork. So she said:

"Well, come in, my dears, and I'll give you some bread and milk, and you shall sit by the fire and get warm."

So they thanked her and went inside, though none of them much liked the idea of having supper with a giant's wife. But she did them no harm, and after eating they felt better, and were just thinking of going off to find somewhere to sleep when there was a great tramping of boots and the giant returned. The little girls were so frightened that they trembled in their shoes, but the giant's wife told them not to be alarmed.

"Come," she said, "hide in this cupboard till he's had his supper. Then perhaps he won't find you."

And she pushed them all three into a great dark cupboard.

The giant strode into the room, threw down his great club, and smelt the air.

"Fee, fi, foh, fum,"

said he,

"I smell the blood of some earthly one."

"Stuff!" said his wife. "You're always smelling things. Sit down like a good boy and have your supper, and afterwards you shall see what a surprise I have for you."

After supper she flung open the door of the cupboard and brought out the three girls.

"Here are three nice little girls," she said. "I have given them supper, and now they are going to stay the night. They can get into the same bed as our own three daughters. It'll be rather a squash, but they must manage as best they can."

So the three little girls went to bed with the giant's three daughters, and how those daughters snored and snuffed in their sleep!

Now the youngest of the three little girls was very smart and clever, and her name was Molly Whipple. She had noticed with her sharp eyes that just before he had come and taken away the candle and bidden his daughters good night, the giant had put three necklaces of gold on their necks. But the necklaces he had put on Molly and her two sisters were of rope. So Molly, tired as she was, managed to stay awake till everyone else was sleeping soundly, and the giant's three daughters were snoring their heads off. Then she quickly took the necklaces of rope from her own and her sisters' necks and put them on the giant's daughters instead of the gold necklaces. These she put on herself and her sisters.

In the dead of night the giant came stalking into the room with his club in his hand. He felt for the necks of the three girls with rope necklaces on, dragged them out of bed and beat them to death with his club. Then he gave a horrible laugh and stalked out.

The two sisters of Molly Whipple awoke crying, but Molly told them to be quiet and get up, for they must leave the house before the giant or his wife awoke. So very early, when it was hardly morning, they crept out of the door and made off as fast as they could.

When morning came, they reached the palace of the King. Molly led her sisters boldly up to the gate and asked to be taken to the King.

"Who are you?" asked His Majesty when he saw them.

"We are three poor sisters," said Molly, "and we have just escaped from a cruel giant. If I may say so, Your Majesty, you ought not to allow such a dreadful creature to live in your kingdom."

"That is easily said," answered the King. "Perhaps you will tell me how I can get rid of him?"

"Well," said Molly Whipple, "you must first get his sword."

"Would you like to get it for me, young lady?" asked the King.

"I can try, Your Majesty," said Molly. "What will you do for me if I get the giant's sword?"

"I will promise my eldest son to your eldest sister," said the King.

"It's a bargain, Your Majesty," said Molly; and after that they were all given a meal in the royal palace.

That evening Molly returned alone to the giant's house, and when it was dark she slipped in unseen and hid under the giant's bed; for she saw that his great sword hung at the bed's head. Presently he came thumping in from his supper, sniffed a little, but was too sleepy to look under the bed, and was soon snoring so that the whole room shook and the banging of the bed nearly drove Molly deaf. Then she crept out and seized hold of the sword, which was hanging behind the giant's head. As she crept towards the door with it, she found it so heavy that she could not help rattling it against the floor; and the noise woke the giant, who instantly sprang out of bed, and without waiting to pick up his club, gave a great roar and followed Molly out of the cottage. He took long strides, but Molly was nimble, and presently they came to the Bridge of One Hair, so called because it is the narrowest and lightest bridge in the world. Molly got across, but the giant could not; she stood on the other side, panting for breath, while he shook his fist at her and shouted:

"Get thee gone, Molly Whipple, get
thee gone!—
If once more thou cross my path,
Thou shalt feel the giant's wrath!"

But Molly only brandished the great sword and called back:

"Twice again, old Fi-Foh-Fee,
I shall come to trouble ye!"

Then she gave a merry laugh and ran off towards the King's palace. When she got there, the King was delighted to have the sword of his enemy, the cruel giant, and he gladly promised Molly's eldest sister the hand of his eldest son in marriage. And there was a solemn feast and great rejoicing.

"Now," said the King, to Molly, "if you could get me the giant's purse, which lies under his pillow, I would promise my second son in marriage to your other sister."

"Very well, Your Majesty," said Molly with a curtsey, "I will do what I can."

So once more Molly went off alone to the giant's house, and when it was dark she crept in and hid under the bed. Before long the giant thumped his way in from supper, flung himself upon the bed, and began to snore like ten thunderstorms. Molly had no difficulty in slipping her hand under the pillow and pulling out the purse. But as she made her way with it towards the door, she tripped over and pulled down a great stone pot, and the noise of its fall woke the giant, who started up and sprang towards the door, just as Molly had darted through it. Well, the giant was a mighty runner, but Molly was nimble, and soon they came to the Bridge of One Hair, which the giant could not cross.

Molly stood on one side, and the giant stood on the other, and once more he shouted:

"Get thee gone, Molly Whipple, get
thee gone!—
If once more thou cross my path,
Thou shall feel the giant's wrath!"

And he shook his great hairy fist at her; but Molly only laughed and waved the purse at him, calling back:

"Once again, old Fi-Foh-Fee,
I shall come to trouble ye!"

And with that she ran off and was gone in a flash.

When she got back to the King's palace, she gave the purse to the King, who was overjoyed. He at once made arrangements for the betrothal of his second son to Molly's elder sister, and a solemn feast was held amidst great rejoicing.

"Now," said the King to Molly, when the ceremony was over, "there is just one more thing I should like you to get for me. It will not be easy; and if you get it, you shall have the hand of my youngest son in marriage, as soon as you are old enough."

"What must I get?" asked Molly.

"You must get," said the King, "the gold ring off the giant's finger."

Well, Molly thought about the cruel giant, and then she thought about the handsome young prince and how she would like to be a princess like her sisters, so she said she would try. Off she went that night, and when it was nearly dark, she slipped into the giant's house and hid under the bed. In a little while the giant thumped his way to bed, and his snoring was like the rumbling of twelve earthquakes. The moon shone through the window, and in the light of the moon Molly could see that the giant's hand was hanging over the side of the bed, and there was the gold ring, shining and sparkling. She put out her hand and took hold of it and gave it a pull. But the ring was stuck tight on the giant's finger, and the whole bed shook with the giant's snoring, and Molly herself was trembling with fear, so that she could hardly shift the ring an inch. But shift it she did, and just as she got it off, the giant gave a great shout, grabbed Molly by the hand in a terrible grip, and jumped out of bed. His fierce eyes shone in the moonlight, and his voice shook with anger.

"Aha, Molly Whipple!" said he. "So I have caught thee at last, have I? Thou saidst thou wouldst come again, didst thou not?"

"Yes, sir," said Molly in a tiny small voice.

"And I said thou shouldst feel the giant's wrath, did I not?"

"Yes, sir," said Molly in an even tinier smaller voice.

"Now then," he said in a very quiet, determined tone, "tell me, Molly Whipple, since thou art so clever, if thou hadst caught me, what wouldst thou do to me, eh?"

"What would I do to thee?" asked Molly.

"Yes," said the giant. "Tell me that now, and be quick about it."

"I'll tell thee what I would do," said Molly. "See that big bag that you have over there for bringing home your dinner in? Well, I would tie you up inside it, together with a cat, a dog, a needle and thread, and a pair of scissors."

"Yes," said the giant. "What then?"

"Then," said Molly, "I would go out into the woods and cut me the biggest stick I could find, and I would beat you with it till you lost your senses."

"So that's what you would do, is it," said the giant, "if you had me in your power, Molly Whipple? And that's just what I'm going to do with you. Into that bag with you, and as soon as it's daylight I'm off to the woods to cut a stick to beat you with."

So he picked Molly up and bundled her into the bag, together with a cat, a dog, a needle and thread, and a great pair of scissors. Then he tied the neck of the bag up tight, hung it on a nail in the wall, and went back to sleep. Inside the bag Molly made friends with the cat and the dog, lay down as comfortably as she could, and waited till morning.

As soon as it was light, the giant stalked off into the woods, leaving Molly safely tied up in the bag.

Presently the giant's wife came in.

"Fee, fi, foh, fum,"

said she, sniffing the air,

"I smell the blood of some earthly one."

"Giant's wife, giant's wife!" called Molly from inside the bag. "Is that you?"

"What are you doing inside that bag?" asked the giant's wife.

"Oh, if only you could see what I see!" said Molly.

"And what can you see in there?" asked the giant's wife.

"Things you'd not believe," answered Molly. "If only you could see them too."

"Let me in," said the giant's wife, "so that I can see what you see."

So quickly Molly cut her way out with the scissors. She took the needle and thread with her and jumped down to the floor. Then she helped the giant's wife up into the bag and began sewing up the hole as fast as she could. She had just got the hole sewn up again when she heard the giant coming back. So she hid behind the door and waited. The giant strode into the room waving a whole tree which he had brought back from the wood.

"Now," shouted he, "where's that impudent girl? Let me get at her! Tie me up in a bag, would she, and beat me with a stick?"

He raised the great stick he had brought from the wood and began beating the bag with it as hard as he was able.

"It's me, not the girl!" shouted the giant's wife inside the bag. "Let me out, can't you! Let me out!"

But the giant could not hear her, for

the cat and the dog set up such a howling and a screeching that her voice was drowned. As for Molly, she crouched behind the door and watched; she did not feel at all sorry for the giant's wife, for she remembered how she had pretended to be kind to her and her sisters and then had opened the cupboard and given them away to her husband. But after a few moments she took her chance and slipped out of the house. Then she ran back to the King's palace and gave him the giant's ring.

The King was overjoyed to see her, for he was afraid that this time the giant might have been too clever for her; besides, she was such a bright, quick-witted girl that he knew she would make an excellent wife for his youngest son.

So Molly and the youngest of the princes were betrothed; and after some years, when they were of age to be married, a great and solemn wedding was held, amidst universal rejoicing. For the prince was beloved by all the people, and Molly, by her quick wits and her brave defiance of the giant, had made herself equally beloved.

As for the cruel giant, after his magic sword, his purse, and his ring had been taken from him, he lost his power to do harm in the land; he pined and became melancholy, and soon was heard of no more. All the mothers and fathers for many miles around had cause to be grateful to Molly for ridding the country of the fierce giant who threatened the lives of all their children.

Literary Folktale

THE WHITE HORSE GIRL AND THE BLUE WIND BOY

Carl Sandburg

This is one of the rare modern American stories in which the girl is as strong and competent as the boy; in which they are clearly portrayed as equals; and in which no special point is made of their equality. Perhaps this is so because Carl Sandburg created his wonderful Rootabaga Stories *for his own little girls. These stories all have a distinctively American flavor, and there are romantic overtones of American Indian legend in this particular story. Sandburg's love of word-sounds is evident in this selection, which should be read aloud.*

When the dishes are washed at night time and the cool of the evening has come in summer or the lamps and fires are lit for the night in winter, then the fathers and mothers in the Rootabaga Country sometimes tell the young people the story of the White Horse Girl and the Blue Wind Boy.

The White Horse Girl grew up far in the west of the Rootabaga Country. All the years she grew up as a girl she liked to ride horses. Best of all things for her was to be straddle of a white horse loping with a loose bridle among the hills and along the rivers of the west Rootabaga Country.

She rode one horse white as snow, another horse white as new washed sheep wool, and another white as silver. And she could not tell because she did not know which of these three white horses she liked best.

"Snow is beautiful enough for me any time," she said, "new washed sheep wool,

Illustrated by Maud and Miska Petersham.

or silver out of a ribbon of the new moon, any or either is white enough for me. I like the white manes, the white flanks, the white noses, the white feet of all my ponies. I like the forelocks hanging down between the white ears of all three—my ponies."

And living neighbor to the White Horse Girl in the same prairie country, with the same black crows flying over their places, was the Blue Wind Boy. All the years he grew up as a boy he liked to walk with his feet in the dirt and the grass listening to the winds. Best of all things for him was to put on strong shoes and go hiking among the hills and along the rivers of the west Rootabaga Country, listening to the winds.

There was a blue wind of day time, starting sometimes six o'clock on a summer morning or eight o'clock on a winter morning. And there was a night wind with blue of summer stars in summer and blue of winter stars in winter. And there was yet another, a blue wind of the times between night and day, a blue dawn and evening wind. All three of these winds he liked so well he could not say which he liked best.

"The early morning wind is strong as the prairie and whatever I tell it I know it believes and remembers," he said, "and the night wind with the big dark curves of the night sky in it, the night wind gets inside of me and understands all my secrets. And the blue wind of the times between, in the dusk when it is neither night nor day, this is the wind that asks me questions and tells me to wait and it will bring me whatever I want."

Of course, it happened as it had to happen, the White Horse Girl and the Blue Wind Boy met. She, straddling one of her white horses, and he, wearing his strong hiking shoes in the dirt and the grass, it had to happen they should meet among the hills and along the rivers of the west Rootabaga Country where they lived neighbors.

And of course, she told him all about the snow white horse and the horse white as new washed sheep wool and the horse white as a silver ribbon of the new moon. And he told her all about the blue winds he liked listening to, the early morning wind, the night sky wind, and the wind of the dusk between, the wind that asked him questions and told him to wait.

One day the two of them were gone. On the same day of the week the White Horse Girl and the Blue Wind Boy went away. And their fathers and mothers and sisters and brothers and uncles and aunts wondered about them and talked about them, because they didn't tell anybody beforehand they were going. Nobody at all knew beforehand or afterward why they were going away, the real honest why of it.

They left a short letter. It read:

To All Our Sweethearts, Old Folks and Young Folks:
We have started to go where the white horses come from and where the blue winds begin. Keep a corner in your hearts for us while we are gone.

The White Horse Girl.
The Blue Wind Boy.

That was all they had to guess by in the west Rootabaga Country, to guess and guess where two darlings had gone.

Many years passed. One day there came riding across the Rootabaga Country a Gray Man on Horseback. He looked like he had come a long ways. So they asked him the question they always asked of any rider who looked like he had come a long ways, "Did you ever see the White Horse Girl and the Blue Wind Boy?"

"Yes," he answered, "I saw them.

"It was a long, long ways from here I saw them," he went on, "it would take years and years to ride to where they are. They were sitting together and talking to each other, sometimes singing, in a place where the land runs high and tough rocks reach up. And they were looking out across water, blue water as far as the eye could see. And away far off the blue waters met the blue sky.

" 'Look!' said the Boy, 'that's where the blue winds begin.'

"And far out on the blue waters, just a little this side of where the blue winds begin, there were white manes, white flanks, white noses, white galloping feet.

" 'Look!' said the Girl, 'that's where the white horses come from.'

"And then nearer to the land came thousands in an hour, millions in a day, white horses, some white as snow, some like new washed sheep wool, some white as silver ribbons of the new moon.

"I asked them, 'Whose place is this?' They answered, 'It belongs to us; this is what we started for; this is where the white horses come from; this is where the blue winds begin.' "

And that was all the Gray Man on Horseback would tell the people of the west Rootabaga Country. That was all he knew, he said, and if there was any more he would tell it.

And the fathers and mothers and sisters and brothers and uncles and aunts of the White Horse Girl and the Blue Wind Boy wondered and talked often about whether the Gray Man on Horseback made up the story out of his head or whether it happened just like he told it.

Anyhow this is the story they tell sometimes to the young people of the west Rootabaga Country when the dishes are washed at night and the cool of the evening has come in summer or the lamps and fires are lit for the night in winter.

Fiction

HARRIET THE SPY

Louise Fitzhugh

Harriet the Spy is a strong-willed, intelligent, disobedient, inventive, humorous, blunt young girl who is avidly curious about other people but insensitive to their feelings—in other words, a reversal of the female stereotype. This characterization is one of the main strengths of the book, which has been extremely popular among youngsters since it was first published in 1964. It is a book about growth and self-discovery, as Harriet tries to break out of the isolation of contemporary society through spying on people. Eventually, she is confronted directly with her need for love and other people, and learns to bend a little in order to draw closer to others. However, the conforming she does is not the kind of submitting that breaks the spirit, but a conforming by choice, which leads to stronger individuality.

When Harriet was ready for bed that night, she took out her notebook. She had a lot to think about. Tomorrow was the beginning of school. Tomorrow she would have a quantity of notes to take on the changes that had taken place in her friends over the summer. Tonight she wanted to think about Mrs. Golly.

I THINK THAT LOOKING AT MRS. GOLLY MUST MAKE OLE GOLLY SAD. MY MOTHER ISN'T AS SMART AS OLE GOLLY BUT SHE'S NOT AS DUMB AS MRS. GOLLY. I WOULDN'T LIKE TO HAVE A DUMB MOTHER. IT MUST MAKE YOU FEEL VERY UNPOPULAR. I THINK I WOULD LIKE TO WRITE A STORY ABOUT MRS. GOLLY GETTING RUN OVER BY A TRUCK EXCEPT SHE'S SO FAT I WONDER WHAT WOULD HAPPEN TO THE TRUCK. I WOULD NOT LIKE TO LIVE LIKE MRS. GOLLY BUT I WOULD LIKE TO KNOW WHAT GOES ON IN HER HEAD.

Harriet put the book down and ran in to Ole Golly's room to kiss her good night. Ole Golly sat in a rocker in the light of an overhead lamp, reading. Harriet flew into the room and bounded right into the center of the billowy yellow quilt which covered the single bed. Everything in the

From Louise Fitzhugh, *Harriet the Spy* (New York: Harper and Row, 1964), pp. 21–48 (all of Chapter 2 and opening of Chapter 3). Illustrated by the author.

room was yellow, from the walls to the vase of chrysanthemums. Ole Golly "took to" yellow, as she put it.

"Take your feet off the bed," Ole Golly said without looking up.

"What does your mother think about?" asked Harriet.

"I don't know," said Ole Golly in a musing way, still looking at her book. "I've wondered that for years."

"What are you reading?" Harriet asked.

"Dostoievsky."

"What's *that?* " asked Harriet in a thoroughly obnoxious way.

"Listen to this," Ole Golly said and got that quote look on her face: " 'Love all God's creation, the whole and every grain of sand in it. Love every leaf, every ray of God's light. Love the animals, love the plants, love everything. If you love everything, you will perceive the divine mystery in things. Once you perceive it, you will begin to comprehend it better every day. And you will come at last to love the whole world with an all-embracing love.' "

"What does that mean?" Harriet asked after she had been quiet a minute. "What do you think it means?"

"Well, maybe if you love everything, then . . . then—I guess you'll know everything . . . then . . . seems like . . . you love everything more. I don't know. Well, that's about it. . . . " Ole Golly looked at Harriet in as gentle a way as she could considering the fact that her face looked like it was cut out of oak.

"I want to know everything, everything," screeched Harriet suddenly, lying back and bouncing up and down on the bed. "Everything in the world, everything, everything. I will be a spy and know everything."

"It won't do you a bit of good to know everything if you don't do anything with it. Now get up, Miss Harriet the Spy, you're going to sleep now." And with that Ole Golly marched over and grabbed Harriet by the ear.

"Ouch," said Harriet as she was led to her room, but it really didn't hurt.

"There now, into bed."

"Will Mommy and Daddy be home in time to kiss me good night?"

"They will not," said Ole Golly as she tucked Harriet in. "They went to a party. You'll see them in the morning at breakfast. Now to sleep, instantly—"

"Hee, hee," said Harriet, "instant sleep."

"And not another word out of you. Tomorrow you go back to school." Ole Golly leaned over and gave her a hard little peck on the forehead. Ole Golly was never very kissy, which Harriet thought was just as well, as she hated it. Ole Golly turned the light out and Harriet listened to her go back into her room which was right across the hall, pick up her book, and sit down in the rocker again. Then Harriet did what she always did when she was supposed to be asleep. She got out her flashlight, put the book she was currently reading under the covers, and read happily until Ole Golly came in and took the flashlight away as she did every night.

The next morning Mrs. Welsch asked, "Wouldn't you like to try a ham sandwich, or egg salad, or peanut butter?" Her mother looked quizzically at Harriet while the cook stood next to the table looking enraged.

"Tomato," said Harriet, not even looking up from the book she was reading at breakfast.

"Stop reading at the table." Harriet put the book down. "Listen, Harriet, you've taken a tomato sandwich to school every day for five years. Don't you get tired of them?"

"No."

"How about cream cheese and olive?"

Harriet shook her head. The cook threw up one arm in despair.

"Pastrami? Roast beef? Cucumber?"

"Tomato."

Mrs. Welsch raised her shoulders and looked helplessly at the cook. The cook grimaced. "Sot in her ways," the cook said firmly and left the room. Mrs. Welsch took a sip of coffee. "Are you looking forward to school?"

"Not particularly."

Mr. Welsch put the paper down and looked at his daughter. "Do you like school?"

"No," said Harriet.

"I always hated it," said Mr. Welsch and went back behind the paper.

"Dear, you mustn't say things like that. I rather liked it—that is, when I was eleven I did." Mrs. Welsch looked at Harriet as though expecting an answer.

Harriet didn't know what she felt about school.

"Drink your milk," said Mrs. Welsch. Harriet always waited until her mother said this, no matter how thirsty she was. It made her feel comfortable to have her mother remind her. She drank her milk, wiped her mouth sedately, and got up from the table. Ole Golly came into the room on her way to the kitchen.

"What do you say when you get up from the table, Harriet?" Mrs. Welsch asked absent-mindedly.

"Excuse me," said Harriet.

"Good manners are very important, particularly in the morning," snapped Ole Golly as she went through the door. Ole Golly was always horribly grumpy in the morning.

Harriet ran very fast all the way up to her room.

"I'm starting the sixth grade," she yelled, just to keep herself company. She got her notebook, slammed her door, and thundered down the steps. "Good-by; good-by," she yelled, as though she were going to Africa, and slammed out the front door.

Harriet's school was called The Gregory School, having been founded by a Miss Eleanore Gregory around the turn of the century. It was on East End Avenue, a few blocks from Harriet's house and across the street from Carl Schurz Park. Harriet skipped away down East End Avenue, hugging her notebook happily.

At the entrance to her school a group of children crowded through the door. More stood around on the sidewalk. They were all shapes and sizes and mostly girls because The Gregory School was a girl's school. Boys were allowed to attend up through the sixth grade, but after that they had to go someplace else. It made Harriet sad to think that after this year Sport wouldn't be in school. She didn't care about the others. In particular about Pinky Whitehead she didn't care, because she thought he was the dumbest thing in the world. The only other boy in her class was a boy Harriet had christened The Boy with the Purple Socks, because he was so boring no one ever bothered to remember his name. He had come to the school last year and everyone else had been there since the first grade. Harriet remembered that first day when he had come in with those purple socks on. Whoever heard of purple socks? She figured it was lucky he wore them; otherwise no one would have even known he was there at all. He never said a word.

Sport came up to her as she leaned against a fire hydrant and opened her notebook. "Hi," he said.

"Hi."

"Anyone else here yet?"

"Just that dumb boy with the purple socks."

Harriet wrote quickly in her notebook:

SOMETIMES SPORT LOOKS AS THOUGH HE'S BEEN UP ALL NIGHT. HE HAS FUNNY LITTLE DRY THINGS AROUND HIS EYES. I WORRY ABOUT HIM.

"Sport, did you wash your face?"

"Huh? Uh . . . no, I forgot."

"Hmmmm," Harriet said disapprovingly, and Sport looked away. Actually Harriet hadn't washed hers either, but you couldn't tell it.

"Hey, there's Janie." Sport pointed up the street.

Janie Gibbs was Harriet's best friend besides Sport. She had a chemistry set and planned one day to blow up the world. Both Harriet and Sport had a great respect for Janie's experiments, but they didn't understand a word she said about them.

Janie came slowly toward them, her eyes apparently focused on a tree across the street in the park. She looked odd walking that way, her head turned completely to the right like a soldier on parade. Both Sport and Harriet knew she did this because she was shy and didn't want to see anyone, so they didn't mention it.

She almost bumped into them.

"Hi."

"Hi."

"Hi."

That over, they all stood there.

"Oh, dear," said Janie, "another year. Another year older and I'm no closer to my goal."

Sport and Harriet nodded seriously. They watched a long black limousine driven by a chauffer. It stopped in front of the school. A small blonde girl got out.

"There's that dreadful Beth Ellen Hansen," said Janie with a sneer. Beth Ellen was the prettiest girl in the class, so everyone despised her, particularly Janie, who was rather plain and freckled.

JANIE GETS STRANGER EVERY YEAR. I THINK SHE *might* BLOW UP THE WORLD. BETH ELLEN ALWAYS LOOKS LIKE SHE MIGHT CRY.

Rachel Hennessey and Marion Hawthorne came walking up together. They were always together. "Good morning, Harriet, Simon, Jane," Marion Hawthorne said very formally. She acted like a teacher, as though she were one minute from rapping on the desk for attention. Rachel did everything Marion did, so now she looked down her nose at them and nodded hello, one quick jerk of the head. The two of them went into the school then.

"Are they not too much?" Janie said and looked away in disgust.

Carrie Andrews got off the bus. Harriet wrote:

CARRIE ANDREWS IS CONSIDERABLY FATTER THIS YEAR.

Laura Peters got out of the station wagon bus. Harriet wrote:

AND LAURA PETERS IS THINNER AND UGLIER. I THINK SHE COULD USE SOME BRACES ON HER TEETH.

"Oh, boy," said Sport. They looked and there was Pinky Whitehead. Pinky was so pale, thin, and weak that he looked like a glass of milk, a tall thin glass of milk. Sport couldn't bear to look at him. Harriet turned away from habit, then looked back to see if he had changed. Then she wrote:

PINKY WHITEHEAD HAS NOT CHANGED. PINKY WHITEHEAD WILL NEVER CHANGE.

Harriet consulted her mental notes on Pinky. He lived on Eighty-eighth Street. He had a very beautiful mother, a father who worked on a magazine, and a baby sister three years old. Harriet wrote:

MY MOTHER IS ALWAYS SAYING PINKY WHITEHEAD'S WHOLE PROBLEM IS HIS MOTHER. I BETTER ASK HER WHAT THAT MEANS OR I'LL NEVER FIND OUT. DOES HIS MOTHER HATE HIM? IF I HAD HIM I'D HATE HIM.

"Well, it's time to go in," said Sport in a tired voice.

"Yeah, let's get this over with," said Janie and turned toward the door.

Harriet closed her notebook and they all went in. Their first period was Assembly in the big study hall.

Miss Angela Whitehead, the present dean, stood at the podium. Harriet scribbled in her notebook as soon as she took her seat:

MISS WHITEHEAD'S FEET LOOK LARGER THIS YEAR. MISS WHITEHEAD HAS BUCK TEETH, THIN HAIR, FEET LIKE SKIS, AND A VERY LONG HANGING STOMACH. OLE GOLLY SAYS DESCRIPTION IS GOOD FOR THE SOUL AND CLEARS THE BRAIN LIKE A LAXATIVE. THAT SHOULD TAKE CARE OF MISS WHITEHEAD.

"Good morning, children." Miss Whitehead bowed as gracefully as a pussy willow. The students rose in a shuffling body. "Good morning, Miss Whitehead," they intoned, an undercurrent of grumbling rising immediately afterward like a second theme. Miss Whitehead made a short speech about gum and candy wrappers being thrown all over the school. She didn't see any reason for this. Then followed the readings. Every morning two or three older girls read short passages from books, usually the Bible. Harriet never listened. She got enough quotes from Ole

Golly. She used this time to write in her book:

OLE GOLLY SAYS THERE IS AS MANY WAYS TO LIVE AS THERE ARE PEOPLE ON THE EARTH AND I SHOULDN'T GO ROUND WITH BLINDERS BUT SHOULD SEE EVERY WAY I CAN. THEN I'LL KNOW WHAT WAY I WANT TO LIVE AND NOT JUST LIVE LIKE MY FAMILY. I'LL TELL YOU ONE THING, I DON'T WANT TO LIVE LIKE MISS WHITEHEAD. THE OTHER DAY I SAW HER IN THE GROCERY STORE AND SHE BOUGHT ONE SMALL CAN OF TUNA, ONE DIET COLA, AND A PACKAGE OF CIGARETTES. NOT EVEN ONE TOMATO. SHE MUST HAVE A TERRIBLE LIFE. I CAN'T WAIT TO GET BACK TO MY REGULAR SPY ROUTE THIS AFTERNOON. I'VE BEEN AWAY ALL SUMMER AND THOSE HOUSES IN THE COUNTRY ARE TOO FAR AWAY FROM EACH OTHER. TO GET MUCH DONE I WOULD HAVE TO DRIVE.

Assembly was over. The class got up and filed into the sixth-grade room. Harriet grabbed a desk right across the aisle one way from Sport and the other way from Janie.

"Hey!" Sport said because he was glad. If they hadn't been able to grab these desks, it would have been hard passing notes.

Miss Elson stood at her desk. She was their homeroom teacher. Harriet looked at her curiously, then wrote:

I THINK MISS ELSON IS ONE OF THOSE PEOPLE YOU DON'T BOTHER TO THINK ABOUT TWICE.

She slammed the notebook shut as though she had put Miss Elson in a box and slammed the lid. Miss Elson called the roll and her voice squeaked: "Andrews, Gibbs, Hansen, Hawthorne, Hennessey, Matthews, Peters, Rocque, Welsch, Whitehead."

Everyone said "Here" dutifully.

"And now, children, we will have the election for officer. Are there any nominations?"

Sport leaped to his feet. "I nominate Harriet Welsch."

Janie yelled, "I second it." They always did this every year because the one that was officer controlled everything. When the teacher went out of the room the officer could write down the names of anyone who was disorderly. The officer also got to be the editor of the Sixth Grade Page in the school paper.

Rachel Hennessey got up. "I nominate Marion Hawthorne," she said in her prissiest voice.

Marion Hawthorne shot Beth Ellen Hansen a look that made Harriet's hair stand on end. Beth Ellen looked terrified, then got timidly to her feet and, almost whispering, managed to stammer, "I second it." It was rigged, the whole thing, every year. There were no more nominations and then came the vote. Marion Hawthorne got it. Every year either Marion or Rachel Hennessey got it. Harriet wrote in her book:

YOU'D THINK THE TEACHERS WOULD SMELL A RAT BECAUSE IT'S FIVE YEARS NOW AND NEITHER ME NOR SPORT NOR JANIE HAS EVER GOTTEN IT.

Marion Hawthorne looked terribly smug. Sport, Janie, and Harriet scowled at each other. Janie whispered, "Our day will come. Just wait." Harriet wondered if she meant that when she blew up the world Marion Hawthorne would see what they were made of. Or maybe Janie meant to blow up Marion Hawthorne first, which wasn't a bad idea.

It was finally three thirty-seven and school was over. Sport came up to Harriet. "Hey, whyncha come over this afternoon?"

"After the spy route, maybe, if I've got time."

"Aw, gee, Janie's working in the lab. You both are always working."

"Why don't you practice? How're you ever going to be a ball player?"

"Can't. Have to clean the house. Come over if you get time."

Harriet said "okay," then "good-by," and ran toward the house. It was time for her cake and milk. Every day at three-forty she had cake and milk. Harriet loved doing everything every day in the same way.

"Time for my cake, for my cake and milk, time for my milk and cake." She ran yelling through the front door of her house. She ran through the front hall past the dining room and the living room and down the steps into the kitchen. There she ran smack into the cook.

"Like a missile you are, shot from that school," screamed the cook.

"Hello cook, hello, cooky, hello, hello, hello, hello," sang Harriet. Then she opened her notebook and wrote:

BLAH, BLAH, BLAH. I ALWAYS DO CARRY ON A LOT. ONCE OLE GOLLY SAID TO ME, "I COULD NEVER LOSE YOU IN A CROWD, I'D JUST FOLLOW THE SOUND OF YOUR VOICE."

She slammed the notebook and the cook jumped. Harriet laughed.

The cook put the cake and milk in front of her. "What you always writing in that dad-blamed book for?" she asked with a sour little face.

"Because," Harriet said around a bit of cake, "I'm a spy."

"Spy, huh. Some spy."

"I *am* a spy. I'm a *good* spy, too. I've never been caught."

Cook settled herself with a cup of coffee. "How long you been a spy?"

"Since I could write. Ole Golly told me if I was going to be a writer I better write down everything, so I'm a spy that writes down everything."

"Hmmmmmmph." Harriet knew the cook couldn't think of anything to say when she did that.

"I know all about you"

"Like fun, you do." The cook looked startled.

"I do too. I know you live with your sister in Brooklyn and that she might get married and you wish you had a car and you have a son that's no good and drinks."

"What do you do, child? Listen at doors?"

"Yes," said Harriet.

"Well, I never," said the cook. "I think that's bad manners."

"Ole Golly doesn't. Ole Golly says find out everything you can cause life is hard enough even if you know a lot."

"I bet she don't know you spooking round this house listening at doors."

"Well, how am I supposed to find out anything?"

"I don't know"—the cook shook her head—"I don't know about that Ole Golly."

"What do you mean?" Harriet felt apprehensive.

"I don't know. I just don't know. I wonder about her."

Ole Golly came into the room. "What is it you don't know?"

Cook looked as though she might hide under the table. She stood up. "Can I get you your tea, Miss Golly?" she asked meekly.

"That would be most kind of you," said Ole Golly and sat down.

Harriet opened her notebook:

I WONDER WHAT THAT WAS ALL ABOUT. MAYBE OLE GOLLY KNOWS SOMETHING ABOUT COOK THAT COOK DOESN'T WANT HER TO KNOW. CHECK ON THIS.

"What do you have in school this year, Harriet?" asked Ole Golly.

"English, History, Geography, French, Math, ugh, Science, ugh, and the Performing Arts, ugh, ugh, ugh." Harriet rattled these off in a very bored way.

"What history?"

"Greeks and Romans, ugh, ugh, ugh."

"They're fascinating."

"What?"

"They are. Just wait, you'll see. Talk about spies. Those gods spied on everybody all the time."

"Yeah?"

" 'Yes,' Harriet, not 'yeah.' "

"Well, *I* wish *I'd* never heard of them."

"Ah, there's a thought from Aesop for you: 'We would often be sorry if our wishes were gratified.' " Ole Golly gave a little moo of satisfaction after she had delivered herself of this.

"I think I'll go now," Harriet said.

"Yes," said the cook, "go out and play."

Harriet stood up. "I do not go out to PLAY, I go out to WORK!" and in as dignified a way as possible she walked from the room and up the steps from the kitchen. Then she began to run, and running furiously, she went past the first floor with the living room and dining room, the second floor with her parents' bedroom and the library, and on up to the third floor to her little room and bath.

Harriet loved her room. It was small and cozy, and the bathroom was a little one with a tiny window which looked out over the park across the street. Her room had a bigger window. She looked around, pleased as always by the order, the efficiency of it. She always picked up everything immediately, not because anyone nagged at her—no one ever had—but because it was her room and she liked to have it just so. Harriet was just so about a lot of things. Her room stood around her pleasantly, waiting for her. Her own small bed next to the window, her bookcase filled with her books, her toy box, which had been filled with toys but which now held her notebooks because it could be locked, her desk and chair at which she did her homework—all seemed to look back at her with affection. Harriet put her books down on the desk and hurriedly began to change into her spy clothes.

Her spy clothes consisted first of all of an ancient pair of blue jeans, so old that her mother had forbidden her to wear them, but which Harriet loved because she had fixed up the belt with hooks to carry her spy tools. Her tools were a flashlight, in case she were ever out at night, which she never was, a leather pouch for her notebook, another leather case for extra pens, a water canteen, and a boy scout knife which had, among other features, a screwdriver and a knife and fork which collapsed. She had never had occasion to eat anywhere, but someday it might come in handy.

She attached everything to the belt, and it all worked fine except that she rattled a little. Next she put on an old dark-blue sweatshirt with a hood which she wore at the beach house in the summer so that it still smelled of salt air in a comforting way. Then she put on an old pair of blue sneakers with holes over each of her little toes. Her mother had actually gone

so far as to throw these out, but Harriet had rescued them from the garbage when the cook wasn't looking.

She finished by donning a pair of black-rimmed spectacles with no glass in them. She had found these once in her father's desk and now sometimes wore them even to school, because she thought they made her look smarter.

She stood back and looked at herself in the full-length mirror which hung on her bathroom door. She was very pleased. Then she ran quickly down the steps and out, banging the front door behind her.

She was particularly excited as she ran along, because today she was adding a new spying place to her route. She had discovered a way into a private house around the corner. Private houses were much more difficult to get into than apartment buildings, and this was the first one Harriet had managed. It belonged to a Mrs. Agatha K. Plumber who was a very strange, rather theatrical lady who had once married a man of considerable means. She was now divorced, lived alone, and apparently talked on the telephone all day. Harriet had found this much out from first listening to several conversations between Mrs. Plumber's maid and an overly friendly garbage man. Harriet had pretended to play ball while the garbage was being picked up.

Just yesterday she had discovered that by timing it exactly she had just enough time to jump in the dumbwaiter and slide the door closed before the maid completed one of her frequent trips up and down the stairs. The dumbwaiter was no longer used but fortunately had not been boarded up. Since there was a small crack in the door, Harriet could see and hear perfectly.

She approached the house, looked through the kitchen windows, and saw the maid preparing a tray. She knew then that the next step would be to take the tray to the second floor. Not a moment to lose. The maid went into the pantry. Harriet stepped through the kitchen door and in one jump was in the dumbwaiter. She barely got the door slid down again before the maid was back in the room. The maid was humming "Miss Am-er-i-ker, look at her, Miss Am-er-i-ker" in a tuneless sort of way.

Then the tray was ready. The maid picked it up and left the room. Simultaneously Harriet started pulling on the ropes that hoisted the dumbwaiter. Terrified, she heard a lot of creaking. This would never do. Maybe she could bring some oil.

She arrived at the second floor. Her heart was beating so fast she was almost unable to breathe. She looked through the crack. The first thing she saw was a huge four-poster bed in the middle of which Mrs. Plumber sat, propped against immense pillows, telephone in hand, surrounded by magazines, books, candy boxes, and a litter of pink baby pillows.

"Well," Mrs. Plumber was saying decisively into the telephone, "*I* have discovered the *secret* of *life.*"

Wow, thought Harriet.

"My dear, it's very simple, you just *take* to your *bed.* You just refuse to leave it for *anything* or *anybody.*"

Some secret, thought Harriet; that's the dumbest thing I ever heard of. Harriet hated bed anyway. In and out was her motto, and the less time there the better.

"Oh, yes, darling, I *know.* I *know* you *can't* run away from life, I *agree* with you. I *loathe* people that do that. But you see, I'm *not.* While I'm lying here I'm actually *working* because, you see, and this is the *divine* part, I'm *deciding* on a profession!"

You must be a hundred and two, thought Harriet; you better get going.

The maid came in with the tray. "Put it down there," said Mrs. Plumber rather crossly, then went back to the phone.

Harriet wrote in her notebook:

IT'S JUST WHAT OLE GOLLY SAYS. RICH PEOPLE ARE BORING. SHE SAYS WHEN PEOPLE DON'T DO ANYTHING THEY DON'T THINK ANYTHING, AND WHEN THEY DON'T THINK ANYTHING THERE'S NOTHING TO THINK ABOUT THEM. IF I HAD A DUMBWAITER I WOULD LOOK IN IT ALL THE TIME TO SEE IF ANYBODY WAS IN IT.

As though she was reading Harriet's mind, Mrs. Plumber said to the maid, "Did you hear a creak just now in that old dumbwaiter?"

"No, ma'am," said the maid.

"It was probably my imagination," She went back to the telephone. "My dear, I have *infinite* possibilities. Now don't you think I would make a *marv-e-lous* actress? Or there's *painting;* I could *paint.* What do you think of that? . . . Well, darling, I'm only *forty,* think of *Gauguin.* . . . "

Harriet started, very slowly, heart pounding, to pull the ropes that would start her downward. It had occurred to her that she'd better exit while Mrs. Plumber was blathering away or she would certainly be heard. There was a tiny creak as she got near the bottom, but she was fairly certain no one heard it. There, the main floor. She peeked into the kitchen. Empty. Could she make it? She scrambled down and ran for her life.

I have never run so fast, she thought as she careened around the corner. Panting, she sat on some steps and took out her book.

I THINK THIS MIGHT BE TOO DANGEROUS AN ASSIGNMENT. BUT I WOULD LIKE TO KNOW WHAT JOB SHE TAKES. BUT HOW CAN YOU WORK LYING DOWN? HOW DOES SHE PAY FOR ANYTHING JUST LYING THERE? I GUESS SHE JUST LIVES ON HER HUSBAND'S MONEY. DOES MY MOTHER MOOCH OFF MY FATHER? I'LL NEVER DO THAT. LOOK AT POOR SPORT. HE HAS TOO MUCH TO DO ALREADY WITHOUT ME LYING UP IN THE BED ALL DAY EATING.

Harriet had three more steps before she was finished for the day, but before she continued she decided to stop by and see Sport. On the way there she got thirsty and stopped in her favorite luncheonette for an egg cream. It was her favorite because it was there that she had first begun to hear what peculiar things people say to each other. She liked to sit at the counter with her egg cream and let the voices from the tables behind her float over her head. Several conversations were always going on at once. Sometimes she would play a game and not look at the people until from listening to them she had decided what they looked like. Then she would turn around and see if she were right.

"A chocolate egg cream, please."

"Certainly, Harriet. How are you?"

"Okay." Harriet sat down, pleased that she was known. She put her twelve cents down and sipped away as she listened.

"My father is a rat."

"So, I have to admit, I handled that case in a perfect way, a really perfect way. I said to the judge . . . "

"He's a rat because he thinks he's perfect."

"Listen, Jane, we have to go to Orchard Street and get that material. I can't live in that house one more minute without shades. Anyone could see in."

Harriet had to restrain herself at this point from looking around at a new possibility for the spy route. If *anyone* could see in . . .

"You know, I've lost very few cases in my time, even if I do say so."

"He's such a rat he never lets my mother open her trap."

Rat trap, thought Harriet.

"You have no idea what it's like to hide all the time. Geez, I can't even walk around in a slip."

Her egg cream finished, Harriet summed up her guesses. The boy with the rat father would be skinny, have black hair, and a lot of pimples. The lawyer who won all his cases would be short, puffy-looking, and be leaning forward. She got no picture of the shadeless girl but decided that she must be fat. She turned around.

At first she couldn't tell. Then she saw the boy with black hair and pimples. She felt a surge of triumph. She looked at what must be the lawyer, one of two men. Then she listened to see if he were the one. No, the other one was the lawyer. He wasn't short and fat, he was long and thin, with a handsome face. She consoled herself with a faint puffiness he had around the eyes.

Well, no wonder she won't walk around in a slip, Harriet thought, looking at the girl with no shades; she's the fattest thing I ever saw.

Enough. Only two out of three. Some days were better than others.

A TASTE OF BLACKBERRIES

Doris Buchanan Smith

Stereotyped sex roles prevail in most of children's literature. Boys are usually presented in roles of adventure and achievement; girls are generally shown in a family situation or in school. It has been considered risky, in terms of the kind of reception a book will get, to describe a boy's need to receive or express affection, or to present him in a situation in which an emotional problem must be solved. This story is a notable exception to this rule, for it presents a boy first holding back, then releasing his grief on the sudden death of a playmate.

Mrs. Houser was holding Jamie's baby brother and Martha sat on the floor with a coloring book and crayons. Everything was dark and cool. Jamie's mother said the house was cooler if it was closed up.

"I'll take the children," Mom said to Mrs. Houser. Mrs. Houser handed over the baby.

"Son, help Martha gather up her crayons and take her over to our play room."

"Jamie got stung," Martha said, barely looking up from her coloring. I reached under her armpits and pulled her to her feet. We left Mom and Mrs. Houser talking in hushed tones.

Martha dropped her crayons in the middle of the yard and we both stooped over to pick them up. I stuffed as many as I could into my pockets.

"That's the color of the am-blance," Martha said, holding the white crayon. "Did you see it? Did you see Jamie get a ride?" Her eyes were bright and excited. We were almost at the spot where the ambulance had parked.

"Yeah," I grunted. I guess I was the only kid in the neighborhood who hadn't been impressed by that ambulance. The whole neighborhood was running and squealing to see what was the matter.

That Jamie. He was an expert attention getter, even when, maybe, he didn't intend to be. I wondered briefly if he had been faking unconsciousness just to keep from grinning at all of us. It would serve him right if he was out cold and didn't even know he was riding in an ambulance.

Something in my conscience kicked me. What if something really was badly wrong. Naw, it couldn't be. What could happen to Jamie the great? He yelled a lot, but he was tough.

If we were wrestling, he would scream sometimes so I thought I had really hurt him, but he would never give up,

From Doris Buchanan Smith, *A Taste of Blackberries* (New York: Thomas Y. Crowell, 1973), Chapters 4–5.

never. And he would do such crazy comic falls that you'd wonder how he kept from breaking his neck. Jamie was a show-off and a clown all right, there was no doubt about that. And most of the time it was funny.

I stretched out on the play room floor and colored a picture for Martha. She could color pretty good for four. She didn't stay inside the lines very well, but the colors she used looked good together. I mean, she didn't dress a lady in black and purple. I colored my entire picture in shades of green and Martha was very impressed.

Mother came in with the baby and I stayed on the floor and started another picture. Part of me wanted to find out all about Jamie; but the other part was afraid to hear.

She lay the baby on the sofa and pushed a chair against it. The baby was asleep, all roses and cream. If I could put that color into a crayon it would be a miracle.

When Mom had the baby settled she called softly for me to come with her. She sat down at the kitchen table and motioned for me to sit down. I couldn't sit. Some awful instinct was hammering on my brain. I tried not to listen.

"Jamie is dead, darling," she said.

"Dead darling" rang in my head. Jamie is dead, darling. Jamie is a dead darling. He didn't look so darling flopping around on the ground, showing off. Jamie was a freak.

"I know," I said bluntly. "I saw the ambulance." I felt trapped. I didn't want to listen to her telling me lies about Jamie.

"Were you out there when it happened?"

"Yes."

"What happened?

"Jamie poked a stick down a bee hole."

"Did you get stung?"

"No, I stood still."

"Then what happened?"

"Everybody ran."

"Did Jamie run?"

It was as though she had punched me in the stomach. I saw Jamie again, falling down and writhing. I closed my eyes. I shouldn't have left. I should have helped him. But how could I know? I swallowed. I thought I was going to be sick.

"Did Jamie run?" she repeated.

"No," I said. "He fell down. I thought he was faking."

She reached out to touch me but I was out of reach and didn't move closer.

"I know," she said. "We all know how Jamie was."

My mind buzzed like that swarm of bees. I hadn't even got stung, and Jamie was dead. Someone had got stung eleven times and it was just like giant mosquito bites, and Jamie was dead.

"How many times was he stung?" I asked. He must have been stung a hundred times.

"Just once or twice. It wasn't the number of stings, it was that Jamie was allergic to them. A few people are allergic to bee stings."

Allergic? I knew about that. A girl at school was allergic to chocolate. It made her sick. We all felt sorry for her. But I didn't know that being allergic could kill you.

"Did Jamie know he was allergic to bee stings?"

"No, he didn't, sweetheart. No one did. He wouldn't have played around a bee hole if he had. It was a freak accident. It hardly ever happens."

"How did they—? Who found him?"

"Mrs. Houser. She looked out to see if you were all working and she saw Jamie on the ground. She ran over and got Jamie's mother."

Mrs. Houser! I would have thought she'd just let you lie there and rot.

"I'm going upstairs," I announced. I went to my room and stood by the window, staring out. Did the world know that Jamie was dead? The sky didn't act like it. It was a blue sky and white cloud day. Horses and lambs and floppy-eared dogs chased across the sky. Was Jamie playing with them?

What kinds of things could you do when you were dead? Or was dead just plain dead and that's all?

I looked across at Jamie's window. He would never flash me a signal again. We had learned Morse code, Jamie and I, and talked to each other at night. Before that we had taken cans and a string and stretched it across from his window to mine.

That had been a funny day. It had been so easy to string up one can and drop the string down from Jamie's window. It wasn't so easy getting the string up to my window.

We dragged the string across the street and Jamie tried to throw the can up to me. I was a little scornful of Jamie's pitching arm until I tried it myself with him upstairs trying to catch.

Finally, I climbed my mother's rose trellis by the kitchen window, careful to keep my foot at the cross pieces of the trellis where it was strongest. I picked my way up through the thorns until I was on the sun deck with the can and string.

"Yeah, smarty," Jamie laughed. "Now, how are you going to get it to your room?"

We felt like engineers trying to set up a communications system, but we figured it out. Then the dumb thing didn't work! We just flopped down exhausted.

"And you know what I just thought of?" Jamie asked when he came back over. "Why didn't we just drop an extra piece of string from your front window and tie onto this one and pull it up?" It was so simple we collapsed again and clapped our arms over our heads. We felt so stupid.

Later, we had got the encyclopedia and looked up Morse code. We saved our money and bought flashlights with blinker buttons. It certainly was easier than that stupid set of cans. And it worked.

So, my mother had told me that Jamie was dead. No more blinks from across the street at night. No more Jamie. Who would we have to make us laugh anymore?

I sat in the bathtub and poked ripples in the water. Soapy whiskers covered my chin. I hadn't eaten lunch before and now hadn't eaten supper. Dad and Mom were getting ready to go to the funeral parlor. They asked me if I wanted to go, but I couldn't do that to Jamie. It seemed that as long as I acted like he wasn't dead, he wouldn't be dead.

The ring of ripples broadened, bounced off the sides of the tub and, larger still, came toward me again. Someone said that ripples go on forever and ever, even when you can't see them anymore.

I thought of me and Jamie throwing stones in a still pond, watching ripples. Jamie wouldn't make ripples anymore. Or shampoo beards.

I grabbed the soap and rubbed up a lather. The soap was my lamp and I was Aladdin. I would rub life back for Jamie. Someone knocked at the door.

"We're going now, sweetheart. We won't be long. If you need anything you go over to Mrs. Mullins."

They were going. They were going to see Jamie. Suddenly, panicky, I yelled.

"Wait. Wait for me." I submerged and let the soap rinse off me. I rubbed my hair as dry as I could and combed it. Mom straightened my part. Usually my hair just hung there, but when it was wet it looked better combed.

I had never been to a funeral parlor before. I had been to a funeral, at a church, when my Dad's Uncle Jonah died. He had tripped with his shotgun and blown off the top of his head. At least that's what they said.

The casket was open during the funeral and, row by row, everyone went by to look. As I went by the casket, I was prepared not to take a good look. But, in just a glance I saw Uncle Jonah's whole head. Then I looked.

He was fixed up just like nothing had happened. He didn't look like he'd been shot. He looked like he was going to wake up any minute and ask us what we were doing, staring at him while he slept.

Of course, nothing like that had happened to Jamie. He had got stung by a couple of bees. It just didn't seem possible that a tiny thing like a bee could kill you. I guess a lot of bees were dead, too, if it was true they died when they stung you, I wasn't glad the bees were dead. I was sorry about anything being dead. Especially Jamie.

When I had popped out of the bathtub and said "Wait for me" I hadn't known why. Now I did. I wasn't going to look at him, but if it was possible that Jamie knew what was going on, I wanted him to know that I was here, thinking about him.

There were people all around, talking in whispers, or not talking. Some were crying. I leaned my back against the door frame, thinking to Jamie.

"I'm here. I'm here, Jamie."

"He looks sweet," a woman said as she came out of the room. "Just like he's asleep, bless his heart."

I remembered how Uncle Jonah looked like he was sleeping. I couldn't imagine Jamie looking like that. I went in and pushed up between my mother and father.

There was Jamie. He was out straight with one hand crossed over his chest. He didn't look like he was asleep to me. Jamie slept all bunched up. Jamie looked dead.

We used to have these staring contests, Jamie and I. We would see who would blink first, or laugh.

It began to sink in that Jamie wasn't going to open his eyes to stare back at me. He wasn't going to blink. He wasn't going to laugh. I ran out of the room and down the hall.

The front yard of the funeral parlor was all green grass and colorful flowers, with lights shining on them. I snatched a yellow bloom from the stem and began tearing it to shreds.

My father called to me and grabbed my shoulder and turned me around.

"Daddy!"

I buried my head into his chest until the buttons on his suit hurt my face.

At home I put on my pajamas. Mother hung around, telling me that sometimes we don't understand why certain things happen. She waited for me to talk. I just lay in bed with my hands behind my head. Finally, she touched my hair and kissed my cheek and left.

I listened to her steps disappear. Then I got up and knelt by the front window. There was my flashlight, in its place on the window sill. Jamie's was probably on his sill, too.

I flicked on my light and shined it over toward Jamie's to see if I could see his flashlight. Of course I couldn't. The beam didn't carry that far. When we signaled we could never see each other, only the dots of light. Unless we put the light up under our chins to make spooky faces.

There was the soft padding of footsteps in the hall and I set my flash down and sprang into bed. They were coming to check. Every night Mother or Dad, or sometimes both, would come check to see if I was asleep.

I pulled the sheet up and scurried around under it to find a comfortable position. I let my head flop down, tilted a little sideways. I raised my arm and tucked my hand along by my cheek. I took a deep breath and let out a big sleepy sigh. I almost convinced myself I was asleep.

The door made the slightest squeak as it opened. I imagined the crack of light slicing across the room. I didn't hear a footstep but something touched my forehead. I almost jumped. I concentrated on keeping my eyeballs from moving around behind my lids.

It must have been my mother. The hand, touching first my head then my cheek, felt soft and smooth. She tucked the sheet up around my shoulders and under my chin, a habit she had even in the summer.

She stopped tucking and I heard the door close.

I opened my eyes. Everything was so black I wondered if she was still in the room, watching me. In a minute, my eyes were used to the dark and I could see she wasn't. I went back to the window.

The front door sounded below me. I didn't look down, I kept staring at Jamie's house. I saw my mother going through Jamie's yard to the door.

The sight of her turned on my tear faucets so suddenly that I was surprised. All day I hadn't cried, even when I pressed my face into my father's coat buttons. The strange thing is I wasn't crying for Jamie, I was crying for me.

I wanted my mother to come back. I wanted her to take care of me. I wished I hadn't pretended to be asleep; then she would have stayed to talk, or just to sit quietly on the side of the bed. I wished I was little and could sit on her lap and be rocked.

The tears kept coming until I had them smeared all over my face. My face was tight where the tears had dried. I was snuffling and fumbling around in the dark for a tissue.

The door opened again and Dad's shadowy form filled most of the crack of light. Out of habit I dove for the bed.

He came over and picked me up as easily as if I were a baby. He sat me on his lap and cradled my head to his chest. Funny, I hadn't thought of Dad's lap, but it was just as good. I cried and cried and cried.

IT'S LIKE THIS, CAT

Emily Neville

The hero of this story is another nonstereotypical male character, an adolescent boy who has human, tender feelings, owns a cat instead of a dog, and is not afraid to form a friendship with an eccentric older woman whom the rest of the neighborhood considers crazy. He is exceptional also in standing up to his father, who tries to push him into the more conventional behavior of a socialized male.

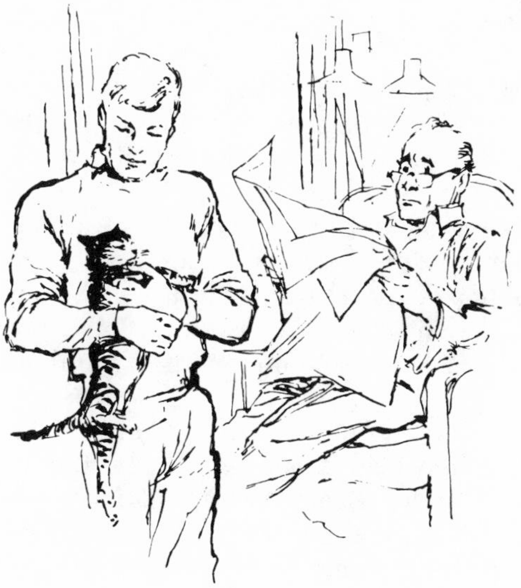

Cat and Kate

My father is always talking about how a dog can be very educational for a boy. This is one reason I got a cat.

My father talks a lot anyway. Maybe being a lawyer he gets in the habit. Also, he's a small guy with very little gray curly hair, so maybe he thinks he's got to roar a lot to make up for not being a big hairy tough guy. Mom is thin and quiet, and when anything upsets her, she gets asthma. In the apartment—we live right in the middle of New York City—we don't have any heavy drapes or rugs, and Mom never

From Emily Neville, *It's Like This, Cat* (New York: Harper and Row, 1963), Chapter 1. Illustrated by Emil Weiss.

fries any food because the doctors figure dust and smoke make her asthma worse. I don't think it's dust; I think it's Pop's roaring.

The big hassle that led to me getting Cat came when I earned some extra money baby-sitting for a little boy around the corner on Gramercy Park. I spent the money on a Belafonte record. This record has one piece about a father telling his son about the birds and the bees. I think it's funny. Pop blows his stack.

"You're not going to play that stuff in this house!" he roars. "Why aren't you outdoors, anyway? Baby-sitting! Baby-talk records! When I was your age, I made money on a newspaper-delivery route, and my dog Jeff and I used to go ten miles chasing rabbits on a good Saturday."

"Pop," I say patiently, "there are no rabbits out on Third Avenue. Honest, there aren't."

"Don't get fresh!" Pop jerks the plug out of the record player so hard the needle skips, which probably wrecks my record. So I get mad and start yelling too. Between rounds we both hear Mom in the kitchen starting to wheeze.

Pop hisses, "Now, see—you've gone and upset your mother!"

I slam the record player shut, grab a stick and ball, and run down the three flights of stairs to the street.

This isn't the first time Pop and I have played this scene, and there gets to be a pattern: When I slam out of our house mad, I go along over to my Aunt Kate's. She's not really my aunt. The kids around here call her Crazy Kate the Cat Woman because she walks along the street in funny old clothes and sneakers talking to herself, and she sometimes has half a dozen or more stray cats living with her. I guess she does sound a little looney, but it's just because she does things her own way, and she doesn't give a hoot what people think. She's sane, all right. In fact she makes a lot better sense than my pop.

It was three or four years ago, when I was a little kid, and I came tearing down our stairs crying mad after some fight with Pop, that I first met Kate. I plunged out of our door and into the street without looking. At the same moment I heard brakes scream and felt someone yank me back by the scruff of my neck. I got dropped in a heap on the sidewalk.

I looked up, and there was a shiny black car with M.D. plates and Kate waving her umbrella at the driver and shouting: "Listen, Dr. Big Shot, whose life are you saving? Can't you even watch out for a sniveling little kid crossing the street?"

The doctor looked pretty sheepish, and so did I. A few people on the sidewalk stopped to watch and snicker at us. Our janitor Butch was there, shaking his finger at me. Kate nodded to him and told him she was taking me home to mop me up.

"Yas'm," said Butch. He says "Yas'm" to all ladies.

Kate dragged me along by the hand to her apartment. She didn't say anything when we got there, just dumped me in a chair with a couple of kittens. Then she got me a cup of tea and a bowl of cottage cheese.

That stopped me snuffling to ask, "What do I put the cottage cheese on?"

"Don't put it on anything. Just eat it. Eat a bowl of it every day. Here, have an orange, too. But no cookies or candy, none of that sweet, starchy stuff. And no string beans. They're not good for you."

My eyes must have popped, but I guess I knew right that first day that you don't argue with Kate. I ate the cottage cheese—it doesn't really have any taste anyway—and I sure have always agreed with her about the string beans.

Off and on since then I've seen quite a lot of Kate. I'd pass her on the street, chirruping to some mangy old stray cat hiding under a car, and he'd always come out to be stroked. Sometimes there'd be a bunch of little kids dancing around jeering at her and calling her a witch. It made me feel real good and important to run them off.

Quite often I went with her to the A & P and helped her carry home the cat food and cottage cheese and fruit. She talks to herself all the time in the store, and if she thinks the peaches or melons don't look good that day, she shouts clear across the store to the manager. He comes across and picks her out an extra good one, just to keep the peace.

I introduced Kate to Mom, and they got along real well. Kate's leery of most people, afraid they'll make fun of her, I guess; my mom's not leery of people, but she's shy, and what with asthma and worrying about keeping me and Pop calmed down, she doesn't go out much or make dates with people. She and Kate would chat together in the stores or sitting on the stoop on a sunny day. Kate shook her head over Mom's asthma and said she'd get over it if she ate cottage cheese every day. Mom ate it for a while, but she put mayonnaise on it, which Kate says is just like poison.

The day of the fight with Pop about the Belafonte record it's cold and windy out and there are no kids in sight. I slam my ball back and forth against the wall where it says "No Ball Playing," just to limber up and let off a little spite, and then I go over to see Kate.

Kate has a permanent cat named Susan and however many kittens Susan happens to have just had. It varies. Usually there are a few other temporary stray kittens in the apartment, but I never saw any father cat there before. Today Susan and her kittens are under the stove, and Susan keeps hissing at a big tiger-striped tomcat crouching under the sofa. He turns his head away from her and looks like he never intended to get mixed up with family life. For a stray cat he's sleek and healthy-looking. Every time he moves a whisker, Susan hisses again, warningly. She believes in no visiting rights for fathers.

Kate pours me some tea and asks what's doing.

"My pop is full of hot air, as usual," I say.

"Takes one to know one," Kate says, catching me off base. I change the subject.

"How come the kittens' pop is around the house? I never saw a full-grown tom here before."

"He saw me buying some cans of cat food, so he followed me home. Susan isn't admitting she ever knew him or ever wants to. I'll give him another feed and send him on his way, I guess. He's a handsome young fellow." Kate strokes him between the ears, and he rotates his head. Susan hisses.

He starts to pull back farther under the sofa. Without stopping to think myself, or giving him time to, I pick him up. Susan arches up and spits. I can feel the muscles in his body tense up as he gets ready to spring out of my lap. Then he changes his mind and decides to take advantage of the lap. He narrows his eyes and gives Susan a bored look and turns his head to take me in. After he's sized me up, he pretends he only turned around to lick his back.

"Cat," I say to him, "how about coming home with me?"

"Hah!" Kate laughs. "Your pop will throw him out faster than you can say 'good old Jeff.' "

"Yeah-h?" I say it slowly and do some thinking. Taking Cat home had been just a passing thought, but right now I decide I'll really go to the mat with Pop about this. He can have his memories of good old Jeff and rabbit hunts, but I'm going to have me a tiger.

Aunt Kate gives me a can of cat food and a box of litter, so Cat can stay in my room, because I remember Mom probably gets asthma from animals, too. Cat and I go home.

Pop does a lot of shouting and sputtering when we get home, but I just put Cat down in my room, and I try not to argue with him, so I won't lose my temper. I promise I'll keep him in my room and sweep up the cat hairs so Mom won't have to.

As a final blast Pop says, "I suppose you'll get your exercise mouse hunting now. What are you going to name the noble animal?"

"Look, Pop," I explain, "I know he's a cat, he knows he's a cat, and his name is Cat. And even if you call him Admiral John Paul Jones, he won't come when you call, and he won't lick your hand, see?"

"He'd better not! And it's not my hand that's going to get licked around here in a minute." Pop snaps.

"All right, all right."

Actually, my pop sometimes jaws so long it'd be a relief if he did haul off and hit me, but he never does.

We call it a draw for that day, and I have Cat.

JULIE OF THE WOLVES
Jean George

Like the young Indian woman in Scott O'Dell's Island of the Blue Dolphins, *Julie of the Wolves is courageous and intelligent—able to cope with a wilderness environment in a terrible survival situation. In presenting strong female characters in the type of adventure that has in the past been limited to boy characters, these two stories have moved far beyond the female stereotype. In the following story, Miyax (Julie is her English name), lost in the Alaskan wilderness, learns to communicate with the great black wolf, Amaroq, through close, careful observation of wolf-language. She is therefore made one of the pack, saving herself from death by starvation.*

Miyax pushed back the hood of her sealskin parka and looked at the Arctic sun. It was a yellow disc in a lime-green sky, the colors of six o'clock in the evening and the time when the wolves awoke. Quietly she put down her cooking pot and crept to the top of a dome-shaped frost heave, one of the many earth buckles that rise and fall in the crackling cold of the Arctic winter. Lying on her stomach, she looked across a vast lawn of grass and moss and focused her attention on the wolves she had come upon two sleeps ago. They were wagging their tails as they awoke and saw each other.

Her hands trembled and her heartbeat quickened, for she was frightened, not so much of the wolves, who were shy and many harpoon-shots away, but because of her desperate predicament. Miyax was lost. She had been lost without food for many sleeps on the North Slope of Alaska. The barren slope stretches for three hundred miles from the Brooks Range to the Arctic Ocean, and for more than eight hundred miles from the Chukchi to the Beaufort Sea. No roads cross it; ponds and lakes freckle its immensity. Winds scream across it, and the view in every direction is exactly the same. Somewhere in this cosmos was Miyax; and the very life in her body, its spark and warmth, depended upon these wolves for

From Jean George, *Julie of the Wolves* (New York: Harper and Row, 1972), first section of book.

survival. And she was not so sure they would help.

Miyax stared hard at the regal black wolf, hoping to catch his eye. She must somehow tell him that she was starving and ask him for food. This could be done she knew, for her father, an Eskimo hunter, had done so. One year he had camped near a wolf den while on a hunt. When a month had passed and her father had seen no game, he told the leader of the wolves that he was hungry and needed food. The next night the wolf called him from far away and her father went to him and found a freshly killed caribou. Unfortunately, Miyax's father never explained to her how he had told the wolf of his needs. And not long afterward he paddled his kayak into the Bering Sea to hunt for seal, and he never returned.

She had been watching the wolves for two days, trying to discern which of their sounds and movements expressed goodwill and friendship. Most animals had such signals. The little Arctic ground squirrels flicked their tails sideways to notify others of their kind that they were friendly. By imitating this signal with her forefinger, Miyax had lured many a squirrel to her hand. If she could discover such a gesture for the wolves she would be able to make friends with them and share their food, like a bird or a fox.

Propped on her elbows with her chin in her fists, she stared at the black wolf, trying to catch his eye. She had chosen him because he was much larger than the others, and because he walked like her father, Kapugen, with his head high and his chest out. The black wolf also possessed wisdom, she had observed. The pack looked to him when the wind carried strange scents or the birds cried nervously. If he was alarmed, they were alarmed. If he was calm, they were calm.

Long minutes passed, and the black wolf did not look at her. He had ignored her since she first came upon them, two sleeps ago. True, she moved slowly and quietly, so as not to alarm him; yet she did wish he would see the kindness in her eyes. Many animals could tell the difference between hostile hunters and friendly people by merely looking at them. But the big black wolf would not even glance her way.

A bird stretched in the grass. The wolf looked at it. A flower twisted in the wind. He glanced at that. Then the breeze rippled the wolverine ruff on Miyax's parka and it glistened in the light. He did not look at that. She waited. Patience with the ways of nature had been instilled in her by her father. And so she knew better than to move or shout. Yet she must get food or die. Her hands shook slightly and she swallowed hard to keep calm.

Miyax was a classic Eskimo beauty, small of bone and delicately wired with strong muscles. Her face was pearl-round and her nose was flat. Her black eyes, which slanted gracefully, were moist and sparkling. Like the beautifully formed polar bears and foxes of the north, she was slightly short-limbed. The frigid environment of the Arctic has sculptured life into compact shapes. Unlike the long-limbed, long-bodied animals of the south that are cooled by dispensing heat on extended surfaces, all live things in the Arctic tend toward compactness, to conserve heat.

The length of her limbs and the beauty of her face were of no use to Miyax as she lay on the lichen-speckled frost heave in the midst of the bleak tundra. Her stomach ached and the royal black wolf was carefully ignoring her.

"*Amaroq, ilaya,* wolf, my friend," she finally called. "Look at me. Look at me."

She spoke half in Eskimo and half in English, as if the instincts of her father and the science of the *gussaks,* the white-faced, might evoke some magical combination that would help her get her message through to the wolf.

Amaroq glanced at his paw and slowly turned his head her way without lifting his eyes. He licked his shoulder. A few matted hairs sprang apart and twinkled individually. Then his eyes sped to each of the three adult wolves that made up his pack and finally to the five pups who were sleeping in a fuzzy mass near the den entrance. The great wolf's eyes softened at the sight of the little wolves, then quickly hardened into brittle yellow jewels as he scanned the flat tundra.

Not a tree grew anywhere to break the monotony of the gold-green plain, for the soils of the tundra are permanently frozen. Only moss, grass, lichens, and a few hardy flowers take root in the thin upper layer that thaws briefly in summer. Nor do many species of animals live in this rigorous land, but those creatures that do dwell here exist in bountiful numbers. Amaroq watched a large cloud of Lapland longspurs wheel up into the sky, then alight in the grasses. Swarms of crane flies, one of the few insects that can survive the cold, darkened the tips of the mosses. Birds wheeled, turned, and called. Thousands sprang up from the ground like leaves in a wind.

The wolf's ears cupped forward and tuned in on some distant message from the tundra. Miyax tensed and listened, too. Did he hear some brewing storm, some approaching enemy? Apparently not. His ears relaxed and he rolled to his side. She sighed, glanced at the vaulting sky, and was painfully aware of her predicament.

Here she was, watching wolves—she, Miyax, daughter of Kapugen, adopted child of Martha, citizen of the United States, pupil at the Bureau of Indian Affairs School in Barrow, Alaska, and thirteen-year-old wife of the boy Daniel. She shivered at the thought of Daniel, for it was he who had driven her to this fate. She had run away from him exactly seven sleeps ago, and because of this she had one more title by gussak standards—the child divorcée.

The wolf rolled to his belly.

"Amaroq," she whispered. "I am lost and the sun will not set for a month. There is no North Star to guide me."

Amaroq did not stir.

"And there are no berry bushes here to bend under the polar wind and point to the south. Nor are there any birds I can follow." She looked up. "Here the birds are buntings and longspurs. They do not fly to the sea twice a day like the puffins and sandpipers that my father followed."

The wolf groomed his chest with his tongue.

"I never dreamed I could get lost, Amaroq," she went on, talking out loud to ease her fear. "At home on Nunivak Island where I was born, the plants and birds pointed the way for wanderers. I thought they did so everywhere . . . and so, great black Amaroq, I'm without a compass."

It had been a frightening moment when two days ago she realized that the tundra was an ocean of grass on which she was circling around and around. Now as that fear overcame her again she closed her eyes. When she opened them her heart skipped excitedly. Amaroq was looking at her!

"Ee-lie," she called and scrambled to her feet. The wolf arched his neck and narrowed his eyes. He pressed his ears forward. She waved. He drew back his lips and showed his teeth. Frightened by what seemed a snarl, she lay down again. When she was flat on her stomach. Amaroq flattened his ears and wagged his tail once. Then he tossed his head and looked away.

Discouraged, she wriggled backward down the frost heave and arrived at her camp feet first. The heave was between herself and the wolf pack and so she relaxed, stood up, and took stock of her home. It was a simple affair, for she had not been able to carry much when she ran away; she took just those things she would need for the journey—a backpack, food for a week or so, needles to mend clothes, matches, her sleeping skin, and ground cloth to go under it, two knives, and a pot.

She had intended to walk to Point Hope. There she would meet the *North Star,* the ship that brings supplies from the States to the towns on the Arctic Ocean in August when the ice pack breaks up. The ship could always use dishwashers or laundresses, she had heard, and so she would work her way to San Francisco where Amy, her pen pal, lived. At the end of every letter Amy always wrote: "When are you coming to San Francisco?" Seven days ago she had been on her way—on her way to the glittering, white, postcard city that sat on a hill among trees, those enormous plants she had never seen. She had been on her way to see the television and carpeting in Amy's school, the glass buildings, traffic lights, and stores full of fruits; on her way to the harbor that never froze and the Golden Gate Bridge. But primarily she was on her way to be rid of Daniel, her terrifying husband.

She kicked the sod at the thought of her marriage; then shaking her head to forget, she surveyed her camp. It was nice. Upon discovering the wolves, she had settled down to live near them in the hope of sharing their food, until the sun set and the stars came out to guide her. She had built a house of sod, like the summer homes of the old Eskimos. Each brick had been cut with her *ulo,* the half-moon shaped woman's knife, so versatile it can trim a baby's hair, slice a tough bear, or chip an iceberg.

Her house was not well built for she had never made one before, but it was cozy inside. She had windproofed it by sealing the sod bricks with mud from the pond at her door, and she had made it beautiful by spreading her caribou ground cloth on the floor. On this she had placed her sleeping skin, a moosehide bag lined with soft white rabbit skins. Next to her bed she had built a low table of sod on which to put her clothes when she slept. To decorate the house she had made three flowers of bird feathers and stuck them in the top of the table. Then she had built a fireplace outdoors and placed her pot beside it. The pot was empty, for she had not found even a lemming to eat.

Last winter, when she had walked to school in Barrow, these mice-like rodents were so numerous they ran out from under her feet wherever she stepped. There were thousands and thousands of them until December, when they suddenly vanished. Her teacher said that the lemmings had a chemical similar to antifreeze in their blood, that kept them active all winter when other little mammals were hibernating. "They eat grass and multiply all winter," Mrs. Franklin had said in her singsong voice. "When there are too many, they grow nervous at the sight of each other. Somehow this shoots too much antifreeze into their bloodstreams and it begins to poison them. They become restless, then crazy. They run in a frenzy until they die."

Of this phenomenon Miyax's father had simply said, "The hour of the lemming is over for four years."

Unfortunately for Miyax, the hour of the animals that prey on the lemmings was also over. The white fox, the snowy owl, the weasel, the jaeger, and the siskin had virtually disappeared. They had no food to eat and bore few or no young. Those that lived preyed on each other. With the passing of the lemmings, however, the grasses had grown high again and the hour of the caribou was upon the land. Healthy fat caribou cows gave birth to many calves. The caribou population increased, and this in turn increased the number of wolves who prey on the caribou. The abundance of the big deer of the north did Miyax no good, for she had not brought a gun on her trip. It had never occurred to her that she would not reach Point Hope before her food ran out.

A dull pain seized her stomach. She pulled blades of grass from their sheaths and ate the sweet ends. They were not very satisfying, so she picked a handful of caribou moss, a lichen. If the deer could survive in winter on this food, why not she? She munched, decided the plant might taste better if cooked, and went to the pond for water.

As she dipped her pot in, she thought about Amaroq. Why had he bared his teeth at her? Because she was young and he knew she couldn't hurt him? No, she said to herself, it was because he was speaking to her! He had told her to lie down. She had even understood and obeyed him. He had talked to her not with his voice, but with his ears, eyes, and lips; and he had even commended her with a wag of his tail.

She dropped her pot, scrambled up the frost heave and stretched out on her stomach.

"Amaroq," she called softly, "I understand what you said. Can you understand me? I'm hungry—very, very hungry. Please bring me some meat."

The great wolf did not look her way and she began to doubt her reasoning. After all, flattened ears and a tail-wag were scarcely a conversation. She dropped her forehead against the lichens and rethought what had gone between them.

"Then why did I lie down?" she asked, lifting her head and looking at Amaroq. "Why did I?" she called to the yawning wolves. Not one turned her way.

Amaroq got to his feet, and as he slowly arose he seemed to fill the sky and blot out the sun. He was enormous. He could swallow her without even chewing.

"But he won't," she reminded herself. "Wolves do not eat people. That's gussak talk. Kapugen said wolves are gentle brothers."

The black puppy was looking at her and wagging his tail. Hopefully, Miyax held out a pleading hand to him. His tail wagged harder. The mother rushed to him and stood above him sternly. When he licked her cheek apologetically, she pulled back her lips from her fine white teeth. They flashed as she smiled and forgave her cub.

"But don't let it happen again," said Miyax sarcastically, mimicking her own elders. The mother walked toward Amaroq.

"I should call you Martha after my stepmother," Miyax whispered. "But you're much too beautiful. I shall call you Silver instead."

Silver moved in a halo of light, for the sun sparkled on the guard hairs that grew out over the dense underfur and she seemed to glow.

The reprimanded pup snapped at a crane fly and shook himself. Bits of lichen and grass spun off his fur. He reeled unsteadily, took a wider stance, and looked down at his sleeping sister. With a yap he jumped on her and rolled her to her feet. She whined. He barked and picked up a bone. When he was sure she was watching, he ran down the slope with it. The sister tagged after him. He stopped and she grabbed the bone, too. She pulled; he pulled; then he pulled and she yanked.

Miyax could not help laughing. The puppies played with bones like Eskimo children played with leather ropes.

"I understand *that,*" she said to the pups. "That's tug-o-war. Now how do you say, 'I'm hungry'?"

Amaroq was pacing restlessly along the crest of the frost heave as if something were about to happen. His eyes shot to Silver, then to the gray wolf Miyax had named Nails. These glances seemed to be a summons, for Silver and Nails glided to him, spanked the ground with their forepaws and bit him gently under the chin. He wagged his tail furiously and took Silver's slender nose in his mouth. She crouched before him, licked his cheek and lovingly bit his lower jaw. Amaroq's tail flashed high as her mouthing charged him with vitality. He nosed her affectionately. Unlike the fox who met his mate only in the breeding season, Amaroq lived with his mate all year.

Next, Nails took Amaroq's jaw in his mouth and the leader bit the top of his nose. A third adult, a small male, came slinking up. He got down on his belly before Amaroq, rolled trembling to his back, and wriggled.

"Hello, Jello," Miyax whispered, for he reminded her of the quivering gussak dessert her mother-in-law made.

She had seen the wolves mouth Amaroq's chin twice before and so she concluded that it was a ceremony, a sort of "Hail to the Chief." He must indeed be their leader for he was clearly the wealthy wolf; that is, wealthy as she had known the meaning of the word on Nunivak Island. There the old Eskimo hunters she had known in her childhood thought the riches of life were intelligence, fearlessness, and love. A man with these gifts was rich and was a great spirit who was admired in the same way that the gussaks admired a man with money and goods.

The three adults paid tribute to Amaroq until he was almost smothered with love; then he bayed a wild note that sounded like the wind on the frozen sea. With that the others sat around him, the puppies scattered between them. Jello hunched forward and Silver shot a fierce glance at him. Intimidated, Jello pulled his ears together and back. He drew himself down until he looked smaller than ever.

Amaroq wailed again, stretching his neck until his head was high above the others. They gazed at him affectionately and it was plain to see that he was their great spirit, a royal leader who held his group together with love and wisdom.

Any fear Miyax had of the wolves was dispelled by their affection for each other. They were friendly animals and so devoted to Amaroq that she needed only to be accepted by him to be accepted by all. She even knew how to achieve this—bite him under the chin. But how was she going to do that?

She studied the pups hoping they had a simpler way of expressing their love for him. The black puppy approached the leader, sat, then lay down and wagged his tail vigorously. He gazed up at Amaroq in pure adoration, and the royal eyes softened.

Well, that's what I'm doing! Miyax thought. She called to Amaroq. "I'm lying down gazing at you, too, but you don't look at *me* that way!"

When all the puppies were wagging his praises, Amaroq yipped, hit a high note, and crooned. As his voice rose and fell, the other adults sang out and the puppies yipped and bounced.

The song ended abruptly. Amaroq arose and trotted swiftly down the slope. Nails followed, and behind him ran Silver, then Jello. But Jello did not run far. Silver turned and looked him straight in the eye. She pressed her ears forward aggressively and lifted her tail. With that, Jello went back to the puppies and the three sped away like dark birds.

Miyax hunched forward on her elbows, the better to see and learn. She now knew how to be a good puppy, pay tribute to the leader, and even to be a leader by biting others on the top of the nose. She also knew how to tell Jello to baby-sit. If only she had big ears and a tail, she could lecture and talk to them all.

Flapping her hands on her head for ears, she flattened her fingers to make friends, pulled them together and back to express fear, and shot them forward to display her aggression and dominance. Then she folded her arms and studied the puppies again.

The black one greeted Jello by tackling his feet. Another jumped on his tail, and before he could discipline either, all five were upon him. He rolled and tumbled with them for almost an hour; then he ran down the slope, turned, and stopped. The pursuing pups plowed into him, tumbled, fell, and lay still. During a minute of surprised recovery there was no action. Then the black pup flashed his tail like a semaphore signal and they all jumped on Jello again.

Miyax rolled over and laughed aloud. "That's funny. They're really like kids."

When she looked back, Jello's tongue was hanging from his mouth and his sides were heaving. Four of the puppies had collapsed at his feet and were asleep. Jello flopped down, too, but the black pup still looked around. He was not the least bit tired. Miyax watched him, for there was something special about him.

He ran to the top of the den and barked. The smallest pup, whom Miyax called Sister, lifted her head, saw her favorite brother in action and, struggling to her feet, followed him devotedly. While they romped, Jello took the opportunity to rest behind a clump of sedge, a moisture-loving plant of the tundra. But hardly was he settled before a pup tracked him to his hideout and pounced on him. Jello narrowed his eyes, pressed his ears forward, and showed his teeth.

"I know what you're saying," she called to him. "You're saying, 'lie down,' " The puppy lay down, and Miyax got on all fours and looked for the nearest pup to speak to. It was Sister.

"Ummmm," she whined, and when Sister turned around she narrowed her eyes and showed her white teeth. Obediently, Sister lay down.

"I'm talking wolf! I'm talking wolf!" Miyax clapped, and tossing her head like a pup, crawled in a happy circle. As she was coming back she saw all five puppies sitting in a row watching her, their heads cocked in curiosity. Boldly the black pup came toward her, his fat backside swinging as he trotted to the bottom of her frost heave and barked.

"You are *very* fearless and *very* smart," she said. "Now I know why you are special. You are wealthy and the leader of the puppies. There is no doubt what you'll grow up to be. So I shall name you after my father Kapugen, and I shall call you Kapu for short."

Kapu wrinkled his brow and turned an ear to tune in more acutely on her voice.

"You don't understand, do you?"

Hardly had she spoken than his tail went up, hs mouth opened slightly, and he fairly grinned.

"Ee-lie!" she gasped. "You do understand. And that scares me." she perched on her heels. Jello whined an undulating note and Kapu turned back to the den.

Miyax imitated the call to come home. Kapu looked back over his shoulder in surprise. She giggled. He wagged his tail and jumped on Jello.

She clapped her hands and settled down to watch this language of jumps and tumbles, elated that she was at last breaking the wolf code. After a long time she decided they were not talking but roughhousing, and so she started home. Later she changed her mind. Roughhousing was very important to wolves. It occupied almost the entire night for the pups.

"Ee-lie, okay," she said. "I'll learn to roughhouse. Maybe then you'll accept me and feed me." She pranced, jumped, and whimpered; she growled, snarled, and rolled. But nobody came to roughhouse.

Sliding back to her camp, she heard the grass swish and looked up to see Amaroq and his hunters sweep around her frost heave and stop about five feet away. She could smell the sweet scent of their fur.

The hairs on her neck rose and her eyes widened. Amaroq's ears went forward aggressively and she remembered that wide eyes meant fear to him. It was not good to show him she was afraid. Animals attacked the fearful. She tried to narrow them, but remembered that was not right either. Narrowed eyes were mean. In desperation she recalled that Kapu had moved forward when challenged. She pranced right up to Amaroq. Her heart beat furiously as she grunt-whined the sound of the puppy begging adoringly for attention. Then she got down on her belly and gazed at him with fondness.

The great wolf backed up and avoided her eyes. She had said something wrong! Perhaps even offended him. Some slight gesture that meant nothing to her had apparently meant something to the wolf. His ears shot forward angrily and it seemed all was lost. She wanted to get up and run, but she gathered her courage and pranced closer to him. Swiftly she patted him under the chin.

The signal went off. It sped through his body and triggered emotions of love. Amaroq's ears flattened and his tail wagged in friendship. He could not react in any other way to the chin pat, for the roots of this signal lay deep in wolf history. It was inherited from generations and generations of leaders before him. As his eyes softened, the sweet odor of ambrosia arose from the gland on the top of his tail and she was drenched lightly in wolf scent. Miyax was one of the pack.

Biography

SOJOURNER TRUTH: A SELF-MADE WOMAN

Victoria Ortiz

One of the most charismatic of American women was Sojourner Truth, the ex-slave who became a powerful voice in the abolitionist and feminist movements of the nineteenth century (and is a heroine to the feminists of our own day). She fought vigorously her entire life for the rights of her people and for an expansion of human understanding.

I'll Keep You Scratching

After her experience at the Northampton community and her contact with the women and men involved in the abolition movement, Sojourner embarked on one of the campaigns which was to be of fundamental importance to her through her life: the struggle for the liberation of the black people of her country, both from bondage and from ignorance and poverty.

The decade leading up to the Civil War was a period of intense and impassioned activity on the part of all those Americans who believed in the words of the Declaration of Independence: "We hold these truths to be self-evident, that all men are created equal. . . . " The issue of slavery was becoming more and more tinged with violence, and government actions served only to aggravate the conflict between supporters and opponents of abolition. The Fugitive Slave Act of 1793, still on the books, was a virtual guarantee to any slaveholder that an escaped slave who was captured would be promptly and legally returned. As if this were insufficient, in 1850 Congress passed a "Compromise," one section of which was known as the Fugitive Slave Law. This infamous statute not only denied the escaping (or allegedly escaping) slave a trial by jury, but also forbade him or her to testify in court and made it a crime for anyone to assist in the escape. Finally, it included the proviso that it be retroactive and thus apply to most of the slaves who had escaped in the past.

With the passage of this law, hundreds if not thousands of blacks fled to Canada and Europe, knowing that it would make little difference to angry slaveholders and complacent judges if they were fugitives or not. For the kidnapping of freed or freeborn blacks had been a frequent occurrence through the earlier part of the century, and now, with the law so fully

From Victoria Ortiz, *Sojourner Truth: A Self-Made Woman* (Philadelphia: J.B. Lippincott, 1974), Chapter 4.

sanctioning the return of slave to master, it seemed likely that such abductions would increase.

The Fugitive Slave Law led also to increased militancy on the part of black and white abolitionists, who began to see that ending slavery would involve much more than mere speech-making and petitioning. Even respected public figures like Frederick Douglass now realized that violence might be the only feasible recourse in the fight for emancipation. Douglass was once moved by his outrage to declare that he would "welcome the intelligence tomorrow . . . that the slaves had risen in the South, and that the sable arms which had been engaged in beautifying and adorning the South, were engaged in spreading death and devastation."

Another harsh cry of wrath from this passionate man encountered the more pacific but equally fervent stance of Sojourner Truth. One day he spoke of the Fugitive Slave Law to an audience and asserted, "Slavery can only end in blood." In the back of the hall arose that dignified black woman. Ever earnest in her faith, she asked: "Frederick, Frederick, is God dead?"

"We were all for a moment brought to a standstill," recalled Douglass as he recreated the incident many years later, "just as we should have been if someone had thrown a brick through the window."

But indeed it did seem to many that Sojourner's kindly and egalitarian God was, if not dead, then at least absent, for the lot of the black American, enslaved or free, had scarcely improved during the first half of the nineteenth century. On the contrary, many laws and acts and compromises in addition to the Fugitive Slave Law made it less and less likely that the slaves would be freed, and even that the freedmen and women would remain so. The Missouri Compromise of 1820, for example, had given the slaveholding forces the entire Louisiana Purchase territory: Missouri and the region south of its southernmost boundary, as far west as what was then the westernmost frontier of the United States. And the Kansas-Nebraska Act of 1854 extended the territory open to slavery beyond the northern boundaries established in 1820, in effect repealing any of the antislavery segments of the original territorial compromise.

Most distressing of all legal decisions, perhaps because it so directly involved a human being and his survival, was the outcome of the Dred Scott case of 1857. Scott, a slave from Missouri, sued for his freedom when his master traveled with him from his home state into Illinois and Minnesota (both free territories) and then back again to Missouri. Scott argued that, having lived in free territories, he should be considered free, and that, according to the law, a resident in a free territory could not be enslaved. In one of the most lamentable decisions in its history, the Supreme Court ruled that since Scott (and therefore every slave) was not a citizen, he could not institute a court proceeding against another person. It further declared even the limited restrictions of the Missouri Compromise unconstitutional, thereby guaranteeing the absolute right of slaveholders to transport their human property anywhere they wanted at any time. Thus, all the territories were opened to slavery, and slaves were legally declared property with no human or civil rights.

The abolitionists, close to the pulse of

antislavery sentiment in the country and alert to the machinations of the slaveholding lobbyists in Washington, were at all times prepared to escalate their struggle for the end of slavery. The earliest abolition groups, virtually all white, had been fundamentally religious and moderate and had supported a colonization plan which called for the settlement of free black Americans in colonies in Africa. But the new abolitionists were radical and militant; included in their ranks blacks and whites, women and men; and stood for immediate uncompensated emancipation and against colonization.

The new brand of abolitionism, loud and demanding, was born officially in 1833 when the American Anti-Slavery Society was formed in Philadelphia. This society and the scores of others which subsequently sprang up across the country undertook the task of bringing to all the American people arguments against slavery and demands for its abolition. Their efforts were seconded by the hundreds of women and men who spoke ardently to small and large gatherings in halls, churches, and courthouses. The period before the Civil War was also marked by eloquence in the written word, as antislavery journals and newspapers proliferated, and the biographies and autobiographies of ex-slaves became popular reading matter.

This was the atmosphere in the antislavery circle which Sojourner Truth joined wholeheartedly in the 1850s. Beginning with her lecture tours in the company of the British parliamentarian George Thompson, and through the period of her most active speech-making, she visited twenty-two states, covering thousands of miles, often on foot, in order to bring her truth to the people. She told anyone who would listen to her about the wrongs of slavery as she herself had endured them and about the rightness of freedom as she knew it and as her God ordained it. Her memories of slavery served her well in all her public appearances, drawing and holding audiences in rapt silence as the starkness of her words moved and angered them. Her background gave her speech a rough-hewn quality whose sincerity drew respect and admiration from even the most educated of listeners.

Sojourner never allowed herself to be intimidated or put down, rising to every occasion and gracefully withdrawing when she felt it judicious. The same courage she had displayed in Northampton when threatened by the obstreperous young men on the meeting ground was to show itself time and time again as she traveled through New York, New Jersey, Ohio, Indiana, Michigan, and all the other states she visited.

Blending tones of pride and modesty, Sojourner often addressed her audience as "children" and individuals as "honey," showing that affection for all sympathizers which endeared her to so many. And the salty wit already characteristic of her speaking style appeared on many occasions, as observers and listeners from the period recall. She was full of amusing sayings, some of which have survived and have been used by other speakers. On one occasion she began a talk by saying: "Children, I've come here like the rest of you to hear what I have to say," an opening gambit which a distinguished lecturer borrowed from her many years later. She coined her own characteristic aphorisms: instead of telling a dependent person to "stand on his own two feet," for example, Sojourner would urge that "every tub has to sit on its own bottom."

It was not only her humor and sharpness that made Sojourner an effective speaker against slavery, nor merely the fact that she spoke as one who had felt the whip's lash ("And now, when I hear them tell of whipping women on the bare flesh, it makes *my* flesh crawl, and my very hair rise on my head"). What also fast converted her into one of the most popular orators of the time was her ability to appeal to the better sentiments of white people by shaming them or encouraging them or even complimenting them. While Frederick Douglass and Harriet Tubman did the vital job of working with their own people, urging them forward and struggling by their side, Sojourner's role was somewhat different. She was one of the few black people of that period who spoke almost exclusively to whites, individually or in groups, and few blacks worked as closely as she did with the white abolitionists. The number of accounts which demonstrate her talent at subduing racist mobs and destroying racist arguments seem to confirm that she truly knew how to "deal with" white people of all persuasions.

One of her favorite reminiscences involved her "finding Jesus." She spoke of the questioning voice within her that wondered at her love for all creatures: " 'There's the white folks that have abused you, and beat you, and abused your people—think of them.' But then there came another rush of love through my soul, and I cried out loud—'Lord, Lord, I can love *even the white folks!*' " And indeed she could confront white people without rancor or bitterness, fear or timidity.

She must have been conscious of her power over white audiences, and clearly she took seriously her responsibility of convincing them to support her and her comrades in their calls for emancipation. At one meeting in Syracuse, in 1850, the crowd had come to hear George Thompson speak and were angered when Sojourner took the floor first. She quieted them by saying: "I'll tell you what Thompson is going to say to you. He's going to argue that the poor Negroes ought to be out of slavery and in the heavenly state of freedom. But, children, I'm against slavery because I want to keep the white folks who hold slaves from getting sent to hell." Sojourner's basic concerns undoubtedly involved her fellow blacks, but it is a testimony to her perceptiveness that she was able, at a difficult moment, to call forth such an astute statement. The meeting was saved, and the crowd listened to Sojourner and to Thompson with interest.

With Rochester as their headquarters, Thompson, Sojourner, and others traveled through western New York during 1851, speaking to audiences of various kinds. Many of these were unruly mobs whose only purpose was to disrupt the meetings and to fluster and perhaps injure the speakers. At all times, it seems, Sojourner maintained her dignity and never showed any fear before the greater strength and numbers of her opponents.

In 1853 her travels took her to the home of Harriet Beecher Stowe, author of *Uncle Tom's Cabin.* Written originally as a serialized novel and published only with reluctance by a Boston publisher, the book had sold 300,000 copies in the first ten months after publication in the United States, and 150,000 copies in England, bringing sudden and lasting fame to its author. (Lincoln even playfully called Stowe "the little lady who wrote the book that made this great war," referring to the Civil War.) So talked about was the novel, and so highly praised by all the activists in the abolitionist camp—while the proslavery forces were enraged by its revelations—that Sojourner soon heard of it, and became curious about its author. Sojourner finally found Stowe in Andover, Massachusetts, and the novelist has left to posterity a detailed account of their visit together.

Sojourner, arriving with a young grandson of hers, settled into the Stowe household with ease and pleasure, entertaining and surprising the other people gathered there with her singing, her preaching, and her reminiscing. Harriet Beecher Stowe wrote of her: "I do not recollect ever to have been conversant with any one who had more of that silent and subtle power which we call personal presence than this woman." Recalling her poise in that white, middle-class household of educated men and women, professors and preachers of renown, Stowe painted this picture of Sojourner: "She seemed perfectly self-possessed and at her ease; in fact, there was almost an unconscious superiority, not unmixed with a solemn twinkle of humor, in the odd, composed manner in which she looked down at me. Her whole air had at times a gloomy sort of drollery which impressed one strangely." And regretting the human loss occasioned by the enslavement of some human beings by others, she observed near the end of her article: "I cannot but think that Sojourner with the same culture might have spoken words as eloquent and undying as the African St. Augustine or Tertullian. How grand and queenly a woman she might have been, with her wonderful physical vigor, her great heaving sea of emotion, her power of spiritual conception, her quick penetration, and her boundless energy!"

As Sojourner Truth continued to travel, this energy carried her across the country, attacking slavery everywhere she went as inhuman, unchristian, and intolerable. She was understandably not always kind and moderate, and she was quite capable of giving vent to feelings of anger when she thought of what slavery had done. On one occasion she was quoted as declaring: "All the gold in California, all the wealth of this nation could not restore to me that which the white people have wrested from me." Although she claimed to be able to love the white people and to pity the slaveholder more than the slave, and even though her closest associates were white, Sojourner remained a spokeswoman for her people, never diluting her criticism of and opposition to the white society which had enslaved her and her fellow blacks. And this firm commitment to freedom and equality carried her over all those miles, bearing with her a white satin banner emblazoned with the words, "Proclaim liberty throughout all the land unto all the inhabitants thereof."

Her staunch belief in her truth enabled her to find retorts and answers when hostile listeners challenged her. Once in Ashtabula, Ohio, in 1855, she was sharing the podium with Parker Pillsbury, who had been sternly criticizing the church in America for its role in supporting the institution of slavery. He was then attacked by a young man in the audience who declared that blacks were closer to the animal kingdom than whites and thus were only useful as slaves. As a thunderstorm broke loudly outside, he went on to say that God was punishing Pillsbury and his adherents for the sacrilegious things he had said. Then Sojourner stood, and Pillsbury reports: "She seemed almost to come up out of the deep darkness or out of the ground. There she stood before us as a vision. Her tall, erect form, dressed in dark green, a white handkerchief crossed over her breast, a white turban on her head . . . a spectacle weird and fearful as an avenger—doubtless to the young man more dreadful than the thunderstorm. . . ."

Sojourner turned to the man who had derided Pillsbury and said in her deep, calm voice: "When I was a slave away down there in New York, and there was some particularly bad work to be done, some colored woman was sure to be called on to do it. And when I heard that man talking away there as he did, almost a whole hour, I said to myself, here's one spot of work sure that's just fit for colored folks to clean up after." Then, after reminding her listeners that she was proud of being pure African in her descent, without a drop of white blood in her, she remarked that the young man should not fear that the storm was God's wrath: "Child, don't be scared; you are not going to be harmed. I don't expect God's ever heard tell of you."

Whatever the rhetorical circumstances, Sojourner had an extraordinary talent for bringing the talk back to slavery. How, she wondered, could those with the power and the opportunity to speak and be heard, talk of anything other than that burning issue while families were still being separated, children being sold away from their mothers? On one occasion, when a religious speaker had been extolling the virtues of family love, Sojourner rose majestically, tears streaking her face. Speaking metaphorically rather than literally, she cried out: "We have heard a great deal about love at home in the family. Now, children, I was a slave, and my husband and my child were sold from me. . . . Now, husband and child are *all* gone, and what has become of the affection I had for them? *That is the question before the house!*"

She saw herself, then, as a sort of reminder or conscience for those who would wander away from what mattered. As long as she could keep the issue alive, keep people's minds on it, she was doing her job. When a northern Ohio man said rudely to her one day, following a meeting, "Old woman, do you think that your talk about slavery does any good? Why, I don't care any more for your talk than I do for the bite of a flea," Sojourner answered with tremendous conciseness and not a little salt: "Perhaps not, but the Lord willing, I'll keep you scratching." And that was what she did. She made people uncomfortable unless they were tackling the problem of slavery and its abolition.

Once she heard someone praise the Constitution and its provisions for equality and justice for all. Sojourner compared that document to the insect-infested wheat of the fields: "Now I hear talk about the Constitution and the rights of man. I come up and I take hold of this Constitution. It looks mighty big. And I feel for my rights. But they aren't there. Then I say, 'God, what ails this Constitution?' And you know what He says to me? God says, 'Sojourner, there's a little weevil in it.' "

In praising as well as in attacking, her remarks were to the point and could be touching or devastating. When a lawyer in the audience at a meeting stood and ranted about the blacks being nothing more than apes and baboons, Sojourner managed to bring the audience's scorn upon him when she replied: "Children, I am one of those monkey tribes. . . . I am going to reply to this creature. Now in the course of my time I have done a great deal of dirty scullion work, but of all the dirty work I ever done, this is the scullionest and the dirtiest. Now, children, don't you pity me?"

She also spoke gently at times, as when she addressed the Children's Mass Meeting at the Methodist Church, during the Annual State Sabbath School Convention in 1863. Facing the young, all-white audience, she said: "Children, who made your skin white? Was it not God? Who made mine black? Was it not the same God? Now, children, remember what Sojourner Truth has told you and thus get rid of your prejudice and learn to love colored children, that you may be all the children of your Father in Heaven. . . . " Her words often succeeded in dissipating the remnants of prejudice and hatred which might have existed at the meeting she was addressing. "She produced a singular effect upon the audience," wrote a New Yorker in 1868, "melting away the prejudice of color and creed. We have seldom witnessed more marked results upon the Soul of an audience. . . . "

Throughout the articles reporting Sojourner's "lectures" and other activities in support of abolition, references are often made to her encounters with "Negro-haters" and "mobocrats," loud-voiced, insolent opponents of black freedom who tried over and over again to disrupt her meetings and drown out her truths. Some of these clashes are described by eyewitnesses, others merely alluded to. Perhaps the most gripping series of confrontations took place in Indiana, where she traveled in the company of the abolitionist Josephine Griffing.

Indiana was a border state, which was at the time undecided on the slavery issue; but clearly the proslavery Democrats were in the majority where lawmaking was concerned, for there were statutes making it illegal for blacks to enter the state and others forbidding white people to entertain blacks in their homes. When it was known that Sojourner Truth, the noted lecturer and outspoken opponent of slavery, a black woman, was coming to speak, mobs formed and crowds gathered, attempting to stop her meetings from being held. On one such occasion, there were threats to burn down the hall in which she was scheduled to speak; hearing this, Sojourner loudly declared that she would speak on the ashes if necessary.

Sojourner and her friends were arrested several times: she for entering and remaining in the state, they for welcoming her into their homes. In each case she managed to outwit the authorities or simply to shame them into releasing her. At one point Union soldiers had to protect her from arrest by the local police; another time the prosecution lawyers, drunk when they entered the courtroom, took one look at the crowd of influential friends surrounding Sojourner, and left again, to be seen entering the tavern across the street!

Sojourner's meetings in Indiana were loudly and insultingly disrupted by shouts of: "Down with you! We think the niggers have done enough! We will not hear you speak! Stop your mouth!" The situation became so fraught with danger that for one meeting Sojourner's friends decided to outfit her in military regalia in order to put the fear of God into her enemies. As she later recalled it, "The ladies thought I should be dressed in uniform as well as the captain of the home guard. So they put upon me a red, white, and blue shawl, a sash and apron to match, a cap on my head with a star in front, and a star on each shoulder. When I was dressed I looked in the glass and was fairly frightened. Said I, 'It seems I am going to battle.' My friends advised me to take a sword or pistol. I replied, 'I carry no weapon; the Lord will preserve me without weapons. I feel safe even in the midst of my enemies; for the truth is powerful and will prevail.' "

Thus dressed, she was taken to the meeting in a carriage, surrounded by armed soldiers. The mob that was gathered around the courthouse, where she was to speak, stood firm at first, but upon seeing the crowd of supporters following Sojourner's carriage, they rapidly dispersed, "looking like a flock of frightened crows, and not one was left but a small boy, who sat upon the fence, crying, 'Nigger, nigger!' " The meeting proceeded as planned, and this time without interruption.

One of her most revealing confrontations also occurred in Indiana and was reported to William Lloyd Garrison by an abolitionist friend who had witnessed it. Wishing to find some means of discrediting Sojourner before she spoke, Democrats in Silver Lake circulated a rumor that she was in fact a man in disguise, a Republican spy sent by the antislavery people to spread dissension in the community. The third meeting she held there, in the hall of a sect called the United Brethren, was attended by a large proslavery crowd led by a Dr. T. W. Strain. At the end of the meeting, this man stood up and asked for silence. He declared that the majority of the people present believed the speaker was a man and felt it just that she allow several women from the crowd to examine her breasts in order to confirm or deny this belief.

In the midst of the tumult that ensued, Sojourner arose and asked above the noise why it was they suspected such a thing. "Your voice is not the voice of a woman, it is the voice of a man, and we believe you are a man," was the answer. Dr. Strain called for a vote to determine whether or not Sojourner was a man, and the ayes won!

The climax of this scene is best described by the eyewitness: "Sojourner told them that her breasts had suckled many a white babe, to the exclusion of her own offspring; that some of those white babies had grown to man's estate; that, although they had sucked her colored breasts, they were, in her estimation, far more manly than they (her persecutors) appeared to be; and she quietly asked them as she disrobed her bosom, if they, too, wished to suck!"

This, then, was the lecturer against slavery, the statuesque, dark, rich-voiced woman who traveled far and wide to spread the truth about slavery and the call for freedom. She was fearless in the face of danger, biting in her wit, sharp in her attacks, pointed in her arguments; tender when necessary, but never weak. As she promised the man who questioned her relevance, she kept the nation scratching at a time when too many people were silent in the presence of the unspeakable wrongs of slavery. Sojourner Truth also joined the ranks of her white sisters in another fight for human justice, when she saw the undeniable link between black rights and women's rights.

Poetry

MARCHING SONG

Robert Louis Stevenson

When children are small, their sex-role differentiation is less distinct than it becomes in adolescence, as this poem shows.

Bring the comb and play upon it!
  Marching, here we come!
Willie cocks his highland bonnet,
  Johnnie beats the drum.

Mary Jane commands the party,
  Peter leads the rear;
Feet in time, alert and hearty,
  Each a Grenadier!

All in the most martial manner
  Marching double-quick;
While the napkin, like a banner,
  Waves upon the stick!

Here's enough of fame and pillage,
  Great commander Jane!
Now that we've been round the village,
  Let's go home again.

A CERTAIN AGE

Phyllis McGinley

This poem represents poignantly the sharp curbing of energies that adolescence has traditionally represented for the girl-child. The poem already feels somewhat dated, since social changes have moved us away from the reality it depicts.

All of a sudden, bicycles are toys,
Not locomotion. Bicycles are for boys
And seventh-graders, screaming when
    they talk.
A girl would rather
Take vows, go hungry, put on last year's
    frock,
Or dance with her own father
Than pedal down the block.

This side of childhood lies a narrow
    land,
Its laws unwritten, altering out of hand,
But, more than Sparta's, savagely severe.
Common or gentry,
The same taboos prevail. One learns, by
    ear,
The customs of the country
Or pays her forfeit here.

No bicycles. No outcast dungarees
Over this season's round and scarless
    knees,
No soft departures from the veering
    norm.
But the same bangle,
Marked with a nickname, now from
    every arm
Identically must dangle,
The speech be uniform—

Uniform as the baubles round the
    throat,
The ill-made wish, the stiffened
    petticoat,
And beauty, blurred but burning in the
    face.
Now, scrubbed and scented.
They move together toward some
    meeting place,
Wearing a regimented,
Unutterable grace.

They travel rapt, each compass pointing
    south—
Heels to the shoes and lipstick on the
    mouth.

MY DOG IS A PLUMBER

Dan Greenburg

This rhyme which appeared originally in Free to Be . . . You and Me *(1974) is written from the point of view of a child grappling with the problems of shifting sex roles.*

My dog is a plumber, he must be a boy.
Although I must tell you his favorite toy
Is a little play stove with pans and with pots
Which he really must like, 'cause he plays with it lots.
So perhaps he's a girl, which kind of makes sense,
Since he can't throw a ball and he can't climb a fence.
But neither can Dad, and I know *he's* a man,
And Mom is a woman, and *she* drives a van.
Maybe the problem is in trying to tell
Just what someone is by what he does well.

Essays

Feminists and Fairy Tales: A Controversy

With the emergence in the 1960s of "the new wave" of feminists, traditional child-rearing practices of all kinds have come under scrutiny, including that of reading fairy tales to children. Feminists and some parents have objected to having their little girls identifying with such female characters as Snow White, Sleeping Beauty, or Cinderella. It is certainly true that fairy tales present many examples of passive, docile females in obviously sex-stereotyped roles and that there is a real danger that girl children will identify with them (and boy children will be negatively impressed with this view of women). But it is also true, as Alison Lurie points out below, that strong women characters are to be found in some tales.

The major points of this important controversy are presented below, both pro and con. In considering the points of the argument, one might also ask the crucial question: Do little girls identify only with female characters and boys with males, or is cross-identification a normal occurrence in the imagination? For a psychologist's opinion, see Bruno Bettelheim's article in "Afterword" ("Vicarious Satisfaction versus Conscious Recognition"), in which Bettelheim argues that although a child cannot identify with a character of the opposite sex on first hearing of a fairy tale, greater familiarity with the story permits identification with characters of the opposite gender. Ultimately this controversy may be a matter of the narrowness or breadth of one's imagination. The best solution would seem to be for children to be encouraged to broaden their own personal horizons through identification with characters of both sexes.

FAIRY TALE LIBERATION

Alison Lurie

Alison Lurie is a novelist and critic. She has a special interest in children's literature, which she teaches at Cornell University.

When I was small it was believed in high-minded progressive circles that fairy tales were unsuitable for children. "Does not Cinderella interject a social and economic situation which is both confusing and vicious? . . . Does not 'Jack and the Beanstalk' delay a child's rationalizing of the world and leave him longer than is desirable without the beginnings of scientific standards?" as one child education expert, Lucy Sprague Mitchell, put it in the Foreword to her *Here and Now Story Book,* which I received for my fifth birthday. It would be much better, she and her colleagues thought, for children to read simple, pleasant, realistic stories which would help to prepare us for the adult world.

Mrs. Mitchell's own contribution to literature was a squat volume, sunny orange in color, with an idealized city scene on the cover. Inside I could read about The Grocery Man ("This is John's Mother. Good Morning, Mr. Grocery Man") and How Spot Found a Home. The children and parents in these stories were exactly like the ones I knew, only more boring. They never did anything really wrong, and nothing dangerous or surprising ever happened to them—no more than it did to Dick and Jane, whom I and my friends were soon to meet in first grade.

New York Review of Books, December 17, 1970, pp. 42 ff.

After we grew up, of course, we found out how unrealistic these stories had been. The simple, pleasant adult society they had prepared us for did not exist. The fairy tales had been right all along—the world was full of hostile, stupid giants and perilous castles and people who abandoned their children in the nearest forest. To succeed in this world you needed some special skill or patronage, plus remarkable luck; and it didn't hurt to be very good-looking. The other qualities that counted were wit, boldness, stubborn persistence, and an eye for the main chance. Kindness to those in trouble was also advisable—you never knew who might be useful to you later on.

The fairy tales were also way ahead of Mrs. Mitchell with respect to women's liberation. In her stories men drove wagons and engines and boats, built houses, worked in stores, and ran factories; women did nothing except look after children and go shopping. The traditional folk tale, on the other hand, is one of the few sorts of classic children's literature of which a radical feminist would approve. Most of these stories are in the literal sense old wives' tales. Throughout Europe (except in Ireland) the storytellers from whom the Grimm Brothers and their followers heard them were most often women; in some areas, they were all women.

Quite logically, writers like Robert

Graves have seen in many familiar fairy tales survivials of an older matriarchal culture and faith. These stories suggest a society in which women are as competent and active as men, at every age and in every class. Gretel, not Hansel, defeats the Witch; and for every clever youngest son there is a youngest daughter equally resourceful. The contrast is greatest in maturity, where women are often more powerful than men. Real help for the hero or heroine comes most frequently from a fairy godmother or wise woman; and real trouble from a witch or wicked stepmother. With a frequency which recalls current feminist polemics, the significant older male figures are either dumb, male-chauvinist giants or malevolent little dwarfs.

To prepare children for women's liberation, therefore, and to protect them against Future Shock, you had better buy at least one collection of fairy tales. . . .

WITCHES AND FAIRIES: FITZGERALD TO UPDIKE

Alison Lurie

I have been thinking lately about the underground connections between fairy tales and modern fiction—between one of the oldest forms of literature and one of the most recent (or, between the first stories that were read or told to us and the novels we read now). What is striking is how often the stock situations and stock characters, especially the female characters, of the fairy tale keep reappearing. They do not appear only in novels, of course. They turn up in films, plays, poetry, comic strips, advertisements, and dreams—and also in real life, which as usual imitates art.

A friend whose parents were divorced when he was eight tells me that on his first paper route he would imagine himself the poor widow's son going out into the world to seek his fortune; and I had a similar experience. I remember those old tales very well, especially the beginnings: "Once upon a time there was a poor woodcutter who had two daughters. The older was ill-tempered, spiteful, and plain; but the younger one was gentle, kind, and pretty. Her name was. . . . " I didn't have to read what her name was; I knew already: it was Jennifer Lurie. My baby sister, who everybody said was as good as she was beautiful, would grow up to marry the prince, while I would be lucky if I didn't end up being rolled downhill in a barrel full of nails.

Some women's liberationists have attacked fairy tales as a male chauvinist form of literature: they feel that giving children stories like "Cinderella" and "Snow White" is a sort of brainwashing, intended to convince them that all little girls must be gentle, obedient, passive, and domestic while they wait for their prince to come.

It is true that some of the tales we know best, those that have been popularized by Disney, have this sort of heroine. But from the point of view of European folklore they are a very unrepresentative selection. They reflect the taste of the refined literary men who edited the first popular collections of fairy tales for children during the Victorian era. Andrew

New York Review of Books, December 2, 1971, pp. 6 ff.

Lang, for instance, chose the tales in his *Blue Fairy Book* (first published in 1889) from among literally thousands known to him as a folklorist; and he chose them—as he explained in the preface to one of his later volumes—partly for their moral lesson. Folk tales recorded in the field by scholars are full of everything Lang leaves out: sex, death, low humor, and female initiative.

In other more recent collections of tales—as well as in Lang's later collections—there are more active heroines. They travel to the world's end, cross oceans on a wild goose's back, climb mountains of glass, enter giants' castles and steal magic objects, outwit false suitors, and defeat all kinds of supernatural enemies. They work for years to release their lovers or relatives from enchantments, and help them to escape from witches and ogres. They are in effect liberated women, who have courage, intelligence, resourcefulness, endurance, and kind hearts.

But even in the favorite fairy tales of the Victorians it is only young girls who are passive and helpless. In the older generation, women often have more power and are more active than men. Is this because folk tales represent survivals of the myths and customs of a matriarchal society, because they are metaphoric statements of the world of the very young child in which Mommy is more important than Daddy, or because they have been traditionally told mostly by women? If you look at fairy-tale themes and characters in modern fiction, you can make out a good case for any one of these explanations. . . .

A REVIEW OF *WOMENFOLK AND FAIRY TALES**

Susan Cooper

Susan Cooper is a writer of books for children. Her books include The Dark Is Rising, *a Newberry honor book in 1974.*

Oh dear, oh dear. . . . The stories, you must understand, are fine. No one could quarrel with an anthology which draws on Andrew Lang and Lafcadio Hearn, Walter de la Mare and the Brothers Grimm. If you want an agreeable collection of fairy tales, you could do a lot worse than this one. It's the motive behind the collecting that seriously bothers me.

That uncomfortable title is soon explained, "Many of us," writes the editor, Rosemary Minard, "are also concerned today that *Woman* be recognized as a full-fledged member of the human race. In the past she has not often been accepted as such, and her role in traditional literature reflects her second-rate position." So here's her prescription: a book of stories with heroines instead of heroes. Little Jane can identify with them; little John can admire.

It's a false premise: an adult neurosis foisted upon children. I don't believe little Jane gives a damn that Jack the Giant Killer is a boy. Lost in the story, she identifies

New York Times Book Review, April 13, 1975, p. 8.

* Edited by Rosemary Minard. Illustrated by Suzanna Klein. 163 pp. Boston: Houghton Mifflin Company. $5.95 (ages 9 to 13).

with him as a *character,* just as little John shares Red Riding Hood's terror of the wolf without reflecting that, of course, she's only a girl. Response to fairy tale, as to all myth, is subconscious, unrelated to such superficial elements. We are all mixtures of male and female; reading stories isn't going to change that.

An anthology based on a feminist approach is fettered by self-consciousness. Clever Grethel, Molly Whipple, Cap o' Rushes are a bright bunch indeed, but their editor has to acknowledge, with regret, a certain distressing sameness in the happy endings of some of their sisters. "Ali Baba was so grateful to Morgiana for thus saving his life that he offered her in marriage to his son, who readily consented."

The bouncier heroines are those who have survived matrimony without eclipse, like the African Unanana swallowed by an elephant and coolly hacking him to death from the inside, or the Three Strong Women from Japan who first flatten and then train a wrestler like a sort of pet. But the three Chinese Red Riding Hoods, though undoubtedly stronger females than the traditional helpless grandchild, have ironically become so only by resembling the Three Little Pigs—who are, alas, male.

I don't mean to knock Rosemary Minard; she isn't a fierce militant lady. Not that I have anything against militant ladies; I'm as ardent for equal pay and opportunity as they are, even if I do believe firmly that Ms. stands for Manuscript, and that "chairperson" is the worst semantic abomination since "nitery." I want only to implore the begetters of books like this not to try so hard. The identification problem burns not in traditional literature, but all around us; 10 television commercials can do more to damage your daughters' image of Woman than 10 centuries of fairy tales.

"SOME DAY MY PRINCE WILL COME": FEMALE ACCULTURATION THROUGH THE FAIRY TALE

Marcia R. Lieberman

A writer and critic, Marcia Lieberman has most recently been a visiting scholar at the College of Letters, Wesleyan University.

In a review of children's stories for a Christmas issue of *The New York Review of Books,* Alison Lurie praised traditional fairy and folk tales as

> one of the few sorts of classic children's literature of which a radical feminist would aprrove. . . . These stories suggest a society in which women are as competent and active as men, at every age and in every class. Gretel, not Hansel, defeats the Witch; and for every clever youngest son there is a youngest daughter equally resourceful. The contrast is greatest in maturity, where women are often more powerful than men. Real help for the hero or heroine comes most frequently from a fairy

College English, December 1972, pp. 383–395.

> godmother or wise woman, and real trouble from a witch or wicked stepmother. . . . To prepare children for women's liberation, therefore, and to protect them against Future Shock, you had better buy at least one collection of fairy tales. . . . [1]

Radical feminists, apparently, bought neither Ms. Lurie's ideas nor the collections of fairy tales. It is hard to see how children could be "prepared" for women's liberation by reading fairy tales; an analysis of those fairy tales that children actually read indicates instead that they serve to acculturate women to traditional social roles.

Ms. Lurie has now repeated her argument in a recent article, in which she objects to the opinion that feminists actually have of such stories as "Cinderella" and "Snow White":

> It is true that some of the tales we know best, those that have been popularized by Disney, have this sort of heroine. But from the point of view of European folklore they are a very unrepresentative selection. They reflect the taste of the refined literary men who edited the first popular collections of fairy tales for children during the Victorian era. Andrew Lang, for instance, chose the tales in his *Blue Fairy Book* (first published in 1889) from among literally thousands known to him as a folklorist; and he chose them . . . partly for their moral lesson. Folk tales recorded in the field by scholars are full of everything Lang leaves out: sex, death, low humor, and female initiative.
>
> In the other more recent collections of tales—as well as in Lang's later collections—there are more active heroines. . . . [2]

No one would disagree with Ms. Lurie that Andrew Lang was very selective in choosing his tales, but to a feminist who wishes to understand the acculturation of women, this is beside the point. Only the best-known stories, those that everyone has read or heard, indeed, those that Disney has popularized, have affected masses of children in our culture. Cinderella, the Sleeping Beauty, and Snow White are mythic figures who have replaced the old Greek and Norse gods, goddesses, and heroes for most children. The "folk tales recorded in the field by scholars," to which Ms. Lurie refers, or even Andrew Lang's later collections, are so relatively unknown that they cannot seriously be considered in a study of the meaning of fairy tales to women.

In this light, *The Blue Fairy Book* is a very fruitful book to analyze, for it contains many of the most famous stories, and has perhaps been the best-known and hence most influential collection of tales. It was compiled by Andrew Lang and first published by Longman's, Green and Co. in London in 1889. It was followed by *The Red Fairy Book,* and then the *Green,* and then by many others, the *Yellow,* the *Brown,* the *Rose,* the *Violet,* etc. In the preface to *The Green Fairy Book,* in 1892, Lang noted that the stories were made not only to amuse children, but also to teach them. He pointed out that many of the stories have a moral, although, he wrote, "we think more as we read them of the diversion than of the lesson."[3] The distinction that Lang drew between diversions and lessons is misleading, for children do not categorize their reading as diverting or instructive, but as interesting or boring. If we are concerned, then, about what our children are being taught, we must pay particular attention to those stories that are so beguiling that children think more as they read them "of the diversion than of the lesson"; perhaps literature is suggestive in direct proportion to its ability to divert. We know that children are socialized or culturally conditioned by movies, television programs, and the stories they read or hear, and we have begun to wonder at the influence that children's stories and entertainments had upon us, though

[1]Alison Lurie, "Fairy Tale Liberation," *The New York Review of Books,* December 17, 1970, p. 42.

[2]Lurie, "Witches and Fairies: Fitzgerald to Updike," *The New York Review of Books,* December 2, 1971, p. 6.

[3]Andrew Lang, ed., *The Green Fairy Book* (New York: McGraw-Hill, 1966), pp. ix-xi.

we cannot now measure the extent of that influence.

Generations of children have read the popular fairy books, and in doing so may have absorbed far more from them than merely the outlines of the various stories. What is the precise effect that the story of "Snow-White and the Seven Dwarfs" has upon a child? Not only do children find out what happens to the various princes and princesses, wood-cutters, witches, and children of their favorite tales, but they also learn behavioral and associational patterns, value systems, and how to predict the consequences of specific act or circumstances. Among other things, these tales present a picture of sexual roles, behavior, and psychology, and a way of predicting outcome or fate according to sex, which is important because of the intense interest that children take in "endings"; they always want to know how things will "turn out." A close examination of the treatment of girls and women in fairy tales reveals certain patterns which are keenly interesting not only in themselves, but also as material which has undoubtedly played a major contribution in forming the sexual role concept of children, and in suggesting to them the limitations that are imposed by sex upon a person's chances of success in various endeavors. It is now being questioned whether those traits that have been characterized as feminine have a biological or a cultural basis: discarding the assumptions of the past, we are asking what is inherent in our nature, and what has become ours through the gentle but forcible process of acculturation. Many feminists accept nothing as a "given" about the nature of female personality; nearly all the work on that vast subject is yet to be done. In considering the possibility that gender has a cultural character and origin we need to examine the primary channels of acculturation. Millions of women must surely have formed their psycho-sexual self-concepts, and their ideas of what they could or could not accomplish, what sort of behavior would be rewarded, and of the nature of reward itself, in part from their favorite fairy tales. These stories have been made the repositories of the dreams, hopes, and fantasies of generations of girls. An analysis of the women in *The Blue Fairy Book* presents a picture that does not accord with Ms. Lurie's hypothesis.

Certain premises and patterns emerge at once, of which only the stereotyped figure of the wicked step-mother has received much general notice. The beauty contest is a constant and primary device in many of the stories. Where there are several daughters in a family, or several unrelated girls in a story, the prettiest is invariably singled out and designated for reward, or first for punishment and later for reward. Beautiful girls are never ignored; they may be oppressed at first by wicked figures, as the jealous Queen persecutes Snow-White, but ultimately they are chosen for reward. Two fundamental conventions are associated here: the special destiny of the youngest child when there are several children in a family (this holds true for youngest brothers as well as for youngest sisters, as long as the siblings are of the same sex), and the focus on beauty as a girl's most valuable asset, perhaps her only valuable asset. Good-temper and meekness are so regularly associated with beauty, and ill-temper with ugliness, that this in itself must influence children's expectations. The most famous example of this associational pattern occurs in "Cinderella," with the opposition of the ugly, cruel, bad-tempered older sisters to the younger, beautiful, sweet Cinderella, but in *The Blue Fairy Book* it also occurs in many other stories, such as "Beauty and the Beast" and "Toads and Diamonds." Even when there is no series of sisters (in "Snow-White and Rose-Red" both girls are beautiful and sweet) the beautiful single daughter is nearly always noted for her docility, gentleness, and good temper.

This pattern, and the concomitant one of reward distribution, probably acts to promote jealousy and divisiveness among girls. The stories reflect an intensely competitive spirit: they are frequently about contests, for which there can be only one winner because there is only one prize. Girls win the prize if they are the fairest of them all; boys win if they are bold, active, and lucky. If a child identifies with the beauty, she may learn to be suspicious of ugly girls, who are portrayed as cruel, sly, and unscrupulous in these stories; if she identifies with the plain girls, she may learn to be suspicious and jealous of pretty girls, beauty being a gift of fate, not something that can be attained. There are no examples of a crossed-pattern, that is, of plain but good-tempered girls. It is a psychological truth that as children, and as women, girls fear homeliness (even attractive girls are frequently convinced that they are plain), and this fear is a major source of anxiety, diffidence, and convictions of inadequacy and inferiority among women. It is probably also a source of envy and discord among them. Girls may be predisposed to imagine that there is a link between the lovable face and the lovable character, and to fear, if plain themselves, that they will also prove to be unpleasant, thus using the patterns to set up self-fulfilling prophecies.

The immediate and predictable result of being beautiful is being chosen, this word having profound importance to a girl. The beautiful girls does not have to *do* anything to merit being chosen; she does not have to show pluck, resourcefulness, or wit; she is chosen because she is beautiful. Prince Hyacinth chooses the Dear Little Princess for his bride from among the portraits of many princesses that are shown to him because she is the prettiest; the bear chooses the beautiful youngest daughter in "East of the Sun & West of the Moon"; at least twenty kings compete to win Bellissima in "The Yellow Dwarf"; the prince who penetrates the jungle of thorns and briars to find the Sleeping Beauty does so because he had heard about her loveliness; Cinderella instantly captivates her prince during a ball that amounts to a beauty contest; the old king in "The White Cat" says he will designate as his heir whichever of his sons brings home the loveliest princess, thereby creating a beauty contest as a hurdle to inheriting his crown; the prince in "The Water-Lily or The Gold Spinners" rescues and marries the youngest and fairest of the three enslaved maidens; the King falls in love with Goldilocks because of her beauty; the enchanted sheep dies for love of the beautiful Miranda in "The Wonderful Sheep"; Prince Darling pursues Celia because she is beautiful; the young king in "Trusty John" demands the Princess of the Golden Roof for her beauty, and so on. This is a principal factor contributing to the passivity of most of the females in these stories (even those few heroines who are given some sort of active role are usually passive in another part of the story). Since the heroines are chosen for their beauty *(en soi),* not for anything they do *(pour soi),* they seem to exist passively until they are seen by the hero, or described to him. They wait, are chosen, and are rewarded.

Marriage is the fulcrum and major event of nearly every fairy tale; it is the reward for girls, or sometimes their punishment. (This is almost equally true for boys, although the boy who wins the hand of the princess gets power as well as a pretty wife, because the princess is often part of a package deal including half or all of a kingdom.) While it would be futile and anachronistic to suppose that these tales could or should have depicted alternate options or rewards for heroines or heroes, we must still observe that marriage dominates them, and note what they show as leading to marriage, and as resulting from it. Poor boys play an active role in winning kingdoms and princesses; Espen Cinderlad, the despised and youngest of the three brothers in so many Norwegian folk tales, wins the Princess on the Glass Hill by riding up a veritable hill of glass. Poor girls are chosen by princes because they have been seen by them.

Marriage is associated with getting rich: it will be seen that the reward basis in fairy and folk tales is overwhelmingly mercenary. Good, poor, and pretty girls always win rich and handsome princes, never merely handsome, good, but poor men. (If the heroine or hero is already rich, she or he may marry someone of equal rank and wealth, as in "The White Cat," "Trusty John," "The Sleeping Beauty," etc.; if poor, she or he marries someone richer.) Since girls are chosen for their beauty, it is easy for a child to infer that beauty leads to wealth, that being chosen means getting rich. Beauty has an obviously commercial advantage even in stories in which marriage appears to be a punishment rather than a reward: "Bluebeard," in which the suitor is wealthy though ugly, and the stories in which a girl is wooed by a beast, such as "Beauty and the Beast," "East of the Sun & West of the Moon," and "The Black Bull of Norroway."

The bear in "East of the Sun & West of the Moon" promises to enrich the whole family of a poor husbandman if they will give him the beautiful youngest daughter. Although the girl at first refuses to go, her beauty is seen as the family's sole asset, and she is sold, like a commodity, to the bear (the family does not know that he is a prince under an enchantment). "Beauty and the Beast" is similar to this part of "East of the Sun," and the Snow-White of "Snow-White and Rose-Red" also becomes rich upon marrying an enchanted prince who had been a bear.[4] Cinderella may be the best-known story of this type.

Apart from the princesses who are served out as prizes in competitions (to the lad who can ride up a glass hill, or slay a giant, or answer three riddles, or bring back some rarity), won by lucky fellows like Espen Cinderlad, a few girls in *The Blue Fairy Book* find themselves chosen as brides for mercantile reasons, such as the girl in "Toads and Diamonds" who was rewarded by a fairy so that flowers and jewels dropped from her mouth whenever she spoke. In "Rumpelstiltzkin," the little dwarf helps the poor miller's daughter to spin straw into gold for three successive nights, so that the King thinks to himself, " 'She's only a miller's daughter, it's true . . . but I couldn't find a richer wife if I were to search the whole world over,' " consequently making her his queen.[5] The system of rewards in fairy tales, then, equates these three factors: being beautiful, being chosen, and getting rich.

Alison Lurie suggests that perhaps fairy tales are the first real women's literature, that they are literally old wives' tales: "throughout Europe . . . the storytellers from whom the Grimm Brothers and their followers heard them were most often women; in some areas they were all women."[6] She wonders if the stories do not reflect a matriarchal society in which women held power, and she mentions Gretel as an example of an active, resourceful young heroine (I will set aside the problem of the power of older women for the moment). An examination of the best-known stories shows that active resourceful girls are in fact rare; most of the heroines are passive, submissive, and helpless. In the story of "Hansel and Gretel" it is true that Gretel pushes the witch into the oven; Hansel is locked up in the stable, where the witch has been fattening him. At the beginning of the story, however, when the children overhear their parents' plan to lose them in the forest, we read that "Gretel wept bitterly and spoke to Hansel: 'Now it's all up with us.' 'No, no, Gretel,' said Hansel, 'don't fret yourself, I'll be able to find a way of escape, no fear.' " (p. 251) It is Hansel who devises the plan of gathering pebbles and dropping them on the path as they are led into the forest. "Later, in the dark forest, Gretel began to cry, and said: 'How are we ever to get out of the wood?' But Hansel comforted her. 'Wait a bit,' he said, 'till the moon is up, and then we'll find our way sure enough.' And when the full moon had risen he took his sister by the hand and followed the pebbles, which shone like

[4]In these stories, the girl who marries a beast must agree to accept and love a beast as a husband; the girl must give herself to a beast in order to get a man. When she is willing to do this, he can shed his frightening, rough appearance and show his gentler form, demonstrating the softening agency of women (as in the story of Jane Eyre and Mr. Rochester). These heroines have an agentive role, insofar as they are responsible for the literal reformation of the male.

[5]Lang, ed., *The Blue Fairy Book* (New York: McGraw-Hill, 1966), p. 98. All quotations are from this edition.

[6]Lurie, "Fairy Tale Liberation."

new threepenny bits, and showed them the path." (p. 252)

After they get home, they overhear their parents scheming to lose them again. Gretel weeps again, and again Hansel consoles her. Gretel does perform the decisive action at the end, but for the first half of the story she is the frightened little sister, looking to her brother for comfort and help.

Even so, Gretel is one of the most active of the girls, but her company is small. The heroines of the very similar "East of the Sun" and "The Black Bull of Norroway" are initially passive, but then undertake difficult quests when they lose their men. The heroine of "East of the Sun" succumbs to curiosity (the common trap for women: this story is derived from the myth of Cupid and Psyche), and attempts to look at her bear-lover during the night, and the second heroine forgets to remain motionless while her bull-lover fights with the devil (good girls sit still). The lovers disappear when their commands are broken. The girls travel to the ends of the earth seeking them, but they cannot make themselves seen or recognized by their men until the last moment. The Master-maid, in a story whose conclusion resembles these other two, is concealed in a back room of a giant's house. A prince, looking for adventure, comes to serve the giant, who gives him tasks that are impossible to accomplish. The Master-maid knows the giant's secrets and tells the prince how to do the impossible chores. She knows what to do, but does not act herself. When the giant tells her to kill the prince, she helps the prince to run away, escaping with him. Without her advice the escape would be impossible, yet apparently she had never attempted to run away herself, but had been waiting in the back room for a prince-escort to show up.

Most of the heroines in *The Blue Fairy Book,* however, are entirely passive, submissive, and helpless. This is most obviously true of the Sleeping Beauty, who lies asleep, in the ultimate state of passivity, waiting for a brave prince to awaken and save her. (She is like the Snow-White of "Snow-White and the Seven Dwarfs," who lies in a death-like sleep, her beauty being visible through her glass coffin, until a prince comes along and falls in love with her.) When the prince does penetrate the tangle of thorns and brambles, enters the castle, finds her chamber, and awakens her, the princess opens her eyes and says, " 'Is it you, my Prince? You have waited a long while.' " (p. 59) This is not the end of the story, although it is the most famous part. The Sleeping Beauty, who was, while enchanted, the archetype of the passive, waiting beauty, retains this character in the second part, when she is awake. She marries the prince, and has two children who look savory to her mother-in-law, an Ogress with a taste for human flesh. While her son is away on a hunting trip the Ogress Queen orders the cook to kill and serve for dinner first one child and then the other. The cook hides the children, serving first a roast lamb and then a kid, instead. When the Ogress demands that her daughter-in-law be killed next, the cook tells her the Queen-mother's orders. The young Queen folds up at once: " 'Do it; do it' (said she, stretching out her neck). 'Execute your orders, and then I shall go and see my children . . . whom I so much and so tenderly loved.' " (p. 62) The compassionate cook, however, decides to hide her too, and the young King returns in time to save them all from the Ogress' wrath and impending disaster.

Cinderella plays as passive a role in her story. After leaving her slipper at the ball she has nothing more to do but stay home and wait. The prince has commanded that the slipper be carried to every house in the kingdom, and that it be tried on the foot of every woman. Cinderella can remain quietly at home; the prince's servant will come to her house and will discover her identity. Cinderella's male counterpart, Espen Cinderlad, the hero of a great many Norwegian folk tales, plays a very different role. Although he is the youngest of the three brothers, as Cinderella is the youngest sister, he is a Cinderlad by choice. His brothers may ridicule and despise him, but no one forces him to sit by the fire and poke in the ashes all day; he elects to do so. All the while, he knows that he is the cleaverest of the three, and eventually he leaves the fireside and wins a princess and half a kingdom by undertaking some adventure or winning a contest.

The Princess on the Glass Hill is the prototype of female passivity. The whole story is in the title; the Princess has been perched somehow on top of a glass hill, and thus made virtually inaccessible. There she sits, a waiting prize for whatever man can ride a horse up the glassy slope. So many of the heroines of fairy stories, including the well-known Rapunzel, are locked up in towers, locked into a magic sleep, imprisoned by giants, or otherwise enslaved, and waiting to be rescued by a passing prince, that the helpless, imprisoned maiden is the quintessential heroine of the fairy tale.

In the interesting story of "The Goose-Girl," an old Queen sends off her beautiful daughter, accompanied by a maid, to be married to a distant prince. The Queen gives her daughter a rag stained with three drops of her own blood. During the journey the maid brusquely refuses to bring the Princess a drink of water, saying " 'I don't mean to be your servant any longer.' " The initimidated Princess only murmurs, " 'Oh! heaven, what am I to do?' " (p. 266) This continues, the maid growing ruder, the Princess meeker, until she loses the rag, whereupon the maid rejoices, knowing that she now has full power over the girl, "for in losing the drops of blood the Princess had become weak and powerless." (p. 268) The maid commands the Princess to change clothes and horses with her, and never to speak to anyone about what has happened. The possession of the rag had assured the Princess' social status; without it she becomes *declassée,* and while her behavior was no less meek and docile before losing the rag than afterward, there is no formal role reversal until she loses it. Upon their arrival the maid presents herself as the Prince's bride, while the Princess is given the job of goose-girl. At length, due solely to the intervention of others, the secret is discovered, the maid killed, and the goose-girl married to the Prince.

The heroine of "Felicia and the Pot of Pinks" is equally submissive to ill-treatment. After their father's death, her brother forbids her to sit on his chairs:

> Felicia, who was very gentle, said nothing, but stood up crying quietly; while Bruno, for that was her brother's name, sat comfortably by the fire. Presently, when suppertime came, Bruno had a delicious egg, and he threw the shell to Felicia, saying:
>
> "There, that is all I can give you; if you don't like it, go out and catch frogs; there are plenty of them in the marsh close by." Felicia did not answer but she cried more bitterly than ever, and went away to her own little room. (p. 148)

The underlying associational pattern of these stories links the figures of the victimized girl and the interesting girl; it is always the interesting girl, the special girl, who is in trouble. It needs to be asked whether a child's absorption of the associational patterns found in these myths and legends may not sensitize the personality, rendering it susceptible to melodramatic self-conceptions and expectations. Because victimized girls like Felicia, the Goose-girl, and Cinderella are invariably rescued and rewarded, indeed glorified, children learn that suffering goodness can afford to remain meek, and need not and perhaps should not strive to defend itself, for if it did so perhaps the fairy godmother would not turn up for once, to set things right at the end. Moreover, the special thrill of persecution, bordering at once upon self-pity and self-righteousness, would have to be surrendered. Submissive, meek, passive female behavior is suggested and rewarded by the action of these stories.

Many of the girls are not merely passive, however; they are frequently victims and even martyrs as well. The Cinderella story is not simply a rags-to-riches tale. Cinderella is no Horatio Alger; her name is partly synonymous with female martyrdom. Her ugly older sisters, who are jealous of her beauty, keep her dressed in rags and hidden at home. They order her to do all the meanest housework. Cinderella bears this ill-treatment meekly: she is the patient sufferer, an object of pity. When the older sisters go off to the ball she bursts into tears; it is only the sound of her weeping that arouses her fairy godmother. Ultimately, her loneliness and her suffering are sentimentalized and become an integral part of her glamor. "Cinderella" and the other stories of this type show children that the girl who is singled out for rejection and bad treatment, and who submits to her lot, weeping but never running away, has a special compensatory destiny awaiting her. One of the pleasures provided by these stories is that the child-reader is free to indulge in pity, to be sorry for the heroine. The girl in tears is invariably the heroine; that is one of the ways the child can identify the heroine, for no one mistakenly feels sorry for the ugly older sisters, or for any of the villains or villainesses. When these characters suffer, they are only receiving their "just deserts." The child who dreams of being a Cinderella dreams perforce not only of being chosen and elevated by a prince, but also of being a glamorous sufferer or victim. What these stories convey is that women in distress are interesting. Fairy stories provide children with a concentrated early introduction to the archetype of the suffering heroine, who is currently alive (though not so well) under the name of Jenny Cavilleri.

The girl who marries Blue Beard is a prime example of the helpless damsel-victim, desperately waiting for a rescuer. She knows that her husband will not hesitate to murder her, because she has seen the corpses of his other murdered wives in the forbidden closet. The enraged Blue Beard announces that he will cut off her head; he gives her fifteen minutes to say her prayers, after which he bellows for her so loudly that the house trembles:

> The distressed wife came down, and threw herself at his feet, all in tears, with her hair about her shoulders.
>
> "This signifies nothing," said Blue Beard: "you must die": then, taking hold of her hair with one hand, and lifting up the sword with the other, he was going to take off her head. The poor lady, turning about to him, and looking at him with dying eyes, desired him to afford her one little moment to recollect herself.
>
> "No, no," said he, "recommend thyself to God," and was just about to strike. . . . (p. 295)

"At this very instant," as the story continues, her brothers rush in and save her.

It is worth noticing that the one Greek legend that Lang included in *The Blue Fairy Book* is the Pereus story, which Lang entitled "The Terrible Head." It features two utterly helpless women, the first being Danae, who is put into a chest with her infant son, Perseus, and thrown out to sea, to drown or starve or drift away. Fortunately the chest comes to land, and Danae and her baby are saved. At the conclusion of the story, as the grown-up Perseus is flying home with the Gorgon's head, he looks down and sees "a beautiful girl chained to a stake at the high-water mark of the sea. The girl was so frightened or so tired that she was only prevented from falling by the iron chain about her waist, and there she hung, as if she were dead." (p. 190) Perseus learns that she has been left there as a sacrifice to a sea-monster; he cuts her free, kills the monster, and carries her off as his bride.

Few other rescues are as dramatic as that of Blue Beard's wife or of Andromeda, but the device of the rescue itself is constantly used. The sexes of the rescuer and the person in danger are almost as constantly predictable; men come along to rescue women who are in danger of death, or are enslaved, imprisoned, abused, or plunged into an enchanted sleep which resembles death. Two well-known stories that were not included in *The Blue Fairy Book,* "Snow-White and the Seven Dwarfs" and "Rapunzel," are notable examples of this type: Snow-White is saved from a sleep which everyone assumes is death by the arrival of a handsome prince; Rapunzel, locked up in a tower by a cruel witch, is found and initially rescued by her prince.

Whatever the condition of younger women in fairy tales, Alison Lurie claims that the older women in the tales are often more active and powerful than men. It is true that some older women in fairy tales have power, but of what kind? In order to understand the meaning of women's power in fairy tales, we must examine the nature, the value, and the use of their power.

There are only a few powerful good women in *The Blue Fairy Book,* and they are nearly all fairies: the tiny, jolly, ugly old fairy in "Prince Hyacinth," the stately fairies in "Prince Darling," "Toads and Diamonds," and "Felicia," and of course Cinderella's fairy godmother. They are rarely on the scene; they only appear in order to save young people in distress, and then they're off again. These good fairies have gender only in a technical sense; to children, they probably appear as women only in the sense that dwarfs and wizards appear as men. They are not human beings, they are asexual, and many of them are old. They are not examples of powerful women with whom children can identify as role models; they do not provide meaningful alternatives to the stereotype of the younger, passive heroine. A girl may hope to become a princess, but can she ever become a fairy?

Powerful, bad older women appear to outnumber powerful, good ones. A certain number of these are also not fully human; they are fairies, witches, trolls, or ogresses. It is generally implied that such females are wicked because of their race: thus the young king in "The Sleeping Beauty" fears his mother while he loves her, "for she was of the race of the Ogres, and the King (his father) would never have married her had it not been for her vast riches; it was even whispered about the Court that she had Orgeish inclinations, and that, whenever she saw little children passing by, she had all the difficulty in the world to avoid falling upon them." (p. 60) Either extra-human race or extreme ugliness is often associated with female wickedness, and in such a way as to suggest that they explain the wickedness. The evil Fairy of the Desert in "The Yellow Dwarf" is described as a "tall old woman, whose ugliness was even more surprising than her extreme old age." (p. 39) The sheep-king in "The Wonderful Sheep" tells Miranda that he was transformed into a sheep by a fairy " 'whom I had known as long as I could remember, and whose ugliness had always horrified me.' " (p. 223) The bear-prince in "East of the Sun" is under a spell cast by a troll-hag, and the fairy who considers herself slighted by the Sleeping Beauty's parents is described as being old: the original illustration for Lang's book shows her to be an ugly old crone, whereas the other fairies are young and lovely.

In the case of wicked but human women, it is also implied that being ill-favored is corollary to being ill-natured, as with Cinderella's step-mother and step-sisters. Cinderella is pretty and sweet, like her dead mother. The step-mother is proud and haughty, and her two daughters by her former husband are like her, so that their ill-temper appears to be genetic, or at least transmitted by the mother. The circumstances in "Toads and Diamonds" are similar: the old widow has two daughters, of whom the eldest resembles her mother "in face and humour. . . . They were both so disagreeable and so proud that there was no living with them. The youngest, who was the very picture of her father for courtesy and sweetness of temper, was withal one of the most beautiful girls ever seen." (p. 274)

Powerful good women are nearly always fairies, and they are remote: they come only when desperately needed. Whether human or extra-human, those women who are either partially or thoroughly evil are generally shown as active, ambitious, strong-willed and, most often, ugly. They are jealous of any woman more beautiful than they, which is not surprising in view of the power deriving from beauty in fairy tales. In "Cinderella" the domineering step-mother and step-sisters contrast with the passive heroine. The odious step-mother wants power, and successfully makes her will prevail in the house; we are told that Cinderella bore her ill-treatment patiently, "and dared not tell her father, who would have rattled her off; for his wife governed him entirely." The wicked maid in "The Goose-Girl" is not described as being either fair or ugly (except that the Princess appears to be fairer than the maid at the end), but like the other female villains she is jealous of beauty and greedy for wealth. She decides to usurp the Princess' place, and being evil she is also strong and determined, and initially successful. Being powerful is mainly associated with being unwomanly.

The moral value of activity thus becomes sex-linked.[7] The boy who sets out to seek his fortune, like Dick Whittington, Jack the Giant-Killer, or Espen Cinderlad, is a stock figure and, provided that he has a kind heart, is assured of success. What is praiseworthy in males, however, is rejected in females; the counterpart of the energetic, aspiring boy is the scheming, ambitious woman. Some heroines show a kind of strength in their ability to endure, but they do not actively seek to change their lot. (The only exceptions to this rule are in the stories that appear to derive from the myth of Cupid and Psyche: "East of the Sun" and "The Black Bull of Norroway," in which the heroines seek their lost lovers. We may speculate whether the pre-Christian origin of these stories diminishes the stress placed on female passivity and acceptance, but this is purely conjectural.) We can remark that these stories reflect a bias against the active, ambitious, "pushy" woman, and have probably also served to instill this bias in young readers. They establish a dichotomy between those women who are gentle, passive, and fair, and those who are active, wicked, and ugly. Women who are powerful and good are never human; those women who are human, and who have power or seek it, are nearly always portrayed as repulsive.

While character depiction in fairy tales is, to be sure, meager, and we can usually group characters according to temperamental type (beautiful and sweet, or ugly and evil), there are a couple of girls who are not portrayed as being either perfectly admirable or as wicked. The princesses in "The Yellow Dwarf," "Goldilocks," and "Trusty John" are described as being spoiled, vain, and willful: the problem is that they refuse to marry anyone. The Queen in "The Yellow Dwarf" expostulates with her daughter:

> "Bellissima," she said, "I do wish you would not be so proud. What makes you despise all these nice kings? I wish you to marry one of them, and you do not try to please me."
>
> "I am so happy," Bellissima answered: "do leave me in peace, madam. I don't want to care for anyone."
>
> "But you would be very happy with any of these princes," said the Queen, "and I shall be very angry if you fall in love with anyone who is not worthy of you."
>
> But the Princess thought so much of herself that she did not consider any one of her lovers clever or handsome enough for her; and her mother, who was getting really angry at her determination not to be married, began to wish that she had not allowed her to have her own way so much. (p. 31)

Princess Goldilocks similarly refuses to consider marriage, although she is not as adamant as Bellissima. The princess in the Grimms' story "King Thrushbeard," which is not included in this collection, behaves like Bellissima; her angry father declares that he will give her to the very next comer, whatever his rank: the next man to enter the castle being a beggar, the king marries his daughter to him. This

[7]Ruth Kelso's *Doctrine for the Lady of the Renaissance* (Urbana: University of Illinois Press, 1956) demonstrates that "the moral ideal for the lady is essentially Christian . . . as that for the gentleman is essentially pagan. For him the ideal is self-expansion and realization. . . . For the lady the direct opposite is prescribed. The eminently Christian virtues of chastity, humility, piety, and patience under suffering and wrong, are the necessary virtues." (p. 36)

princess suffers poverty with her beggar-husband, until he reveals himself as one of the suitor kings she had rejected. Bellissima is punished more severely; indeed, her story is remarkable because it is one of the rare examples outside of H.C. Andersen of a story with a sad ending. Because Bellissima had refused to marry, she is forced by a train of circumstances to promise to marry the ugly Yellow Dwarf. She tries to avoid this fate by consenting to wed one of her suitors at last, but the dwarf intervenes at the wedding. Ultimately the dwarf kills the suitor, whom Bellissima had come to love, and she dies of a broken heart. A kind mermaid transforms the ill-fated lovers into two palm trees.

These princesses are portrayed as reprehensible because they refuse to marry; hence, they are considered "stuck-up," as children would say. The alternate construction, that they wished to preserve their freedom and their identity, is denied or disallowed (although Bellissima had said to her mother, " 'I am so happy, do leave me in peace, madam.' ") There is a sense of triumph when a willful princess submits or is forced to submit to a husband.

The Blue Fairy Book is filled with weddings, but it shows little of married life. It contains thirty stories in which marriage is a component, but eighteen of these stories literally end with the wedding. Most of the other twelve show so little of the marital life of the hero or heroine that technically they too may be said to end with marriage. Only a few of the stories show any part of the married life of young people, or even of old ones. The Sleeping Beauty is a totally passive wife and mother, and Blue Beard's wife, like the Sleeping Beauty, depends on a man to rescue her. Whereas the Sleeping Beauty is menaced by her mother-in-law who, being an Ogress, is only half-human, Blue Beard's wife is endangered by *being* the wife of her ferocious husband. (Her error may be ascribed to her having an independent sense of curiosity, or to rash disobedience.) This widely known story established a potent myth in which a helpless woman violates her husband's arbitrary command and then is subject to his savage, implacable fury. It is fully the counterpoise of the other stock marital situation containing a scheming, overbearing wife and a timid, hen-pecked husband, as in "Cinderella"; moreover, whereas the domineering wife is always implicitly regarded as abhorrent, the helpless, threatened, passive wife is uncritically viewed and thus implicitly approved of. As Andromeda, Blue Beard's wife, or the imperiled Pauline, her function is to provide us with a couple of thrills of a more or less sadistic tincture.

The other peculiar aspect of the depiction of marriage in these stories is that nearly all the young heroes and heroines are the children of widows or widowers; only five of the thirty-seven stories in the book contain a set of parents: these include "The Sleeping Beauty," in which the parents leave the castle when the hundred-year enchantment begins, and the two similar tales of "Little Thumb" and "Hansel and Gretel," in both of which the parents decide to get rid of their children because they are too poor to feed them. (In "Little Thumb" the husband persuades his reluctant wife, and in "Hansel and Gretel" the wife persuades her reluctant husband.) Cinderella has two parents, but the only one who plays a part in the story is her step-mother. In general, the young people of these stories are described as having only one parent, or none. Although marriage is such a constant event in the stories, and is central to their reward system, few marriages are indeed shown in fairy tales. Like the White Queen's rule, there's jam tomorrow and jam yesterday, but never jam today. The stories can be described as being preoccupied with marriage. without portraying it; as a real condition, it's nearly always off-stage.

In effect, these stories focus upon courtship, which is magnified into the most important and exciting part of a girl's life, brief though courtship is, because it is the part of her life in which she most counts as a person herself. After marriage she ceases to be wooed, her consent is no longer sought, she derives her status from her husband, and her personal identity is thus snuffed out. When fairy tales show courtship as exciting, and conclude with marriage, and the vague statement that "they lived happily ever after," children may develop a deep-seated desire always to be courted, since marriage is literally the end of the story.

The controversy about what is biologically determined and what is learned has just begun. These are the questions now being asked, and not yet answered: to what extent is passivity a biological attribute of females; to what extent is it culturally determined? Perhaps it will be argued that these stories show archetypal female behavior, but one may wonder to what extent they reflect female attributes, or to what extent they serve as training manuals for girls? If one argued that the characteristically passive behavior of female characters in fairy stories is a reflection of an attribute inherent in female personality, would one also argue, as consistency would require, that the mercantile reward system of fairy stories reflects values that are inherent in human nature? We must consider the possibility that the classical attributes of "femininity" found in these stories are in fact imprinted in children and reinforced by the stories themselves. Analyses of the influence of the most popular children's literature may give us an insight into some of the origins of psycho-sexual identity.

Sugar 'n Spice 'n Snips 'n Snails: The Social-Sexual Role in Children's Fiction

Anne Devereaux Jordan

Anne Devereaux Jordan is founder and former executive secretary of the Children's Literature Association.

Since the inception of the idea of "childhood" in the seventeenth century, social and biological sexual identification has been, and still remains, a prime concern of children's books. Until recently the social and biological aspects of sexual identification were inextricably linked and rigidly defined: the female child being traditionally associated with dolls, cooking, sewing, submissiveness, and passivity; the male with animals, outdoor games, machines, dominance, and action. In many contemporary children's books, however, and particularly in the area of fiction, there appears a separation of the biological role from the social role, with a resultant shift from an emphasis on the traditional biological-social modes and mores of behavior to those which would in the past have been considered perverted or, at the very least, improper.

Sheila Egoff, in her article "Precepts and Pleasure: Changing Emphases in the Writing and Criticism of Children's Literature," points out that "as society in general does not seem to know what to say to its children and cannot express itself with one voice, we have both a literature of 'personal decision,' which suggests that each young person has to come to terms with life on an individual basis, and a literature of conformity."[1] It is the former type of literature which is attacking the traditional views of social sexual identification and offering the child the freedom to determine his or her own behavior. The choice is one of passivity or activity, or a combination, without reference to biological sex. The literature of conformity, as Egoff terms it, does not offer this choice. It is the literature of the past, espousing the traditional social-sexual view. It is the literature which the literature of "personal decision" is attempting to combat.

Children's fiction, particularly that of the eighteenth and nineteenth centuries, has long been preoccupied with portraying "right" and "wrong" behavior. "Right" behavior was that which conformed with the social mores of the day, which were linked with biological sexual identification. "Right" behavior was praised; "wrong" was censured. The eighteenth and nineteenth centuries praised the passive and submissive in the female, the active in the male. In the H. W. Hewet publication *Goody Two-Shoes* (c. 1855), for example, Margery (Goody) and Tommy, her brother, are orphaned and then befriended by a kindly relative of Mr. Smith, the clergyman:

> The gentleman ordered little Margery a new pair of shoes, gave Mr. Smith some money to buy her clothes, and said he would take Tommy, and make him a little sailor; and, accordingly, had a jacket, and trowsers made for him.[2]

Tommy is given the opportunity of a career; Goody Two-Shoes stays home, with new clothes as a consolation prize. There is no protest from either. It is Goody's role, as a female, to remain quietly at home. Likewise, Tommy isn't asked if he wishes to go to sea: being a sailor is a "manly" occupation, therefore he will love it.

Books which did not illustrate these traditional roles were the exception rather than the rule in the eighteenth and nineteenth centuries. Perhaps it is for this reason that the exceptions have continued to be popular into the twentieth century. Lewis Carroll's Alice is not "ladylike" nor is she passive. A lady does not slide down rabbit holes or upset a jury box in exasperation. Alice was a pleasant vacation from the stilted "good deeds" and "modest looks" standard observed in girl's fiction at that time, and she remains an enjoyable diversion today.

As children's books moved toward and into the twentieth century, the passive female character underwent a change toward a more active participation in the events within a book, reflecting the more active interest women in reality were taking in business, politics, and society in general. Series books were produced with girls as the main characters doing things formerly thought the province of the male. Starting, in the United States, with such books as *The Little Colonel* series, and followed by series like *The Motor Girls, The Corner House Girls, The Girl Aviators, The Outdoor Girls,* and *The Moving Picture Girls,* the series books culminate with the most popular series character, Nancy Drew. The *Nancy Drew* series is still popular and read avidly by girls today because Nancy is daring and successful in areas usually left to the male. The other series fell by the way because the devices upon which they were based —the motor car, the biplane—became commonplace or obsolete; they were victims of technological advancement.

In the series books for girls, characters were often described as "boyish," as if to explain their daring, but this was rigidly circumscribed by author qualifications. In *The Outdoor Girls at Ocean View* by Laura Lee Hope (Edward Stratemeyer), a character nicknamed "Billy" is described:

1. Sheila, Egoff, "Precepts and Pleasures," *Only Connect,* ed. by Sheila Egoff, G. T. Stubbs, and L. F. Ashley (New York: Oxford University Press, 1969), p. 433.

2. *Goody Two-Shoes* (New York: H. W. Hewet, c.1855), p. 3.

> . . . at a glance you could understand why she was called so. There was such a wholesome, frank and comrade-like quality about her, though she was not at all masculine, that "Billy" just suited.[3]

The descriptive language—"frank," "comrade-like"—is that typical of male characters. Stratemeyer hastens to qualify it, however, lest any taint of perversion be attached to his character. Even with these qualifications, however, female characters were leaving the passive role behind, breaking from the traditional social role given to females.

From being described as "boyish," characters in books for girls progressed to become "tomboys," and the tomboy theme has persisted in popularity to contemporary times. However, while the term "tomboy" implies that the female character will assume a more active role in the denouement, it also, as with "boyish," implies limitation. A "tomboy," it is assumed, will grow out of this behavior and, at a later age, put on the stereotypic mantle of femininity, adjusting to being a wife and mother. Zena Sutherland points out in her article "Make No Mystique About It," in the *Saturday Review:*

> One of the most oft-repeated patterns in books for older readers is the tomboy who, at the end of the story, adjusts to her traditional role, conceding that her mother was right and dresses can be pretty, or that it is possible to enjoy a girls' club as much as playing shortstop with the boys.[4]

A girl could be a tomboy but, until the 1960s, there was a cutoff point whereupon she would metamorphose to the passive role.

While tomboyism is an open move toward active participation in events by the female, at the same time there was a more covert move toward this goal in other children's books. The most striking example is Watty Piper's *The Little Engine That Could.* Here is a picture book which children have read and loved since its publication in 1930, yet few realize that the Little Engine is female, and that she is doing something which all the other engines—who are male—cannot or will not do. Read from one perspective, *The Little Engine That Could* is a delightful piece of propaganda advocating the assumption of the active role by the female.

While the female was making this progress toward more active participation in events, the male seemed to be left behind. The image of boys in children's books, traditionally seen as active and dominant, admitted no element of passivity without strong censure. As with Tommy, in *Goody Two-Shoes,* there is no choice. Those characters who were passive were usually billed as "sissies" and more often than not provided a comic relief from the "masculine" action of the main characters. Any element of the passive—"feminine"—in the main character is shunned. In an early example, *Tom Brown at Oxford* (1861), Tom makes up with his friend, Jack Hardy, after an arguement:

> . . . Tom rushed across to his friend, dearer than ever to him now, and threw his arm round his neck; and, if the un-English truth must out, had three parts of a mind to kiss the rough face which was working with strong emotion.[5]

This "un-English" idea—"un-English" implying "feminine"—is *quickly* dropped by both character and author, such emotions in men being reserved solely for their relations with the opposite sex.

This stress on the active, "masculine" character has continued to our own times in much of the fiction for boys. In the 1940s and 1950s, however, slow progress was made toward the admission of a passive side to the male character. Elizabeth

3. Laura Lee Hope (Edward Stratemeyer), *The Outdoor Girls at Ocean View* (New York: Grosset and Dunlap, 1915), p. 2.

4. Zena Sutherland, "Make No Mystique About It," *Saturday Review,* 20 March 1971, p. 30.

5. Thomas Hughes, *Tom Brown at Oxford* (New York: A. L. Burt Publishers, 1870), p. 222.

Enright, in her books about the Melendy family, allows this in her two boy characters, Rush and Oliver. Besides liking the typical "masculine" activities, Rush likes to play the piano and wishes to be a composer; Oliver enjoys cooking. Enright has added an element of realism to her characters that was lacking in earlier books. The rather disappointing feature of this, however, is that, because the male image was so strongly inculcated, books which admitted a passive side to the male character were read primarily by girls rather than boys.

During the 1960s authors became interested in developing the whole child rather than maintaining stereotypes. One author, Nat Hentoff, comments, "I began to read what other writers in the field were doing and agreed with the young critics that little of relevance is being written about what it is to be young now." [6] Both children and the writers for children were becoming aware of the fact that an individual is more than a societal stereotype; that girls and women are not necessarily passive and submissive, boys and men, active and dominant. For the first time the passive element in boys was allowed and dealt with realistically. Such "new" books as *The Teddy Bear Habit or How I Became a Winner* by James L. Collier, were written and, more importantly, published. In this very humorous book, the main character has a secret: he, a normal boy otherwise, cannot attempt achievement without having his childhood teddy bear with him. Ten years earlier such a book would never have been written, let alone published. More to the point, this book was accepted and read by *both* girls and boys.

In contemporary children's fiction there is evidence that today's authors are attempting to give children a knowledge of the human experience, something adult fiction has long been doing but children's books have not, to any great extent. There is an awareness being expressed of the social and biological sexual nature of both children and adults, and an effort being made to help the child understand this. Opposite views are presented, rather than just one side, and the child is allowed to come to a personal decision as to how he or she views these opposites and himself or herself in relation to them. One side effect is a better literature being written: fuller and richer.

The passive side of human nature is now presented without censure. One instance is Charlotte Zolotow's *William's Doll.* William wishes to have a doll "to love" so that he will know what to do when he grows up and becomes a father. While presenting William's position with sensitivity and understanding, Zolotow also presents the opposite view—William is called a "sissy"—allowing the young reader to see all sides of the issue and choose. *William's Doll* is one of a number of picture books showing boys enjoying what formerly was the territory of girls; others include Betsy Byar's *Go and Hush the Baby* and Eve Merriam's *Boys and Girls, Girls and Boys.* The argument implicit in these books is that behavior is not a sex-linked characteristic but is often a matter of choice.

For older boys, equally important, but often more complex issues are presented. The literature being written is no longer the "let's win the big game!" type, but rather deals with the psychology of an individual and the choices he must make. One very powerfully written example is Robert Cormier's *The Chocolate War.* The main character, Jerry Renault, refuses to be bullied into selling chocolates for the school's secret society, the Vigils. When it comes to a showdown, Jerry is seriously beaten by a stooge of Archie Costello, leader of the Vigils, and,

> He had to tell Goober to play ball, to play football, to run, to make the team, to sell the chocolates, to sell whatever they wanted you to sell, to do whatever they wanted you to do. . . . Don't disturb the universe,

6. Nat Hentoff, "Fiction for Teenagers," *Only Connect,* p. 400.

Goober, no matter what the posters say.[7]

The "good guy" doesn't win; there's more to good and bad. Issues aren't always clear-cut.

Cormier's book deals with the complexity of individual decision in relation to the situations a person must face. The result of this type of book is more realistic characters and plots, a breakdown of stereotype and of sterotypic language. Words such as "frank" and "comrade-like" and "wholesome" have, for the most part, dropped any sexual implication, or been eliminated entirely. Cormier's *The Chocolate War* is merely one book that deals with a boy confronting choices socially. George A. Woods's *Vibrations* and *To Catch a Killer,* Maia Wojciechowska's *Don't Play Dead Before You Have To,* or Susan Hinton's *The Outsiders* are among the many books now available for boys which confront situations realistically without didacticism.

In fiction for older girls similar changes have occurred. The female in fiction is no longer the vapid do-gooder and bystander. She is now active, interested, and interesting. Spurred in part by the various equality-for-women groups, contemporary books in which the female is the initiator of action in nontraditional ways are numerous. Books such as Norma Klein's *Mom, the Wolfman and Me,* Madeleine L'Engle's *Wrinkle in Time,* or any of Virginia Hamilton's books call to mind entertaining and interesting female characters who, like Robert Cormier's Jerry Renault, are individuals dealing with the human condition. These books present insight and knowledge to the reader so that the reader can better deal with herself and experience.

7. Robert Cormier, *The Chocolate War* (New York: Pantheon Books, 1974), p. 248.

Zena Sutherland points out, in regard to literature for girls, "They do want an open door, an equal chance, and female characters who are intelligent and active."[8] Girls do want this, but boys want it equally. The cry is sexless. It is one for realistic characters, a break from the "literature of conformity" toward a literature of human experience. And contemporary writers are providing this. The writers of contemporary books for children that deal with life directly and honestly are espousing the idea of a certain type of freedom: a freedom to choose between activity or passivity regardless of sex or pre-existing sexual stereotypes. They have recognized, as Sigmund Freud did,

> The result of this [observation of activity or passivity in male and female individuals] in man is that there is no pure masculinity or femininity either in the biological or psychological sense. On the contrary, every individual person shows a mixture of his own biological sex characteristics with the biological traits of the other sex and a union of activity and passivity; this is the case whether these psychological characteristic features depend on biological elements or whether they are independent of them.[9]

Social roles and behavior are not dependent upon sex. Contemporary writers for children recognize this and are attempting to bring to the child an awareness of roles other than those traditionally linked with sex, and to show these without censure. The stereotypes of the past are falling by the way; what is left are people.

8. Sutherland, p. 30.

9. Dr. A. A. Brill, ed., *The Basic Writings of Sigmund Freud* (New York: The Modern Library, 1938), p. 613n.

Explorations

STORYTELLING AND ACTING OUT

1. *(Atalanta)* A good way to involve children in storytelling is to stop before the end of the story and have them predict what the ending is to be. Try asking for predictions for the ending of this story. After all the predictions are in (and don't be surprised if most of them reflect the traditional sex-role stereotypes), tell the children the real ending. If it surprises them, or they disagree with it, encourage them to express their feelings on the subject—then explain why the ending is a good one in human terms.
2. *(Nana Miriam)* This is a story that depends on skilled storytelling for effectiveness. It is a good one on which to practice your developing storytelling skills. If you like the story and want to share it with children, tell it over to yourself until it feels as if it belongs to you. Remember to adjust the words to the age and comprehension of your audience and to keep certain choice phrases from the original. Use as many of your available resources of expression as you can: an expressive voice, mobile face, natural gestures.

   The drama of the story lies in the struggle it depicts between good and evil (the magic of Nana Miriam is used to protect the people of the tribe against the devouring hippopotamus). This dramatic conflict should be brought out and heightened wherever possible. Try to do it mainly with your voice—letting it rise and fall in loudness and pitch, pacing the story slower at some points and faster at others.
3. *(Three Strong Women/Molly Whipple)* Present one of these stories in a puppet play. They both contain plenty of action, which makes them entertaining choices. "The Strong Women" should concentrate on the women's feats of physical strength—on wrestling, tugging, and tree hurling—while "Molly Whipple," because it has a more detailed plot, will depend more heavily on a good, expressive narrator telling the story in the background.

   Present "Three Strong Women" as a shadow puppet story (see Explorations in "Masks and Shadows" for instructions on how to do this). Be sure to make the figure of Forever-Mountain big and strong, and the figures of Maru-me, Mother, and Grandmother small to emphasize the humor of their superior strength.
4. *(Master-Maid)* Tell this story to a group of children, concentrating on the highlights of the story: the arrival of the prince at the giant's house, the first appearance of the Master-Maid, her instructions to the prince on how to outwit the giant, the reactions of the giant to being outwitted, the escape of the Master-Maid and the prince, the apparent abandonment of the Master-Maid in a strange land, the happy resolution. Since the story depends to some degree on reversal of sex roles, discuss with the

children their feelings about the story. Did they think it was "realistic"? Would they have changed the story in any way? If the Master-Maid was so clever, why didn't she escape before the prince arrived? As in Exploration 1, encourage them to express their feelings fully—especially on the subject of sex-role stereotyping—then show them how the balance between the sexes suggested by the story is an accurate representation of the human situation.

5. *(White Horse Girl . . . Blue Wind Boy)* This story is a favorite of storytellers. Because of its poet-author's skillful use of word-sounds and powerful images, it has a unique and haunting quality. Here is a story from which you will want to choose certain key phrases to preserve in your storytelling. Try to bring the sound of the wind into your voice and to evoke a feeling for the faraway land where the girl and boy go together. You must feel a story as you tell it or you can't expect others to feel it. This story is particularly appreciated by older children, though younger ones enjoy it too.
6. *(Harriet the Spy)* Read this selection aloud to some children. Would they like to have Harriet as a friend? What do they think of her behavior? Would they like to be like her? When their concept of Harriet as a person is clear in their minds, have them imagine further adventures she might have. You might read a later chapter from the book to them (perhaps the chapter in which Harriet's friends turn on her after they find her notebook) and see if it fits with their idea of Harriet.
7. *(It's Like This, Cat)* Read this selection to older children, then ask for two volunteers to play the roles of the boy and his father. Have the others create situations in which the two are likely to find themselves in disagreement. Choose one or two of the best ones for your volunteers to act out. Whose side is the audience on? Do they resent the father's trying to force his son into a sex-stereotyped role? Are they aware of this aspect of the conflict between father and son? If not, it should be called to their attention.
8. *(Julie of the Wolves)* The scene in this selection in which Miyax (Julie) observes the ritual approach of the wolf pack to their leader and imitates it in order to receive his protection is a fascinating glimpse into the world of animals. After reading the selection to some children, have them pantomime this scene. One child should be chosen to play Miyax, another to play Amaroq, leader of the wolves, and the rest of the children, the wolf pack. To help the children get into their wolf parts, do some more reading about wolves—perhaps Rudyard Kipling's poem "The Law of the Jungle," his story of Mowgli in the *Jungle Books,* and "How St. Francis Tamed the Very Fierce Wolf of Gubbio" (from *The Little Flowers of St. Francis*), as well as a nonfiction description of wolf behavior from a book about animals. (There are also phonograph records of wolf calls.) You will learn that wolves are intelligent animals with a strongly developed social sense. The dignity of the animal world is conveyed beautifully by Jean George in the story. Encourage the children to embody that same dignity in their pantomime of the wolves.

PARTICIPATING IN OTHER WAYS

1. *(Atalanta)* With a group of children, make a mural of the race between Atalanta and her suitors. The figures in the mural may be colored or

painted separately by the children (in addition to the running figures, there are spectators and a king to be put into the picture), so that each child makes an individual contribution to the mural. The separate drawings may be cut out and then fastened in place (use staples or glue) on a long sheet of wrapping paper. Everybody can then join in to create a colorful background—suggesting the excitement of the race—using crayons, chalk, or tempera.

2. *(White Horse Girl... Blue Wind Boy)* Choosing music that expresses the mood of a story is a good way to help children become sensitive to mood as a factor in their response to literature. Help some children choose music to go with this story. You might choose several records that seem appropriate to you and let the children pick the ones that they like best. Instrumental arrangements of American folk songs might be a good place to start looking. Watch the several swings of mood to be found in this story and match them with appropriate music.
3. *(Harriet the Spy)* By pretending to be a reporterlike spy, a child might try to duplicate Harriet's experience. If a tape recorder is available, people's conversations might be taped and played back (be sure to let the people know they're being taped). If one isn't available, just record in writing short bits of overheard conversation (again, letting people know). Are the recorded conversations as interesting as Harriet's?
4. *(Taste of Blackberries)* The emotions this selection arouses may be difficult for a child to express except in a private way. Children to whom you read it might try to express their feelings about it in a poem or short piece of prose writing, or in a drawing.
5. There are many strong characters in this section. Have a child pick one with whom he or she identifies (not necessarily of the same sex) and write one week's entries in a diary the character might have kept. When the week is completed, make an appropriate cover for the diary. If children are interested in each other's diaries, they can be traded.
6. Children can write their own poems about boys and girls and the problems of sex roles. Read the three poems in the book to children to start them off.

Selected Readings

READINGS FOR CHILDREN

Blume, Judy. *Are You There God? It's Me Margaret.* Scarsdale, N.Y.: Bradbury, 1970. Fiction.

______. *Then Again, Maybe I Won't.* Scarsdale, N.Y.: Bradbury, 1971. Fiction.

Brink, Carol Ryrie. *Caddie Woodlawn.* Illustrated by Kate Seredy. New York: Macmillan, 1936. Historical fiction.

______. *Caddie Woodlawn.* Illustrated by Trina Schart Hyman. New York: Macmillan, 1973. Historical fiction.

Buckmaster, Henrietta. *Women Who Shaped History.* New York: Macmillan, 1966. Biography.

Burch, Robert. *Queenie Peavy.* Illustrated by Jerry Lazare. New York: Viking, 1966. Fiction.

Burnett, Frances Hodgson. *The Secret Garden.* Philadelphia: Lippincott, 1911. Fiction.

Byars, Betsy. *Go and Hush the Baby.* Illustrated by Emily A. McCully. New York: Viking, 1971. Fiction (picture book).

Carlson, Dale. *Girls Are Equal Too: The Women's Movement for Teenagers.* New York: Atheneum, 1973. Informational book.

Cleaver, Vera and Bill. *Ellen Grae.* Illustrated by Ellen Raskin. Philadelphia: Lippincott, 1967. Fiction.

______. *Where the Lilies Bloom.* Philadelphia: Lippincott, 1969. Fiction.

______. *The Whys and Wherefores of Littabelle Lee.* New York: Atheneum, 1973. Fiction.

Clifton, Lucille. *Don't You Remember?* Illustrated by Evaline Ness. New York: Dutton, 1973. Fiction (picture book).

______. *Some of the Days of Everett Anderson.* Illustrated by Evaline Ness. New York: Holt, 1970. Poetic fiction (picture book).

Clymer, Eleanor. *Luke Was There.* Illustrated by Diane de Groat. New York: Holt, 1973. Fiction.

Credle, Ellis. *Down, Down the Mountain.* Illustrated by the author. New York: Nelson, 1934. Fiction.

Donovan, John. *I'll Get There. It Better Be Worth the Trip.* New York: Harper, 1969. Fiction.

Farmer, Penelope. *The Summer Birds.* Illustrated by James Spanfeller. New York: Harcourt, 1962. Fantasy.

Fitzhugh, Louise. *The Long Secret.* New York: Harper, 1965. Fiction.

______. *Nobody's Family Is Going to Change.* New York: Farrar, 1974. Fiction.

Garner, Alan. *The Owl Service.* New York: Walck, 1968. Fantasy.

Goffstein, M. B. *Goldie the Dollmaker.* New York: Farrar, 1969. Fantasy (picture book).

Greene, Constance C. *Isabelle the Itch.* Illustrated by Emily A. McCully. New York: Viking, 1973. Fiction.

______. *The Unmaking of Rabbit.* New York: Viking, 1972. Fiction.

Hamilton, Virginia. *Zeely.* Illustrated by Symeon Shimin. New York: Macmillan, 1967. Fiction.

Haskins, James. *Fighting Shirley Chisholm.* New York: Dial, 1975. Biography.

Hill, Elizabeth Starr. *Evan's Corner.* Illustrated by Nancy Grossman. New York: Holt, 1967. Fiction (picture book).

Howard Moses L. *The Ostrich Chase.* Illustrated by Barbara Seuling. New York: Holt, 1974. Fiction.

Jewell, Nancy. *Try and Catch Me.* Illustrated by Leonard Weisgard. New York: Harper, 1972. Fiction.

Jordan, June. *Fannie Lou Hamer.* Illustrated by Albert Williams. New York: Thomas Crowell, 1972. Biography.

Keats, Ezra Jack. *Peter's Chair.* New York: Harper, 1967. Fiction (picture book).

Keller, Gail Faithfull. *Jane Addams.* Illustrated by Frank Aloise. New York: Thomas Crowell, 1971. Biography.

Kingman, Lee. *Georgina and the Dragon.* Illustrated by Leonard Shortall. Boston: Houghton Mifflin, 1972. Fiction.

Klein, Norma. *Girls Can Be Anything.* Illustrated by Roy Doty. New York: Dutton, 1973. Fiction (picture book).

______. *Mom, the Wolf Man and Me.* New York: Pantheon, 1972. Fiction.

Konigsburg, E. L. *From the Mixed-Up Files of Mrs. Basil E. Frankweiler.* New York: Atheneum, 1967. Fiction.

Larrick, Nancy, and Merriam, Eve, eds. *Male and Female Under 18.* New York: Avon, 1973. Comments and poems about sex roles by boys and girls.

Lawrence, Jacob. *Harriet and the Promised Land.* New York: Simon & Schuster, 1968. Biography (picture book about Harriet Tubman).

L'Engle, Madeleine. *A Wrinkle in Time.* New York: Farrar, 1962. Fantasy.

Lindgren, Astrid. *Pippi Longstocking.* Illustrated by Louis Glanzman. New York: Viking, 1950. Fantasy.

Lionni, Leo. *Fish Is Fish.* Illustrated by the author. New York: Pantheon, 1970. Fantasy (picture book).

Lofts, Norah. *The Maude Reed Tale.* Illustrated by Anne and Janet Grahame Johnstone. Nashville: Thomas Nelson, 1972. Fiction.

Longsworth, Polly. *Emily Dickinson: Her Letter to the World.* New York: Thomas Crowell, 1965. Biography.

______. *I, Charlotte Forten, Black and Free.* New York: Thomas Crowell, 1970. Biography.

Mann, Peggy. *Amelia Earhart: First Lady of Flight.* Illustrated by Kiyo Komoda. New York: Coward, McCann, 1970. Biography.

Meltzer, Milton. *Tongue of Flame: The Life of Lydia Maria Child.* New York: Thomas Crowell, 1965. Biography.

Merriam, Eve. *Boys and Girls, Girls and Boys.* New York: Holt, 1972. Informational book (picture book).

______. *Mommies at Work.* Illustrated by Beni Montresor. New York: Knopf, 1961. Informational book (picture book).

Minard, Rosemary, ed. *Womenfolk and Fairy Tales.* Illustrated by Suzanna Klein. Boston: Houghton Mifflin, 1975. Folktales.

Montgomery, Lucy Maud. *Anne of Green Gables.* Illustrated by M. A. and W. A. Claus. Boston: L. C. Page, 1908. Fiction.

Nathan, Dorothy. *Women of Courage.* Illustrated by Carolyn Cather. New York: Random House, 1964. Biography.

Neilson, Winthrop and Francis. *Seven Women: Great Painters.* Philadelphia: Chilton, 1967. Biography.

Ness, Evaline, ed. and illus. *Amelia Mixed the Mustard and Other Poems.* New York: Scribner, 1975. Poetry (a collection featuring heroines and dedicated to all females).

Noble, Iris. *Emmeline and Her Daughters: The Pankhurst Suffragettes.* New York: Messner, 1974. Biography.

O'Dell, Scott. *Island of the Blue Dolphins.* Illustrated by Evaline Ness. Boston: Houghton Mifflin, 1960. Fiction.

———. *Sing Down the Moon.* Boston: Houghton Mifflin, 1970. Fiction.

Ransome, Arthur. *Swallowdale.* London: Jonathan Cape, 1931. Fiction.

Rodgers, Mary. *Freaky Friday.* New York: Harper, 1972. Fantasy.

Sachs, Marilyn. *Peter and Veronica.* Illustrated by Louis Glanzman. Garden City, N.Y.: Doubleday, 1969. Fiction.

———. *Veronica Ganz.* Illustrated by Louis Glanzman. Garden City, N.Y.: Doubleday, 1968. Fiction.

Speare, Elizabeth George. *The Witch of Blackbird Pond.* Boston: Houghton Mifflin, 1958. Historical fiction.

Thane, Elswyth. *Dolley Madison: Her Life and Times.* New York: Macmillan, 1970. Biography.

Thomas, Marlo, and others. *Free to Be You and Me.* New York: McGraw, 1974. Collection of stories, poems, and songs (picture book).

Wagner, Jane. *J. T.* Illustrated by G. Parks, Jr. New York: Van Nostrand, 1969. Fiction.

Wersba, Barbara. *The Dream Watcher.* New York: Atheneum, 1968. Fantasy.

Wilder, Laura Ingalls. *Little House in the Big Woods.* Illustrated by Helen Sewell. New York: Harper, 1932. Fiction.

———. *Little House on the Prairie.* Illustrated by Helen Sewell. New York: Harper, 1935. Fiction.

Yashima, Taro. *Crow Boy.* New York: Viking, 1955. Fiction (picture book).

Zindel, Paul. *I Never Loved Your Mind.* New York: Harper, 1970. Fiction.

Zolotow, Charlotte. *William's Doll.* Illustrated by William Pène du Bois. New York: Harper, 1972 Fiction (picture book).

REFERENCES FOR ADULTS

Adell, Judith, and Klein, Hilary Dale, comp. *A Guide to Non-Sexist Children's Books.* Edited by Walter Schacher. Introduction by Alan Alda. Chicago: Academy, 1976.

Cohen, Martha. *Stop Sex Role Stereotypes in Elementary Education: A Handbook for Parents and Teachers.* Hartford, Conn.: Connecticut Public Interest Research Group, 1974. Pamphlet.

Damon, Jean, and Stuart, Lee. *The Lesbian in Literature.* San Francisco, Calif.: Daughters of Belitis, 1967.

Feminists on Children's Literature. "A Feminist Look at Children's Books." *School Library Journal* 18 (January 1971): 19–24.

Feminists on Children's Media. *Little Miss Muffet Fights Back: Recommended Non-Sexist Books about Girls for Young Readers.* Rev. ed. New York: Feminists on Children's Media, 1974.

Franz, Marie-Luise von. *Problems of the Feminine in Fairy Tales.* New York: Spring Publications, 1972.

Frazier, Nancy, and Sadker, Myra. *Sexism in School and Society.* New York: Harper, 1973.

Garsoni-Stavn, Diane. *Sexism and Youth.* New York: Bowker, 1974.

Howe, Florence. "Educating Women: No More Sugar and Spice." *Saturday Review,* 16 October 1971, pp. 76–77.

———. "Sexual Stereotypes Start Early." *Saturday Review,* 16 October 1975, pp. 76–93.

Nilsen, Alleen Pace. "Women in Children's Literature." *College English* 32, no. 8 (May 1971): 918–26.

Rudman, Masha Kabakow. *Children's Literature: An Issues Approach.* Lexington, Mass.: Heath, 1976.

Weitzman, Lenore J., and others. "Sex Role Socialization in Picture Books for Pre-School Children." *American Journal of Sociology* 77, no. 6 (May 1972): 1125–50.

Women on Words and Images. *Dick and Jane as Victims: Sex Stereotyping in Children's Readers.* Princeton, N.J.: National Organization for Women, 1972.

V. Circles

The circle is one of the most important symbols known to human beings. It is usually interpreted as a symbol of psychic wholeness. When one thinks of circles, one thinks of wedding rings, of such natural circle forms as the sun and the full moon, or of life cycles from birth to death to rebirth. One may also think of seasonal cycles or the movement of the earth and the planets.

The circle is related to another important psychological symbol, the cross. The circle by itself and the cross bisecting a circle are mandala shapes (*mandala* is Sanskrit, meaning "magic circle") that are often seen in primitive drawings and carvings. A charming native American folktale is told to account for the remarkable little crystals in the shape of perfect Roman or Maltese crosses that are found in clods of earth on a mountain plateau in Patrick County, Virginia, and are regarded as lucky stones. According to the tale, the Indians were dancing on the plateau when a messenger from the Holy Land brought them word that

Christ had died. They stopped in their dance and their tears fell down and became tiny stone crosses. In this story round tears are the circumference of the crosses that lie at the heart of circles.

The circle and crossed circle forms are deeply rooted in the human psyche and are the first intelligible shapes to appear in children's earliest drawings. In all countries, these early drawings follow the same pattern. At the age of three and a half, the child begins to produce in drawings the circle, the crossed circle, and the circle containing several circles, and produces these forms in a frequency that is significant. What is interesting about this phenomenon is that these symbolic drawings are made spontaneously and are not modeled on the objects of the outside world. As outer reality becomes more important, the circle and the crossed circle become the sun (the crosses move outside the circle to become "rays") and, eventually, human figures (the circle becomes the head; the rays, arms and legs).

The source of the circle archetype in the human psyche is perhaps related to the fact that circles occur so often in nature—in the circular movements and forms of the sun and moon, in the circular movement of the seasons. Many myths undertake to explain the change of the seasons, but the Greek myth of Demeter grieving for her lost daughter Persephone is one of the most beautiful. The Bible, particularly in Ecclesiastes, includes magnificent passages on the rotation of the seasons, the circular movement of life: "The sun rises, the sun sets." The ancient fertility rites performed around the May pole also had a circular motion—perhaps still recalled in such children's game dances as "Round the Mulberry Bush" and "Ring Around the Rosie."

It is believed that the medieval mummers' play *St. George and the Dragon*—which, though English, has Eastern origins—is associated as a ritual with the circular motion of the seasons. It is sometimes still put on in English villages at Easter, as a testimony to the death of winter and the rebirth of spring, and a charm as well to ensure the continuance of this seasonal rotation. Like the seasons, the plot of the play is cyclical in nature. St. George kills the Turkish knight, who rises to life again.

Modern children's literature offers many examples of stories concerned with the importance of the cycle of the seasons. Generally, these are stories about farming people or those for whom the passing of the seasons is a crucial matter. Such stories as Laura Armer's *Waterless Mountain,* about the Navaho people, and Joseph Krumgold's *. . . and now Miguel,* about a sheepherding family in New Mexico, re-create for children a world in which life revolves around seasonal change.

Another important natural circular form is the island. The island, like the circle, can represent psychic wholeness, in the sense of being self-contained and separate. At times, the island seems to represent independence of parent figures, or places of retreat where psychic wholeness can be obtained. Like the circle the Greeks drew around a sacred place in ancient times, the island is an area of safety. Though there is no room to include them here (the best known are easily available), many stories have to do with life on islands, notably Daniel Defoe's *Robinson Crusoe,* from which hundreds of stories have descended, including Johann David Wyss's *Swiss Family Robinson* and Robert Louis Stevenson's *Treasure Island.*

Circular movement, as well as circular form, is an important aspect of circle symbolism. Love, because it transforms those whom it touches, has the power to set life in motion, acting in a static situation like the impetus that sets a ball or hoop to rolling—and to continue rolling, once started. This "circular" power of love can be seen very often in folktales, where love frequently awakens a character to maturity, or redeems or restores someone to life. The classical Greek myth of "Cupid and Psyche," from which such old folktales as "East of the Sun and West of the Moon" appear to descend, is a tribute to the transformative power of love, which can overcome all difficulties. In the folktale of "Rapunzel," there is a couple who are like Adam and Eve in the Garden of Eden. The curse upon their daughter Rapunzel comes from the wife's eating something forbidden in a garden, but ultimately, through the redemptive power of love, Rapunzel is found in the desert where she has been banished, and the blinded prince can see again.

Antoine de Saint-Exupéry's *The Little Prince* and E. B. White's *Charlotte's Web,* two fantasies excerpted here, attest in their beautiful treatment of death to the circular movement of life.

Next comes roundness commented on with surface humor but inner seriousness: Gertrude Stein's poetic fiction *The World Is Round,* in which roundness is shown to hold certain terrors.

Myth

DEMETER

(Greek)

Retold by Edith Hamilton

One of the Homeric Hymns, of the eighth or beginning of the seventh century B.C.*, is the earliest recorded source we have for this ancient myth, whose roots extend even farther into the past. At one level, it is the story of the grief of a mother—Demeter, the great Goddess of the Corn—who is separated from her daughter, Persephone, and who wanders through the earth, disguised as an old woman, searching for her. At another level, it is a beautiful explanation for the changing round of the seasons.*

Demeter had an only daughter, Persephone (in Latin Proserpine), the maiden of the spring. She lost her and in her terrible grief she withheld her gifts from the earth, which turned into a frozen desert. The green and flowering land was icebound and lifeless because Persephone had disappeared.

The lord of the dark underworld, the king of the multitudinous dead, carried her off when, enticed by the wondrous bloom of the narcissus, she strayed too far from her companions. In his chariot drawn by coal-black steeds he rose up through a chasm in the earth, and grasping the maiden by the wrist set her beside him. He bore her away, weeping, down to the underworld. The high hills echoed her cry and the depths of the sea, and her mother heard it. She sped like a bird over sea and land seeking her daughter. But no one would tell her the truth, "no man nor god, nor any sure messenger from the birds." Nine days Demeter wandered, and all that time she would not taste of ambrosia or put sweet nectar to her lips. At last she came to the Sun and he told her all the story: Persephone was down in the world beneath the earth, among the shadowy dead.

Then a still greater grief entered Demeter's heart. She left Olympus; she dwelt on earth, but so disguised that none knew her, and, indeed, the gods are not easily discerned by mortal men. In her desolate wanderings she came to Eleusis and sat by the wayside near a wall. She seemed an aged woman, such as in great houses care for the children or guard the storerooms. Four lovely maidens, sisters, coming to draw water from the well, saw her and asked her pityingly what she did there. She answered that she had fled from pirates who had meant to sell her as a slave, and that she knew no one in this strange land to go to for help. They told her that any house in the town would welcome her, but that they would like best to bring her to their own if she would wait there while they went to ask their mother. The goddess bent her head in assent, and the girls, filling their shining pitchers with water, hurried home. Their mother, Metaneira, bade them return at once and invite the stranger to come, and speeding back they found the glorious goddess still sitting there, deeply veiled and covered to her slender feet by her dark robe. She followed them, and as she crossed the threshold to the hall where the mother sat holding her young son, a divine radiance filled the doorway and awe fell upon Metaneira.

She bade Demeter be seated and herself offered her honey-sweet wine, but the goodess would not taste it. She asked instead for barley-water flavored with mint, the cooling draught of the reaper at harvest time and also the sacred cup given the worshipers at Eleusis. Thus refreshed she took the child and held him to her fragrant bosom and his mother's heart was glad. So Demeter nursed Demophoön, the son that Metaneira had borne to wise Celeus. And the child grew like a young god, for daily Demeter anointed him with ambrosia and at night she would place him in the red heart of the fire. Her purpose was to give him immortal youth.

Something, however, made the mother uneasy, so that one night she kept watch and screamed in terror when she saw the child laid in the fire. The goddess was angered; she seized the boy and cast him on the ground. She had meant to set him free from old age and from death, but that was not to be. Still, he had lain upon her knees and slept in her arms and therefore he should have honor throughout his life.

Then she showed herself the goddess manifest. Beauty breathed about her and a lovely fragrance; light shone from her so that the great house was filled with brightness. She was Demeter, she told the awestruck women. They must build her a great temple near the town and so win back the favor of her heart.

Thus she left them, and Metaneira fell speechless to the earth and all there trembled with fear. In the morning they told Celeus what had happened and he called the people together and revealed to them the command of the goddess. They worked willingly to build her a temple, and when it was finished Demeter came to it and sat there—apart from the gods in Olympus, alone, wasting away with longing for her daughter.

That year was most dreadful and cruel for mankind over all the earth. Nothing grew; no seed sprang up, in vain the oxen drew the plowshare through the furrows. It seemed the whole race of men would die of famine. At last Zeus saw that he must take the matter in hand. He sent the gods to Demeter, one after another, to try to turn her from her anger, but she listened to none of them. Never would she let the earth bear fruit until she had seen her daughter. Then Zeus realized that his brother must give way. He told Hermes to go down to the underworld and to bid the lord of it let his bride go back to Demeter.

Hermes found the two sitting side by side, Persephone shrinking away, reluctant because she longed for her mother. At Hermes' words she sprang up joyfully, eager to go. Her husband knew that he must obey the word of Zeus and send her up to earth away from him, but he prayed her as she left him to have kind thoughts of him and not be so sorrowful that she was the wife of one who was great among the immortals. And he made her eat a pomegranate seed, knowing in his heart that if she did so she must return to him.

He got ready his golden car and Hermes took the reins and drove the black horses straight to the temple where Demeter was. She ran out to meet her daughter as swiftly as a Maenad runs down the mountainside. Persephone sprang into her arms and was held fast there. All day they talked of what had happened to them both, and Demeter grieved when she heard of the pomegranate seed, fearing that she could not keep her daughter with her.

Then Zeus sent another messenger to her, a great personage, none other than his revered mother Rhea, the oldest of the gods. Swiftly she hastened down from the heights of Olympus to the barren, leafless earth, and standing at the door of the temple she spoke to Demeter.

Come, my daughter, for Zeus,
far-seeing, loud-thundering, bids you.
Come once again to the halls of the
gods where you shall have honor,
Where you will have your desire, your
daughter, to comfort your sorrow
As each year is accomplished and
bitter winter is ended.
For a third part only the kingdom of
darkness shall hold her.
For the rest you will keep her, you
and the happy immortals.
Peace now. Give men life which
comes alone from your giving.

Demeter did not refuse, poor comfort though it was that she must lose Persephone for four months every year and see her young loveliness go down to the world of the dead. But she was kind; the "Good Goddess," men always called her. She was sorry for the desolation she had brought about. She made the fields once more rich with abundant fruit and the whole world bright with flowers and green leaves. Also she went to the princes of Eleusis who had built her temple and she chose one, Triptolemus, to be her ambassador to men, instructing them how to sow the corn. She taught him and Celeus and the others her sacred rites, "mysteries which no one may utter, for deep awe checks the tongue. Blessed is he who has seen them; his lot will be good in the world to come."

Queen of fragrant Eleusis,
Giver of earth's good gifts,
Give me your grace, O Demeter.
You, too, Persephone, fairest,
Maiden all lovely, I offer
Song for your favor.

In the stories of both goddesses, Demeter and Persephone, the idea of sorrow was foremost. Demeter, goddess of the harvest wealth, was still more the divine sorrowing mother who saw her daughter die each year. Persephone was the radiant maiden of the spring and the summertime, whose light step upon the dry, brown hillside was enough to make it fresh and blooming, as Sappho writes,

I heard the footfall of the flower
spring . . .

—Persephone's footfall. But all the while Persephone knew how brief that beauty was; fruits, flowers, leaves, all the fair growth of earth, must end with the coming of the cold and pass like herself into the power of death. After the lord of the dark world below carried her away she was never again the gay young creature who had played in the flowery meadow without a thought of care or trouble. She did indeed rise from the dead every spring, but she brought with her the memory of where she had come from; with all her bright beauty there was something strange and awesome about her. She was often said to be "the maiden whose name may not be spoken."

The Olympians were "the happy gods," "the deathless gods," far removed from suffering mortals destined to die. But in their grief and at the hour of death, men could turn for compassion to the goddess who sorrowed and the the goddess who died.

CUPID AND PSYCHE

(Greek)

Retold by Edith Hamilton

The story of Cupid and Psyche, based on ancient Greek myth, is taken from Metamorphoses, or The Golden Ass, *a long romance by the second-century* A.D. *Roman writer Apuleius. It is a love story that is also a depiction of the ordeal a young girl must undergo before she becomes a woman. Psyche's life with Cupid passes like a dream until, at the instigation of her two envious sisters, she does the forbidden—takes a lamp and looks at the real man who is her husband. Instantly Cupid flees from her, and Psyche must then perform four labors for the goddess Venus before she can gain him back. Because the love must be struggled for, it becomes more mature and enduring. Love clearly sets life in motion in this myth, as it moves Psyche from girlhood to womanhood.*

There was once a king who had three daughters, all lovely maidens, but the youngest, Psyche, excelled her sisters so greatly that beside them she seemed a very goddess consorting with mere mortals. The fame of her surpassing beauty spread over the earth, and everywhere men journeyed to gaze upon her with wonder and adoration and to do her homage as though she were in truth one of the immortals. They would even say that Venus herself could not equal this mortal. As they thronged in ever-growing numbers to worship her loveliness no one any more gave a thought to Venus herself. Her temples were neglected; her altars foul with cold ashes; her favorite towns deserted and falling in ruins. All the honors once hers were now given to a mere girl destined some day to die.

It may well be believed that the goddess would not put up with this treatment. As always when she was in trouble she turned for help to her son, that beautiful winged youth whom some call Cupid and others Love, against whose arrows there is no defense, neither in heaven nor on the earth. She told him her wrongs and as always he was ready to do her bidding. "Use your power," she said, "and make the hussy fall madly in love with the vilest and most despicable creature there is in the whole world." And so no doubt he would have done, if Venus had not first shown him Psyche, never thinking in her jealous rage what such beauty might do even to the God of Love himself. As he looked upon her it was as if he had shot one of his arrows into his own heart. He said nothing to his mother, indeed he had no power to utter a word, and Venus left him with the happy confidence that he would swiftly bring about Psyche's ruin.

What happened, however, was not what she had counted on. Psyche did not fall in love with a horrible wretch, she did not fall in love at all. Still more strange, no one fell in love with her. Men were content to look and wonder and worship—and then pass on to marry someone else. Both her sisters, inexpressibly inferior to her, were splendidly married, each to a king. Psyche, the all-beautiful, sat sad and solitary, only admired, never loved. It seemed that no man wanted her.

This was, of course, most disturbing to her parents. Her father finally traveled to an oracle of Apollo to ask his advice on how to get her a good husband. The god answered him, but his words were terrible. Cupid had told him the whole story and had begged for his help. Accordingly Apollo said that Psyche, dressed in deepest mourning, must be set on the summit of a rocky hill and left alone, and that there her destined husband, a fearful winged serpent, stronger than the gods themselves, would come to her and make her his wife.

The misery of all when Psyche's father brought back this lamentable news can be imagined. They dressed the maiden as though for her death and carried her to the hill with greater sorrowing than if it had been to her tomb. But Psyche herself kept her courage. "You should have wept for me before," she told them, "because of the beauty that has drawn down upon me the jealousy of Heaven. Now go, knowing that I am glad the end has come." They went in despairing grief, leaving the lovely helpless creature to meet her doom alone, and they shut themselves in their palace to mourn all their days for her.

On the high hilltop in the darkness Psyche sat, waiting for she knew not what terror. There, as she wept and trembled, a soft breath of air came through the stillness to her, the gentle breathing of Zephyr, sweetest and mildest of winds. She felt it lift her up. She was floating away from the rocky hill and down until she lay upon a grassy meadow soft as a bed and fragrant with flowers. It was so peaceful there, all her trouble left her and she slept. She woke beside a bright river; and on its bank was a mansion stately and beautiful as though built for a god, with pillars of gold and walls of silver and floors inlaid with precious stones. No sound was to be heard; the place seemed deserted and Psyche drew near, awestruck at the sight of such splendor. As she hesitated on the threshold, voices sounded in her ear. She could see no one, but the words they spoke came clearly to her. The house was for her, they told her. She must enter without fear and bathe and refresh herself. Then a banquet table would be spread for her. "We are your servants," the voices said, "ready to do whatever you desire."

The bath was the most delightful, the food the most delicious, she had ever enjoyed. While she dined, sweet music breathed around her: a great choir seemed to sing to a harp, but she could only hear, not see, them. Throughout the day, except for the strange companionship of the voices, she was alone, but in some inexplicable way she felt sure that with the coming of the night her husband would be with her. And so it happened. When she felt him beside her and heard his voice softly murmuring in her ear, all her fears left her. She knew without seeing him that here was no monster or shape of terror, but the lover and husband she had longed and waited for.

This half-and-half companionship could not fully content her; still she was happy and the time passed swiftly. One night, however, her dear though unseen husband spoke gravely to her and warned her that danger in the shape of her two sisters was approaching. "They are coming to the hill where you disappeared, to weep for you," he said; "but you must not let them see you or you will bring great sorrow upon me and ruin to yourself." She promised him she would not, but all the next day she passed in weeping, thinking of her sisters and herself unable to comfort them. She was still in tears when her husband came and even his carresses could not check them. At last he yielded sorrowfully to her great desire. "Do what you will," he said, "but you are seeking your own destruction." Then he warned her solemnly not to be persuaded by anyone to try to see him, on pain of being separated from him forever. Psyche cried out that she would never do so. She would die a hundred times over rather than live without him. "But give me this joy," she said: "to see my sisters." Sadly he promised her that it should be so.

The next morning the two came, brought down from the mountain by Zephyr. Happy and excited, Psyche was waiting for them. It was long before the three could speak to each other; their joy was too great to be expressed except by tears and embraces. But when at last they entered the palace and the elder sisters saw its surpassing treasures; when they sat at the rich banquet and heard the marvelous music, bitter envy took possession of them and a devouring curiosity as to who was the lord of all this magnificence and their sister's husband. But Psyche kept faith; she told them only that he was a young man, away now on a hunting expedition. Then filling their hands with gold and jewels, she had Zephyr bear them back to the hill. They went willingly enough, but their hearts were on fire with jealousy. All their own wealth and good fortune seemed to them as nothing compared with Psyche's, and their envious anger so worked in them that they came finally to plotting how to ruin her.

That very night Psyche's husband warned her once more. She would not listen when he begged her not to let them come again. She never could see him, she reminded him. Was she also to be forbidden to see all others, even her sisters so dear to her? He yielded as before, and very soon the two wicked women arrived, with their plot carefully worked out.

Already, because of Psyche's stumbling and contradictory answers when they asked her what her husband looked like, they had become convinced that she had never set eyes on him and did not really know what he was. They did not tell her this, but they reproached her for hiding her terrible state from them, her own sisters. They had learned, they said, and knew for a fact, that her husband was not a man, but the fearful serpent Apollo's oracle had declared he would be. He was kind now, no doubt, but he would certainly turn upon her some night and devour her.

Psyche, aghast, felt terror flooding her heart instead of love. She had wondered so often why he would never let her see him. There must be some dreadful reason. What did she really know about him.? If he was not horrible to look at, then he was cruel to forbid her ever to behold him. In extreme misery, faltering and stammering, she gave her sisters to understand that she could not deny what they said, because she had been with him only in the dark. "There must be something very wrong," she sobbed, "for him so to shun the light of day." And she begged them to advise her.

They had their advice all prepared beforehand. That night she must hide a sharp knife and a lamp near her bed. When her husband was fast asleep she must leave the bed, light the lamp, and get the knife. She must steel herself to plunge it swiftly into the body of the frightful being the light would certainly show her. "We will be near," they said, "and carry you away with us when he is dead."

Then they left her torn by doubt and distracted what to do. She loved him; he was her dear husband. No; he was a horrible serpent and she loathed him. She would kill him—She would not. She must have certainty—She did not want certainty. So all day long her thoughts fought with each other. When evening came, however, she had given the struggle up. One thing she was determined to do: she would see him.

When at last he lay sleeping quietly, she summoned all her courage and lit the lamp. She tiptoed to the bed and holding the light high above her she gazed at what lay there. Oh, the relief and the rapture that filled her heart. No monster was revealed, but the sweetest and fairest of all creatures, at whose sight the very lamp seemed to shine brighter. In her first shame at her folly and lack of faith, Psyche fell on her knees and would have plunged the knife into her own breast if it had not fallen from her trembling hands. But those same unsteady hands that saved her betrayed her, too, for as she hung over him, ravished at the sight of him and unable to deny herself the bliss of filling her eyes with his beauty, some hot oil fell from the lamp upon his shoulder. He started awake: he saw the light and knew her faithlessness, and without a word he fled from her.

She rushed out after him into the night. She could not see him, but she heard his voice speaking to her. He told her who he was, and sadly bade her farewell. "Love cannot live where there is no trust," he said, and flew away. "The God of Love!" she thought. "He was my husband, and I, wretch that I am, could not keep faith with him. Is he gone from me forever? . . . At any rate," she told herself with rising courage, "I can spend the rest of my life searching for him. If he has no more love left for me, at least I can show him how much I love him." And she started on her journey. She had no idea where to go; she knew only that she would never give up looking for him.

He meanwhile had gone to his mother's chamber to have his wound cared for, but when Venus heard his story and learned that it was Psyche whom he had chosen, she left him angrily alone in his pain, and went forth to find the girl of whom he had made her still more jealous. Venus was determined to show Psyche what it meant to draw down the displeasure of a goddess.

Poor Psyche in her despairing wanderings was trying to win the gods over to her side. She offered ardent prayers to them perpetually, but not one of them would do anything to make Venus their enemy. At last she perceived that there was no hope for her, either in heaven or on earth, and she took a desperate resolve. She would go straight to Venus; she would offer herself humbly to her as her servant, and try to soften her anger. "And who knows," she thought, "if he himself is not there in his mother's house." So she set forth to find the goddess who was looking everywhere for her.

When she came into Venus' presence the goddess laughed aloud and asked her scornfully if she was seeking a husband since the one she had had would have nothing to do with her because he had almost died of the burning wound she had given him. "But really," she said, "you are so plain and ill-favored a girl that you will never be able to get you a lover except by the most diligent and painful service. I will therefore show my good will to you by training you in such ways." With that she took a great quantity of the smallest of the seeds, wheat and poppy and millet and so on, and mixed them all together in a heap. "By nightfall these must all be sorted," she said. "See to it for your own sake." And with that she departed.

Psyche, left alone, sat still and stared at the heap. Her mind was all in a maze because of the cruelty of the command; and, indeed, it was of no use to start a task so manifestly impossible. But at this direful moment she who had awakened no compassion in mortals or immortals was pitied by the tiniest creatures of the field, the little ants, the swift-runners. They cried to each other, "Come, have mercy on this poor maid and help her diligently." At once they came, waves of them, one after another, and they labored separating and dividing, until what had been a confused mass lay all ordered, every seed with its kind. This was what Venus found when she came back, and very angry she was to see it. "Your work is by no means over," she said. Then she gave Psyche a crust of bread and bade her sleep on the ground while she herself went off to her soft, fragrant couch. Surely if she could keep the girl at hard labor and half starve her, too, that hateful beauty of hers would soon be lost. Until then she must see that her son was securely guarded in his chamber where he was still suffering from his wound. Venus was pleased at the way matters were shaping.

The next morning she devised another task for Psyche, this time a dangerous one. "Down there near the riverbank," she said, "where the bushes grow thick, are sheep with fleeces of gold. Go fetch me some of their shining wool." When the worn girl reached the gently flowing stream, a great longing seized her to throw herself into it and end all her pain and despair. But as she was bending over the water she heard a little voice from near her feet, and looking down saw that it came from a green reed. She must not drown herself, it said. Things were not as bad as that. The sheep were indeed very fierce, but if Psyche would wait until they came out of the bushes toward evening to rest beside the river, she could go into the thicket and find plenty of the golden wool hanging on the sharp briars.

So spoke the kind and gentle reed, and Psyche, following the directions, was able to carry back to her cruel mistress a quantity of the shining fleece. Venus received it with an evil smile. "Someone helped you," she said sharply. "Never did you do this by yourself. However, I will give you an opportunity to prove that you really have the stout heart and the singular prudence you make such a show of. Do you see that black water which falls from the hill yonder? It is the source of the terrible river which is called hateful, the river Styx. You are to fill this flask from it." That was the worst task yet, as Psyche saw when she approached the waterfall. Only a winged creature could reach it, so steep and slimy were the rocks on all sides, and so fearful the onrush of the descending waters. But by this time it must be evident to all the readers of this story (as, perhaps, deep in her heart it had become evident to Psyche herself) that although each of her trials seemed impossibly hard, an excellent way out would always be provided for her. This time her savior was an eagle, who poised on his great wings beside her, seized the flask from her with his beak and brought it back to her full of the black water.

But Venus kept on. One cannot but accuse her of some stupidity. The only effect of all that had happened was to make her try again. She gave Psyche a box which she was to carry to the underworld and ask Proserpine to fill with some of her beauty. She was to tell her that Venus really needed it, she was so worn-out from nursing her sick son. Obediently as always Psyche went forth to look for the road to Hades. She found her guide in a tower she passed. It gave her careful directions how to get to Proserpine's palace, first through a great hole in the earth, then down to the river of death, where she must give the ferryman, Charon, a penny to take her across. From there the road led straight to the palace. Cerberus, the three-headed dog, guarded the doors, but if she gave him a cake he would be friendly and let her pass.

All happened, of course, as the tower had foretold. Proserpine was willing to do Venus a service, and Psyche, greatly encouraged, bore back the box, returning far more quickly than she had gone down.

Her next trial she brought upon herself through her curiosity and, still more, her vanity. She felt that she must see what that beauty-charm in the box was; and, perhaps, use a little of it herself. She knew quite as well as Venus did that her looks were not improved by what she had gone through, and always in her mind was the thought that she might suddenly meet Cupid. If only she could make herself more lovely for him! She was unable to resist the temptation; she opened the box. To her sharp disappointment she saw nothing there; it seemed empty. Immediately, however, a deadly languor took possession of her and she fell into a heavy sleep.

At this juncture the God of Love himself stepped forward. Cupid was healed of his wound by now and longing for Psyche. It is a difficult matter to keep Love imprisoned. Venus had locked the door, but there were the windows. All Cupid had to do was to fly out and start looking for his wife. She was lying almost beside the palace, and he found her at once. In a moment he had wiped the sleep from her eyes and put it back into the box. Then waking her with just a prick from one of his arrows, and scolding her a little for her curiosity, he bade her take Proserpine's box to his mother and he assured her that all thereafter would be well.

While the joyful Psyche hastened on her errand, the god flew up to Olympus. He wanted to make certain that Venus would give them no more trouble, so he went straight to Jupiter himself. The Father of Gods and Men consented at once to all that Cupid asked—"Even though," he said, "you have done me great harm in the past—seriously injured my good name and my dignity by making me change myself into a bull and a swan and so on. . . . However, I cannot refuse you."

Then he called a full assembly of the gods, and announced to all, including Venus, that Cupid and Psyche were formally married, and that he proposed to bestow immortality upon the bride. Mercury brought Psyche into the palace of the gods, and Jupiter himself gave her the ambrosia to taste which made her immortal. This, of course, completely changed the situation. Venus could not object to a goddess for her daughter-in-law; the alliance had become eminently suitable. No doubt she reflected also that Psyche, living up in heaven with a husband and children to care for, could not be much on the earth to turn men's heads and interfere with her own worship.

So all came to a most happy end. Love and the Soul (for that is what Psyche means) had sought and, after sore trials, found each other; and that union could never be broken.

Biblical Writing

The Bible contains many passages using the metaphor of natural cycles to convey thoughts that lie too deep for words. Here are three famous ones.

"The earth abideth forever"

(*Ecclesiastes* 1)

The earth abideth forever.
The sun also ariseth, and the sun goeth
down,
And hasteth to his place where he arose.

The wind goeth toward the south,
And turneth about unto the north;
It whirleth about continually,
And the wind returneth again according
to his circuits.

All the rivers run into the sea;
Yet the sea is not full;
Unto the place whence the rivers come,
Thither they return again.

"To everything there is a season . . . "

(*Ecclesiastes* 3)

To every thing there is a season, and a time to every purpose under the heaven:

A time to be born, and a time to die; a time to plant, and a time to pluck up that which is planted;

A time to kill, and a time to heal; a time to break down, and a time to build up;

A time to weep, and a time to laugh; a time to mourn, and a time to dance;

A time to cast away stones, and a time to gather stones together; a time to embrace, and a time to refrain from embracing;

A time to get, and a time to lose; a time to keep, and a time to cast away;

A time to rend, and a time to sew; a time to keep silence, and a time to speak;

A time to love, and a time to hate; a time of war, and a time of peace.

"The voice of the turtle . . . "

(*The Song of Songs* 2)

For, lo, the winter is past,
The rain is over and gone;
The flowers appear on the earth;
The time of the singing of birds is come,
And the voice of the turtle* is heard in
our land.

* The word "turtle" refers to turtledove.

Folk Songs

ROUND THE MULBERRY BUSH

Circle songs are among the most ancient of children's games and appear in all cultures. This is one of the most popular in English.

mf
Here we go round the mul-berry bush, the mul-berry bush, the mul-berry bush;
Here we go round the mul-berry bush, All on a frost - y morn - ing.
This is the way we clap our hands, This is the way we clap our hands,
This is the way we clap our hands, All on a frost - y morn - ing.

RING-A-RING O' ROSES

*Although the lines "Cusha! Cusha!/ All fall down," accompanied by sneezing and falling-down actions, have led to the notion that this circle song dates back to the Great Plague of the Middle Ages, the words of the rhyme have not been found in children's literature before 1881, according to Iona and Peter Opie (*The Oxford Dictionary of Nursery Rhymes*, 1951). The fall itself was probably a version of a curtsy.*

mf
Ring - a - ring o' ros - es, A pock - et full of pos - ies.
Cush - a, Cush - a! All fall down.

Folk Play

ST. GEORGE AND THE DRAGON

Retold by Diana John

The theme of St. George and the Dragon *is repeated in folk plays all over the world. Such plays always present a symbolic contest in which a champion is killed and then revived, representing the victory of spring over winter, life over death. It is customary for a clown figure to restore the hero to life and ensure the victory. The audience usually participates in some way in these performances, by sharing food or contributions with the actors, or by singing and dancing together at the end of the play.*

FOOL: I open the door, I enter in;

I hope your favour we shall win.
Stir up the fire and strike a light
And see my merry boys act tonight.
Whether we stand or whether we fall
We'll do our best to please you all.

Enter the ACTORS.

Room, room, brave gallants all,
Pray give us room to rhyme;
We've come to show activity
This merry Christmas time;
Activity of youth,
Activity of age,

The like was never seen

Illustrated by Diana John.

Upon a common stage.
And if you don't believe what I say,
Step in the Turkish Knight and clear the way.

Enter SLASHER.

SLASHER: In come I, the Turkish Knight,
Come from afar to try this fight;
I mean to fight St George,
That man of courage bold,
And if his blood is hot,
I soon shall make it cold.

Enter ST GEORGE.

ST GEORGE: Here come I, St George,
From Britain did I spring;
I'll fight the Dragon Bold,
My wonders to begin.
I'll cut his wings, he shall not fly,
I'll cut him down or else I die.

Enter DRAGON.

DRAGON: Who's he that seeks the Dragon's blood

And calls so angry and so loud?
That English Dog will he before me stand;
I'll cut him down with my courageous hand.

With my long teeth and scurvy jaw
Of such I'd break up half a score
And stay my stomach till I'd more.

ST GEORGE *fights and kills the Dragon.*

ST GEORGE: Here am I, St George,
The man of courage bold,
With my broad axe and sword
I won a crown of gold.
I fought the fiery dragon
And brought him down in slaughter,
And by these deeds I won
The King of Egypt's daughter.

The PRINCESS SABRA *appears.*
ST GEORGE *kisses her hand then speaks again.*

ST GEORGE: Show me the man that bids me stand; I'll cut him down with my courageous hand.

FOOL: Step up, bold Slasher, come this way,
Sir George is ready for the fray.

Enter SLASHER.

SLASHER: In come I, the Turkish Knight,
Come from the Turkish land to fight.
I'll fight St George, who is my foe,
I'll make him yield before I go.

ST GEORGE: Stand off, stand off, Bold Slasher,
And let no more be said,
For if I draw my sword and strike
I'm sure to break your head.
You speak so bold you cannot know
The man that you defy.
I'll cut you up in little bits
And make your buttons fly.

SLASHER: My head is made of iron strong,
My body's made of steel,
My arms and legs of beaten brass,
No man can make me feel.

ST GEORGE: Then draw your sword and fight,
Or draw your purse and pay,
For satisfaction I must get
Before I go away.

SLASHER: No satisfaction shall you get,
I do not shrink to hear your threat.

ST GEORGE: Battle to Battle then let's cry
And see which one first will die.

SLASHER: Battle to Battle let us sound
And see which falls to bite the ground.

ST GEORGE: Then guard your body and guard your head
Or else my sword will strike you dead.

They fight and SLASHER *falls.*

Enter KING OF EGYPT.

KING OF EGYPT: O cruel George, what have you done?
You've wounded and killed my only son

ST GEORGE: It's true I killed the Turkish Knight
But he first challenged me to fight.

KING OF EGYPT: Is there a doctor who can save
My son from lingering in the grave?
Doctor, Doctor, come I beg,
My son is wounded in the heart,
A thousand golden pounds I give
The doctor who could make him live.

Enter DOCTOR.

DOCTOR: Yes there's a doctor who can save
Your son from lingering in the grave,
For all my medicines are sure
And death's a sickness I can cure.

KING OF EGYPT: Where do you come from? Tell me plain

DOCTOR: Italy, Sicily, France and Spain—
All round the world and back again.
There's no disease I haven't seen
And nowhere that I haven't been.

KING OF EGYPT: A thousand pounds I'll give—
Make my poor son live.

DOCTOR: That I'll do, please have no doubts;
The itch, the stitch, the palsy and gout,
Pains within and pains without,
If the devil were in I'd fetch him out.
See this small bottle at my side,

The fame of it is spread far and wide,
Its name El-e-can-pin-pom-pane
And it brings the dead to life again.

He sprinkles SLASHER *with it.*

A drop on his head, a drop on his heart,
Rise up, bold boy, and take your part.

SLASHER *rises.*

SLASHER: Father, your face I'm glad to see,
I thought it was the end of me.

ST GEORGE: And now that I've my duty done, I'll return to the dear bride I've won.

He goes to SABRA. *All cheer.*

FOOL: Now that St George has cleared the way, Come in you others and have your say.

Enter BIG-HEAD.

BIG-HEAD: In come I who hasn't been yet,
With my big head and little wit,
With head so big and wit so small,
I'll dance a jig to please you all.

He dances, the others join in.

Enter JOHNNY JACK.

JOHNNY JACK: In come I, little Johnny Jack,
With my wife and family at my back,
My family's large and I am small,
A little if you please will help us all.

Enter BEELZEBUB.

BEELZEBUB: In come I, old Beelzebub,
On my shoulder I carry a club,
In my hand a frying-pan,
Don't you think I'm a jolly old man?

Enter DEVIL DOUT.

DEVIL DOUT: In come I, little Devil Dout,
If you don't give me money, I'll sweep you out.
Money I want and money I crave,
If you don't give me money, I'll sweep you to the grave.

FOOL: Gentlemen and ladies, your sport is done and I can no longer stay.
Remember still St George will bear the sway.
Gentlemen and ladies all, I hope you will be free
For to subscribe a little part to pay the Doctor's fee.

All hold hands and come to the front of the stage.

ALL: We wish you a Merry Christmas and a Happy New Year,
A pocket full of money and a cellar full of beer,
And a good fat pig to last you all the year.

Folktales

EAST OF THE SUN AND WEST OF THE MOON

(Scandinavian)

Retold by Gwyn Jones

This is a Scandinavian version of the Greek myth "Cupid and Psyche." The folktale contains some obvious motifs derived from the northern setting into which it has been transplanted—walls that go "whiff-whaff-whuff" when the wind blows, a big White Bear that is the beast the beautiful youngest daughter must marry, and a North Wind that blows the woodcutter's daughter to the castle that lies East of the Sun and West of the Moon. Again, though, the central theme of the story consists of the awakening of a young girl through the power of love. The woodcutter's daughter is transformed from a helpless young girl who does her father's bidding into a young woman who dares to search for her young prince all the way to the faraway castle where he is kept under an enchantment.

Once upon a time there was a poor woodcutter who had so many children, he and his wife, that he didn't know what to do. Of food they had little, and of raiment still less, but there was one good thing about them: they were all the prettiest children you ever saw, and the youngest daughter was the prettiest of all.

Illustrated by Joan Kiddell-Monroe.

One evening late in the fall of the year the weather turned so cruel outside, with wind and rain and dark, that there was nothing for them to do but sit as snug as they could indoors, knitting and stitching, and watching the walls go whiff-whaff-whuff with the wind. Just then they heard something give three loud taps on the window-pane. This happened three times before the father thought he had better go out and see what was to do. When he came outside, what should he see but a big White Bear.

"Good evening, woodcutter," said the White Bear.

"Good evening, Bear. Is there anything I can do for you?

"As a matter of fact there is. Will you give me your youngest daughter? If you will, I can make you just as rich as you are at this moment poor."

"That will be very rich indeed," replied the woodcutter. "But I think I should have a word with my daughter first. Would you mind waiting?"

"Not at all," said the Bear. So back inside went the father and explained how there was a fine White Bear waiting outside who had given him his word to make them rich as rich if only he would give him his youngest daughter.

"Oh, no," cried the daughter, "oh no, no!" But he went on to explain just how poor he was and how hard he found it, and what a difference it would make to her brothers and sisters, and how the White Bear was the politest and handsomest creature in the whole wide world, and so on, till at length she changed her mind, and having washed her face and combed her hair, and with all her rags about her, declared herself ready and went out to meet the Bear.

"Are you afraid?" he asked. "There is no need to be. Just climb on my back with your bundle and we shan't be long."

So on she climbed, and off they went, and when they had been some time on their way he again asked her whether she was afraid. "There is no need to be," he assured her. "Just hold tight to this shaggy coat of mine and we shan't be long."

But they rode what seemed a very long way indeed till they came to a big steep hill. There the White Bear gave a knock-knock-knock, just as you or I might knock on a door, and sure enough there was a door in the hill which opened to him, and in they went, as it were into a great castle, with walls and a roof and windows, and rooms where the candlelight sparkled on silver and gold, and other rooms which were studded with crystal and bright gems. They walked on into the castle and came to a room where there was a table laid with precious food and drink, and, "Are you hungry?" asked the White Bear. "There is no need to be. Just eat and drink all you want from this table and then we shan't be long."

The next thing he did was to give her a soft silver bell. "Whatever you want," he said, "you have only to ring this bell, and it will be yours on the instant."

When she had eaten and drunk her fill, she felt so sleepy after her meal and her journey that she thought no place could be so pleasant as bed. So she rang the bell, and before it finished ringing she found herself in a lovely bedchamber, with a bed as soft and white as the heart's desire, its pillows of down and its curtains silken, and all the fringes of thread of gold. There was nothing in the room that was not gold or silver, save what was satin and silk. When she had gone to bed and put out the light, someone came and lay down beside her, but who it was she did not know. In fact it was the White Bear, who threw off his beast-shape by night, when it was dark, but was up and away and a bear again before she could wake in the morning. After this fashion she lived for a while and was happy, but then there came a day when she grew silent and sad. For at home she would be talking to her father and mother, with her brothers and sisters about her, but here she was all alone; so when the White Bear asked her one day what might make her happy again, she told him how she longed to go home, if only for a month, or a week, or a day, or just one hour.

"There is no need to be sad," said the

White Bear. "Go home by all means. Promise me one thing, though: never to talk alone with your mother, but only when the rest of the family are near. For if you let her get you on your own, there is no telling what bad luck may follow."

She promised, and next Sunday along came the White Bear and said, "Well, shall we be off?" Once more she climbed on to his back, and held tight to his shaggy coat, and when they had travelled a long, long way they came to a fine big house where her sisters ran in and out and her brothers round and about, and where her father and mother sat at ease in the parlour, and everything was fine as only fine can be.

The White Bear said he wouldn't come in and intrude. "But don't forget your promise." And with that away he trundled.

At home there was such joy as defeats the telling. For a start they just couldn't thank her enough for making them rich, and there were their dresses to talk about too. Besides, they wanted to know what sort of life she was leading with the White Bear. But she was as clever as she was pretty, and the more she seemed to tell them the less they really knew. Even when her mother tried to get her alone in her bedroom, she remembered what the White Bear had told her, and for a time found excuses for not going upstairs.

But what will be, shall be, and somehow or other her mother got round her at last, till she had blabbed out the whole story, how when she had gone to bed and the light was out someone came and lay down beside her, but before morning-light he would be up and away, so that she had never a glimpse of him, and how unhappy this made her, and how all day she lived alone, and her life was dull and dreary.

"The good Lord defend us!" cried her mother. "Why, it might be a troll you are living with. Luckily, I know a trick worth two of his. Take this piece of candle, daughter, which you can carry home in your bosom. If you want a good look at him, light it while he is still asleep, but take care, such great care, not to drop the tallow on his shirt."

She promised, and hid the candle in her bosom, and before nightfall the White Bear came to fetch her.

"Have you been talking to your mother?" he asked. "For if you have, we face nothing short of disaster."

Not she, she vowed. Why should she talk to her mother? "Why indeed?" sighed the White Bear, and his sigh struck her heart like a stone. But she said nothing to undeceive him, and soon after dark they were back in the hill.

Here, it was the old story all over again. When she had gone to bed and the light was out someone came and lay down beside her; but there was this much of change, that in the blackest minute after midnight, when she could hear how hard he slept, she rose from bed, and lighting the candle let it shine gently upon him. What she saw was a prince so young and handsome that she felt she must then and there kiss him or die. But as she bent over him to do so the candle tilted, so that three drops of tallow fell on to his shirt, and as they touched him he woke up.

"Alas," he cried, "what have you done? Had you been resolute for just one year I should have been freed from my enchantment. It is my step-mother who has laid a spell on me, so that I am a White Bear by day and a Man by night. Now all is over between us, and I must return to where she is dwelling in a castle which stands East of the Sun and West of the Moon. A Princess lives there too, whose nose is three feet long, and rosy into the bargain, and she is the one I shall have to marry now."

"Forgive me, forgive me," she cried to him, weeping; but there was no help for it: off he must go.

"Let me go with you, please let me go!"

There was no chance of that, he told her sadly. He must go as he came, alone.

"Tell me the way, then," she pleaded. "Surely I may know that, and come looking for you?"

Unhappily, he told her, there was no way thither. The castle lay East of the Sun and West of the Moon, and that was all about it.

So she cried herself to sleep, and next morning when she woke up the Prince and the castle had gone into thin air, and she was lying on a small green mound in the middle of the forest, and all she had to wear were the rags she had worn the day she left her father the woodcutter's home. But because she was as brave as she was pretty, she stood up and determined to go looking for the castle that lay East of the Sun and West of the Moon.

She had been walking almost a day when she came to where an old crone, with three loose teeth in her head, was sitting under a high rock, playing with a golden apple. When she had greeted this crone, she asked her whether she knew the way to the Prince and his step-mother in the castle that lay East of the Sun and West of the Moon, where there lived also a Princess with a red nose three feet long whom the Prince might have to marry.

"Why do you ask?" asked the crone, and her teeth went shiggle-shiggle-shiggle. "Are you the girl for him?"

"I would be, if I could find him again."

"I believe you," said the crone. "But all I know is what you know for yourself already. But here, have the loan of my horse, who will carry you to my sister's. Maybe she can tell you more than I can. When you get there, just give the horse a flick under the right ear, and he'll come trotting home of himself. Oh, and take this golden apple with you."

She climbed on the horse and away she went, and in time she came upon another crone with two loose teeth in her head, sitting under another rock, carding with a golden carding-comb. Her too she asked whether she knew the way to her Prince and his step-mother and the long-nosed Princess in the castle that lay East of the Sun and West of the Moon.

"I doubt whether I know more than you do," said the crone, and her teeth went shiggle-shiggle. "But here, have the loan of my horse, who will carry you to my sister's. Maybe she can tell you more than I can. Just give the horse a flick under the right ear when you get there, and he will come cantering home of himself. Oh, and you had better take this golden carding-comb with you."

Once more she climbed on the horse and away she went, and after a long and weary journey she came upon yet a third crone, with just one loose tooth in her head, spinning with a golden spinning-wheel. Again she asked much the same question, and again she had much the same answer.

"But I'll lend you this horse of mine," promised the crone, and her one tooth went shiggle. "Ride on and find the East Wind and ask him to help you. He has been about a good deal. And you need only give the horse a flick under the right ear when you have done with him, and he'll come galloping home of himself. Oh, and why not take this golden spinning-wheel with you?"

And now she had to ride for many days, a hard and weary time, before she reached the East Wind's home. He was in, as it happened, and told her, yes, he had heard of that place, but where it was he could not say, for he had never had breath to blow so far.

"But let us go along to my brother the West Wind. He may well have been there, for he blows much more strongly than I."

She climbed on his back, and it is enough to say that they travelled like the East Wind and reached the West Wind's house in no time at all. The West Wind was in, as it happened, but though he had been around a good deal he had never blown as far as that castle. "But perhaps our brother the South Wind is your man. He is much stronger than I, and has flapped his wings from the front to the back of beyond. He has a good memory too, and if he has seen that Three-Foot Rosy-Nosy will be sure to remember so inflammable yet dismal a sight."

She climbed on his back, and need we say more than that they travelled like the West Wind and reached the South Wind's house in no time at all? The South Wind too was at home, getting his breath back after a long blow round the southern rim of the world, but while he admitted, and admitted with pride, that he had blustered round more than most, he had never blown to the castle that lay East of the Sun and West of the Moon. "Your only chance now is to catch our brother the North Wind. He is the oldest and strongest of us all, and the only places he has never blown on are the places that aren't there. So just you climb on my back and we'll be there in a whiffy."

And so they were, or in two at the most. As they drew near the North Wind's house she could hear fluster and bluster, and the icy puffs of his breath blew on her small pretty face.

"Oh blow, blast, and blither!" roared the North Wind, as they arrived at his door. "Blow off, the pair of you, I say."

"Don't storm so," said the South Wind. "It is only I your brother and the woodcutter's daughter, who ought by rights to marry the Prince who lives in the castle that lies East of the Sun and West of the Moon—the one that may have to marry the Three-Foot Rosy-Nosy instead. All we want to know is whether you have been there and could find the way there again."

"Oh whiff, whaff, and whuffle!" roared the North Wind, but more gently. "Once upon a time I blew an aspen-leaf there, and for weeks thereafter I couldn't raise a puff. Still, little sweetheart, if you really want to go there, and aren't afraid of my roaring, just climb on my back tomorrow morning and we ought to arrive before dark."

All night long she heard the North Wind snoring to draw his puff together; and then as day broke he so blew himself up for the journey that she was afraid to look at him. Oh, but he was big and stout and blustery! Still, she climbed on his back when he was ready, and then, whuff! away they went, high into the air and far over the sea, as though no bound of the world lay before them. Down below, what a storm they had! Forests fell to the ground, and ships swirled to the ocean-bottom. And all the while they drove on further and faster, till even the North Wind began to get tired, and at last had hardly a fistful of breath left. And as he grew tired the air left his feathers, so that they drooped and drave and drifted, and the sea-spray wetted his wings, and the crests of the waves washed over his heels.

"Are you afraid?" asked the North Wind. And when, trembling, she gasped out No, "That's just as well," he added, "for I am!"

But they were now in sight of land, and he had just enough blow in him to bring her ashore under the castle that lay East of the Sun and West of the Moon. By that time he was so weary that he lay on the sand gasping, and it was days before he had puff enough to blow himself home.

Next morning she sat herself down before the castle and began to play with her golden apple. In a twinkling someone appeared and threw up the window. You didn't have to look twice to know that this was the Three-Foot Rosy-Nosy.

"Hey, you, creature that you are," shouted the Long-nose, "what do you want for your apple?"

"Neither gold nor silver, neither price nor hire. But if I may see the Prince who lives here, and be with him tonight, it shall be yours."

Well, that could be arranged, no trouble at all. So the Princess got the gold apple, and the girl whom the North Wind had brought was taken up to the Prince's chamber when he was asleep. She called to him and shook him, and all the time her tears ran like rain, but the harder she tried to wake him the harder he slept—and no wonder, for the Long-nose had given him a sleep-sleepy drink. And at daylight up came the Long-nose and drove her flying out.

Once more she sat herself down before the castle, and began to card with her golden carding-comb. It was the same story all over again. The Princess asked what she wanted for it, and she made the same answer, and that night again she went to the Prince's chamber and found him asleep. And the faster she tried to wake him the faster he slept. And at daybreak in came the Long-nose and drove her flying out.

So there she was the third time, sitting before the castle and spinning with her golden spinning-wheel, and a third time the Princess asked what she wanted for it, and a third time she drove the same bargain, only this time there was a difference; for a servant who was there, and who very properly disliked the Long-nose who was always being cruel to her, told the Prince that a girl had been there twice running to see him, and had wept and prayed over him right till daybreak. So this time, when the Long-nose brought him the sleep-sleepy drink, though he pretended to drain it as usual, in fact he threw it over his left shoulder. And that, as the saying says, was that.

A third time she came to the Prince's chamber, the girl whom the North Wind had brought, and now she found him awake. There are no words to describe their happiness, but at last he begged her to tell him how she had managed to find him and the castle that lay East of the Sun and West of the Moon.

"Nor have you come one moment too soon," he informed her, the minute her recital was over. "For tomorrow was to have been my wedding day with the Princess. If only we could think of a plan!" He thought, and she thought, till her head ached for him. "I have it," he announced at last. "Before the wedding can take place I shall say that I want to make certain what my wife is fit for in the housekeeping line. Take washing, for instance. I'll ask her to wash the shirt which has the three drops of tallow on it. She is sure to say yes, for she has no idea who put them there. It was a Christian candle, don't forget, and no troll will get far with *that.* Finally you will hear me swear that no woman shall be my bride who cannot wash those spots clean, and that is where you come in, through the window or the door, just as you prefer."

This seemed such a good plan that they were there in joy all night. Then next morning, when the Princess had powdered her three-foot nose for the wedding, the Prince suddenly announced: "Before I marry, I want to see what my wife is fit for in the housekeeping line. Is that fair, step-mother?"

"Fair enough," said the step-mother, who was a big ugly trollop.

"Just look at this shirt," continued the Prince. "It was to have been my wedding shirt, and somehow or other it has picked up three drops of tallow. I swear, step-mother, that no woman shall be my bride who cannot wash them clean."

The words were hardly clear of his mouth when the Three-Foot Rosy-Nosy was over the tub and into the suds, but the longer she rubbed and the harder she scrubbed, the bigger the spots became.

"What a useless thing I bred you!" shouted the old trollop her mother. "Here, let me try."

And try she did, but with no better luck, for the further she lathered and farther she slithered, the dirtier the shirt became.

Then all the rest of them rushed at the tub, and such washing and drying and sloshing and crying was never beheld before or be-since. But for all they could do, the shirt looked at last as though it had been dropped down two chimneys and pulled up three.

"I'm a lucky man I married none of you," the Prince told them. "But look, there's a beggar girl outside the window, and I am sure she can wash better than all you trolls put together. Come inside, girl!" he called to her, and she came.

"Can you wash this shirt clean, do you think?"

"I can try," she said. And as she put it into the water it turned white as milk, and as she plucked it forth it grew white as snow.

"This is the girl for me, and always has been," said the Prince, and he kissed her in sight of them all.

At this the old trollop so swelled with rage that she burst with a loud report. Then the Three-Foot Rosy-Nosy burst with a still louder one, and there were the rest of the trolls and the trollops, one after the other, bursting as though they had practised at it all their lives. And when the last report was over, and the birds were settling to the boughs, the Prince made the woodcutter's daughter his own Princess, and they carried off with them all the gold and silver, and lived happily thereafter, for three years short of three hundred, as far off as they could get from the castle that lay East of the Sun and West of the Moon.

RAPUNZEL
(German)

Because a woman believes she cannot live without eating rampion from a witch's garden—and her husband caters to her—their daughter Rapunzel (meaning rampion) must be given to the witch when she is born. Thus Rapunzel's long imprisonment in a tower begins, to be ended finally by the love of a prince. The power of the witch in this haunting tale is very great—and so the love of the prince must be also, as he wanders blind and poor for years in his search for Rapunzel. The "circular" power of love can only be set in motion by a strong, mature love that has the quality of endurance.*

Once upon a time there lived a man and his wife who were very unhappy because they had no children. These good people had a little window at the back of their house, which looked into the most lovely garden, full of all manner of beautiful flowers and vegetables; but the garden was surrounded by a high wall, and no one dared to enter it, for it belonged to a witch of great power, who was feared by the whole world. One day the woman stood at the window overlooking the garden, and saw there a bed full of the finest rampion: the leaves looked so fresh and green that she longed to eat them. The desire grew day by day, and just because she knew she couldn't possibly get any, she pined away and became quite pale and wretched. Then her husband grew alarmed and said:

"What ails you, dear wife?"

"Oh," she answered, "if I don't get some rampion to eat out of the garden behind the house, I know I shall die."

The man, who loved her dearly, thought to himself, "Come! rather than let your wife die you shall fetch her some rampion, no matter the cost." So at dusk he climbed over the wall into the witch's garden, and, hastily gathering a handful of rampion leaves, he returned with them to his wife. She made them into a salad, which tasted so good that her longing for the forbidden food was greater than ever. If she were to know any peace of mind, there was nothing for it but that her hus-

"Rapunzel" is one of the fairy tales collected by the Grimm brothers. This version is from *The Red Fairy Book,* edited by Andrew Lang.

* Each spring in Appalachia, in Cosby, Tennessee, there is a "rampion" festival, celebrating the emergence of this leafy plant with the strong onion taste. Some doctors think it has medicinal powers.

band should climb over the garden wall again, and fetch her some more. So at dusk over he got, but when he reached the other side he drew back in terror, for there, standing before him, was the old witch.

"How dare you," she said, with a wrathful glance, "climb into my garden and steal my rampion like a common thief? You shall suffer for your foolhardiness."

"Oh!" he implored, "pardon my presumption; necessity alone drove me to the deed. My wife saw your rampion from her window, and conceived such a desire for it that she would certainly have died if her wish had not been gratified." Then the Witch's anger was a little appeased, and she said:

"If it's as you say, you may take as much rampion away with you as you like, but on one condition only—that you give me the child your wife will shortly bring into the world. All shall go well with it, and I will look after it like a mother."

The man in his terror agreed to everything she asked, and as soon as the child was born the Witch appeared, and having given it the name of Rapunzel, which is the same as rampion, she carried it off with her.

Rapunzel was the most beautiful child under the sun. When she was twelve years old the Witch shut her up in a tower, in the middle of a great wood, and the tower had neither stairs nor doors, only high up at the very top a small window. When the old Witch wanted to get in she stood underneath and called out:

"Rapunzel, Rapunzel,
Let down your golden hair,"

for Rapunzel had wonderful long hair, and it was as fine as spun gold. Whenever she heard the Witch's voice she unloosed her plaits, and let her hair fall down out of the window about twenty yards below, and the old Witch climbed up by it.

After they had lived like this for a few years, it happened one day that a Prince was riding through the wood and passed by the tower. As he drew near it he heard someone singing so sweetly that he stood still spell-bound, and listened. It was Rapunzel in her loneliness trying to while away the time by letting her sweet voice ring out into the wood. The Prince longed to see the owner of the voice, but he sought in vain for a door in the tower. He rode home, but he was so haunted by the song he had heard that he returned every day to the wood and listened. One day, when he was standing thus behind a tree, he saw the old Witch approach and heard her call out:

"Rapunzel, Rapunzel,
Let down your golden hair."

Then Rapunzel let down her plaits, and the Witch climbed up by them.

"So that's the staircase, is it?" said the Prince. "Then I too will climb it and try my luck."

So on the following day, at dusk, he went to the foot of the tower and cried:

"Rapunzel, Rapunzel,
Let down your golden hair,"

and as soon as she had let it down the Prince climbed up.

At first Rapunzel was terribly frightened when a man came in, for she had never seen one before; but the Prince spoke to her so kindly, and told her at once that his heart had been so touched by her singing, that he felt he should know no peace of mind till he had seen her. Very soon Rapunzel forgot her fear, and when he asked her to marry him she consented at once. "For," she thought, "he is young and handsome, and I'll certainly be happier with him than with the old Witch." So she put her hand in his and said:

"Yes, I will gladly go with you, only how am I to get down out of the tower? Every time you come to see me you must bring a skein of silk with you, and I will make a ladder of them, and when it is finished I will climb down by it, and you will take me away on your horse."

They arranged that, till the ladder was ready, he was to come to her every evening, because the old woman was with her during the day. The old Witch, of course, knew nothing of what was going on, till one day Rapunzel, not thinking of what she was about, turned to the Witch and said:

"How is it, good mother, that you are so much harder to pull up than the young Prince? He is always with me in a moment."

"Oh! you wicked child," cried the Witch. "What is this I hear? I thought I had hidden you safely from the whole world, and in spite of it you have managed to deceive me."

In her wrath she seized Rapunzel's beautiful hair, wound it round and round her left hand, and then grasping a pair of scissors in her right, snip snap, off it came, and the beautiful plaits lay on the ground. And, worse than this, she was so hard-hearted that she took Rapunzel to a lonely desert place, and there left her to live in loneliness and misery.

But on the evening of the day in which she had driven poor Rapunzel away, the Witch fastened the plaits on to a hook in the window, and when the Prince came and called out:

"Rapunzel, Rapunzel,
Let down your golden hair,"

she let them down, and the Prince climbed up as usual, but instead of his beloved Rapunzel he found the old Witch, who fixed her evil, glittering eyes on him, and cried mockingly:

"Ah, ah! you thought to find your lady love, but the pretty bird has flown and its song is dumb; the cat caught it, and will scratch out your eyes too. Rapunzel is lost to you for ever—you will never see her more."

The Prince was beside himself with grief, and in his despair he jumped right down from the tower, and, though he escaped with his life, the thorns among which he fell pierced his eyes out. Then he wandered, blind and miserable, through the wood, eating nothing but roots and berries, and weeping and lamenting the loss of his lovely bride. So he wandered about for some years, as wretched and unhappy as he could well be, and at last he came to the desert place where Rapunzel was living. Of a sudden he heard a voice which seemed strangely familiar to him. He walked eagerly in the direction of the sound, and when he was quite close, Rapunzel recognised him and fell on his neck and wept. But two of her tears touched his eyes, and in a moment they became quite clear again, and he saw as well as he had ever done. Then he led her to his kingdom, where they were received and welcomed with great joy, and they lived happily ever after.

THE BLANKET

(French)

Retold by Francelia Butler

The circle of life extends from birth to death, from childhood to old age. We tend to be prejudiced favorably toward the young and prejudiced unfavorably toward the old. This story raises the serious question of cruelty to the old. Versions of this folktale are found in several countries, including India and the United States.

On a small farm in the South of France lived a man, his wife, and his son. With them lived his old father. This arrangement was not satisfactory to the wife. She was constantly complaining about the old man.

"When he eats, he slurps his soup," she said. "And he lets it drizzle down his beard. It makes me sick at my stomach and I cannot digest my food properly."

Her husband yielded to her demands and asked his father to eat his food in the adjoining room. But her complaints continued.

"Every time I look up from my plate," she said, "he is always staring out in my direction. I can't stand his eyes on me."

Finally, she made an ultimatum: "Either he goes or I do."

The son, sad about the affair, but having no choice but to lose either his wife or his father, chose to send his father away.

"I know it's winter, father," he said, "but my wife simply won't stand your presence here any longer. I must ask you to leave."

The father nodded. "Of course, son, I will go."

Remorseful at sending his father out in the middle of winter, the son asked his little boy to go to the barn and fetch the horseblanket.

"At least, father, the blanket will help to keep you warm."

The little boy left and was gone a long time. Finally, he returned, but he had only half the blanket. He had cut it jaggedly in two.

"What have you done that for?" the father demanded. "You have ruined a perfectly good blanket."

"Father," the little boy replied, "I was saving half of it for you and mother when you get old."

Literary Folktale

ESARHADDON, KING OF ASSYRIA

Leo Tolstoy

There is a mystical circle that unites us all. In this story, the joining circle is lived out when King Esarhaddon becomes King Lailie. Suffering all that he had made Lailie suffer, Esarhaddon learns what it is to put oneself into the position of one's fellow human being and to understand his point of view. "Esarhaddon, King of Assyria," is one of Tolstoy's last group of tales, which together represent a synthesis of Tolstoy's philosophy at the culmination of his life. First published in Yiddish, the story was sent by Tolstoy to Sholem Aleichem in 1903 to help raise funds for the victims of an anti-Jewish pogrom.

Esarhaddon, the Assyrian king, had conquered King Lailie's dominion; he ravaged and burned all the cities, drove the inhabitants back to his own country, slaughtered the warriors, and put King Lailie himself into a cage.

One night King Esarhaddon lay in bed thinking how he would put Lailie to death, when all at once he heard a rustling, and opening his eyes he beheld an old man with a long gray beard and gentle eyes.

"Do you wish to kill Lailie?" asked the old man.

"Yes," the king answered, "but I cannot decide by what means to execute him."

"But you are Lailie," the old man said.

"That is not true," replied the king. "I am I, and Lailie is Lailie."

"You and Lailie are one," said the old man. "It only seems to you that you are not Lailie and that Lailie is not you."

"What do you mean—seems?" said the king. "Here I lie on a soft bed, surrounded by my obedient slaves, and tomorrow, as today, I shall feast with my friends; whereas Lailie sits like a bird in a cage, and tomorrow he will be squirming on a stake with his tongue hanging out till he dies, his body torn to pieces by dogs."

"You cannot destroy his life," said the old man.

"And what of the fourteen thousand warriors I killed—with whose bodies I built a tumulus?" asked the king. "I am alive and they are not; therefore I can destroy life."

Translated by Ann Dunnigan.

"How do you know they are not alive?"

"Because I do not see them. And, moreover, they were tortured, not I. It was bad for them, but good for me."

"This, too, seems so to you. You tortured yourself, not them."

"I do not understand," said the king.

"Do you want to understand?"

"I do."

"Come here," said the old man, pointing to a font full of water.

Esarhaddon did as the old man bade him.

"Now, as soon as I begin to pour this water over you," said the old man, dipping a jug into the water, "submerge your head."

As he tipped the jug over him, the king submerged his head.

No sooner was his head under water than he felt that he was no longer Esarhaddon, but someone else. And, feeling himself to be that other man, he saw himself lying on a luxurious bed beside a beautiful woman. He had never seen this woman before, but he knew she was his wife. The woman raised herself and said to him:

"My dear husband, Lailie, you were tired by yesterday's work and have slept longer than usual, and I have watched over your rest and have not roused you. But now the princes await you in the great hall. Dress and go out to them."

And Esarhaddon, understanding from these words that he was Lailie, not only felt no surprise, but even wondered that he had not known this before. And he rose and dressed himself and went to the great hall where the princes attended him.

Bowing to the ground the princes greeted Lailie, their king, then rose, and at his command seated themselves before him. The eldest of them began to speak, saying that it was no longer possible to bear the affronts of the wicked King Esarhaddon, and that they must wage war against him. But Lailie did not agree with them, and commanded that emissaries be sent to Esarhaddon to exhort him, and he dismissed the princes. He then appointed eminent men to act as ambassadors, carefully instructing them in what to say to Esarhaddon.

Having finished these matters, Esarhaddon, feeling himself to be Lailie, rode up into the hills to hunt wild asses. The hunt was successful, the king himself killing two asses, and, when he returned home he feasted with his friends while watching his slave girls dance.

The following day, as was his custom, he went to court, where he was awaited by petitioners, litigants, and prisoners brought to trial, and he judged the cases brought before him. When he had finished, he again rode out to his favorite pastime, hunting. And on that day he succeeded in killing an old lioness and capturing her two cubs. After the hunt he again feasted with his friends, diverting himself with music and dancing, after which he spent the night with his beloved wife.

Thus he lived for days and weeks, while waiting for the return of the ambassadors he had sent to that King Esarhaddon whom he once had been. Only after a month had gone by did they return—and then with their noses and ears cut off.

King Esarhaddon had instructed them to tell Lailie that what had been done to his ambassadors would be done to him too, unless he immediately sent the specified tribute of silver, gold, and cypress wood, and came in person to pay homage to him.

Lailie, formerly Esarhaddon, again called the princes together and took counsel with them. With one accord they declared that instead of waiting for Esarhaddon to attack them they must go to war against him.

The king agreed, and, taking his place at the head of his army, he set out on the campaign. The march lasted seven days. Each day the king rode among his men, inspiring them to valor. On the eighth day they met Esarhaddon's army in a broad valley on the bank of a river. Lailie's warriors fought bravely, but Lailie, formerly Esarhaddon, saw the enemy swarming down from the mountain like ants, overrunning the valley and vanquishing his army, and he sped his chariot into the midst of the battle, slashing and hewing at the enemy. But Lailie's warriors numbered hundreds, while Esarhaddon's were in the thousands. And Lailie felt that he was wounded, and that they had taken him prisoner.

He marched for nine days with the other captives, bound, and surrounded by Esarhaddon's soldiers. On the tenth day he was brought to Nineveh and put into a cage.

Lailie suffered not so much from his wound and hunger as from shame and impotent rage. He felt powerless to avenge himself for all the evil he was suffering. The one thing he could do was to deprive his enemies of the joy of watching his agony, and he firmly resolved to endure courageously and without a murmur all that happened to him.

For twenty days he sat in the cage awaiting execution. He saw his relatives and friends led out to death, and heard their groans; some had their arms and legs cut off, others were flayed alive, but he showed no agitation, no pity, no fear. He saw his beloved wife bound by two eunuchs, and he realized that she was being taken to Esarhaddon as a slave. And this too he bore in silence.

At last two executioners unlocked the door of his cage, and, after tying his arms behind his back with thongs, they led him to the gory execution site. Lailie saw the sharp, bloodstained stake from which the dead body of one of his friends had just been torn, and he realized that this stake had been cleared for his own execution.

They took off his clothes. Lailie was horrified at the gauntness of his once strong and handsome body. The two executioners seized that body by its scrawny thighs, lifted it up, and were about to impale it on the stake.

"Now death, extinction," Lailie thought, and forgetting his resolution to remain courageously calm to the end, he sobbed and prayed for mercy. But no one listened to him.

"But this cannot be! Surely I am asleep—it is a dream!" And he made an effort to rouse himself, thinking, "I am not Lailie, I am Esarhaddon."

"You are both Lailie and Esarhaddon," he heard a voice saying, and he felt that now his execution was going to begin.

He cried out, at the same instant raising his head from the font. The old man was standing over him, pouring the last drops of water from the jug onto his head.

"Oh, how terribly I have suffered! And how long!" said Esarhaddon.

"Long?" replied the old man. "You have only just dipped your head under water and raised it again. See, all the water has not yet been poured out of the jug. Do you understand?"

Esarhaddon did not reply, but only looked in terror at the old man.

"Do you understand," the old man continued, "that Lailie is you, that the warriors you put to death also were you? And not only the warriors, but the animals you hunted and slew and afterwards devoured at your feasts, they too were you. You thought life dwelt in you alone, but I have drawn aside the veil of delusion, and you have seen that in doing evil to others you have done it to yourself as well. Life is one in everything, and within yourself you manifest but a portion of this one life. And only in that portion that is within you can you make life better or worse, magnify or diminish it. You can make life better within yourself only by destroying the barriers that divide your life from that of other beings, and by regarding others as yourself and loving them. To destroy the life that dwells in others is not within your power. The life that was in those you have slain has not been destroyed: it has merely vanished from before your eyes. You thought to prolong your own life and to shorten the lives of others, but you cannot do this. For life there is neither time nor space. The life of a moment and the life of thousands of years, your life and the lives of all creatures seen and unseen, is one. To destroy life, even to alter it, is impossible, for life alone exists. All else only seems to be."

Having said this, the old man vanished.

The next morning King Esarhaddon commanded that Lailie and all the prisoners be freed and the executions stopped. And on the following day he summoned his son, Ashurbanipal, and gave over the kingdom into his hands. He himself withdrew into the wilderness to meditate on all that he had learned. Later he went as a pilgrim through the towns and villages, preaching to the people that all life is one, and that men do evil only to themsleves in desiring to do evil to others.

Fantasy

THE LITTLE PRINCE

Antoine de Saint-Exupéry

This beloved poetic fantasy tells the story of a prince who visits the earth, leaving his tiny planet home in the stars to do so. Having gone through a lifetime of experiences, with a rose, whom he loves, and with a succession of materialists whose spirits are imprisoned by their egos—except for a lamplighter—the Little Prince meets a wise fox and a stranded airplane pilot with whom he forms ties. Now it is time to say good-bye. It is a sad time, but it will not be the end. "In one of the stars I shall be living," the Little Prince tells the pilot. "In one of them I shall be laughing. And so it will be as if all the stars were laughing, when you look at the sky at night . . . You—only you—will have stars that can laugh!" The quiet close to the Little Prince's existence shows beautifully for children the natural circular movement from life to death.

Beside the well there was the ruin of an old stone wall. When I came back from my work, the next evening, I saw from some distance away my little prince sitting on top of this wall, with his feet dangling. And I heard him say:

"Then you don't remember. This is not the exact spot."

Another voice must have answered him, for he replied to it:

"Yes, yes! It is the right day, but this is not the place."

From Antoine de Saint-Exupéry, *The Little Prince* (New York: Harcourt, Brace and World, 1943), Chapter 26. Translated by Katherine Woods. Illustrated by the author.

I continued my walk toward the wall. At no time did I see or hear anyone. The little prince, however, replied once again:

"—Exactly. You will see where my track begins, in the sand. You have nothing to do but wait for me there. I shall be there tonight."

I was only twenty meters from the wall, and I still saw nothing.

After a silence the little prince spoke again:

"You have good poison? You are sure that it will not make me suffer too long?"

I stopped in my tracks, my heart torn asunder; but still I did not understand.

"Now go away," said the little prince.

"I want to get down from the wall."

I dropped my eyes, then, to the foot of the wall—and I leaped into the air. There before me, facing the little prince, was one of those yellow snakes that take just thirty seconds to bring your life to an end. Even as I was digging into my pocket to get out my revolver I made a running step back. But, at the noise I made, the snake let himself flow easily across the sand like the dying spray of a fountain, and, in no apparent hurry, disappeared, with a light metallic sound, among the stones.

I reached the wall just in time to catch my little man in my arms; his face was white as snow.

"What does this mean?" I demanded. "Why are you talking with snakes?"

I had loosened the golden muffler that he always wore. I had moistened his temples, and had given him some water to drink. And now I did not dare ask him any more questions. He looked at me very gravely, and put his arms around my neck. I felt his heart beating like the heart of a dying bird, shot with someone's rifle. . . .

"I am glad that you have found what was the matter with your engine," he said. "Now you can go back home—"

"How do you know about that?"

I was just coming to tell him that my work had been successful, beyond anything that I had dared to hope.

He made no answer to my question, but he added:

"I, too, am going back home today. . . ."

Then, sadly—

"It is much farther. . . . It is much more difficult . . ."

I realized clearly that something was happening. I was holding him close in my arms as if he were a little child; and yet it seemed to me that he was rushing headlong toward an abyss from which I could do nothing to restrain him. . . .

His look was very serious, like some one lost far away.

"I have your sheep. And I have the sheep's box. And I have the muzzle . . .

And he gave me a sad smile.

I waited a long time. I could see that he was reviving little by little.

"Dear little man," I said to him, "You are afraid. . . . "

He was afraid, there was no doubt about that. But he laughed lightly.

"I shall be much more afraid this evening. . . . "

Once again I felt myself frozen by the sense of something irreparable. And I knew that I could not bear the thought of never hearing that laughter any more. For me, it was like a spring of fresh water in the desert.

"Little man," I said, "I want to hear you laugh again."

But he said to me:

"Tonight, it will be a year. . . . My star, then, can be found right above the place where I came to the Earth, a year ago. . . ."

"Little man," I said, "tell me that it is only a bad dream—this affair of the snake, and the meeting-place, and the star . . . "

But he did not answer my plea. He said to me, instead:

"The thing that is important is the thing that is not seen. . . . "

"Yes, I know. . . . "

"It is just as it is with the flower. If you love a flower that lives on a star, it is sweet to look at the sky at night. All the stars are a-bloom with flowers. . . . "

"Yes, I know. . . . "

"It is just as it is with the water. Because of the pulley, and the rope, what you gave me to drink was like music. You remember—how good it was."

"Yes, I know. . . . "

"And at night you will look up at the stars. Where I live everything is so small that I cannot show you where my star is to be found. It is better, like that. My star will be just one of the stars, for you. And so you will love to watch all the stars in the heavens. . . . They will all be your friends. And, besides, I am going to make you a present. . . ."

He laughed again.

"Ah, little prince, dear little prince! I love to hear that laughter!"

"That is my present. Just that. It will

be as it was when we drank the water. . . . "

"What are you trying to say?"

"All men have the stars," he answered, "but they are not the same things for different people. For some, who are travelers, the stars are guides. For others they are no more than little lights in the sky. For others, who are scholars, they are problems. For my businessman they were wealth. But all these stars are silent. You—you alone—will have the stars as no one else has them—"

"What are you trying to say?"

"In one of the stars I shall be living. In one of them I shall be laughing. And so it will be as if all the stars were laughing, when you look at the sky at night . . . You—only you—will have stars that can laugh!"

And he laughed again.

"And when your sorrow is comforted (time soothes all sorrows) you will be content that you have known me. You will always be my friend. You will want to laugh with me. And you will sometimes open your window, so, for that pleasure. . . . And your friends will be properly astonished to see you laughing as you look up at the sky! Then you will say to them, 'Yes, the stars always make me laugh!' And they will think you are crazy. It will be a very shabby trick that I shall have played on you. . . . "

And he laughed again.

"It will be as if, in place of the stars, I had given you a great number of little bells that knew how to laugh. . . . "

And he laughed again. Then he quickly became serious:

"Tonight—you know. . . . Do not come."

"I shall not leave you," I said.

"I shall look as if I were suffering. I shall look a little as if I were dying. It is like that. Do not come to see that. It is not worth the trouble. . . . "

"I shall not leave you."

But he was worried.

"I tell you—it is also because of the snake. He must not bite you. Snakes—they are malicious creatures. This one might bite you just for fun. . . . "

"I shall not leave you."

But a thought came to reassure him:

"It is true that they have no more poison for a second bite."

That night I did not see him set out on his way. He got away from me without making a sound. When I succeeded in catching up with him he was walking along with a quick and resolute step. He said to me merely:

"Ah! You are there. . . . "

And he took me by the hand. But he was still worrying.

"It was wrong of you to come. You will suffer. I shall look as if I were dead; and that will not be true. . . . "

I said nothing.

"You understand. . . . It is too far. I cannot carry this body with me. It is too heavy."

I said nothing.

"But it will be like an old abandoned shell. There is nothing sad about old shells. . . . "

I said nothing.

He was a little discouraged. But he made one more effort:

"You know, it will be very nice. I, too, shall look at the stars. All the stars will be wells with a rusty pulley. All the stars will pour out fresh water for me to drink. . . . "

I said nothing.

"That will be so amusing! You will have five hundred million little bells, and I shall have five hundred million springs of fresh water. . . . "

And he too said nothing more, because he was crying. . . .

"Here it is. Let me go on by myself."

And he sat down, because he was afraid. Then he said, again:

"You know—my flower . . . I am responsible for her. And she is so weak! She is so naïve! She has four thorns, of no use at all, to protect herself against all the world. . . . "

I too sat down, because I was not able to stand up any longer.

"There now—that is all. . . . "

He still hesitated a little; then he got

up. He took one step. I could not move.

There was nothing there but a flash of yellow close to his ankle. He remained motionless for an instant. He did not cry out. He fell as gently as a tree falls. There was not even any sound, because of the sand.

CHARLOTTE'S WEB

E. B. White

A combination of fantasy and bittersweet realism, E. B. White's Charlotte's Web *has been popular since it was first published in 1952 and has received universal critical acclaim. Children as well as adults respond to the true-to-life characterizations, and to the wit and accuracy of White's observations about personal relationships.*

Wilbur is a runt pig who was raised by a little girl named Fern until he grows so big he must be returned to the barnyard. Charlotte the spider becomes a true friend to Wilbur, and

From E. B. White, *Charlotte's Web* (New York: Harper and Row, 1952), Chapters 21–22. Illustrated by Garth Williams.

through her ingenuity and the aid of Templeton the rat, has saved his life. Now her own life has run its course. At first Wilbur cannot reconcile himself to the loss of his friend, but as he grows wiser, he knows that she is still with him through his memory of her and through her children and grandchildren.

Last Day

Charlotte and Wilbur were alone. The families had gone to look for Fern. Templeton was asleep. Wilbur lay resting after the excitement and strain of the ceremony. His medal still hung from his neck; by looking out of the corner of his eye he could see it.

"Charlotte," said Wilbur after a while, "why are you so quiet?"

"I like to sit still," she said. "I've always been rather quiet."

"Yes, but you seem specially so today. Do you feel all right?"

"A little tired, perhaps. But I feel peaceful. Your success in the ring this morning was, to a small degree, *my* success. Your future is assured. You will live, secure and safe, Wilbur. Nothing can harm you now. These autumn days will shorten and grow cold. The leaves will shake loose from the trees and fall. Christmas will come, then the snows of winter. You will live to enjoy the beauty of the frozen world, for you mean a great deal to Zuckerman and he will not harm you, ever. Winter will pass, the days will lengthen, the ice will melt in the pasture pond. The song sparrow will return and sing, the frogs will awake, the warm wind will blow again. All these sights and sounds and smells will be yours to enjoy, Wilbur—this lovely world, these precious days . . ."

Charlotte stopped. A moment later a tear came to Wilbur's eye. "Oh, Charlotte," he said. "To think that when I first met you I thought you were cruel and bloodthirsty!"

When he recovered from his emotion, he spoke again.

"Why did you do all this for me?" he asked. "I don't deserve it. I've never done anything for you."

"You have been my friend," replied Charlotte. "That in itself is a tremendous thing. I wove my webs for you because I liked you. After all, what's a life, anyway? We're born, we live a little while, we die. A spider's life can't help being something of a mess, with all this trapping and eating flies. By helping you perhaps I was trying to lift up my life a trifle. Heaven knows anyone's life can stand a little of that."

"Well," said Wilbur. "I'm no good at making speeches. I haven't got your gift for words. But you have saved me, Charlotte, and I would gladly give my life for you—I really would."

"I'm sure you would. And I thank you for your generous sentiments."

"Charlotte," said Wilbur. "We're all going home today. The Fair is almost over. Won't it be wonderful to be back home in the barn cellar again with the sheep and the geese? Aren't you anxious to get home?"

For a moment Charlotte said nothing. Then she spoke in a voice so low Wilbur could hardly hear the words.

"I will not be going back to the barn," she said.

Wilbur leapt to his feet. "Not going back?" he cried. "Charlotte, what are you talking about?"

"I'm done for," she replied. "In a day or two I'll be dead. I haven't even strength enough to climb down into the crate. I doubt if I have enough silk in my spinnerets to lower me to the ground."

Hearing this, Wilbur threw himself down in an agony of pain and sorrow. Great sobs racked his body. He heaved and grunted with desolation. "Charlotte," he moaned. "Charlotte! My true friend."

"Come now, let's not make a scene," said the spider. "Be quiet, Wilbur. Stop thrashing about!"

"But I can't *stand* it," shouted Wilbur. "I won't leave you here alone to die. If you're going to stay here I shall stay, too."

"Don't be ridiculous," said Charlotte. "You can't stay here. Zuckerman and Lurvy and John Arable and the others will be back any minute now, and they'll shove you into that crate and away you'll go. Besides, it wouldn't make any sense for you to stay. There would be no one to feed you. The Fair Grounds will soon be empty and deserted."

Wilbur was in a panic. He raced round and round the pen. Suddenly he had an idea—he thought of the egg sac and the five hundred and fourteen little spiders that would hatch in the spring. If Charlotte herself was unable to go home to the barn, at least he must take her children along.

Wilbur rushed to the front of his pen. He put his front feet up on the top board and gazed around. In the distance he saw the Arables and the Zuckermans approaching. He knew he would have to act quickly.

"Where's Templeton?" he demanded.

"He's in that corner, under the straw, asleep," said Charlotte.

Wilbur rushed over, pushed his strong snout under the rat, and tossed him into the air.

"Templeton!" screamed Wilbur. "Pay attention!"

The rat, surprised out of a sound sleep, looked first dazed then disgusted.

"What kind of monkeyshine is this?" he growled. "Can't a rat catch a wink of sleep without being rudely popped into the air?"

"Listen to me!" cried Wilbur. "Charlotte is very ill. She has only a short time to live. She cannot accompany us home, because of her condition. Therefore, it is absolutely necessary that I take her egg sac with me. I can't reach it, and I can't climb. You are the only one that can get it. There's not a second to be lost. The people are coming—they'll be here in no time. Please, please, *please,* Templeton, climb up and get the egg sac."

The rat yawned. He straightened his whiskers. Then he looked up at the egg sac.

"So!" he said, in disgust. "So it's old Templeton to the rescue again, is it? Templeton do this, Templeton do that, Templeton please run down to the dump and get me a magazine clipping, Templeton please lend me a piece of string so I can spin a web."

"Oh, hurry!" said Wilbur. "Hurry up, Templeton!"

But the rat was in no hurry. He began imitating Wilbur's voice.

"So it's 'Hurry up, Templeton,' is it?" he said. "Ho, ho. And what thanks do I ever get for these services, I would like to know? Never a kind word for old Templeton, only abuse and wisecracks and side remarks. Never a kind word for a rat."

"Templeton," said Wilbur in desperation, "if you don't stop talking and get busy, all will be lost, and I will die of a broken heart. Please climb up!"

Templeton lay back in the straw. Lazily he placed his forepaws behind his head and crossed his knees, in an attitude of complete relaxation.

"Die of a broken heart," he mimicked. "How touching! My, my! I notice that it's always me you come to when in trouble. But I've never heard of anyone's heart breaking on *my* account. Oh, no. Who cares anything about old Templeton?"

"Get up!" screamed Wilbur. "Stop acting like a spoiled child!"

Templeton grinned and lay still. "Who made trip after trip to the dump?" he asked. "Why, it was old Templeton! Who saved Charlotte's life by scaring that

Arable boy away with a rotten goose egg? Bless my soul, I believe it was old Templeton. Who bit your tail and got you back on your feet this morning after you had fainted in front of the crowd? Old Templeton. Has it ever occurred to you that I'm sick of running errands and doing favors? What do you think I am, anyway, a rat-of-all-work?"

Wilbur was desperate. The people were coming. And the rat was failing him. Suddenly he remembered Templeton's fondness for food.

"Templeton," he said, "I will make you a solemn promise. Get Charlotte's egg sac for me, and from now on I will let you eat first, when Lurvy slops me. I will let you have your choice of everything in the trough and I won't touch a thing until you're through."

The rat sat up. "You mean that?" he said.

"I promise. I cross my heart."

"All right, it's a deal," said the rat. He walked to the wall and started to climb. His stomach was still swollen from last night's gorge. Groaning and complaining, he pulled himself slowly to the ceiling. He crept along till he reached the egg sac. Charlotte moved aside from him. She was dying, but she still had strength enough to move a little. Then Templeton bared his long ugly teeth and began snipping the threads that fastened the sac to the ceiling. Wilbur watched from below.

"Use extreme care!" he said. "I don't want a single one of those eggs harmed."

"Thith thtuff thticks in my mouth," complained the rat. "It'th worth than caramel candy."

But Templeton worked away at the job, and managed to cut the sac adrift and carry it to the ground, where he dropped it in front of Wilbur. Wilbur heaved a great sigh of relief.

"Thank you, Templeton," he said. "I will never forget this as long as I live."

"Neither will I," said the rat, picking his teeth. "I feel as though I'd eaten a spool of thread. Well, home we go!"

Templeton crept into the crate and buried himself in the straw. He got out of sight just in time. Lurvy and John Arable and Mr. Zuckerman came along at that moment, followed by Mrs. Arable and Mrs. Zuckerman and Avery and Fern. Wilbur had already decided how he would carry the egg sac—there was only one way possible. He carefully took the little bundle in his mouth and held it there on top of his tongue. He remembered what Charlotte had told him—that the sac was waterproof and strong. It felt funny on his tongue and made him drool a bit. And of course he couldn't say anything. But as he was being shoved into the crate, he looked up at Charlotte and gave her a wink. She knew he was saying good-bye in the only way he could. And she knew her children were safe.

"Good-bye!" she whispered. Then she summoned all her strength and waved one of her front legs at him.

She never moved again. Next day, as the Ferris wheel was being taken apart and the race horses were being loaded into vans and the entertainers were packing up their belongings and driving away in their trailers, Charlotte died. The Fair Grounds were soon deserted. The sheds and buildings were empty and forlorn. The infield was littered with bottles and trash. Nobody, of the hundreds of people that had visited the Fair, knew that a grey spider had played the most important part of all. No one was with her when she died.

A Warm Wind

And so Wilbur came home to his beloved manure pile in the barn cellar. His was a strange homecoming. Around his neck he wore a medal of honor; in his mouth he held a sac of spider's eggs. There is no place like home, Wilbur thought, as he placed Charlotte's five hundred and fourteen unborn children carefully in a safe corner. The barn smelled good. His friends the sheep and the geese were glad to see him back.

The geese gave him a noisy welcome.

"Congratu-congratu-congratulations!" they cried. "Nice work."

Mr. Zuckerman took the medal from Wilbur's neck and hung it on a nail over the pigpen, where visitors could examine it. Wilbur himself could look at it whenever he wanted to.

In the days that followed, he was very happy. He grew to a great size. He no longer worried about being killed, for he knew that Mr. Zuckerman would keep him as long as he lived. Wilbur often thought of Charlotte. A few strands of her old web still hung in the doorway. Every day Wilbur would stand and look at the torn, empty web, and a lump would come to his throat. No one had ever had such a friend—so affectionate, so loyal, and so skillful.

The autumn days grew shorter, Lurvy brought the squashes and pumpkins in from the garden and piled them on the barn floor, where they wouldn't get nipped on frosty nights. The maples and birches turned bright colors and the wind shook them and they dropped their leaves one by one to the ground. Under the wild apple trees in the pasture, the red little apples lay thick on the ground, and the sheep gnawed them and the geese gnawed them and foxes came in the night and sniffed them. One evening, just before Christmas, snow began falling. It covered house and barn and fields and woods. Wilbur had never seen snow before. When morning came he went out and plowed the drifts in his yard, for the fun of it. Fern and Avery arrived, dragging a sled. They coasted down the lane and out onto the frozen pond in the pasture.

"Coasting is the most fun there is," said Avery.

"The most fun there is," retorted Fern, "is when the Ferris wheel stops and Henry and I are in the top car and Henry makes the car swing and we can see everything for miles and miles and miles."

"Goodness, are you still thinking about that ol' Ferris wheel?" said Avery in disgust. "The Fair was weeks and weeks ago."

"I think about it all the time," said Fern, picking snow from her ear.

After Christmas the thermometer dropped to ten below zero. Cold settled on the world. The pasture was bleak and frozen. The cows stayed in the barn all the time now, except on sunny mornings when they went out and stood in the barnyard in the lee of the straw pile. The sheep stayed near the barn, too, for protection. When they were thirsty they ate snow. The geese hung around the barnyard the way boys hang around a drug store, and Mr. Zuckerman fed them corn and turnips to keep them cheerful.

"Many, many, many thanks!" they always said, when they saw food coming.

Templeton moved indoors when winter came. His ratty home under the pig trough was too chilly, so he fixed himself a cozy nest in the barn behind the grain bins. He lined it with bits of dirty newspapers and rags, and whenever he found a trinket or a keepsake he carried it home and stored it there. He continued to visit Wilbur three times a day, exactly at mealtime, and Wilbur kept the promise he had made. Wilbur let the rat eat first. Then, when Templeton couldn't hold another mouthful, Wilbur would eat. As a result of overeating, Templeton grew bigger and fatter than any rat you ever saw. He was gigantic. He was as big as a young woodchuck.

The old sheep spoke to him about his size one day. "You would live longer," said the old sheep, "if you ate less."

"Who wants to live forever?" sneered the rat. "I am naturally a heavy eater and I get untold satisfaction from the pleasures of the feast." He patted his stomach, grinned at the sheep, and crept upstairs to lie down.

All winter Wilbur watched over Charlotte's egg sac as though he were guarding his own children. He had scooped out a special place in the manure for the sac, next to the board fence. On very cold nights he lay so that his breath would warm it. For Wilbur, nothing in life was so important as this small round object—nothing else mattered. Patiently he awaited the end of winter and the coming of the little spiders. Life is always a rich and steady time when you are waiting for something to happen or to hatch. The winter ended at last.

"I heard the frogs today," said the old sheep one evening. "Listen! You can hear them now."

Wilbur stood still and cocked his ears. From the pond, in shrill chorus, came the voices of hundreds of little frogs.

"Springtime," said the old sheep, thoughtfully. "Another spring." As she walked away, Wilbur saw a new lamb following her. It was only a few hours old.

The snows melted and ran away. The streams and ditches bubbled and chattered with rushing water. A sparrow with a streaky breast arrived and sang. The light strengthened, the mornings came sooner. Almost every morning there was another new lamb in the sheepfold. The goose was sitting on nine eggs. The sky seemed wider and a warm wind blew. The last remaining strands of Charlotte's old web floated away and vanished.

One fine sunny morning, after breakfast, Wilbur stood watching his precious sac. He wasn't thinking of anything much. As he stood there, he noticed something move. He stepped closer and stared. A tiny spider crawled from the sac. It was no bigger than a grain of sand, no bigger than the head of a pin. Its body was grey with a black stripe underneath. Its legs were grey and tan. It looked just like Charlotte.

Wilbur trembled all over when he saw it. The little spider waved at him. Then Wilbur looked more closely. Two more little spiders crawled out and waved. They climbed round and round on the sac, exploring their new world. Then three more little spiders. Then eight. Then ten. Charlotte's children were here at last.

Wilbur's heart pounded. He began to squeal. Then he raced in circles, kicking manure into the air. Then he turned a back flip. Then he planted his front feet and came to a stop in front of Charlotte's children.

"Hello, there!" he said.

The first spider said hello, but its voice was so small Wilbur couldn't hear it.

"I am an old friend of your mother's," said Wilbur. "I'm glad to see you. Are you all right? Is everything all right?"

The little spiders waved their forelegs at him. Wilbur could see by the way they acted that they were glad to see him.

"Is there anything I can get you? Is there anything you need?"

The young spiders just waved. For several days and several nights they crawled here and there, up and down, around and about, waving at Wilbur, trailing tiny draglines behind them, and exploring their home. There were dozens and dozens of them. Wilbur couldn't count them, but he knew that he had a great many new friends. They grew quite rapidly. Soon each was as big as a BB shot. They made tiny webs near the sac.

Then came a quiet morning when Mr. Zuckerman opened a door on the north side. A warm draft of rising air blew softly through the barn cellar. The air smelled of the damp earth, of the spruce woods, of the sweet springtime. The baby spiders felt the warm updraft. One spider climbed to the top of the fence. Then it did something that came as a great surprise to Wilbur. The spider stood on its head, pointed its spinnerets in the air, and let loose a cloud of fine silk. The silk formed a balloon. As Wilbur watched, the spider let go of the fence and rose into the air.

"Good-bye!" it said, as it sailed through the doorway.

"Wait a minute!" screamed Wilbur. "Where do you think you're going?"

But the spider was already out of sight. Then another baby spider crawled to the top of the fence, stood on its head, made a balloon, and sailed away. Then another spider. Then another. The air was soon filled with tiny balloons, each balloon carrying a spider.

Wilbur was frantic. Charlotte's babies were disappearing at a great rate.

"Come back, children!" he cried.

"Good-bye!" they called. "Good-bye, good-bye!"

At last one little spider took time enough to stop and talk to Wilbur before making its balloon.

"We're leaving here on the warm updraft. This is our moment for setting forth. We are aeronauts and we are going out into the world to make webs for ourselves."

"But *where* ?" asked Wilbur.

"Wherever the wind takes us. High, low. Near, far. East, west. North, south. We take to the breeze, we go as we please."

"Are *all* of you going?" asked Wilbur. "You can't *all* go. I would be left alone, with no friends. Your mother wouldn't want that to happen, I'm sure."

The air was now so full of balloonists that the barn cellar looked almost as though a mist had gathered. Balloons by the dozen were rising, circling, and drifting away through the door, sailing off on the gentle wind. Cries of "Good-bye, good-bye, good-bye!" came weakly to Wilbur's ears. He couldn't bear to watch any more. In sorrow he sank to the ground and closed his eyes. This seemed like the end of the world, to be deserted by Charlotte's children. Wilbur cried himself to sleep.

When he woke it was late afternoon. He looked at the egg sac. It was empty. He looked into the air. The balloonists were gone. Then he walked drearily to the doorway, where Charlotte's web used to be. He was standing there, thinking of her, when he heard a small voice.

"Salutations!" it said. "I'm up here."

"So am I," said another tiny voice.

"So am I," said a third voice. "Three of us are staying. We like this place, and we like *you*."

Wilbur looked up. At the top of the doorway three small webs were being constructed. On each web, working busily was one of Charlotte's daughters.

"Can I take this to mean," asked Wilbur, "that you have definitely decided to live here in the barn cellar, and that I am going to have *three* friends?"

"You can indeed," said the spiders.

"What are your names, please?" asked Wilbur, trembling with joy.

"I'll tell you my name," replied the first little spider, "if you'll tell me why you are trembling."

"I'm trembling with joy," said Wilbur.

"Then my name is Joy," said the first spider.

"What was my mother's middle initial?" asked the second spider.

"A," said Wilbur.

"Then my name is Aranea," said the spider.

"How about me?" asked the third spider. "Will you just pick out a nice sensible name for me—something not too long, not too fancy, and not too dumb?"

Wilbur thought hard.

"Nellie?" he suggested.

"Fine, I like that very much," said the third spider. "You may call me Nellie." She daintily fastened her orb line to the next spoke of the web.

Wilbur's heart brimmed with happiness. He felt that he should make a short speech on this very important occasion.

"Joy! Aranea! Nellie!" he began. "Welcome to the barn cellar. You have chosen a hallowed doorway from which to string your webs. I think it is only fair to tell you that I was devoted to your mother. I owe my very life to her. She was brilliant, beautiful, and loyal to the end. I shall always treasure her memory. To you, her daughters, I pledge my friendship, forever and ever."

"I pledge mine," said Joy.

"I do, too," said Aranea.

"And so do I," said Nellie, who had just managed to catch a small gnat.

It was a happy day for Wilbur. And many more happy, tranquil days followed.

As time went on, and the months and years came and went, he was never without friends. Fern did not come regularly to the barn any more. She was growing up, and was careful to avoid childish things, like sitting on a milk stool near a pigpen. But Charlotte's children and grandchildren and great grandchildren, year after year, lived in the doorway. Each spring there were new little spiders hatching out to take the place of the old. Most of them sailed away, on their balloons. But always two or three stayed and set up housekeeping in the doorway.

Mr. Zuckerman took fine care of Wilbur all the rest of his days, and the pig was often visited by friends and admirers, for nobody ever forgot the year of his triumph and the miracle of the web. Life in the barn was very good—night and day, winter and summer, spring and fall, dull days and bright days. It was the best place to be, thought Wilbur, this warm delicious cellar, with the garrulous geese, the changing seasons, the heat of the sun, the passage of swallows, the nearness of rats, the sameness of sheep, the love of spiders, the smell of manure, and the glory of everything.

Wilbur never forgot Charlotte. Although he loved her children and grandchildren dearly, none of the new spiders ever quite took her place in his heart. She was in a class by herself. It is not often that someone comes along who is a true friend and a good writer. Charlotte was both.

Fiction

WATERLESS MOUNTAIN

Laura Adams Armer

In the culture of the Navaho Indian, the circle motif is an important one, appearing over and over in ritual dances and in sand paintings. In this description of Navaho ritual from Laura Armer's beautiful and carefully researched story of an Indian boy who is going to become a medicine man (the 1932 Newbery Medal winner), the motif is used to represent two natural circles: the physical circle the sun makes in the sky and the recurrent metaphorical circle of the seasons.

. . . all were kept busy, planning and working for the great ceremony. It was to be held near Mother's hogan, but far enough back so that no road passed it.

The medicine lodge was built and a roadway about thirty feet wide extended eastward three hundred feet. On this level ground the dances of the ninth night would be held.

The lodge was left alone for one day before Uncle arrived. He came in the evening, blessed the lodge inside, and started the ceremonies.

For four days everyone in the lodge was busy making sacred cigarettes and round rings of twigs with feathers attached. Uncle sang songs, the patient was given sweat baths out of doors, and something happened every minute. Younger Brother stayed close to Uncle, watching everything that was done and helping where he could.

On the fourth night about nine o'clock, Uncle's assistant laid blankets on the ground, northwest of the fire. On top of the blankets they spread a buffalo robe. On top of that, many yards of new calico were laid, and on top of all, a fine white buckskin.

Then the twenty precious masks, which Uncle's uncle had saved in the jars, were placed in two rows on the buckskin. They were face up, with their tops toward the fire. By the side of the masks, the assistants placed rattles, a basket of plumes, fox skins, and medicine bags.

The patient, Hasteen Sani, sprinkled pollen on the masks, while he prayed in a low voice. After that was done, everyone sat back in his place. There were about

From Laura Adams Armer, *Waterless Mountain* (New York: Longmans, Green, 1931), Chapter 29 (pp. 180–183), Chapter 30 (pp. 184, 187–188), Chapter 31 (pp. 189–193).

fifteen friends of Hasteen Sani in the medicine lodge. All were very quiet, sitting around the edge of the sacred lodge, with its fire in the middle, and Uncle sitting on the west.

Younger Brother was worshipful and intense. This was one of the most important moments in his life—sitting next to Uncle and the twenty buckskin masks.

While everyone waited expectantly in the firelight, a crier outside the medicine lodge called:

"Bike hatali haku—Come on the trail of song."

Younger Brother saw the curtain at the doorway thrown aside and he saw a woman enter with two bowls in her hand. She was followed by many more women, all bearing old pottery bowls or modern dishes filled with food.

The women, dressed in brilliantly colored plush waists and full calico skirts, with their black, shining hair knotted at the back of their heads, walked in single file, slowly around the fire. They walked sunwise and the leader went as far as the door on its northern side. There were enough women to form a circle around the fire, leaving the eastern side open.

When the circle had been formed, the leader of the procession put one bowl of food on the floor in the north. Then the last woman put her two bowls down in the south and then the leader placed her second dish by the side of the first one.

After these four dishes had been placed, the other women put theirs down in a circle around the fire, then they sat down with the rest of the company.

The food in the bowls was prepared after an ancient recipe. There was corn meal mush made without the usual cedar ashes, and there were bee-weed greens, and greens of another plant, and there was thin corn wafer bread.

The circle of dishes stood alone while the next part of the ceremony was held. This was most important because it honored the masks.

A girl and a boy, about ten years old, who had come in with the food bearers, now dipped wands of turkey plumes into the basket of sacred water and sprinkled the masks while Uncle and other medicine men sang.

Younger Brother watched every motion of the two children. He saw the little boy pour water from a wicker jar into a gourd. He saw the little girl put four handfuls of corn meal into an earthen bowl. He watched the boy pour the water on the meal while the girl stirred it. Everyone kept very still. The masks were to be fed.

The boy put a little of the corn meal mush on the mouth of every mask and tasted some himself four times. The little girl also tasted and so did Hasteen Sani and Uncle, Younger Brother, and everyone else in the lodge.

It was a love feast, a communion, promising new life to the tribe. Younger Brother, who knew so well the legends of his people, felt the power and the peace that comes through fellowship with men and gods.

He liked to think how long the masks had lived in beauty in the cliff where the little Pack Rat had guarded them.

Younger Brother was happy and content as he listened to the songs, which lasted throughout the night. . . .

On the morning of the sixth day, the first sand painting was made. Uncle sat in his place on the west, directing twelve young men, who poured the colored sand. All day an old man ground sandstone on a metate, for the young men to use.

He ground red, yellow and white from rocks gathered from the cliffs of the Waterless Mountain. He ground charcoal for black and mixed black and white for blue. . . .

For three days, paintings were made, songs were sung, and there was no time to grow lazy. The old masks were repainted and dressed with spruce collars. They were all ready for the dancers to wear on the ninth night.

Every now and then a clattering wagon, drawn by horses with their winter coats on, would stop, and camps would be made on both sides of the roadway leading east from the lodge. The brightly colored blankets hooding the smiling faces of the women, the happy children packed in the back of the wagon with hay for the horses, and sheepskins and pots and pans for the camp, added to the excitement of the festival.

From far and near, bands of horsemen rode through the crisp winter air. Sometimes a couple of young men would leave the group and race wildly down a canyon to the cry of "Yego, yego" from the other riders.

The people rode past Standing Rock, rising like a towering island from a sea of sagebrush. They passed the hole in the mountain made by the mighty Children of the Sun when they shot their bolts of lightning.

Hundreds came, on horseback and in wagons, and in old Fords that hardly ever hit on all four cylinders. Temporary corrals were made for a few sheep that were brought along for the feast. Everyone used the water from the tank and there was enough for all.

Wagons, saddles, blankets and people made a barricade on each side of the dancing space which led from the lodge to a green bough room where the performers were to dress.

Everything was in readiness for the all-night dance of the Yays. . . . *

The night was cold and frosty, and the little campfires were most welcome. Particularly welcome was the hot coffee and tea kept ready all the time for anyone that wished it.

In the silence of the chilly night, everyone waited for the Yays to leave the green bough shelter. Finally they appeared, preceded by Uncle, who wore a handsome red blanket, with a mountain lion skin draped over his shoulders.

The white-masked god followed him. Uncle walked slowly, uttering a benediction and scattering corn meal on the ground before the four masked dancers as they moved quietly forward, shaking their gourd rattles.

*"Yays" is the Navaho word for a god or holy being.

They sang so softly as they moved toward the west that the audience could hardly hear them. Stealthily they entered the dance ground between the little fires, while Hasteen Sani, the patient, appeared from the lodge.

He was wearing a splendid blanket of red and orange and green. In his hands he carried a basket of meal to be blessed by Uncle, while the dancers moved their feet in continuous rhythm.

While all the thousand spectators sat silently watching, and the thin smoke of the cedar fires rose toward the stars, Uncle spoke softly, line by line, the ancient prayer of his people.

You who dwell in the House of Dawn
And evening twilight,
You who dwell in the House of Cloud
And darkening mist;
The house of rain
Strong as man;
The house of rain
Soft as woman;
You who dwell in the House of Pollen
And of grasshoppers,
Whose door is made of the dark mist,
Whose trail is the rainbow,
Where zigzag lightning
Stands high above,
Where virile rain
Stands high above,
You who dwell there, come to us.

Absolute silence hovered over the thousand Navahos gathered to hear the holy words of their fathers. The dancers kept up the hypnotic rhythm of their feet and swaying heads, throughout the long prayer that ended with a plea for the happiness of the tribe.

Hasteen Sani, standing solemnly in the firelight, spoke the last words:

In beauty I walk.
With beauty before me,
Behind me, above me
And all around.
It is finished in beauty.
It is finished in beauty.
It is finished in beauty.
It is finished in beauty.

When the prayer was finished, the four Yays started their dance for growing things. One dancer represented corn, one was vegetation, one was soft grain, and the fourth was pollen.

It was a song of growing things and the Yays bent to the ground, singing:

The corn comes up,
The rain descends.

All night the little fires were kept burning. At regular intervals, different groups of masked singers entered the dance ground to sing and dance in the ancient custom of their people.

When dawn came with its bluebird song, everyone stirred himself to listen. The Navaho voices, in weird, falsetto tones, greeted the morning with the words:

He sings in gladness,
Bluebird sings in gladness,
As daylight comes,
As morning comes.

After the song of dawn, all the Indians packed their goods in covered wagons, Fords and saddle bags and started for home, remembering in their hearts the words of Uncle:

May they all reach home in peace.

Younger Brother had enjoyed the whole ceremony and had been so impressed with the idea of growing things that he decided to plant a garden when the right time came. He went to the trading post to tell the Big Man about it.

"Grandfather, I need some seeds."

"What kind of seeds do you need?"

"The kind the Yays sang about in the farming songs."

"Tell me what they sang, child. What were the songs about?"

"They were about that young man who floated down the river to the lake. He had a pet turkey."

"What did the turkey do?"

"The turkey followed the young man and when they came to a good place for a farm, the young man sang the first farm song. He sang, *I wish I had some seed.*

"The turkey listened to that song and then he gobbled and shook white corn seed out of his wings. Then he shook all the colored corn seeds, and beans, and muskmelon seeds, and then he shook out tobacco seeds. He was a good pet."

"He sounds like a good pet," said the Big Man. "What else did he do?"

"He was a very good pet," repeated Younger Brother. "When night came and the young man lay down on the ground to sleep, he was cold. He spoke to the turkey roosting in the cedar tree above him. He said, 'My pet, I am cold.'

"Soon after, he fell asleep and while he slept, the turkey jumped down from the tree and covered the young man with his right wing. He slept soundly all night and when he awoke in the morning, the turkey wing was over him and he was all warm."

Younger Brother continued, "I wish I had a pet like that, but I have none, so I ask you for beans and muskmelon seeds, and watermelon seeds. I would like the kind that grows big and fast."

The Big Man smiled and said:

"I will send for them and when they come, you must plant them in the right season."

"I will do it, Grandfather. That will be when the Planting Stars are two fingers above the western horizon, when the sun has set."

. . . AND NOW MIGUEL

Joseph Krumgold

The circle of the seasons is of tremendous significance to the New Mexican sheepherding family portrayed in . . . and now Miguel, *winner of the 1954 Newbery Medal. Each spring the men of the Chavez family must take the sheep up into the summer feeding grounds in the Mountains of the Sangre de Cristo. Twelve-year-old Miguel's great wish is to prove himself ready to be allowed to go on this spring journey. The first two chapters are included here.*

I am Miguel. For most people it does not make so much difference that I am Miguel. But for me, often, it is a very great trouble.

It would be different if I were Pedro. He is my younger brother, only seven years old. For Pedro everything is simple. Almost all the things that Pedro wants, he has—without much worry.

I wanted to find out how it was with him one day when we were in our private place near the Rio Pueblo, the river that goes through our farm. I asked him "Pedro, suppose you could have anything you want. Is there anything you want?"

"Ai, of course." He looked up from reaching below a rock in the river. In this way we catch trout, slowly feeling around in the quiet places beneath big stones. If the fish comes by, sliding soft against your hand, you can catch him. Pedro was just learning to fish like this. He looked up, not wishing to talk. "Of course, sure I want something."

From Joseph Krumgold, . . . *and now Miguel* (New York: Thomas Y. Crowell, 1953), Chapters 1–2. Illustrated by Jean Charlot.

"Like what?"

"Like not so much school."

"School—yes. But that is something that you do not want."

"Like I say—not so much."

"Then what is it that you do want?"

"Shh!" He closed his eyes, moving his hand slowly, slowly in the water, holding his breath, with his tongue between his teeth.

Of a sudden he grabbed, splashing. He made a big commotion in the water. It was no good. Even before he took his hand out of the water, I knew it was empty.

"A good big trout, that's what I do want." Pedro looked at me like he was mad at me, like I spoiled his chance for the fish. "A good one, six inches big!"

He was mad. He took a stone and threw it into the water with all his might.

So I caught him a trout. It is not so hard. You lay down with your hand in the water, in a place where there are shadows below the bank. You leave your hand there for a long time, until the fish see that it is nothing strange. Until they come by, even touching you. Until you can touch them, even rub them very lightly. They seem to like this, the fish, for you to rub them this way. Then when you feel them coming through your fingers, slowly you hold on to them, slowly but tight. Without any sudden move. And that's that.

I gave the fish to Pedro. It was almost six inches. He was happy with me again.

That's the way it is with Pedro. One such fish, not too big after all, and he is happy.

It is enough for him for everything to be like it is.

When the sun shines hot and dry and he can go swimming in the pool where the river goes around the farm of my Uncle Eli, that for Pedro is enough.

And when it rains, that too is enough. He is a great artist, Pedro. He sits in the kitchen when there is thunder outside, and all the pictures in his book he turns yellow and red and blue with his crayons.

If there is a ball, he will play ball. And if there is not, he will roll an old tire. No matter which, he is content.

It would be good to be Pedro. But how long can you stay seven years old? The trouble with me is that I am Miguel.

It would be good to be Gabriel. He is also my brother, and he is nineteen years old. Next to my Grandfather, and my Uncle Bonifacio, and my Uncle Eli, and next to my father who is called Old Blas, and my biggest brother who is called Young Blas and who wears a badge and drives the school bus, Gabriel is the greatest man in the world.

Everything that Gabriel wants, he can get. He explained this to me one Friday last winter.

All week long Gabriel goes to the high school in Taos, which is very big town eight miles away, of one thousand people and many stores that sell marshmallow candy. This year Gabriel will graduate from high school. And that will be too bad for the basketball team and the baseball team as well as for the Future Farmers of America, a club of which he is president. From Monday to Friday Gabriel goes to school and wins the games there and is a president. But on Friday he forgets all these things and helps my uncles and my father with the sheep.

In our family there is always one thing, and that is the sheep. The summer passes and the winter comes and soon it is Easter and the time for spring; but all the time, no matter when, there is the sheep. In our house we may be very happy. Like the time my littlest sister, Faustina, was born. Or very sad. Like when Young Blas was hurt by the mowing machine. But these things they come and go. Everything comes and goes. Except one thing. The sheep.

For that is the work of our family, to raise sheep. In our country, wherever you find a man from the Chavez family, with him will be a flock of sheep. It has been this way for many years, even hundreds, my grandfather told me. Long before the Americans came to New Mexico, long before there was any such thing here called the United States, there was a Chavez family in this place with sheep. It was even so in Spain where our family began. It is even so today.

And so when Gabriel finishes school for the week, on Friday, he goes out to the sheep camp. There he takes the place of one of my uncles or my father, and the older man can come home for a day or two.

In the winter we pasture our sheep on the big mesa that stretches from the cliffs on the other side of our river, far, far north, flat and straight almost into Colorado. This wide plain spreads out to the west to the Rio Grande river where there is a deep arroyo, a great canyon that goes down, down into the earth to where the big river flows. The land is owned by the Indians of the Taos Pueblo and my father pays the war chief of these Indians ten cents every month for each sheep that we pasture. We are very good friends with the Indians. It was not always so, my father tells me, but now we are good friends.

The sheep camp is built into a wagon, so that it can be moved as the sheep are driven from where they have eaten to new pasture. It has a bed built in, and shelves, and a stove. No matter how hard it snows or how cold it gets, inside the sheep wagon it is always tight against the wind and dry and warm.

On this Friday the wagon was in a place very near to the Rio Grande canyon, almost twelve miles from our house. Gabriel went there with the pick-up truck, and he took me along. Driving the truck is very hard. There are no roads. You drive right across the mesa through the mesquite bushes, keeping away from the big holes and the big rocks. It is wise to drive slow and be careful.

But Gabriel did not drive slow, yet he was still careful. He swung the big truck from side to side like it was a little stick, and all the time he sang a beautiful song about a red flower.

"Miguel," he turned to me after he had finished with the song, "what's up with you? You haven't opened your mouth since we left the house."

"Me?" I stopped looking at the bushes and the rocks. "As for me, I've been thinking."

"About what?"

"About how easy it is for you—" Gabriel swung the wheel, and the truck skidded in the snow away from a big hole. "Well, how easy it is for you—to be Gabriel."

Gabriel laughed. "Easier for me than anyone else in the world. After all, that's who I am."

"But it is not so easy for me—to be Miguel."

"Maybe not." Gabriel smiled, watching the snow ahead. "It takes a little time. Wait a year or two, and it'll be easier."

"Only to wait? Isn't there something else I can do? Like—practice?"

"Being Miguel—it's not like playing basketball. No, it's a hard thing to train for."

The truck was going faster. Gabriel was looking through the windshield, his eyes a little closed and tight, like he was looking into the wind. But now that we were talking about such important things, there was much that I wanted to know.

"There must be a secret! Some kind of a special secret, isn't there?"

"For what?" It was hard to talk now, the truck was roaring so much because we were going so fast.

"How to get to be a president." I had to yell. "So easy. And when you want a deer, you take a horse and in a day or two you come back with a deer. And the house?"

"What house?" Gabriel yelled back at me.

"The house by the cottonwood tree. You're going to build such a house of adobe?"

"Sure. Someday."

"And you're going to become an engineer? At the college?"

"Uh-huh."

"How?" I had to shout real loud. "How is all this done—so easy—to get what you wish?" I took him by the arm because he didn't seem to be hearing. "How?"

"Mike!" He shoved me away, back into the corner of the seat. "Lay off. Coyote."

I looked off to one side where Gabriel nodded with his head. And there it was, racing away for the edge of the mesa, no bigger than a dog, than our sheep dog Cyclone. He was just a speck, the coyote, moving against the snow. They are terrible animals for the sheep. Every year they kill many lambs, sometimes more than two dozen. They are smart and they are faster than a bird.

But with Gabriel driving we were getting closer. There was no more time to be careful. Into holes and over rocks we went, and I held on or else I would hit the ceiling of the truck with my head. We pulled closer. I could watch the coyote, moving like a fist that opens and closes quicker than you can blink your eyes. A shadow sliding across the snow.

"Reach down," Gabriel spoke quick. "In back of the seat."

I got the rifle that was there and held it. At just the right moment, Gabriel stamped on the brakes. Before the car even stopped skidding in the snow, Gabriel had pulled off one of his gloves, grabbed the gun and was sighting it. I hardly knew he'd taken it out of my hands before I heard it crack.

The coyote stopped in the middle of a leap. As if a tight wire was stretched in his path and caught him. But when he dropped he continued on his way, not so fast but he still kept going.

Gabriel took his time, carefully holding the animal in the sights of the rifle. He actually hummed the song about the red flower as he took his time. He tightened his finger on the trigger.

The second bullet stopped the coyote for good. And Gabriel laughed. It was good to kill a coyote. With two bullets, many lambs were saved. Gabriel laughed because it was good and because it was so easy.

That's the way it was with Gabriel. Everything that he wants he can get. With Pedro, it is the opposite. Everything that he has is enough.

Both of them, they are happy.

But to be in between, not so little anymore and not yet nineteen years, to be me, Miguel, and to have a great wish—that is hard.

I had such a wish. It was a secret and yet not a secret. For how secret can you keep high mountains that one can see for hundreds of miles around, mountains that face me when I first open my eyes every morning and are the last thing I see in the night.

This was my wish, to go up there—into those mountains that are called the Mountains of the Sangre de Cristo.

There is one thing to say right away about the Sangre de Cristo Mountains and it is this. They are wonderful.

I don't know if it is true but I have been told that if you are good all the time and if sometimes you pray, then you will go to heaven. Maybe this is so and maybe not.

But about the Sangre de Cristo Mountains I know for sure. If you are ready and the time comes, then that's all. You will go.

To get to be ready, it is first necessary to be of my family, a Chavez, and that I have come to be without even trying. Then, one must be a shepherd and know all about how to take care of the sheep. It is likewise a help to know how to bake bread and be a good cook as well as to ride a horse and shoot a gun and catch fish. When you can do these things then you are ready.

And all that must be done then is to wait until the time comes.

And it always does. Every year. It comes as sure as the time for the lambs to be born, and the time for the Fiesta de San Ysidro, and then the shearers arrive and the wool is clipped. Just so sure as all these things happen, comes the time for the flock to go up into the Mountains of the Sangre de Cristo.

Then you will go along. If, that is, everyone knows you are ready.

But if they don't, then you must wait again for another whole year. And even another year and another.

Each year, after the last heavy snows are over, the time comes to show that I am ready and that it is different this year for me, Miguel, than it was last year. It is in this early part of the year that the new lambs are born. Then the sheep are brought in from the pueblo land of the Indians, from the big mesa where they have spent the winter. The sheep wagon is brought in too. Now the flock must stay close to the house so that everyone can help with the birth of the lambs.

At this time there is no question of who is Pedro and who is Gabriel and who am I. Everyone helps without it making any difference who he is.

Even in the middle of the night someone can come into the bedroom where Faustina sleeps in one bed and me and Pedro in another. This one can say, "Come on, they need water."

There is no question who asks for the water or who goes to fetch it. We are quick to find our clothes and run to the spring, which is down the hill behind the tool shed. We carry the water to where it is needed, to the lambing pens where the fires are kept going all night and the men must help the newest lambs who are having a hard time to get born. Or to the kitchen where my mother is always cooking, during this time, because someone is always eating.

The lambs come at all different hours, and all our uncles and cousins stay at our house to be ready to help, and there is no breakfast time or dinner time or bed time. Everyone sleeps and eats when he can, no matter who he is, as long as he is ready when something is needed.

I would like it to matter who he is, especially if it's me, Miguel. But that has never happened.

"Behind the tractor," my father will talk to me without even turning around, "in the tool shed there on the shelf is the liniment. The brown bottle. Hurry!"

My father will be busy bending over a ewe who tries hard to give birth to a lamb, working together with Uncle Eli. He will not even look up when I bring the medicine and put it into his hand.

Once I tried to make my father see who I am. When he asked for some burlap bags to wrap one small lamb who was cold, I brought him the bags. When he took them from me, I said, "Here are the bags."

My father said nothing. He rubbed the lamb and wrapped it up.

"All right?" I said. "Okay?"

My father felt the neck of the lamb. "He'll be all right. It'll live."

"No," I shook my head. "I ask about the bags."

"What about the bags?"

"Are they all right?"

"What can be wrong with bags?"

"Wrong? Nothing. Except sometimes —." This was not what I wanted to talk about at all. "There can be holes in them."

"For our purpose, to wrap up new lambs, holes make no difference. That's why we use old bags."

I knew all this. But I couldn't stop him from saying it.

"If we wanted to put something into them, like grain or wool, then we use new bags without holes." My father stood up now, looking down at me. "You didn't bring me any of the new wool bags, those that are in the corner of the shearing shed?"

"Me?" I said quickly. "Not me!" This is why it is hard for me to be Miguel sometimes, getting people to understand.

"Then what is all this talk about bags?" My father put his hands in the back pockets of his pants and waited.

"I'm sorry." I looked around trying to find some way to leave. But it was too late.

"Miguel, what's the trouble?"

"Nothing." When my father looks at you then there is no place to go. "It's only that I wanted you to know that it was me—I brought you the bags when you asked for them."

"Of course. They were needed. That's why I asked."

"I know, but—" It was no use. It could not get any better. "That's all."

"Ai Blas." Uncle Bonifacio yelled to my father from across the corral. "This ewe here, with twins. Look's bad.""Be right with you," my father called to him, but he looked back. "Let me understand this, Miguel. This is nothing but a question of bags, yes?"

"That's all."

"Nothing else?"

"No."

"Very well," said my father, and he hurried through the sheep to the other side of the corral.

It is different in school. There when the teacher asks you to write in your book the capital of the State of New Mexico, and you write "Sante Fe," the matter does not come to an end. If you do what she asks, then you get a star in your book. And after you get enough stars you get a *G* on your report card instead of an *F.*

To be sure it is always good to have a card with a *G* instead of an *F.* Though, to tell the real truth, I never found it made so much difference from one day to the next what kind of letter you had on the card.

But here with the family and with the sheep, where it makes a big difference, to bring an old bag is nothing but the question of a bag. And if you talk about it, all you do is to get into trouble. And liniment is nothing else but liniment. And when you bring water that is the end of it. There are no stars.

And here, too, it makes a big difference from one day to the next. For soon the days pass and all the lambs are born, and then the shearers arrive and not many days are left.

And even though everyone gets busy again at the shearing, it's not like when the lambs come. To shear and to bag the wool, to tie the fleeces, you have to be an expert to do these things. Even a little mistake is bad. All I can do is to sit on a fence, with Pedro, and watch the others hard at work under the shearing sheds.

"And after so many years," like I once told Pedro, "it's not enough, just to watch anymore."

"Why?" said Pedro. "This is fine. Nothing to do. No school. What could be better than this?"

"It would be better to help, like our brother Blas over there, pushing the sheep into the pen for the shearers."

"Such hard work. What for?"

I had not told Pedro, or anyone else, about my wish to go to the Sangre de Cristo. Nor did I tell him now. Instead I said, "When we work with the others, as at the lambing, we are less by ourselves. It is not so lonesome."

"We're together," said Pedro. "That's not lonesome."

"I mean alone by ourselves. When the others are working."

"You know as good as I do," said Pedro, "when we run and fetch and help at lambing time, no one even knows we're there."

This is true, as I have said. "But even so, it would be better to help," I said once again. "Much better."

"It is better to be sitting here on the fence," said Pedro, "just watching and doing nothing else."

That's the way it is with Pedro. Everything he has is enough. But for me, I have the wish to be part of everything that happens, even if it is not happening to me. Like when the shearers leave and the day comes for the men to leave with the flock, to start for the Mountains. Even though I have never gone with the others, that day for me is a bigger day than Christmas.

Hardly anyone goes to sleep because the start is very early in the morning, before it gets light, and because there is so much to prepare. We all work to get everything together the men will need—the horses and a tent, the blankets and the food and the guns and a stove. Each man who is going must have everything for the whole time he is away.

And I, too, in secret, have for many years now prepared a bundle for myself which I keep underneath the bed without anyone knowing. In it I put all my clothes of the winter though it is by then summer, because it is cold, they have told me, on the high ridges and on the top peaks. In it, too, I pack my best fish hooks, the luckiest ones. I put this bundle beneath my bed because you never know. It could happen at the very last that my father, or my brother Blas, or Uncle Eli will say, "One moment, Miguel. It has been decided among us that you are ready and that this year you will come with the flock, with the rest of us, to the Sangre de Cristo. You are needed."

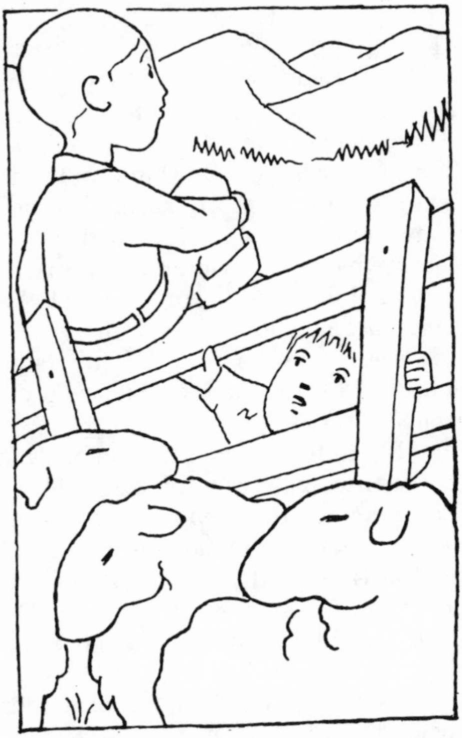

"If I am needed," I will say, "then of course I will be glad to go."

Then they will say, "The only trouble is we forgot to tell you until it is late. Can you get ready in time?"

And because my bundle is already under the bed, I will say, "Yes. Sure. No trouble."

It could happen this way. Though it never has. But until the very last minute, until the very start, the chance remains that it might. And until then it is good to be in our house. For everyone talks of nothing but the Mountains of the Sangre de Cristo. And because the men are going away for so long, not less than three months, they like to talk to the rest of us who are staying. Even when Faustina cries because they are leaving my father will stop his work and take her on his lap.

"Tinga mia," he will tell her. "It is not forever. At the end of the summer we will be back."

"Why?" Faustina squeaks very high like a lamb when she cries. "Why don't you stay here, in the house?"

"We must feed the sheep. There is good grass, the best in the world, on the Sangre de Cristo."

"Here is grass. On the farm is grass. What's grass?"

My father always has to wipe her nose. It runs like a spring when she cries. "There's not enough, Tinga," he tells her. "For so many sheep. On this farm we can feed no more than fifty sheep. We have many hundreds and each one with a lamb. That's why in the winter we must rent from the Indians to pasture the flock. You remember how it is in the winter?"

"Yes," says Faustina. If my father holds her long enough on his lap pretty soon she quiets down.

"But in the summer the pueblo lands on the mesa get very dry. There is very little grass for the sheep to eat. We are lucky we have the mountains so close. Up there it is never dry. The grass is always green and rich. It makes the sheep and the lambs fat and healthy. Isn't that good, Tinga?"

"Okay," says Faustina, as if she understood what it was all about.

The truth is we are lucky indeed to be able to take the sheep to the Sangre de Cristo. Not everyone can go there for pasture. All this was explained to me by Uncle Bonifacio.

"No one owns the mountains." We were packing flour and bacon and all kinds of food in bags when he told me this. "No one except the government. And the government name for the Sangre de Cristo is the Carson National Forest."

"Carson—he is part of the government."

"No, he's just a man by the name Kit Carson who fought with the Indians and killed buffaloes and was a soldier, and now he is dead. So instead of putting up a statue for him where the birds can sit when they get tired of sitting in trees, they set aside the mountains so that no one can own them and gave his name, Carson, to the whole place." Uncle Bonifacio smiled as we kept putting food into the bags. Often he smiles, my Uncle Bonifacio, but I have never seen him laugh.

"Now people come from far away to go up in the mountains because it is beautiful there."

"Like I say," I said. "Wonderful."

"That's also true." Uncle Bonifacio nodded. "Wonderful. Almost anything you like, you can find in the mountains. Great sights to see. Good fishing, bass in the lakes and trout everywhere. Animals to hunt, in the proper season, even bears and wolf and deer."

"And lions and tigers?"

"There are mountain lions. But tigers? This is the Sangre de Cristo after all, Miguel, not a traveling circus. And there are trees everywhere, good for making lumber if one gets permission from the government and promises not to cut down all the trees. In which case the birds would have to go back to the statues after all. And fine pasture for cattle and sheep. But in order to graze your stock on the mountains you must also get permission, and this is difficult."

"With the mountains so big? Stretching as far as you can see?"

"Even so, there are men in the government who say even less sheep should graze in the Sangre de Cristo than now. For there is a danger if all the grass is eaten. Then when it rains on the bare earth the dirt will wash away, and the water will run off the hills as from a roof, making one day a flood and the next day dry, bare rocks under the sun. That is why only a few are given the permit to pasture their sheep in the mountains. And that is why we of the Chavez family are lucky to have such a permit."

"Thank goodness we are lucky!"

"Thank goodness if you wish," Uncle Bonifacio closed the bag now and tied it up, "but also thank your grandfather for being such a wise man. It was he, many years ago, who got the permit for our flock. If not for him you would have to be a policeman when you grow up, or an airplane pilot," he smiled.

I don't think to be a policeman or an airplane pilot is anything so terrible. But still I am glad that I was growing up to be a shepherd, if only it doesn't take too long. And so, as Uncle Bonifacio said, I thanked my grandfather.

It was during the last hour of the night. I helped my grandfather tie the canvas bag filled with blankets onto the mule, Herman. My grandfather is almost eighty years, which is as old as most people get. He no longer goes to the mountains but nothing is done without his help. Tying the pack, he worked very slow and every knot was tight. He stopped and shook his head when I thanked him.

"The permit, it is only a piece of paper of the government. The paper will go and the government will go, but still the mountains will remain where the good Lord put them. It is He you should thank."

"Yes, Padre de Chavez," I said. "I will, next Sunday when we go to Mass."

"Be sure to thank him for everything," he said. He turned from the mule and slowly he pointed with his hand from north to the south. It was not yet dawn, but already the sky looked to be in two parts. The part that was really the sky was not so dark, and the part that was the mountains still black. "When you wish to see what is ahead, in the time to come, you look to the mountains. If it is white on their peaks with snow, like blessed white clouds that have come to rest, it will be a good year. There will be much water all through the months from the snows that melt, and we and the sheep will have it good, here and far from here. All down the Rio Grande valley, they will rejoice. Even in Texas and Arizona and in Old Mexico they will give thanks to the Lord that he has placed here the Mountains of the Sangre de Cristo. Give thanks, too, Miguel, for the year that is ahead."

"Next Sunday," I promised. "For sure."

And I did. Though last year, when we spoke, it was not the year for which I wanted to thank anybody. Last year it happened like all the years before.

When the time came, my father kissed my mother and then each one of us. Then we all went outside, and everybody hugged everybody else and said goodbye. No one said anything special to me, not even at the last moment.

One could see the mountains with the tops all white as they started out, for it was getting day. Gabriel was on his horse Blackie, leading the three pack horses. And Uncle Eli, too, was on a horse. My father, my brother Blas, and Uncle Bonifacio went on foot, driving the flock with the dog Cyclone.

We stood watching them. My mother stood with my grandfather, and my big sisters were with the little ones, Faustina and Pedro. And me, not big or little, I stood there alongside the others.

The flock sent up a big cloud of dust as it started out. And after awhile there was nothing to watch but this brown, dirty cloud coming up and moving slowly toward the high mountains. By then the others had gone back into the house. Soon, even the dust of the cloud disappeared, and nothing was left to look at except the tops of the Mountains of the Sangre de Cristo, standing clean and shining and high in the sun. At the end it was no good to stand there any more looking up at them. It made you to feel more little than you are.

So I went back into the house. I took the bundle out from underneath the bed.

I put everything back in its place.

It happened this way last year. And that is the last time, I have promised myself, it will happen in such a way. For now it is a new year, with the winter coming to an end, and I have become twelve.

Poetic Fiction

THE WORLD IS ROUND

Gertrude Stein

J. D. O'Hara's essay "Gertrude Stein's The World Is Round" *(which appears at the end of this section) should help to sort out the meaning of this story, which belongs to the realm of emotion rather than logic. Gertrude Stein is less interested in what happened to Rose than in how what happened to her* felt *as it was happening.*

The following suggestions on how to read The World Is Round *appeared on the jacket flap of the original version of the story, published by William R. Scott in 1939:*

> *This book was written to be enjoyed. It is meant to be read aloud a few chapters at a time. . . . Don't bother about the commas which aren't there, read the words. Don't worry about the sense that is there, read the words faster. If you have any trouble read faster and faster until you don't. . . . This book was written to be enjoyed.*

The complete text is included here.

Rose Is A Rose

Once upon a time the world was round and you could go on it around and around.

Everywhere there was somewhere and everywhere there they were men and women children dogs cows wild pigs little rabbits cats lizards and animals. That is the way it was. And everybody dogs cats sheep rabbits and lizards and children all wanted to tell everybody all about it and they wanted to tell all about themselves.

And then there was Rose.

Rose was her name and would she have been Rose if her name had not been Rose. She used to think and then she used to think again.

Would she have been Rose if her name had not been Rose and would she have been Rose if she had been a twin.

Rose was her name all the same and her father's name was Bob and her mother's name was Kate and her uncle's name was William and her aunt's name was Gloria and her grandmother's name was Lucy. They all had names and her name was Rose, but would she have been she used to cry about it would she have been Rose if her name had not been Rose.

I tell you at this time the world was all round and you could go on it around and around.

Rose had two dogs a big white one called Love, and a little black one called Pépé, the little black one was not hers but she said it was, it belonged to a neighbor and it never did like Rose and there was a reason why, when Rose was young, she was nine now and nine is not young no Rose was not young, well anyway when she was young she one day had little Pépé and she told him to do something, Rose liked telling everybody what to do, at least she liked to do it when she was young, now she was almost ten so now she did not tell every one what they should do but then she did and she told Pépé, and Pépé did not want to, he did not know what she wanted him to do but even if he had he would not have wanted to, nobody does want to do what anybody tells them to do, so Pépé did not do it, and Rose shut him up in a room. Poor little Pépé he had been taught never to do in a room what should be done outside but he was so nervous being left all alone he just did, poor little Pépé. And when he was let out and there were a great many people about but little Pépé made no mistake he went straight among all the legs until he found those of Rose and then he went up and he bit her on the leg and then he ran away and nobody could blame him now could they. It was the only time he ever bit any one. And he never would say how do you do to Rose again and Rose always said Pépé was her dog although he was not, so that she could forget that he never wanted to say how do you do to her. If he was her dog that was alright he did not have to say how do you do but Rose knew and Pépé knew oh yes they both knew.

Rose and her big white dog Love were pleasant together they sang songs together, these were the songs they sang.

Love drank his water and as he drank, it just goes like that like a song a nice song and while he was doing that Rose sang her song. This was her song

I am a little girl and my name is
Rose
Rose is my name.
Why am I a little girl
And why is my name Rose
And when am I a little girl
And when is my name Rose
And where am I a little girl
And where is my name Rose
And which little girl am I
Am I the little girl named Rose
Which little girl named Rose.

And as she sang this song and she sang it while Love did his drinking

Why am I a little girl
Where am I a little girl
When am I a little girl
Which little girl am I

And singing that made her so sad she began to cry.

And when she cried Love cried he lifted up his head and looked up at the sky and he began to cry and he and Rose and Rose and he cried and cried and cried until she stopped and at last her eyes were dried.

And all this time the world just continued to be round.

Willie Is Willie

Rose had a cousin named Willie and once he was almost drowned. Twice he was almost drowned.

That was very exciting.

Each time was very exciting.

The world was round and there was a lake on it and the lake was round. Willie went swimming in the lake, there were three of them they were all boys swimming and there were lots of them they were all men fishing.

Lakes when they are round have bottoms to them and there are water-lilies pretty water-lilies white water-lilies and yellow ones and soon very soon one little boy and then another little boy was caught right in by them, water-lilies are pretty to see but they are not pretty to feel not at all.

Willie was one and the other little boy was the other one and the third boy was a bigger one and he called to them to come and they, Willie and the other boy they couldn't come, the water-lilies did not really care but they just all the same did not let them.

Then the bigger boy called to the men *come and get them they cannot come out from the water-lilies and they will drown come and get them.*

But the men they had just finished eating and you eat an awful lot while you are fishing you always do and you must never go into the water right after eating, all this the men knew so what could they do.

Well the bigger boy he was that kind he said he would not leave Willie and the other behind, so he went into the water-lilies and first he pulled out one little boy and then he pulled out Willie and so got them both to the shore.

And so Willie was not drowned although the lake and the world were both all round.

That was one time when Willie was not drowned.

Another time he was not drowned was when he was with his father and his mother and his cousin Rose they were all together.

They were going up a hill and the rain came down with a will, you know how it comes when it comes a heavy and fast it is not wet it is a wall that is all.

So the car went up the hill and the rain came down the hill and then and then well and then there was hay, you know what hay is, hay is grass that is cut and when it is cut it is hay. Well anyway.

The hay came down the way it was no way for hay to come anyway. Hay should stay until it is taken away but this hay, the rain there was so much of it the hay came all the way and that made a dam so the water could not go away and the water went into the car and somebody opened the door and the water came more and more and Willie and Rose were there and there was enough water there to drown Willie certainly to drown Willie and perhaps to drown Rose.

Well anyway just then the hay went away, hay has that way and the water went away and the car did stay and neither Rose nor Willie were drowned that day.

Much later they had a great deal to say but they knew of course they knew that it was true the world was round and they were not drowned.

Now Willie liked to sing too. He was a cousin to Rose and so it was in the family to sing, but Willie had no dog with whom to sing so he had to sing with something and he sang with owls, he could only sing in the evening but he did sing in the evening with owls. There were three kinds of owls a Kew owl a chuette owl and a Hoot owl and every evening Willie sang with owls and these are the songs he sang.

My name is Willie I am not like Rose
I would be Willie whatever arose,
I would be Willie if Henry was my name
I would be Willie always Willie all the same.

And then he would stop and wait for the owls.

Through the moon the Q. owl blew

Who are you who are you.

Willie was not like his cousin Rose singing did not make him cry it just made him more and more excited.

So there was a moon and the moon was round.

Not a sound.

Just then Willie began to sing

Drowning
Forgetting
Remembering
I am thinking

And the chuette owl interrupted him

Is it
His it
Any eye of any owl is round.

Everything excited Willie, he was more excited and he sang

Once upon a time
The world was round
The moon was round
The lake was round
And I
I was almost drowned.

And the hoot owl hooted

Hullo Hullo
Willie is your name
And Willie is your nature
You are a little boy
And that is your stature
Hullo Hullo.

SILENCE

Willie was asleep
And everything began to creep around
Willie turned in his sleep and murmured
Round drowned.

Eyes A Surprise

Rose did not care about the moon, she liked stars.

Once some one told her that the stars were round and she wished that they had not told her.

Her dog Love did not care about the moon either and he never noticed the stars. He really did not notice the moon not even when it was all round, he liked the lights of automobiles coming in and out. That excited him and even made him bark, Love was not a barker although little Pépé was. Pépé could always bark, he really did say bow wow really he did, when you listened he really did.

Well once they were out in the evening in an automobile, not Pépé, Pépé was not Rose's dog, you remember that, but Rose and Love and the lights of the automobile were alight so who could listen to the bright moon-light, not Rose nor Love nor the rabbit, not they.

It was a little rabbit and there he was right in front and in the light and it looked as if he meant it but he really could not help it, not he not the little rabbit.

Bob, Rose's father was driving and he stopped but that did not help the little rabbit.

Light is bright and what is bright will confuse a little rabbit who has not the habit.

So the little rabbit danced from one light to the other light and could never get alright, and then Bob the father said *let out Love perhaps he will help the rabbit to run away,* so they let out the white dog Love and he saw first the light and then he saw the rabbit and he went up to say how do you do to the rabbit, that is the way Love was, he always went up and said how do you do he said it to a dog or a man or a child or a lamb or a cat or a cook or a cake or anything he just said how do you do and when he said how do you do to the little rabbit the little rabbit forgot all about the light being bright he just left that light and Love the dog Love disappointed because the little rabbit had not said how do you do, back again, he went after him, of course any little rabbit can run quicker than any white dog and even if the white dog is nice and kind and Love is, so that was all of that. It was a lovely night and Love came back into the car and Bob the father drove on home and of course Rose sang as the rabbit ran and her song began

My
What a sky
And then the glass pen

Rose did have a glass pen

When oh When
Little glass pen
Say when
Will there not be that little rabbit.
When
Then
Pen

And Rose burst into tears.
She did then she burst into tears.

A little later it was decided that Rose should go to school. She went to school where mountains were high, they were so high she never did see them. Rose was funny that way.

There at the school were other girls and Rose did not have quite as much time to sing and cry.

The teachers taught her
That the world was round
That the sun was round
That the moon was round
That the stars were round
And that they were all going around and around
And not a sound.
It was so sad it almost made her cry
But then she did not believe it
Because mountains were so high,
And so she thought she had better sing
And then a dreadful thing was happening
She remembered when she had been young
That one day she had sung,
And there was a looking-glass in front of her

And as she sang her mouth was round and was going around and around.

Oh dear oh dear was everything just to be round and go around and around. What could she do but try and remember the mountains were so high they could stop anything.

But she could not keep on remembering and forgetting of course not but she could sing of course she could sing and she could cry of course she could cry.

Oh my.

Willie And His Singing

All this time Willie was living along
Of course he could always make a song
The thing that bothered Willie the most
Was that when there was no wind blowing
A twig in a bush would get goin
Just as if the wind was blowing.
He knew when he ran
And he knew when he sang
And he knew who
Who was Willie
He was Willie
All through.

Willie went away not to stay.
Willie never went away to stay
That was not Willie.

But once when he went away it was to stay there where he had seen it.

He saw it.
It was a little house and two trees near it.
One tree sometimes makes another tree.
Willie
Will he.

In a little while nobody wondered that thunder rumbled in winter, lightning struck and thunder rumbled in winter.

Oh Willie.
Of course Willie never went away to stay.
But Willie could sing.
Oh yes he sang a song.

He sang a little song about a house two trees and a rabbit

He sang a little song about a lizard.

A lizard climbed up the side of the house, it climbed out on the roof of the house and then the poor little lizard fell off of it.

Plump it fell off of it.
Willie saw it.

And Willie said, if the earth is all round can a lizard fall off it.

And the answer was yes if there is a roof over it.
Little lizard it lost its tail but it was not dead.
Willie sat down to rest.

It's funny he said, a lizard does not fall off a wall, it is funny and Willie sat down again to rest.

One of the things Willie did was to sit down and rest.

He liked cats and lizards, he liked frogs and pigeons he liked butter and crackers, he liked flowers and windows.

Once in a while they called for him and when they did he would talk to them.

And then he began to sing.
He sang

Bring me bread
Bring me butter
Bring me cheese
And bring my jam
Bring me milk
And bring me chicken
Bring me eggs
And a little ham.

This is what Willie sang.
And then all at once
The world got rounder and rounder.
The stars got rounder and rounder
The moon got rounder and rounder
The sun got rounder and rounder

And Willie oh Willie was ready to drown her, not Rose dear me not Rose but his sorrows.

He loved to sing and he was exciting
This is what Willie sang

Believe me because I tell you so
When I know yes when I know
Then I am Willie and Willie oh
Oh Willie needs Willie to tell them so.

Yes he said, he said *yes.*
Then Willie began to sing again

Once upon a time I met myself and ran.
Once upon a time nobody saw how I ran.
Once upon a time something can
Once upon a time nobody sees
But I I do as I please
Run around the world just as I please.
I Willie.

Willie stopped again and again he began to sing.

He sang.

It was time Willie did something, why not when the world was all so full anywhere, Willie went on, he saw how many there were there.

Funny said Willie *that a little dog sees another little dog far far away and I,* said Willie, *I see a little boy.*

Well well said the dog *little dogs are interesting.*

Well well said Willie *little boys are interesting.*

Undoubtedly Willie had something to do and now was the time to do it.

Willie And His Lion

Willie had a father and Willie had a mother

That was Willie.

Willie went with his father to a little place where they sold wild animals.

If the world is round can wild animals come out of the ground.

In the place that his father took Willie wild animals did not grow there, they were not always sold there but they were always there. Everybody there had them. Wild animals were with them on the boats on the river and they went with every one in the garden and in the house. Everybody there had a wild animal and they always had them with them.

Nobody knows how the wild animals came there. If the world is round can they come out of the ground but anyway everybody had one and sometimes somebody sold one, quite often everybody sold one.

Willie's father went to get one. Which one. That was for Willie to say. It was funny seeing wild animals in a boat, one wild animal in a rowing boat, one wild animal in a sail boat, one wild animal in a motor boat.

It was a funny place this town that is it would not have been a funny place it was just like any place only that every one always had a wild animal with them, men women and children and very often they were in the water in a boat and the wild animal with them and of course wild animals are wild, of course they are wild.

It was a funny place.

Willie went everywhere so of course he was there, besides his father had taken him there. It was a funny place. And Willie always took whatever he was given. So he hoped he would have one. Any one. Everybody had one so of course Willie would come to have one, any wild animal will do, if it belongs to you.

And Willie did come to have one.

Which one.

There were elephants, an elephant in a rowing boat, Willie did not get that one.

And a tiger in a sail boat, Willie did not get that one. Willie got a lion, not a very little one, one who looked like Rose's dog Love only the Lion was terrifying. Any lion is, even a quite small one and this was a pretty big one. Willie began to sing, it was exciting and Willie sang and sang he did not sing to the lion but he sang about lions being exciting, about cats and tigers and dogs and bears about windows and curtains and giraffes and chairs. The giraffe's name was Lizzie, it really was.

Willie was so excited he almost stopped singing but as soon as he saw his own lion again he began singing again. Singing and singing. This was the song he sang

Round is around.
Lions and tigers
Kangaroos and canaries abound
They are bound to be around.
Why
Because the world is round
And they are always there.
Any little dog is afraid of there.

Then he sang in a whisper

Suppose it should rain
Suppose it should never be the
same

And then Willie's voice rose

The lion is what I chose.

After a long moment he sat down to cry

He said *there, here I am just like my cousin Rose.*

Which was true
He was.
He almost was not Willie.
Oh will he again be Willie.
Not as long as he has a lion.
Not as long.

And it was getting worse and worse and then suddenly he said *there were only two baskets of yellow peaches and I have them both.*

He whispered very low *and I have them both.*

And Willie had, they were lovely round yellow peaches really round really yellow really peaches and there were only two baskets of them and Willie had them both.

And so he cheered up and decided to give the lion to his cousin Rose.

Is A Lion Not A Lion

It is not easy to give a lion away
What did you say
I said it is not easy to give a lion away.

Rose And Willie's Lion

There is a lion its name is lion and lion lion is its name.

Rose began to cry.
Just try
Not to make Rose cry
Just try.

That is what Willie said to the lion
When he gave Rose the lion
His lion.
Oh yes his lion.
Well there was more to it than that.

When Rose knew about a lion his lion Willie's lion she remembered her dog Love. He was clipped like a lion but it was not that. It was when Love was only three months old and had never seen a lion.

Love was not a barker, he neither barked nor bit and when he was three months old he never had barked.

They began to be worried lest he

could not bark, like children who will not talk. Well anyway.

One day Rose and her father Bob and her mother Kate and her grandmother Lucy and her uncle William were out riding and little Love was with them. Love had a pink nose and bright blue eyes and lovely white hair. When he ate asparagus and he liked to eat asparagus his rosy nose turned red with pleasure, but he never barked, not even at a cat or at asparagus. And then that day suddenly that day he stood up he was astonished and he barked. What was he astonished at. There in the middle of the open country was a big truck and on the truck were cages and the sides were down and there they were lions tigers bears and monkeys and Love just could not stand it and he barked.

Rose was very young then quite young too young then to sing a song but she sang one all the same.

This was the song she sang

How does Love know how wild they are
Wild and wild and wild they are
How does Love know who they are
When he never ever had seen them before.

And then she went on

If a cat is in a cage
Does that make him rage.
If a dog is on a roof
Does that make him aloof
Or is there any proof
That he is a dog and on a roof.
And so
Oh
How could Love know
That wild animals were wild.
Wild animals yes wild.
Are they wild if they are wild,
If oh I am wild if you are wild
Are you wild are you wild

Rose began to cry.
She began to try
She began to deny
The wild animals could lie.
Lie quietly not die but just lie.
And then Rose once more began to sing
I know, she said, *I knew I would sing*
And this is everything.
I wish, she said, *I wish I knew*
Why wild animals are wild.
Why are they wild why why,
Why are they wild oh why
And once more Rose began to cry.
Love was asleep he knew he could bark,
So why stay awake to hear Rose cry and sing
And sing and cry. Why.
That is what Love said.
Why.

And then later on when Love saw a wild animal he sometimes did anybody sometimes did, he did not bark he just turned his head away as much as to say, I did once but not again, wild animals are not interesting.

Love mostly barked in his sleep.
He dreamed.
And when he dreamed, he made a strangled bark,
Like anybody dreaming.

Love never said whether he liked to dream or not, but he did dream and when he dreamed he barked.

Rose was thinking all about everything when she heard that her cousin Willie had a lion.

Rose Thinking

If the world is round
would a lion
fall
o
f
f.

A Favorite Color

Rose certainly made a noise when no one was found

Rose oh Rose look down at the ground

And what do you see

You see that the world is not round.

That is what Rose said when she knew that it was true that a lion is not blue.

Of course she knew that a lion is not blue but blue is her favorite color.

Her name is Rose and blue is her favorite color. But of course a lion is not blue. Rose knew that of course a lion is not blue but blue was her favorite color.

Bringing Billie Back

The lion had a name, his color was not blue but he had a name too just as any one has a name and his name was Billie. Willie was a boy and Billie was a lion.

Bringing Back Billie To Willie

That is what happened.

Of course Rose could not keep a lion in school, she could not have kept him even if he had been blue which was her favorite color but she certainly could not keep him when he was yellow brown which is the natural color for a lion to be even if the lion has a name as well as a mane and that name is Billie.

In fact you might say really say that Rose had never had him, the lion had never come in, of course not if a lamb can not come into a school how certainly not can a lion.

So outside the school was a man with a drum, he was on a bicycle and the drum was on a bicycle and he was drumming and when Rose heard him drumming she went to the door and the man was calling out *either or either or, either there is a lion here or there is no lion here, either or, either or.*

Rose began to sing she just could not help herself, tears were in her eyes, she just could not help herself and she began to sing, she just could not help herself.

The drumming went on, *either or,* cried the man, *neither nor,* cried Rose *he is neither here nor there, no no lion is here, no lion is there, neither nor,* cried Rose *he is neither here nor there.* The man began to drum and the drumming went further and further away and the drum was round and the wheels of the bicycle were round and they went around and around and as they went around and around the man whose mouth was round kept saying *either or, either or,* until there was no more no more drumming no more bicycle no more man any more.

So Rose was left at the door and she knew no more about the lion about Billie the lion than she had known before and slowly she began to sing

Billie is going back to Willie,
Willie is getting back Billie,
No lion is blue
So there is no lion for me
There is a lion for you

Oh Willie Willie yes there is a lion for you, a brown lion for you a real lion for you, neither will you nor will you ever know how little I wanted to take away the lion from you, dear Willie sweet Willie, take back oh take back your lion to you, because, and she began to whisper to herself as if she herself was Willie, *because if a lion could be blue I would like a lion to come from you, either from you or to you, dear Willie sweet Willie, there is no blue lion in blue no blue in lion, neither nor,* wailed Rose *neither nor,* and as she said *neither nor* there, there was a door, and filled with sobs Rose went through the door and never any more never any more would she remember that it had been a lion that she saw, either or.

Once Upon A Time

Once upon a time Willie was always there of course he was that was where Willie was and the lion he had almost forgotten that there had been a lion and he had almost forgotten that it had a name and Willie was getting very interested in knowing whether a lizard could or could not be a twin and just then he heard a bell ring and it was the lion Billie the lion back again and Willie just could not help it he just had to begin to sing and he sang a song called

Bringing Billie back again.

Bringing Billie back.
How could Billie come back.

How if there was no h in how. That is what Willie said. *How could Billie come back, how, how.*

And Billie was back. *Was Billie a lion when he was back. No,* said Willie, *Billie was not a lion when he was back. Was he a kitten when Billie was back. No,* said Willie, *Billie was not a kitten when he was back. Was he a rat when he was back. No,* said Willie, *he was not a rat. Well what,* said Willie, *what was Billie when he was back. He was a twin,* said Willie, *that is what Billie was when he got back.*

And Willie began to laugh and by the time he stopped laughing he had begun again to laugh. That was Willie not Billie, Billie never had had to laugh not Billie because Billie was a lion and a lion had never had to laugh.

So that was all there was about Billie the lion and he was never there any more anywhere neither here nor there neither there nor here, Billie the lion never was anywhere. The end of Billie the lion.

A Chair On The Mountain

When mountains are really true they are blue.

Rose knew they were blue and blue was her favorite color. She knew they were blue and they were far away or near just as the rain came or went away. The rain came or the rain went away any day.

And so Rose would look and see and deary me the mountains would be blue.

And then one day she saw a mountain near and then it was all clear.

This was the way Rose knew what to say.

Listen.

Mountains are high
Up there is a sky
Rain is near
Mountains are clear
Mountains are blue
That is true
And one mountain two mountains
three mountains or four
When there are mountains there
always are more
Even from the door

So Rose would say when every day she came that way.

Rose was at school there.

There the mountains were and they were blue, oh dear blue blue just blue, dear blue sweet blue yes blue.

And then Rose began to think. It was funny about Rose she always could just begin to think. She would say to her father Bob *Father I have a complaint to make, my dog Love does not come when I call.*

Rose was always thinking. It is easy to think when your name is Rose. Nobody's name was ever Blue, nobody's, why not. Rose never thought about that. Rose thought she thought a lot but she never did think about that.

But mountains yes Rose did think about mountains and about blue when it was on the mountains and feathers when clouds like feathers were on the mountains and birds when one little bird and two little birds and three and four and six and seven and ten and seventeen and thirty or forty little birds all came flying and a big bird came flying and the little birds came flying and they flew higher than the big bird and they came down and one and then two and then five and then fifty of them came picking down on the head of the big bird and slowly the big bird came falling down between the mountain and the little birds all went home again. Little birds do go home again after they have scared off the big bird.

How Rose thought when she was thinking. Rose would get all round thinking her eyes her head her mouth her hands, she would get all round while she was thinking and then to relieve her hearing her thinking she would sing.

She sang a song of the mountain.
She sang.

Dear mountain tall mountain real mountain blue mountain yes mountain high mountain all mountain my mountain, I will with my chair come climbing and once there mountain once there I will be thinking, mountain so high, who cares for the sky yes mountain no mountain yes I will be there.

Tears came to her eyes.

Yes mountain she said *yes I will be there.*

And then as she looked she saw that one mountain had a top and the top was a meadow and the meadow came up to a point and on the point oh dear yes on the point yes Rose would put a chair and she would sit there and yes she did care yes there she would put a chair there there and everywhere she would see everywhere and she would sit on that chair, yes there.

And she did and this was how she did it. All alone she did it. She and the chair there there, and it was not blue there, no dear no it was green there, grass and trees and rocks are green not blue there no blue was there but blue was her favorite color all through.

The Going Up With The Chair

The first thing about which Rose had to make up her mind was what kind of a chair would she want way up there. She might take a camp stool that would be easiest to carry but that would not look very well up there.

She would want one that would look well way up there and that would be comfortable to sit in because she would be sitting a long time once she really did get all the way up there and it would have to be one that the rain would not harm because clouds are rain and surely there would be clouds up there. No matter how many things Rose thought about there would always be some way it could be done better and a chair dear me, a chair well a chair just had to be there.

When Rose knew she had to climb and climb all the time she knew she would have to go away all day and she knew no matter how she tried that that would not do. She knew she did not know the name of the mountain she would climb she knew it had a nice name, any name is a nice name, just have it be a name and it is a nice name, but the mountain perhaps the mountain did not have a name and if it did not have a name would it be a nice name. And if it had no name could a chair stay there right on top of a mountain that did not have a name.

As Rose thought of this she began to feel very funny she just naturally did begin to feel very very funny.

Do you suppose that Rose is a rose
If her favorite color is blue
Noses can be blue but not roses but Rose was a rose and her favorite color was blue.

And now she had to make up her mind what to do.

Would the chair be a green chair or a blue
The chair she was to take up there
There where
She was to sit on the mountain so high
Right up under the sky

But always remember that the world is round no matter how it does sound. Remember.

So Rose had to do so many things too beside deciding whether her chair should be green or blue.

She had to think about number 142. Why.

Numbers are round.

All she took was the blue chair to go there.

It was a long way to go
And so
From morning to evening she did not get there.
But from evening to morning she did get there she and the blue chair.

The Trip

It was not a trip she had to grip the blue chair and sometimes it hung by a hair not Rose's hair but any hair so great had been Rose's scare.

This Was Her Trip

She had decided about the chair it was a blue chair a blue garden chair otherwise scratches and rain and dew and being carried all through would do a chair harm but not a blue garden chair.

So Rose left early so no one saw her and her chair she held before her and the mountain was high and so was the sky and the world was round and was all ground and she began to go, even so it was a very long way to go even if a mountain does not grow even so, climb a mountain and you will know even if there is no snow. Oh no.

Well shall I go Rose said as she was going, nobody does like to go nobody does say no and so Rose did go, even so she did go.

As she began to go it was early morning you know.

The birds began to stir

And then she heard some birds making funny screams as they flew.

And she thought of cousin Willie but that would not do.

Did the blue garden chair have arms or was it without arms, I am wondering.

Up The Hill

A hill is a mountain, a cow is a cat,

A fever is heating and where is she at.

She is climbing the mountain a chair in her arms, and always around her she is full of alarms. Why not, a chair is something but not to talk to when it is too cold to be bold too hot to be cold a lot too white to be blue, too red to be wed. *Oh Willie* she said and there was no Willie but there was a simple noise just a noise and with a noise there were eyes and with the eyes there was a tail and then from Rose there was a wail *I wish I was not dead* said Rose *but if I am I will have torn my clothes, blackberries are black and blueberries are blue strawberries are red and so are you,* said Rose to Rose and it was all true. She could not sit down on her chair because if she did sit down on her chair she would think she was already there and oh dear she just could not see how high it all could be but she knew oh dear yes she knew and when those birds flew she just could not do so too and she could not sing and cry no matter how much she could try because she was there right in the middle of everything that was around her and how little she could move just a little and a little and the chair was sticking and she was sticking and she could not go down because she would not know where, going down might be anywhere, going up had to be there, oh dear where was Rose she was there really she was there not stuck there but very nearly really very nearly really stuck there. And now everything began and if it had not been on a mountain and if it had not been a chair there where she was she would not care but she did not run she never ran, there was no tin can, she was not hungry oh never that, but everything helped to hold her back, but if she stayed she was afraid, run ran a chair can be a man, *oh dear chair do dear chair be a man so I will not be all scare,* that is what Rose said trying not to see her own hair. Dear me hair chair ran man, Rose is beginning to feel as funny as she can. Anybody try to climb a mountain all alone with only a blue garden chair to hold there and everything on a mountain that is there and then see what it is that ran. Water yes and birds yes and rats yes and snakes yes and lizards yes and cats yes and cows yes, and trees yes and scratches yes, and sticks yes, and flies yes, and bees yes but not a Rose with a chair, all a Rose with a chair can dare is just not stare but keep on going up there.

She did.

Day And Night

Was she awake or did she dream that her cousin Willie heard her scream.

She was asleep right there with her arms around her chair.

She never dragged the chair she carried it before and in a way it was a cane, she leaned upon it all the same and she went on climbing and then it was all still, she heard a sound like a trill and then she thought of her cousin Willie and his lion Billie who was never still but it was not that, no not that, it was nothing completely nothing like that, it was something moving perhaps it was just fat. It, fat can burn like that to make a trill and to be all still and to smell like the lion of cousin Will. Anything can happen while you are going up hill. And a mountain is so much harder than a hill and still. Go on.

The Night

Rose did go on smelling and breathing and pushing and shoving and rolling, she sometimes just rolled, and moving. Anything on a mountain side is moving, rocks are rolling, stones are turning, twigs are hitting, trees are growing, flowers are showing and animals are glowing that is their eyes are and everywhere there oh dear everywhere there well Rose was there and so was her chair.

How many minutes go around to make a second how many hours go round to make a minute how many days go around to make an hour how many nights go round to make a day and was Rose found. She never had been lost and so how could she be found even if everything did go around and around.

The Night

It all grew rosy they call it an alpine glow when it does so but Rose well Rose is her name and blue is her favorite color.

And then she knew yes she had heard it too,

Red at night is a sailor's delight

Red in the morning is a sailor's warning,

And said she *is it rose or red*

And said she *is it morning or evening*

And said she *am I awake or am I in bed,*

And said she *perhaps a sailor does not know perhaps somebody just told him so.*

And then she remembered everything she had heard it was not about a bird it was about a spider,

A spider at night is a delight a spider in the morning is an awful warning,

And then she remembered about if you put shoes on a table it makes awful trouble, but she had not a table she only had a chair and after all she could not take off her shoes there up upon the mountain so high and that funny black that first was blue and then grey up there in the sky, and then she remembered about the moon, if you see the new moon through a window with glass not any trouble will ever pass no it will not and then she remembered just when she was about to be scared that after all she had never cared no she never had cared for any moon so what was the use how it was seen. And then,

Then she remembered if you see a girl or a woman dwarf it is awful more awful than any cough it is just awful awful all awful and then she remembered just before she began to cry, not that she really would cry, she only cried when she sang, and climbing a mountain was too occupying ever to sing so then she remembered that it was true if you saw a female dwarf everything was through everything was over there was nothing to do. And then she remembered if she saw a boy or a man dwarf not a fairy nothing so foolish as that but a dwarf something little that should have been big and then if she saw it and it was not a female but a man then everything would be better and better and she would get the mountain the mountain would not get her.

And just then was it a pen was it a cage was it a hut but anyway there was no but, she saw it was a dwarf, and it was not a woman it was a man and if it knew how, and it did, away it ran, so Rose oh Rose was as happy then as any hen and she fell on her chair and embraced it there the blue chair.

And then she said perhaps it was not a dwarf perhaps it was a little boy and I could have it for a toy, she knew what a little boy was because she had her cousin whose name was Willie even if he was a little silly. That is the way Rose felt about it but not on the mountain up there, there she would not care if Willie was silly if he would only be there.

Night

Rose did not want Willie, it was at night and she was not really resting and yet why did she think Willie was singing about what a day it was when Rose was not there. As she thought of that she almost let go her chair and went and went down and not up there. And then of course Willie never came. Why not when Willie was his name. Why not.

And so Rose went on again.

And now it was really night and when she could see them the stars were bright, and she remembered then that they say when the stars are bright rain comes right away and she knew it the rain would not hurt the chair but she would not like it to be all shiny there. Oh dear oh dear where was that dwarf man, it is so easy to believe whatever they say when you are all alone and so far away.

Rose Saw It Close

What did Rose see close, that is what she never can tell and perhaps it is just as well, suppose she did tell oh dear oh dear what she saw when she fell. Poor dear Rose. She saw it close. Never again would she stay on that spot, the chair quick the chair anywhere but there.

Rose and the chair went on, it was dark at least it would have been if it had not been so bright, alright, alright it was alright of course it was alright it was just night, that is all it was just at night.

Night

What is it that water does do.

It falls it does too.

It rises up that is when it is dew but when it falls, it is a water-fall and Rose knew all about that too, Rose knew almost everything that water can do, there are an awful lot when you think what, dew lakes rivers oceans fogs clouds and water-falls too, the thing that Rose heard it was night and Rose heard what she heard, dear little bird dear little water and dear little third, not dew, not a few but a water otter, a brown water otter, a long water otter and Rose said not you no not you you cannot frighten me no not you.

So then Rose was frightened all through Rose and the chair which was blue and the otter the brown otter, Rose would have liked him better if he had been blue, and then the water-fall, the water-fall, the water-fall, the water was full of water-fall. Rose carrying the chair went to look behind there to see if there was room for the blue chair. There always is room behind a water-fall when it is tall, and this water-fall even in the night was quite tall.

So Rose went in there it was all dark darker than out there and then she put down the chair and then she saw she did not know but it was so, she did see it there behind the water-fall, although it was all dark there. It was written three times just how it looked as if it was done with a hair on a chair, and it said, oh dear yes it said, *Devil, Devil Devil,* it said Devil three times right there. There was no devil there of course there was no devil there there is no devil anywhere devil devil devil where. But just there where there might be a chair and written in large writing and clear in the black there it was written there.

Dear me, Rose came out with her blue chair she decided no she would not sit down there. She decided she did not like water to fall, water fall water fall, that is what cows call but there was no cow there there was only writing there. It was too bad that Rose could read writing otherwise she would not have known that it said devil three times there. There are people who cannot read writing, but Rose was not one of them. Oh no.

So Rose and the blue chair went away from there she never could go down not there not ever again there, she could never go anywhere where water is falling and water does fall even out of a faucet, poor Rose dear Rose sweet Rose only Rose, poor Rose alone with a blue chair there.

So she went on climbing higher and higher and higher and blinking, the stars were blinking and she had to think of something. If she did not she would think of seeing that, was the Devil round, was he around, around round, round around, oh dear no think of Pépé, do not think of cousin Willie, he could go around and around, Willie did, and do not think of the blue chair after all the seat of a chair, might it be round oh dear around and around, and Pépé Pépé the little dog who bit her, no he was not round, well his eyes were but not his teeth, they bit oh dear she just thought of that, they had told her that little dogs like Pépé when there are many they bite at the back of the legs of little donkeys and the donkeys fall and the little dogs eat them and do they when they eat a donkey get round like a ball, and there was the moon it was setting a little flat but it was a little round oh dear and it looked as if there was a little girl way up there in the moon with its hair flying and partly lying and she had no chair oh dear oh dear up there.

What a place a mountain could be it looked so steep and its sides so straight and the color so blue and now one two three all out but she and red white and blue all out but you and if there was a cock it was the time when it crew, but no there was no cock, there was no hen there was no glass pen, there was only Rose, Rose Rose, Rose and all of a sudden Rose knew that in Rose there was an o and an o is round, oh dear not a sound.

The Morning

Rose was a rose, she was not a dahlia, she was not a butter-cup (that is yellow), she was not a fuchsia or an oleander, well Rose wake Rose, Rose had not been asleep oh dear no, the dawn comes before the sun, and the dawn is the time to run, it is easy to run before the sun and Rose did. She was now not among the bushes which scratched but among trees which have nuts and she liked that, anybody would, and she did.

It was wonderful how many trees there are when they are all there and just then all the trees were all there, tree trunks are round that is if you go around but they are not round up into the air. Rose drew a deep breath of relief, and she lifted up her chair and she was almost glad she was there there where she was.

The Trees And The Rocks Under Them

The dawn is not rosy but it is quite cosy and in the woods it really is so, they did once say the woods the poor man's overcoat, and it is true there in the woods no rain comes through no sun comes through no snow comes through no dust comes through, there has to be a lot of anything before in a thick wood it does come through, and this was so and now Rose could know that this was so so early in the morning before there is a morning, and so Rose began to think of singing she thought how nice it would be to sing there in the woods where there were only trees and nothing, perhaps rocks and leaves and nuts and mushrooms but really not anything and perhaps she would like to begin singing, singing with her blue chair. And then she thought of course it always did happen as soon as she began to sing she began to cry and if she began to cry well no matter how much she would try when she began to sing she would begin to cry. And then there she was in the woods, they said the woods were a covering and she had her blue chair and she had to think of something but if she began to sing or if she began to say something. Well when you are all alone alone in the woods even if the woods are lovely and warm and there is a blue chair which can never be any harm, even so if you hear your own voice singing or even just talking well hearing anything even if it is all your own like your own voice is and you are all alone and you hear your own voice then it is frightening.

Rose Does Something

So Rose did not sing but she had to do something.

And what did she do well she began to smile she was climbing all the while climbing not like on a stair but climbing a little higher everywhere and then she saw a lovely tree and she thought yes it is round but all around I am going to cut *Rose is a Rose is a Rose* and so it is there and not anywhere can I hear anything which will give me a scare.

And then she thought she would cut it higher, she would stand on her blue chair and as high as she could reach she would cut it there.

So she took out her pen-knife, she did not have a glass pen she did not have a feather from a hen she did not have any ink she had nothing pink, she would just stand on her chair and around and around even if there was a very little sound she would carve on the tree *Rose is a Rose is a Rose is a Rose is a Rose* until it went all the way round. Suppose she said it would not go around but she knew it would go around. So she began.

She put the chair there she climbed on the chair it was her blue chair but it excited her so, not the chair but the pen-knife and putting her name there, that she several times almost fell off of the chair.

It is not easy to carve a name on a tree particularly oh yes particularly if the letters are round like R and O and S and E, it is not easy.

And Rose forgot the dawn forgot the rosy dawn forgot the sun forgot she was only one and all alone there she had to carve and carve with care the corners of the Os and Rs and Ss and Es in a *Rose is a Rose is a Rose is a Rose.*

Well first she did one and then the pen-knife seemed not to cut so well so she thought she would find a shell or a stone and if she rubbed her knife hard on it until it shone it would cut again just as it did before the knife began to groan. So she had to climb up and down on the chair and she had to find a stone and she had to go on and on, and at last well was it still dawn was there a sun well anyway at last it was more than begun it was almost done and she was cutting in the last *Rose* and just then well just then her eyes went on and they were round with wonder and alarm and her mouth was round and she had almost burst into a song because she saw on another tree over there that some one had been there and had carved a name and the name dear me the name was the same it was Rose and under Rose was Willie and under Willie was Billie.

It made Rose feel very funny it really did.

Rose And The Bell

She climbed on and on and she could not tell not very well whether it was night or day but she knew it was day and not night because it was really quite bright, it might though yes it might have been night. But was it.

Well anyway she was climbing away she and the chair and she almost thought that she was almost there and then was it that she fell but anyway she did hear a bell, it was a tinkle and she heard it clearly it might be that a stone had stumbled and hit the garden chair, it might be that the chair had hit something right there or it might be that it was a cat that had a bell or it might be that it was a cow that had a bell or a sheep or a bird or even a little dog that might be running there chasing a low flying crow, or it might be a telephone, not very likely but it might, or it might be a dinner bell, or it might not be a bell at all it might be just a call, or it might be a lizard or a frog or it might be dear me it might be a log, rolling over rocks and water, but no it was a bell how can you tell if a bell is a bell.

There are so many things that are just funny it might just be silver money, anyway Rose was there and she certainly did think she knew she had heard a bell. Did she hear a bell. And would she know it was a bell if it was a bell. Did it come nearer and did she go nearer and was it just perhaps lightning and thunder.

All around the sun was shining and the bell was ringing and the woods were thinning and the green was shining. Please Rose please she was remembering. That is the way it was. It made her feel a little lonesome, until then she had been busy climbing but now she was beginning beginning hearing everything and it was a little lonesome.

Rose was a little lonesome, she had her blue chair. She was a little lonesome.

Rose And The Bell

The bell was ringing but there was no singing and Rose went climbing up and on. And then gradually she came out of the trees and there she saw an enormous green meadow going up to a point and in the middle of the meadow green, it was green as grass, there was a little black dog way up all alone and shaking himself like a dog does. *Oh* said Rose and she almost sat down. It was the first word she had said of all the many that had come into her head since she first began to climb. And of course it was a round one. Oh is a round one. For the first time since she began to climb Rose did not know what to do next.

Once Upon A Time

Once upon a time way back, there were always meadows with grass on them on top of every mountain. A mountain looked as if it had rocks way up there but really way up there there was always grass and the grass always made it look elegant and it was nice.

Grass is always the most elegant more elegant than rocks and trees, trees are elegant and so are rocks but grass is more so.

And here way up there was grass and it was going on and on and it is so much harder to climb up and up and up on grass than on rocks and under trees.

And to carry a blue chair way up there on and on through the grass because grass is steep steeper than rocks are, it was a very difficult day that day and that was the way Rose went on her way.

She had to what else could she do she had to see it through getting up there to be all the way there and to sit on her chair.

And when you are walking on grass it is harder to see where there is. And anyway what did it say. The grass did not say anyway, it was green and nothing green ever has anything to say.

Rose knew that that is why she always did prefer blue.

The Green Grass Meadow

Rose was now going up and up the green grass meadow that went right on to the top. She did not say oh again she just went on. It was hot, and the green grass was hot and underneath the green grass there was ground and in that ground oh dear Rose almost stepped on it there was something round.

Rose had courage everywhere she just went on going up there.

The Last Hour

It is hard to go on when you are nearly there but not nearly enough to hurry up to get there. That is where Rose was and she well she hardly could go on to get there. And where was there. She almost said it she almost whispered it to herself and to the chair. Where oh where is there.

But she went on and the grass was shorter and the slant was steeper and the chair was bluer and heavier and the clouds were nearer and the top was further because she was so near she could not see which way it was and if she went one way and the top was the other way could it be that she would never see what she could see. Oh deary me oh deary me what did she see. She did see and her eyes were round with fright and her hands and arms did hold her chair tight and suddenly green became blue and she knew that one would become two and three would become four and never again no never again would there ever be a door for her to go through.

But Rose was not like that, stumbling would be the beginning of tumbling and she would not tumble up but tumble down if she began to stumble and so she began to frown and she knew she would have to begin to count, one two one two one two one two.

Close your eyes and count one two open your eyes and count one two and then green would not be blue. So Rose began counting *one two one two* and she knew that she was counting *one two one two* and so her eyes were blue although her name was Rose. Of course her eyes were blue even though her name was Rose. That is the reason she always did prefer blue because her eyes were blue. And she had two eyes and each one of her two eyes was blue, one two one two.

And sooner than it could be true there she saw something that was not green nor blue, it was violet and other colors it was high up as high as the sky it was where she could cry it was a rain-bow. Oh yes oh no it was a rain-bow.

And Rose just went right through, she went right through the rain-bow and she did know that was what she would do. She had it to do and she went right through the rain-bow and then there she was right on the top so that there was no other top there just the top with room for the blue chair and Rose put the blue chair there and she sat upon the chair. And Rose was there.

There

She was all alone on the top of everything and she was sitting there and she could sing.

This was the song she sang,
It began

Here I am.
When I wish a dish
I wish a dish of ham.
When I wish a little wish
I wish that I was where I am.

She stopped and sat awhile not that she ever got up, she was so pleased with sitting she just sat.

And then she sang

When I see I saw I can
I can see what I saw
I saw where I am sitting.
Yes I am sitting.

She sighed a little.

Yes I can see I am sitting.

She sighed again.

Yes I can.
Once when five apples were red,
They never were
It was my head.
No said she
No it was not my head
It was my bed.

So she began again.

Once when apples were red
When all is said when all is said
Are apples red
Or is it said
That I know which which I have.

She stopped to think
Rose stopped to think,

I think said Rose and she wriggled a little on her chair.

She was alone up there.
I think said Rose.
And then she began to sing

Am I asleep or am I awake
Have I butter or have I cake,
Am I here or am I there,
Is the chair a bed or is it a chair.
Who is where.

Once more Rose began to sing.

It was getting a little dark and once more Rose began to sing

I am Rose my eyes are blue
I am Rose and who are you
I am Rose and when I sing
I am Rose like anything.

I am Rose said Rose and she began to sing

I am Rose but I am not rosy
All alone and not very cosy
I am Rose and while I am Rose
Well well Rose is Rose.

It was a little darker.

Rose was a little tighter on her blue chair. She really was up there. She really was.

She began to sing

Once upon a time I knew
A chair was blue.
Once upon a time
I knew whose chair was blue.
My chair was blue
Nobody knew but I knew
I knew my chair was blue.

Rose went on singing it was getting darker. *Once upon a time there was a way to stay to stay away, I did not stay away I came away I came away away away*

And I am here
And here is there
Oh where oh where is there
Oh where.

And Rose began to cry *oh where where where is there. I am there oh yes I am there oh where oh where is there.*

It was darker and darker and the world was rounder and rounder and the chair the blue chair was harder and harder and Rose was more there than anywhere. Oh dear yes there.

And once more Rose began to sing

When I sing I am in a ring
And a ring is round
And there is no sound
And the way is white
And pepper is bright and Love
my dog Love
He is away alright

Oh dear wailed Rose *oh dear oh dear I never did know I would be here, and here I am all alone all night and I am in a most awful fright.*

Oh chair dear chair
Dear hard blue chair
Do hold me tight
I'll sit in you with all my might.

It was getting darker and darker and there was no moon, Rose never had cared about the moon but there were lots of stars and somebody had told her that stars were round, they were not stars, and so the stars were not any comfort to her and just then well just then what was it just then well it was just that it was just then.

Just then wailed Rose *I wish just then had been a hen.*

A Light

Well it was night and night well night can be all night that is just what a night can be it can be all night. And Rose knew that. Rose knew so much it made her clutch the blue chair closer as she sat on it there.

And then just then what was it, it was not lightning it was not a moon it was not a star not even a shooting star it was not an umbrella it was not eyes eyes in the dark oh dear no it was a light, a light and oh so bright. And there it was way off on another hill and it went round and round and it went all around Rose and it was a search light surely it was and it was on a further hill and surely Will her cousin Will surely he was on another hill and he made the light go round and round and made the ground green not black and made the sky white not black and Rose oh Rose just felt warm right through to her back.

And she began to sing

A little boy upon a hill
Oh Will oh Will.
A little boy upon a hill
He will oh will.
Oh Will oh Will.

And I am here and you are there, and I am here and here is there and you are there and there is here oh Will oh Will on any hill.

Oh Will oh Will oh Will
Oh Will oh Will.
Will you sang Rose *oh yes you will.*

And she sang *oh Will oh Will* and she cried and cried and cried and cried and the search light went round and round and round and round.

The End

Willie and Rose turned out not to be cousins, just how nobody knows, and so they married and had children and sang with them and sometimes singing made Rose cry and sometimes it made Willie get more and more excited and they lived happily ever after and the world just went on being round.

Poetry

In the following group of poems, the circle motif appears directly, as a governing image of the poem, or indirectly (as in Blake's "The Lamb"), in repetitive, circular movement.

THERE WAS A CHILD WENT FORTH

Walt Whitman

The circle motif can be seen both in the life cycle that is depicted in this poem and in the repetition of words, whose circling motion magically suggests the knitting together that takes place as the child takes in a multitude of impressions and makes them part of himself.

There was a child went forth every day,
And the first object he look'd upon, that object he became,
And that object became part of him for the day or a certain part of the day,
Or for many years or stretching cycles of years.

The early lilacs became part of this child,
And grass and white and red morning-glories, and white and red clover, and the song of the phoebe-bird,
And the Third-month lambs and the sow's pink-faint litter, and the mare's foal and the cow's calf,
And the noisy brood of the barnyard or by the mire of the pond-side,
And the fish suspending themselves so curiously below there, and the beautiful curious liquid,
And the water-plants with their graceful flat heads, all became part of him.

The field-sprouts of Fourth-month and Fifth-month became part of him,
Winter-grain sprouts and those of the light-yellow corn, and the esculent roots of the garden,
And the apple-trees cover'd with blossoms and the fruit afterward, and wood-berries, and the commonest weeds by the road,
And the old drunkard staggering home from the outhouse of the tavern whence he had lately risen,
And the schoolmistress that pass'd on her way to the school,
And the friendly boys that pass'd, and the quarrelsome boys,
And the tidy and fresh-cheek'd girls, and the barefoot negro boy and girl,
And all the changes of city and country wherever he went.

His own parents, he that had father'd him and she that had conceiv'd him in her womb and birth'd him,
They gave this child more of themselves than that,
They gave him afterward every day, they became part of him.

The mother at home quietly placing the dishes on the supper-table,
The mother with mild words, clean her cap and gown, a wholesome odor falling off her person and clothes as she walks by,
The father, strong, self-sufficient, manly, mean, anger'd, unjust,
The blow, the quick loud word, the tight bargain, the crafty lure,
The family usages, the language, the company, the furniture, the yearning and swelling heart,
Affection that will not be gainsay'd, the sense of what is real, the thought if after all it should prove unreal,
The doubts of day-time and the doubts

of night-time, the curious whether and how,
Whether that which appears so is so, or is it all flashes and specks?
Men and women crowding fast in the streets, if they are not flashes and specks what are they?
The streets themselves and the façades of houses, and goods in the windows,
Vehicles, teams, the heavy-plank'd wharves, the huge crossing at the ferries,
The village on the highland seen from afar at sunset, the river between,
Shadows, aureola and mist, the light falling on roofs and gables of white or brown two miles off,
The schooner near by sleepily dropping down the tide, the little boat slack-tow'd astern,
The hurrying tumbling waves, quick-broken crests, slapping,
The strata of color'd clouds, the long bar of maroon-tint away solitary by itself, the spread of purity it lies motionless in,
The horizon's edge, the flying sea-crow, the fragrance of salt marsh and shore mud,
These became part of that child who went forth every day, and who now goes, and will always go forth every day.

DREAM VARIATION

Langston Hughes

To fling my arms wide
In some place of the sun,
To whirl and to dance
Till the white day is done.
Then rest at cool evening
Beneath a tall tree
While night comes on gently,
Dark like me—
That is my dream!

To fling my arms wide
In the face of the sun,
Dance! Whirl! Whirl!
Till the quick day is done.
Rest at pale evening . . .
A tall, slim tree . . .
Night coming tenderly
Black like me.

A TRAGIC STORY

William Makepeace Thackeray

There lived a sage in days of yore,
And he a handsome pigtail wore;
But wondered much, and sorrowed more,
Because it hung behind him.

He mused upon this curious case,
And swore he'd change the pigtail's place,
And have it hanging at his face,
Not dangling there behind him.

Says he, "The mystery I've found—
I'll turn me round,"—he turned him round;
But still it hung behind him.

Then round and round, and out and in,
All day the puzzled sage did spin;
In vain—it mattered not a pin—
The pigtail hung behind him.

And right, and left, and round about,
And up, and down, and in, and out
He turned; but still the pigtail stout
Hung steadily behind him.

And though his efforts never slack,
And though he twist, and twirl, and tack,
Alas! still faithful to his back,
The pigtail hangs behind him.

ROUNDELAY FROM THE AUGUST ECLOGUE

(The Shepheardes Calendar)

Edmund Spenser

Spenser was a great admirer of the earlier poet Chaucer, and this "roundelay," or "roundel" (something forming a circle or a ring, such as a round dance or a song with a refrain) contains archaisms deliberately used to give the poem an antique feeling, much as we might use expressions from colonial times to give a piece of writing an old flavor.

The roundelay has a circular motion, as the name suggests. It is full of the joy of life in nature and is so musical that the words scarcely matter. Two shepherds, Willie and Perigot, are engaged in a musical duel, each chanting an alternate line. They do so well that their friend Cuddie declares that they are both winners: one gets a lamb for a prize and the other, a carved wooden cup, or "mazer."

Four hundred years ago, in simpler times, such competitive singing or chanting was thought to be fun. A group of people can still enjoy it. A leader with a strong voice and sense of rhythm acts as Perigot, and the poem is read as a responsive reading, with the group members forming a composite Willie. The responsive reading encourages playing with words that convey not so much the meaning as the rhythm of the language. The language says, "Isn't life fun?" (For the curious, some of the words are glossed at the foot of the page.)

PERIGOT. It fell upon a holy eve,
WILLIE. hey ho holiday,
PER. When holy fathers wont[1] to shrieve,[2]
WIL. now beginneth this roundelay.

PER. Sitting upon a hill so high
WIL. hey ho the high hill,
PER. The while my flock did feed thereby
WIL. the while the shepherd himself did spill.[3]

PER. I saw the bouncing Bellibone,[4]
WIL. hey ho Bonibell,[5]
PER. Tripping over the dale alone,
WIL. she can trip it very well.

PER. Well decked in a frock of gray,
WIL. hey ho gray is greete,[6]
PER. And in a kirtle[7] or green say,[8]
WIL. the green is for maidens meet.[9]

PER. A chaplet[10] on her head she wore,
WIL. hey ho chaplet,
PER. Of sweet violets therein was store,[11]
WIL. she sweeter than the violet.

PER. My sheep did leave their wonted food,
WIL. hey ho silly sheep,
PER. And gazed on her, as they were wood,[12]

1. *wont,* were accustomed 2. *shrieve,* to administer the sacrament of penance 3. *spill,* waste or squander time 4., 5. *Bellibone, Bonibell,* punning on the French words *bonne,* good, upright, and *belle,* beautiful—meaning a fair or bonny maid

6. *is greete,* stands for weeping and complaint 7. *kirtle,* a long gown or dress 8. *say,* a fine cloth, in the sixteenth century sometimes partly of silk 9. *meet,* proper 10. *chaplet,* a garland of flowers or leaves 11. *store,* plenty, abundance 12. *as they were wood,* as if

WIL. wood as he, that did them
keep.
PER. As the bonny lass passed by,
WIL. hey ho bonny lass,
PER. She roued[13] at me with
glancing eye,
WIL. as clear as the crystal
glass.
PER. Just as the sunny beam so
bright,
WIL. hey ho the sun beam,
PER. Glances from Phoebus'[14]
face forthright,
WIL. so love into thy heart did
stream.
PER. Or as the thunder cleaves
the clouds,
WIL. hey ho the thunder,
PER. Wherein the lightsome levin
shrouds.[15]
WIL. so cleaves thy soul
asunder.
PER. Or as Dame Cynthia's[16]
silver ray,
WIL. hey ho the moonlight,
PER. Upon the glittering wave
doth play—
WIL. such play is a piteous
plight.
PER. The glance into my heart
did glide,
WIL. hey ho the glider,
PER. Therein my soul was sharply
gryde,[17]
WIL. such wounds soon wexen[18]
wider.
PER. Hasting to wrench the arrow
out,
WIL. hey ho Perigot.
PER. I left the head in my
heart-root—
WIL. it was a desperate shot.
PER. There it rankleth more and
more,
WIL. hey ho the arrow,
PER. Nor can I find salve for my
sore—
WIL. love is a cureless sorrow.
PER. And though my bale[19] with
death I bought,
WIL. hey ho heavy cheer,
PER. Yet should this lass not from
my thought—
WIL. so you may buy gold too
dear.
PER. But whether in painful love
I pine,
WIL. hey ho pinching pain,
PER. Or thrive in wealth, she
shall be mine—
WIL. but if[20] thou can her
obtain.
PER. And if for graceless grief I
die,
WIL. hey ho graceless grief,
PER. Witness, she slew me with
her eye—
WIL. let thy folly be the proof.
PER. And you that saw it, simple
sheep,
WIL. hey ho the fair flock,
PER. For proof thereof, my death
shall weep,
WIL. and moan with many a
mock.
PER. So learned I love on a holy
eve,
WIL. hey ho holiday.
PER. That ever since my heart
did grieve—
now endeth our
roundelay.

Cuddie

Certainly such a roundel never heard I
none.
Little lacketh Perigot of the best.
And Willie is not greatly overgone,
So were his undersongs well addressed.

they were crazy 13. *roued,* shot with an arrow 14. *Phoebus',* the sun god, Apollo 15. *the lightsome levin shrouds,* the radiant lightning lies hid 16. *Dame Cynthia,* the moon 17. *gryde,* pierced 18. *wexen,* grow 19. *bale,* sorrow 20. *but if,* unless

Willie

Herdgroom,[21] I fear me, thou have a
 squint eye.[22]
Aread[23] uprightly, who has the victory?

Cuddie

Faith of my soul, I deem each have
 gained.
Therefore let the lamb be Willie's his
 own.
And for Perigot so well hath him
 pained,[24]
To him be the wroughten mazer[25]
 alone.

21. *Herdgroom*, herdsman 22. *squint eye*, partial judgment 23. *Aread*, advise me 24. *pained*, taken pains, exerted himself 25. *mazer*, a drinking cup made of hard maple

THE PLEASURES OF MERELY CIRCULATING
Wallace Stevens

The garden flew round with the angel,
The angel flew round with the clouds,
And the clouds flew round and the
 clouds flew round
And the clouds flew round with the
 clouds.

Is there any secret in skulls,
The cattle skulls in the woods?
Do the drummers in black hoods
Rumble anything out of their drums?

Mrs. Anderson's Swedish baby
Might well have been German or
 Spanish,
Yet that things go round and again go
 round
Has rather a classical sound.

THE LAMB
William Blake

In Songs of Innocence (1789), from which this poem was taken, Blake was deliberately using simple rhyming verse such as that in Isaac Watts's Divine Songs Attempted in Easy Language for the Use of Children (1715) and Mother Goose rhymes, as well as singing games and ballads, to say profound things about life. Note the simple circular motion of "The Lamb."

Little Lamb, who made thee?
 Dost thou know who made thee?
Gave thee life, & bid thee feed
By the stream & o'er the mead;
Gave thee clothing of delight,
Softest clothing, wooly, bright;
Gave thee such a tender voice,
Making all the vales rejoice?
 Little Lamb, who made thee?
 Dost thou know who made thee?

Little Lamb, I'll tell thee,
 Little Lamb, I'll tell thee:
He is called by thy name,
For he calls himself a Lamb.
He is meek, & he is mild;
He became a little child.
I a child, & thou a lamb,
We are called by his name.
 Little Lamb, God bless thee!
 Little Lamb, God bless thee!

THE SECRET SITS
Robert Frost

We dance round in a ring and suppose,
But the Secret sits in the middle and
 knows.

THE CAT AND THE MOON

William Butler Yeats

The cat went here and there
And the moon spun round like a top,
And the nearest kin of the moon,
The creeping cat, looked up.
Black Minnaloushe stared at the moon,
For, wander and wail as he would,
The pure cold light in the sky
Troubled his animal blood.
Minnaloushe runs in the grass
Lifting his delicate feet.
Do you dance, Minnaloushe, do you
dance?
When two close kindred meet,
What better than call a dance?
Maybe the moon may learn,
Tired of that courtly fashion,
A new dance turn.
Minnaloushe creeps through the grass
From moonlit place to place,
The sacred moon overhead
Has taken a new phase.
Does Minnaloushe know that his pupils
Will pass from change to change,
And that from round to crescent,
From crescent to round they range?
Minnaloushe creeps through the grass
Alone, important and wise,
And lifts to the changing moon
His changing eyes.

THE WORLD

Henry Vaughan

This powerful image of a ring of pure light—the circle as a symbol of spiritual perfection—appears in the opening lines of a four-stanza poem by the seventeenth-century metaphysical poet Henry Vaughan.

I saw Eternity the other night
Like a great *Ring* of pure and endless
light,
All calm, as it was bright,
And round beneath it, Time in hours,
days, years
Driv'n by the spheres
Like a vast shadow mov'd, In which the
world
And all her train were hurl'd.

WHERE THE HAYFIELDS WERE

Archibald MacLeish

Coming down the mountain in the
twilight—
April it was and quiet in the air—
I saw an old man and his little daughter
Burning the meadows where the
hayfields were.

Forksful of flame he scattered in the
meadows.
Sparkles of fire in the quiet air
Burned in their circles and the silver
flowers
Danced like candles where the hayfields
were,—

Danced as she did in enchanted circles,
Curtseyed and danced along the quiet
air:
Slightly she danced in the stillness, in
the twilight,
Dancing in the meadows where the
hayfields were.

THE CREATION
James Weldon Johnson

This poem presents the story of creation in the imaginative, powerful style of an old-time black preacher. It should be read aloud to create the effect intended by the poet. There are many circles in the poem—circle forms like balls and circle movements like rolling—all used to suggest the tremendously active principle that was released in the creation.

And God stepped out on space,
And he looked around and said:
I'm lonely—
I'll make me a world.

And as far as the eye of God could see
Darkness covered everything,
Blacker than a hundred midnights
Down in a cypress swamp.

Then God smiled,
And the light broke,
And the darkness rolled up on one side,
And the light stood shining on the other,
And God said: That's good!

Then God reached out and took the light in his hands,
And God rolled the light in his hands
Until he made the sun;
And he set that sun a-blazing in the heavens.
And the light that was left from making the sun
God gathered it up in a shining ball
And flung it against the darkness,
Spangling the night with the moon and stars.
Then down between
The darkness and the light
He hurled the world;
And God said: That's good!

Then God himself stepped down—
And the sun was on his right hand,
And the moon was on his left;
The stars were clustered about his head,
And the earth was under his feet.
And God walked, and where he trod
His footsteps hollowed the valleys out
And bulged the mountains up.

Then he stopped and saw
That the earth was hot and barren.
So God stepped over to the edge of the world
And he spat out the seven seas—
He batted his eyes, and the lightnings flashed—
He clapped his hands, and the thunders rolled—
And the waters above the earth came down,
The cooling waters came down.

Then the green grass sprouted,
And the little red flowers blossomed,
The pine tree pointed his finger to the sky,
And the oak spread out his arms,
The lakes cuddled down in the hollows of the ground,
And the rivers ran down to the sea;
And God smiled again,
And the rainbow appeared,
And curled itself around his shoulder.

Then God raised his arm and waved his hand,
Over the sea and over the land,
And he said: Bring forth! Bring forth!
And quicker than God could drop his hand,
Fishes and fowls
And beasts and birds
Swam the rivers and the seas,
Roamed the forests and the woods,
And split the air with their wings.
And God said: That's good!

Then God walked around,
And God looked around
On all that he had made.
He looked at his sun,
And he looked at his moon,
And he looked at his little stars;

He looked on his world
With all its living things,
And God said: I'm lonely still.

Then God sat down—
On the side of a hill where he could
think;
By a deep, wide river he sat down;
With his head in his hands,
God thought and thought,
Till he thought; I'll make me a man!

Up from the bed of the river
God scooped the clay;
And by the bank of the river
He kneeled him down;
And there the great God Almighty
Who lit the sun and fixed it in the sky,
Who flung the stars to the most far
corner of the night,
Who rounded the earth in the middle of
his hand;
This great God,
Like a mammy bending over her baby,
Kneeled down in the dust
Toiling over a lump of clay
Till he shaped it in his own image;

Then into it he blew the breath of life,
And man became a living soul.
Amen. Amen.

Countless poems in all cultures celebrate the circle of the seasons. Here is a brief sampling.

Issa (Japanese, 1762–1826)

Even as the snow fell
Through it there came whispering
A breath of spring!

WRITTEN IN MARCH

William Wordsworth

The Cock is crowing,
The stream is flowing,
The small birds twitter,
The lake doth glitter,
The green field sleeps in the sun;
The oldest and youngest
Are at work with the strongest;
The cattle are grazing,
Their heads never raising;
There are forty feeding like one!

Like an army defeated
The snow hath retreated,
And now doth fare ill
On the top of the bare hill;
The ploughboy is
whooping—anon—anon:
There's joy in the mountains;
There's life in the fountains;
Small clouds are sailing,
Blue sky prevailing;
The rain is over and gone!

James Russell Lowell

And what is so rare as a day in June?*
Then, if ever, come perfect days;
Then Heaven tries earth if it be in tune,
And over it softly her warm ear lays:
Whether we look, or whether we listen,
We hear life murmur, or see it glisten;
Every clod feels a stir of might,
An instinct within it that reaches and
towers,
And, groping blindly above it for light,
Climbs to a soul in grass and flowers;

* From Prelude to *The Vision of Sir Launfal.*

The flush of life may well be seen
  Thrilling back over hills and valleys;
The cowslip startles in meadows green,
  The buttercup catches the sun in its chalice,
And there's never a leaf nor a blade too mean
  To be some happy creature's palace;
The little bird sits at his door in the sun,
  Atilt like a blossom among the leaves,
And lets his illumined being o'errun
  With the deluge of summer it receives;
His mate feels the eggs beneath her wings,
And the heart in her dumb breast flutters and sings;
He sings to the wide world, and she to her nest,—
In the nice ear of Nature which song is the best?

Now is the high-tide of the year,
  And whatever of life hath ebbed away
Comes flooding back with a ripply cheer,
  Into every bare inlet and creek and bay;
Now the heart is so full that a drop overfills it,
We are happy now because God wills it;
No matter how barren the past may have been,
'Tis enough for us now that the leaves are green;
We sit in the warm shade and feel right well
How the sap creeps up and the blossoms swell;
We may shut our eyes, but we cannot help knowing
That skies are clear and grass is growing;
The breeze comes whispering in our ear,
That dandelions are blossoming near,
  That maize has sprouted, that streams are flowing,
That the river is bluer than the sky,
That the robin is plastering his house hard by;
And if the breeze kept the good news back,
For other couriers we should not lack;
  We could guess it all by yon heifer's lowing,—
And hark! how clear bold chanticleer,
Warmed with the new wine of the year,
  Tells all in his lusty crowing!

Rhyme

A ROUNDABOUT TURN

Robert H. Charles

As the Toad who wanted to see the World discovered, circles are fun. It is fun to whirl round and round on a merry-go-round ("roundabout" in England)—if you get off before you become dizzy.

A toad that lived on Albury Heath
Wanted to see the World.

"It isn't that I dislike the Heath,
"It's a perfectly charming Heath, of course—
"All this heather, and all this gorse,
"All this bracken to walk beneath,
"With its feathery fronds to the sky uncurled—
"It's as jolly a Heath as ever was found,
"But it's flat, and the World, they say, is round.
"Yes, fancy," he said, "it's round, they tell me.
"And wouldn't I like to go and see!
"But there—it's a long way down the road
"For a fellow that walks as slow as a Toad.
"If I had a horse, I'd go," said he,
"If only I had a horse!
"Who's got a horse," he cried, "to sell me?"

Well, nobody had, you see.

But horses came to the Heath one day,
Mettlesome steeds in brave array,
With prancing legs and staring eyes,
And crimson saddles that fall and rise
As round the galloping squadron flies,
And tents, and swings, and cokernut shies,
And a hoop-la stall with many a prize,
And races, and a band, and cheering.

"Hark!" said the Toad, "what's this I'm hearing?
"It must be the World arrived, by the sound;
"*Now* I'll see if it's really round!"

Off he crawled to the thick of things,
And the crowds made crawling rather tiring.
"Dear me," he said, "I wish I'd wings!
"If this is the World," said he, perspiring,
"It's inconveniently full of Feet."

When a sudden voice said, "Look—how sweet!
"Mummy, a toad! Let's give him a treat.
"It's not very safe for him on the ground,
"So I'll put him up——
——on the merry-go-round."

And before the Toad could answer the floor began to slide,
The horses started prancing, and the riders settled to ride,
And they all moved faster, and the band began to play,
And away round he went with them, away and away and away.
Hooray! . . .

So the Toad rode the Roundabout
Round and round and round;
No one minded him, he sat without a sound:
He rather liked the movement, he rather liked the tune,
He just rode the Roundabout
All the afternoon.

When the time to pay came
What did he do?
"Tuppence a ride! Tuppence a ride! How much for you?"
Some had ridden for one ride, some had ridden for two—
"Seventy-nine," the Toad cried;

Illustrated by L. Leslie Brooke.

The Boy said, "Coo!"
"But never you mind," the Toad replied
"Here's an I.O.U."

"And now," he said, "I'll go, thanks,
"I want to get home to tea.
"Another for nothing? *No,* thanks,
"*Not* any more for me."

Home, holding the grasses,
Crawling a crooked road,
Slowly there passes
A very unsteady
Toad.

"Well, and what have you found, dear?
"And what have you seen and heard?
"Is the World really round, dear?"
"Round?" he said. "My word!
"Round?" said he; "you should feel it spin!
"Roundest place I ever was in!—
"Round!" he chuckled; "it's that!
"But it's rather," he said with a knowing wink—
"It's rather a *giddy* place, I think.
"Give me a drop of the dew to drink,
"And give me the Heath;
it's flat!"

Essays

WEBS OF CONCERN: THE LITTLE PRINCE AND CHARLOTTE'S WEB

Laurence Gagnon

Laurence Gagnon, a former Woodrow Wilson Fellow, teaches in the Department of Philosophy and Religion, Colgate University.

I

Any literary work is susceptible to an indefinite variety of interpretations. In this respect works of literature are like formal systems. Our understanding of the sequences of words in a novel, poem, etc., or the sequences of symbols in a logico-mathematical system is not completely determined by those sequences of words or symbols, still less by any intentions of the author(s). We achieve an understanding of a literary work or a formal system when we associate with it some model of the way things are or, at least, of a way they could be. Sometimes in order to do this we may have to suspend (temporarily) some of our beliefs about what is the case. But such are the demands of imaginative interpretation.

One type of model which can be used with great success in interpreting works of children's literature and adult fantasy is a Heideggerian model. By associating parts of Martin Heidegger's philosophy with certain parts of these literary works, we can achieve a novel, if not profound, understanding of them. Two cases in point are *The Little Prince* by A. de Saint-Exupéry and *Charlotte's Web* by E. B. White.[1] It has even been reported that Heidegger himself once considered *The Little Prince* to be "one of the great existentialist books of this century."[2]

Stated as simply and untechnically as possible, the particular Heideggerian model appealed to here is one concerned with persons and their capabilities.[3] Now persons are capable of many things, of flying planes and watering flowers, of eating leftovers and killing insects. Yet these are rather superficial capabilities, not being characteristic of persons as such but rather only of persons as pilots or gardeners, omnivores or killers. Among the more fundamental capabilities are those of being

1. All references cited in the text will be to the following editions of these works: A. de Saint-Exupéry, *The Little Prince,* trans. by K. Woods (New York: Harcourt Brace Jovanovich, 1971); E. B. White, *Charlotte's Web* (New York: Harper & Row, 1952).

2. C. Cate, *Antoine de Saint-Exupéry* (New York: G. P. Putnam's Sons, 1970), p. 465.

3. Some of the passages in M. Heidegger's *Sein und Zeit,* which are relevant to the present model are: pp. 12, 42–43, 53–57, 121–130, 142–145, 175–176, 191–196, 231-236, 245–280, 296–310, 325–326, 386, 424–426. These are indicated in the margins of J. Macquarrie and E. Robinson's translation of the work (New York: Harper & Row, 1962). Of course, if other passages are emphasized or other works used, different Heideggerian models will result.

aware of oneself, of being concerned about things in the world, of dreading one's death, and ultimately of living authentically. Since each person as such is unique and irreplaceable, this ultimate capability is also the ultimate personal obligation: to live authentically. Under the present interpretation, *The Little Prince* and *Charlotte's Web* are about various personal struggles to live authentically. In each of these works there are characters who find themselves thrown into existence, as it were, amidst other beings with whom they end up being concerned, all the while being confronted with the difficult and inescapable task of truly becoming what they alone can be—even unto death. This is precisely the task of living authentically. The ever-present danger here is that of losing one's sense of personal identity by becoming part of the crowd or by becoming overly concerned with other beings.[4]

II

In *The Little Prince,* neither the stranded pilot nor the prince himself have succumbed to the temptation of becoming a people-self; i.e., a faceless, anonymous part of a crowd. Since he was six years old, the time at which he produced his famous drawings of a boa constrictor digesting an elephant, the stranded pilot has been of the opinion that grown-ups are not only concerned with inconsequential "matters of consequence," such as bridge and golf, politics and neckties, but also terribly dense when it comes to discussing such important matters as boa constrictors, primeval forests, and stars. "So," he says, "I have lived my life alone, without anyone that I could really talk to . . . " (p. 5).

The little prince has not been so lonely, having his flower to talk to. However, his opinion of grown-ups is much the same as that of the stranded pilot. They are not merely strange, nor even "very, very odd," but rather "altogether extraordinary" in their denseness and their concerns (pp. 47, 50, 52, 57). The king who has no subjects except a rat, the conceited man who has no admirers except himself, the tippler who drinks to forget that he is ashamed of drinking, the businessman who values his accounts but not what they are of, the geographer who knows nothing in particular about geography—none of these receives nor deserves the admiration of the little prince, for none are living authentically. Worse yet there is little hope that they will change, since they neither take care of things nor care for persons. What interest they take in the little visitor is selfish. Living on their respective planets, the little prince would at best be treated as an extension of themselves, not as a distinct individual worthy of their concern. It is not just physically that they lead isolated lives.

Only on asteroid 329 does the little prince find a man whom he could possibly befriend—the lamplighter—who at least takes care of his lamp. "But his planet is indeed too small. There is no room on it for two people . . . " (p. 61). On earth there is at least room. Here, of course, the little prince finds friendship. He tames the willing fox. He establishes ties with the not-so-willing, stranded pilot. He becomes forever responsible for them, and they in turn for him.

But there is always a danger here; one can lose oneself to the things one takes care of and the persons one cares for. One can become so concerned with other beings that one identifies with them rather than striving for the unique identity proper to oneself. As long as one does this, one cannot live authentically. Before he began his wanderings, the little prince was too concerned with his rose; in his conscientiousness he had become a slave to her and she in her vanity and pride encouraged his servitude. This was not good for either of them. At that time it was important to both that she be the only flower of her kind in the whole universe. Because

4. The details of the model are worked out in the subsequent interpretations of the two works. For a lucid exposition of the model, see J. Demske, *Being, Man, and Death* (Lexington: University of Kentucky, 1970).

of all this, his agony in the garden is inevitable, when he discovers that there are thousands upon thousands of roses like his own. Yet none are his rose. This the tamed fox enables him to see. What makes his rose precious is not its physical appearance but the time he has "wasted" on it. "It is only with the heart that one can see rightly; what is essential is invisible to the eye" (p. 87). This truth, which men have forgotten, sets the little prince free; while he still has ties with his rose, he is no longer tied down to her.

In this regard the stranded pilot has much to learn. Although his initial concerns are taking care of his damaged plane and caring for himself, he eventually manages to become deeply concerned for his little visitor. But in this new concern, he becomes overly attached to his new friend. He understands that the little prince must leave but he cannot accept it as the fox has done. He asks for comfort and implores his readers to send him word of the little man's return. Yet this is understandable, for the stranded pilot is neither as wise and patient as the fox nor as young and innocent as the little prince. He requires more time.

The wisdom of the fox is not the only wisdom which the little prince discovers on earth. He also learns that while taking care of one's possessions and caring for others are necessary for one to live authentically, they alone are not sufficient, even when done without attachment. One must also recognize that life, especially one's own life, necessarily involves death, not as a termination of these concerns but rather as a culmination of them. This is the wisdom of the snake who always speaks in riddles. With a certain resoluteness, the little prince advances toward his own death, even though he is somewhat afraid and anxious. As the stranded pilot discovers, it was not by chance that little man was "strolling along like that, all alone, a thousand miles from any inhabited region" (p. 98). Death is always a solitary experience.

But since the little prince is a star-child, innocent and true, there is a resurrection. His "was not such a heavy body" after all (p. 109). Yet even with the element of resurrection, the question of what comes after death ought not to arise. For dying is the ultimate individual act of which a person is capable. The stranded pilot cannot quite accept this. He still ponders the mystery of what happens afterward: "What is happening on his planet?"; "Has the sheep eaten the flower?" (pp. 109, 111).

These questions are not important in themselves, but only in so far as they symbolize the ties which have been established between the little prince and the stranded pilot. What is important is stated by the star-child:

> In one of the stars I shall be living. In one of them I shall be laughing. And so it will be as if all the stars were laughing, when you look at the sky at night . . . You—only you—will have stars that can laugh! . . . And when your sorrow is comforted (time soothes all sorrows) you will be content that you have known me. You will always be my friend. (p. 104)

And this would be true, even if there were no resurrection.

III

In *Charlotte's Web,* a rat, a pig, and a spider find themselves thrown into existence together, inescapably confronted with the task of truly becoming what they can be—even unto death. The rat, Templeton, commits himself to an inauthentic existence. In a miserly fashion he acquires things without thereafter tending to them. Merely storing rotten eggs like banking stars does not involve taking care of one's possessions. Not having developed even this capacity, he cannot develop his capacity of caring for others. He must be enticed to go to the fair and bribed to pick up the egg sac. He could not care less whether Wilbur, the pig, died of a broken heart or whether Charlotte, the spider, died of exhaustion and old age (pp. 168–169). Nor does he really confront the possibility of his own death. He lives for the present, especially when it is "full of life" in the form of feasting and carousing (pp. 147, 175). Of course, his death will come sometime. But he sees it as coming in the distant future, as the end of his life, rather than as a distinctive part of his life. "Who wants to live forever?" he sneers (p. 175).

Wilbur, on the other hand, is not committed to inauthentic existence, but he is tempted in a variety of ways to live inauthentically. As a young pig, he does not have an especially strong personality. His attitudes and opinions can easily be swayed by outside influences: a few words from the goose, a pail of slops, a rainy day, the bad news from the old sheep, the reassuring promise of Charlotte. As a result he is always in danger of becoming a people-self rather than a distinctive person. If Charlotte's web says that he is "some pig" and people believe it, Wilbur believes it. If it says that he is "terrific" and people believe it, he not only believes it but also really feels terrific. If it's "radiant," then radiant Wilbur is. (Only with the last, prophetic message is there a genuineness in Wilbur's attitude—he has finally become more of himself, a humble pig.)

Wilbur refuses to face the fact that he might be killed next Christmas-time and turned into smoked bacon and ham. " 'I don't *want* to die . . . ' " he moans, " ' . . . I want to stay alive, right here in my comfortable manure pile with all my friends' " (p. 51). He does not see his dying as an integral part of his life. He sees it as the end of it all.

Left to his own devices, the selfish and insecure Wilbur would remain a people-self. But "out of the darkness, came a small voice he had never heard before. . . . " 'Do you want a friend, Wilbur?' it said. 'I'll be a friend to you' " (p. 31). Charlotte tames him. From the ties thus established, Wilbur gradually grows to care for the large grey spider, who lives in the upper part of the barn doorway. Since he naturally tends toward being a people-self, his initial reaction is to identify himself with his new-found friend by imitating her. So he tries in vain to spin a web, ignoring Charlotte's profound observation, " ' . . . you and I lead different lives' " (p. 56). When Charlotte says she's glad she's a sedentary spider, Wilbur replies, " 'Well, I'm sort of sendentary myself, I guess' " (p. 61).

Gradually Wilbur realizes that he and Charlotte are different, even though friends. They are different not merely generically, as pig and spider, but also individually, as distinctive persons. But persons are beings-unto-death. So Wilbur and Charlotte must also differ in their dying.

It is only after the Fair has ended, the crowd dispersed, and Wilbur's hour of triumph over that he turns his attention away from himself toward his dying friend. " 'Why did you do all this for me? . . . I don't deserve it. I've never done anything for you' " (p. 169). With her characteristic wisdom, Charlotte replies, " 'You have been my friend . . . That in itself is a tremendous thing' " (p. 164).

Now more than ever, Wilbur wants to preserve the ties that have been established between him and the lovely grey spider. He throws "himself down in an agony of pain and sorrow," sobbing " . . . 'I can't *stand* it . . . I won't leave you here alone to die' " (p. 165). But Wilbur is being ridiculous. He can't stay with Charlotte. For if he stayed, he would not be true either to Charlotte or himself. His call of conscience is to return to the farm with Charlotte's egg sac. With amazing agility (for a pig) Wilbur accepts this call to authenticity. "All winter Wilbur watched over Charlotte's egg sac as though he were guarding his own children" (pp. 175–176).

In the spring the young spiders came. But there is sorrow in this resurrection. Being unique themselves, none can live the life Charlotte did. So Charlotte's children sail away. "This is our moment for setting forth" (p. 180). However, Wilbur is not left totally alone. Three of them stay. To them Wilbur pledges his friendship, "forever and ever" (p. 183). Yet "Wilbur never forgot Charlotte. Although he loved her children and grandchildren dearly, none of the new spiders ever quite took her place in his heart. She was in a class by herself" (p. 184). From the beginning

Charlotte had resolutely advanced toward her own solitary death, all the while taking care of her magnificent web and caring for her humble friend. She saves Wilbur from an undistinctive death and gives him both the situation and the time to heed his own call of concern.

> Nobody, of the hundreds of people that had visited the Fair, knew that a grey spider had played the most important part of all. No one was with her when she died. (p. 171)

IV

Thus a stranded pilot and a little prince, a young pig, and a grey spider struggled to live authentically, each necessarily in his own way and time. Because of them, laughing stars illuminate webs of concern in the dead of night.

GERTRUDE STEIN'S THE WORLD IS ROUND

J. D. O'Hara

J. D. O'Hara, who received his Ph.D. from Harvard University, has made a special study of modern and romantic literature. He has published in Book World, Saturday Review, New Yorker, *the* New York Times, *and elsewhere.*

Gertrude Stein (1874–1946) was well past her own youthful bloom when the bud of an earlier Rose story blossomed into *The World Is Round* (1939), dedicated to a little French girl named Rose. Like many children's stories, this one is a fake: pretending to be a mere tots' tale about childish dream adventures, told in a cheerful kind of baby talk, it is actually the Halloween skeleton of a series of often grim psychological experiences—a skeleton that occasionally fleshes itself out and clatters through a spooky *danse macabre.* The sugary surface is to fool the adults. The story inside is what the children want.

It begins quite cheerily with nine-year-old Rose wondering about her possibly detachable name and nature, but things darken quickly. Although Love is a big white dog, tame and loving, Pépé is a dog of another color; little black Pépé bites, and Rose has to keep him at bay with a lie: "Rose always said Pépé was her dog although he was not. . . . If he was her dog that was alright he did not have to say how do you do but Rose knew and Pépé knew oh yes they both knew." So things are not always what they seem, especially when they seem good. The water-lilies, for instance: "water-lilies are pretty to see but they are not pretty to feel not at all." Even Willie is questionable—will he rescue Rose?—and at the end he turns out not to be what we all thought he was.

Pépé the dog is bad enough—his fantasy reappearance on the mountaintop as a whole pack of little biting Pépés almost does Rose in—but Billie the terrifying lion is worse. (Why does silly Willie try to give him to Rose?) Only the magic word-game of neither/nor can make the lion neither here nor there. But when he disappears more remains, much more: spooky things in the night; the little birds who make the big bird fall; the waterfall, with *"Devil Devil Devil"* written behind it. ("There was no devil there of course," Rose lectures herself in a rationalist's panic, "there was no devil there there is no devil anywhere"; but she soon finds herself wondering "was the Devil round, was he around, around round, round around, oh dear. . . . ")

Water drags people down (like the boys in the round pond), just as the Devil does. Water also falls . . . and so does Rose, once. That moment when she becomes a fallen woman is so awful that she can never tell what she "saw close" then, never never. It was a fall so awful that the waterfall right afterward was traumatic: "she could never go anywhere where water is falling and water does fall even out of a faucet." Dangerous animals and falling and drowning and always some dreadful roundness surrounding her. A fine children's story this is turning out to be.

Yes. "Fair seed-time had my soul," William Wordsworth remembered, "and I grew up/Fostered alike by beauty and by fear"—especially fear. It is trouble that urges us onward and upward. Growing pains accompany the growth of the mind —look at the Alice books—and Gertrude Stein knew all too well that unusual people may have especially tough childhoods. That is why O Rose thou art sick, at least by conventional standards. She doesn't like her surroundings, infested as they are with dangers. Roundness gets her down; she refuses to fall for it. Better to follow your inclinations upward and risk a fall than stay grounded and a kid; better to grow up and go up.

Up, because "the mountains were so high they could stop anything." If anything can stop the world from being round it's a mountain pointing out of the ground, and if anything has a point and a view it has to be a mountain too. And a mountain is blue. Or so Rose thought—Rose who so liked blue, that color of space, hope, imagination, and dreams. But if distance lends blue enchantment to the view, facts discolor it: "it was not blue there, no dear no it was green there, grass and trees and rocks are green not blue there no blue was there but blue was her favorite color all through." But even though its beauty is only in the blue eye of the beholder, the mountain is valuable still. It has a point to it. "Going down might be anywhere, going up had to be there." Up is aimed, down around the base is just whirled. ("Whirled without aimed amen," says *Finnegans Wake,* giddily.) Mounting up is Rose's aim in life: "She had to what else could she do she had to see it through getting up there to be all the way there and to sit on her chair."

Her achievement evokes many another trial and quest. Rose is tested physically by the climb, psychologically by nightmarish threats, and morally by temptations to sit and quit. It is a learning experience too. She outgrows her tags of conventional wisdom—"if you put shoes on a table it makes awful trouble" and jingly stuff like that. She acquires sensibly phrased knowledge, such as that "it is hard to go on when you are nearly there but not nearly enough to hurry up to get there." And finally she overcomes her hallucinations at the summit; she gets beyond blue and green and through the rainbow, "and Rose put the blue chair there and she sat upon the chair. And Rose was there," where she learns painfully what success and achievement and superiority can teach her.

Before we turn to that, though, let's look closely at Rose and Willie. Willie is easily Willie ("My name is Willie I am not like Rose/I would be Willie whatever arose"), and when a lion enters his life he accepts it easily as another self with his own name. Why fuss about the arrival of wildness in the form of a lion? "Everybody had one so of course Willie would come to have one." But then Willie gets cold feet. He tries to foist Billie the lion off on Rose, and they both suppress Billie flat. This works for silly Willie, but Rose is left with problems that she can't exorcise, internal ones, herself. A rosy morning, for instance, is a sailor's warning; a rose that prefers blue may not be a real rose; and "all of a sudden Rose knew that in Rose there was an o and an o is round, oh dear not a sound." Willie shed Billie by the old kids' trick of calling him a twin, a trick that Gertrude Stein herself used more than once to detach scapegoats from herself and exile them into the wilderness. But Rose has to live with her double self. Though the world is round, the lions don't fall off. They'll always be around, and so will the dangers inside Rose. No wonder she's afraid to be alone and afraid of her own voice, even singing. She combines rosy danger and blue delight, and at her peak and the mountain's she is a very exciting mixture:

I am Rose my eyes are blue
I am Rose and who are you
I am Rose and when I sing
I am Rose like anything.

The "who are you" is rather nervous; night is coming and she is alone with the round stars. But help of sorts is at hand. Along comes not questionable Will-he but purposeful Will, and "Rose oh Rose just felt warm right through to her back . . . and she sang *oh Will oh Will* and she cried and cried and cried and cried and the search light went round and round and round and round." It is sadly ambivalent, this rescue by marriage at the age of nine, with all that crying and roundness. There may be a touch of autobiographical wish fulfillment when Rose and Will's relationship is made legitimate. ("Willie and Rose turned out not to be cousins, just how nobody knows.") What's more, "they lived happily ever after." But Rose still cried when she sang, and "the world just went on being round," and we . . . well, we are likely to remember best not the precociously maternal Mrs. Willie, but that image of Rose triumphantly enthroned on the hill, solidly planted up there on her chair—like Gertrude Stein herself in Picasso's portrait—back then when "she was all alone on the top of everything and she was sitting there and she could sing."

Now let's get around to the roundness. A zero is nothing with a hole in it. If you follow it around, like an inchworm on the rim of a glass, then ever and never become clear and depressing ideas. Never is oh no; with two circles put together, mathematicians multiply never into the ever of infinity (∞); another way of going on forever is to imagine a serpent with its tail in its mouth. Cube a circle and you have a ball—but a ball black as Pépé, with a ∞ on it and you behind it. Scared? When you're scared your eyes and mouth grow round and you say oh! Pomologists deny that there were apples in Eden, but *some* thing round was around—olives? oranges? Omens of eternal nothingness.

"Numbers are round" and words go round, especially when they rhyme, and soon the mind goes around too: "Dear me hair chair ran man, Rose is beginning to feel as funny as she can." The world is also round, as the skeptical farmer found when he climbed the hill to see—round as a pie plate—and the world is ominous. Going up the mountain, Rose finds that even sky-pointing trees hold circles: "tree trunks are round that is if you go around but they are not round up into the air." So Rose tries to neutralize the tree's roundness by carving it into "Rose is a Rose is a Rose"—circular reasoning, necessarily, but at least "as high as she could reach." It is a brave effort. Unfortunately, the world's writing says something different: *"Devil Devil Devil"* lurks behind the falling water, and on another tree

Rose
Willie
Billie

leads us down, not up, and links Rose to the animals and the round world below.

There are good roundnesses too, of course. The circle and the sphere are traditional images of perfection. But no perfections appear in Gertrude Stein's story, or in reality. The world is not round but flat on the ends, and its orbit is elliptical.

Despite all our bouncing baby boys, a well-rounded man remains hard to find. Even eggs are only egg-shaped. The perfect circle is only an ideal, a bullseye for mothers to aim at, like the round musical notes of perfect sound that our singers imitate in pear-shaped tones. Like Rose, we live somewhere between Alpha's mountain peak and the perfection (which may amount to nothing at all) of Omega.

Explorations

STORYTELLING AND ACTING OUT

1. *("Earth abideth . . . "/"To everything . . . ")* Perform these as choral readings, letting a child who can read do the alternate lines. You might play the song "Sunrise, Sunset" from the musical *Fiddler on the Roof* softly as a background.
2. *(St. George)* Act out this folk play with a group of children. It is still sometimes done traditionally in English villages. Read it several times, then do it in your own words. You can double up on the parts, if need be.
3. *(Cupid and Psyche/East of the Sun)* Read these two stories to some older children and ask them if they can see how the two are alike. In particular, ask them to compare Cupid (Love) and the White Bear, and Psyche (the Soul) and the poor man's daughter. Is Cupid enthralled by a bad mother image or is Psyche the only one with problems? Explain that the Greek story is an ancient ancestor of the later Scandinavian story.

   Perform "East of the Sun and West of the Moon" either in pantomime or as a puppet play, making sure you have a good narrator who can huff and puff well in the background as the four winds.
4. *(Blanket)* This story makes a good play. Try acting it out with a group of children using the present ending, then suggest that the children create a new ending for it and act out the new version. Ask them why they gave it the ending they did. Which ending did they prefer?
5. *(Esarhaddon)* After telling this story to some children, ask them to think of someone they have hurt. Have them try to imagine what it would feel like to be that person (or another person they know). You might then read them Eleanor Estes' *The Hundred Dresses* (1944), a short modern story about a little girl who was rejected because some other children judged her by outer appearances only.
6. *(Charlotte's Web)* Tell this selection to a group of children, encouraging them to interrupt and question. If you have a tape recorder, listen to how you sound. Listen also to the questions, comments, and reactions of the children. You will learn a lot about how they think and feel.
7. *(Waterless Mountain)* Read this selection out loud to some children, taking particular care with the poetic chants. This is a first-person story and difficult to read. Don't imitate the Spanish accent unless you can do it accurately and naturally.
8. *(World Is Round)* The headnote to this selection already instructs one on how to read it. In small doses it can be very funny. Before sharing it with children, read J. D. O'Hara's essay about it to deepen your understanding.

   After introducing Gertrude Stein's writing to some children, read them a chapter from a children's biography of her (e.g., Ellen Wilson's

They Named Me Gertrude Stein, for ages twelve and up—see "Selected Readings").

9. *(Creation)* Read this poem out loud as if you were an old-time preacher.
10. Now that you have had so much practice in storytelling from the first section on, you might arrange a storytelling session for children and grown-ups. Look over the stories in this book that you have read and told, decide which are your favorites, and practice and polish them. Always be aware of the audience to which the stories are directed. Some stories are more interesting, as you can see, to young children; others, to the middle group; and still others, to teenagers. Many would appeal to the sick or to the old, and you might plan to share them with such groups.
11. Make up a story that goes in a circle—in that it ends where it begins.
12. Our culture is a death-phobic one, and this psychological situation has created disturbance for children as well as adults. The symbol of the circle can be used to introduce the child to the idea of the naturalness and significance of death in a positive way. Weave in this idea when you are reading or telling some of the selections from this section to children, especially the excerpts from Ecclesiastes and the selections from *The Little Prince* and *Charlotte's Web.*

PARTICIPATING IN OTHER WAYS

1. To launch yourself in the "Circles" section, sing a round of "Row, row, row your boat" or "Three blind mice." You need only three people to do it.
2. *(Demeter)* Make up your own song to "Come, my daughter, for Zeus, far seeing. . . . " Or, if making up tunes isn't your forte, read the lines to the soft accompaniment of music.

   Have you ever tasted Greek food? Imbue yourself in the spirit of Demeter by making a casserole of moussaka, a delicious and inexpensive dish of ground meat, eggplant, cheese, eggs, nutmeg. Find the recipe in a Greek cookbook. A child could help to make it. To top it off, get some honey cakes or baklava at an international food counter. You can pretend you are Metaneira serving the goddess Demeter. Food is important imagery in children's stories, and children love to work side-by-side with adults. Since Demeter was the Greek goddess of agriculture, this is a good point at which to combine literature with lunch.
3. *(Round the Mulberry Bush/Ring-a-Ring o' Roses)* Sing and dance these two folk songs in circle dances of your own invention.

   These particular folk songs are also two of the best-known children's games, so they fit in "Toys and Games" as well as in "Circles." How many other circular folk games do you know? Are any of them contemporary versions of old games? If you are interested in the games and special lore of children, the books of Iona and Peter Opie are good ones to consult (see "Selected Readings").
4. *(Rapunzel)* In the early spring I always think of Rapunzel, a name derived from rampion. A variety of this plant grows in various parts of the United States, including the Washington, D.C., area, along the Potomac River, and in the Great Smokies of Tennessee. If you are in an area where rampion grows, pick some and put a little in an omelet or a stew.
5. *(Waterless Mountain)* Note how the themes of Masks and Circles interre-

late in this selection. You have probably already observed that major themes have this tendency. Get a record of an Indian dance and try performing it with some children (in masks, if you like), moving in slow circles around the room.

6. *(There Was a Child)* Notice that all the senses are to be found in this poem: hearing, seeing, smelling, tasting, and touching. Read the poem to some children and have them notice where the senses are mentioned in the imagery.
7. *(The World)* Draw a picture of Eternity as Henry Vaughan pictures it in his poem.
8. *(Where the Hayfields Were)* Make a crayon drawing or painting (tempera, watercolor) of the picture evoked by this poem—of the old man burning the grass and the little girl dancing.
9. *(Dream Variations)* With a soft, appropriate musical accompaniment, do a dance to this poem.
10. *(A Tragic Story)* This poem would fit as well in "Fools" as in "Circles." It is another example of how themes tend to interrelate. Draw a picture of the "sage"—who, like many sages, is a fool—and his pigtail.
11. *(A Roundabout Turn)* Read this rhyming story out loud with a calliope record or a music box softly playing to accompany it. After the reading, draw a picture of a merry-go-round with a Toad on it.
12. The circle is one of the most important organizing forms in folk dancing. Learn one or two circle dances, such as the well-known Israeli *hora.*

Selected Readings

READINGS FOR CHILDREN

Benary-Isbert, Margot. *The Ark.* Translated by Clara and Richard Winston. New York: Harcourt, 1953. Fiction

Blake, William. *Songs of Innocence.* Illustrated by Harold Jones. New York: Barnes & Noble, 1961. Poetry.

______. *Songs of Innocence.* Illustrated by Ellen Raskin. Garden City, N.Y.: Doubleday, 1966. Poetry.

Blyton, Enid. *Five on a Treasure Island.* Illustrated by Vera Neville. New York: Atheneum, 1942. Fiction (island story).

Bradbury, Bianca. *Two on an Island.* Illustrated by Robert MacLean. Boston: Houghton Mifflin, 1965. Fiction (island story).

Brewton, Sara and John E., eds. *Sing a Song of Seasons.* Illustrated by Vera Bock. New York: Macmillan, 1955. Poetry.

Brown, Margaret Wise. *The Dead Bird.* Illustrated by Remy Charlip. Reading, Mass.: W. R. Scott, 1958. Fiction (circles of life—picture book).

______. *The Runaway Bunny.* Illustrated by Clement Hurd. New York: Harper, 1942. Fantasy (picture book).

Buck, Pearl. *The Big Wave.* New York: John Day, 1947. Fiction (circles of life).

Burningham, John. *Seasons.* Indianapolis, Ind.: Bobbs-Merrill, 1970. Informational book (cycle of seasons—picture book).

Burton, Virginia. *The Little House.* Illustrated by the author. Boston: Houghton Mifflin, 1937. Fantasy (picture book).

Byars, Betsy. *The House of Wings.* Illustrated by Daniel Schwartz. New York: Viking, 1972. Fiction (circles of life—boy's relationship with grandfather).

Clark, Ann Nolan. *Circle of Seasons.* Illustrated by W. T. Mars. New York: Farrar, 1970. Informational book (description of the ceremonies and rituals that mark the Pueblo Indian year).

Cleaver, Vera and Bill. *Where the Lilies Bloom.* Illustrated by James Spanfeller. Philadelphia: Lippincott, 1969. Fiction (circles of life).

Clymer, Eleanor. *The Spider, the Cave and the Pottery Bowl.* Illustrated by Ingrid Fetz. New York: Atheneum, 1971. Fiction (circles of life—learning old traditions).

Cole, William, ed. *Poems for Seasons and Celebrations.* Illustrated by Johannes Troyer. Cleveland: World, 1961. Poetry.

Corcoran, Barbara. *Sam.* Illustrated by Barbara McGee. New York: Atheneum, 1967. Fiction (island story).

Defoe, Daniel. *Robinson Crusoe.* Illustrated by Roger Duvoisin. Cleveland: World, 1946. Fiction (island story).

______. *Robinson Crusoe.* Illustrated by N. C. Wyeth. New York: Scribner,

1957. Fiction (island story).

Farjeon, Eleanor. *Around the Seasons.* Illustrated by Jane Paton. New York: Walck, 1969. Poetry.

Fisher, Aileen. *Valley of the Smallest: The Life Story of a Shrew.* Illustrated by Jean Zallinger. New York: Thomas Crowell, 1966. Informational book (life cycle).

Gage, Wilson. *Big Blue Island.* Illustrated by Glen Rounds. Cleveland: World, 1964. Fiction.

George, Jean. *Spring Comes to the Ocean.* Illustrated by John Wilson. New York: Thomas Crowell, 1965. Informational book.

Holm, Anne. *North to Freedom.* Translated by L. W. Kingsland. New York: Harcourt, 1965. Historical fiction.

Hopkins, Lee Bennett, ed. *I Think I Saw a Snail: Young Poems for City Seasons.* Illustrated by Harold James. New York: Crown, 1969. Poetry.

Hurd, Edith Thatcher. *The Mother Owl.* Illustrated by Clement Hurd. Boston: Little, Brown, 1974. Informational book (life-cycle picture book). See also *The Mother Beaver,* 1971; *The Mother Deer,* 1972; *The Mother Whale,* 1973.

Jarrell, Randall. *The Animal Family.* Illustrated by Maurice Sendak. New York: Pantheon, 1965. Fantasy (island story).

Kantrowitz, Mildred. *Maxie.* Illustrated by Emily A. McCully. New York: Parents', 1970. Fiction (picture book).

Lamorisse, Albert. *The Red Balloon.* Garden City, N.Y.: Doubleday, 1956. Fantasy (picture book).

L'Engle, Madeleine. *Meet the Austins.* New York: Vanguard, 1960. Fiction (circles of life—coping with a death).

______. *A Wrinkle in Time.* New York: Farrar, 1962. Science fiction.

McDermott, Gerald. *Arrow to the Sun.* New York: Viking, 1974. Folktale (picture book).

MacDonald, George. *The Golden Key.* Illustrated by Maurice Sendak. Afterword by W. H. Auden. New York: Farrar, 1967. Fantasy.

McGraw, Eloise Jarvis. *Master Cornhill.* New York: Atheneum, 1973. Historical fiction.

McIlwraith, Maureen [Mollie Hunter]. *The Haunted Mountain: A Story of Suspense.* Illustrated by Laszlo Kubinyi. New York: Harper, 1972. Fantasy.

Malcolmson, Anne, ed. *William Blake: An Introduction.* With illustrations from Blake's paintings and engravings. London: Constable Young, 1967. Biography.

Mazer, Norma Fox. *A Figure of Speech.* New York: Delacorte, 1973. Fiction (circles of life—problem of aging).

Miles, Miska. *Annie and the Old One.* Illustrated by Peter Parnall. Boston: Little, Brown, 1971. Fiction (circles of life—Navajo grandmother dies).

Newsome, Arden J. *Egg Craft.* New York: Lothrop, 1973. Informational book.

O'Dell, Scott. *Island of the Blue Dolphins.* Boston: Houghton Mifflin, 1960. Historical fiction (island story).

Proudfit, Isabel. *The Treasure Hunter: The Story of Robert Louis Stevenson.* Illustrated by Hardie Gramatky. New York: Julian Messner, 1939. Biography.

Ransome, Arthur. *Swallows and Amazons.* London: Jonathan Cape, 1930. Fiction (island story).

Ravielli, Anthony. *The World Is Round.* Illustrated by the author. New York: Viking, 1963. Informational book.

Rhoads, Dorothy M. *The Corn Grows Ripe.* Illustrated by Jean Charlot. New York: Viking, 1956. Fiction (circles of life).

Selsam, Millicent E. *Birth of an Island.* Illustrated by Winifred Lubell. New York: Harper, 1959. Informational book.

Slobodkin, Florence. *Sarah Somebody.* Illustrated by Louis Slobodkin. New York: Vanguard, 1969. Fiction (circles of life—death of a grandmother).

Slote, Alfred. *Hang Tough, Paul Mather.* Philadelphia: Lippincott, 1973. Fiction (circles of life—a boy dying of leukemia).

Sonneborn, Ruth. *Friday Night Is Papa Night.* Illustrated by Emily McCully. New York: Viking, 1970. Fiction (picture book).

Stevenson, Robert Louis. *Treasure Island.* Illustrated by N. O. Wyeth. New York: Scribner, 1911; text originally published in 1883. Fiction.

Taylor, Theodore. *The Cay.* Garden City, N.Y.: Doubleday, 1969. Fiction (island story).

Thackeray, W. M. *The Rose and the Ring or The History of Prince Giglio and Prince Bulbo.* Harmondsworth, Middlesex, England: Penguin, 1964; first published in 1855. Pantomime.

Thurber, James. *Many Moons.* Illustrated by Louis Slobodkin. New York: Harcourt, 1943. Fantasy (picture book).

______. *The Wonderful O.* Illustrated by Marc Simont. New York: Simon & Schuster, 1957. Fantasy.

Tresselt, Alvin. *It's Time Now.* Illustrated by Roger Duvoisin. New York: Harper, 1969. Informational book (cycle of seasons in a city—picture book).

______. *Sun Up.* Illustrated by Roger Duvoisin. New York: Lothrop, 1949. Informational book (the cycle of a summer day—picture book).

Udry, Janice May. *The Moon Jumpers.* Illustrated by Maurice Sendak. New York: Harper, 1959. Fantasy (picture book).

Viorst, Judith. *The Tenth Good Things About Barney.* Illustrated by Erik Blegvad. New York: Atheneum, 1971. Fiction (circles of life—picture book).

Warburg, Sandol Stoddard. *The Growing Time.* Illustrated by Leonard Weisgard. New York: Harper, 1969. Fiction (circles of life—child's first experience with death).

Whitney, Thomas P., trans. *The Story of Prince Ivan, the Firebird and the Gray Wolf.* Illustrated by Nonny Hogrogian. New York: Scribner, 1968. Folktale.

Wilson, Ellen. *They Named Me Gertrude Stein.* New York: Farrar, 1973. Biography.

Wyss, Johann David. *The Swiss Family Robinson.* Illustrated by Jeanne Edwards. Cleveland: World, 1947. Fiction (island story).

______. *The Swiss Family Robinson.* Illustrated by Charles Folkard. New York: Dutton, 1951. Fiction (island story).

REFERENCES FOR ADULTS

Bachelard, Gaston. *The Poetics of Space.* Translated by Maria Jolas. New York: Orion Press, 1964.

Brunvand, Jan Harold. *The Study of American Folklore.* New York: Norton, 1968.

Cate, Curtis. *Antoine de Saint-Exupéry.* New York: Putnam's, 1970. Biography.

Campbell, Joseph. "The Universal Round." In *The Hero with a Thousand Faces.* New York: Pantheon, 1949. The Bollingen Series 17. Pp. 261–69.

Di Leo, Joseph H. *Young Children and Their Drawings.* New York: Brunner/Mazel, 1970.

Franz, Marie-Luise von. *An Introduction to the Interpretation of Fairy Tales.* Zurich, Switzerland: Spring Publications, 1970.

Fried, Frederick. *A Pictorial History of the Carousel.* New York: Bonanza, 1964.

Heuscher, Julius E. *A Psychiatric Study of Myths and Fairy Tales: Their Origin, Meaning and Usefulness.* An enlarged and thoroughly revised 2nd ed. of *A Psychiatric Study of Fairy Tales.* Springfield, Ill.: Thomas, 1974.

Hillman, James. "A Note on Story." *Children's Literature* 3 (1974): 9–11.

Jung, C. G. *Man and His Symbols.* Garden City, N.Y.: Doubleday, 1964. See discussion of circle symbol.

Kellogg, Rhoda. *Analyzing Children's Art.* Palo Alto, Calif.: Mayfield, 1969.

Munari, Bruno. *The Discovery of the Circle.* Translated by Marcello and Edna Maestro. New York: G. Wittenborn, 1965.

Opie, Iona and Peter. *Children's Games in Street and Playground.* New York: Oxford, 1969.

———. *The Lore and Language of Schoolchildren.* New York: Oxford, 1959.

Travers, Pamela L. *About the Sleeping Beauty.* Illustrated by Charles Keeping. New York: McGraw, 1975.

Wolff, Robert Lee. *The Golden Key: A Study of the Fiction of George MacDonald.* New Haven, Conn.: Yale University Press, 1961.

Afterword on Fantasy and the Child

That the world is full of fantasy and that fantasy is a favored domain of children are obvious things, but as everyone knows, the most obvious things—and their consequences—are often lost sight of. Fantasy is one step beyond imagination: something that happens to us when our imagination goes dramatic, when we make a static scene dynamic. An instrument of rare usefulness, its essential role in the lives of developing children is to help them toward adulthood by, paradoxically, uncovering the real and by accommodating the psyche to the real. Even more interesting is that fantasy very often discovers realities which no one had suspected before.

For the past few generations, adults have been brainwashed into thinking that children always want to be children and that their fantasies are identical with the bland imaginings of Walt Disney. They don't want to be children, and their fantasies are more valuable than we adults sometimes think. Often their fantasies put them in touch with adult roles and smooth out the perilous paths of maturation. Occasionally a child's or adolescent's fantasy breaks through to profound understanding.

The role of fantasy in the development of a child's understanding and mastery of his experiences and his human and physical environment has been studied by a number of psychologists, including L. Vygotsky, E. Klinger, and J. Singer.* Specifically, Klinger has suggested three possible functions: to permit exploration of goals or desired outcomes that the child cannot as yet achieve; to permit emotional integration of overwhelming events; and (in summary) to provide continuity between known and new experiences. Free exploration of experience (that is, without the irrevocable consequences of overt behavior) may provide genuinely new combinations and thus new meanings of events for the child.

The psychologists are in effect telling us what we have known all along. As soon as a little girl can walk, she steps into her mother's shoes and shuffles about until she breaks the arches. A little boy claps on his father's hat or trails his father's overcoat. If a child draws a picture or writes a story, it is frequently a picture or story about adults. Obviously, the happenings children put on—"doctor," "nurse" (whether male or female)—and the games they play are ways of fantasizing their future roles as adults and also ways of working out current problems.

As children grow older and their fantasy about reaching adulthood becomes a reality, they begin to realize other fantasies—still children's fantasies, for children and adults are not separate life forms, but people in different stages of development. Their fantasies then lead them in various directions to discovery of the meaning of their adult roles—sociological, ethical, artistic, scientific.

Copernicus as a youth studied astronomy at Jagellonian University, Cracow, Poland. Later, with virtually no instruments available except an astrolabe to assist him in his calculations about the heavenly bodies, he imagined that the sun, not the earth, was the center of the universe. Finally, in the center of the concentric circles where scholars had always put the earth, he drew a small circle and wrote "Sol" (sun). That fantasy of his (his findings were published in the mid-sixteenth century)—that small circle—changed all philosophy, psychology, astronomy, and brought us into the modern world. Of course, the fantasy was reality all along, but no one had noticed.

Fantasy likewise may lead a young person to discover profound philosophical truth and to embody that perception in art,

*Lev Semenovich Vygotsky, "Play and Its Role in the Mental Development of the Child," *Soviet Psychology* 5, no. 3 (1967): 6–18; Jerome L. Singer, *The Child's World of Make Believe: Experimental Studies of Imaginative Play,* with chapters by Ephraim Bibliow and others (New York: Academic Press, 1973); Eric Klinger, "Development of Imaginative Behavior: Implications of Play for a Theory of Fantasy," *Psychological Bulletin* 72, no. 4 (1969): 277–298.

As a boy in Frankfurt, Germany, Goethe saw a puppet show of Faust. Later he recorded that "the thoughts of this marionette play echoed and hummed about me in every key." Throughout his literary life, he devoted himself to his great work, *Faust,* only completing it in 1832, the year of his death. In it, he pondered how man could cope with the problem of evil within himself.

Evidence points to the childhood origins of John Ruskin's fantasies about social injustice, which led him to write several books on the subject, books which in turn stimulated the formation around the turn of the century of numerous communal societies named after him. As a rich and lonely little boy of eight, Ruskin read and copied Grimms' fairy tales. He was totally absorbed by these simple tales, some of which are allegories of the tribulations of peasants in confrontation with the rich and powerful. Later, when Ruskin was a young and famous art critic, he wrote *The King of the Golden River,* a fairy tale modeled on Grimm. In this tale, two brothers exploit those who work for them. Nature retaliates: there is a dreadful flood. All ends well for the workers and badly for the exploiters. Through his tale and his prose writings on social problems, Ruskin's fantasy became reality in the lives of many people, and still has immeasurable influence.

Fantasy in the lives of children of all ages has a circular movement. First, children rehearse in fantasy their approaching roles as adults, and when these roles are clearly becoming realities, they move on to develop early fantasies about more complex facts of adulthood—art, science, philosophy, and so on. Ultimately, as adults, they tend to try to recapture the simple fantasy world of childhood, as Carl Jung theorized. Recapturing the innocence and vulnerability of childhood supplies a resource enabling the adult to cope better by sorting out the real values of things.

Since fantasy is such a natural vehicle for children's growing awareness, it is no surprise that one of the most effective ways of communicating the deepest truths to children is through fantasy.

Alice in Wonderland is liberating to children and reassuring to adults because it helps us, through fantasy, to see the way the world really is—that it is not a logical, seriously important place but a place full of silly contradictions. Upside down, it makes just as much sense. We take comfort in the tales of Hans Christian Andersen, the ugly duckling in his childhood who spent his life reenacting the fantasy of turning into a swan.

When the child becomes an adult, recollection of his or her childhood fantasies can have great value. To arrive at a better understanding of the roots of human behavior, Carl Jung attempted to reestablish the vivid inner life he had experienced as a child. On the Zurich lake shore, he played childish games. He collected stones and built a miniature village, including a castle, cottages, and a church. The building game had the desired effect and released a stream of fantasies that helped him to open himself to the materials originating in the collective unconscious.

James Hillman, a depth psychologist in Zurich and one of the major followers of Jung, has observed that fantasy is the dominant force in life.* "Fantasy in our view is the attempt of the psyche itself to re-mythologize consciousness. . . . As Owen Barfield and Norman Brown have written: 'Literalism is the enemy.' I would add: 'Literalism is sickness. . . . '" Hillman goes on to say that "children need less convincing of the importance of story than do adults. To be adult has come to mean to be adulterated with rationalist explanations, and to shun such childishness as we find in fairy stories." Because of this difference in emphasis on the importance of the imagination, "adult and child have come to be set against each other: childhood tends to mean wonder, imagination, creative spontaneity, while adulthood, the loss of these perspectives." According to Hillman, the first task in "restorying" the adult is to restore the imagination to a primary place in consciousness.

W. H. Auden also understood adults' need to return to the primary world of fantasy. Shortly before his death, he said that "it is only in play acting that human beings can approximate the moral innocence of animals."

Given the importance of fantasy for human existence, one wonders about the motives of those parents determined to suppress the fantasy lives of their children. The modern attempt to suppress or control the fantasy lives of children began with the Puritans, who must bear the responsibility for the development of "children's literature" as a separate field, so much of which is propagandistic in nature. Originally evangelical, designed to save children, all of whom were believed to be "conceived in sin," the purpose became distorted as Puritans became less religious and more mercantile. A strong affinity existed between Calvinism and capitalism: the virtuous will profit. Puritans were often of the merchant class in seventeenth-century England. In that century, they began turning out their "Warnings to Apprentices," in which they used religion as a tool to force compliance with their strictures on labor. Drinking and smoking, malingering and loitering, were crimes against God because they lessened the time an apprentice could spend on the job and caused him to demand more money to support his habits.

From the young apprentices, the Puritans moved rapidly into the "Joyous Death" books, by which they controlled even smaller children. The instrument they employed was in effect fantasy-control. In deathbed "confessions," children acknowledged their deficiencies in their "duties" to employer or parent. These confessions proved so effective that they were even translated into

*James Hillman, "A Note on Story," *Children's Literature,* Journal of the Modern Language Association Seminar on Children's Literature and the Children's Literature Association, 3 (1974): 9–11.

Indian languages in America and used to control the Indians (along with firewater and gunpowder).

Out of these confessions grew the Sunday school movement, begun by Robert Raikes, a shipowner in Gloucester, England, to keep poverty-stricken children busy on Sundays so that they would not damage his ships. He even paid them a penny or so to go to Sunday school and get their weekly booster shot of guilt. (A biographer of Raikes expressed shock that the children had to be paid to go to the funeral of their "benefactor"!) With the enthusiastic support of businessmen in America, then sometimes termed the "guardians of moral prosperity," American ministers took up the movement. In the middle of the nineteenth century, a Presbyterian minister in Philadelphia attested to the success of the idea in cutting down on vandalism.

Through this brief backward look, we can see that the suppression of fantasy has deep historical roots. Bruno Bettelheim, in *The Uses of Enchantment*,* suggests a modern cause for the suppression of fantasy: the distress of adults at the discovery by psychoanalysis of the violence and destructiveness of the child's imagination and the accompanying belief that suppression of fantasy and fairy tales with violent themes would discourage these upsetting feelings in children. In fact, the opposite is true. The child who can project his violent feelings onto fairy-tale figures like the wicked stepmother or the ogre who devours children is much less likely to be overwhelmed by those feelings than the child who represses those feelings because he has no outlet for them.

Fantasy, then, would seem to be in part a vehicle for the working out of problems of varying degrees of seriousness. If the child can identify with the problem projected in a literary fantasy, it may help that child attain a psychic balance. Since, as J. R. R. Tolkien pointed out, fairy tales are like soup at the back of an old French stove—a broth enriched by centuries of tossing in new ingredients—they encompass all human situations. Thus, in reading them, children may derive comfort, may find a solution for an unexpressed conflict. The stories can operate like a shotgun remedy or one-drug *materia medica*—an aspirin for the psyche.

A psychologist who works with the mountaineers in Tennessee has noted that there is very little mental illness among those mountaineers, children and adults, who still spend most of Sunday together in church, re-creating scenes from the Bible. Here, for instance, a preacher who cannot read gets a volunteer from his audience to read about the Tower of Babel. Then he says, "We're a goin' to build a tower." And everyone runs forward—Brother Henry with an imaginary brick, his little Sally with some imaginary mortar, young Jessie spreading it smooth, while the

*Bruno Bettelheim, "Fear of Fantasy," *The Uses of Enchantment: The Meaning and Importance of Fairy Tales* (New York: Alfred A. Knopf, 1976), pp. 116–123.

imaginary tower grows so high that the preacher has to stand on a chair on his tiptoes to reach the top. And all the time he is saying, "My, don't them people in the valley wish they had a tower like our'n!" Then finally, with a great heave of a shape-note book (old hymn books with notes in the shape of squares, triangles, etc., each representing a particular pitch), Preacher knocks the tower down and commands the people to "think about what God is thinkin' about you and not what yer neighbors is thinkin'."

Here children and adults share a fantasy. If this were so more often, the child would no longer be surrounded by crucifixions. "Lo," says the Adult, "This is my Money and my Time which I have given to Thee. Play with those toys, watch those Saturday morning TV shows so I can get some sleep, and read those Sesame Street books, damn it!"

We should truly embrace children and not shut ourselves off from their fantasy world, not try to manipulate them by imposing our own unhealthy fantasies on them. In dress and in literature and in life experience, they should be allowed to come as close to realizing their fantasies—to dress and share life experience with adults—as common sense dictates.

Each of the four essays that follows suggests that fantasy has value for adults as well as children, and that rational adults can best experience its value when they get in touch with their "hidden child" within. Bettelheim writes: "If an adult was not exposed as a child to fairy tales, his dreams may be less rich in content and meaning and thus serve him less well in restoring the ability to master life." Chesterton tells us that fairy tales "make rivers run with wine only to make us remember, for one wild moment, that they run with water." Fadiman tries, as a grandfather, to dissolve a part of himself into his own childhood: "However evanescent the experience, it is necessary." And Tolkien observes that beyond the values they share with other literary forms, fairy stories offer adults fantasy, recovery, escape, and consolation—"all things of which children have, as a rule, less need than older people."

In order for adults to get in touch with the "hidden child," there must occur some sort of suspension of rational consciousness. This can happen either through active participation in story through acting the story out in some way (singing, dancing, mime) or through *passive receptiveness* to the story material (giving oneself over to its magic without the adult critical faculty taking over and creating the barrier of "but it's only a story"). Each essayist in turn notes the importance of this process—to obtain what Tolkien calls "an enchanted state" so that the adult can enter the Secondary World which the storymaker has created. By so doing, one is not mesmerizing oneself into a false world. Rather, one is entering what Chesterton calls "a reasonable" world. As

Bettelheim writes: "Chesterton is speaking of [fairy tales] as experiences, as mirrors of inner experience. . . . "

The real good of sharing a story comes about only when the adult experiences the story in this way—which is similar to that in which the child experiences it. If an adult tells a story to a child in a manner that is at all superior or patronizing, the child will sense it and the magic of sharing cannot take place. Of course, the problem is: how can adults suspend their "superior" rationality?

Much depends on the attitude of the adult. If adults are truly eager to communicate, they will naturally call forth the child from within. One must remember that the child can't become an adult for the sake of communication, but the adult who tries can become a child. True communication, in other words, takes place only between equals.

The literature must enter one's being if it is to refresh. To help this process to occur, the Explorations were added at the end of each section. Call it antirational if you wish, but my experience has been that such simple, expressive activities can add elements of beauty and joy to the rational approach to literature. In fact, if one thinks about it, all four of these thoughtful human beings whose essays follow actually are arguing *against* the rationalists who would forbid fantasy and folktale. Bettelheim and Chesterton are doing it by arguing *for* the psychological and ethical value of fairy tales. Fadiman describes the "hidden child" phenomenon very well; and Tolkien presents the case for adult and child relating to fairy tales on an equal, or peer, basis.

THE USES OF ENCHANTMENT

Bruno Bettelheim

Bruno Bettelheim, the eminent child psychologist, is most deeply interested in the therapeutic rather than the aesthetic aspects of fairy tales. The storyteller, he feels, should give the children plenty of time to reflect on the story and talk about it with adults. "Later conversation reveals that the story offers a great deal emotionally and intellectually, at least to some children." He adds that "like the patients

From Bruno Bettelheim, *The Uses of Enchantment: The Meaning and Importance of Fairy Tales* (New York: Alfred A. Knopf, 1976), pp. 53–66.

of Hindu medicine men who were asked to contemplate a fairy tale to find a way out of the inner darkness which beclouded their minds, the child, too, should be given the opportunity to slowly make a fairy tale his own by bringing his own associations to and into it." In the following selection, Bettelheim concentrates chiefly on what the fairy tales can do for young human beings.

Vicarious Satisfaction Versus Conscious Recognition

Like all great art, fairy tales both delight and instruct; their special genius is that they do so in terms which speak directly to children. At the age when these stories are most meaningful to the child, his major problem is to bring some order into the inner chaos of his mind so that he can understand himself better—a necessary preliminary for achieving some congruence between his perceptions and the external world.

"True" stories about the "real" world may provide some interesting and often useful information. But the way these stories unfold is as alien to the way the prepubertal child's mind functions as the supernatural events of the fairy tale are to the way the mature intellect comprehends the world.

Strictly realistic stories run counter to the child's inner experiences; he will listen to them and maybe get something out of them, but he cannot extract much personal meaning from them that transcends obvious content. These stories inform without enriching, as is unfortunately also true of much learning in school. Factual knowledge profits the total personality only when it is turned into "personal knowledge."[1] Outlawing realistic stories for children would be as foolish as banning fairy tales: there is an important place for each in the life of the child. But a fare of realistic stories only is barren. When realistic stories are combined with ample and psychologically correct exposure to fairy tales, then the child receives information which speaks to both parts of his budding personality—the rational and the emotional.

Fairy tales contain some dreamlike features, but these are akin to what happens in the dreams of adolescents or adults, not of children. Startling and incomprehensible as an adult's dreams may be, all their details make sense when analyzed and permit the dreamer to understand what preoccupies his unconscious mind. By analyzing his dreams, a person can gain a much better understanding of himself through comprehending aspects of his mental life which had escaped his notice, were distorted or denied—not recognized before. Considering the important role such unconscious desires, needs, pressures, and anxieties play in behavior, new insights into oneself from dreams permit a person to arrange his life much more successfully.

Children's dreams are very simple: wishes are fulfilled and anxieties are given tangible form. For example, in a child's dream an animal beats him up, or devours some person. A child's dreams contain unconscious content that remains practically unshaped by his ego; the higher mental functions hardly enter into his dream production. For this reason, children cannot and should not analyze their dreams. A child's ego is still weak and in the process of being built up. Particularly before school age, the child has to struggle con-

1. "The act of knowing includes an appraisal, a personal coefficient which shapes all factual knowledge," writes Michael Polanyi. If the greatest scientist has to rely to a considerable degree on "personal knowledge," it seems obvious that children cannot acquire knowledge truly meaningful to them unless they have first shaped it by introducing their personal coefficients.

tinually to prevent the pressures of his desires from overpowering his total personality—a battle against the powers of the unconscious which he loses more often than not.

This struggle, which is never entirely absent from our lives, remains a dubious battle well into adolescence, although as we grow older we also have to contend with the irrational tendencies of the superego. As we mature, all three institutions of the mind—id, ego, and superego—become ever more clearly articulated and separated from each other, each able to interact with the other two without the unconscious overpowering the conscious. The repertoire of the ego for dealing with id and superego becomes more varied, and the mentally healthy individual exercises, in the normal course of events, effective control over their interaction.

In a child, however, whenever his unconscious comes to the fore, it immediately overwhelms his total personality. Far from being strengthened by the experience of his ego recognizing the chaotic content of his unconscious, the child's ego is weakened by such direct contact, because it is overwhelmed. This is why a child has to externalize his inner processes if he is to gain any grasp—not to mention control—of them. The child must somehow distance himself from the content of his unconscious and see it as something external to him, to gain any sort of mastery over it.

In normal play, objects such as dolls and toy animals are used to embody various aspects of the child's personality which are too complex, unacceptable, and contradictory for him to handle. This permits the child's ego to gain some mastery over these elements, which he cannot do when asked or forced by circumstances to recognize these as projections of his own inner processes.

Some unconscious pressures in children can be worked out through play. But many do not lend themselves to it because they are too complex and contradictory, or too dangerous and socially disapproved. For example, the feelings of the Jinny while it was sealed into the jar are so ambivalent, violent, and potentially destructive that a child could not act these out on his own in play because he could not comprehend these feelings sufficiently to externalize them through play, and also because the consequences might be too dangerous. Here, knowing fairy tales is a great help to the child, as illustrated by the fact that many fairy stories are acted out by children, but only after the children have become familiar with the story, which they never could have invented on their own.

For example, most children are delighted to act out "Cinderella" in dramatic form, but only after the fairy tale has become part of their imaginary world, including especially its happy ending to the situation of intense sibling rivalry. It is impossible for a child to fantasize on his own that he will be rescued, that those who he is convinced despise him and have power over him will come to recognize his superiority. Many a girl is so convinced at moments that her bad (step)mother is the source of all her troubles that, on her own, she is not likely to imagine that it could all suddenly change. But when the idea is presented to her through "Cinderella," she can believe that at any moment a good (fairy) mother may come to the rescue, since the fairy tale tells her in a convincing fashion that this will be the case.

A child can give body to deep desires, such as the oedipal one of wanting to have a baby with mother or father, indirectly by taking care of a toy or real animal as if it were a baby. In doing so, the child is satisfying a deeply felt need by externalizing the wish. Helping the child to become aware of what the doll or animal represents to him, and what he is acting out in his play with it—as would happen in adult psychoanalysis of his dream material—throws the child into deep confusion beyond his years. The reason is that a child does not yet possess a secure sense of identity. Before a masculine or feminine identity is well established, it is easily shaken or destroyed by recognition of complicated, destructive, or oedipal wishes that are contrary to a firm identity.

Through play with a doll or animal, a child can vicariously satisfy a desire for giving birth to and caring for a baby, and a boy can do this as much as a girl. But, unlike a girl, a boy can derive psychological comfort from baby-doll playing only as long as he is not induced to recognize what unconscious desires he is satisfying.

It might be argued that it would be good for boys to recognize consciously this wish to bear children. I hold that a boy's being able to act on his unconscious desire by playing with dolls is good for him, and that it should be accepted positively. Such externalization of unconscious pressures can be valuable, but it becomes dangerous if recognition of the unconscious meaning of the behavior comes to consciousness before sufficient maturity has been achieved to sublimate desires which cannot be satisfied in reality.

Many girls of an older age group are deeply involved with horses; they play with toy horses and spin elaborate fantasies around them. When they get older and have the opportunity, their lives seem to rotate around real horses, which they take excellent care of and seem inseparable from. Psychoanalytic investigation has revealed that overinvolvement in and with horses can stand for many different emotional needs which the girl is trying to satisfy. For example, by controlling this powerful animal she can come to feel that she is controlling the male, or the sexually animalistic, within herself. Imagine what it would do to a girl's enjoyment of riding, to her self-respect, if she were made conscious of this desire which she is acting out in riding. She would be devastated—robbed of a harmless and enjoyable sublimation, and reduced in her own eyes to a bad person. At the same time, she would be hard-pressed to find an equally suitable outlet for such inner pressures, and therefore might not be able to master them.

As to fairy tales, one might say that the child who is not exposed to this literature is as badly off as the girl who is anxious to discharge her inner pressures through horseback riding or taking care of horses, but is deprived of her innocent enjoyment. A child who is made aware of what the figures in fairy tales stand for in his own psychology will be robbed of a much-needed outlet, and devastated by having to realize the desires, anxieties, and vengeful feelings that are ravaging him. Like the horse, fairy tales can and do serve children well, can even make an unbearable life seem worth living, as long as the child doesn't know what they mean to him psychologically.

While a fairy tale may contain many dreamlike features, its great advantage over a dream is that the fairy tale has a consistent structure with a definite beginning and a plot that moves toward a satisfying solution which is reached at the end. The fairy tale also has other important advantages when compared to private fantasies. For one, whatever the content of a fairy tale—which may run parallel to a child's private fantasies whether these are oedipal, vengefully sadistic, or belittling of a parent—it can be openly talked about, because the child does not need to keep secret his feelings about what goes on in the fairy tale, or feel guilty about enjoying such thoughts.

The fairy-tale hero has a body which can perform miraculous deeds. By identifying with him, any child can compensate in fantasy and through identification for all the inadequacies, real or imagined, of his own body. He can fantasize that he too, like the hero, can climb into the sky, defeat giants, change his appearance, become the most powerful or most beautiful person—in short, have his body be and do all the child could possibly wish for. After his most grandiose desires have thus been satisfied in fantasy, the child can be more at peace with his body as it is in reality. The fairy tale even projects this acceptance of reality for the child, because while extraordinary transfigurations in the hero's body occur as the story unfolds, he becomes a mere mortal again once the struggle is over. At the fairy story's end we hear no more about the hero's unearthly beauty or strength. This is quite unlike the mythical hero, who retains his superhuman characteristics forever. Once the fairy-tale hero has achieved his true identity at the story's ending (and with it inner security about himself, his body, his life, his position in society), he is happy the way he is, and no longer unusual in any respect.

For the fairy tale to have beneficial externalization effects, the child must remain unaware of the unconscious pressures he is responding to by making fairy-story solutions his own.

The fairy story begins where the child is at this time in his life and where, without the help of the story, he would remain stuck: feeling neglected, rejected, degraded. Then, using thought processes which are his own—contrary to adult rationality as these may be—the story opens glorious vistas which permit the child to overcome momentary feelings of utter hopelessness. In order to believe the story, and to make its optimistic outlook part of his world experience, the child needs to hear it many times. If in addition he acts it out, this makes it that much more "true" and "real."

The child *feels* which of the many fairy tales is true to his inner situation of the moment (which he is unable to deal with on his own), and he also feels where the story provides him with a handle for coming to grips with a difficult problem. But this is seldom an immediate recognition, achieved upon hearing a fairy tale for the first time. For that, some elements of the fairy story are too strange—as they must be in order to speak to deeply hidden emotions.

Only on repeated hearing of a fairy tale, and when given ample time and opportunity to linger over it, is a child able to profit fully from what the story has to offer him in regard to understanding himself and his experience of the world. Only then will the child's free associations to the story yield the tale's most personal meaning to him, and thus help him to cope with problems that oppress him. On the first hearing of a fairy tale, for example, a child cannot cast himself in the role of a figure of the other sex. It takes distance and personal elaboration over time before a girl can identify with Jack in "Jack and the Beanstalk" and a boy with Rapunzel.[2]

I have known parents whose child reacted to a fairy story by saying "I like it," and so they moved on to telling another one, thinking that an additional tale would increase the child's enjoyment. But the child's remark, as likely as not, expresses an as yet vague feeling that this story has something important to tell him—something that will get lost if the child is not given repetition of the story and time to grasp it. Redirecting the child's thoughts prematurely to a second story may kill the impact of the first, while doing so at a later time may increase it.

When fairy tales are being read to children in classes, or in libraries during story hour, the children seem fascinated. But often they are given no chance to contemplate the tales or otherwise react; either they are herded immediately to some other activity, or another story of a different kind is told to them, which dilutes or destroys the impression the fairy story had

2. Here once more fairy tales may be compared with dreams, though this can be done only with great caution and many qualifications, the dream being the most personal expression of the unconscious and the experiences of a particular person, while the fairy tale is the imaginary form that more or less universal human problems have attained as a story has been passed on over generations.

Hardly ever does a dream that goes beyond the most direct wish-fulfilling fantasies permit understanding of its meaning on first recall. Dreams which are the result of complex inner processes need repeated mulling over before comprehension of the dream's latent meaning is arrived at. Frequent and leisurely contemplation of all of the dream's features, rearranging these in a different order from that first recalled; changes in emphasis; and much else is required to find deep meaning in what at first appeared senseless, or quite simple. Only as one goes over the same material repeatedly do features which for some time seemed merely distracting, pointless, impossible, or otherwise nonsensical begin to offer up important clues for grasping what the dream was all about. More often than not, for a dream to yield its deeper meaning, other imaginative material has to be called on to enrich the understanding. Such was the recourse taken by Freud to fairy tales, to elucidate the dreams of the Wolf Man.

In psychoanalysis, free associations are one method to provide additional clues for what one or another detail may signify. In fairy tales, too, the child's associations are needed to have the story gain its full personal importance. Here other fairy tales the child has heard provide additional fantasy material, and can become more meaningful.

created. Talking with children after such an experience, it appears that the story might as well not have been told, for all the good it has done them. But when the storyteller gives the children ample time to reflect on the story, to immerse themselves in the atmosphere that hearing it creates in them, and when they are encouraged to talk about it, then later conversation reveals that the story offers a great deal emotionally and intellectually, at least to some of the children.

Like the patients of Hindu medicine men who were asked to contemplate a fairy tale to find a way out of the inner darkness which beclouded their minds, the child, too, should be given the opportunity to slowly make a fairy tale his own by bringing his own associations to and into it.

This, incidentally, is the reason why illustrated storybooks, so much preferred by both modern adults and children, do not serve the child's best needs. The illustrations are distracting rather than helpful. Studies of illustrated primers demonstrate that the pictures divert from the learning process rather than foster it, because the illustrations direct the child's imagination away from how he, on his own, would experience the story. The illustrated story is robbed of much content of personal meaning which it could bring to the child who applied only his own visual associations to the story, instead of those of the illustrator.[3]

Tolkien, too, thought that "however good in themselves, illustrations do little good to fairy stories. . . . If a story says, 'He climbed a hill and saw a river in the valley below,' the illustrator may catch, or nearly catch, his own vision of such a scene, but every hearer of the words will have his own picture, and it will be made out of all the hills and rivers and dales he has ever seen, but especially out of The Hill, The River, The Valley which were for him the first embodiment of the word."[4] This is why a fairy tale loses much of its personal meaning when its figures and events are given substance not by the child's imagination, but by that of an illustrator. The unique details derived from his own particular life, with which a hearer's mind depicts a story he is told or read, make the story much more of a personal experience. Adults and children alike often prefer the easy way of having somebody else do the hard task of imagining the scene of the story. But if we let an illustrator determine our imagination, it becomes less our own and the story loses much of its personal significance.

Asking children, for example, what a monster they have heard about in a story looks like, elicits the widest variations of embodiment: huge human-like figures, animal-like ones, others which combine certain human with some animal-like features, etc.—and each of these details has great meaning to the person who in his mind's eye created this particular pictorial realization. On the other hand, seeing the monster as painted by the artist in a particular way, conforming to his imagination, which is so much more complete as compared to our own vague and shifting image, robs us of this meaning. The idea of the monster may then leave us entirely cold, having nothing of importance to tell us, or may scare us without evoking any deeper meaning beyond anxiety.

The Importance of Externalization

Fantasy Figures and Events. A young child's mind contains a rapidly expanding collection of often ill-assorted and only partially integrated impressions: some correctly seen aspects of reality, but many

3. While I do not know of any studies showing how distracting the illustrations in fairy stories are, this is amply demonstrated for other reading matter. See, for example, S. J. Samuels, "Attention Process in Reading: The Effect of Pictures on the Acquisition of Reading Responses," *Journal of Educational Psychology* 58 (1967); and his review of many other studies of this problem: "Effects of Pictures on Learning to Read, Comprehension, and Attitude," *Review of Educational Research* 40 (1970).

4. J. R. R. Tolkien, *Tree and Leaf* (Boston: Houghton Mifflin, 1965).

more elements completely dominated by fantasy. Fantasy fills the huge gaps in a child's understanding which are due to the immaturity of his thinking and his lack of pertinent information. Other distortions are the consequence of inner pressures which lead to misinterpretations of the child's perceptions.

The normal child begins his fantasizing with some more or less correctly observed segment of reality, which may evoke such strong needs or anxieties in him that he gets carried away by them. Things often become so muddled in his mind that he is not able to sort them out at all. But some orderliness is necessary for the child to return to reality not weakened or defeated, but strengthened by this excursion into his fantasies.

Fairy tales, proceeding as the child's mind does, help the child by showing how a higher clarity can and does emerge from all this fantasy. These tales, like the child in his own imagining, usually start out in a quite realistic way: a mother telling her daughter to go all by herself to visit grandmother ("Little Red Riding Hood"); the troubles a poor couple are having feeding their children ("Hansel and Gretel"); a fisherman not catching any fish in his net ("The Fisherman and the Jinny"). That is, the story begins with a real but somewhat problematic situation.

A child presented with perplexing everyday problems and events is stimulated by his schooling to understand the how and why of such situations, and to seek solutions. But since his rationality has as yet poor control over his unconscious, the child's imagination runs away with him under the pressure of his emotions and unsolved conflicts. A child's barely emerging ability to reason is soon overwhelmed by anxieties, hopes, fears, desires, loves, and hates—which become woven into whatever the child began thinking about.

The fairy story, although it may begin with the child's psychological state of mind—such as feelings of rejection when compared to siblings, like Cinderella's—never starts with his physical reality. No child has to sit among the ashes, like Cinderella, or is deliberately deserted in a dense wood, like Hansel and Gretel, because a physical similarity would be too scary to the child, and "hit too close to home for comfort" when giving comfort is one of the purposes of fairy tales.

The child who is familiar with fairy tales understands that these speak to him in the language of symbols and not that of everyday reality. The fairy tale conveys from its inception, throughout its plot, and by its ending that what we are told about are not tangible facts or real persons and places. As for the child himself, real events become important through the symbolic meaning he attaches to them, or which he finds in them.

"Once upon a time," "In a certain country," "A thousand years ago, or longer," "At a time when animals still talked," "Once in an old castle in the midst of a large and dense forest"—such beginnings suggest that what follows does not pertain to the here and now that we know. This deliberate vagueness in the beginnings of fairy tales symbolizes that we are leaving the concrete world of ordinary reality. The old castles, dark caves, locked rooms one is forbidden to enter, impenetrable woods all suggest that something normally hidden will be revealed, while the "long ago" implies that we are going to learn about the most archaic events.

The Brothers Grimm could not have begun their collection of fairy tales with a more telling sentence than the one which introduces their first story, "The Frog King." It starts, "In olden times when wishing still helped, there lived a king whose daughters were all beautiful, but the youngest was so beautiful that the sun itself, which has seen so much, was astonished whenever it shone in her face." This beginning locates the story in a unique fairy-tale time: the archaic period when we all believed that our wishes could, if not move mountains, change our fate; and when in our animistic view of the world, the sun took notice of us and reacted to events. The unearthly beauty of the child, the effectiveness of wishing, and the sun's astonishment signify the absolute uniqueness of this event. Those are the coordinates which place the story not in time or place of external reality, but in a state of mind—that of the young in spirit. Being placed there, the fairy tale can cultivate this spirit better than any other form of literature.

Soon events occur which show that normal logic and causation are suspended, as is true for our unconscious processes, where the most ancient and most unique and startling events occur. The content of the unconscious is both most hidden and most familiar, darkest and most compelling; and it creates the fiercest anxiety as well as the greatest hope. It is not bound by a specific time or location or a logical sequence of events, as defined by our rationality. Without our awareness, the unconscious takes us back to the oldest times of our lives. The strange, most ancient, most distant, and at the same time most familiar locations which a fairy tale speaks about suggest a voyage into the interior of our mind, into the realms of unawareness and the unconscious.

The fairy tale, from its mundane and simple beginning, launches into fantastic events. But however big the detours—unlike the child's untutored mind, or a dream—the process of the story does not get lost. Having taken the child on a trip into a wondrous world, at its end the tale returns the child to reality, in a most reassuring manner. This teaches the child what he needs most to know at this stage of his development: that permitting one's fantasy to take hold of oneself for a while is not detrimental, provided one does not remain permanently caught up in it. At the story's end the hero returns to reality—a happy reality, but one devoid of magic.

As we awake refreshed from our dreams, better able to meet the tasks of reality, so the fairy story ends with the hero returning, or being returned, to the real world, much better able to master life. Recent dream research has shown that a person deprived of dreaming, even though not deprived of sleep, is nevertheless impaired in his ability to manage reality; he becomes emotionally disturbed because of being unable to work out in dreams the unconscious problems that beset him.[5] Maybe someday we will be able to demonstrate the same fact experimentally for fairy tales: that children are much worse off when deprived of what these stories can offer, because the stories help the child work through unconscious pressures in fantasy.

If the dreams of children were as complex as those of normal, intelligent adults, where the latent content is much elaborated, then the child's need for fairy tales would not be so great. On the other hand, if an adult was not exposed as a child to fairy tales, his dreams may be less rich in content and meaning and thus serve him less well in restoring the ability to master life.

The child, so much more insecure than an adult, needs assurance that his need to engage in fantasy, or his inability to stop doing so, is not a deficiency. By telling fairy tales to his child, a parent gives the child an important demonstration that he or she considers the child's inner experiences as embodied in fairy tales worthwhile, legitimate, in some fashion even "real." This gives the child the feeling that since his inner experiences have been accepted by the parent as real and important, he—by implication—is real and important. Such a child will feel later in life like Chesterton, who wrote: "My first and last philosophy, that which I believe in with unbroken certainty, I learnt in the nursery. . . . The things I believed most in then, the things I believe most now, are the things called fairy tales." The philosophy which Chesterton and any child can derive from fairy tales is "that life is not only a pleasure but a kind of eccentric privilege." It is a view of life

5. There is considerable literature on the consequences of dream deprivation—for example, Charles Fisher, "Psychoanalytic Implications of Recent Research on Sleep and Dreaming," *Journal of the American Psychoanalytic Association* 13 (1965); and Louis J. West, Herbert H. Janszen, Boyd K. Lester, and Floyd S. Cornelison, Jr., "The Psychosis of Sleep Deprivation," *Annals of the New York Academy of Science* 96 (1962).

very different from that which "true-to-reality" stories convey, but one more apt to sustain one undaunted when meeting the hardships of life.

In the chapter of Chesterton's *Orthodoxy* from which these quotations come, titled "The Ethics of Elfland," he stresses the morality inherent in fairy tales: "There is the chivalrous lesson of 'Jack the Giant Killer,' that giants should be killed because they are gigantic. It is a manly mutiny against pride as such. . . . There is the lesson of 'Cinderella,' which is the same as that of the Magnificat—*exaltavit humiles* (He lifted up the humble). There is the great lesson of 'Beauty and the Beast,' that a thing must be loved *before* it is loveable. . . . I am concerned with a certain way of looking at life, which was created in me by fairy tales." When he says that fairy tales are "entirely reasonable things," Chesterton is speaking of them as experiences, as mirrors of inner experience, not of reality; and it is as such that the child understands them.[6]

After the age of approximately five—the age when fairy tales become truly meaningful—no normal child takes these stories as true to external reality. The little girl wishes to imagine she is a princess living in a castle and spins elaborate fantasies that she is, but when her mother calls her to dinner, she knows she is not. And while a grove in a park may be experienced at times as a deep, dark forest full of hidden secrets, the child knows what it really is, just as a little girl knows her doll is not really her baby, much as she calls it that and treats it as such.

Stories which stay closer to reality by starting in a child's living room or backyard, instead of in a poor woodcutter's hut hard by a great forest; and which have people in them very much like the child's parents, not starving woodcutters or kings and queens; but which mix these realistic elements with wish-fulfilling and fantastic devices, are apt to confuse the child as to what is real and what is not. Such stories, failing to be in accord with the child's inner reality, faithful though they may be to external reality, widen the gap between the child's inner and outer experience. They also separate him from his parents, because the child comes to feel that he and they live in different spiritual worlds; as closely as they may dwell in "real" space, emotionally they seem to live temporarily on different continents. It makes for a discontinuity between the generations, painful for both parent and child.

If a child is told only stories "true to reality" (which means false to important parts of his inner reality), then he may conclude that much of his inner reality is unacceptable to his parents. Many a child thus estranges himself from his inner life, and this depletes him. As a consequence he may later, as an adolescent no longer under the emotional sway of his parents, come to hate the rational world and escape entirely into a fantasy world, as if to make up for what was lost in childhood. At an older age, on occasion this could imply a severe break with reality, with all the dangerous consequences for the individual and society. Or, less seriously, the person may continue this encapsulation of his inner self all through his life and never feel fully satisfied in the world because, alienated from the unconscious processes, he cannot use them to enrich his life in reality. Life is then neither "a pleasure" nor "a kind of eccentric privilege." With such separation, whatever happens in reality fails to offer appropriate satisfaction of unconscious needs. The result is that the person always feels life to be incomplete.

When a child is not overwhelmed by his internal mental processes and he is well taken care of in all important respects, then he is able to manage life in his age-appropriate manner. During such times he can solve the problems that arise. But watching young children on a playground, for example, shows how limited these periods are.

Once the child's inner pressures take over—which happens frequently—the only way he can hope to get some hold

6. G. K. Chesterton, *Orthodoxy* (London: John Lane, 1909).

over these is to externalize them. But the problem is how to do so without letting the externalizations get the better of him. Sorting out the various facets of his outer experience is a very hard job for a child; and unless he gets help, it becomes impossible, once the outer experiences get muddled up with his inner experiences. On his own, the child is not yet able to order and make sense of his internal processes. Fairy tales offer figures onto which the child can externalize what goes on in his mind, in controllable ways. Fairy tales show the child how he can embody his destructive wishes in one figure, gain desired satisfactions from another, identify with a third, have ideal attachments with a fourth, and so on, as his needs of the moment require.

When all the child's wishful thinking gets embodied in a good fairy; all his destructive wishes in an evil witch; all his fears in a voracious wolf; all the demands of his conscience in a wise man encountered on an adventure; all his jealous anger in some animal that pecks out the eyes of his archrivals—then the child can finally begin to sort out his contradictory tendencies. Once this starts, the child will be less and less engulfed by unmanageable chaos.

THE ETHICS OF ELFLAND

G. K. Chesterton

It is not surprising to learn that the mathematician Alfred North Whitehead chose this essay on fantasy to include in a collection of important essays on science, for on a philosophical level, it is both logical and scientific. Says Chesterton, "We cannot say why an egg can turn into a chicken any more than we can say why a bear could turn into a fairy prince. As ideas, the egg and the chicken are further off from each other than the bear and the prince; for no egg in itself suggests a chicken, whereas some princes do suggest bears. . . . It is no argument for unalterable law (as Huxley fancied) that we count on the ordinary course of things. We do not count on it; we bet on it."

Though G. K. Chesterton, English journalist and critic, wrote at the turn of the century or long before Einstein, he already intuits the concept of relativity. He also foresees the paradox of the exploration of outer space at a

From G. K. Chesterton, "The Ethics of Elfland," in *Orthodoxy* (New York: Dodd, Mead, 1957; first published in 1909), pp. 87–100.

time when man is in the Dark Ages in his understanding of himself. "One may understand the cosmos," writes Chesterton, "but never the ego; the self is more distant than any star."

My first and last philosophy, that which I believe in with unbroken certainty, I learnt in the nursery. I generally learnt it from a nurse; that is, from the solemn and star-appointed priestess at once of democracy and tradition. The things I believed most then, the things I believe most now, are the things called fairy tales. They seem to me to be the entirely reasonable things. They are not fantasies: compared with them other things are fantastic. Compared with them religion and rationalism are both abnormal, though religion is abnormally right and rationalism abnormally wrong. Fairyland is nothing but the sunny country of common sense. It is not earth that judges heaven, but heaven that judges earth; so for me at least it was not earth that criticised elfland, but elfland that criticised the earth. I knew the magic beanstalk before I had tasted beans; I was sure of the Man in the Moon before I was certain of the moon. This was at one with all popular tradition. Modern minor poets are naturalists, and talk about the bush or the brook; but the singers of the old epics and fables were supernaturalists, and talked about the gods of brook and bush. That is what the moderns mean when they say that the ancients did not "appreciate Nature," because they said that Nature was divine. Old nurses do not tell children about the grass, but about the fairies that dance on the grass; and the old Greeks could not see the trees for the dryads.

But I deal here with what ethic and philosophy come from being fed on fairy tales. If I were describing them in detail I could note many noble and healthy principles that arise from them. There is the chivalrous lesson of "Jack the Giant Killer"; that giants should be killed because they are gigantic. It is a manly mutiny against pride as such. For the rebel is older than all the kingdoms, and the Jacobin has more tradition than the Jacobite. There is the lesson of "Cinderella," which is the same as that of the Magnificat — *exaltavit humiles*. There is the great lesson of "Beauty and the Beast"; that a thing must be loved *before* it is loveable. There is the terrible allegory of the "Sleeping Beauty," which tells how the human creature was blessed with all birthday gifts, yet cursed with death; and how death also may perhaps be softened to a sleep. But I am not concerned with any of the separate statutes of elfland, but with the whole spirit of its law, which I learnt before I could speak, and shall retain when I cannot write. I am concerned with a certain way of looking at life, which was created in me by the fairy tales, but has since been meekly ratified by the mere facts.

It might be stated this way. There are certain sequences or developments (cases of one thing following another), which are, in the true sense of the word, reasonable. They are, in the true sense of the word, necessary. Such are mathematical and merely logical sequences. We in fairyland (who are the most reasonable of all creatures) admit that reason and that necessity. For instance, if the Ugly Sisters are older than Cinderella, it is (in an iron and awful sense) *necessary* that Cinderella is younger than the Ugly Sisters. There is no getting out of it. Haeckel may talk as much fatalism about that fact as he pleases: it really must be. If Jack is the son of a miller, a miller is the father of Jack. Cold reason decrees it from her awful throne: and we in fairyland submit. If the three brothers all ride horses, there are six animals and eighteen legs involved: that is true rationalism, and fairyland is full of it. But as I put my head over the hedge of the elves and began to take notice of the natural world, I observed an extraordinary thing. I observed that learned men in spectacles were talking of the actual things that happened—dawn and death and so on—as if *they* were rational and inevitable. They talked as if the fact that trees bear fruit were just as *necessary* as the fact that two and one trees make three. But it is not. There is an enormous difference by the test of fairyland; which is the test of the imagination. You cannot *imagine* two and one not making three. But you can easily imagine trees not growing fruit; you can imagine them growing golden candlesticks or tigers hanging on by the tail. These men in spectacles spoke much of a man named Newton, who was hit by an apple, and who discovered a law. But they could not be got to see the distinction between a true law, a law of reason, and the mere fact of apples falling. If the apple hit Newton's nose, Newton's nose hit the apple. That is a true necessity: because we cannot conceive the one occurring without the other. But we can quite well conceive the apple not falling on his nose; we can fancy it flying ardently through the air to hit some other nose, of which it had a more definite dislike. We have always in our fairy tales kept this sharp distinction between the science of mental relations, in which there really are laws, and the science of physical facts, in which there are no laws, but only weird repetitions. We believe in bodily miracles, but not in mental impossibilities. We believe that a Bean-stalk climbed up to Heaven; but that does not at all confuse our convictions on the philosophical question of how many beans make five.

Here is the peculiar perfection of tone and truth in the nursery tales. The man of science says, "Cut the stalk, and the apple will fall"; but he says it calmly, as if the one idea really led up to the other. The witch in the fairy tale says, "Blow the horn, and the ogre's castle will fall"; but she does not say it as if it were something in which the effect obviously arose out of the cause. Doubtless she has given the advice to many champions, and has seen many castles fall, but she does not lose either her wonder or her reason. She does not muddle her head until it imagines a necessary mental connection between a horn and a falling tower. But the scientific men do muddle their heads, until they imagine a necessary mental connection between an apple leaving the tree and an apple reaching the ground. They do really talk as if they had found not only a set of marvellous facts, but a truth connecting those facts. They do talk as if the connection of two strange things physically connected them philosophically. They feel that because one incomprehensible thing constantly follows another incomprehensible thing the two together somehow make up a comprehensible thing. Two black riddles make a white answer.

In fairyland we avoid the word "law"; but in the land of science they are singularly fond of it. Thus they will call some interesting conjecture about how forgotten folks pronounced the alphabet, Grimm's Law. But Grimm's Law is far less intellectual than Grimm's Fairy Tales. The tales are, at any rate, certainly tales; while the law is not a law. A law implies that we know the nature of the generalisation and enactment; not merely that we have noticed some of the effects. If there is a law that pick-pockets shall go to prison, it implies that there is an imaginable mental connection between the idea of prison and the idea of picking pockets. And we know what the idea is. We can say why we take liberty from a man who takes liberties. But we cannot say why an egg can turn into a chicken any more than we can say why a bear could turn into a fairy prince. As *ideas*, the egg and the chicken are further off from each other than the bear and the prince; for no egg in itself suggests a chicken, whereas some princes do suggest bears. Granted, then, that certain transformations do happen, it is essential that we should regard them in the philosophic manner of fairy tales, not in the unphilosophic manner of science and the "Laws of Nature." When we are asked why eggs turn to birds or fruits fall in autumn, we must answer exactly as the fairy godmother would answer if Cinderella asked her why mice turned to horses or her clothes fell from her at twelve o'clock. We must answer that it is *magic.* It is not a "law," for we do not understand its general formula. It is not a necessity, for though we can count on it happening practically, we have no right to say that it must always happen. It is no argument for unalterable law (as Huxley fancied) that we count on the ordinary course of things. We do not count on it; we bet on it. We risk the remote possibility of a miracle as we do that of a poisoned pancake or a world-destroying comet. We leave it out of account, not because it is a miracle, and therefore an impossibility, but because it is a miracle, and therefore an exception. All the terms used in the science books, "law," "necessity," "order," "tendency," and so on, are really unintellectual, because they assume an inner synthesis, which we do not possess. The only words that ever satisfied me as describing Nature are the terms used in the fairy books, "charm," "spell," "enchantment." They express the arbitrariness of the fact and its mystery. A tree grows fruit because it is a *magic* tree. Water runs downhill because it is bewitched. The sun shines because it is bewitched.

I deny altogether that this is fantastic or even mystical. We may have some mysticism later on; but this fairy-tale language about things is simply rational and agnostic. It is the only way I can express in words my clear and definite perception that one thing is quite distinct from another; that there is no logical connection between flying and laying eggs. It is the man who talks about "a law" that he has never seen who is the mystic. Nay, the ordinary scientific man is strictly a sentimentalist. He is a sentimentalist in this essential sense, that he is soaked and swept away by mere associations. He has so often seen birds fly and lay eggs that he feels as if there must be some dreamy, tender connection between the two ideas, whereas there is none. A forlorn lover might be unable to dissociate the moon from lost love; so the materialist is unable to dissociate the moon from the tide. In both cases there is no connection, except that one has seen them together. A sentimentalist might shed tears at the smell of apple-blossom, because, by a dark association of his own, it reminded him of his boyhood. So the materialist professor (though he conceals his tears) is yet a sentimentalist, because, by a dark association of his own, apple-blossoms remind him of apples. But the cool rationalist from fairyland does not see why, in the abstract, the apple tree should not grow crimson tulips; it sometimes does in his country.

This elementary wonder, however, is not a mere fancy derived from the fairy tales; on the contrary, all the fire of the fairy tales is derived from this. Just as we all like love tales because there is an instinct of sex, we all like astonishing tales because they touch the nerve of the ancient instinct of astonishment. This is proved by the fact that when we are very young children we do not need fairy tales: we only need tales. Mere life is interesting enough. A child of seven is excited by being told that Tommy opened a door and saw a dragon. But a child of three is excited by being told that Tommy opened a door. Boys like romantic tales; but babies like realistic tales—because they find them romantic. In fact, a baby is about the only person, I should think, to whom a modern realistic novel could be read without boring him. This proves that even nursery tales only echo an almost pre-natal leap of interest and amazement. These tales say that apples were golden only to refresh the forgotten moment when we found that they were green. They make rivers run with wine only to make us remember, for one wild moment, that they run with water. I have said that this is wholly reasonable and even agnostic. And, indeed, on this point I am all for the higher agnosticism; its better name is Ignorance. We have all read in scientific books, and, indeed, in all romances, the story of the man who has forgotten his name. This man walks about the streets and can see and appreciate everything; only he cannot remember who he is. Well, every man is that man in the story. Every man has forgotten who he is. One may understand the cosmos, but never the ego; the self is more distant than any star. Thou shalt love the Lord thy God; but thou shalt not know thyself. We are all under the same mental calamity; we have all forgotten our names. We have all forgotten what we really are. All that we call common sense and rationality and practicality and positivism only means that for certain dead levels of our life we forget that we have forgotten. All that we call spirit and art and ecstacy only means that for one awful instant we remember that we forget.

But though (like the man without memory in the novel) we walk the streets with a sort of half-witted admiration, still it is admiration. It is admiration in English and not only admiration in Latin. The wonder has a positive element of praise. This is the next milestone to be definitely marked on our road through fairyland. I shall speak in the next chapter about optimists and pessimists in their intellectual aspect, so far as they have one. Here I am only trying to describe the enormous emotions which cannot be described. And the strongest emotion was that life was as precious as it was puzzling. It was an ecstacy because it was an adventure; it was an adventure because it was an opportunity. The goodness of the fairy tale was not affected by the fact that there might be more dragons than princesses; it was good to be in a fairy tale. The test of all happiness is gratitude; and I felt grateful, though I hardly knew to whom. Children are grateful when Santa Claus puts in their stockings gifts of toys or sweets. Could I not be grateful to Santa Claus when he put in my stockings the gift of two miraculous legs? We thank people for birthday presents of cigars and slippers. Can I thank no one for the birthday present of birth?

There were, then, these two first feelings, indefensible and indisputable. The world was a shock, but it was not merely shocking; existence was a surprise, but it was a pleasant surprise. In fact, all my first views were exactly uttered in a riddle that stuck in my brain from boyhood. The question was, "What did the first frog say?" And the answer was, "Lord, how you made me jump!" That says succinctly all that I am saying. God made the frog jump; but the frog prefers jumping. But when these things are settled there enters the second great principle of the fairy philosophy.

Any one can see it who will simply read "Grimm's Fairy Tales" or the fine collections of Mr. Andrew Lang. For the pleasure of pedantry I will call it the Doctrine of Conditional Joy. Touchstone talked of much virtue in an "if"; according to elfin ethics all virtue is in an "if." The note of the fairy utterance always is, "You may live in a palace of gold and sapphire, *if* you do not say the word 'cow' "; or "You may live happily with the King's daughter, *if* you do not show her an onion." The vision always hangs upon a veto. All the dizzy and colossal things conceded depend upon one small thing withheld. All the wild and whirling things that are let loose depend upon one thing that is forbidden. Mr. W. B. Yeats, in his exquisite and piercing elfin poetry, describes the elves as lawless; they plunge in innocent anarchy on the unbridled horses of the air—

"Ride on the crest of the dishevelled tide,
And dance upon the mountains like a flame."

It is a dreadful thing to say that Mr. W. B. Yeats does not understand fairyland. But I do say it. He is an ironical Irishman, full of intellectual reactions. He is not stupid enough to understand fairyland. Fairies prefer people of the yokel type like myself; people who gape and grin and do as they are told. Mr. Yeats reads into elfland all the righteous insurrection of his own race. But the lawlessness of Ireland is a Christian lawlessness, founded on reason and justice. The Fenian is rebelling against something he understands only too well; but the true citizen of fairyland is obeying something that he does not understand at all. In the fairy tale an incomprehensible happiness rests upon an incomprehensible condition. A box is opened, and all evils fly out. A word is forgotten, and cities perish.

A lamp is lit, and love flies away. A flower is plucked, and human lives are forfeited. An apple is eaten, and the hope of God is gone.

A MEDITATION ON CHILDREN AND THEIR LITERATURE

Clifton Fadiman

Clifton Fadiman, American writer and editor, is concerned in this selection with the "hidden child" phenomenon, especially as it appears in writers of children's literature. He suggests that "the ideal author of the volume [of children's literature] you are reading should be a chimera, half grownup, half child—or perhaps a super-child. . . . He should be able concurrently to feel as child and as grownup. . . ."

The Hidden Child

The child, we know, is something more, or less, but in any case other, than an embryonic "civilized" adult. At times—Golding's implacable *Lord of the Flies* makes this clear—he gives the impression of a small savage. In their classic *Children's Games in Street and Playground* the Opies cite Bertrand Russell's " . . . it is biologically natural that [children] should, in imagination, live through the life of remote savage ancestors." Sometimes the child looks like part of a weird non-Darwinian evolutionary process: such enchanting freaks as those disguised children, the Hobbits and the Moomins, represent another order of creation. Or again, the child seems akin to an animal: the most persuasive animal stories have either been written for children (Beatrix Potter, *The Jungle Books)* or appropriated by them (*The Yearling*). And there are even times when the child (though rarely after the age of eight or nine) identifies with inanimate nature itself. Think of those moments of union in which Huck is as much river as boy; and there are similar instances from Book I of Wordsworth's *Prelude*. Freud's related "oceanic feeling" is not unfamiliar to sensitive children. Indeed parents are often exasperated by the de-individualizing stupor into which the child occasionally seems to fall. He is, we complain, absent-minded. That is, he diffuses into a brown study where mind does not matter. (Today's young people who try hallucinogens may be seeking a gateway to the oceanic trance of childhood, preferring it to the apparently unrewarding bustle of adulthood.)

Why is fantasy a favorite genre in children's literature? Surely in part because it is rooted in the notion of transformation. The plasticity of our early years goes very

From Clifton Fadiman, "Prologue: A Meditation on Children and Their Literature," introduction to a book to be published by Little, Brown and Company.

deep. Whitman tells us:

> There was a child went forth every
> day,
> And the first object he look'd upon,
> that object he became,
> And that object became part of him
> for the day or a certain part of the
> day,
> Or for many years or stretching cycles
> of years.

As children we are princes in disguise; we are stones and plants, beasts and winds; we are jet planes and jet pilots; we are the toys in a shop, we are the shop, we are the shopkeeper; we are the dancer and the dance. If I question the child, he dutifully reports that he is "playing," returning to me the word I have taught him. But "playing" only roughly describes it, because multiple-being is larger than mere doing, deeper than let's-pretend. Of course the child does not "believe" he is Snoopy. Momentarily, however, he can empty his consciousness of all except Snoopy feelings. " 'Making believe' is the gist of his whole life," says Robert Louis Stevenson, "and he cannot so much as take a walk except in character."

Now this protean, quicksilver being, we all know, must lie couched and callupable within the masters of children's literature. We do not really understand how Lewis Carroll can also at will be Alice, or Meindert DeJong be Siebran in *The Journey from Peppermint Street,* or Sanchez-Silva become a little boy who in turn becomes an ant in *Ladis and the Ant.* Even the process by which Shakespeare is at once a sane playwright and a mad king is less mystifying. At least both Shakespeare and Lear are adults, dwelling in the same age-zone. But the author of a first-rate children's book breaks the laws of time, being at the same time old and young, master of his mature, static identity, yet somehow also in phase with the shifting identity-in-formation of the child.

In her twenties Ann Taylor was one of the authors of *Original Poems for Infant Minds* (1804). At eighty she spoke for many writers of children's books and to some degree for all their appreciative adult readers: "The feeling of being a grown woman, to say nothing of an *old* woman, does not come naturally to me." A century after Ann Taylor we find Erich Kästner putting the matter explicitly. The child hidden within the grownup "stands on a footstool and looks out upon the world through the man's eyes, as if they were windows." Such a man "contemplates the world, stories, dreams, the great and small adventures of life, language itself, with two pairs of eyes. He has a large pair of ears, and a small. Inside his head is another head, a child's head. He laughs, he weeps with two voices. His curiosity, his astonishment are twofold." Again and again we find the masters in agreement on this point. Thus Maurice Sendak: "Reaching the kids is important, but secondary. First, always, I have to reach and keep hold of the child in me."

There is no other branch of literature that requires of the writer quite such a queer bifurcation. His seems a crazy business, almost literally so, for as he writes he must be beside himself. Part of the fascination of children's literature for the grownup—a fascination lost on the child—lies precisely in this property of doubleness. Those who write it are compounds. Their shingle should read: *Monster at Work.*

Much in the same way the ideal author of the volume you are reading should be a chimera, half grownup, half child—or perhaps a super-child. He should properly, not merely conventionally, use the first person plural. He should be able to read with double vision, absorbing two books in one, the book as the child perceives it, the book as the knowledgeable adult perceives it. He should be able concurrently to feel as child and as grownup; to remember, yet to repress the sensation of remembering; to enjoy without judging, yet to judge without blunting the edge of enjoyment. The aims of this study can never be achieved except by such a monster as I have described. All books about children's literature are fated to fail. Mission Impossible.

Still, we keep trying to square the circle. What else can we do? After all, children cannot write about what they read. Indeed, they are not even reading what *we* read. We read "literature," they a book. It is we antiques who must make a rural pen, and stain the water clear. And yet it is not all frustration. As suggested, even I, a grandfather, can at times dissolve a part of me into my own childhood. Only a part, only at times, for a flashing interval, the mini-life of the glowing coal. Yet, however evanescent the experience, it is necessary. Not sufficient. But necessary.

How is the trick performed, the hidden child called forth? No one quite knows. The masters merely tell us that it happens, and, being creators, not introspective psychologists, they are themselves puzzled by the phenomenon. The critic or historian is in even worse case, because in him the hidden child is far less alive than in a Pamela Travers, a Josef Guggenmos, a Marcel Aymé. What we need is some odd creative genius who can do for the *élan vital* of children's literature what Henri Poincaré did for mathematical insight; or some great scholar who will devote a whole book to the subject as Hadamard did, again for mathematics, or John Livingston Lowes for poetry. Even trial essays, similar to those by Valéry and Housman, which also deal with the making of poetry, would help.

We feel, of course, that the evocation of the hidden child is linked to Coleridge's "streamy nature of association, which thinking curbs and rudders." But it is not merely a matter of remembering concrete events of our childhood. All of us can do that. It is recreating the thick, specific tone, the how-it-felt, of the event, and manipulating the child of long ago so that it is *he*, not *you*, that does the feeling.

Ten minutes before the above lines were written, I received a letter from a friend, a learned art critic and philosopher of esthetics, acknowledging the receipt of a study of children's literature I had done. He writes: " . . . you made me remember what I thought I had forgotten. A hot summer afternoon around 1920, for instance, in Fulton, Illinois. I was barefooted, and picking my way across a freshly oiled dirt street to the public library to return *The Water Babies*." The streamy associative faculty that can put together Kingsley and the feel of bare feet is required for anyone daring to write about the literature of childhood.

For Proust his madeleine; and for each of us perhaps some other secret charm or mental amulet to draw us back along the path to our beginnings. I do not know why, but if I repeat to myself, "Turn again, Dick Whittington, thrice Lord Mayor of London," or "How many miles to Babylon?" I at once find that I can enter a child's book with a shade more sensibility than if I open it without the aid of the incantation. Yes, this curious business has its serendipities. Backing the basin in my bathroom is an oblong looking-glass. By sheer accident I discovered a year or two ago that it was so hinged it could open like a little door; and that, opening it, I suddenly looked out upon the hitherto unsuspected street. Not an earth-shattering discovery? True—yet for me a useful one. I felt, if but for a moment, that vibration of other worlds to which children respond when they poke about in an attic or an abandoned, cluttered lot. It is the magic casement thrill of a thousand children's books, *Alice* being merely the most famous. But note that the looking-glass worked only once. I am used to it now. That is, I am old, I get used to things all too quickly. Furthermore, objects, being palpable, have only limited talismanic powers. They generate weaker fields of force than memories.

Permit me one other illustration. Sometimes, in the course of my reading, I find it advisable to feel four years old. This is not easy. I use a certain charm of which all I can say is that it helps a little. When I was four, I slept in the same bed with my nine-year-old brother. It was an ancient four-poster with brass knobs on the posts. My brother would gravely assure me that, if he looked at one of those brass knobs long enough, he could "see the whole world in it." I tried too, and failed, but nevertheless had an uneasy feeling that, as

I knew my brother to be extremely wise, there must be *something* to it. And so, drifting toward sleep, I would keep my eyes fixed on the knob, feeling a bit scared, a bit hopeful of the miracle, a bit many other things that do not lend themselves to words. Whatever I felt, I felt as a four-year-old. But even today, recalling that knob, that bedpost and that brother, I can sense my remote past thickening somewhere within me. And—though you need not believe this—that makes it easier for me to understand why the authors of *Mother Goose*, for example, are very fine writers indeed. It makes it possible for me to remember how funny Peter the Pumpkin-eater seemed when I first heard about him, and thus refresh my pleasure today in his domestic problem.

I must at once state that the process I have so clumsily described has little to do with nostalgia. I am not in love with my childhood (which, as I know now, though I did not know it then, was not a happy one) nor with the child I was. My talismanic devices include memories that have little to do with wonder or any "romantic" emotion. At six I watched a policeman put a bullet through the head of a horse that had broken its leg on the icy street. At once I became aware that life's underside was crawling with pain and violence. In consequence such tragic books as George MacDonald's *At The Back of the North Wind* (for tragic it is) could be better internalized by my small self.

No, one need not love one's childhood. Nor, shocking as it may sound, need the writer of or about children's literature love children, except in the most general way. (Obviously one who *dis*likes, or more often *fears*, children cannot write about them.) What he must love, if he is a storyteller, are his child *characters*, which is different from loving children. For example, in reading Professor Tolkien's discussions of fairy tales, one hardly gets the impression that he is in love with children. What counts is that he cares deeply for his Hobbits. Despite the sweetness of her letters to children, there is little evidence that Beatrix Potter really loved them; her stories are often tender, her personality was tough. In his sensitive study Roger Lancelyn Green writes of C. S. Lewis: ". . . the Narnian stories were not told to actual children; nor had he any but the most superficial acquaintance with the species at the time of writing." Some of the best writers of children's books resent being so called. They are not writing love-letters to the little ones, but trying to fashion works of art. Love in excess may even harm the writer. What he must be is not in love with children but, even if at a distance, *interested* in them—and unreservedly interested in the child hidden within himself.

Some first-rate writers have been "good with youngsters," as clearly Lewis Carroll was, though his affections were limited to pre-adolescent girls. Some, equally clearly, have not been "good," with no harmful effect on their work. Jules Verne probably belongs in the latter category.

Nor does being a parent help. Many outstanding living writers have chosen to remain unmarried. As for the dead, one could make a long list of members of the Celibates' Club. Among them, to name only a handful, were Edward Lear, Lewis Carroll, Louisa May Alcott, Collodi, Maria Edgeworth, Lucretia Peabody Hale, Hans Christian Andersen, Selma Lagerlöf, Jean Ingelow, Charles and Mary Lamb, Christina Rossetti, Anna Sewell, Frances Browne, Charlotte Yonge, Kate Greenaway, Elinor Mure (author of the earliest extant written version of *The Three Bears*), Sarah Orne Jewett, Palmer Cox, Susan Coolidge (*What Katy Did*), Mary Howitt, Catherine Sinclair, Dr. Isaac Watts, Jane Taylor, and Oliver Goldsmith (if indeed he wrote *Goody Two-Shoes*, which is far from established). Jacob Grimm was a bachelor; James Catnach, the nineteenth-century printer of chapbooks for the young, was one also, as was the Swedish anthologist Henrik Reuterdahl. Anna Carroll Moore, among the greats in the field of children's librarianship, remained single. Finally the reader may draw any conclusion he cares to from the circumstance that at least three famous names associated with children's stories apparently had little, if any, sexual vitality: Carroll, Ruskin, Barrie.

A great many writers, of course, did love children and wrote with a specific favorite child, or favorite children, in mind. The classic examples are Lear and Carroll, as well as Milne, Hugh Lofting, and Jean de Brunhoff. Even forbidding (and childless) Mrs. Barbauld wrote most of her stories for her adopted nephew Charles, just as the (also childless) Maria Edgeworth read her first tales to her little brothers and sisters. And it was to the little convalescent Edith Story that the "great benevolent giant" Thackeray read, chapter by chapter, *The Rose and The Ring.* Despite these instances the heart of the matter seems to lie less in the writer's relationship to the live children about him than to the live child within him.

This familiar but basic proposition emerges as soon as we pass in rapid chronological review the whole procession of children's literature. One feature stands out immediately: the historic shift from a body of ephemeral work produced by unalloyed adults to one of higher quality produced by adults alloyed in varying degrees by their childhood. It is hard to determine when the shift began—in England perhaps with Catherine Sinclair, perhaps with Edward Lear. But it is fair to say that from about 1920 we see clearly the emergence of a numerous class of writers who are conservators of their childhood, as were in an earlier generation such rare specimens as Alcott, Mark Twain, and a few others. They represent a true mutation, almost inconceivable in the days of Thomas Day, Arnaud Berquin, and Joachim Heinrich Campe. Crass theories of the marketplace or those based on the mere expansion of the field do not explain the mutation. It has to do with a nebulous but profound socio-psychic movement, involving the "discovery" of the child, a matter we discuss later. It is as though the tribe of children's writers suddenly began to rid themselves of repressions that for long had hindered their imaginative freedom.

One thinks at once, of course, of Freud. The fact is that his emphasis on the importance of infancy and early childhood has had only a modest effect on the literature itself. (As we shall note, children's literature lags behind grownup literature in its sensitivity to intellectual revolutions.) But Freud, or rather the whole Freudian ambiance of our day, may well have stimulated the children's writer to retrospective self-analysis and so to the evocation of the child hidden within himself.

The Hidden Child and the Mainstream

This study restricts itself to measuring the dimensions and estimating the depths of what is admittedly only a tributary literature. But the relationship between mainstream and tributary is not quite exhausted when we identify it as one of ancestor and descendant. If, as we have seen, children's literature is directly associated with memories of childhood, and if it can be shown that mainstream literature is to any significant extent indirectly so associated, then the link between the two becomes more interesting.

We think at once of Freud's preoccupation with the child's repressed traumas and their later expression or sublimation in neurosis and art. But it is best not to make too much of this, best to refrain from a glib application of the jargon, beginning with the Oedipus complex. Freud himself warns us: "Whence the artist derives his creative capacities is not a question for psychology." We males may resent our fathers to the point of potential patricide; but most of us, unable to profit from the resentment, turn out to be not Dostoevsky but mere bookkeepers, salesmen, and literary historians.

Nevertheless, one or two of Freud's insights bear on our theme. He speaks, for example, of the "foster child" phantasy, the feeling a child often has that he is really the scion of mysterious, other, perhaps even royal parents. The phantasy, Freud correctly points out, lies at the root of much mainstream literature. We shall see that this is even more markedly the case with children's literature. In "The Creative Writer and Daydreaming" (1908) Freud speculates on whether certain writers may not be triggered by an experience linked to a forgotten childhood memory. In this essay he also discusses children's play, connecting it with daydreaming, which in turn he connects with the writer's activity. The bond between literature, especially poetry, and play has been remarked by many others, especially Huizinga and Sewell. "In any true man," says Nietzsche, "hides a child who wants to play." Is not the dancing, singing Zarathustra something of a great child? Speaking of the British General Strike of 1926, Richard Hughes writes:

> This was no nation grimly enduring a crisis, but one unexpectedly let out of school and enjoying a lovely romp—which just went to show what a crass mistake it is to suppose that the grown-up has any less need of play than the child! He probably needs even more; and the fact that he mostly gets less is the likeliest reason he's often so much more badly behaved.

How far may we venture in tracing these links? If children's literature is the overt expression of the child, is mainstream literature his covert expression? Common sense tells us the answer is No: where is the child in *Père Goriot, Measure for Measure, Le Misanthrope*? Yet the suspicion persists that just as there is an easily detected child in Hugh Lofting, there may be one almost impossible to detect in T.S. Eliot. If this were totally untrue, it would be hard to explain why through the centuries literally scores of highly intelligent creators have stressed the connection between the child and the mature poet or novelist. The linkage is suggested in its most cautious form by Doudan: "There is a certain *enfantillage* (child's play, childishness) of the imagination that we must retain all our lives."

With Wordsworth's more insistent feeling on this point we are familiar, as with the somewhat similar view of De Quincey who was influenced by him. Carried to excess, it is the heart of Novalis's cry: "All poetry must be fairy tale-ish *(märchenhaft).*" Says Baudelaire: "Genius is childhood rediscovered," and again: " . . . genius is nothing but childhood distinctly formulated, but now endowed, in order to express itself, with virile and powerful organs. Still, I do not claim to offer this idea to physiology as anything better than a pure conjecture." The Franco-American novelist Julian Green says, "The child dictates, the man writes it down." Says Rainer Maria Rilke: "Never believe fate's more than the condensation of childhood." (Rilke here has in mind his own, the poet's "fate.") It was Jean Cocteau who divided people into two kinds: poets and grownups. And there is Picasso's frequently quoted remark, uttered as he examined some children's drawings: "When I was their age I could draw like Raphael; but it has taken me my whole life to learn to draw like them."

The reader may demur on the ground that these are mere enthusiastic proclamations, some of them by romantics—in Baudelaire's phrase, "pure conjecture." I do not claim they are "the truth." But, to be fair, I draw attention to a close and systematic formulation, by a reputable scholar, of the idea we have been considering.

The scholar is Jean-Paul Weber, a leading French critic and esthetician. His "esthétique des profondeurs" turns on a basic proposition which he applies not only to literature. The proposition is: "Art is the remembrance of childhood." In his instructive introduction to Weber's *The Psychology of Art*, Robert Emmet Jones summarizes the complex Weberian thesis thus: " . . . the entire work of an author is the result of a memory or a situation largely forgotten since childhood." Weber does not reject the Freudian approach, but his notion of the dominating "themes" or obsessions in the artist's work appears to go beyond Freud. "Let me say only that every writer, every dramatist seems to me to write only to symbolize, modulate, unconsciously, a childhood theme, sometimes two, rarely three; and that every work—including the existence of the artist —is a modulation, more or less clear. more or less firmly structured, of one or another aspect of this theme, or of this counterpoint of themes." His book concludes with a detailed analysis of "the Nose," which Weber claims as one of the dominant themes in all of Gogol's work and which "appears in this author in such a way that it would be impossible to find its source other than in the childhood of the author.

I find the thesis "Art is the remembrance of childhood," though brilliantly argued, far too sweeping. Yet one cannot read Weber, or reflect on the long line of creative men who have expressed similar ideas, without wondering whether there is not at least some truth in the notion. Certain writers to whom it clearly applies at once spring to mind: Mark Twain; Proust, of course; Dickens, as Edmund Wilson classically demonstrated in "Dickens: The Two Scrooges"; Nabokov, who, speaking of the stimuli back of his Russian poems, refers to his "never-resolved childhood." The reader will think almost effortlessly of other instances.

If children's literature and mainstream literature are linked by the child concealed, in different ways, in both, the study of either should cast light on the other. Our own task in this book thus gains in interest, in seriousness—and in difficulty. We are not exploring a back eddy, but part of the broad current of moving language on which civilization, that of the child and that of the man who is also partly a child, floats.

TREE AND LEAF

J. R. R. Tolkien

J.R.R. Tolkien, author of The Hobbit *and* The Lord of the Rings, *warns in this essay that children are not a separate race. In Tolkien's opinion, moreover, fairy stories should not be especially associated with an audience comprised exclusively of children. All those who have retained the heart of a child can find recovery and solace in them. "Collections of fairy-stories are, in fact, by nature attics and lumber-rooms, only by temporary and local custom play-rooms. Their contents are disordered, and often battered, a jumble of different dates, purposes, and tastes; but among them may occasionally be found a thing of permanent virtue; an old work of art, not too*

From J. R. R. Tolkien, *Tree and Leaf* (Boston: Houghton Mifflin, 1965), pp. 33–46.

much damaged, that only stupidity would ever have stuffed away."

Children

. . . what, if any, are the values and functions of fairy-stories *now?* It is usually assumed that children are the natural or the specially appropriate audience for fairy-stories. In describing a fairy-story which they think adults might possibly read for their own entertainment, reviewers frequently indulge in such waggeries as: "this book is for children from the ages of six to sixty." But I have never yet seen the puff of a new motor-model that began thus: "this toy will amuse infants from seventeen to seventy"; though that to my mind would be much more appropriate. Is there any *essential* connexion between children and fairy-stories? Is there any call for comment, if an adult reads them for himself? *Reads* them as tales, that is, not *studies* them as curios. Adults are allowed to collect and study anything, even old theatre programmes or paper bags.

Among those who still have enough wisdom not to think fairy-stories pernicious, the common opinion seems to be that there is a natural connexion between the minds of children and fairy-stories, of the same order as the connexion between children's bodies and milk. I think this is an error; at best an error of false sentiment, and one that is therefore most often made by those who, for whatever private reason (such as childlessness), tend to think of children as a special kind of creature, almost a different race, rather than as normal, if immature, members of a particular family, and of the human family at large.

Actually, the association of children and fairy-stories is an accident of our domestic history. Fairy-stories have in the modern lettered world been relegated to the "nursery," as shabby or old-fashioned furniture is relegated to the play-room, primarily because the adults do not want it, and do not mind if it is misused.[1] It is not the choice of the children which decides this. Children as a class—except in a common lack of experience they are not one—neither like fairy-stories more, nor understand them better than adults do; and no more than they like many other things. They are young and growing, and normally have keen appetites, so the fairy-stories as a rule go down well enough. But in fact only some children, and some adults, have any special taste for them; and when they have it, it is not exclusive, nor even necessarily dominant.[2] It is a taste, too, that would not appear, I think, very early in childhood without artificial stimulus; it is certainly one that does not decrease but increases with age, if it is innate.

It is true that in recent times fairy-stories have usually been written or "adapted" for children. But so may music be, or verse, or novels, or history, or scientific manuals. It is a dangerous process, even when it is necessary. It is indeed only saved from disaster by the fact that the arts and sciences are not as a whole relegated to the nursery; the nursery and schoolroom are merely given such tastes and glimpses of the adult thing as seem fit for them in adult opinion (often much mistaken). Any one of these things would, if left altogether in the nursery, become gravely impaired. So would a beautiful ta-

1. In the case of stories and other nursery lore, there is also another factor. Wealthier families employed women to look after their children, and the stories were provided by these nurses, who were sometimes in touch with rustic and traditional lore forgotten by their "betters." It is long since this source dried up, at any rate in England; but it once had some importance. But again there is no proof of the special fitness of children as the recipients of this vanishing "folk-lore." The nurses might just as well (or better) have been left to choose the pictures and furniture.

2. See Note C at end.

ble, a good picture, or a useful machine (such as a microscope), be defaced or broken, if it were left long unregarded in a schoolroom. Fairy-stories banished in this way, cut off from a full adult art, would in the end be ruined; indeed in so far as they have been so banished, they have been ruined.

The value of fairy-stories is thus not, in my opinion, to be found by considering children in particular. Collections of fairy-stories are, in fact, by nature attics and lumber-rooms, only by temporary and local custom play-rooms. Their contents are disordered, and often battered, a jumble of different dates, purposes, and tastes; but among them may occasionally be found a thing of permanent virtue: an old work of art, not too much damaged, that only stupidity would ever have stuffed away.

Andrew Lang's *Fairy Books* are not, perhaps, lumber-rooms. They are more like stalls in a rummage-sale. Someone with a duster and a fair eye for things that retain some value has been round the attics and box-rooms. His collections are largely a by-product of his adult study of mythology and folk-lore; but they were made into and presented as books for children.[3] Some of the reasons that Lang gave are worth considering.

The introduction to the first of the series speaks of "children to whom and for whom they are told." "They represent," he says, "the young age of man true to his early loves, and have his unblunted edge of belief, a fresh appetite for marvels." " 'Is it true?' " he says, "is the great question children ask."

I suspect that *belief* and *appetite for marvels* are here regarded as identical or as closely related. They are radically different, though the appetite for marvels is not at once or at first differentiated by a growing human mind from its general appetite. It seems fairly clear that Lang was using *belief* in its ordinary sense: belief that a thing exists or can happen in the real (primary) world. If so, then I fear that Lang's words, stripped of sentiment, can only imply that the teller of marvellous tales to children must, or may, or at any rate does trade on their *credulity*, on the lack of experience which makes it less easy for children to distinguish fact from fiction in particular cases, though the distinction in itself is fundamental to the sane human mind, and to fairy-stories.

Children are capable, of course, of *literary belief*, when the story-maker's art is good enough to produce it. That state of mind has been called "willing suspension of disbelief." But this does not seem to me a good description of what happens. What really happens is that the story-maker proves a successful "sub-creator." He makes a Secondary World which your mind can enter. Inside it, what he relates is "true": it accords with the laws of that world. You therefore believe it, while you are, as it were, inside. The moment disbelief arises, the spell is broken; the magic, or rather art, has failed. You are then out in the Primary World again, looking at the little abortive Secondary World from outside. If you are obliged, by kindliness or circumstance, to stay, then disbelief must be suspended (or stifled), otherwise listening and looking would become intolerable. But this suspension of disbelief is a substitute for the genuine thing, a subterfuge we use when condescending to games or make-believe, or when trying (more or less willingly) to find what virtue we can in the work of an art that has for us failed.

A real enthusiast for cricket is in the enchanted state: Secondary Belief. I, when I watch a match, am on the lower level. I can achieve (more or less) willing suspension of disbelief, when I am held there and supported by some other motive that will keep away boredom: for instance, a wild, heraldic, preference for dark blue rather than light. This suspension of disbelief may thus be a somewhat tired, shabby, or sentimental state of mind, and so lean to the "adult." I fancy it is often the state of adults in the presence of a fairy-story. They are held there and supported by sentiment (memories of

3. By Lang and his helpers. It is not true of the majority of the contents in their original (or oldest surviving) forms.

childhood, or notions of what childhood ought to be like); they think they ought to like the tale. But if they really liked it, for itself, they would not have to suspend disbelief: they would believe—in this sense.

Now if Lang had meant anything like this there might have been some truth in his words. It may be argued that it is easier to work the spell with children. Perhaps it is, though I am not sure of this. The appearance that it is so is often, I think, an adult illusion produced by children's humility, their lack of critical experience and vocabulary, and their voracity (proper to their rapid growth). They like or try to like what is given to them: if they do not like it, they cannot well express their dislike or give reasons for it (and so may conceal it); and they like a great mass of different things indiscriminately, without troubling to analyse the planes of their belief. In any case I doubt if this potion—the enchantment of the effective fairy-story—is really one of the kind that becomes "blunted" by use, less potent after repeated draughts.

" 'Is it true?' is the great question children ask," Lang said. They do ask that question, I know; and it is not one to be rashly or idly answered.[4] But that question is hardly evidence of "unblunted belief," or even of the desire for it. Most often it proceeds from the child's desire to know which kind of literature he is faced with. Children's knowledge of the world is often so small that they cannot judge, off-hand and without help, between the fantastic, the strange (that is rare or remote facts), the nonsensical, and the merely "grown-up" (that is ordinary things of their parents' world, much of which still remains unexplored). But they recognize the different classes, and may like all of them at times. Of course the borders between them are often fluctuating or confused; but that is not only true for children. We all know the differences in kind, but we are not always sure how to place anything that we hear. A child may well believe a report that there are ogres in the next county; many grown-up persons find it easy to believe of another country; and as for another planet, very few adults seem able to imagine it as peopled, if at all, by anything but monsters of iniquity.

Now I was one of the children whom Andrew Lang was addressing—I was born at about the same time as the *Green Fairy Book*—the children for whom he seemed to think that fairy-stories were the equivalent of the adult novel, and of whom he said: "Their taste remains like the taste of their naked ancestors thousands of years ago; and they seem to like fairy-tales better than history, poetry, geography, or arithmetic."[5] But do we really know much about these "naked ancestors," except that they were certainly not naked? Our fairy-stories, however old certain elements in them may be, are certainly not the same as theirs. Yet if it is assumed that we have fairy-stories because they did, then probably we have history, geography, poetry, and arithmetic because they liked these things too, as far as they could get them, and in so far as they had yet separated the many branches of their general interest in everything.

And as for children of the present day, Lang's description does not fit my own memories, or my experience of children. Lang may have been mistaken about the children he knew, but if he was not, then at any rate children differ considerably, even within the narrow borders of Britain, and such generalizations which treat them as a class (disregarding their individual talents, and the influences of the countryside they live in, and their upbringing) are delusory. I had no special "wish to believe." I wanted to know. Belief depended on the way in which stories were presented to me, by older people, or by the authors, or on the inherent tone and quality of the tale. But at no time can I remember that the enjoyment of a story was dependent on belief that such things could happen, or had happened, in "real life."

4. Far more often they have asked me: "Was he good? Was he wicked?" That is, they were more concerned to get the Right side and the Wrong side clear. For that is a question equally important in History and in Faërie.

5. Preface to the *Violet Fairy Book.*

Fairy-stories were plainly not primarily concerned with possibility, but with desirability. If they awakened *desire*, satisfying it while often whetting it unbearably, they succeeded. It is not necessary to be more explicit here, for I hope to say something later about this desire, a complex of many ingredients, some universal, some particular to modern men (including modern children), or even to certain kinds of men. I had no desire to have either dreams or adventures like *Alice*, and the account of them merely amused me. I had very little desire to look for buried treasure or fight pirates, and *Treasure Island* left me cool. Red Indians were better: there were bows and arrows (I had and have a wholly unsatisfied desire to shoot well with a bow), and strange languages, and glimpses of an archaic mode of life, and, above all, forests in such stories. But the land of Merlin and Arthur was better than these, and best of all the nameless North of Sigurd of the Völsungs, and the prince of all dragons. Such lands were pre-eminently desirable. I never imagined that the dragon was of the same order as the horse. And that was not solely because I saw horses daily, but never even the footprint of a worm.[6] The dragon had the trade-mark *Of Faërie* written plain upon him. In whatever world he had his being it was an Other-world. Fantasy, the making or glimpsing of Other-worlds, was the heart of the desire of Faërie. I desired dragons with a profound desire. Of course, I in my timid body did not wish to have them in the neighbourhood, intruding into my relatively safe world, in which it was, for instance, possible to read stories in peace of mind, free from fear.[7] But the world that contained even the imagination of Fáfnir was richer and more beautiful, at whatever cost of peril. The dweller in the quiet and fertile plains may hear of the tormented hills and the unharvested sea and long for them in his heart. For the heart is hard though the body be soft.

All the same, important as I now perceive the fairy-story element in early reading to have been, speaking for myself as a child, I can only say that a liking for fairy-stories was not a dominant characteristic of early taste. A real taste for them awoke after "nursery" days, and after the years, few but long-seeming, between learning to read and going to school. In that (I nearly wrote "happy" or "golden," it was really a sad and troublous) time I liked many other things as well, or better: such as history, astronomy, botany, grammar, and etymology. I agreed with Lang's generalized "children" not at all in principle, and only in some points by accident: I was, for instance, insensitive to poetry, and skipped it if it came in tales. Poetry I discovered much later in Latin and Greek, and especially through being made to try and translate English verse into classical verse. A real taste for fairy-stories was wakened by philology on the threshold of manhood, and quickened to full life by war.

I have said, perhaps, more than enough on this point. At least it will be plain that in my opinion fairy-stories should not be *specially* associated with children. They are associated with them: naturally, because children are human and fairy-stories are a natural human taste (though not necessarily a universal one); accidentally, because fairy-stories are a large part of the literary lumber that in latter-day Europe has been stuffed away in attics; unnaturally, because of erroneous sentiment about children, a sentiment that seems to increase with the decline in children.

It is true that the age of childhood-sentiment has produced some delightful books (especially charming, however, to adults) of the fairy kind or near to it; but it has also produced a dreadful undergrowth of stories written or adapted to what was or is conceived to be the measure of children's minds and needs. The old stories are mollified or bowdlerized, instead of being reserved; the imitations are

6. See Note D at end.

7. This is, naturally, often enough what children mean when they ask: "Is it true?" They mean: "I like this, but is it contemporary? Am I safe in my bed?" The answer: "There is certainly no dragon in England today," is all that they want to hear.

often merely silly, Pigwiggenry without even the intrigue; or patronizing; or (deadliest of all) covertly sniggering, with an eye on the other grown-ups present. I will not accuse Andrew Lang of sniggering, but certainly he smiled to himself, and certainly too often he had an eye on the faces of other clever people over the heads of his child-audience—to the very grave detriment of the *Chronicles of Pantouflia.*

Dasent replied with vigour and justice to the prudish critics of his translations from Norse popular tales. Yet he committed the astonishing folly of particularly *forbidding* children to read the last two in his collection. That a man could study fairy-stories and not learn better than that seems almost incredible. But neither criticism, rejoinder, nor prohibition would have been necessary if children had not unnecessarily been regarded as the inevitable readers of the book.

I do not deny that there is a truth in Andrew Lang's words (sentimental though they may sound): "He who would enter into the Kingdom of Faërie should have the heart of a little child." For that possession is necessary to all high adventure, into kingdoms both less and far greater than Faërie. But humility and innocence—these things "the heart of a child" must mean in such a context—do not necessarily imply an uncritical wonder, nor indeed an uncritical tenderness. Chesterton once remarked that the children in whose company he saw Maeterlinck's *Blue Bird* were dissatisfied "because it did not end with a Day of Judgement, and it was not revealed to the hero and the heroine that the Dog had been faithful and the Cat faithless." "For children," he says, "are innocent and love justice; while most of us are wicked and naturally prefer mercy."

Andrew Lang was confused on this point. He was at pains to defend the slaying of the Yellow Dwarf by Prince Ricardo in one of his own fairy-stories. "I hate cruelty," he said, " . . . but that was in fair fight, sword in hand, and the dwarf, peace to his ashes! died in harness." Yet it is not clear that "fair fight" is less cruel than "fair judgement"; or that piercing a dwarf with a sword is more just than the execution of wicked kings and evil stepmothers—which Lang abjures: he sends the criminals (as he boasts) to retirement on ample pensions. That is mercy untempered by justice. It is true that this plea was not addressed to children but to parents and guardians, to whom Lang was recommending his own *Prince Prigio* and *Prince Ricardo* as suitable for their charges.[8] It is parents and guardians who have classified fairy-stories as *Juvenilia.* And this is a small sample of the falsification of values that results.

If we use *child* in a good sense (it has also legitimately a bad one) we must not allow that to push us into the sentimentality of only using *adult* or *grown-up* in a bad sense (it has also legitimately a good one). The process of growing older is not necessarily allied to growing wickeder, though the two do often happen together. Children are meant to grow up, and not to become Peter Pans. Not to lose innocence and wonder, but to proceed on the appointed journey: that journey upon which it is certainly not better to travel hopefully than to arrive, though we must travel hopefully if we are to arrive. But it is one of the lessons of fairy-stories (if we can speak of the lessons of things that do not lecture) that on callow, lumpish, and selfish youth peril, sorrow, and the shadow of death can bestow dignity, and even sometimes wisdom.

Let us not divide the human race into Eloi and Morlocks: pretty children—"elves" as the eighteenth century often idiotically called them—with their fairy-tales (carefully pruned), and dark Morlocks tending their machines. If fairy-story as a kind is worth reading at all it is worthy to be written for and read by adults. They will, of course, put more in and get more out than children can. Then, as a branch of a genuine art, children may hope to get fairy-stories fit for them to read and yet within their measure; as they may hope to get suitable introductions to poetry, his-

8. Preface to the *Lilac Fairy Book.*

tory, and the sciences. Though it may be better for them to read some things, especially fairy-stories, that are beyond their measure rather than short of it. Their books like their clothes should allow for growth, and their books at any rate should encourage it.

Very well, then. If adults are to read fairy-stories as a natural branch of literature—neither playing at being children, nor pretending to be choosing for children, nor being boys who would not grow up—what are the values and functions of this kind? That is, I think, the last and most important question. I have already hinted at some of my answers. First of all: if written with art, the prime value of fairy-stories will simply be that value which, as literature, they share with other literary forms. But fairy-stories offer also, in a peculiar degree or mode, these things: Fantasy, Recovery, Escape, Consolation, all things of which children have, as a rule, less need than older people. Most of them are nowadays very commonly considered to be bad for anybody.

Note C

As far as my knowledge goes, children who have an early bent for writing have no special inclination to attempt the writing of fairy-stories, unless that has been almost the sole form of literature presented to them; and they fail most markedly when they try. It is not an easy form. If children have any special leaning it is to Beast-fable, which adults often confuse with Fairy-story. The best stories by children that I have seen have been either "realistic" (in intent), or have had as their characters animals and birds, who were in the main the zoomorphic human beings usual in Beast-fable. I imagine that this form is so often adopted principally because it allows a large measure of realism: the representation of domestic events and talk that children really know. The form itself is, however, as a rule, suggested or imposed by adults. It has a curious preponderance in the literature, good and bad, that is nowadays commonly presented to young children: I suppose it is felt to go with "Natural History," semi-scientific books about beasts and birds that are also considered to be proper pabulum for the young. And it is reinforced by the bears and rabbits that seem in recent times almost to have ousted human dolls from the play-rooms even of little girls. Children make up sagas, often long and elaborate, about their dolls. If these are shaped like bears, bears will be the characters of the sagas; but they will talk like people.

Note D

I was introduced to zoology and palaeontology ("for children") quite as early as to Faërie. I saw pictures of living beasts and of true (so I was told) prehistoric animals. I liked the "prehistoric" animals best: they had at least lived long ago, and hypothesis (based on somewhat slender evidence) cannot avoid a gleam of fantasy. But I did not like being told that these creatures were "dragons." I can still re-feel the irritation that I felt in childhood at assertions of instructive relatives (or their gift-books) such as these: "snowflakes are fairy jewels," or "are more beautiful than fairy jewels"; "the marvels of the ocean depths are more wonderful than fairyland." Children expect the differences they feel but cannot analyse to be explained by their elders, or at least recognized, not to be ignored or denied. I was keenly alive to the beauty of "Real things," but it seemed to me quibbling to confuse this with the wonder of "Other things." I was eager to study Nature, actually more eager than I was to read most fairy-stories; but I did not want to be quibbled into Science and cheated out of Faërie by people who seemed to assume that by some kind of original sin I should prefer fairy-tales, but according to some kind of new religion I ought to be induced to like science. Nature is no doubt a life-study, or a study for eternity (for those so gifted); but there is a part of man which is not "Nature," and which therefore is not obliged to study it, and is, in fact, wholly unsatisfied by it.

INDEX